Disciples'

Literal

New Testament

Disciples' Literal New Testament

Serving modern disciples
by more fully reflecting
the writing style
of the ancient disciples

Michael Magill

Reyma Publishing

Published by Reyma Publishing, P.O. Box 173, Beaverton, Oregon 97075
    Email: Reyma@LiteralNewTestament.com
    Website: www.ReymaPublishing.com

Library of Congess Control Number: 2011932205

ISBN 978-1-937368-07-4 Hardback
ISBN 978-1-937368-03-6 Paperback

The translation contained in this book was previously published in outline format in the *New Testament TransLine*, Copyright © 2002 Michael J. Magill.

Reyma is a phonetic spelling of the Greek word rendered 'Word' in Eph 6:17:
And take ... the sword of the Spirit, which is the Word of God

May the blessing of the Father of Lights rest on all readers and expounders of his inspired Word, and move us all, in these proud and dangerous days, to yield up our high thoughts unto him who 'of God is made unto us wisdom,' and to determine, even as an inspired apostle determined amid the skeptical disputants of his own times, 'not to know anything save Jesus Christ and Him crucified.'

—Charles Ellicott, September 1861, England

Contents

Introduction. ix

Matthew 1

Mark 57

Luke. 91

John 146

Acts 188

Romans 242

1 Corinthians 271

2 Corinthians 296

Galatians 313

Ephesians 322

Philippians 331

Colossians 338

1 Thessalonians 345

2 Thessalonians 351

1 Timothy. 355

2 Timothy 362

Titus. 367

Philemon 371

Hebrews 373

James 394

1 Peter 401

2 Peter 409

1 John. 414

2 John 422

3 John. 423

Jude 424

Revelation 427

Appendix: Details About This Translation. 455

Introduction

The goal of the *Disciples' Literal New Testament* is to help all Bible readers better understand the New Testament from the original writers' point of view. This is accomplished in two primary ways. First, the translation reflects the Greek forms, grammar, and sentence structure, rather than using elegant English like our standard translations. Second, the paragraphs are arranged to display the flow of thought in the Apostles' minds as revealed in their Greek writings, rather than the artificial 460 year old chapter and verse structure we are used to seeing. The New Testament is opened up to English readers in a depth formerly available only to those who carefully studied their Greek New Testament. Used together with your standard Bible version, you will now have the best of both languages.

This is the companion volume to the 1025 page *New Testament TransLine*, which presents this same translation in outline format. First published by Zondervan in 2002, it includes extensive notes on the meaning and usage of the words of the New Testament, notes that explain the meaning of a passage where needed, notes that list the different interpretations when the meaning is not clear, and notes on over 3000 textual variations in the Greek manuscripts that lie behind all English translations. Pastors and Bible students wanting more depth and detail will find it useful.

Features of the *Disciples' Literal New Testament*.

Outline. The first thing you see is the detailed outline of the book, which directly corresponds to the paragraphing and indentation of the translation that follows. The words of the outline are taken directly from the words of the book itself. This gives you a thorough overview of the book, a big picture view of what the writer intends to communicate.

Interpretive Headings. Next you will notice that each paragraph has a heading in *italics*. These are descriptive, interpretive headings intended to make the original writer's flow of thought more explicit to you by summarizing the main point of the paragraph in its context in the book. In fact, if you read through a book's paragraph headings first, you will get a solid picture of the flow of the book.

Intelligent Paragraphing. The arrangement of the text is broken into thought paragraphs reflecting the Apostle's flow of thought. The paragraphs are indented in a kind of outline grouping so that major thoughts and subordinate thoughts can easily be seen. This will help you follow the main points and see the tangents! Greek is so different from English that some mechanism like this is needed in order to clearly display the connections of thought contained in the Greek. To help you see how far a paragraph has been indented so that you can connect the points, there is a grey baseline down the left side of the page.

Chapter And Verse Numbers. As you may know, after the invention of the printing press, the chapter and verse numbers were added to the New Testament in 1551 by Robert Stephanus. Unfortunately, as often pointed out from the pulpit, they are sometimes not at all helpful in following the thought contained in the Greek writings. They sometimes prevent you from easily seeing the flow of thought in the author's mind, and hinder you from even asking the right questions. This hurdle to our understanding has been eliminated in the *Disciples' Literal New Testament*. The verse numbers are still included for your reference, but the paragraphing and sentence structure reflects what was originally written.

Literal Translation. The *Disciples' Literal New Testament* is a literal reflection of writing style, ways of speaking, sentence and thought structures, and word patterns of the New Testament writers. It is not intended to be an elegant English translation like the NASB, NKJV, ESV, NRSV, or to recast itself in even more natural English like the NIV or NLT or *The Message*. But using the *Disciples' Literal New Testament* you will be able see more deeply into the minds of the original writers, and understand their intent more clearly than ever. And you will be able to see how those translations transformed the Greek ways of speaking into pleasing and effective English ways of speaking.

Italics, Brackets, Bold Type, Hyphenated Words. *Italics* are used for words not in the Greek, but implied by the grammar of the Greek word, phrase, or sentence structure, or required in normal English grammar. Don't skip over them; they are part of the literal translation. [Brackets] are used for words added to clarify the meaning of a word, phrase or sentence. Skip over these words if you like, and what remains will be the literal translation. **Bold** type is used for words actually emphasized in the Greek by the biblical writer. For example, sometimes a subject is emphasized, "But **I** say to you," or, "**they** will be comforted." Sometimes the Greek word order is arranged so as to place emphasis on a word. Hyphenated words are single Greek words translated by multiple English words. For example, "announced-as-good-news" represents a single Greek word. Such words are hyphenated when linked to notes and on some other occasions, but not on every occurrence.

Notes. Each page has some translation and interpretive notes at the bottom of the page. These will help you better understand the text, the meaning, and the Greek ways of speaking. You can find much more detail on these matters in the *New Testament TransLine*.

What is a literal translation?

Translations such as the NASB, NKJV, ESV, RSV, mean by 'literal' that their translation reflects the *words and grammar* of the Greek as much as possible in an elegant English translation. They seek to strike the perfect balance between what was said in Greek and how we would say it in beautiful English. In technical terms, there is a significant degree of 'formal equivalence' between the Greek and the English. In layman's terms, these are word-for-word translations, within the bounds of pleasing and proper English. We like these translations because we feel they are the most accurate.

Other versions seek to literally communicate the *meaning* intended by the original writers to an English speaking audience, using normal and pleasing English ways of speaking. In doing this, these translations rephrase sentences and clarify thoughts as needed so that the intended *meaning* in the Greek is conveyed to the English reader. This is done to various degrees depending on how far the focus is moved from the Greek to the English, and how much 'interpretation' is added to the 'translation.' At one extreme the translation remains close to the Greek, but enhances or clarifies the meaning in English. The NRSV is an example. At the other extreme the translation is a paraphrase completely rewritten into words and phrases chosen by the translator. *The Message* is an example. In technical terms, this method is called 'dynamic equivalence.' In layman's terms, these are thought-for-thought translations. We like these translations because they feel so natural to us. They speak to us in a way we can more easily understand, or even in an exciting and thought-provoking manner.

How does the *Disciples' Literal New Testament* compare to other translations?

Imagine a translation scale of zero to ten, where zero is the Greek New Testament and ten is an exciting paraphrase such as *The Message*. A one would be a Greek-English interlinear. A five would be a translation that seeks to perfectly balance the Greek and English. The NASB, NKJV, RSV and ESV would be examples of a five. The NRSV would be a six; the NIV a seven. There are many wonderful translations available between five and ten. The *Disciples' Literal New Testament* would be a three, opening a new view into the New Testament for English readers.

Is the *Disciples' Literal New Testament* better than the other translations?

Better as your standard English translation? No. Since it more closely follows the Greek ways of speaking, it is of course more foreign-sounding, and therefore inferior as an *English* translation to all the versions mentioned above. But as a reflection of the Greek mind and thought processes and intent of the original writers, it is indeed a fuller display of the ancient writings. To get any closer to the mind of those writers, you would have to learn Greek! And as a basis from which to evaluate and understand the adjustments made to accomodate the English language by the translations in the five to ten range mentioned above, it is superior.

Every translation strives to accomplish a certain balance of translation goals, a balance of Greek accuracy and English expression. There can be no perfect translation. To illustrate, the NIV expresses the thoughts contained in the Greek using the full breadth and beauty of English, foregoing strict conformity to the Greek phraseology. The *Disciples' Literal New Testament* expresses much more of the breadth and beauty of the Greek phraseology, sacrificing normal English idiom. So 'better' is not really a proper question, because each translation serves its purpose. The *Disciples' Literal New Testament,* the NASB, the NIV, and *The Message,* to use these four as examples, are each better at what they are trying to do than the others. Which is better for you depends on what you are trying to accomplish at the time.

Can a one-man translation be any good?

Many have been done, all along the scale above from five to ten. But a team of Greek and English scholars is certainly essential for an *authoritative* translation seeking to perfectly balance the Greek and English, or an *accurate* thought-for-thought translation like the NIV. But a translation such as the *Disciples' Literal New Testament* can indeed be done well by one person. Why? Consider how the translation process takes place. First you would make a straightforward translation that accurately reflects the Greek as your starting point. Then you would revise this initial translation from the English point of view, making the adjustments and adding the nuances that would transform it into a polished English translation. It is precisely at the stage of making these adjustments and nuances that a team of people is superior to a single individual. But the initial translation from the Greek could be made by any one of the team members. The *Disciples' Literal New Testament* is consistently and accurately and thoroughly done at that initial level of translation, deliberately stopping short of smoothing and nuancing in English. That is its strength. It allows you to see the Greek ways of writing and expressing thoughts before the translation is adjusted into better English sentences. Those wanting more detail on the translation methods can find it in the Appendix.

Matthew

A. The book of the genealogy of Jesus Christ, son of David, son of Abraham   1:1-17
B. The birth of Jesus Christ was as follows— He was fathered in Mary by the Holy Spirit   1:18-25
C. After His birth, magi worshiped Him, Herod tried to kill Him, God protected Him   2:1-23
D. During those days John the Baptist comes, proclaiming, Repent, the kingdom is near   3:1-12
E. Then Jesus comes from Galilee to the Jordan to John to be baptized by him   3:13-17
F. Then Jesus was led up into the wilderness by the Spirit to be tempted by the devil   4:1-11
G. Jesus went back to Galilee. From then on, He proclaimed the kingdom in all Galilee   4:12-24
H. Large crowds followed Him. And having seen them, He was teaching them, saying   4:25-5:2

   1. Blessed are the poor in spirit, mourners, gentle, hungry, merciful, and others   5:3-12
   2. You are the salt of the earth. You are the light of the world   5:13-16
   3. I came to fulfill the Law. Unless your righteousness abounds, you will not enter. Murder 5:17-48
      and anger, adultery and lust, divorce, oaths, eye for an eye, love and hate
   4. But take heed not to do your righteousness before people— almsgiving, praying, fasting   6:1-18
   5. Do not treasure up treasures on earth, but seek His kingdom. You cannot serve both   6:19-34
   6. Do not judge others. With what judgment you judge, you will be judged. Pearls and pigs   7:1-6
   7. Ask and you will receive. Seek and you will find. Knock and it will be opened   7:7-11
   8. Therefore, everything you want others to be doing to you, you be doing to them   7:12
   9. Enter through the narrow gate on the narrow road leading to life   7:13-14
   10. Beware of the false prophets. You will know them by their fruits   7:15-20
   11. Not everyone saying "Lord, Lord" will enter the kingdom. Only the doer of God's will   7:21-27

I. When He finished these words, the crowds were astounded and followed Him   7:28-8:1

   1. A leper said, If You are willing, You are able to cleanse me. I am willing. Be cleansed 8:2-4
   2. Having entered Capernaum, He healed a centurion's paralyzed servant. Great faith   8:5-13
   3. He healed Peter's mother-in-law. They brought Him many, and He healed them all   8:14-17
   4. They departed for the other side. On the sea, He calmed the storm   8:18-27
   5. At the other side of the sea, Jesus cast demons into a herd of pigs   8:28-34
   6. He crossed back over the sea, and forgave and healed a paralytic. Which is easier?   9:1-8
   7. While eating at Matthew's house, the Pharisees objected. The ill need a physician   9:9-13
   8. John's disciples come and ask why Jesus' disciples are not fasting. New wine   9:14-17
   9. An official asked Him to raise his daughter. While going, He healed a woman   9:18-26
   10. Passing on from there, two blind men followed Him. Jesus healed them   9:27-31
   11. He healed a mute man. The crowds marveled, the Pharisees called it Satanic   9:32-34

J. Jesus was going through all the villages teaching, proclaiming and curing. Having seen the 9:35-38
   crowds, He had deep feelings for them. Ask the Lord of the harvest to send out workers

   1. Having summoned the twelve, Jesus gave them authority over demons and diseases   10:1-4
   2. Jesus sent out the twelve, after instruction, to proclaim the kingdom to Israel and heal 10:5-15

      a. Jesus prewarns them about coming persecution. You will be hated and killed   10:16-31
      b. I came to divide the world, not to bring peace. Take up your cross and follow Me   10:32-42

   3. When He finished giving directions to the twelve, He passed on to teach and proclaim   11:1

K. John, having heard in prison of His works, sent his disciples to ask— Are you the One? Jesus 11:2-6
   said, Report to John what you are hearing and seeing

   1. While proceeding, Jesus spoke of John. If you will accept it, John is Elijah   11:7-19

2.	Then Jesus began to reproach the cities in which He did miracles for not repenting	11:20-24
3.	Jesus praised God for hiding these things from the wise. Come to Me, all	11:25-30
4.	The Pharisees objected to the disciples picking grain. I am Lord of the Sabbath	12:1-8
5.	In the synagogue, Jesus healed on the Sabbath. The Pharisees plotted against Him	12:9-21
6.	Jesus healed and the Pharisees said He did it by Beelzebub. It will not be forgiven	12:22-37
7.	Some scribes and Pharisees said, We want to see a sign. No sign will be given	12:38-45
8.	His family came. He said, My family is whoever does God's will	12:46-50
9.	On that day, from a boat, He spoke to the crowds in parables about the kingdom	13:1-35
10.	Then having left the crowds, He explained and spoke parables to the disciples	13:36-52
11.	When He finished these parables, He went to His hometown. They took offense	13:53-58
12.	At that time, Herod said Jesus is John the Baptist, risen from the dead	14:1-12
13.	Having heard of it, Jesus withdrew. Crowds followed. He fed 5000	14:13-21
14.	He sent the disciples away in a boat. At night, He walked out to them on water	14:22-33
15.	Having crossed, He healed the sick. All who touched His garment were healed	14:34-36
16.	Pharisees objected to a lack of hand-washing. What comes out of the heart defiles	15:1-20
17.	Jesus withdrew to Tyre and Sidon. He healed the daughter of a Canaanite woman	15:21-28
18.	He went beside the Sea of Galilee, where He healed large crowds and fed 4000	15:29-38
19.	Having crossed to Magadan, the Pharisees asked for a sign from heaven	15:39-16:4
20.	Having crossed, Jesus said to the disciples, Beware of the leaven of the Pharisees	16:4-12
21.	Jesus asks, Who do you say I am? You are the Christ, the Son of God	16:13-20

L.	From that time on, Jesus began to show them He must suffer, die, and rise again. Having taken Him aside, Peter said, This shall never happen to You. Get behind Me, Satan	16:21-23

1.	Jesus said to them, Deny yourself and follow Me. Some here will see My glory	16:24-28
2.	After six days, Jesus was transfigured before Peter, James and John	17:1-8
3.	Coming down from the mountain, Jesus said, Tell no one. They asked about Elijah	17:9-13
4.	Having come to the crowd, Jesus healed a person that the disciples could not heal	17:14-21
5.	Being gathered in Galilee, Jesus said He would be killed, and raised the third day	17:22-23
6.	Having come to Capernaum, Peter got their tax money from the mouth of a fish	17:24-27
7.	The disciples asked, Who is greater in the kingdom? Jesus said, the childlike believer	18:1-4

	a.	Woe to whoever causes one of My children to fall	18:5-9
	b.	Do not look down on My little ones. It is not God's will that one be lost	18:10-14
	c.	But if your brother sins against you, expose the sin and seek to restore him	18:15-20
	d.	Always forgive one another from the heart, seventy times seven	18:21-35

M.	When He finished these words, He left Galilee for Judea. He healed large crowds there	19:1-2

1.	Pharisees came to Him, testing Him regarding divorce and the Law of Moses	19:3-12
2.	Then children were brought to Him, and He laid His hands upon them	19:13-15
3.	What should I do to have eternal life? It is hard for the rich to enter. As for you disciples, you will sit on twelve thrones. But many first will be last	19:16-20:16
4.	While going to Jerusalem, He said, I will be crucified, and raised on the third day	20:17-19
5.	Then the mother of James and John asked that they sit on His right hand and left	20:20-28
6.	While leaving Jericho, Jesus healed two blind men	20:29-34
7.	Near Jerusalem, Jesus sent the disciples to get a donkey. He enters with hosannas	21:1-9

N.	And having entered Jerusalem, the whole city said, Who is this? It is the prophet, Jesus	21:10-11

1.	Jesus entered the temple and threw out those buying and selling. Priests objected	21:12-17
2.	In the morning, Jesus cursed a barren fig tree. It withered	21:18-22

3. Having come into the temple, the priests asked, By what authority do you do this?   21:23-27
Jesus said, Tell me first the source of John's baptism. They refused

    a. Which son did the will of his father? Those who repent from sin will enter   21:28-32
    b. You are like tenant farmers who killed the owner's son. But the rejected stone   21:33-44
became the cornerstone. The kingdom will be taken from you
    c. The king will destroy those who refuse the invitation to his son's wedding   21:45-22:14

4. The Pharisees tried to snare Him, saying, Is it lawful to pay a poll tax to Caesar?   22:15-22
5. On that day, the Sadducees asked, Whose wife will she be in the resurrection?   22:23-33
6. A Pharisee asked, Which is the great commandment in the Law?   22:34-40
7. Jesus asked, If the Christ is the son of David, why does David call him Lord?   22:41-46
8. Jesus rebuked the Pharisees. Woe to you. Your house is left to you desolate   23:1-39
9. Jesus prophesies the destruction of the temple. What is the sign of Your coming?   24:1-4

    a. Many will come claiming to be the Messiah: Don't be deceived. There will be   24:4-14
birthpains: Don't be alarmed. The good news will be proclaimed to the whole
world, and then the end will come
    b. When you see the abomination spoken of by Daniel the prophet, flee. For then   24:15-28
there will be a great affliction. Don't be deceived by false Christs, for My
coming will be as visible as lightning in the sky
    c. After that affliction, Jesus will come on the clouds of heaven in great glory   24:29-31
    d. The parable of the fig tree: When the leaves grow out, summer is near   24:32-35
    e. No one knows the day or hour, so keep watch. It will be like the days of Noah   24:36-44
    f. The faithful and wise slave is the one doing the master's will when he comes   24:45-51
    g. The wise bridesmaids are the ones prepared for the coming of the groom   25:1-13
    h. The good slave works with his master's resources to produce a return for him   25:14-30
    i. When Jesus comes, He will sit on His throne and send people to their destinies   25:31-46

O. When Jesus finished all these words, He said, After two days, I will be crucified   26:1-2

1. Then the priests gathered to plot to seize and kill Jesus. But not during the Feast   26:3-5
2. A woman anoints Jesus with costly perfume. She is preparing Me for burial   26:6-13
3. Judas asks, What are you willing to give me to betray Jesus? Thirty silver coins   26:14-16
4. They eat the Passover. One of you will betray Me. The bread and the cup   26:17-29
5. On the Mount of Olives, Jesus said, You all will be caused to fall. Peter said, not me!   26:30-35
6. At Gethsemane, Jesus prays, they sleep. Jesus is seized. The disciples flee   26:36-56
7. The priests and elders condemn Him to death. Peter denies Him three times   26:57-75
8. Having become morning, they led Him away bound, to Pilate   27:1-2
9. Then Judas, having seen that He was condemned, regretted it. He hanged himself   27:3-10
10. Pilate asked, Are You King of the Jews? Jesus or Barabbas? Crucify Him!   27:11-26
11. Then they mocked Him, crucified Him, blasphemed Him. Jesus let His spirit go   27:27-56
12. Having become evening, Joseph asks for His body and places it in his new tomb   27:57-61
13. On the next day, the priests ask Pilate to guard the tomb. They seal it   27:62-66

P. On Sunday, an angel moved the stone and told the women Jesus arose. Tell His disciples   28:1-7

1. While running to report this, the women see the risen Jesus and worship Him   28:8-10
2. The guards report to the chief priests, and are bought off   28:11-15
3. Jesus commissions the eleven to make disciples of all nations   28:16-20

1:1 *The* book *of the* genealogy^A *of* Jesus Christ, son *of* David, son *of* Abraham—

² Abraham fathered^B Isaac, and Isaac fathered Jacob, and Jacob fathered Judah and his brothers, ³ and Judah fathered Perez and Zerah by Tamar, and Perez fathered Hezron, and Hezron fathered Ram, ⁴ and Ram fathered Aminadab, and Aminadab fathered Nahshon, and Nahshon fathered Salmon, ⁵ and Salmon fathered Boaz by Rahab, and Boaz fathered Obed by Ruth, and Obed fathered Jesse, ⁶ and Jesse fathered David the king.

And David fathered Solomon by the *one of* Uriah, ⁷ and Solomon fathered Rehoboam, and Rehoboam fathered Abijah, and Abijah fathered Asaph, ⁸ and Asaph fathered Jehoshaphat, and Jehoshaphat fathered Joram, and Joram fathered Uzziah, ⁹ and Uzziah fathered Jotham, and Jotham fathered Ahaz, and Ahaz fathered Hezekiah, ¹⁰ and Hezekiah fathered Manasseh, and Manasseh fathered Amos, and Amos fathered Josiah, ¹¹ and Josiah fathered Jeconiah and his brothers at the time of the deportation *of* Babylon.

¹² And after the deportation *of* Babylon, Jeconiah fathered Shealtiel, and Shealtiel fathered Zerubbabel, ¹³ and Zerubbabel fathered Abihud, and Abihud fathered Eliakim, and Eliakim fathered Azor, ¹⁴ and Azor fathered Zadok, and Zadok fathered Achim, and Achim fathered Eliud, ¹⁵ and Eliud fathered Eleazar, and Eleazar fathered Matthan, and Matthan fathered Jacob, ¹⁶ and Jacob fathered Joseph the husband *of* Mary— by whom^C Jesus was born, the *One* being called Christ.

¹⁷ So all^D the generations from Abraham to David *are* fourteen generations, and from David to the deportation *of* Babylon *are* fourteen generations, and from the deportation *of* Babylon to the Christ *are* fourteen generations.

The Birth of The King: Jesus Is Born To a Virgin In Fulfillment of Isaiah
¹⁸ Now the birth *of* Jesus Christ was as follows: His mother Mary having been promised-in-marriage^E *to* Joseph, before they came-together she was found having *a child* in *the* womb by *the* Holy Spirit. ¹⁹ And Joseph her husband^F, being righteous and not wanting to publicly-expose^G her, intended to send her away^H secretly^I. ²⁰ And he having pondered these *things*, behold— *an* angel *of the* Lord appeared *to* him in *a* dream saying "Joseph, son *of* David, do not fear to take Mary *as* your wife, for the *child* having been fathered^J in her is by *the* Holy Spirit. ²¹ And she will give-birth to *a* Son. And you shall call His name Jesus, for **He** will save His people from their sins. ²² And^K this entire *thing* has taken place in order that the *thing* might be fulfilled having been spoken by *the* Lord through the prophet saying ²³ 'Behold— the virgin will have *a child* in *the* womb, and she will give-birth to *a* Son. And they will call His name "Immanuel" ' " [Isa 7:14], which being translated is "God with us". ²⁴ And Joseph, having arisen from the sleep, did as the angel *of the* Lord commanded him and took *her as* his wife. ²⁵ And he was not knowing^L her until which *time* she gave-birth to *a* Son. And he called His name Jesus.

A. Or, generation, account, taking this as a title for the whole book. **B.** Or, caused to be born, became the father of, begat. **C.** This word is feminine, referring to Mary. **D.** That is, all the ones Matthew names above. He limits his list to fourteen in each group. **E.** That is, by her parents, according to their custom. **F.** A man would be regarded as such even during the betrothal period. **G.** Or, make a public example of, disgrace. **H.** That is, divorce, a term used in that culture even during the period of betrothal. **I.** Or, privately, quietly. **J.** Same word as in v 2-16. **K.** This may be Matthew's comment; or, still the angel's. **L.** That is, in a sexual sense.

Magi Arrive Seeking The Newborn King. King Herod Sends Them To Bethlehem

2:1 Now Jesus having been born in Bethlehem *of* Judea in *the* days *of* Herod[A] the king, behold— magi[B] from *the* east arrived in Jerusalem, **2** saying "Where is the *One* having been born King *of* the Jews? For we saw His star in the east[C] and came to pay-homage *to* Him". **3** And having heard *it*, King Herod was disturbed, and all Jerusalem with him. **4** And having gathered-together all the chief priests and scribes *of* the people, he was inquiring from them *as to* where the Christ was [to be] born. **5** And the *ones* said *to* him, "In Bethlehem *of* Judea. For thus it has been written through the prophet [in Mic 5:2]: **6** 'And **you**, Bethlehem, land *of* Judah, are by no means least among the rulers *of* Judah. For *One* ruling[D] will come out of you Who will shepherd My people Israel' ". **7** Then Herod, having called the magi secretly, learned-accurately from them the time *of* the appearing *of the* star. **8** And having sent them to Bethlehem, he said, "Having gone, search-out accurately[E] concerning the Child. And when you find *Him*, report *to* me so that **I** also, having come, may pay-homage *to* Him".

A Star Leads Them To The Child, To Whom They Give Gifts

9 And the *ones,* having heard the king, proceeded. And behold— the star which they saw in the east was going-ahead-of them, until having come, it stood[F] over where the Child was. **10** And having seen the star, they rejoiced *an* extremely great rejoicing. **11** And having come into the house[G], they saw the Child with Mary His mother. And having fallen-*down*, they paid homage *to* Him. And having opened their treasure-chests, they offered gifts *to* Him— gold and frankincense and myrrh. **12** And having been warned in *a* dream not to return to Herod, they went back to their country by another way.

An Angel Tells Joseph To Flee From Herod To Egypt, Fulfilling Hosea

13 And they having gone away, behold— *an* angel *of the* Lord appears *to* Joseph in *a* dream saying, "Having arisen, take the Child and His mother and flee into Egypt, and be there until I tell you. For Herod is about to seek-*for* the Child *that he might* destroy Him". **14** And the *one*, having arisen, took the Child and His mother *by* night and withdrew into Egypt, **15** and was there until the end[H] *of* Herod— in order that the *thing* might be fulfilled having been spoken by *the* Lord through the prophet saying "I called My Son out of Egypt" [Hos 11:1].

Herod Kills The Boys In Bethlehem, Bringing Another Fulfillment of Jeremiah

16 Then Herod, having seen that he was tricked[I] by the magi, became very furious. And having sent-out *men*, he killed all[J] the boys— the *ones* in Bethlehem and in all its districts from two years old and under— in accordance with the time which he learned-accurately from the magi. **17** Then the *thing* was fulfilled having been spoken through Jeremiah the prophet saying **18** "*A* voice was heard in Ramah[K], weeping and great mourning— Rachel weeping-*for* her children. And she was not willing to be comforted, because they are no *more*" [Jeremiah 31:15].

A. That is, Herod the Great, king of Israel from 37 to 4 B.C. **B.** That is, wise men/priests/seers/astrologers at least similar (their country is not given) to those in Daniel 2:48. Perhaps their knowledge came from Daniel's prophecies. **C.** That is, while they were in the east. **D.** Or, leading, governing. **E.** Or, carefully. **F.** Or, stopped, stood still. **G.** Joseph would have moved his family from the stable (Lk 2:7) to a house as soon as possible. **H.** That is, the death. **I.** Or, made a fool, mocked. **J.** Some think this might have involved up to twenty infants. **K.** This town is about 6 miles or 9 kilometers north of Jerusalem. In Jeremiah 31:15, Rachel, representing the mother of the nation, weeps over the ten tribes killed or taken captive by the Assyrians. Matthew sees another fulfillment of this here when some of her children are again taken in violence.

After Herod Dies, Joseph Returns To Israel And Settles In Nazareth
19 And Herod having come-to-an-endᴬ, behold— *an* angel *of the* Lord appears *to* Joseph in *a* dream in Egypt **20** saying, "Having arisen, take the Child and His mother and proceed into *the* land *of* Israel. For the *ones* seeking the life *of* the Child are dead". **21** And the *one*, having arisen, took the Child and His mother and entered into *the* land *of* Israel. **22** But having heard that Archelausᴮ was king *of* Judea in place of his father Herod, he feared to go there. And having been warned in *a* dream, he withdrew into the regions *of* Galilee. **23** And having ⸱come, he dwelled in *a* city being called Nazareth— so that the *thing* having been spoken through the prophets might be fulfilled, becauseᶜ He will be called *a* Nazarene.

In Fulfillment of Isaiah, John The Baptist Prepares The Nation For The Messiah
3:1 Now during those days John the Baptist comesᴰ, proclaiming in the wilderness *of* Judea **2** and saying, "Repent, for the kingdom *of* the heavens has drawn-near". **3** For this *one* is the *one* having been spoken *of* through Isaiah the prophet saying [in Isa 40:3], "*A* voice *of one* shouting in the wilderness: 'Prepare the way *of the* Lord, be making His paths straight' ". **4** Now John himself was havingᴱ his clothing [made] of camel's hair, and *a* belt made-of-leather around his waist. And his food was locusts and wild honey. **5** At that time Jerusalem and all Judea and all the surrounding-region *of* the Jordan was going out to him. **6** And they were being baptized in the Jordan River by him while confessing-outᶠ their sins.

John Says To Produce Fruit Worthy of Repentance, Because The Chaff Will Be Burned
7 But having seen many *of* the Pharisees and Sadducees coming toᴳ his baptism, he said *to* them, "Brood *of* vipers— who showedᴴ you to flee from the coming wrath? **8** Therefore produce fruit worthy *of* repentance. **9** And do not think *that you may* say withinᴵ yourselves, 'We have Abraham *as our* father'. For I say *to* you that God is able to raise-up children *for* Abraham from these stones! **10** And the axe is **already** lyingᴶ at the root *of* the trees. Therefore every tree not producing good fruit is cut down and thrown into *the* fire. **11** I am baptizing you withᴷ water for repentance, but the *One* coming after me is more powerful *than* me, *of* Whom I am not fit to carry the sandals. **He** will baptize you withᴸ *the* Holy Spirit and fireᴹ— **12** Whose winnowing-tool *is* in His hand, and He will cleanse-out His threshing floor and gather His wheat into the barn. But He will burn up the chaff *with an* inextinguishable fire".

When Jesus Is Baptized, The Spirit Descends Upon Him And His Father Expresses His Pleasure
13 Then Jesus comes from Galilee to the Jordan to John *that He might* be baptized by him. **14** But John was preventing Him, saying, "**I** have *a* need to be baptized by You, and **You** are coming to me?" **15** But having responded, Jesus said to him, "Permit *it* at this time. For it is fittingᴺ *for* us to fulfill all righteousness in this manner". Then he permits Him. **16** And having been baptized, Jesus immediately ascendedᴼ fromᴾ the water. And behold— the heavens were opened *to* Him,

---

A. That is, having died. **B.** This son of Herod the Great ruled part of his father's kingdom from 4 B.C. until A.D. 6, when the Romans deposed him. **C.** Matthew may be referring to the prophets who say Messiah will be despised and lowly. He sees this as partially fulfilled in that Jesus is called a Nazarene. Or, 'that', if what follows is a summary quote to this effect. **D.** Or, arrives, appears publicly. **E.** That is, was habitually having. **F.** Or, acknowledging, openly admitting. **G.** Or, upon, for. **H.** Or, indicated to, warned. **I.** Or, among. **J.** Or, being laid. **K.** Or, in. **L.** Or, in. **M.** This fire of judgment may be with regard to unbelievers, the chaff mentioned next, or with regard to the purifying work of the Spirit on believers. **N.** That is, for Jesus as a devout son of Israel; or, for Jesus as an inauguration of His own ministry. **O.** Or, went up, came up. **P.** Or, away from.

and he^A saw the Spirit *of* God descending as-if^B *a* dove, and coming upon Him. **¹⁷** And behold— *a* voice from the heavens saying, "This is My beloved Son with Whom I was^C well-pleased".

Satan Tempts The Son of God To Act Contrary To His Father's Will
4:1 Then Jesus was led-up into the wilderness by the Spirit to be tempted by the devil. **²** And having fasted *for* forty days and forty nights, afterward He was hungry. **³** And having come to *Him*, the *one* tempting said *to* Him, "If You are^D God's **Son**, say that these stones should become loaves-of-bread". **⁴** But the *One*, having responded, said, "It has been written [in Deut 8:3]: 'Mankind^E shall live not on bread alone, but on every word proceeding-out through *the* mouth *of* God' " **⁵** Then the devil takes Him into the holy city. And he stood Him on the pinnacle *of* the temple. **⁶** And he says *to* Him, "If You are God's **Son**, throw Yourself down. For it has been written: 'Because^F He will command His angels concerning You, and they will lift You up on *their* hands that You may not ever strike Your foot against *a* stone' " [Ps 91:11-12]. **⁷** Jesus said *to* him, "Again^G, it has been written: 'You shall not put *the* Lord your God to the test' " [Deut 6:16]. **⁸** Again, the devil takes Him to *a* very high mountain and shows Him all the kingdoms *of* the world and their glory. **⁹** And he said *to* Him, "I will give all these *things to* You if, having fallen-*down*, You give-worship *to* me". **¹⁰** Then Jesus says *to* him, "Go-away, Satan! For it has been written: 'You shall worship *the* Lord your God, and serve Him only' " [Deut 6:13]. **¹¹** Then the devil leaves Him. And behold— angels came to *Him* and were ministering *to* Him.

Jesus Begins His Ministry In Capernaum of Galilee, Fulfilling Isaiah
¹² And having heard that John was handed-over^H [to prison], He went-back^I into Galilee. **¹³** And having left-behind Nazareth, having come, He dwelled in Capernaum, the *one* by-the-sea in the districts *of* Zebulun and Naphtali, **¹⁴** in order that the *thing* might be fulfilled having been spoken through Isaiah the prophet saying **¹⁵** "Land *of* Zebulun and land *of* Naphtali, *the* way *of the* sea, beyond the Jordan, Galilee *of* the Gentiles— **¹⁶** the people sitting in darkness saw *a* great Light. And *for* the *ones* sitting in *the* region and shadow *of* death, *a* Light rose *for* them" [Isa 9:1-2]. **¹⁷** From that time *on* Jesus began to proclaim and say, "Repent, for the kingdom *of* the heavens has drawn-near".

Jesus Calls Peter And Andrew And Then James And John To Follow Him
¹⁸ And while walking beside the Sea *of* Galilee He saw two brothers— Simon (the *one* being called Peter) and Andrew, his brother— throwing *a* casting-net into the sea, for they were fishermen. **¹⁹** And He says *to* them, "Come after Me and I will make you fishermen *of* people". **²⁰** And immediately the *ones*, having left the nets, followed Him. **²¹** And having gone on from there He saw two other brothers— James (the *son of* Zebedee) and John, his brother— preparing^J their nets in the boat with Zebedee their father. And He called them. **²²** And immediately the *ones*, having left the boat and their father, followed Him.

Jesus Goes Around All Galilee Teaching And Healing Every Disease
²³ And He was going around in all Galilee— teaching in their synagogues and

A. That is, John. **B.** Or, like. **C.** Or, I delighted, I took pleasure. This may have an eternal sense, 'I was well pleased' to choose and send Him for this task (as in Isa 42:1; Lk 9:35; Mt 12:18); or, a timeless sense, 'I am well pleased'; or, a historical sense, 'I have become well pleased' in His obedience. **D.** That is, Assuming You are, as God said in 3:17. **E.** Or, Man, The person, The human, Humankind. **F.** This is part of the quote from Ps 91. Or, written that, 'He will. **G.** That is, For the second time I say; or, On the other hand. **H.** That is, by Herod Antipas, Mt 14:3. **I.** Or, withdrew. **J.** Or, putting in order, restoring.

proclaiming the good-news *of* the kingdom and curing every disease and every infirmity among the people. **24** And the report[A] *of* Him went into all Syria[B]. And they brought to Him all the *ones* being ill, being gripped[C] *with* various diseases and torments, and being demon-possessed, and having seizures[D], and paralytics. And He cured them.

The Teachings of The King: True Righteousness Expounded With Divine Authority
25 And large crowds from Galilee and Decapolis and Jerusalem and Judea and beyond the Jordan followed Him. **5:1** And having seen the crowds, He went up on the mountain. And He having sat-*down*, His disciples[E] came to Him. **2** And having opened His mouth He was teaching[F] them[G], saying—

These Are The Ones God Considers Blessed
3 "Blessed[H] *are* the poor *in* spirit, because the kingdom *of* the heavens is theirs. **4** Blessed *are* the *ones* mourning, because **they**[I] will be comforted. **5** Blessed *are* the gentle *ones*, because **they** will inherit the earth. **6** Blessed *are* the *ones* hungering and thirsting *as to* righteousness, because **they** will be filled-to-satisfaction. **7** Blessed *are* the merciful *ones*, because **they** will be shown-mercy. **8** Blessed *are* the pure *in* heart, because **they** will see God. **9** Blessed *are* the peacemakers, because **they** will be called sons *of* God[J]. **10** Blessed *are* the *ones* having been persecuted for the sake of righteousness, because the kingdom *of* the heavens is theirs. **11** You are blessed *ones* whenever they reproach you and persecute *you* and speak every [kind of] evil against you while lying, because-of[K] Me. **12** Be rejoicing and be overjoyed, because your reward *is* great in the heavens. For in this manner they persecuted the prophets before you.

You Are Salt And Light. Salt Must Be Tasty. Light Must Shine
13 "**You** are the salt *of* the earth. But if the salt should become-tasteless, with what will it be salted[L]? It no longer has strength for anything except, having been thrown outside, to be trampled-underfoot by people. **14 You** are the light *of* the world. *A* city lying on *a* hill is not able to be hidden. **15** Nor do they burn *a* lamp and put it under the basket, but on the lampstand— and it shines *on* all the *ones* in the house. **16** In this manner, let your light shine in front of people so that they may see your good works and glorify your Father in the heavens.

I Came To Fulfill The Law. Your Righteousness Must Abound More Than The Pharisees
17 "Do not think that I came to abolish[M] the Law or the Prophets. I did not come to abolish, but to fulfill[N]. **18** For truly I say *to* you, until heaven and earth pass away, one iota[O] or one

---

A. Or, news. **B.** That is, the Roman province that included all the regions mentioned in v 25. **C.** Or, held *by*, ruled *by*, oppressed *with*. **D.** Or, being a lunatic (out of control of oneself). **E.** That is, the twelve; or, the larger group from which the twelve were chosen, Lk 6:13, 17, 20. **F.** Chapters 5-7 may represent the attainable standard of righteousness necessary to enter the kingdom; or, the unattainable standard that drives us to Christ, the premier application of the Law; or, the standard of conduct for those who have entered the kingdom. **G.** That is, the crowds (note 7:28); or, the disciples. **H.** Or, Fortunate, Happy, from God's point of view. **I.** Or, they themselves (and in each case below). This word has the emphasis. **J.** That is, children characterized by the same trait as their Father. **K.** That is, from the persecutor's point of view. Or, for the sake of, from the believer's point of view. **L.** Or, seasoned. **M.** Or, destroy, do away with, annul. **N.** Or, complete, finish. That is, to perfectly fulfill the Law's requirements; or, to fill out its true meaning and intent in His teaching; or, to bring it to its completion and conclusion in His death. **O.** That is, the smallest letter, like our i.

stroke[A] will by no means pass away from the Law until all *things* take-place[B]. **19** Therefore, whoever breaks[C] one *of* the least *of* these commandments and in this manner teaches people— he will be called least in the kingdom *of* the heavens. But whoever does and teaches *them*— this *one* will be called great in the kingdom *of* the heavens. **20** For I say *to* you that unless your righteousness abounds more[D] *than* [that of] the scribes and Pharisees, you will by-no-means[E] enter into the kingdom *of* the heavens!

Some Say Do Not Murder. I Say Do Not Get Angry
21 "You heard that it was said *to*[F] the ancient *ones*, 'You shall not murder', and 'Whoever murders shall be liable[G] *to* the judgment'. **22** But **I** say *to* you that everyone being angry *with* his brother shall be liable *to* judgment. And whoever says *to* his brother, 'Raca'[H], shall be liable *to* the Sanhedrin. And whoever says, 'Fool'[I], shall be liable to the Gehenna[J] *of* [K] fire. **23** Therefore if you are offering your gift at the altar, and there you remember that your brother has something against you, **24** leave your gift there in front of the altar, and go. First be reconciled *to* your brother, and then, having come, be offering your gift. **25** Be settling *with* your adversary quickly— until[L] you are with him on the way [to court]— that *your* adversary might not perhaps hand you over *to* the judge, and the judge *to* the officer, and you be thrown into prison. **26** Truly I say *to* you, you will by no means come out from there until you pay the last quadrans[M].

Some Say Do Not Commit Adultery. I Say Do Not Desire Another Woman
27 "You heard that it was said, 'You shall not commit-adultery'. **28** But **I** say *to* you that everyone looking-*at a* woman so-as to desire[N] her already committed-adultery-*with* her in his heart. **29** And if your right eye is causing you to fall, tear it out[O] and throw *it* from you. For it is better[P] *for* you that one *of* your body-parts perish and your whole body not be thrown into Gehenna. **30** And if your right hand is causing you to fall, cut it off and throw *it* from you. For it is better *for* you that one *of* your body-parts perish and your whole body not go into Gehenna.

Some Say Get a Legal Divorce. I Say Divorcees Who Remarry Commit Adultery
31 "And it was said, 'Whoever sends-away[Q] his wife, let him give her *a* divorce[R] certificate'. **32** But **I** say *to* you that everyone sending-away his wife except for *a* matter[S] *of* sexual-immorality is causing her to commit-adultery[T]. And whoever marries *a woman* having been sent-away [from her husband] is committing-adultery.

A. That is, the single stoke that distinguishes one letter from another, like an E from an F, or a Q from an O. **B.** Or, happen, come about. **C.** That is, annuls the authority of, does away with, repeals. **D.** As seen in what follows, Jesus means it must not merely be an external righteousness. **E.** Or, never. **F.** Or, *by*. **G.** Or, answerable, subject. **H.** That is, empty one; numbskull, blockhead. **I.** This may have the same meaning as Raca; or, Raca may insult the intellect, Fool the character. **J.** Or, hell. **K.** That is, characterized by fire; the fiery Gehenna. **L.** Lit, up to which *time*. Or, while, in which case '[to court]' can be omitted. **M.** This is the smallest Roman coin, 1/64th of a denarius (a day's wage). That is, once you enter the judicial system, this world's or God's, the full penalty must be paid. **N:** so as to desire. This expresses the purpose of the looking. **O.** Take whatever action is necessary to avoid sinning. **P.** The eternal consequences of sin are far worse that losing physical eyesight. **Q.** Or, dismisses. This refers to the physical separation aspect of divorce. The legal aspect is referred to next. **R.** This legal document was to protect the woman and make it possible for her to remarry. **S.** Or, word, account. **T.** Or, become-an-adulteress. That is, when she remarries.

Some Say Do Not Break Your Oath. I Say Do Not Swear an Oath At All
33 "Again, you heard that it was said *to* the ancient *ones*, 'You shall not break-*your-*oath[A], but you shall pay your oaths *to* the Lord'. **34** But I say *to* you not to swear-with-an-oath[B] at all— **35** neither by heaven, because it is *the* throne *of* God; nor by earth, because it is *a* footstool *of* His feet; nor with reference to Jerusalem, because it is *the* city *of* the great King; **36** nor may you swear-with-an-oath by your head, because you are not able to make one hair white or black. **37** But let your statement be, 'Yes, yes', [or] 'No, no'. And the *thing* beyond these is from[C] the evil *one*.

Some Say Avenge an Eye For an Eye. I Say Do Not Retaliate, But Do The Opposite
38 "You heard that it was said, '*An* eye for[D] *an* eye, and *a* tooth for *a* tooth'. **39** But I say *to* you not to resist[E] the evil *person*. But whoever slaps[F] you on your right cheek, turn the other *to* him also. **40** And *to* the *one* wanting to sue you and take your tunic[G], permit him also the cloak. **41** And whoever will press you into service[H] *for* one mile, go with him two. **42** Give *to* the *one* asking you, and do not turn away from the *one* wanting to borrow from you.

Some Say Hate Your Enemies. I Say Love Them And Pray For Them
43 "You heard that it was said, 'You shall love your neighbor and hate your enemy'. **44** But I say *to* you, be loving your enemies, and be praying for the *ones* persecuting you, **45** so that you may prove-to-be[I] sons *of* your Father[J] in *the* heavens— because He causes His sun to rise upon evil and good *ones*, and He sends rain upon righteous and unrighteous *ones*. **46** For if you love the *ones* loving you, what reward do you have? Are not even the tax-collectors doing the same? **47** And if you greet your brothers only, what extraordinary *thing* are you doing? Are not even the Gentiles[K] doing the same?

Be Perfect Reflections of Your Heavenly Father
48 "Therefore **you** shall be perfect, as your heavenly Father is perfect.

But Do Not Merely Put On a Show of Righteousness For Others
6:1 "But take-heed not to do your righteousness[L] in-front-of people so-as to be seen[M] *by* them. Otherwise indeed, you do not have *a* reward with your Father in the heavens.

Don't Give Money To Glorify Yourself. Give Without Thinking of Yourself At All
2 "So whenever you do almsgiving[N], do not trumpet *it* before you as-indeed the hypocrites do in the synagogues and in the lanes[O] so that they may be glorified by people. Truly I say *to* you, they are receiving their reward[P] in full. **3** But while **you** *are* doing almsgiving, do not let your left *hand* know what your right *hand* is doing,

A. Or, swear-falsely, make-false-oaths. **B.** Or, affirm, confirm with an oath, such as saying 'I swear by heaven...'. **C.** Or, *of* evil; that is, of evil origin. **D.** That is, let your revenge be in proportion to the offense. **E.** Or, oppose, stand against. Leave vengeance to God. Do not return evil for evil, Rom 12:17. **F.** A slap is a personal affront. **G:** tunic... cloak. The Law did not permit Jews to take the outer cloak, but they could sue for the tunic, the undergarment. **H.** Soldiers would compel people to carry their things. Simon was pressed into service to carry the cross, Mt 27:32. **I.** Or, be, become. **J.** That is, children characterized by the same trait as your Father. **K.** That is, the non-believers. **L.** That is, your righteous deeds. **M.** That is, for the purpose of being seen. **N.** That is, give to the poor as charity. **O.** Or, narrow streets, alleys. **P.** Their reward is glory from people.

[4] so that your almsgiving may be in secret. And your Father, the *One* seeing in secret, will reward you.

Don't Pray To Impress Others. Always Pray As If Alone With Your Heavenly Father
[5] "And whenever you pray, do not be like the hypocrites. Because standing in the synagogues and on the corners *of* the wide-roads, they **love** to pray so that they may make-an-appearance[A] *to* people. Truly I say *to* you, they are receiving their reward in full. [6] But whenever **you** pray, enter into your inner-room, and having shut your door, pray *to* your Father, the *One* in secret. And your Father, the *One* seeing in secret, will reward you.

Don't Babble On In Prayer. Pray As a Child of God, Aligned With His Purposes
[7] "And while praying, do not babble as-indeed the Gentiles *do*. For they are thinking that they will be heard by means of their many-words[B]. [8] So do not be like them, for your Father knows *of the things* which you have *a* need before you ask Him. [9] Therefore, **you** be praying as follows, 'Our Father in the heavens: [10] let[C] Your name be treated-as-holy. Let Your kingdom come. Let Your will be done[D]— as in heaven, also on earth. [11] Give us today our daily bread. [12] And forgive us our debts, as **we** also forgave[E] our debtors. [13] And do not bring us into *a* temptation[F], but deliver[G] us from the evil *one*[H]'. [14] For if you forgive people their trespasses, your heavenly Father will also forgive you. [15] But if you do not forgive people *their trespasses*, neither will your Father forgive your trespasses.

Don't Display Yourself As Fasting. Fast In Secret
[16] "And whenever you fast, do not be like the sad-faced hypocrites. For they disfigure[I] their faces so that they may appear *to* people *as ones* fasting. Truly I say *to* you, they are receiving their reward in full. [17] But while **you** *are* fasting, anoint your head and wash your face [18] so that you may not appear *to* people *as one* fasting, but *to* your Father, the *One* in secret. And your Father, the *One* seeing in secret, will reward you.

Build Your Storehouse of Treasure In Heaven, Not On Earth
[19] "Do not be treasuring-up treasures *for* yourselves on earth, where moth and eating[J] destroy, and where thieves break-in and steal. [20] But be treasuring up treasures *for* yourselves in heaven, where neither moth nor eating destroys, and where thieves do not break in nor steal.

Your Heart Will Be Where Your Treasure Is. You Cannot Serve God And Money
[21] "For where your treasure is, there your heart also will be. [22] The lamp[K] *of* the body

---

A. Or, are-visible. **B.** Or, wordiness, much talking. **C.** That is, make it reality that your name is treated as holy (it does not mean 'let' in the sense of 'allow'). All six requests are in the form of a command (as usual), but the grammar changes with the fourth request. **D.** Or, take place, come about, happen, become *reality*. **E.** Forgiveness is assumed to be a characteristic part of a believer's life. **F.** That is, a situation in which we will be tempted by the evil one. Or, testing, trial. Compare Lk 22:40. **G.** Or, rescue, save. **H.** Or, from evil. Some manuscripts add 'Because Yours is the kingdom and the power and the glory forever, amen'. **I.** These people blackened their faces with ashes so they would be seen by others as ones fasting. **J.** That is, the consumption of all kinds of treasures by all kinds of natural processes, of which moth-eating is a specific example. Or, eating *by rust*, corroding (a meaning not found elsewhere in Greek), if Jesus specifically has in view here a different category of treasure than that eaten by moths, metal treasures. **K.** That is, the source of light.

is the eye. Therefore if your eye is single[A], your whole body will be full-of-light[B]. **23** But if your eye is bad[C], your whole body will be full-of-darkness. If then the light in you is darkness[D], how great *is* the darkness! **24** No one can be serving[E] two masters. For either he will hate the one and love the other, or he will be devoted-to one and disregard[F] the other. You cannot be serving God and wealth[G].

Don't Be Anxious About Your Earthly Life. Seek God's Kingdom And Righteousness
25 "For this reason I say *to* you— do not be anxious[H] *for* your life *as to* what you may eat or what you may drink, nor *for* your body *as to* what you may put-on. Is not life more *than* food, and the body *more than* clothing? **26** Look at the birds *of* the heaven— that they do not sow, nor reap, nor gather into barns. And your heavenly Father feeds them. Are **you** not worth more *than* they? **27** And which of you while being anxious is able to add one cubit[I] upon his life-span? **28** And why are you anxious about clothing? Observe-closely the lilies *of* the field, how they grow— they do not labor nor spin. **29** But I say *to* you that not even Solomon in all his glory clothed *himself* like one *of* these. **30** But if God dresses in this manner the grass *of* the field existing today and being thrown into *an* oven tomorrow, *will He* not *by* much more *care for* you— *ones* of-little-faith? **31** Therefore, do not be anxious[J], saying, 'What may we eat?' or 'What may we drink?' or 'What may we put-on?' **32** For the Gentiles are seeking-after all these *things.* For your heavenly Father knows that you have need *of* all these *things.* **33** But be seeking first the kingdom *of* God and His righteousness, and all these *things* will be added *to* you. **34** Therefore do not be anxious for tomorrow, for tomorrow will be anxious *for* itself. Sufficient *for* the day *is* the trouble[K] *of* it.

Don't Be Judgmental of Others. But Use Discernment In Your Actions Toward Others
7:1 "Do not be judging[L], in order that you may not be judged. **2** For with what judgment you judge, you will be judged; and with what measure you measure, it will be measured *to* you. **3** And why do you look-*at* the speck in the eye *of* your brother, but do not consider[M] the log in **your** eye? **4** Or how will you say *to* your brother, 'Permit me to take out the speck from your eye', and behold— the log *is* in your eye? **5** Hypocrite! First take out the log from your eye, and then you will see-clearly to take out the speck from the eye *of* your brother. **6** Do not give the holy *thing to* the dogs[N], nor throw your pearls in front of the pigs, so that they will not perhaps trample them with their feet, and having turned, tear you to pieces.

Keep Pursuing What You Need From God. He Will Give You Good Things
7 "Be asking, and it will be given *to* you; be seeking, and you will find; be knocking, and

---

A. Or, sincere, simple. That is, single-focused on God; or, spiritually healthy. **B.** Or, illuminated. **C.** That is, double-focused on wealth and God; or, sick, spiritually diseased. **D.** That is, if the spiritual 'light' your eye allows in is in fact darkness. **E.** That is, be serving as slave to. **F.** The slave will internally hate or love one master over the other, or he will express this in action, devoting himself to serving one while disregarding the other. **G.** Or, property, money. **H.** Or, be worried *about*, be concerned *about*. The grammar implies, stop being anxious, or, do not be in the habit of being anxious. **I.** That is, add 18 inches, one step, to his life's path. **J.** The grammar implies, do not become anxious, as also in v 34, addressing the issue as a whole. **K.** Or, misfortune, evil, badness. **L.** That is, in the sense of finding fault with, criticizing, passing judgment on. **M.** Or, notice, perceive. **N.** That is, unholy persons, God-rejecters, as in Rev 22:15. This statement balances v 1 and 3, since this requires a proper kind of judging.

it will be opened *to* you. [8] For everyone asking receives; and the *one* seeking finds; and *to* the *one* knocking, it will be opened. [9] Or what person is there from-*among* you whom his son will ask-*for* bread— he will not give him *a* stone[A], *will he?* [10] Or indeed he will ask-*for a* fish— he will not give him *a* snake[B], *will he?* [11] Therefore if **you**, being evil, know-*how* to give good gifts *to* your children, how much more will your Father in the heavens give good *things to* the *ones* asking Him!

Treat Others As You Yourself Want To Be Treated
[12] "Therefore, everything that you want[C] people to be doing *to* you, thus also **you** be doing *to* them. For this is the Law and the Prophets.

Enter God's Kingdom Through The Narrow Gate, Which Is Found By Few
[13] "Enter through the narrow gate, because wide *is* the gate and broad[D] *is* the road leading-away to destruction— and many are the *ones* entering through it. [14] How narrow *is* the gate and constricted[E] *is* the road leading-away to life— and few are the *ones* finding it.

Beware of False Prophets. The Nature of What They Produce Will Reveal Them
[15] "Beware of the false-prophets— who come to you in *the* clothing *of* sheep, but inside are ravenous[F] wolves. [16] You will know them by their fruits. They do not collect grapes from thorns, or figs from thistles, *do they?* [17] Thus, every good tree produces good fruit, but the bad tree produces bad[G] fruit. [18] *A* good tree is not able to produce bad fruit, nor *is a* bad tree *able* to produce good[H] fruit. [19] Every tree not producing good fruit is cut down and thrown into *the* fire. [20] So indeed, you will know them by their fruits.

Not Everyone Talking About God Knows Him. Only Those Doing His Will Enter His Kingdom
[21] "Not everyone saying *to* Me, 'Lord, Lord', will enter into the kingdom *of* the heavens, but the *one* doing the will *of* My Father in the heavens. [22] Many will say *to* Me on that day, 'Lord, Lord, did we not prophesy *in* Your name, and cast-out demons *in* Your name, and do many miracles[I] *in* Your name?' [23] And then I will declare[J] *to* them that 'I never knew[K] you. Depart from Me, *ones* working lawlessness'. [24] Therefore everyone who hears these words *of* Mine and is doing them will be-like *a* wise[L] man who built his house upon the bed-rock. [25] And the rain came down, and the rivers[M] came, and the winds blew— and they fell against that house. And it did not fall, for it had been founded upon the bed-rock. [26] And everyone hearing these words *of* Mine and not doing them will be like *a* foolish man who built his house upon the sand. [27] And the rain came down, and the rivers came, and the winds blew— and they struck-against that house. And it fell, and the falling[N] *of* it was great".

A. That is, something useless. **B.** That is, something harmful. **C.** Or, wish, desire, intend. **D.** Or, spacious, roomy. **E.** Or, pressed in, compressed. **F.** Or, thieving, vicious. **G:** good ... good... bad... bad. Two different words are used for 'good' and 'bad' here. Jesus may mean every 'beneficial' type of tree (like a fruit tree) produces fruit 'fit' to eat, but every 'unusable' type of tree produces 'useless' fruit or none at all. Or, He may mean every 'good' fruit tree produces 'healthy' fruit, but the 'rotten' fruit tree produces 'bad' fruit or none at all. **H:** good... bad... bad... good. That is, the 'beneficial' type of tree cannot produce 'useless' fruit, nor the 'unusable' tree fruit 'fit' to eat; or, the 'good' fruit tree cannot produce 'bad' fruit, nor can the 'rotten' fruit tree produce 'healthy' fruit. **I.** Or, *works of* power. **J.** Or. confess. **K.** That is, as one of My family. **L.** Or, prudent, sensible. **M.** That is, rivers of flood waters. **N.** Or, collapse, downfall.

The Works of The King: Divine Power In Action

28 And it came about *that* when Jesus finished these words, the crowds were astounded[A] at His teaching. **29** For He was teaching them as *One* having authority, and not as their scribes. **8:1** And[B] He having come down from the mountain, large crowds followed Him.

Because Jesus Is Willing And Able To Heal, He Heals a Man With Leprosy

2 And behold— *a* leper having come to *Him* was prostrating-*himself before* Him, saying, "Master, if You are willing, You are able to cleanse me". **3** And having stretched-out *His* hand, He touched him, saying, "I am willing[C]. Be cleansed". And immediately his leprosy was cleansed. **4** And Jesus says *to* him, "See *that* you tell no one. But go, show yourself *to* the priest, and offer the gift which Moses commanded, for *a* testimony *to* them".

Because of a Master's Faith, Jesus Heals a Paralyzed Servant Who Is Not Even Present

5 And He having entered into Capernaum, *a* centurion[D] came to Him, appealing-to Him **6** and saying, "Master, my servant has been put in the house paralyzed, being terribly tormented". **7** And He says *to* him, "Having come, I will[E] cure him". **8** And having responded, the centurion said, "Master, I am not fit that You should come-in under my roof. But only speak *it in a* word[F] and my servant will be healed. **9** For I also am *a* man under authority, having soldiers under myself. And I say *to* this *one*, 'Go!' and he goes; and *to* another, 'Come!' and he comes; and *to* my slave, 'Do this!' and he does *it*". **10** Now having heard, Jesus marveled, and said *to* the *ones* following, "Truly I say *to* you, with no one in Israel did I find so-great *a* faith! **11** And I say *to* you that many will come from east and west, and will lie-back [to eat] with Abraham and Isaac and Jacob in the kingdom *of* the heavens. **12** But the sons *of*[G] the kingdom will be thrown out into the outer darkness. In that place, there will be the weeping and the grinding *of* teeth". **13** And Jesus said *to* the centurion, "Go. Let it be done *for* you as you believed". And his servant was healed at that hour.

The Healings Done By Jesus Fulfill What Was Predicted of Him In Isaiah

14 And Jesus, having come into the house *of* Peter, saw his mother-in-law having been put *in bed*, and being sick-with-fever. **15** And He touched her hand, and the fever left her. And she arose, and was serving Him. **16** And having become evening, they brought to Him many being demon-possessed. And He cast-out the spirits *with a* word and cured all the *ones* being ill, **17** so that the *thing* might be fulfilled having been spoken through Isaiah the prophet saying "**He** took our weaknesses[H], and carried *our* diseases" [Isa 53:4].

Jesus Calls His Followers To Set Aside Earthly Goals And Limitations

18 Now Jesus, having seen *a* crowd around Him, gave-orders to depart to the other side. **19** And having come to *Him*, one scribe said *to* Him, "Teacher, I will follow You wherever You go". **20** And Jesus says *to* him, "The foxes have holes and the birds *of* the heaven *have* nests, but the Son *of* Man does not have[I] *a place* where He may lay *His* head". **21** And

---

A. Or, overwhelmed, amazed, astonished. **B.** Matthew now turns to the miracles of the King, giving samples from various periods of Christ's ministry. **C.** Jesus alone heals in His own name, without calling upon God. **D.** That is, a Roman commander of a hundred soldiers. **E:** Having come, I will cure him. Or, Shall I, having come, cure him? **F.** That is, a word of command. **G.** That is, those who appeared to be destined to inherit the kingdom; the Jews. **H.** Or, infirmities, sicknesses. Christ's physical healings point to His identity as the One in Isa 53. This prophecy is ultimately fulfilled in His healing of our spiritual disease. **I.** That is, Jesus is not going to an earthly home or destiny to which this man can follow Him.

another *of* His disciples said *to* Him, "Master, permit me first to go and bury[A] my father". [22] But Jesus says *to* him, "Be following Me, and allow the dead to bury their *own* dead".

Even The Winds And Sea Obey Jesus

[23] And He having gotten into the boat, His disciples followed Him. [24] And behold— *a* great shaking took place in the sea, so that the boat *was* being covered by the waves. But **He** was sleeping. [25] And having gone to *Him*, they woke Him, saying, "Master, save *us*. We are perishing". [26] And He says *to* them, "Why are you afraid, *ones* of-little-faith?" Then having arisen, He rebuked the winds and the sea. And there was *a* great calm. [27] And the men marveled, saying, "What kind of *man* is this *One*, that[B] even[C] the winds and the sea obey Him?"

Demons Recognize Jesus As The Son of God, And Submit To His Authority Over Them

[28] And He having come to the other side, to the country *of* the Gadarenes, two *men* being demon-possessed met Him, coming out of the tombs. *They were* very violent[D], so that no one *was* strong-*enough* to pass through that way. [29] And behold— they cried-out, saying, "What do we have to do with You[E], Son *of* God? Did You come here to torment us before *the* time?" [30] Now there was *a* herd *of* many pigs feeding far away from them. [31] And the demons were begging Him, saying, "If You are casting us out, send us out into the herd *of* pigs". [32] And He said *to* them, "Go!" And the *ones,* having come out, went into the pigs. And behold— the whole herd rushed down the steep-bank into the sea and died in the waters. [33] And the *ones* feeding[F] *them* fled. And having gone into the city, they reported everything— even the *things about* the *ones* being demon-possessed. [34] And behold— the whole city came out to meet *with* Jesus. And having seen Him, they begged that He pass on from their districts.

Jesus Heals a Paralyzed Man To Prove He Has The Authority To Forgive Sins

9:1 And having gotten into *a* boat, He crossed-over and came to *His* own city[G]. [2] And behold— they were bringing to Him *a* paralytic having been put on *a* bed. And Jesus, having seen their faith, said *to* the paralytic, "Take-courage, child. Your sins are forgiven". [3] And behold— some *of* the scribes said within themselves, "This *One* is blaspheming". [4] And Jesus, having seen their thoughts, said "Why are you thinking evil *things* in your hearts? [5] For which is easier: to say 'Your sins are forgiven', or to say 'Arise, and walk'? [6] But in order that you may know that the Son *of* Man has authority on earth to forgive sins"— then He says *to* the paralytic, "Having arisen, pick up your bed and go to your house". [7] And having arisen, he went to his house. [8] And having seen *it*, the crowds were awed[H]. And they glorified God, the *One* having given such authority *to* humans[I].

Jesus Calls Matthew The Tax Collector And Eats With His Friends. I Came For Sinners

[9] And while Jesus *was* passing on from there, He saw *a* man sitting at the tax-office, being called Matthew. And He says *to* him, "Be following Me!" And having stood up, he followed Him. [10] And it came about while He *was* reclining-back [to eat] in the[J] house that behold— many tax-collectors and sinners[K], having come, were reclining-back-with

---

A. This man's father may have just died; or, he may mean 'Let me fulfill my duty to my father. When he dies, I will follow You.' **B.** Or because. **C.** Or, both. **D.** Or, troublesome. **E.** Lit, What *is there for* us and *for* You? **F.** Or, tending, grazing, driving to pasture. **G.** That is, Capernaum, 4:13. **H.** Or, afraid. **I.** Or, people, men, mankind. **J.** That is, Matthew's house, Lk 5:29. **K.** That is, irreligious people, living outside of God's laws.

Jesus and His disciples. **11** And having seen *it*, the Pharisees were saying *to* His disciples, "For what reason is your Teacher eating with the tax-collectors and sinners?" **12** And the *One*, having heard *it*, said, "The *ones* being strong have no need *of a* physician, but the *ones* being ill. **13** But having gone, learn what it means [in Hos 6:6]: 'I desire mercy, and not *a* sacrifice'. For I did not come to call righteous *ones*, but sinners".

Jesus Did Not Come To Patch Up The Old System, But To Inaugurate a New One
14 Then the disciples *of* John come to Him, saying "For what reason are we and the Pharisees fasting^A often, but Your disciples are not fasting?" **15** And Jesus said *to* them, "The sons *of* the wedding-hall^B cannot be mourning as long as the bridegroom is with them, *can they*? But days will come when the bridegroom is taken-away from them, and then they will fast. **16** And no one puts *a* patch *of* unshrunk cloth on *an* old garment. For the fullness *of* it takes^C from the garment and *a* worse tear takes place. **17** Nor do they put new wine into old wineskins. Otherwise indeed the wineskins are burst, and the wine spills out and the wineskins are ruined. But they put new wine into fresh^D wineskins, and both are preserved".

Jesus Raises a Girl After a Public Request, And Heals a Woman With a Secret Request
18 While He *was* speaking these *things to* them, behold— one [synagogue] official, having come, was prostrating-*himself before* Him, saying that "My daughter just-now came-to-an-end^E. But having come, lay Your hand on her, and she will live". **19** And having arisen, Jesus followed him, and [so did] His disciples. **20** And behold— *a* woman having-a-bloody-discharge^F *for* twelve years, having approached from behind, touched the tassel *of* His garment. **21** For she was saying within herself, "If I only touch His garment, I will be restored^G". **22** But Jesus, having turned and having seen her, said, "Take-courage, daughter. Your faith has restored you". And the woman was restored from that hour. **23** And Jesus, having come into the house *of* the official, and having seen the flute-players and the crowd being thrown-into-a-commotion^H, **24** was saying "Go away. For the little-girl did not die, but is sleeping". And they were laughing-scornfully *at* Him. **25** But when the crowd was put out, having gone in, He took-hold-of her hand and the little girl arose. **26** And this news went out into that whole land.

Jesus Gives Sight To The Blind
27 And while Jesus *was* passing on from there, two blind *men* followed Him, crying-out and saying, "Have-mercy-on us, Son *of* David!" **28** And *He* having gone into the house, the blind *men* came to Him. And Jesus says *to* them, "Do you believe that I am able to do this?" They say *to* Him, "Yes, Master". **29** Then He touched their eyes, saying, "Let it be done *to* you according-to^I your faith". **30** And their eyes were opened. And Jesus

A. John's disciples may have been fasting regarding his imprisonment or their own repentance and preparation. Some Pharisees fasted twice a week, Lk 18:12. **B.** That is, the groomsmen, the attendants of the groom, representing the disciples. **C.** During washing, the new patch 'takes' from the old garment, tearing it. Jesus is not a patch repairing the Jewish system. He is a new garment, so His disciples behave in a new way. **D.** Jesus, the new and fresh, cannot be contained within the old worn out Jewish system of that day. **E.** That is, died. **F.** Or, hemorrhaging, suffering a loss of blood. **G.** Or, saved (from this disease). **H.** That is, Jesus saw the funeral crowd expressing itself in the customary way. **I.** Or, in agreement with, corresponding to, based on.

sternly-commanded^A them, saying, "See *that* no one knows *it*". **31** But the *ones*, having gone forth, widely-spread [the news about] Him in that whole land.

Jesus Heals The Mute
32 And while they *were* going forth, behold— they brought to Him *a* mute man being demon-possessed. **33** And the demon having been cast-out, the mute *man* spoke. And the crowds marveled, saying, "It never was visible^B like this in Israel!" **34** But the Pharisees were saying, "He is casting out the demons by^C the ruler *of* the demons".

The King Sends Out Messengers To The Nation: Divine Compassion Reaches Out To The People
35 And Jesus was going around all the cities and the villages, teaching in their synagogues, and proclaiming the good-news *of* the kingdom, and curing every disease and every infirmity. **36** And having seen the crowds, He felt-deep-feelings [of compassion] concerning them, because they had been troubled^D and thrown-forth^E like sheep not having *a* shepherd. **37** Then He says *to* His disciples, "The harvest *is* great, but the workers *are* few! **38** Therefore ask the Lord *of* the harvest that He send-out workers into His harvest".

Jesus Grants The Twelve Power Over Demons And Every Disease
10:1 And having summoned His twelve disciples, He gave them authority *over* unclean spirits so as to be casting them out, and to be curing every disease and every infirmity. **2** Now the names *of* the twelve apostles are these— first, Simon (the *one* being called Peter) and Andrew (his brother), and James (the *son of* Zebedee) and John (his brother), **3** Philip and Bartholomew, Thomas and Matthew (the tax-collector), James (the *son of* Alphaeus) and Thaddaeus, **4** Simon (the Cananaean^F) and Judas the Iscariot^G (the *one* also having handed Him over).

Jesus Instructs The Twelve On Where To Go, What To Say, What To Do, How To Live
5 Jesus sent out these twelve, having instructed^H them, saying— "Do not go into *the* path *of* Gentiles, and do not enter into *a* city *of* Samaritans. **6** But be proceeding instead to the lost^I sheep *of the* house *of* Israel. **7** And while proceeding, be proclaiming, saying that 'The kingdom *of* the heavens has drawn near'. **8** Be curing *ones* being sick, raising dead *ones,* cleansing lepers, casting out demons. You received freely— give freely. **9** Do not acquire^J gold nor silver nor copper [money] for your [money] belts— **10** not *a* [traveler's] bag for *the* journey, nor two^K tunics, nor sandals, nor *a* staff. For the worker *is* worthy *of* his food. **11** And into whatever city or village you enter, search-out^L who is worthy in it, and stay there until you go forth. **12** And while entering into the house, greet^M it. **13** And if the house is worthy let your peace come upon it, but if it is not worthy let your peace return to you. **14** And whoever does not welcome you nor listen-to your words— shake-out the dust *from* your feet while going outside *of* that house or city. **15** Truly I say *to* you, it will be more-tolerable^N *for the* land *of* Sodom and Gomorrah on *the* day *of* judgment than *for* that city.

A. Or, sternly-warned. Jesus commanded them with intense emotion. **B:** was visible. Or, appeared. That is, nothing like this was done before. **C.** Or, in union with. **D.** Or, harassed, bothered. **E.** That is, scattered. Or, thrown down, as wounded or helpless. **F.** That is, the zealot. **G.** This may mean the one from Kerioth, a town in southern Judea or Moab. **H.** Or, commanded, ordered. **I.** Lit, having gotten lost, having become lost. **J.** Or, get, obtain, procure. **K.** That is, an extra undergarment, an extra pair of sandals, an extra staff (walking stick). Take no extra provisions, nor the means to buy or carry them. **L.** Or inquire into. **M.** That is, express good wishes and God's blessing toward the house and the people in it. **N.** Or, more endurable, more bearable.

Jesus Pre-Warns The Twelve About The Persecution They Will Face In The Future

16 "Behold— **I** am sending^A you out as sheep in *the* midst *of* wolves. Therefore be shrewd^B as the snakes, and innocent^C as the doves. **17** And beware of people. For they will hand you over to councils^D and whip you in their synagogues. **18** And you will even be brought before governors and kings for My sake— for *a* testimony *to* them^E and *to* the Gentiles. **19** But whenever they hand you over, do not be anxious-*about* how or what you should speak. For what you should speak will be given *to* you in that hour. **20** For **you** are not the *ones* speaking, but the Spirit *of* your Father *is* the *One* speaking in you. **21** And brother will hand-over brother to death, and *a* father *his* child. And children will rise-up-in-rebellion^F against parents and they will put them to death. **22** And you will be being hated by all because of My name. But the *one* having endured to *the* end^G, this *one* will be saved. **23** But whenever they persecute you in this city, flee to another. For truly I say *to* you— you will by no means finish the cities *of* Israel until the Son *of* Man comes^H.

Proclaim The Truth Boldly; Do Not Fear Them. God Will Watch Over You

24 "*A* disciple^I is not above the teacher, nor *is a* slave above his master. **25** *It is* enough *for* the disciple that he become like his teacher, and the slave like his master. If they called the Household-Master^J Beelzebul^K, how much more His household-members! **26** So do not fear^L them. For nothing has been covered which will not be revealed, and *is* secret which will not be known. **27** What I am saying *to* you in the darkness, speak in the light. And what you are hearing in *your* ear, proclaim upon the housetops. **28** And do not be fearing^M *anything* from the *ones* killing the body but not being able to kill the soul. But be fearing instead the *One* being able to destroy both soul and body in Gehenna^N. **29** Are not two sparrows sold *for an* assarion^O? And one of them will not fall on the ground apart from^P your Father. **30** But even the hairs *of* **your** head have all been numbered! **31** So do not be fearing. **You** are more valuable *than* many sparrows.

Jesus Instructs Them About His Mission: I Came To Divide The World Over Myself

32 "Everyone therefore who will confess Me in front of people, **I** also will confess him in front of My Father in the heavens. **33** But whoever denies^Q Me in front of people, **I** also will deny him in front of My Father in the heavens. **34** Do not suppose that I came to cast peace over the earth. I did not come to cast peace, but *a* sword. **35** For I came to cause-a-separation^R— *a* man against his father, and *a* daughter against her mother, and *a* daughter-in-law against her mother-in-law. **36** And *the* enemies *of* the person *will be* his household-members. **37** The *one* loving father or mother above Me is not worthy *of* Me. And the *one* loving son or daughter above Me is not worthy *of* Me. **38** And he

---

A. This section is prophetic, looking beyond this mission to their life ministry and beyond. **B.** Or, wise, prudent. **C.** Or, pure. **D.** That is, local Jewish courts, local sanhedrins. **E.** That is, the Jews. **F.** Or, stand-up against. **G.** That is, the end of his life, or the second Coming, whichever comes first. **H.** That is, comes to you at the end of this preaching tour; or, comes as Messiah in Jerusalem in 21:9; or, the coming may refer to His transfiguration, or resurrection, or to the day of Pentecost, or to His coming to destroy Jerusalem in A.D. 70, or to His second Coming. **I.** Or, learner, pupil, student. **J.** That is, Jesus. **K.** That is, the devil. **L.** The grammar implies, Do not become fearful of them. **M.** The grammar implies, Stop fearing or, Do not be in the habit of fearing. **N.** That is, hell. **O.** This Roman coin was worth 1/16th of a denarius (a day's wage). **P.** That is, without His consent. **Q.** Or, repudiates. **R.** Or, divide in two, separate, disunite.

who is not taking his cross^A and following after Me is not worthy *of* Me. **39** The *one* having found his life will lose it, and the *one* having lost his life for My sake will find it. **40** The *one* welcoming^B you is welcoming Me. And the *one* welcoming Me is welcoming the One having sent Me forth. **41** The *one* welcoming *a* prophet in *the* name^C *of a* prophet will receive *the* reward *of a* prophet. And the *one* welcoming *a* righteous *one* in *the* name *of a* righteous *one* will receive *the* reward *of a* righteous *one*. **42** And whoever gives one *of* these little *ones* only *a* cup *of* cold *water* to drink in *the* name *of a* disciple— truly I say *to* you he will by no means lose his reward".

After Commissioning The Twelve, Jesus Moves On To Teach In Other Cities
11:1 And it came about *that* when Jesus finished giving-directions *to* His twelve disciples, He passed-on from there *that He might* teach and proclaim in their cities.

John The Baptist Asks, Are You The King? Jesus Points Him To His Works
2 Now John^D, having in prison heard-*of* the works *of* the Christ, having sent through his disciples, **3** said *to* Him, "Are **You** the *One* coming^E, or should we be looking-for *a* different *one*?" **4** And having responded, Jesus said *to* them, "Having gone, report *to* John *the things* which you are hearing and seeing^F— **5** blind *ones* are seeing-again and lame *ones* are walking. Lepers are being cleansed and deaf *ones* are hearing. And dead *ones* are being raised and poor *ones* are having-good-news-announced^G *to them*. **6** And blessed is whoever does not take-offense^H in Me".

Jesus Says John The Baptist Is The Fulfillment of The Prophecies of Malachi
7 And while these *ones were* proceeding, Jesus began to speak *to* the crowds about John— "What^I did you go out into the wilderness to look-*at*? *A* reed being shaken by *the* wind? **8** But what did you go out to see? *A* man having been dressed in soft *garments*? Behold— the *ones* wearing the soft *garments* are in the houses *of* kings! **9** But what did you go out to see? *A* prophet? Yes, I say *to* you, and more *than a* prophet. **10** This *one* is about whom it has been written [in Mal 3:1]: 'Behold— **I** am sending-forth My messenger ahead *of* Your presence, who will make Your way ready in front of You'. **11** Truly I say *to* you, *a* greater^J *one than* John the Baptist has not arisen among *ones* born *of* women. But the least^K *one* in the kingdom *of* the heavens is greater^L *than* he. **12** But the kingdom *of* the heavens is being treated-violently^M from the days *of* John the Baptist until now, and violent *ones*

A. That is, carrying the instrument of his death, his suffering loss for Him, his death to self for Him. In this context, rejection by family members is in view. Note that this is an ongoing, life-long matter. **B.** Or, accepting. **C.** That is, because he is a prophet. **D.** Matthew now uses John to 'prepare the way' again by asking the key question, Are You the One? What follows details how Jesus both hid and revealed the answer as He responded to opposition and continued His words of revelation, culminating in the response of Peter in 16:16. **E.** Or, the coming *One*. That is, the Messiah. **F.** As His answer, Jesus lists things Isaiah prophesied that Messiah would do. His works answer John's question. **G.** Or, are being evangelized, are being told good news. **H.** Or, is not caused to fall by Me. **I.** Or, Why. In this case the three questions would be punctuated this way: Why did you go out into the wilderness? To look-*at a* reed...? **J.** That is, greater in character, in obedience to God; or, greater in what John would know and do with regard to the Messiah. **K.** Or, lesser. **L.** That is, in privilege, as adult family members, co-heirs with the King. John belongs to the OT period of childhood. **M:** treated violently... violent *ones* are snatching it away. That is, the kingdom is being attacked by enemies like Herod and the Pharisees, who are snatching away the people and the message of the kingdom; or, the kingdom is 'forcefully advancing' (or passively, is being forced, taken by storm), and the 'forceful' (in a positive sense, the spiritually bold) are 'seizing hold' of it; or, the kingdom is 'suffering violence', and the violent ones (like the Zealots) are trying to establish it by force.

are snatching it away. **13** For all the prophets and the Law prophesied until John. **14** And if you are willing to accept *it*, he himself is Elijah— the *one* going-to^A come. **15** Let the *one* having ears hear^B.

But This Generation Rejects Both The One Preparing And The One Who Came
16 "But *to* what will I liken this generation? It is like children sitting in the marketplaces who, calling to the others, **17** say 'We played the flute *for* you and you did not dance. We lamented^C and you did not beat-your-breast^D'. **18** For John came neither eating nor drinking^E, and they say 'He has *a* demon'. **19** The Son *of* Man came eating and drinking, and they say 'Behold— *a* man *who is a* glutton and drunkard^F, *a* friend *of* tax-collectors and sinners'. And wisdom was vindicated^G by her works^H".

Woe To You Cities Who Have Seen My Works And Not Repented
20 Then He began to reproach^I the cities in which most-of ^J His miracles took place, because they did not repent. **21** "Woe *to* you, Chorazin! Woe *to* you, Bethsaida! Because if the miracles having taken place in you had taken place in Tyre and Sidon, they would have repented long ago in sackcloth and ashes. **22** Nevertheless^K I say *to* you— it will be more tolerable *for* Tyre and Sidon on *the* day *of* judgment than *for* you. **23** And you, Capernaum, will you be exalted up to heaven? You will go-down as far as Hades. Because if the miracles having taken place in you had been done in Sodom, it would have remained until today. **24** Nevertheless I say *to* you that it will be more tolerable *for* the land *of* Sodom on *the* day *of* judgment than *for* you".

It Pleases God To Hide The Kingdom From The Wise And Reveal It To The Childlike
25 At that time, having responded, Jesus said, "I praise You, Father, Lord *of* heaven and earth, that^L You hid these *things* from wise *ones* and intelligent *ones,* and You revealed them *to* children^M. **26** Yes, Father, because^N in-this-manner it became well-pleasing in Your sight. **27** All *things* were handed-over *to* Me by My Father. And no one knows^O the Son except the Father. Nor does anyone know the Father except the Son, and *anyone to* whom^P the Son wills^Q to reveal *Him*. **28** Come to Me, all the *ones* being weary and having been burdened^R, and **I** will give you rest. **29** Take My yoke upon you and learn from Me, because I am gentle and humble *in* heart, and you will find rest *for* your souls. **30** For My yoke *is* easy^S, and My burden^T is light".

Regarding The Sabbath, Jesus Makes Himself The Issue: I Am Lord of The Sabbath
12:1 At that time Jesus went through the grainfields *on* the Sabbath. And His disciples

---

A. That is, according to Mal 4:5-6. **B.** If John is Elijah, then Jesus is Messiah. **C.** Or, sang a funeral song. **D.** That is, in mourning. **E.** That is, John did not socialize with them. Jesus did the opposite, eating and drinking with all the people. The Jews rejected them both. **F.** Jesus associates with people who eat and drink too much, so He must be guilty of the same! Yet He was no more guilty of this than that John had a demon. **G.** Or, declared right. **H.** That is, the results it produced. **I.** Or, scold, reprimand. **J.** Or, His very great miracles. **K.** That is, in spite of the fact that they did not repent and were judged by God, I say to you by comparison. Or, But. But in contrast to what you may think about them, I say to you. **L.** Or, because. **M.** Or, childlike *ones.* **N.** Or, that; Yes, Father, *I praise you* that. **O.** Or, understands, fully-knows; knows as a family member. **P.** Or, *to* whomever. **Q.** Or, wishes, wants, desires. **R.** That is, loaded down with burdens to carry, given a heavy yoke to pull. **S.** Lit, good, with the sense of what one carrying a load would consider good: easy, pleasant. **T.** Or, load, cargo.

were hungry and began to pluck[A] heads [of grain] and eat. [2] And the Pharisees, having seen *it*, said *to* Him, "Behold— Your disciples are doing what is not lawful to be doing on *a* Sabbath". [3] And the *One* said *to* them, "Did you not read [in 1 Sam 21:1-6] what David did when he was hungry, and the *ones* with him— [4] how he entered into the house *of* God and they ate the Bread *of* Presentation[B] which it was not lawful *for* him to eat, nor *for* the *ones* with him, but *for* the priests alone? [5] Or did you not read in the Law that *on* the Sabbaths, the priests in the temple profane[C] the Sabbath and are guiltless[D]? [6] But I say *to* you that *a* greater-*thing than* the temple is here. [7] But if you had known what it means [in Hos 6:6]— 'I desire mercy, and not *a* sacrifice'— you would not have condemned the guiltless *ones*. [8] For the Son *of* Man is **Lord** *of* the Sabbath[E]".

Jesus Deliberately Heals a Man On The Sabbath, Inflaming The Pharisees

[9] And having passed-on from there, He went into their synagogue. [10] And behold— *there was a* man having *a* withered hand. And they questioned Him, saying, 'Is it lawful to cure *on* the Sabbath?'— in order that they might accuse Him. [11] And the *One* said *to* them, "What person will there be from-*among* you who will have one sheep, and if this *sheep* falls into *a* pit *on* the Sabbath, will not take hold of it and raise *it*? [12] How much then is *a* person more-valuable *than a* sheep! So then, it is lawful to be acting commendably[F] *on* the Sabbath". [13] Then He says *to* the man, "Stretch-out your hand". And he stretched *it* out, and it was restored, healthy like the other. [14] And having gone out, the Pharisees took counsel against Him, so that they might destroy Him.

Jesus Speaks By His Actions. He Does Not Quarrel Or Shout, Fulfilling Isaiah

[15] But Jesus, having known *it*, withdrew from there. And large crowds followed Him, and He cured them all. [16] And He warned them that they should not make Him known, [17] in order that the *thing* might be fulfilled having been spoken through Isaiah the prophet saying [18] "Behold My servant Whom I chose, My Beloved in Whom My soul was[G] well-pleased: I will put My Spirit upon Him, and He will announce[H] justice *to* the Gentiles. [19] He will not quarrel, nor shout, nor will anyone hear His voice in the wide-roads. [20] He will not break *a* reed having been bruised, and He will not quench *a* smoldering wick, until He leads-out[I] justice[J] to victory. [21] And *the* Gentiles will put-hope *in* His name" [Isa 42:1-4].

The Crowds Call Jesus The Messiah. The Pharisees Attribute His Power To The Devil

[22] Then *a* blind and mute *man* being demon-possessed was brought to Him. And He cured him, so that the mute *man was* speaking and seeing. [23] And all the crowds were astonished, and were saying, "This *One* is not the Son *of* David, *is He*?" [24] But the Pharisees, having heard *it*, said, "This *One* is not casting out the demons except by Beelzebul, *the ruler of* the demons!"

Such Blasphemy Against The Spirit Will Not Be Forgiven

[25] And knowing their thoughts, He said *to* them— "Every kingdom having been

---

A. The Law permitted this, Deut 23:25. **B.** That is, the bread 'presented to' or 'set-before' God, Lev 24:6-9. See Mk 2:26. **C.** That is, treat as common, as an ordinary work day. In other words, the temple ministry is more important than the Sabbath. And Jesus is more important than the temple. **D.** Or, innocent, without accusation. **E.** Compare Mk 2:27. **F.** Or, rightly, appropriately, well. God did not forbid doing good on the Sabbath. Compare Mk 3:4. **G.** See 3:17. **H.** Or, declare, proclaim. **I.** Or, brings out, sends out, takes out. **J.** Or, judgment.

divided against itself is desolated, and every city or house having been divided against itself will not stand; **26** and if Satan is casting-out Satan, he was divided against himself. How then will his kingdom stand? **27** And if **I** am casting out the demons by Beelzebul, by whom^A are **your sons** casting *them* out? For this reason **they** will be your judges; **28** but if **I** am casting out the demons by *the* Spirit *of* God, then the kingdom *of* God came^B upon you. **29** Or how can anyone enter into the house *of* the strong *man* and snatch-away his things unless he first binds the strong *man*? And then he will plunder his house. **30** The *one* not being with Me^C is against Me. And the *one* not gathering with Me is scattering. **31** For this reason I say *to* you— every sin and blasphemy will be forgiven *to* people. But the blasphemy *against* the Spirit will not be forgiven^D. **32** And whoever speaks *a* word against the Son *of* Man, it will be forgiven *to* him. But whoever speaks against the Holy Spirit, it will not be forgiven *to* him— neither in this age nor in the *one* coming. **33** Either make the tree good and its fruit good, or make the tree bad and its fruit bad^E. For the tree is known by the fruit. **34** Brood *of* vipers! How are you able to speak good *things,* being evil? For the mouth speaks out of the abundance *of* the heart— **35** the good person brings out good *things* from *his* good treasure^F, and the evil person brings out evil *things* from *his* evil treasure. **36** And I say *to* you that every useless^G word which people will speak— they will render *an* account for it on *the* day *of* judgment. **37** For by your words you will be declared-righteous, and by your words you will be condemned".

Pharisees Ask Jesus For a Sign. He Offers Only The Sign of Jonah: Three Days In a Grave
38 Then some *of* the scribes and Pharisees responded *to* Him, saying "Teacher, we want to see *a* sign from You". **39** But the *One*, having responded, said *to* them— "*An* evil and adulterous^H generation is seeking-for *a* sign. And *a* sign will not be given *to* it, except the sign *of* Jonah the prophet. **40** For just as Jonah was three days and three nights in the belly *of* the sea-creature^I, so the Son *of* Man will be three days and three nights^J in the heart *of* the earth.

The Ninevites Will Condemn This Generation, For They Repented At Jonah's Message
41 "Ninevite men will rise-up at the judgment with this generation, and they will condemn it. Because they repented at the proclamation *of* Jonah, and behold— *a* greater *thing than* Jonah *is* here. **42** The Queen *of the* South will be raised at the judgment with this generation, and she will condemn it. Because she came from the ends *of* the earth to hear the wisdom *of* Solomon, and behold— *a* greater *thing than* Solomon *is* here.

The Demons I Cast Out Now Will Return Later, And You Will Be Worse Off
43 "Now when the unclean spirit departs from the person, it goes through waterless

---

A. The reasoning required to prove that the Jews are not using the power of Satan to cast out demons will also prove it in the case of Jesus. **B.** Or arrived. **C.** That is, not standing with Me. **D.** To attribute the works and power of Jesus to Satan is to speak against the Spirit empowering Him. **E:** make the tree good... or... bad. That is, either make the tree (Jesus) good and the fruit (His works) good... or bad. You can't say that His miracles are good and He is from Satan. Or, either make the tree (you Pharisees) good and its fruit (repentance, believing Jesus) good... or bad. Make your choice about Me! **F.** Or, treasury, treasure house. **G.** Or, unproductive, idle, not working, and therefore, non-edifying, unprofitable, worthless. **H.** That is, spiritually unfaithful to God. **I.** Or, huge fish. This is a generic term used of large sea creatures. **J.** A day and a night is one day, as in Gen 1:5. This is another way of saying 'three days'. It does not mean 72 hours.

places seeking rest[A], and does not find *it*. **44** Then it says, 'I will return to my house from where I came-out'. And having come, it finds *it* being unoccupied, having been swept and put-in-order[B]. **45** Then it proceeds and takes along with itself seven other spirits more evil *than* itself. And having gone in, they dwell there, and the last[C] *state of* that person becomes worse *than* the first. So it will be[D] also *with* this evil generation".

Jesus Says That Whoever Does The Will of God Is His Brother And Sister And Mother
46 While He *was* still speaking *to* the crowds, behold— His mother and brothers were standing outside, seeking to speak *to* Him. **47** And someone said *to* Him, "Behold— Your mother and Your brothers are standing outside, seeking to speak *to* You". **48** But the *One*, having responded, said *to* the *one* speaking *to* Him, "Who is My mother and who are My brothers?" **49** And having stretched-out His hand toward His disciples, He said "Behold— My mother and My brothers! **50** For whoever does the will *of* My Father in *the* heavens— **he** is My brother and sister and mother".

Jesus Teaches The Crowds Using Parables
13:1 On that day Jesus, having gone out *of* the house, sat beside the sea. **2** And large crowds were gathered-together with Him so that He, having gotten into *a* boat, sits-*down* [to teach]. And the whole crowd was standing on the shore. **3** And He spoke many *things to* them in parables, saying—

The Sower's Seed Falls On Different Kinds of Soil. Only The Good Soil Produces Fruit
"Behold— the *one* sowing went out *that he might* sow. **4** And during his sowing, some *seeds* fell along the road. And having come, the birds ate them up. **5** And others fell on the rocky[E] *places* where they were not having much soil. And immediately they sprang-up, because of not having *a* depth *of* soil. **6** But *the* sun having risen, they were scorched. And because of not having *a* root, they were dried-up. **7** And others fell on the thorns. And the thorns came up and choked[F] them. **8** And others fell on the good soil and were giving fruit— one *a* hundred, and another sixty, and another thirty. **9** Let the *one* having ears, hear".

Jesus Tells His Disciples He Uses Parables To Both Hide And Reveal The Truth
10 And having come to *Him*, the disciples said *to* Him, "For what reason are You speaking *to* them in parables?" **11** And the *One*, having responded, said *to* them, "Because it has been given *to* you to know[G] the mysteries[H] *of* the kingdom *of* the heavens. But it has not been given *to* those *ones*. **12** For whoever has— it will be given *to* him, and he will be caused to abound. But whoever does not have— even what he has will be taken-away from him. **13** For this reason I am speaking *to* them in parables— because while seeing, they are not seeing; and while hearing, they are not hearing, nor understanding. **14** And the prophecy *of* Isaiah is being fulfilled *in* them, the *one*[I] saying [in Isa 6:9-10]: '*In* hearing, you will

---

A. Or, *a* resting place. **B.** Or, adorned, decorated. **C.** Lit, last *things*. **D.** Jesus is casting out demons and putting Israel's house in order. But upon this evil generation's rejection of Him, the demons will return and Israel will be worse off. **E.** That is, bedrock or rocky outcroppings. **F.** Or, strangled, suffocated. **G.** Or, understand. **H.** That is, the things formerly hidden, but now being revealed by Jesus. **I.** That is, the prophecy saying.

hear and by no means understand. And while seeing, you will see and by no means perceive. [15] For the heart *of* this people became dull[A], and they hardly[B] heard *with their* ears, and they closed their eyes that[C] they might not ever see *with their* eyes, and hear *with their* ears, and understand *in their* heart and turn-back, and I shall heal[D] them'. [16] But blessed[E] *are* **your** eyes because they are seeing, and your ears, because they are hearing. [17] For truly I say *to* you that many prophets and righteous *ones* desired to experience[F] *the things* which you are seeing, and they did not experience *them*, and to hear *the things* which you are hearing, and they did not hear *them.*

Jesus Explains The Parable of The Sower To His Disciples

[18] "**You** therefore, hear the parable *of* the *one* having sown: [19] Anyone hearing the word[G] *of* the kingdom and not understanding *it*— the evil *one* comes and snatches-away the *thing* having been sown in his heart. This *person* is the *one* having been sown *the seed* along the road. [20] And the *one* having been sown *the seed* on the rocky *places*— this *person* is the *one* hearing the word and immediately receiving it with joy. [21] And he does not have *a* root in himself, but is temporary[H]. And affliction or persecution having come about because of the word— immediately he is caused-to-fall. [22] And the *one* having been sown *the seed* into the thorns— this *person* is the *one* hearing the word, and the anxiety[I] *of the* age[J] and the deceitfulness[K] *of* riches is choking the word, and it becomes unfruitful. [23] And the *one* having been sown *the seed* on the good soil— this *person* is the *one* hearing the word and understanding[L] *it,* who indeed[M] is bearing-fruit[N] and producing: one *a* hundred, and another sixty, and another thirty".

A Field Is Sown With Good And Bad Seed: At Harvest The Weeds Will Be Burned

[24] He put-before them another parable, saying, "The kingdom *of* the heavens became-like[O] *a* man having sown good seed in his field. [25] But during the men's sleeping, his enemy came and re-sowed[P] darnel[Q] between the wheat, and went away. [26] Now when the grass budded and produced fruit[R], then the darnel appeared also. [27] And having come to *him*, the slaves *of* the house-master said *to* him, 'Master, did you not sow good seed in your field? Then from where does it have *the* darnel?' [28] And the *one* said *to* them, '*A* hostile man did this'. And the slaves say *to* him, 'Then do you want us, having gone, to collect them?' [29] But the *one* says, 'No, that while collecting the darnel, you may not perhaps uproot the wheat together with them. [30] Permit both to grow together until the harvest. And at *the* time *of* the harvest I will say *to* the harvesters, "Collect first the darnel, and bind them into bundles so-as to burn them up. But gather the wheat into my barn" ' ".

A. Or, thick, fat, insensitive. **B.** That is, with difficulty. They are spiritually hard of hearing. **C.** This expresses the purpose of the people. They willfully closed their eyes to God that they might not ever see what they did not want to see, and never have to change their ways and return to God. **D.** Or, would heal. This is what God would do if they saw, heard, understood, and turned back, but they refuse to take this path. **E.** Or, fortunate. **F.** Or, see, but not the same word as next. **G.** Or, message. **H.** Or, transitory. **I.** Or, concern, care. **J.** Or, world; that is, this life. **K.** Or, deception. **L.** This is in contrast with the first soil, v 19. **M.** Or, now, at this time; or, therefore. **N.** This is in contrast with the second two soils. **O.** Or, was like. Jesus may be speaking prophetically from the point of view of the end of the age; or, He may mean this in a timeless sense, 'is like'. **P.** Or, over-sowed. **Q.** This is a weed that is indistinguishable from wheat in its early stages. **R.** That is, heads of grain.

The Mustard Seed: God's Kingdom Will Start Very Small And Grow Very Large

31 He put-before them another parable, saying, "The kingdom *of* the heavens is like *a* seed *of a* mustard-plant, which having taken, *a* man sowed in his field— **32** which is smaller *than* all the seeds, but when it grows is larger *than* the garden-plants. And it becomes *a* tree^A, so that the birds *of* the heaven come and are nesting in its branches".

Like Leaven In Bread, God's Kingdom Will Permeate The World

33 He spoke another parable *to* them, "The kingdom *of* the heavens is like leaven, which having taken, *a* woman concealed^B into three measures^C *of* wheat-flour until which *time the* whole *thing* was leavened".

Jesus Spoke In Parables In Fulfillment of Psalm 78:2

34 Jesus spoke all these *things to* the crowds in parables. And He was speaking nothing *to* them apart from *a* parable, **35** so that the *thing* might be fulfilled having been spoken through the prophet saying "I will open My mouth in parables. I will utter *things* having been hidden since *the* foundation *of the* world" [Ps 78:2].

Jesus Teaches His Disciples Using Parables

36 Then, having left the crowds, He went into the house. And His disciples came to Him, saying, "Make-clear *to* us the parable *of* the darnel *of* the field". **37** And the *One*, having responded, said—

Jesus Explains The Parable of The Good And Bad Seed Sown In The Field

"The *one* sowing the good seed is the Son *of* Man. **38** And the field is the world. And the good seed— these are the sons *of* ^D the kingdom. And the darnel are the sons *of* the evil *one*. **39** And the enemy having sown them is the devil. And the harvest is *the* conclusion *of the* age. And the harvesters are angels. **40** Therefore, just as the darnel is collected and burned up *with* fire, so it will be at the conclusion *of* the age. **41** The Son *of* Man will send out His angels, and they will collect out of His kingdom all the causes-of-falling and the *ones* doing lawlessness. **42** And they will throw them into the furnace *of* ^E fire. In that place, there will be the weeping and the grinding *of* teeth. **43** Then the righteous *ones* will shine-forth like the sun in the kingdom *of* their Father. Let the *one* having ears, hear.

God's Kingdom Is Like a Hidden Treasure Worth Selling All You Have To Obtain

44 "The kingdom *of* the heavens is like *a* treasure having been hidden in the field, which having found, *a* man hid. And from his joy^F, he goes and sells all that he has and buys that field. **45** Again, the kingdom *of* the heavens is like *a* man *who is a* merchant seeking fine pearls. **46** And having found one very-valuable pearl, having gone, he has sold all that he was having, and he bought it.

A. That is, in relative size. Compare Mk 4:32. **B.** Or, hid in. Normally, we would say 'mixed into', but this puts emphasis on the mixer and the mixing. Jesus is putting emphasis on the hiddenness of the leaven within the flour, and its transforming of the whole from within. **C.** Or seah, a Hebrew measure, amounting here to about six gallons or 25 liters, a batch size seen in Gen 18:6. **D.** That is, belonging to. **E.** That is, characterized by fire; the fiery furnace. **F.** Or, from the joy *of* it.

God's Kingdom Is Like a Net Catching Every Kind of Fish. The Bad Are Thrown Out
47 "Again, the kingdom *of* the heavens is like *a* drag-net^A having been cast into the sea and having gathered *fish* of every kind— **48** which, when it was filled, having pulled *it* up on the shore, and having sat-*down*, they collected the good *ones* into containers and threw the bad^B *ones* outside. **49** So it will be at the conclusion *of* the age. The angels will go forth and separate the evil *ones* out of *the* midst *of* the righteous *ones*. **50** And they will throw them into the furnace *of* fire. In that place, there will be the weeping and the grinding *of* teeth.

Teachers in My Kingdom Will Expound From a Treasure of Old And New Things
51 "Did you understand all these *things*?" They say *to* Him, "Yes". **52** And the *One* said *to* them, "For this reason^C, every scribe^D having become-a-disciple^E in^F the kingdom *of* the heavens is like *a* man *who is a* house-master, who brings out new *things* and old^G *things* from his treasure".

The Hometown People Are Astounded At Jesus, But Unbelieving
53 And it came about *that* when Jesus finished these parables, He went-away from there. **54** And having come into His hometown^H, He was teaching them in their synagogue, so that they were astounded and saying "From where *did* this wisdom and the miracles *come to* this *One*? **55** Is not this *One* the son *of* the carpenter? Is not His mother called Mary, and His brothers, James and Joseph and Simon and Jude^I? **56** And His sisters, are they not all with us? From where then *did* all these *things come to* this *One*?" **57** And they were taking-offense^J at Him. But Jesus said *to* them, "*A* prophet is not without-honor except in *his* hometown and in *his* house". **58** And He did not do many^K miracles there because of their unbelief.

Herod Says The Miracles of Jesus Mean He Is John The Baptist Back From The Dead
14:1 At that time, Herod the tetrarch^L heard the report *about* Jesus **2** and said *to* his servants, "This *One* is John the Baptist. He himself arose from the dead, and for this reason the *miraculous*-powers^M are at-work in him".

For Herod Had Beheaded John The Baptist
3 For^N Herod, having seized John, bound him and put *him* away in prison because of Herodias^O, the wife *of* Philip^P his brother. **4** For John was saying *to* him, "It is not lawful *for* you to have her". **5** And while wanting to kill him, he feared the crowd, because they were holding him as *a* prophet. **6** But *at* Herod's birthday-celebrations

A. That is, a large fishing net deployed from a boat. **B:** good... bad. That is, the 'fit' to eat versus the 'unusable'. **C.** That is, because the disciples now understand these new truths. **D.** That is, expert on the OT. **E.** Or, having been discipled, made a disciple. **F.** Or, *for*. **G.** His treasure now contains old truths and new (previously hidden) truths about the kingdom of Messiah. This scribe can now expound both. **H.** That is, Nazareth. **I.** Or, Judas, Judah. **J.** Or, being caused to fall. **K.** Or, great. **L.** Or governor, appointed by Rome. That is, Herod Antipas, a son of Herod the Great (Mt 2:1). He was governor of Galilee and Perea from 4 B.C. to A.D. 39, when he was exiled. His capital was Tiberius, on the western shore of the Sea of Galilee. He divorced the daughter of Aretas (2 Cor 11:32) to marry Herodias, v 3. **M.** Or, the Powers, the supernatural beings who were the source of these miracles in Herod's mind. **N.** Matthew now explains what happened to John at some time previous to this (see Mk 1:14), then continues in v 13. **O.** She was a grand-daughter of Herod the Great, daughter of Aristobulus, sister of Agrippa I (Act 12:1). **P.** That is, Philip I, a private citizen in Rome. Antipas, Aristobulus, and Philip were sons of Herod the Great from three different wives.

having come about, the daughter^A *of* Herodias danced in *their* midst. And she pleased Herod. **7** Hence, he declared with *an* oath to give her whatever she asked. **8** And the *one,* having been prompted^B by her mother, says, "Give me here on *a* platter the head *of* John the Baptist". **9** And [although] having been grieved, the king ordered *that it* be given, because of the oaths and the *ones* reclining-back-with *him* [to eat]. **10** And having sent, he beheaded John in the prison. **11** And his head was brought on *a* platter and given *to* the girl, and she brought *it to* her mother. **12** And having come to *him,* his disciples took away the corpse and buried him. And having gone^C, they reported *it to* Jesus.

Jesus Creates More Than Enough Bread And Fish To Feed 5000 Men
13 And having heard-*of it*^D, Jesus withdrew from there privately in *a* boat to *a* desolate place. And having heard-*of it*, the crowds followed Him *on* foot from the cities. **14** And having gone-out^E, He saw *a* large crowd and felt-deep-feelings [of compassion] for them. And He cured their sick *ones*. **15** And having become evening^F, the disciples came to Him saying, "*This* place is desolate and the hour already passed. Send-away the crowds in order that having gone away into the villages, they may buy themselves food". **16** But Jesus said *to* them, "They have no need to go away— **you** give them *something* to eat". **17** But the *ones* say *to* Him, "We do not have *anything* here except five loaves and two fish!" **18** But the *One* said, "Bring them here *to* Me". **19** And having ordered the crowds to lie-back on the grass, having taken the five loaves and the two fish, having looked up to heaven, He blessed^G *them*. And having broken *them*, He gave the loaves *to* the disciples, and the disciples *gave them to* the crowds. **20** And they all ate and were filled-to-satisfaction. And they picked up the *amount of* the fragments being left over— twelve full baskets. **21** And the *ones* eating were about five-thousand men, apart from women and children.

Jesus Walks Across The Raging Sea To His Disciples. They Say, Truly You Are God's Son
22 And immediately He compelled^H the disciples to get into the boat and to be going ahead of Him to the other side while^I He sent-away the crowds. **23** And having sent-away the crowds, He went up on the mountain privately to pray. And having become evening^J, He was there alone. **24** And the boat was already many stades^K distant from the land, being tormented by the waves. For the wind was contrary. **25** And He came to them *in the* fourth watch^L *of* the night, walking across^M the sea. **26** But the disciples, having seen Him walking on the sea, were frightened, saying that "It is *a* phantom^N". And they cried-out from the fear. **27** But immediately Jesus spoke *to* them, saying, "Take-courage, **I** am^O *the One*. Do not be afraid^P". **28** But having responded *to* Him, Peter said, "Master, if **You** are^Q *the One*, order me to come to You across the waters". **29** And the *One* said, "Come". And having gone down from the boat, Peter walked across the waters and came^R to Jesus. **30** But seeing the strong wind, he became afraid. And having begun to sink, he cried-out, saying,

---

A. Herodias had a daughter named Salome when she was married to Philip I. This may be the girl mentioned here. **B.** Or, put forward, coached, instructed. See Mk 6:22. **C.** Or, come. **D.** That is, heard that Herod said Jesus was John raised from the dead, v 1-2. Perhaps Jesus also heard of John's death at this time. Matthew does not tell us how long prior to v 1-2 John's death occurred. **E.** Or, come-out. **F.** That is, late in the day before sundown, between 3 and 6 P.M. **G.** That is, the loaves. Or, blessed *God,* spoke a blessing. **H.** Jn 6:15 explains why. **I.** Or, until which *time*. **J.** That is, later on since v 15, between 6 and 9 P.M. **K.** A stade is 607 feet or 185 meters. Compare Jn 6:19. **L.** That is, between 3 and 6 A.M. **M.** Or, over. **N.** Or, ghost. **O.** That is, It is Me. **P.** That is, Stop being afraid. **Q.** That is, if it is You. **R.** Or, went.

"Master, save me!" **31** And immediately Jesus, having stretched-out *His* hand, took-hold-of him. And He says *to* him, "*One* of-little-faith, for what *purpose*^A did you doubt?" **32** And they having gone-up^B into the boat, the wind stopped. **33** And the *ones* in the boat gave-worship^C *to* Him, saying, "Truly^D You are God's Son".

In Gennesaret, All Who Just Touch The Tassel of His Garment Are Healed
34 And having crossed-over, they came on land in Gennesaret. **35** And having recognized Him, the men *of* that place sent out into that whole surrounding-region. And they brought to Him all the *ones* being ill. **36** And they were begging Him that they might only touch the tassel *of* His garment. And all-who touched *it* were restored.

Jesus Condemns The Pharisees For Obeying Their Traditions Instead of God's Commands
15:1 Then Pharisees and scribes come to Jesus from Jerusalem, saying, **2** "For what reason are Your disciples transgressing the tradition *of* the elders? For they are not washing^E their hands when they eat bread". **3** But the *One*, having responded, said *to* them, "For what reason indeed are **you** transgressing the commandment *of* God for the sake of your tradition? **4** For God said [in Ex 20:12]: 'Be honoring *your* father and *your* mother', and [in Ex 21:17] 'Let the *one* speaking-evil-of father or mother come-to-an-end^F *by a* death'. **5** But **you** say, 'Whoever says *to* his father or *his* mother: "Whatever you might be benefitted from me *is a* gift^G [to God]" **6** shall by-no-means honor^H his father'. And you nullified^I the word *of* God for the sake of your tradition. **7** Hypocrites! Isaiah prophesied rightly concerning you, saying [in Isa 29:13]: **8** 'This people honors Me *with their* lips, but their heart is far distant from Me. **9** But they are worshiping Me in-vain^J— teaching *as* teachings *the* commandments *of* humans' ". **10** And having summoned the crowd, He said *to* them, "Listen and understand. **11** The *thing* entering into the mouth does **not** defile^K the person. But the *thing* proceeding out of the mouth— this defiles the person".

The Pharisees Focus On What Goes Into The Body Versus What Comes From The Heart
12 Then having come to *Him*, the disciples say *to* Him, "Do You know that the Pharisees, having heard *Your* statement, took-offense^L? **13** But the *One*, having responded, said, "Every plant which My heavenly Father did not plant will be uprooted. **14** Leave them *alone*. They are blind guides *of* blind ones. And if *a* blind *one* guides *a* blind *one*, both will fall into *a* pit". **15** And having responded, Peter said *to* Him, "Explain this parable *to* us". **16** And the *One* said, "Are **you**^M even yet also without-understanding? **17** Do you not perceive that everything proceeding into the mouth advances into the stomach and is expelled into *a* latrine? **18** But the *things* proceeding out of the mouth come out of the heart. And those *things* defile the person. **19** For out of the heart come evil thoughts^N, murders, adulteries, sexual-immoralities,

---

A. Or, to what *end*. What was the point of doubting? **B.** Or, come up. **C.** Or, prostrated-*themselves before*. **D.** Or, Really, Actually. **E.** See Mark's explanation of this in Mk 7:3-4. **F.** That is, die. 'Come to an end by a death' imitates a Hebrew idiom meaning, 'Let him surely die'. **G.** Or, offering. **H.** In other words, if you vow to give your estate to God when you die, then you must no longer honor the request of your parent to have some present benefit from it. **I.** Or, voided, invalidated, annulled. **J.** Or, to no end, pointlessly, futilely. **K.** Or, make unclean or impure. It is disobedience to God's Law that defiles. Their rules about ritual defilement are not part of God's Law. **L.** Or, were caused to fall, were offended. This is because v 3-11 are a direct attack on the Pharisees as teachers, and on their traditions. **M.** This is plural, addressing them all. **N.** Or, reasonings.

thefts, false-testimonies[A], blasphemies. **20** These are the *things* defiling the person. But the eating *with* unwashed hands does not defile the person".

A Gentile Woman Begs For Crumbs From The Master's Table

21 And having gone out from there, Jesus withdrew into the regions *of* Tyre and Sidon. **22** And behold— *a* Canaanite woman having come out from those districts was crying out, saying, "Have mercy on me, Master, Son *of* David. My daughter is badly demon-possessed". **23** But the *One* did not respond *a* word *to* her. And having come to *Him*, His disciples were asking Him, saying, "Send her away, because she is crying-out after us". **24** But the *One*, having responded, said, "I was not sent-forth except for[B] the lost[C] sheep *of the* house *of* Israel". **25** But the *one*, having come, was prostrating-*herself before* Him, saying, "Master, help me". **26** And the *One*, having responded, said, "It is not good to take the bread *of* the children and throw *it to* the little-dogs[D]". **27** But the *one* said, "Yes, Master. For indeed the little-dogs eat from the crumbs falling from the table *of* their masters!" **28** Then, having responded, Jesus said *to* her, "O woman, your faith *is* great. Let it be done *for* you as you wish". And her daughter was healed from that hour.

Jesus Again Creates Bread And Fish For a Group of 4000 Men

29 And having passed on from there, Jesus went beside the Sea *of* Galilee. And having gone up on the mountain, He was sitting there. **30** And large crowds came to Him, having with them lame *ones*, blind *ones*, crippled *ones*, mute *ones*, and many others. And they threw[E] them at His feet. And He cured them, **31** so that the crowd marveled— seeing mute *ones* speaking, crippled *ones* healthy, and lame *ones* walking, and blind *ones* seeing. And they glorified the God *of* Israel. **32** And Jesus, having summoned His disciples, said, "I feel-deep-feelings [of compassion] toward the crowd, because *it is* already three days they are remaining-with Me and they do not have anything they may eat. And I do not want to send them away hungry, so that they may not perhaps become-exhausted[F] on the way". **33** And the disciples say *to* Him, "From where *are there* so many loaves *for* us in *a* desolate place so as to fill-to-satisfaction so large *a* crowd?" **34** And Jesus says *to* them, "How many loaves do you have?" And the *ones* said, "Seven, and *a* few small-fish". **35** And having ordered the crowd to fall-back on the ground [to eat], **36** He took the seven loaves and the fish. And having given-thanks, He broke *them* and was giving *them to* the disciples, and the disciples *to* the crowds. **37** And they all ate and were filled-to-satisfaction. And they picked up the *amount of* the fragments being left-over— seven full large-baskets. **38** And the *ones* eating were four-thousand men, apart from women and children.

The Pharisees Ask For a Sign From Heaven. No Sign Will Be Given Except Jonah's

39 And having sent away the crowds, He got into the boat and went to the districts *of* Magadan. **16:1** And having come to *Him*, the Pharisees and Sadducees— testing *Him*— asked Him to show them *a* sign out-of heaven. **2** But the *One*, having responded, said *to* them, "Having become evening, you say, 'Fair weather!— for the heaven is red'; **3** and early-in-the-morning, 'Stormy-weather today!— for the lowering[G] heaven is red'. You[H] know-*how* to discern the appearance *of* the heaven but cannot *discern* the signs *of* the

---

A. Or, perjuries, if in a courtroom setting. **B.** Or, to. **C.** That is, having gotten lost. **D.** Or, house dogs, lap dogs. Jesus answers her with a proverbial-type statement, and she responds in the same way. **E.** Or, hurled, flung, tossed. This indicates not violence, but haste and urgency. **F.** Or, faint, give out. **G.** Or, gloomy, overcast. **H.** Or, this may be a question, Do you know-*how*?

times! **⁴** *An* evil and adulterous^A generation is seeking-for *a* sign. And *a* sign will not be given *to* it, except the sign *of* Jonah".

Jesus Warns His Disciples To Beware of The Leaven of The Pharisees: Their Teachings
And having left them behind, He went away. **⁵** And the disciples, having come to the other side, forgot to take bread. **⁶** And Jesus said *to* them, "Watch-out and beware of the leaven *of* the Pharisees and Sadducees". **⁷** And the *ones* were discussing among themselves, saying that^B "We did not take bread". **⁸** But having known *it*, Jesus said, "Why are you discussing among yourselves, *ones* of-little-faith, that you do not have bread? **⁹** Do you not yet perceive? Do you not-even^C remember the five loaves *of* the five-thousand, and how many baskets you received? **¹⁰** Not even the seven loaves *of* the four-thousand, and how many large-baskets you received? **¹¹** How *is it* you do not perceive that I did not speak *to* you concerning bread? But beware of the leaven *of* the Pharisees and Sadducees". **¹²** Then they understood that He did not say to beware of the leaven *of* bread, but of the teaching *of* the Pharisees and Sadducees.

Who Do You Say That I Am? Peter Says, You Are The Messiah, The Son of The Living God
¹³ And Jesus, having come into the regions *of* Philip's^D Caesarea, was asking His disciples, saying, "Who do people say *that* the Son *of* Man is?" **¹⁴** And the *ones* said, "Some, John the Baptist. And others, Elijah. And different *ones*, Jeremiah or one *of* the prophets". **¹⁵** He says *to* them, "But who do **you** say *that* I am?" **¹⁶** And having responded, Simon Peter said "**You** are the Christ, the Son *of* the living God". **¹⁷** And having responded, Jesus said *to* him, "You are blessed, Simon Bar-Jonah^E, because flesh and blood did not reveal *it to* you, but My Father in the heavens. **¹⁸** And **I** also^F say *to* you that **you** are *a* rock^G and upon this bed-rock^H I will build My church— and *the* gates^I *of* Hades will not prevail-against^J it. **¹⁹** I will give you the keys^K *of* the kingdom *of* the heavens. And whatever you^L bind^M on earth will have been bound^N in the heavens, and whatever you loose on earth will have been loosed in the heavens". **²⁰** Then He gave-orders *to* the disciples that they should tell no one that **He** is the Christ^O.

A. That is, spiritually unfaithful to God. **B.** Or, saying, "*It is* because we did not take bread". **C.** Or, perceive, nor remember. **D.** That is, the Caesarea that was the capital city of Herod Philip II (see Lk 3:1), north of the Sea of Galilee. **E.** That is, son of Jonah. **F.** That is, I also reveal in addition to what the Father revealed; or, I also bless you, in addition to this blessing you have received from the Father. **G.** Or, Peter, as this is always rendered elsewhere. Jesus has both his name and the meaning of his name in view. 'A rock' shows the flow of thought, 'Peter' the connection to the apostle. Jesus had long ago given him this name, Jn 1:42. **H.** That is, Peter himself, as the leader described in v 19; or, Peter's confession, the human confession of Christ as Son of God; or, the Father's revelation of Him to humans; or, Christ may be pointing to Himself. **I.** That is, the gates all humans pass through at death; death will not defeat the church. Or, the forces of evil coming through those gates to attack the church; they will not be victorious. **J.** Or, win the victory over. **K.** Keys are for opening and closing. Peter may be using these keys when he opens the kingdom to the Jews, Samaritans, and Gentiles, in Acts. **L.** This is singular. This power may have been held by Peter exclusively; or, by all the apostles; or, it may have passed on to other believers. Compare 18:18. **M:** bind... loose. Some think this means forbidding and permitting things, as the Rabbis used these terms; others, forgiving and retaining sins, Jn 20:23; others, the power of excommunication, Mt 18:18. **N:** will have been bound... loosed. Lit, will be having been bound... loosed. God does not second what Peter binds, but what Peter binds will correspond to what has been bound in heaven. In other words, Peter will speak with God's authority, with divine guidance. **O.** That is, Messiah. This term had political overtones Jesus did not want to fan at this time.

The King Begins To Predict His Death And Resurrection
21 From that time^A *on,* Jesus began to show His disciples that He must go to Jerusalem, and suffer many *things* from the elders and chief priests and scribes, and be killed, and be raised *on* the third day. **22** And having taken Him aside, Peter began to rebuke Him, saying, "*God be* merciful^B *to* You, Lord! This shall never happen *to* You". **23** But the *One,* having turned, said *to* Peter, "Get behind Me, Satan! You are *a* cause-of-falling *to* Me, because you are not thinking the *things of* God, but the *things of* humans".

Deny Yourself, Take Up Your Cross, And Follow Me. Some Here Will See Me In My Kingdom
24 Then Jesus said *to* His disciples, "If anyone wants to come after Me, let him deny^C himself, and take up his cross^D, and be following Me. **25** For whoever wants to save^E his life^F will lose it. But whoever loses his life for My sake will find it. **26** For what will *a* person be profited if he gains the whole world, but forfeits his life^G? Or what will *a* person give in-exchange-for his life? **27** For the Son *of* Man is going to come in the glory *of* His Father with His angels. And then He will render *to* each *one* according to his practice^H. **28** Truly I say *to* you that there are some *of* the *ones* standing here who will by no means taste death until^I they see the Son *of* Man coming in His kingdom".

Three Disciples See Jesus Transformed, And Hear God Tell Them To Listen To Jesus
17:1 And after six days, Jesus takes-along Peter and James and John his brother, and brings them up on *a* high mountain privately. **2** And He was transfigured^J in front of them. And His face shined like the sun, and His garments became white as the light. **3** And behold— Moses and Elijah appeared *to* them, talking with Him. **4** And having responded, Peter said *to* Jesus, "Lord, it is good *that* we are here. If You wish, I will make three dwellings^K here— one *for* You, and one *for* Moses, and one *for* Elijah". **5** While he *was* still speaking, behold— *a* bright^L cloud overshadowed^M them. And behold— *a* voice out of the cloud saying "This is My beloved Son, with Whom I was^N well-pleased. Be listening-to Him". **6** And having heard *it,* the disciples fell on their face and became extremely afraid. **7** And Jesus came to *them,* and having touched them, said, "Arise, and do not be afraid". **8** And having lifted up their eyes, they saw no one except Jesus Himself alone.

Jesus Tells The Three Disciples That John The Baptist Was Elijah
9 And while they *were* coming down from the mountain, Jesus commanded them, saying, "Tell the sight^O *to* no one until which *time* the Son *of* Man is raised from *the* dead". **10** And the disciples questioned Him, saying, "Why^P then do the scribes say that Elijah must come first?" **11** And the *One,* having responded, said, "Elijah is coming^Q and will restore all

---

A. Matthew reaches a turning point. Jesus now speaks directly about His death and resurrection for the first time, and begins to prepare the disciples for that event and their life and mission after it. **B.** That is, May God mercifully spare You from this. **C.** That is, disown and refuse to follow the impulses of self. **D.** That is, the instrument of his or her death to self. **E.** That is, by avoiding his cross, and refusing to deny himself. **F.** That is, life in an earthly sense. **G.** That is, life in an eternal sense. **H.** Or, doing, activity, course of action. **I.** Jesus may be referring to the three with Him at the transfiguration next, where they saw the King in His glory; or, to the eleven who saw Him after the resurrection or experienced the coming of the Spirit on Pentecost; or, to those who remained alive to see the destruction of Jerusalem in A.D. 70, the judgment of the King on Israel. **J.** Or, transformed. **K.** Or, tents, tabernacles. **L.** Or, full of light. **M.** Or, covered, hovered over. **N.** Or, am well pleased. See 3:17. **O.** Or, vision, what was seen. **P.** That is, since you are the Messiah, where is Elijah, whom Mal 4:5 says comes before You? **Q:** coming... came. Jesus may mean Elijah is coming in the future, but already came in John the Baptist; there are two comings of Elijah, just as with the Messiah. Or, the scribes rightly teach *things*— **12** but I say *to* you that Elijah already came. And they did not recognize him, but did with^A him whatever they wanted. So also the Son *of* Man is going to suffer by them". **13** Then the disciples understood that He spoke *to* them about John the Baptist.

Jesus Heals a Boy His Disciples Could Not Heal Because of Their Little Faith
14 And *they* having come to the crowd, *a* man came to Him, kneeling-before Him, **15** and saying, "Master, have mercy on my son, because he has seizures and is suffering badly. For he often falls into the fire, and often into the water. **16** And I brought him to Your disciples and they were not able to cure him". **17** But having responded, Jesus said, "O unbelieving^B and perverted generation! How long will I be with you? How long will I bear-with you? Bring him here *to* Me". **18** And Jesus rebuked it, and the demon departed from him, and the boy was cured from that hour. **19** Then the disciples, having come to Jesus privately, said, "For what reason were **we** not able to cast it out?" **20** And the *One* says *to* them, "Because of your little-faith. For truly I say *to* you, if you have faith like *a* seed^C *of a* mustard-plant, you will say *to* this mountain, 'Pass from-here to-there', and it will pass. And nothing will be impossible *for* you. **21^D**

Jesus Again Predicts His Death And Resurrection
22 And while they *were* being gathered^E in Galilee, Jesus said *to* them, "The Son *of* Man is going to be handed-over into *the* hands *of* men. **23** And they will kill Him. And He will be raised *on* the third day". And they were extremely grieved.

Jesus Pays His Temple Tax With a Coin From a Fish He Sent Peter To Catch
24 And they having come to Capernaum, the *ones*^F taking the double-drachmas^G came to Peter and said, "Does not your teacher pay the double-drachmas?" **25** He says, "Yes". And *Peter* having come into the house, Jesus anticipated him, saying, "What seems *right to* you, Simon— from whom do the kings *of* the earth take taxes^H or *a* poll-tax^I, from their sons^J or from the strangers?" **26** And *Peter* having said "From the strangers", Jesus said *to* him, "Then indeed, the sons^K are free! **27** But in order that we may not offend^L them— having gone to *the* sea, cast *a* hook. And take the first fish having come up. And having opened its mouth, you will find *a* stater^M. Having taken that, give *it to* them for Me and you".

Who Is The Greatest In The Kingdom? Whoever Will Humble Himself Like This Child
18:1 At that hour the disciples came to Jesus, saying, "Who then^N is greater^O in the kingdom *of* the heavens?" **2** And having summoned *a* child, He stood him^P in *the* middle *of* them, **3** and said, "Truly I say *to* you, unless you are turned-*around*^Q and become like

---

that Elijah is coming, but in fact he has already come in John; just as Jesus was not what the Jews expected, so with Elijah. Compare Mk 9:12. **A.** Lit, in, in connection with, in his case. **B.** Or, faithless. **C.** That is, the tiniest amount, since it is God that does the work. But their 'little faith' did not issue in them using any at all on this occasion. **D.** Some manuscripts add as v 21, But this kind does not go out except by prayer and fasting. **E.** Or, gathering-*themselves*. **F.** These are Jews commissioned by the Temple, not the hated 'tax collectors'. **G.** This was the yearly half-shekel (equivalent to two drachmas, the silver double-drachma coin) temple tax required of all male Jews 20 to 50 years old throughout the world. One Greek drachma was equivalent to one Roman denarius (one day's wage). **H.** That is, local taxes. **I.** That is, a tax paid to the Emperor, based on a census. **J.** Does the king's family pay taxes, or the families of his subjects? **K.** That is, the sons of the Father, Jesus and the disciples, are exempt from their Father's temple tax. **L.** Or, cause them to fall. **M.** This Greek silver coin was worth four drachmas, enough for both of them. **N.** That is, since You are Messiah, how will we rank in Your kingdom? **O.** Or, greatest. **P.** Or, her. Lit, it (the child). **Q.** Or, changed, converted, turned (from your ways to God).

children^A, you will never enter into the kingdom *of* the heavens. **4** Therefore whoever will humble himself like this child, this *one* is the greater *one* in the kingdom *of* the heavens.

But Woe To Whoever Causes One of My Children Believing In Me To Fall

5 "And whoever welcomes^B one such^C child on the basis of My name, welcomes Me. **6** But whoever causes one *of* these little *ones* believing in Me to fall— it *would* be better^D *for* him that *a* donkey's millstone^E be hung around his neck and he be sunk in the deep-part^F *of* the sea.

Woe To The World Because of Causes of Falling. Better To Tear Out Your Eye

7 "Woe *to* the world because of the causes-of-falling. For *it is a* necessity *that* causes-of-falling *should* come; nevertheless, woe *to* the person through whom the cause-of-falling comes. **8** But if your hand or your foot is causing you to fall, cut it off and throw *it* from you. It is better *for* you to enter into life crippled or lame than to be thrown into the eternal fire having two hands or two feet. **9** And if your eye is causing you to fall, tear it out and throw *it* from you. It is better *for* you to enter into life one-eyed than to be thrown into the Gehenna^G *of* fire having two eyes.

Don't Look Down On These Little Ones. God Does Not Want One of Them Lost

10 "See *that* you do not look-down-upon^H one *of* these little *ones*. For I say *to* you that their angels in *the* heavens are continually seeing^I the face *of* My Father in *the* heavens. **11** ^J **12** What seems *right to* you? If *a* hundred sheep belong *to* any man and one of them went-astray, will he not leave the ninety nine on the mountains, and having gone, be seeking the *one* going astray? **13** And if it comes about *that he* finds it, truly I say *to* you that he rejoices over it more than over the ninety nine not having gone astray. **14** So it is not *the* will in-the-sight-of^K your Father in *the* heavens that one *of* these little *ones* should be-lost.

If Your Brother Sins Against You, Seek To Restore Him

15 "But if your brother sins against you^L, go, expose^M him between you and him alone. If he listens-to you, you gained^N your brother. **16** But if he does not listen, take-along with you one or two more in order that every word may be established based-on *the* mouth *of* two or three witnesses. And if he refuses-to-listen-to them, tell *it to* the church. **17** And if he even refuses^O to listen to the church, let him be *to* you just like the Gentile^P and the tax-collector^Q. **18** Truly I say *to* you, whatever you^R binds^S on earth

---

A. That is, dependent and helpless before God, as this child is before adults and God. **B.** Having answered their question, Jesus goes on to draw another lesson from this child. **C.** That is, one such physical child like this one before them; or, one such spiritual child of any age who humbles himself in the way just mentioned. **D.** It is better to be killed (a one-time event) than to face the consequences of this (an eternal loss). **E.** That is, a large millstone which donkeys would turn. **F.** Lit, open-sea *of* the sea. **G.** That is, fiery hell, equivalent to eternal fire in v 8. **H.** Or, despise, disregard, treat with contempt, because you think of yourself as greater than them. **I.** That is, they have continual access to God. **J.** Some manuscripts add as v 11, For the Son *of* Man came to save the lost. **K.** Or, in the presence of. This is a reverential way of saying it is not God's will. **L.** Now Jesus turns to the opposite case. What should be done when you are suffering an injury, not inflicting one. **M.** Or, convict, rebuke. **N.** That is, gained him for the kingdom. **O.** The church focuses the individual on the impact of his sin on his relationship with Christ and the Christian community. He must choose between his sin and Christ. **P.** That is, the non-believer. **Q.** That is, the traitor to the community, the outcast. **R.** This is plural. Some think it refers to the church; others, to the apostles. Compare 16:19. **S:** bind... loose. See 16:19.

will have been bound[A] in heaven. And whatever you loose on earth will have been loosed in heaven. **19** Again[B], truly I say *to* you that if two of you on earth agree concerning any matter which they may ask, it will be done *for* them by My Father in *the* heavens. **20** For[C] where two or three have been gathered-together in[D] My name, I am there in *the* midst *of* them".

Always Forgive One Another From The Heart, As God Has Forgiven You
21 Then having come to *Him*, Peter said *to* Him, "Lord, how often[E] will my brother sin against me and I will forgive him? Up to seven-times?" **22** Jesus says *to* him, "I do not say *to* you up to seven-times, but up to seventy-times[F] [and][G] seven. **23** For this reason, the kingdom *of* the heavens became-like[H] *a* man *who was a* king, who wished to settle *the* account with his slaves. **24** And he having begun to settle *it*, one debtor *of* ten-thousand talents[I] was brought to him. **25** But he not having *the means* to pay, the master ordered *that* he be sold— and *his* wife and *his* children and all that he has— and *that it* be paid. **26** Then the slave, having fallen, was prostrating-*himself before* him, saying, 'Be patient with me and I will pay everything *to* you'. **27** And having felt-deep feelings [of compassion], the master *of* that slave released him and forgave him the loan. **28** But having gone out, that slave found one *of* his fellow-slaves who owed him *a* hundred denarii. And having seized him, he was choking *him,* saying, 'Pay *me,* since you are owing *me* something'. **29** Then his fellow slave, having fallen, was begging him, saying, 'Be patient with me and I will pay *it to* you'. **30** And the *one* was not willing, but having gone, he threw him into prison until he should pay the *amount* being owed. **31** Then his fellow slaves, having seen the *things* having taken place, were extremely grieved. And having come, they made-clear *to* their master all the *things* having taken place. **32** Then, having summoned him, his master says *to* him, 'Evil slave! I forgave you all that debt because you begged me. **33** Should not you also have had mercy on your fellow slave, as I also had mercy on you?' **34** And having become angry[J], his master handed him over *to* the tormenters[K] until[L] which *time* he should pay all the *amount* being owed. **35** So also My heavenly Father will do *to* you if you do not forgive— each *one* his brother— from your hearts".

The King Leaves Galilee For Judea. Large Crowds Follow Him And He Heals Them
19:1 And it came about *that* when Jesus finished[M] these words, He went-away from Galilee and came into the districts[N] *of* Judea, beyond the Jordan. **2** And large crowds followed Him, and He cured them there.

The Pharisees Test Jesus With a Question About Divorce. Divorce Is Not God's Will
3 And Pharisees came to Him— testing Him, and saying, "Is it lawful *for a* man[O] to send-

A. Lit, will be having been bound. Likewise with 'loosed' next. Divine guidance is promised to the church. **B.** Some think v 19-20 are in regard to the disciplinary decisions just mentioned, even if the church is two or three. Others think this is a separate point regarding prayer in general, unrelated to what precedes. **C.** The promised divine guidance is now made explicit. **D.** Or, with reference to. **E.** Peter is responding to v 15, 'If he listens to you'. **F.** That is, seventy-occasions, as also with 'seven-times' in v 21. **G.** For a total of seventy-seven. Or, [times], making 490. **H.** Or, is like. Same grammar as in 13:24. **I.** A silver talent is 6000 denarii, 6000 days wages, the wages of 20 years for a laborer. Ten thousand talents is a huge amount of money, 600,000 times more than a hundred denarii in v 28. Such is our debt to God compared to anyone's debt to us. **J.** Or, wrathful. **K.** Or, torturers. **L.** The man would never be able to repay it. **M.** This marks the end of the ministry of Jesus in Galilee. **N.** Or, boundaries. **O.** This question is asked from the Jewish husband's perspective. Jesus refutes the

away^A his wife for any reason^B?" **4** And the *One*, having responded, said, "Did you not read [in Gen 1:27] that the *One* having created from *the* beginning^C 'made them male and female'? **5** And He said [in Gen 2:24], 'For this reason^D *a* man will leave-behind *his* father and *his* mother and will be joined^E *to* his wife. And the two will be one flesh'. **6** So then, they are no longer two, but one flesh. Therefore what God paired-together^F, let *a* person^G not separate". **7** They say *to* Him, "Why then did Moses command *us* to give *a* certificate^H *of* divorce and send her away?" **8** He says *to* them that "Moses permitted^I you to send-away your wives because of your hardness-of-heart. But from the beginning it has not been so^J. **9** And I say *to* you that whoever sends-away his wife not based on sexual-immorality, and marries another, is committing-adultery".

The Disciples Conclude It Is Better Not To Marry. Jesus Says This Is Right For Some
10 His disciples say *to* Him, "If the case *of* the man with the wife is like this, it is not expedient^K to marry!" **11** But the *One* said *to* them, "Not all give-way-to^L this statement, but [only] ones *to* whom it has been given. **12** For there are eunuchs^M who were born thus from *a* mother's womb. And there are eunuchs who were made-eunuchs by people. And there are eunuchs who made themselves eunuchs for the sake of the kingdom *of* the heavens. Let the *one* being able to give way, give way".

Don't Forbid The Children To Come To Me. Of Such Is The Kingdom of God
13 Then children were brought to Him in order that He might lay *His* hands on them and pray. But the disciples rebuked them^N. **14** But Jesus said, "Permit^O the children, and do not be forbidding them to come to Me. For the kingdom *of* the heavens is *of*^P such *ones*". **15** And having laid *His* hands on them, He proceeded from there.

A Rich Man Asks What To Do To Enter Heaven. Jesus Says, Sell Everything And Follow Me
16 And behold— one having come to Him said, "Teacher, what good *thing* should I do in order that I may have eternal life?" **17** And the *One* said *to* him, "Why do you ask Me about *what is* good? There is One *Who is* good. But if you wish to enter into life, keep the commandments". **18** He says *to* Him, "Which *ones*?" And Jesus said, "You shall not murder. You shall not commit-adultery. You shall not steal. You shall not give-false-testimony. **19** Be honoring *your* father and *your* mother". And, "You shall love your neighbor as yourself". **20** The young man says *to* Him, "I kept all these *things*. What am I still lacking?" **21** Jesus said *to* him, "If you wish to be perfect^Q, go, sell your possessions and give *it* *to* the poor, and you will have treasure in *the* heavens. And come, be following

---

Jewish man's commonly held view of divorce. **A.** That is, divorce. **B.** Or, for all grounds, for every cause. That is, for any fault the husband might find with her. **C.** That is, created, made them from *the* beginning. Or, created *them* at the beginning, made them. **D.** That is, because God made them to be a complementary pair. This is God's intent. **E.** Or, join-*himself*. **F.** Or, yoked together, joined as a pair. **G.** Or, man (generically speaking), a human. The broader sense is clear in Mk 10:9-12. Do not divorce your wives. **H.** This document was to protect the wife and make it possible for her to remarry. **I.** Jesus corrects the Pharisees. Deut 24:1 does not command divorce. **J.** That is, it has not been God's plan and intent that you divorce your wives. **K.** Or, advantageous, profitable. This direct attack of Jesus upon male authority is shocking even to the disciples. **L.** Or, make room for, accept. Not all have the ability to live in an unmarried state. This is an understatement, since God made them to be a pair, v 4-5. But Jesus validates singleness as also a gift from God, in contradiction to the views of that day. **M.** That is, celibate or castrated males. Some are born with this disposition, some are forced into it, some choose to remain unmarried. **N.** That is, those who brought the children. **O.** Or, Leave the children *alone*. **P.** That is, made up of; or, belonging to. **Q.** That is, complete, so as not to 'lack' anything.

Me". ²² But having heard the statement, the young man went away grieving. For he was having many properties.

It Is Hard For The Rich To Enter. But All Who Leave Anything Will Inherit More
²³ And Jesus said *to* His disciples, "Truly I say *to* you that *a* rich *one* will enter with-difficulty into the kingdom *of* the heavens. ²⁴ And again I say *to* you, it is easier *that a* camel go through *a* hole *of a* needle^A than^B *that a* rich *one* enter into the kingdom *of* God". ²⁵ And having heard *it*, the disciples were extremely astounded, saying, "Who then can be saved?" ²⁶ And having looked at *them*, Jesus said *to* them, "With humans, this is impossible. But with God, all *things are* possible". ²⁷ Then Peter, having responded, said *to* Him, "Behold— **we** left everything and followed You. What then will there be *for* us?" ²⁸ And Jesus said *to* them, "Truly I say *to* you that you, the *ones* having followed Me— at the regeneration^C when the Son *of* Man sits on *the* throne^D *of* His glory, **you** also will sit on twelve thrones, judging^E the twelve tribes *of* Israel. ²⁹ And everyone who left houses or brothers or sisters or father or mother or children or fields for the sake of My name will receive *a* hundred-fold^F, and will inherit eternal life.

The First In This World Will Be Last And The Last Will Be First
³⁰ "But many first^G *ones* will be last, and last *ones,* first. **20:1** For the kingdom *of* the heavens is like *a* man *who is a* house-master, who went out together-with early-morning to hire workers into his vineyard. ² And having made-an-agreement with the workers for *a* denarius^H *for* the day, he sent them out into his vineyard. ³ And having gone out around *the* third^I hour, he saw others standing idle in the marketplace. ⁴ And *to* those he said, '**You** also go into the vineyard, and I will give you whatever may be right'. ⁵ And the *ones* went. And again having gone out around *the* sixth and *the* ninth hour, he did similarly. ⁶ And having gone out around the eleventh^J *hour,* he found others standing *there*. And he says *to* them, 'Why are you standing here idle the whole day? ⁷ They say *to* him, 'Because no one hired us'. He says *to* them, '**You** also go into the vineyard'. ⁸ And having become evening, the master *of* the vineyard says *to* his manager^K, 'Call the workers, and pay them the wages— beginning from the last *ones*, up to the first *ones*'. ⁹ And having come, the *ones hired* around the eleventh hour received *a* denarius apiece. ¹⁰ And having come, the first *ones* thought that they would receive more. And they also themselves received the denarius apiece. ¹¹ And having received *it,* they were grumbling against the house-master, ¹² saying, 'These last *ones* did one hour, and you made them equal *to* us— the *ones* having

---

A. Lit, bored-hole *of a* sewing-needle. **B.** In other words, it is impossible, as Jesus says next. This is another shocking statement. Wealth was considered a clear sign of God's blessing. **C.** Or, rebirth [of the world]. **D.** Or, His throne *of* glory; His glorious throne. **E.** That is, administering justice to. **F.** That is, a hundred times as much. Or this may be a hyperbole meaning 'many times as much', as in Lk 18:30. **G.** Or, foremost, chief. That is, first in time; or first in status. The parable that follows illustrates this point. In answer to Peter's question in v 27, Jesus says God will reward based on His own will, not what we think we deserve; and based on completion of the work assigned to us, not based on comparison to the work done by others or in proportion to our part of the total work performed. Compare the parable at 25:14. Thus from the human viewpoint, some seeming to have done the least will seem to be rewarded the most; some who appear to deserve more will receive the same as others who appear to deserve less. **H.** A Roman silver coin. A day's wage for a laborer. **I.** That is, 9 A.M. **J.** That is, 5 P.M. They worked until 6 P.M. **K.** Or, foreman.

borne the burden *of* the day and the burning-heat'. **¹³** But the *one*, having responded, said *to* one *of* them, 'Friend, I am not wronging you. Did you not make-an-agreement *with* me *for a* denarius? **¹⁴** Take what *is* yours and go. But I want to give *to* this last one as *I* also *gave to* you. **¹⁵** Or is it not lawful *for* me to do what I want with my *things*? Or is your eye^A evil because I am good?' **¹⁶** Thus the last *ones* will be first, and the first *ones*, last".

Jesus Predicts His Death And Resurrection For The Third Time

¹⁷ And while going up to Jerusalem, Jesus took aside the twelve disciples privately and said *to* them on the road, **¹⁸** "Behold— we are going up to Jerusalem. And the Son *of* Man will be handed-over *to* the chief priests and scribes. And they will condemn Him *to* death, **¹⁹** and will hand Him over *to* the Gentiles so that *they might* mock and whip and crucify *Him*. And He will be raised *on* the third day".

Two Disciples Jockey For Position In The Kingdom. Jesus Says, It Is Not Mine To Give

²⁰ Then the mother *of* the sons *of* Zebedee came to Him with her sons^B, prostrating-*herself* and asking something from Him. **²¹** And the *One* said *to* her, "What do you want?" She says *to* Him, "Say that these two sons *of* mine may sit one on Your right *side* and one on Your left *side* in Your kingdom". **²²** But having responded, Jesus said, "You^C do not know what you are asking. Are you able to drink the cup which I am about to drink?" They say *to* Him, "We are able". **²³** He says *to* them, "You will drink My cup— but the sitting on My right *side* and on *the* left *side*, this is not Mine to give, but *it is for* whom it has been prepared by My Father".

Whoever Wants To Be First Shall Be Your Slave. Even I Came To Serve

²⁴ And having heard-*of it*, the ten were indignant about the two brothers. **²⁵** But Jesus, having summoned them, said, "You know that the rulers *of* the Gentiles are lording-over^D them, and the great *ones* are exercising-authority-over^E them. **²⁶** It shall not be so among you. But whoever wants to become great among you shall be your servant, **²⁷** and whoever wants to be first among you shall be your slave— **²⁸** just as the Son *of* Man did not come to be served, but to serve, and to give His life *as a* ransom for many".

Two Blind Men Appeal To The Messiah For Their Sight, And Are Healed

²⁹ And while they *were* proceeding out from Jericho, *a* large crowd followed Him. **³⁰** And behold— two blind *men* sitting beside the road, having heard that Jesus was going by, cried-out saying, "Have-mercy-on us, Master, Son *of* David!" **³¹** But the crowd rebuked them in order that they might keep-silent. But the *ones* cried out louder, saying, "Have mercy on us, Master, Son *of* David!" **³²** And having stopped, Jesus called them and said, "What do you want Me to do *for* you?" **³³** They say *to* Him, "Master— that our eyes might be opened!" **³⁴** And having felt-deep-feelings [of compassion], Jesus touched their eyes. And they immediately saw-again. And they followed Him.

The King Rides Into Jerusalem On a Donkey, As Predicted In Zechariah

21:1 And when they drew-near to Jerusalem and came to Bethphage, to the Mount *of*

A. That is, are you envious. **B.** That is, James and John. **C.** This word is plural. Jesus answers all three. **D.** Or, domineering over. They reign as masters over their subjects. **E.** They lead and rule by authority.

Olives, then Jesus sent forth two disciples, [2] saying *to* them, "Proceed to the village before you, and immediately you will find *a* donkey having been tied, and *a* colt with her. Having untied *them,* bring *them to* Me. [3] And if someone says something *to* you, you shall say that 'The Lord has need *of* them', and immediately he will send them forth". [4] Now this has taken place in order that the *thing* might be fulfilled having been spoken through the prophet saying:[5] "Say *to* the daughter *of* Zion, 'Behold, your King is coming *to* you— gentle, and mounted upon *a* donkey, even upon *a* colt, *a* foal *of a* beast-of-burden' " [Zech 9:9]. [6] And the disciples— having proceeded, and having done just as Jesus directed them— [7] brought the donkey and the colt. And they put *their* cloaks on them. And He sat on them[A]. [8] And most-of the crowd[B] spread their cloaks in the road. And others were cutting branches from the trees and spreading *them* in the road. [9] And the crowds going ahead of Him, and the *ones* following *Him,* were crying out, saying, "Hosanna[C] *to* the Son *of* David. Blessed *is* the *One* coming in *the* name *of the* Lord. Hosanna in the highest [heavens]".

The King Arrives In Jerusalem, And The Whole City Is Shaken

[10] And He having entered into Jerusalem, the whole city was shaken[D], saying, "Who is this?" [11] And the crowds were saying, "This is the prophet Jesus from Nazareth *of* Galilee".

Jesus Cleanses The Temple And Accepts Praises From Boys. The Chief Priests Object

[12] And Jesus entered into the temple. And He threw-out all the *ones* selling and buying in the temple, and overturned the tables *of* the money-changers[E] and the seats *of* the *ones* selling the doves[F]. [13] And He says *to* them, "It has been written [in Isa 56:7]: 'My house shall be called *a* house *of* prayer'. But **you** are making it *a* den *of* robbers[G]". [14] And blind *ones* and lame *ones* came to Him in the temple, and He cured them. [15] But the chief priests and the scribes— having seen the marvelous *things* which He did, and the boys[H] crying-out in the temple and saying "Hosanna *to* the Son *of* David"— were indignant [16] and said *to* Him, "Do You hear what these *boys* are saying?" And Jesus says *to* them, "Yes— did you never read [in Ps 8:2] that 'You prepared-*Yourself* praise out of *the* mouth[I] *of* children and nursing *ones*'?" [17] And having left them behind, He went outside *of* the city to Bethany and spent-the-night there.

Jesus Curses a Fruitless Fig Tree

[18] Now early-in-the-morning while returning to the city, He was hungry. [19] And having seen one fig tree near the road, He went to it and found nothing on it except leaves only[J]. And He says *to* it, "May fruit no longer come from you— forever". And the fig tree was dried-up at-once. [20] And having seen *it,* the disciples marveled, saying, "How was the fig tree dried up at once?" [21] And having responded, Jesus said *to* them, "Truly I say *to* you— if you have faith and do not doubt, you will not only do the *thing of* the fig tree, but even if you say *to* this mountain, 'Be taken up and be thrown into the sea', it will be done. [22] And you will receive all that you ask in prayer, believing".

A. That is, the garments. **B.** Or, the very-large crowd. **C.** This transliterated Hebrew word means 'Save *us,* we pray' or 'Help *us,* we pray', as in Ps 118:25. It was used as a shout of praise. They are calling out to Jesus as their Messiah. **D.** Or, agitated, stirred up. **E.** They changed foreign currency into Jewish currency for use in the temple. **F.** That is, the doves used in the sacrifices commanded by God. **G.** Or, plunderers, bandits. **H.** Perhaps these were twelve-year-olds like Jesus in Lk 2:43. **I.** If God accepts praise from the first words of the smallest children in Ps 8, why not these boys now? He will bring it from the stones, if necessary (Lk 19:40). **J.** This is a parable of Israel. They had the appearance of life, but no fruit. Jesus curses them.

The Priests Ask, By What Authority Do You Do This?

²³ And He having come into the temple, the chief priests and the elders *of* the people came to Him while *He was* teaching, saying, "By what-kind-of^ authority are You doing these *things*, and who gave You this authority?" ²⁴ And having responded, Jesus said *to* them, "I also will ask you one thing, which if you tell Me, I also will tell you by what-kind-of authority I am doing these *things*— ²⁵ From where was the baptism *of* John, from heaven or from humans?" And the *ones* were discussing among themselves, saying, "If we say, 'From heaven', He will say *to* us, 'Then for what reason did you not believe him?' ²⁶ But if we say, 'From humans', we fear the crowd. For they all are holding John as *a* prophet". ²⁷ And having responded *to* Jesus, they said, "We do not know". **He** also said *to* them, "Nor am I telling you by what-kind-of authority I am doing these *things*.

One Son Feigns Obedience, One Disobeys But Repents. Which Did The Father's Will?

²⁸ "But what seems *right to* you?— *A* man had two children. And having gone to the first he said, 'Child, go, work today in the vineyard'. ²⁹ And the *one*, having responded, said, 'I will not'. But having regretted^B *it* later, he went. ³⁰ And having gone to the other, he spoke similarly. And the *one*, having responded, said, 'I *will*, sir', and he did not go. ³¹ Which of the two did the will *of* the father?" They say, "The first".

You Priests Feign Obedience To God, But Did Not Believe John, God's Messenger

Jesus says *to* them, "Truly I say *to* you that the tax-collectors and the prostitutes are going-ahead-of you into the kingdom *of* God. ³² For John came to you in^C *the* way *of* righteousness and you did not believe him. But the tax collectors and the prostitutes believed him. And **you**, having seen *it*, did not-even regret *it* later, *that you might* believe him.

You Priests Are Like Farmers Who Killed The Owner's Messengers And Son

³³ "Listen-to another parable. There was *a* man *who was a* house-master, who planted *a* vineyard and put *a* fence around it and dug *a* winepress in it and built *a* tower. And he rented it *to* farmers and went-on-a-journey. ³⁴ And when the time *of* the fruits drew-near, he sent forth his slaves to the farmers to receive his fruits. ³⁵ And the farmers, having taken his slaves, beat one, and killed another, and stoned another. ³⁶ Again he sent-forth other slaves— more *than* the first. And they did similarly *to* them. ³⁷ But finally he sent forth his son to them, saying, 'They will have-regard-for my son'. ³⁸ But the farmers, having seen the son, said among themselves, 'This is the heir. Come, let us kill him and let us have his inheritance'. ³⁹ And having taken him, they threw *him* outside *of* the vineyard and killed *him*. ⁴⁰ Therefore when the owner *of* the vineyard comes, what will he do *to* those farmers?" ⁴¹ They say *to* Him, "He will miserably destroy *the* miserable *ones* themselves! And he will rent the vineyard *to* other farmers who will give-back the fruits *to* him in their seasons".

The Kingdom Will Be Taken Away Because You Rejected God's Cornerstone

⁴² Jesus says *to* them, "Did you never read in the Scriptures, '*The* stone which the *ones* building rejected, this became *the* head^D *of the* corner. This came about

---

A. Or, what authority. That is, a prophet's authority? Messiah's? **B.** Or, changed *his* mind. **C.** That is, in connection with. **D.** That is, the headstone belonging to the corner. This may mean the cornerstone of a foundation; or, the capstone in the arch.

from *the* Lord, and it is marvelous in our eyes'? [Ps 118:22-23]. ⁴³ For this reasonᴬ I say *to* you that the kingdom *of* God will be taken-away from you, and will be given *to a* nationᴮ producing its fruits. ⁴⁴ And the *one* having fallen upon this stone will be broken-to-piecesᶜ. And upon whomever it may fall, it will crushᴰ him".

When The Invited Refuse To Attend The Wedding Of The King's Son, They Are Destroyed
⁴⁵ And having heard His parables, the chief priests and the Pharisees knew that He was speaking about them. ⁴⁶ And while seeking to seize Him, they feared the crowds, because they were holding Him for *a* prophet. **22:1** And having responded, Jesus again spoke in parables *to* them, saying, ² "The kingdom *of* the heavens became-likeᴱ *a* man *who was a* king, who made wedding-celebrations *for* his son. ³ And he sent out his slaves to call the *ones* having been invitedᶠ to the wedding-celebrations, and they were not willing to come. ⁴ Again he sent out other slaves saying, 'Say *to* the *ones* having been invited, "Behold— I have prepared my luncheonᴳ, my bulls and fatted-cattle having been slaughtered, and everything *is* prepared. Come to the wedding-celebrations" '. ⁵ But the *ones*, having paid-no-concernᴴ, departed— one to *his* own field, and another on his business. ⁶ And the rest, having seized his slaves, mistreated *them* and killed *them*. ⁷ And the king became angryᴵ. And having sent his troops, he destroyed those murderers and set their city on fire. ⁸ Then he says *to* his slaves, 'The wedding-celebration is prepared— but the *ones* having been invited were not worthy! ⁹ Therefore go to the outletsᴶ *of* the roads, and invite all-that you find to the wedding-celebrations'. ¹⁰ And having gone out into the roads, those slaves gathered-together all whom they found, both evilᴷ and good. And the wedding-hall was filled *with ones* reclining-back [to eat]. ¹¹ And the king, having come in to seeᴸ the *ones* reclining-back [to eat], saw there *a* person not having dressed-inᴹ *the* clothing *of* ᴺ *a* wedding. ¹² And he says *to* him, 'Friend, how did you come in here, not having *the* clothing *of a* wedding?' But the *one* was silenced. ¹³ Then the king said *to* the servants, 'Having bound his feet and hands, throw him out, into the outer darkness'. In that place, there will be the weeping and the grinding *of* teeth. ¹⁴ For many are called *ones*, but few *are* chosen *ones*".

The Pharisees Try To Snare Jesus: Shall We Pay Taxes To Caesar?
¹⁵ Then the Pharisees, having gone, took counsel so that they might snare Him in *a* statement. ¹⁶ And they send-forth their disciples *to* Him, with the Herodiansᴼ, saying, "Teacher, we know that You are truthful, and You teach the way *of* God in truth. And You

are not concerned about [pleasing] anyone, for You do not look at *the* face^A *of* people. ^17 Tell us then, what seems *right to* You? Is it lawful to give *a* poll-tax^B *to* Caesar, or not?" ^18 But having known their evilness^C, Jesus said, "Why are you testing Me, hypocrites? ^19 Show Me the coin *for* the poll-tax". And the *ones* brought to Him *a* denarius^D. ^20 And He says *to* them, "Whose *is* this image and inscription?" ^21 They say *to* Him, "Caesar's". Then He says *to* them, "Then give-back^E the *things of* Caesar *to* Caesar, and the *things of* God *to* God". ^22 And having heard *it*, they marveled. And having left Him, they went away.

The Sadducees Try To Snare Jesus On The Resurrection of a Wife With Seven Husbands
^23 On that day Sadducees came to Him— *ones* saying *that* there is not *a* resurrection. And they questioned Him, ^24 saying, "Teacher, Moses said [in Deut 25:5] 'If someone dies not having children, his brother shall as-next-of-kin-marry^F his wife and raise-up *a* seed^G *for* his brother'. ^25 Now there were seven brothers with us. And the first, having married, came-to-an-end^H. And not having *a* seed, he left his wife *to* his brother. ^26 Likewise also the second, and the third, up to the seventh. ^27 And last *of* all, the woman died. ^28 In the resurrection, therefore, *of* which *of* the seven will she be *the* wife? For they all had her!" ^29 But having responded, Jesus said *to* them, "You are mistaken^I, not knowing the Scriptures, nor the power *of* God. ^30 For in the resurrection, they neither marry nor are given-in-marriage, but are like angels^J in heaven. ^31 And concerning the resurrection *of* the dead, did you not read the *thing* having been spoken *to* you by God^K, saying [in Ex 3:15] ^32 'I am the God *of* Abraham, and the God *of* Isaac, and the God *of* Jacob'? He is not the God *of* dead *ones*, but *of* living *ones*". ^33 And having heard *it*, the crowds were astounded at His teaching.

A Scribe Tests Jesus: Which Is The Great Commandment?
^34 And the Pharisees, having heard that He silenced the Sadducees, were gathered-together at the same *place.* ^35 And one of them, *a* Law-expert, asked *Him*— testing Him— ^36 "Teacher, which *is the* great^L commandment in the Law?" ^37 And the *One* said *to* him: " 'You shall love *the* Lord your God with your whole heart, and with your whole soul, and with your whole mind' [Deut 6:5]— ^38 this is the great and foremost^M commandment. ^39 And *the* second *is* like it, 'You shall love your neighbor as yourself' [Lev 19:18]. ^40 The whole Law and the Prophets hang^N on these two commandments".

Jesus Asks The Pharisees, If David Calls The Messiah His Lord, How Can He Be His Son?
^41 Now the Pharisees having^O been gathered-together, Jesus questioned them, ^42 saying, "What seems *right to* you concerning the Christ— Whose son is He?" They say *to* Him, "David's". ^43 He says *to* them, "How then does David by^P *the* Spirit call Him 'Lord', saying [in Ps 110:1], ^44 '*The* Lord said *to* my Lord, "Be sitting on My right *side*, until I put Your

A. That is, You show no partiality toward anyone in Your teaching. **B.** That is, taxes based on a census and paid to the Emperor. Is it lawful to pay taxes to a foreign king? **C.** Or, maliciousness. **D.** This is a Roman silver coin. **E.** Or, render, pay. **F.** This marriage-as-next-of-kin is called 'levirite' marriage (from a Latin word meaning 'brother-in-law'). **G.** That is, offspring; and thus, a posterity. **H.** That is, died. **I.** Or, deceived, going astray; or, deceiving-*yourselves*. **J.** That is, not subject to death (and so not needing to marry and procreate), and members of God's family, not separate families. See Lk 20:36. **K.** God spoke to you about the resurrection when He said 'I am the God of Abraham'. **L.** Or by implication, the greatest. **M.** Or, first. **N.** That is, like a door on its hinges. **O.** That is, since the Pharisees had gathered-together (in v 34). **P.** Or, in. That is, under the inspiration of the Spirit.

enemies under Your feet"'? [45] Therefore if David calls Him 'Lord', how[A] is He his son?" [46] And no one was able to answer Him *a* word, nor did anyone dare from that day to question Him any more.

Jesus Tells The Crowds: Do Not Act Like The Scribes And Pharisees
23:1 Then Jesus spoke *to* the crowds and *to* His disciples, [2] saying— "The scribes and the Pharisees sat-*down*[B] on *the* seat *of* Moses. [3] Therefore, do and be keeping all that they tell you. But do not be acting[C] in accordance with their works. For they say *things* and do not do *them*. [4] And they bind-up heavy and hard-to-bear burdens[D] and lay them on the shoulders *of* people. But **they** are not willing to move[E] them *with* their finger. [5] And they do all their works so-as to be seen *by* people. For they widen their phylacteries[F] and lengthen *their* tassels[G]. [6] And they love the place-of-honor[H] at the banquets, and the seats-of-honor[I] in the synagogues, [7] and the greetings in the marketplaces, and to be called 'Rabbi'[J] by people. [8] But you— do not be called[K] 'Rabbi'. For One is your Teacher, and **you** are all brothers. [9] And do not call[L] *one* on earth your father. For One is your Father— the heavenly *One*. [10] Nor be called master-teachers[M], because your master-teacher is One— the Christ. [11] But the greater[N] *of* you shall be your servant. [12] And whoever will exalt himself will be humbled, and whoever will humble himself will be exalted.

Woe To You, Scribes And Pharisees. You Are Blind Guides. How Will You Escape Hell?
[13] "But woe *to* you, scribes and Pharisees, hypocrites, because you are shutting the kingdom *of* the heavens in-front-of[O] people. For **you** are not entering, nor are you permitting the *ones* entering to enter. [14] [P]   [15] Woe *to* you, scribes and Pharisees, hypocrites, because you go-around the sea and the dry *land* to make one proselyte. And when he becomes *one*, you make him *a* son *of* Gehenna[Q] double-more *than* you. [16] Woe *to* you, blind guides— the *ones* saying, 'Whoever swears-an-oath by the temple, it is nothing. But whoever swears-an-oath by the gold *of* the temple, he is obligated'. [17] Foolish and blind *ones*! For which is greater, the gold, or the temple having sanctified[R] the gold? [18] And, 'Whoever swears-an-oath by the altar, it is nothing. But whoever swears-an-oath by the gift[S] on it, he is obligated'. [19] Blind *ones*! For which *is* greater, the gift, or the altar sanctifying the gift? [20] Therefore, the *one* having sworn by the altar is swearing by it and by all the *things* on it. [21] And the *one*

A. If Messiah is David's own Lord, how can He be his distant physical descendant? Jesus is God's Son (David's Lord) and Mary's son (David's descendant). **B.** That is, they took their seat as teachers of the Law. **C.** Lit, doing. That is, Do what they teach you from the Law, but do not be doing what they do. **D.** Jesus is referring to their traditions, their man-made rules of conduct. **E.** That is, to help those carrying them; or, to carry them themselves. **F.** That is, the small leather boxes worn on the forehead and arm, containing Ex 13:1-10, 11-16; Deut 6:4-9; 11:13-21. This symbolized guarding oneself to keep the commandments, in literal obedience to Ex 13:9, 16; Deut 6:8; 11:18. But the Pharisees made them bigger for show. **G.** That is, the tassels the Jews wore on the four corners of their garments in obedience to Num 15:38-41. Jesus Himself wore them, Mt 9:20; 14:36. But they lengthened them for show. **H.** Lit, the first reclining place (they reclined to eat); the foremost place to eat. **I.** Lit, first seats, foremost seats. **J.** Or, Teacher. **K.** Do not accept the title of 'teacher', elevating you above your brothers and sisters. God is your teacher. **L.** Do not give out such honor to others by calling them 'father'. **M.** That is, the honored teaching expert who leads the way in a thing. **N.** Or, greatest. **O.** You pull the door shut from the outside before they can enter. **P.** Some manuscripts have here, 'And woe *to* you scribes and Pharisees, hypocrites, because you devour the houses *of* the widows, and *are* praying long *for a* pretense. Because of this, you will receive *a* greater condemnation'. **Q.** That is, hell. You make converts to Phariseeism, not to God. **R.** Or, consecrated, made holy. **S.** That is, the sacrificial offering.

having sworn by the temple is swearing by it and by the *One* dwelling-in^A it. **22** And the *one* having sworn by heaven is swearing by the throne *of* God and by the *One* sitting on it. **23** Woe *to* you, scribes and Pharisees, hypocrites, because you are giving-a-tenth-of the mint and the dill and the cummin, and you neglected^B the weightier *things of* the Law— the justice, and the mercy, and the faithfulness^C. But *you* ought-to-have done these *things*, and not be neglecting those *things*. **24** Blind guides— the *ones* straining-out^D the gnat, but swallowing^E the camel! **25** Woe *to* you, scribes and Pharisees, hypocrites, because you cleanse the outside *of* the cup and the dish, but inside they are full from^F [your] plundering and self-indulgence. **26** Blind Pharisee— first cleanse the inside *of* the cup, in order that the outside *of* it may also become clean! **27** Woe *to* you, scribes and Pharisees, hypocrites, because you are similar *to* burial-places having been whitewashed^G, which outside appear beautiful, but inside are full *of* bones *of* dead *ones* and all impurity! **28** So also you outside appear righteous *to* people— but inside you are full *of* hypocrisy and lawlessness! **29** Woe *to* you, scribes and Pharisees, hypocrites, because you build the burial-places *of* the prophets and adorn^H the tombs *of* the righteous *ones,* **30** and say, 'If we had been in the days *of* our fathers, we would not have been their partners in the blood *of* the prophets'. **31** So then, you are testifying *concerning* yourselves that you are sons^I *of* the *ones* having murdered the prophets. **32** And **you**— fill-up^J the measure *of* your fathers! **33** Snakes, brood *of* vipers, how may you escape from the condemnation *of* ^K Gehenna?

God Will Avenge The Blood of All The Righteous On You. Your House Is Left Desolate
34 "For this reason behold, **I** am sending-forth prophets and wise *ones* and scribes^L to you— *some* of them you will kill and crucify, and *some* of them you will whip in your synagogues and persecute from city to city— **35** so that all *the* righteous blood being shed on the earth^M may come upon you^N: from the blood *of* Abel^O the righteous *one*, up to the blood *of* Zechariah, son *of* Berechiah, whom you murdered between the temple and the altar. **36** Truly I say *to* you, all these *things* will come upon this generation. **37** Jerusalem, Jerusalem, the *one* killing the prophets and stoning the *ones* having been sent-forth to her. How often I wanted to gather together your children the way *a* hen gathers together her chicks under *her* wings, and you did not want *it*. **38** Behold— your house is being left *to* you desolate^P. **39** For I say *to* you, you will by no means see Me^Q from now *on* until you say, 'Blessed *is* the *One* coming in *the* name *of the* Lord' ".

A. Or, inhabiting. God dwelled in this temple in the same way as in all the earth, not in a local sense, as said in Act 7:48; 17:24. Yet He also dwelled in it as the place where He chose to be worshiped by His people Israel in accordance with the Law He gave them. **B.** Or, let go, left behind. **C.** That is, fidelity, being trustworthy. Or, faith. **D.** Or, filtering. **E.** Gnats and camels were both unclean under the Law of Moses. Jesus does not fault the Pharisees for their over-attention to micro-matters (they actually filtered the gnats out of their drinks), but for their under-attention to the big issues (they figuratively swallowed camels). **F.** Or, of. The cup is full with the things resulting from your greedy and self-indulgent actions. **G.** A month before Passover, burial places were whitewashed to prevent pilgrims from accidentally coming in contact with them and becoming ceremonially unclean. **H.** Or, decorate, put in order. **I.** That is, you share the traits of your fathers who murdered the prophets. Compare Lk 11:48. **J.** This is a command. Do what is in your hearts! Do what your fathers did! **K.** That is, consisting of. The sentence consisting of hell. **L.** Jesus is referring to the apostles and others whom He will send after His death. **M.** Or, land. **N.** That is, so that the bloodguilt of your fathers may be avenged upon you as you repeat their crimes on those I send. **O:** Abel to Zechariah. That is, from the first recorded murder in the OT to the last (in the Hebrew order of books). **P.** Or, deserted, empty. **Q.** That is, as Messiah, son of God. These

Jesus Tells His Disciples That The Temple Will Be Destroyed. They Ask, When?

24:1 And having departed from the temple, Jesus was proceeding. And His disciples came to *Him* to show Him the buildings *of* the temple. **2** But the *One*, having responded, said *to* them, "Do you see all these *things*? Truly I say *to* you— *a* stone upon *a* stone will by no means be left here which will not be torn-down^A". **3** And while He *was* sitting on the Mount *of* Olives, the disciples came to Him privately, saying, "Tell us— when will these^B *things* happen? And what *will be* the sign *of* Your coming and *the* conclusion^C *of* the age?" **4** And having responded, Jesus said *to* them—

There Will Be Birthpangs, But The Gospel Will Reach The Whole World Before The End

"Be watching out *that* no one may deceive you. **5** For^D many will come on the basis of My name, saying, 'I am the Christ'. And they will deceive many. **6** And you will-certainly^E hear-*of* wars and rumors *of* wars. See^F *that* you are not alarmed! For *they* must take place, but it is not yet the end. **7** For nation will arise against nation, and kingdom against kingdom. And there will be famines and earthquakes in various places. **8** But all these *things are*^G *a* beginning *of* birth-pains. **9** Then^H they will hand you over to affliction, and they will kill you. And you will be being hated by all the nations because of My name. **10** And then^I many will be caused-to-fall, and will hand one another over, and will hate one another. **11** And many false-prophets will arise and deceive many. **12** And the love *of* the majority will grow cold because of lawlessness being multiplied. **13** But the *one* having endured to *the* end^J— this *one* will be saved. **14** And this good-news *of* the kingdom will be proclaimed in the whole world for *a* testimony *to* all the nations. And then the end^K will come.

When You See Daniel's Abomination, Flee. For There Will Be a Great Affliction

15 "Therefore when you see^L the abomination *of* desolation^M— the *thing* having been spoken through Daniel the prophet— standing in *the* holy place^N (let the *one* reading understand), **16** then let the *ones* in Judea be fleeing to the mountains. **17** Let the *one* upon the housetop not go down to take the *things* out of his house. **18** And let the *one* in the field not turn behind to take his cloak. **19** And woe *to* the *ones* having *a child* in *the* womb, and *to* the *ones* nursing in those days. **20** And be praying that your flight may not take place *in* winter, nor *on a* Sabbath. **21** For then^O there will be *a* great affliction^P such as has not taken place since *the* beginning *of the* world until now, nor

words represent the end of the public ministry of Jesus to Israel. **A.** Or, destroyed, demolished, done away with. **B.** That is, the tearing down of the temple (24:3), the things coming upon this generation (23:34-36), the house being left desolate (23:38). **C.** Or, consummation, completion, finish, end. **D.** Some think v 5-14 refer to events prior to the destruction of Jerusalem in A.D. 70; others, to birth-pains that started in the apostles' day and continue until the end, which begins in v 14b; others, that Jesus intended a double meaning, one for the apostles' day and one for the end-time when these birth-pains will precede the end. **E.** Or, must hear, **will** hear. **F.** Or, Watch out! Do not be alarmed! **G.** Or, *will be*. **H.** That is, next in time (some amount of time after v 6-8); or, next in sequence without reference to time (Next, as the birth-pains continue). Or, At that time (at the time of the birth-pains). The meaning can be affected by which rendering is chosen. This word is also in 24:10, 14, 16, 21, 23, 30, 40; 25:1, 7, 31, 34, 37, 41, 44, 45. **I.** Or, at that time. **J.** That is, the end of his life, or the coming of Christ, whichever comes first. **K.** That is, the coming of Christ; or, the beginning of the end time. **L.** Some think that this is the sign of the destruction of Jerusalem, as in Lk 21:20-24; others, that it is the sign of the beginning of the end time, as in 2 Thes 2:3-4; others, both. **M.** That is, an act of sacrilege *characterized by* or *consisting of* or *resulting in* desolation. The term comes from Dan 9:27; 11:31; 12:11. **N.** This could refer to the A.D. 70 temple or an end-time temple of God, or to Jerusalem, or to Judea. **O.** Or, at that time. **P.** Or, distress, trouble, tribulation.

ever will take place. [22] And if those days had not been shortened[A], no[B] flesh would have been saved. But those days will be shortened for the sake of the chosen *ones*.

Do Not Be Deceived. My Coming Will Be As Visible To All As Lightning
[23] Then[C] if someone says *to* you, 'Behold— here *is* the Christ,' or 'Here', do not believe *it*. [24] For false-christs and false-prophets will arise and give great signs and wonders, so as to deceive, if possible, even the chosen *ones*. [25] Behold— I have told you beforehand. [26] Therefore, if they say *to* you, 'Behold— He is in the wilderness', do not go out; 'Behold— *He is* in the inner-rooms', do not believe *it*. [27] For just as the lightning comes out from *the* east and is visible[D] as far as *the* west, so will the coming *of* the Son *of* Man be. [28] Wherever the corpse[E] may be, there the vultures will be gathered.

After That Affliction, The Powers Will Be Shaken. I Will Come On The Clouds In Glory
[29] "And immediately after the affliction *of* those days, the sun[F] will be darkened, and the moon will not give its glow, and the stars will fall from the heaven, and the powers *of* the heavens will be shaken. [30] And then[G] the sign *of* the Son *of* Man will appear in *the* heaven. And at-that-time all the tribes *of* the earth will beat-their-breasts. And they will see the Son *of* man coming on the clouds *of* heaven with power and great glory. [31] And He will send-out His angels with *a* loud trumpet. And they will gather together His chosen *ones* from the four winds, from *the* ends[H] *of* the heavens to their [other] ends.

The Parable of The Fig Tree: When You See These Things, You Know I Am Near
[32] "Now learn the parable from the fig-tree[I]: when its branch already becomes tender and grows-out *its* leaves, you know that the summer *is* near. [33] So also you— when you see all[J] these *things,* you know[K] that He[L] is near, at *the* doors. [34] Truly I say *to* you that this[M] generation will by no means pass away until all these *things* take place. [35] Heaven and earth will pass away, but My words will by-no-means pass away.

But No One Knows The Day And Hour, So Keep Watching And Be Prepared Always
[36] "But no one knows about that day and hour— not even the angels *of* the heavens, nor the Son— except the Father alone. [37] For just as the days *of* Noah *were*, so will

---

A. Or, curtailed, cut short. **B.** Lit, all flesh would not have. Some think all flesh means all humanity; others, all those in Judea, v 16. **C.** Or, At that time. **D.** Or, shines. **E.** The corpses may be those killed at the return of Christ; both His coming and its aftermath will be unmistakable. Or, linking this with v 24, the false prophets (the vultures) will gather upon the spiritually dead (the corpses). Or, linking this with v 15-26, Jerusalem (the corpse) will attract the Roman 'eagles' (as 'vultures' can also be rendered). Or, this may be a general rule: As corpses attract vultures, so the spiritually dead will attract judgment. **F:** sun... moon... stars... powers. Some take these as literal end-time events; others, as symbolic of the fall of political rulers. **G.** Or, at that time. **H.** Or, extremities. That is, from horizon to horizon; or, from all earth (the four winds) and all heaven. **I.** Some think that this has reference to Israel; others, that it is simply an illustration for which any fruit tree would have worked, as in Lk 21:29. **J.** When you see all of v 5-29 or 15-29, you are seeing the tree leafed out. **K.** Or, know that (a command). **L.** Or, it, Christ's coming. **M.** Some think Jesus means the apostles' generation, which would see all these things (v 5 or 15 to v 28 or 29) fulfilled in the destruction of Jerusalem (compare 23:36). Since that day, He is at the door. Others think He means the generation alive to see all these things in the end-time. Others think 'this generation' refers to unbelieving Israel (as often in the Gospels). Such persons will continue until He returns.

the coming *of* the Son *of* Man be. **38** For as in those days before the flood they were eating and drinking, marrying and giving-in-marriage, until which day Noah entered into the ark, **39** and did not know until the flood came and took-away everyone, so also^A will the coming *of* the Son *of* Man be. **40** At-that-time there will be two *men* in the field— one is taken, and one is left; **41** two *women* grinding at the mill— one is taken^B, and one is left. **42** Therefore keep-watching, because you do not know *on* which day your Lord is coming. **43** And you know^C that *saying*, that if the house-master had known *on* which watch^D the thief was coming, he would have kept-watch^E and would not have allowed his house to be broken-into. **44** For this reason **you** also be prepared *ones*— because the Son *of* Man is coming *at an* hour which you do not expect.

Wise Servants Found Working When The Master Returns Will Be Put In Charge of More
45 "Who then^F is the faithful and wise slave whom *his* master put-in-charge^G over his body-of-servants^H *that he might* give them *their* food at *the* proper-time? **46** Blessed *is* that slave whom his master, having come, will find so doing. **47** Truly I say *to* you that he will put him in charge over all his possessions. **48** But if that bad slave says in his heart, 'My master is delaying', **49** and begins to strike his fellow-slaves, and is eating and drinking with the *ones* being drunk— **50** the master *of* that slave will come on *a* day which he does not expect, and at *an* hour which he does not know. **51** And he will cut him in two, and assign *him* his part^I with the hypocrites. In that place, there will be the weeping and the grinding *of* teeth.

Wise Bridesmaids Will Keep Watch And Stay Prepared For The Coming of The Groom
25:1 "At-that-time^J, the kingdom *of* the heavens will be-like ten virgins, who, having taken their lamps^K, went out to meet the bridegroom. **2** Now five of them were foolish, and five *were* wise. **3** For the foolish *ones*, having taken their lamps, did not take oil with them. **4** But the wise *ones* took oil in jars with their lamps. **5** And while the bridegroom *was* delaying, they all became drowsy and were sleeping. **6** And *in the* middle *of the* night, *a* shout has come— 'Behold, the bridegroom! Come out to meet him!' **7** Then all those virgins arose and put their lamps in-order. **8** And the foolish *ones* said *to* the wise *ones*, 'Give us from your oil, because our lamps are going-out^L'. **9** But the wise *ones* responded, saying, 'There will not by any means ever^M be enough *for* us and *for* you. Go instead to the *ones* selling and buy *for* yourselves'. **10** And while they *were* going away to buy, the bridegroom came. And the prepared *ones* entered with him into the wedding-celebrations. And the door was shut. **11** And later, the other virgins also come, saying, 'Sir, sir, open *for* us'. **12** But the *one*, having

---

A. That is, life was going on as normal, and God suddenly and unexpectedly intervened into human history. **B.** Or, taken along... left behind. Some think believers are taken, referring either to protection on earth (as with Noah) or in heaven (through the rapture); unbelievers are left for judgment. Others think unbelievers are taken in judgment, believers are left on earth (like Noah). **C.** Or, know that (a command to understand). **D.** That is, watch of the night. The night was divided into four watches. **E.** That is, he would have been prepared for the thief when he came. Since he does not know when the thief is coming, he must be prepared at all times. **F.** In view of the sudden nature of Christ's return, who is the wise slave among those left to lead when the master left? The wise one is the one doing his will when he returns. **G.** Or, appointed, set. **H.** That is, the master's group of servants which he left to do whatever tasks he had assigned to them. **I.** Or, share, place. **J.** That is, when Jesus comes unexpectedly. **K.** Or, torches. **L.** Or, being quenched. **M:** There will not by any means ever be enough. Or, No! There will by no means be enough.

responded, said, 'Truly I say *to* you, I do not know^A you'. ^13 Therefore, keep-watching, because you do not know the day nor the hour.

Wise Servants Will Put Their Talents To Work For The Master While He Is Gone
^14 "For *it*^B *is* just like *a* man going-on-a-journey— he called *his* own slaves and handed over his possessions *to* them. ^15 And he gave five talents^C *to* one, and two *to* another, and one *to* another— *to* each according to *his* own ability. And he went on *his* journey. ^16 Immediately^D having gone, the *one* having received the five talents worked with them and gained another five. ^17 Similarly, the *one having received* the two *talents* gained another two. ^18 But the *one* having received the one *talent*, having gone, dug [a hole in] *the* ground and hid his master's silver *talent.* ^19 Now after much time, the master *of* those slaves comes and settles *the* account with them. ^20 And having come to *him*, the *one* having received the five talents brought another five talents, saying, 'Master, you handed-over five talents *to* me. Look, I gained another five talents'. ^21 His master said *to* him, 'Well^E *done*, good and faithful slave. You were faithful over *a* few *things.* I will put you in charge over many *things.* Enter into the joy *of* your master'. ^22 And also having come to *him*, the *one having received* the two talents said, 'Master, you handed over two talents *to* me. Look, I gained another two talents'. ^23 His master said *to* him, 'Well *done*, good and faithful slave. You were faithful over *a* few *things.* I will put you in charge over many *things.* Enter into the joy *of* your master'. ^24 And also having come to *him*, the *one* having received^F the one talent said, 'Master, I knew you— that you are *a* hard man, reaping where you did not sow and gathering from where you did not scatter^G [threshings]. ^25 And having become afraid, having gone, I hid your talent in the ground. Look, you have what *is* yours'. ^26 But having responded, his master said *to* him, 'Evil and lazy slave! You knew that I reap where I did not sow and gather from where I did not scatter^H! ^27 Therefore you should-have put my money *with* the bankers. And having come, **I** would have received-back what *was* mine with interest. ^28 Therefore take the talent away from him, and give *it to* the *one* having the ten talents. ^29 For *to* everyone having, it will be given, and he will be caused-to-abound. But *from* the *one* not having, even what he has will be taken away from him. ^30 And throw-out the unprofitable^I slave into the outer darkness'. In that place, there will be the weeping and the grinding *of* teeth.

When The King Comes In Glory, Mankind Will Be Sent To Their Eternal Destinies
^31 "Now when^J the Son *of* Man comes in His glory, and all the angels with Him, at-that-time He will sit on *the* throne^K *of* His glory, ^32 and all the nations will be gathered in front of Him. And He will separate them^L from one another, just as the shepherd

A. Thus they were also foolish because they thought of themselves as friends of the bridegroom, yet he did not even know them. **B.** That is, the kingdom of the heavens, v 1. Or, For *He*, the Son of Man. **C.** One silver talent was equivalent to 6000 denari, 6000 days wages for a laborer. This large sum of money represents our individual gifts and abilities, spiritual and natural. **D:** journey. Immediately having gone. Or, journey immediately. Having gone. **E.** Or, *It is* good; or, Excellent! **F.** This is a different tense of this word, implying here 'having received and still having'. **G.** Or, winnow. Or, scatter [seed], repeating the previous statement. This one did nothing with what he was given, and seeks to excuse himself by blaming it on the master— Because you are they way you are, I did not invest what you gave me. **H:** scatter! Therefore. Or, scatter? Then. **I.** Or, worthless, useless, good-for-nothing. He brought no gain to the master. **J.** Jesus returns to where He left off in 24:31. **K.** Or, His throne *of* glory; or, His glorious throne. **L.** Grammatically this does not refer to 'nations', but to the people in the nations,

separates the sheep from the goats. **33** And He will make the sheep stand^A on His right *side*, and the goats on *the* left *side*. **34** Then the King will say *to* the *ones* on His right *side*, 'Come, the *ones* having been blessed *of* ^B My Father— inherit the kingdom having been prepared *for* you since *the* foundation *of the* world. **35** For I was hungry, and you gave Me *something* to eat. I thirsted, and you gave-a-drink-*to* Me. I was *a* stranger, and you brought^C Me in; **36** naked^D, and you clothed Me. I was sick, and you looked-after Me. I was in prison, and you came to Me'. **37** Then the righteous *ones* will respond *to* Him, saying, 'Lord, when did we see You hungering and we fed *You*, or thirsting and we gave-a-drink? **38** And when did we see You *a* stranger and we brought *You* in, or naked and we clothed *You*? **39** And when did we see You being sick or in prison and we came to You?' **40** And having responded, the King will say *to* them, 'Truly I say *to* you, in-as-much-as^E you did *it to* one *of* the least *of* these My brothers^F, you did *it to* Me'. **41** Then He will also say *to* the *ones* on *the* left *side*, 'Depart from Me, the *ones* having been cursed, into the eternal fire having been prepared *for* the devil and his angels. **42** For I was hungry, and you did not give Me *something* to eat. I thirsted, and you did not give-a-drink-*to* Me. **43** I was *a* stranger, and you did not bring Me in; naked, and you did not clothe Me; sick, and in prison, and you did not look after Me'. **44** Then **they** also will respond, saying, 'Lord, when did we see You hungering, or thirsting, or *a* stranger, or naked, or sick, or in prison, and we did not serve You?' **45** Then He will respond *to* them, saying, 'Truly I say *to* you, in as much as you did not do *it to* one *of* the least *of* these, neither did you do *it to* Me'. **46** And these will go to eternal punishment, but the righteous *ones* to eternal life".

The King Is Put To Death
26:1 And it came about *that* when Jesus finished all^G these words, He said *to* His disciples, **2** "You know that after two days the Passover [Feast] comes^H, and the Son *of* Man is handed-over so as to be crucified".

The Priests Plot To Seize And Kill Jesus
3 Then the chief priests and the elders *of* the people were gathered together in the courtyard^I *of* the high priest, the *one* being called Caiaphas. **4** And they plotted in order that they might seize Jesus *by* deceit^J and kill *Him*. **5** But they were saying, "Not during the Feast, in order that no uproar may take place among the people".

Jesus Is Anointed With Oil In Preparation For His Burial
6 Now Jesus having come-to-be in Bethany at *the* house *of* Simon the leper, **7** *a* woman came to Him having *an* alabaster-jar *of* very-expensive perfume^K. And she poured *it* down upon His head while *He was* reclining-back [to eat]. **8** But having seen *it*, the disciples were indignant, saying, "For what *purpose is* this waste? **9** For this could have been sold *for* much and given *to* poor one^s". **10** But having known *it*, Jesus said *to* them, "Why are you causing troubles *for* the woman? For she worked *a* good work^L for^M Me. **11** For you

---

who are referred to next as sheep and goats. **A.** Or, put the sheep, set the sheep. **B.** That is, *by*. **C.** Or, took Me with *you*; that is, into your house or with you on your way. Or, gathered Me in with *yourself*; that is, to help Me. **D.** That is, without adequate clothing. **E.** Or, to the extent that, in so far as. **F.** That is, family-members. **G.** That is, all the words spoken in chapters 24-25; or, that day (21:23-25:46); or, in the public ministry (4:17-25:46). **H.** Or, takes place. **I.** Or, palace. **J.** Or, treachery, cunning. **K.** Or, fragrant oil. **L.** Or, did a good deed. **M.** Or, to, with reference to.

always have the poor with you, but you do not always have **Me.** [12] For this *one* having put this perfume on My body did *it* so as to[A] prepare Me for burial. [13] Truly I say *to* you, wherever this good-news is proclaimed in the whole world, what this *one* did will also be spoken for *a memorial of* her".

Jesus Is Betrayed By One of The Twelve
[14] Then one *of* the twelve, the *one* being called Judas Iscariot, having gone to the chief priests, [15] said, "What are you willing to give me, and **I** will hand Him over *to* you?" And the *ones* set[B] thirty silver-coins *for* him. [16] And from that time *on,* he was seeking *a* favorable-opportunity in order that he might hand Him over.

Jesus Celebrates Passover With The Twelve
[17] Now *on* the first *day of* the *Feast of* Unleavened-Bread, the disciples came to Jesus, saying, "Where do You want us to prepare *for* You to eat the Passover [meal]?" [18] And the *One* said, "Go into the city to so-and-so[C], and say *to* him, 'The Teacher says, "My time is near. I am doing[D] the Passover [meal] with you, along-with My disciples"'" [19] And the disciples did as Jesus directed them. And they prepared the Passover [meal]. [20] And having become evening, He was reclining back [to eat] with the twelve.

The Betrayer Is Exposed
[21] And while they *were* eating, He said, "Truly I say *to* you that one of you will hand Me over". [22] And while being extremely grieved, each one began to say *to* Him, "**I** am not *the one, am I,* Lord?" [23] And the *One,* having responded, said, "The *one* having dipped *his* hand with[E] Me in the bowl— this *one* will hand Me over. [24] The Son *of* Man is going just as it has been written about Him— but woe *to* that man by whom the Son *of* Man is being handed-over! It *would have* been better *for* him if that man had not been born". [25] And having responded, Judas, the *one* handing Him over, said, "**I** am not[F] *the one, am I,* Rabbi?" He says *to* him, "**You** said[G] *it* ".

The Bread And The Wine Are Given a New Meaning
[26] And while they *were* eating, having taken bread and having blessed *it*[H], Jesus broke *it*. And having given *it to* the disciples, He said, "Take, eat. This is My body". [27] And having taken *a* cup and given-thanks, He gave *it to* them, saying, "Drink from it, everyone. [28] For this is My blood *of*[I] the covenant— the *blood* being poured-out for many for forgiveness *of* sins. [29] And I say *to* you, I will by-no-means drink of this fruit *of* the grapevine from now *on* until that day when I drink it new with you in the kingdom *of* My Father".

A. Jesus may mean that she knowingly did it for this purpose; or, that she did so without realizing it. **B.** This may mean 'set on a scale', and thus, weighed out, paid; Or, set as the price, intending to pay upon delivery. **C.** Some think Jesus did not name the person so that Judas would not know in advance; others think Matthew did not name the person to protect him from the Jews. **D.** That is, observing, performing. **E.** That is, It is one of the ones eating with Me. **F.** When his turn arrives, Judas asks the same question, which expects a 'No' answer. **G.** This may simply mean 'Yes'; or, it may be intentionally ambiguous, leaving the hearers to take it one way (You said it *rightly;* you are not the one'), but meaning the opposite (You said it *falsely*; you are the one). The eleven thought Jesus meant the former; Jesus and Judas knew He meant the latter. **H.** Or, blessed *God.* **I.** That is, inaugurating the new covenant.

You Will All Be Scattered In Fulfillment of Zechariah. Peter's Denial Is Predicted
30 And having sung-a-hymn, they went out to the Mount *of* Olives. **31** Then Jesus says *to* them, "**You** all will be caused-to-fall in-connection-with Me^A during this night. For it has been written [in Zech 13:7]: 'I will strike the Shepherd, and the sheep *of* the flock will be scattered'. **32** But after I am raised, I will go ahead of you to Galilee". **33** But having responded, Peter said *to* Him, "If all^B will be caused-to-fall in connection with You, **I** will never be caused to fall". **34** Jesus said *to* him, "Truly I say *to* you that during this night, before *a* rooster crows, you will deny Me three-times". **35** Peter says *to* Him, "Even if I have-to die with You, I will never deny You". All the disciples also spoke likewise.

Jesus Waits And Prays In The Garden of Gethsemane
36 Then Jesus comes with them to *a* place being called Gethsemane. And He says *to* the disciples, "Sit here while^C I pray, having gone there". **37** And having taken-along Peter and the two sons^D *of* Zebedee, He began to be grieved and distressed. **38** Then He says *to* them, "My soul is deeply-grieved, to the point of death. Stay here and keep-watching with Me". **39** And having gone ahead *a* little, He fell on His face while praying and saying, "My Father, if it is possible, let this cup pass from Me. Yet not as **I** want^E, but as You *want* ". **40** And He comes to the disciples and finds them sleeping. And He says *to* Peter, "So were you^F [three] not strong-*enough*^G to keep watch with Me *for* one hour? **41** Keep watching, and be praying that^H you may not enter into temptation^I. The spirit *is* willing^J, but the flesh *is* weak". **42** Again having gone away for *a* second *time,* He prayed, saying, "My Father, if this cannot pass unless I drink it, let Your will be done". **43** And having come, He again found them sleeping. For their eyes had been weighed-down. **44** And having left them again, having gone away, He prayed for *a* third *time*, having spoken the same thing^K again. **45** Then He comes to the disciples and says *to* them, "Are you sleeping and resting^L from-now-on^M? Behold— the hour has drawn-near, and the Son *of* Man is being handed-over into *the* hands *of* sinners. **46** Arise, let us be going. Behold— the *one* handing Me over has drawn near".

Jesus Is Betrayed With a Kiss And Arrested
47 And while He *was* still speaking, behold— Judas, one *of* the twelve, came. And with him *was a* large crowd from the chief priests and elders *of* the people with swords and clubs. **48** Now the *one* handing Him over gave them *a* sign, saying, "Whomever I kiss is He. Seize Him". **49** And immediately having gone to Jesus, he said, "Greetings, Rabbi", and kissed Him. **50** And Jesus said *to* him, "Friend, *it is* for what^N you are here". Then, having come to *Him*, they put *their* hands on Jesus and seized Him. **51** And behold— one *of* the *ones* with Jesus, having stretched-out *his*

A. That is, in connection with what is going to happen to Me tonight. **B.** The grammar means 'Assuming that all'. **C.** Or, as long as. Or, until (until I pray and return). **D.** That is, James and John. **E.** Or, wish, will. **F.** This word is plural. **G.** Or, did you not have strength, were you not able. **H.** Or, Keep watching and praying, in order that. **I.** Jesus may mean the temptation to deny Him as He predicted; or, to sleep. **J.** Or, *is* eager, ready. This willingness may refer to their promise in v 35. Their weak flesh needs spiritual strength if they are to stand firm. Pray for strength so that the upcoming trial does not become a cause of falling for you. Or, Jesus may mean that they want to stay awake, but their body is tired. **K.** Or, statement, word *of prayer*. This word is singular. That is, the same request. **L.** Or, Sleep and rest (a command). **M.** Or, henceforth, for the remaining time. That is, are you going to sleep away all the remaining time? This sentence may be viewed as a reproach, or as fatherly sympathy. **N.** Or, *This is* for what you are here (just as it has been written, v 24, 56). Or, *Is this* for what you

hand, withdrew his sword. And having struck the slave *of* the high priest, he took-off his ear. **52** Then Jesus says *to* him, "Return your sword into its place. For all the *ones* having taken *the* sword will perish by *the* sword. **53** Or do you think[A] that I am not able to appeal-to My Father, and He will provide[B] Me right-now more *than* twelve legions[C] *of* angels? **54** How then would the Scriptures *saying* that it must take place in this manner be fulfilled?" **55** At that hour, Jesus said *to* the crowds, "Did you come out to arrest Me with swords and clubs as-*if* against *a* robber? Daily I was sitting in the temple teaching, and you did not seize Me. **56** But this entire *thing* has taken place in order that the Scriptures *of* the prophets might be fulfilled". Then all the disciples, having left[D] Him, fled.

Jesus Is Led Before The High Priest And The Sanhedrin. Peter Follows

57 Now the *ones* having seized Jesus led *Him* away to Caiaphas the high priest, where the scribes and the elders were gathered together. **58** And Peter was following Him at *a* distance, as far as the courtyard *of* the high priest. And having entered inside, he was sitting with the officers[E] to see the outcome.

Jesus Swears Under Oath That He Is The Messiah, The Son of God

59 Now the chief priests and the whole Sanhedrin were seeking false-testimony against Jesus, so that they might put Him to death. **60** And they did not find *it*, many false-witnesses having come-forward. But finally, two having come-forward **61** said, "This *One* said, 'I am able to tear-down the temple *of* God, and to build *it* in three days' ". **62** And having stood up, the high priest said *to* Him, "Are You answering nothing? What *is it* these[F] *ones* are testifying against You?" **63** But Jesus was being silent. And the high priest said *to* Him, "I am putting You under oath[G] by the living God that You tell us if **You** are the Christ, the Son *of* God". **64** Jesus says *to* him, "**You** said[H] *it*. Nevertheless, I say *to* you— from-now-on[I] you will see the Son *of* Man sitting on *the* right *side of* the Power[J], and coming on the clouds[K] *of* heaven". **65** Then the high priest tore his garments, saying, "He blasphemed! What further need do we have *of* witnesses? See— now you heard the blasphemy. **66** What seems *right to* you?" And the *ones*, having responded, said, "He is subject-to[L] death!" **67** Then they spat in His face and beat Him. And the[M] *ones* slapped *Him*, **68** saying, "Prophesy *to* us, Christ— who is the *one* having hit You?"

---

are here?; or, *Do that* for which you are here. **A.** Or, suppose, imagine, presume. **B.** Or, put at My disposal, place beside Me. **C.** A Roman legion had about 6000 soldiers, plus horsemen and auxiliaries. Rather than a literal number of angels, Jesus may simply mean 'a huge, overwhelming force'. **D.** Or, abandoned. **E.** That is, the temple guards. **F.** Or, Are You answering nothing *as to* what these. **G.** Or, causing You to swear. That is, Tell us under oath. **H.** Jesus answers them as He did Judas in v 25. Some think it simply means 'Yes'. Others think its meaning depends on the context. In any case, Jesus does not leave His meaning at all unclear, because He goes on to say 'Nevertheless'. No matter what you think, I say to you. Then He directly and unequivocally states that He is exactly the Messiah coming in power and glory to carry out judgment that they were expecting. Mk 14:62 says 'I am', giving the intent of what is said here. **I:** from now *on*. Or, henceforth. After today, this is how you will next see Me. **J.** That is, of God. Or, *of* power; that is, of God's power. **K:** sitting on *the* right *side*... and coming on the clouds. Jesus is claiming to be the fulfillment of Ps 110:1 and Dan 7:13. **L.** Or, liable to, deserving of. **M.** Matthew may mean 'And others', another group besides the priests and elders in the previous sentence; or, 'And some' of the ones in the previous sentence.

Peter Denies That He Even Knows Jesus

69 Now Peter was sitting outside in the courtyard. And one servant-girl came to him, saying, "**You** also were with Jesus the Galilean". **70** But the *one* denied *it* in front of everyone, saying, "I do not know what you are saying". **71** And *he* having gone out to the gate[A], another saw him. And she says *to* the *ones* there, "This *one* was with Jesus the Nazarene". **72** And again he denied *it* with *an* oath that "I do not know the man". **73** And having come to *him* after *a* little *while*, the *ones* standing *there* said *to* Peter, "Truly **you** also are *one* of them, for even your speaking[B] makes you evident". **74** Then he began to curse[C], and to swear-with-an-oath[D] that "I do not know the man". And immediately *a* rooster crowed. **75** And Peter remembered the word Jesus *had* spoken[E]— that "Before *a* rooster crows, you will deny Me three-times". And having gone outside, he wept bitterly.

Jesus Is Led Before The Roman Governor, Pilate

27:1 Now having become early-morning, all the chief priests and the elders *of* the people took counsel against Jesus so as to put Him to death. **2** And having bound Him, they led *Him* away and handed *Him* over *to* Pilate the governor.

The Betrayer Kills Himself

3 Then Judas (the *one* handing Him over)— having seen that He was condemned, having regretted *it*— returned the thirty silver-coins *to* the chief priests and elders, **4** saying, "I sinned, having handed-over innocent blood!" But the *ones* said, "What *is it* to us? **You** shall see *to it*". **5** And having thrown the silver-coins into[F] the temple, he departed. And having gone away, he hanged *himself.* **6** But the chief priests, having taken the silver-coins, said, "It is not lawful to put them into the temple-treasury, since it is *the* price *of* blood". **7** And having taken counsel, they bought the field *of* the potter with[G] them, for *a* burial-place *for* strangers. **8** For this reason[H], that field was called *the* Field *of* Blood up to today. **9** Then the *thing* was fulfilled having been spoken through Jeremiah[I] the prophet saying "And they took the thirty silver-coins— the price *of* the One having been priced[J], Whom they from *the* sons *of* Israel priced— **10** and they gave them for the field *of* the potter, just as *the* Lord directed me".

The Roman Governor Offers To Free Jesus, But The Crowd Demands He Be Crucified

11 Now Jesus was stood[K] in front of the governor. And the governor questioned Him, saying, "Are **You** the King *of* the Jews?" And Jesus said, "**You** are saying[L] *it*". **12** And during His being accused by the chief priests and elders, He answered nothing. **13** Then Pilate says *to* Him, "Do You not hear how many *things* they are testifying against You?" **14** And He

---

A. That is, the gate from the street into the courtyard. **B.** That is, your Galilean accent or manner of speaking. **C.** That is, to put under a curse, such as, May I be cursed if I know Him. **D.** For example, By the heavens, I do not know Him. **E.** Or, the word *of* Jesus, *who had* said that. **F.** Or, in the temple. Matthew may mean into the holy place; or, in the temple area. **G.** Lit, for them, for [the value of] them. **H.** That is, because it was bought with blood money. **I.** The paraphrase that follows comes from Jeremiah and Zechariah. Matthew attributes it to the better known prophet. **J.** That is, the price of the One having had a price set for Him by these sons of Israel. **K.** Or, was made to stand. **L.** Some think this simply means 'Yes'. Others think it is deliberately understated. Though Jesus means 'you are saying it correctly', He leaves Pilate to supply this intent, which he does based on the Jewish accusers. Jesus may have answered this way because 'King of the Jews' meant something different to Pilate than to Jesus.

did not answer him with-regard-to even one charge^A, so that the governor *was* marveling greatly. **15** Now at *the* Feast, the governor was accustomed to release *for* the crowd one prisoner whom they were wanting. **16** And at that time they were holding *a* notorious prisoner being called Jesus^B Barabbas. **17** So they^C having been gathered together, Pilate said *to* them, "Whom do you want me to release *for* you? Jesus Barabbas, or Jesus, the *One* being called Christ?" **18** For he knew that they^D handed Him over because of envy. **19** And while he *was* sitting on the judgment-seat, his wife sent out *a message* to him, saying, "Have nothing to do with that righteous^E *One*. For I suffered greatly today in *a* dream because of Him". **20** But the chief priests and the elders persuaded the crowds that they should ask-*for* Barabbas and destroy Jesus. **21** Now having responded, the governor said *to* them, "Which of the two do you want me to release *for* you?" And the *ones* said, "Barabbas". **22** Pilate says *to* them, "Then what should I do *as to* Jesus, the *One* being called Christ?" They all say, "Let Him be crucified!" **23** But the *one* said, "What indeed^F did He do wrong?" But the *ones* were crying out even more, saying, "Let Him be crucified!" **24** And Pilate— having seen that he^G is profiting nothing, but rather *an* uproar is taking place— having taken water, washed-off *his* hands in front of the crowd, saying, "I am innocent of the blood^H *of* this *One*. **You** shall see *to it*. **25** And having responded, all the people said, "His blood *be* upon us and upon our children". **26** Then he released Barabbas *to* them. But having flogged^I Jesus, he handed *Him* over in order that He might be crucified.

The King of The Jews Is Mocked, Spit On, Beaten And Crucified
27 Then the soldiers *of* the governor, having taken Jesus into the Praetorium^J, gathered the whole [Roman] cohort^K to^L Him. **28** And having stripped Him, they put *a* scarlet cloak^M on Him. **29** And having woven *a* crown out of thorns, they put *it* on His head, and *they put a* staff^N in His right *hand*. And having knelt in front of Him, they mocked Him, saying, "Hail^O, King *of* the Jews!" **30** And having spat on Him, they took the staff and were striking *Him* on His head. **31** And when they mocked Him, they stripped the cloak off Him and put His garments on Him. And they led Him away so as to crucify *Him*. **32** And while going forth, they found *a* Cyrenian^P man, Simon *by* name. They pressed this *one* into service in order that he might take-up His cross. **33** And having come to *a* place being called Golgotha^Q (which is meaning "*The* Place *of a* Skull"), **34** they gave Him wine having been mixed with gall^R to drink. And having tasted *it*, He did not want to drink. **35** And having crucified Him, they divided His garments among *themselves*, casting *a* lot. **36** And sitting-down, they were guarding Him there. **37** And above His head they put on His charge, having been written, "This is Jesus, the King *of* the Jews". **38** Then two robbers^S are crucified with Him, one on *the* right *side* and one on *the* left *side*.

A. Or, up-to even one word. **B.** Some manuscripts omit this word here and in v 17. **C.** That is, the crowd, v 15, 20. **D.** That is, the chief priests and elders, v 12, 20. **E.** Lit, *Let there be* nothing *for* you and *for* that righteous *One*. **F.** Or, Why? What evil did He do? Pilate is incredulous. **G.** Or, it. **H.** Or, of this blood. **I.** Or, scourged. That is, whipped with a whip. This was the common Roman practice before a crucifixion. **J.** That is, governor's palace, fortress, headquarters. **K.** This word was used of a Roman battalion (one tenth of a legion, about 600 soldiers), and of a 'tactical unit' or 'detachment' of soldiers. The portion of the cohort then on duty came to watch. **L.** Or, against. **M.** This refers to a short cloak worn by soldiers, officers, and officials. **N.** Or, stick, walking stick, in imitation of a kingly scepter. **O.** Or, Greetings, Farewell. This was a common greeting. **P.** That is, from the city of Cyrene on the coast of Africa. **Q.** This is a transliterated Hebrew word meaning 'skull'. In Latin, 'Skull' is calvariae, from which we get 'Calvary'. **R.** The soldiers may have added gall to make it taste bitter, another insult; or, this is the drink noble Jewish women provided to victims of crucifixion to dull the senses. In any case, Jesus refused to drink it. **S.** Or, insurrectionists.

The King of Israel Is Mocked While Hanging On The Cross

39 And the *ones* passing by were blaspheming Him while shaking their heads **40** and saying, "The *One* tearing-down the temple and building *it* in three days, save Yourself— if [A] You are God's **Son**— and come down from the cross". **41** Likewise also the chief priests, mocking *Him* with the scribes and elders, were saying, **42** "He saved others— Himself He is not able to save! He is King *of* Israel— let Him come down now from the cross and we will put-faith upon Him! **43** He trusts in God— let Him deliver *Him* now, if He wants[B] Him. For He said that 'I am **God's** Son' ". **44** And even[C] the robbers, the *ones* having been crucified with Him, were reproaching Him the same.

Jesus Dies

45 And from *the* sixth hour, *a* darkness came over all the land[D] until *the* ninth[E] hour. **46** And around the ninth hour Jesus shouted-out *with a* loud voice, saying, "Eli, Eli, lema sabachthani?", that is, "My God, My God, why[F] did you forsake[G] Me?" **47** And some *of* the *ones* standing there, having heard, were saying that "This *One* is calling Elijah". **48** And immediately one of them— having run, and having taken *a* sponge, and having filled *it with* sour-wine[H], and having put *it* on *a* stick[I]— was giving-a-drink-*to* Him. **49** But the others were saying, "Leave *Him* alone. Let us see if Elijah comes *to* save Him". **50** And Jesus, again having cried-out[J] *with a* loud voice, let *His* spirit go[K].

The Temple Curtain Is Torn. The Earth Quakes. Tombs Are Opened, Bodies Raised

51 And behold— the curtain *of* the temple was torn[L] in two from top to bottom. And the earth was shaken and the rocks were split. **52** And the tombs were opened. And many bodies *of* the saints having fallen-asleep were raised. **53** And having come out from the tombs after[M] His resurrection, they entered into the holy city and appeared *to* many. **54** And the centurion and the *ones* with him guarding Jesus— having seen the earthquake and the *things* having taken place— became extremely afraid, saying, "Truly this *One* was God's[N] Son!"

Many Women Followers of Jesus Watch At a Distance

55 And many women were there watching at *a* distance, who followed Jesus from Galilee while serving Him, **56** among whom was Mary the Magdalene[O], and Mary the mother *of* James and Joseph, and the mother[P] *of* the sons *of* Zebedee.

A. That is, assuming that, since, spoken in a mocking way. **B.** Or, delights *in* Him, if they are quoting Ps 22:8, where this same word is used in the Septuagint. Matthew may intend his readers to recognize this reference here. Both renderings make good sense. **C.** Or, the robbers also. **D.** Or, earth. Or, the whole land. **E.** That is, from noon to 3 P.M. **F.** Or, for what purpose; in order that what might happen. **G.** Or, abandon, desert. Jesus is quoting Ps 22:1. **H.** Or, wine-vinegar (watered down). This was a favorite beverage of the soldiers and common people. **I.** Or, rod, staff. **J.** The words Jesus cried out are recorded in Lk 23:46 and Jn 19:30. **K.** Or, sent away *His* spirit. **L.** Or, split, divided. This may symbolize that the way into God's presence is now open; and/or, that God has abandoned the Jewish temple. **M.** Matthew may mean the dead ones arose when Jesus died on Friday, but came out on Sunday; or, that the tombs were opened on Friday and the dead were raised and came out on Sunday. This is indicative of the fact that Jesus conquered death for all believers. **N.** The centurion could mean 'a divine person', or be expressing genuine faith. The words do not make explicit what was in his heart. **O.** That is, the one from Magdala, on the Sea of Galilee. **P.** If Mark 15:40 is referring to the same person, her name was Salome.

Jesus Is Laid In a Rich Man's Tomb

⁵⁷ Now having become evening^A, *a* rich man from Arimathea came, Joseph *as to* the-name, who also himself became-a-disciple *to* Jesus. ⁵⁸ This *one*, having gone to Pilate, asked-*for* the body *of* Jesus. Then Pilate ordered *that it* be given-back. ⁵⁹ And having taken the body, Joseph wrapped it in clean linen-cloth ⁶⁰ and laid it in his new tomb which he hewed in the rock. And having rolled *a* large stone to the door *of* the tomb, he departed. ⁶¹ And Mary the Magdalene was there, and the other^B Mary, sitting in front of the burial-place.

The Tomb Is Secured And Roman Guards Posted

⁶² Now *on* the next-day^C which is after the Preparation^D *day*, the chief priests and the Pharisees were gathered together with Pilate, ⁶³ saying, "Sir, we remembered that that deceiver said while still alive, 'I am arising after three days'. ⁶⁴ Therefore, give-orders *that* the burial-place be made-secure until the third day, so that His disciples, having come, might not at any time steal Him and say *to* the people, 'He arose from the dead', and the last deception will be worse *than* the first". ⁶⁵ Pilate said *to* them, "Have^E *a* guard^F. Go, make *it* secure as you know-*how*". ⁶⁶ And the *ones*, having gone, made the burial-place secure, having sealed the stone along-with^G the guard.

The King Rises From The Dead. An Angel Moves the Stone And Announces, He Is Risen.

28:1 Now after *the* Sabbath^H, *in* the dawning toward *the* first *day of the* week, Mary the Magdalene and the other Mary went to see the burial-place. ² And behold— *a* great earthquake took place. For *an* angel *of the* Lord— having come down from heaven, and having gone to *it*— rolled away the stone and was sitting on it. ³ And his appearance was like lightning, and his clothing *was* white as snow. ⁴ And the *ones* guarding were shaken from the fear *of* him, and became like dead *men*. ⁵ And having responded^I, the angel said *to* the women, "Don't **you**^J be fearing, for I know that you are seeking **Jesus**, the *One* having been crucified. ⁶ He is not here, for He arose, just as He said. Come, see the place where He was lying. ⁷ And having gone quickly, tell His disciples that 'He arose from the dead. And behold— He is going-ahead-of you to Galilee. You will see Him there'. Behold— I told you".

While Running To Report This To The Disciples, The Women See The Risen Jesus

⁸ And having quickly departed from the tomb with fear and great joy, they ran to report *it* to His disciples. ⁹ And behold— Jesus met them, saying "Greetings". And the *ones*, having gone to *Him*, took-hold-of His feet and gave-worship *to* Him. ¹⁰ Then Jesus says *to* them, "Do not be fearing. Go, report *to* My brothers that^K they should go to Galilee. And there they will see Me".

A. That is, between 3 and 6 P.M., before the Sabbath began at dark. **B.** That is, the other one mentioned in v 56. **C.** That is, Saturday. **D.** That is, Friday. **E.** Or, You have. This could be a command or a statement. Pilate grants their request. **F.** This is a transliterated Latin word referring to a detachment of Roman soldiers. It is only used here in v 65-66, and in 28:11. **G.** Or, by-means-of. Matthew may mean that the priests sealed the stone "together-with" the Romans, making the site secure; or, that the priests sealed the stone "by-means-of" the Roman detachment, making the site secure; or, that the priests made the site secure by sealing the stone "along-with" placing the Roman detachment. **H.** That is, Sunday morning near sunrise they went to see the burial-place. Or, late *on the* Sabbath, *in* the dawning. That is, late in the day on Saturday, just before the beginning of the new Jewish day at sundown, they went to 'see' the grave. After sundown, they went to buy spices (Mk 16:1). Then they returned to the grave Sunday morning to anoint the body (Mk 16:2), where Matthew continues next. **I.** That is, to the arrival of the women. **J.** The emphasis may mean 'you' in contrast to the guards; or, 'you' of all people, you who love Him. **K.** Or, report *it to* My brothers so that they will go.

The Roman Guards Are Bought Off, And The Priests Plot Out Their Story

11 And while they *were* going, behold— some *of* the guard[A], having come into the city, reported all the *things* having taken place *to* the chief priests. **12** And having been gathered together with the elders, and having taken counsel, they gave sufficient[B] money *to* the soldiers[C], **13** saying, "Say that 'His disciples, having come *by* night, stole Him while we *were* sleeping'. **14** And if this should be heard[D] before the governor, **we** will persuade him. And we will make **you** free-from-concern". **15** And the *ones*, having taken the money, did as they were instructed. And this statement was spread-widely among Jews, until this very day[E].

Jesus Commissions The Eleven To Make Disciples of All Nations

16 And the eleven disciples proceeded to Galilee, to the mountain where Jesus ordered them. **17** And having seen Him, they worshiped *Him*. But the[F] *ones* doubted[G]. **18** And having come to *them*, Jesus spoke *to* them, saying, "All authority in heaven and on earth was given *to* Me. **19** Therefore having gone, make-disciples-of[H] all the nations, baptizing them in the name *of* the Father and the Son and the Holy Spirit, **20** teaching them to keep all that I commanded you. And behold— **I** am with you all the days until the conclusion *of* the age".

A. That is, the Roman detachment. **B.** Or, considerable. **C.** That is, Roman soldiers, as this word is always used in the Gospels and Acts. **D.** That is, in a judicial sense. If you are put on trial for losing the body, we will persuade Pilate to spare you (perhaps with a bribe). **E.** Lit, the today day. **F.** As in 26:67, this could mean 'others doubted'; or, 'some *of the eleven* doubted'. Some think this is the appearance to 500 people mentioned in 1 Cor 15:6. **G.** Or, hesitated. Perhaps Matthew means they were unsure it was really Jesus, until He came to them, v 18. **H.** This is the command. Included in the carrying out of this command is the going, the baptizing, and the teaching.

Mark

The beginning of the good news of Jesus Christ, the Son of God		1:1

A.   As Isaiah wrote, John came— making ready the way, proclaiming a baptism of repentance   1:2-8

B.   In those days Jesus came and was baptized by John. Then He was tempted in the wilderness   1:9-13

C.   After John was handed over, Jesus went to Galilee proclaiming the good news of God   1:14-15

1.   While passing beside the Sea of Galilee, He called Simon, Andrew, James, John   1:16-20
2.   They go into Capernaum. He teaches and heals. Peter's mother-in-law   1:21-38
3.   He went proclaiming in their synagogues in all Galilee. He heals a leper   1:39-45
4.   In Capernaum Jesus forgave and healed a paralytic on the Sabbath. Some objected   2:1-12
5.   He went out by the sea and taught. He called Levi and ate at his house. Some objected   2:13-17
6.   Why are Your disciples not fasting? The bridegroom is here. New wine and wineskins   2:18-22
7.   The disciples picked grain on the Sabbath. Some objected. I am Lord of the Sabbath   2:23-28
8.   He healed a man on the Sabbath. Pharisees and Herodians plotted to destroy Him   3:1-6
9.   Jesus withdrew to the sea. A great multitude followed. He cured many   3:7-12
10.   He goes up into the mountain and appoints twelve to be with Him and to proclaim   3:13-19
11.   He goes into a house. Some say He cast out demons by Satan. His family comes   3:20-35
12.   He was teaching in parables. The sower. The lamp. The mustard seed. He explains   4:1-34
13.   That evening, they left in a boat, and He calmed the sea. They said, Who is this One?   4:35-41
14.   At the other side, He cast demons into a herd of pigs, and sent the man to proclaim it   5:1-20
15.   He crossed back over and healed a woman and raised Jairus's daughter from the dead   5:21-6:1
16.   He comes to His hometown and teaches in the synagogue. They took offense at Him   6:1-6
17.   He was going around the villages, teaching. And He sent out the twelve, two by two   6:6-13
18.   King Herod heard of Him and said He was John the Baptist risen from the dead   6:14-29
19.   The apostles gather and report all that they did. They go to rest. Jesus feeds 5000   6:30-44
20.   He sends the disciples away in a boat. Later, He comes to them walking on the sea   6:45-52
21.   Having crossed over to Gennesaret, He healed people wherever He went   6:53-56
22.   Pharisees accuse His disciples. He says, It is what comes out of the heart that defiles   7:1-23
23.   Jesus departed to Tyre, and healed a Gentile's daughter— crumbs from the table   7:24-30
24.   He went to the Sea of Galilee in Decapolis and healed a deaf mute   7:31-37
25.   In those days, there again being large crowd, Jesus fed about 4000   8:1-9
26.   He left for Dalmanutha. The Pharisees asked for a sign. None will be given   8:10-12
27.   He left for the other side. They forgot bread. Jesus said, Do you not yet understand?   8:13-21
28.   They come to Bethsaida. Jesus heals a blind man in two steps   8:22-26
29.   On the way to Caesarea, Jesus asked, Who do you say I am? You are the Christ   8:27-30

D.   And He began to teach His disciples that He must suffer, be rejected, be killed, and rise up.   8:31-33
    Peter rebuked Him. Jesus said, You are not thinking the things of God, but of humans

1.   Jesus said, If any want to follow Me, let him deny himself and take up his cross   8:34-9:1
2.   After six days, Jesus takes Peter, James, and John up a mountain, and is transfigured   9:2-8
3.   While coming down from the mountain, they asked about Elijah   9:9-13
4.   Having come back to the disciples, Jesus healed one the disciples could not   9:14-29
5.   Passing through Galilee, Jesus was teaching them that He must be killed, and arise   9:30-32
6.   At Capernaum they were discussing who was greater. Jesus said, the servant, the child   9:33-50

E.   He went from there into the districts of Judea. Crowds gathered and He was teaching them   10:1

1.   Pharisees asked, Is lawful for a man to divorce a wife— testing Him   10:2-12
2.   They were bringing children to Him. You must welcome the kingdom like a child   10:13-16
3.   What should I do to inherit eternal life? Sell, follow me. It is not easy for the rich   10:17-31

	4.	Jesus took aside the twelve and said He will be killed, and will rise again	10:32-34
	5.	James and John ask to sit next to Him in the kingdom. It is not mine to give	10:35-45
	6.	At Jericho, Jesus healed Bartimaeus, a blind beggar	10:46-52
	7.	At Bethany Jesus sent two disciples to get a colt. He road it, and they cried out Hosanna!	11:1-10
F.		Jesus entered into Jerusalem, into the temple. He looked around, and went out to Bethany	11:11
	1.	On the next day, He cursed a fig tree	11:12-14
	2.	He entered the temple and drove out those buying and selling. The priests plotted	11:15-19
	3.	Passing by the next day, they saw the fig tree withered. Be having faith in God	11:20-26
	4.	By what authority are you doing these things? The parable of the vineyard	11:27-12:12
	5.	Pharisees try to trap Him. Is it lawful to give a poll-tax to Caesar?	12:13-17
	6.	Sadducees come questioning Him about the resurrection. Whose wife is she?	12:18-27
	7.	A scribe ased, What is the foremost commandment? Love God. Love your neighbor	12:28-34
	8.	Jesus asked them, David calls the Christ "Lord". In what way is He his son?	12:34-37
	9.	In His teaching, He was saying, Beware of the scribes seeking honor and money	12:37-40
	10.	He was observing those giving to the temple, and praised a widow who gave all	12:41-44
	11.	Jesus prophesies the destruction of the temple. What is the sign of Your coming?	13:1-5
		a. Many will come claiming to be the Messiah: Don't be deceived. There will be birthpains: Do not be alarmed. Watch yourselves, you will be persecuted. The good news will be proclaimed to all the nations	13:5-13
		b. When you see the abomination of desolation, flee. For then there will be a great affliction. False Christs will arise: do not believe them	13:14-23
		c. After that affliction, Jesus will come on the clouds in great glory	13:24-27
		d. The parable of the fig tree: When the leaves grow out, summer is near	13:28-31
		e. No one knows the day or hour, so keep watch	13:32-37
G.		Now the Passover was two days away and the priests planned how to seize and kill Him	14:1-2
	1.	At Bethany a woman poured perfume on Jesus. He said, She has anointed Me for burial	14:3-9
	2.	Judas went to the priests in order that He might hand Him over to them	14:10-11
	3.	They ate the Passover meal. One will betray Me. This is My body, My blood	14:12-25
	4.	They went to the Mount of Olives. Jesus said they would fall away. Peter said, Not me	14:26-31
	5.	They come to Gethsemane. Jesus prayed, they slept. Judas comes, Jesus is taken	14:32-52
	6.	Jesus is led to the high priest, and condemned for blasphemy. Peter denies Him	14:53-72
	7.	The Jews lead Him to Pilate. Pilate offers to free Jesus or Barabbas. Crucify Him!	15:1-15
	8.	The soldiers mock Him, and crucify Him. The Jews blaspheme Him. He expires	15:16-41
	9.	Joseph of Arimathea asked Pilate for the body, and placed it in a tomb	15:42-47
H.		After the Sabbath, three women bought spices. Jesus arose. Go tell His disciples	16:1-8
	1.	Jesus appears to His disciples	16:9-14
	2.	He commissions them to proclaim the gospel to all creation	16:15-18
	3.	Jesus is taken up into heaven	16:19-20

1:1 *The*[A] beginning *of* the good-news *of* [B] Jesus Christ, God's Son

As Predicted By Isaiah, John The Baptist Came To Prepare The Way For The Messiah
2 Just as it has been written in Isaiah[C] the prophet— "Behold, I am sending-forth My messenger ahead *of* Your presence[D], who will make Your way ready: **3** *A* voice *of one* shouting in the wilderness, 'Prepare the way *of the* Lord; be making His paths straight' "— **4** John came[E], the *one* baptizing in the wilderness and proclaiming *a* baptism *of* repentance for *the* forgiveness *of* sins. **5** And the whole Judean country[F] was going out to him, and all the people-of-Jerusalem. And they were being baptized by him in the Jordan River while confessing-out[G] their sins. **6** And John was dressed-in camel's hair and *a* belt made-of-leather around his waist, and *was* eating locusts and wild honey. **7** And he was proclaiming, saying "The *One* more powerful *than* me is coming after me— *of* Whom I am not fit, having stooped, to untie the strap *of* His sandals. **8** **I** baptized you *with*[H] water, but **He** will baptize you with[I] *the* Holy Spirit".

Jesus Is Baptized By John. God Expresses His Pleasure. Jesus Is Tempted By Satan
9 And it came about during those days *that* Jesus came from Nazareth *of* Galilee and was baptized in the Jordan by John. **10** And immediately while ascending[J] out-of the water, He saw the heavens being divided[K] and the Spirit like *a* dove descending to[L] Him. **11** And *a* voice came from the heavens— "**You** are My beloved Son. With You I was[M] well-pleased". **12** And immediately the Spirit sends Him out[N] into the wilderness. **13** And He was in the wilderness forty days being tempted by Satan. And He was with the wild-beasts. And the angels were ministering[O] *to* Him.

After John Is Arrested, Jesus Comes To Galilee Proclaiming The Good News of God
14 Now after John *was* handed-over[P] [to prison], Jesus came to Galilee proclaiming the good-news *of* [Q] God **15** and saying that "The time has been fulfilled, and the kingdom *of* God has drawn-near. Repent, and put-faith in the good-news".

Jesus Calls The First Disciples
16 And while passing-by beside the Sea *of* Galilee, He saw Simon and Andrew (the brother *of* Simon), casting-a-net in the sea. For they were fishermen. **17** And Jesus said *to* them, "Come after Me, and I will make you become fishermen *of* people". **18** And immediately, having left the nets, they followed Him. **19** And having gone on *a* little, He saw James (the son *of* Zebedee) and John (his brother)— they also in *their* boat, preparing[R] the nets. **20** And immediately He called them. And having left their father Zebedee in the boat with the hired *ones*, they went after Him.

Jesus Casts Out a Demon. They Are All Astonished. The News of Him Spreads
21 And they proceed into Capernaum. And immediately, having entered into the synagogue *on* the Sabbath, He was teaching. **22** And they were astounded[S] at His teaching, for He was teaching them as *one* having authority, and not as the scribes. **23** And immediately there

---

A. This may be the title for the whole book; or, for v 2-8; or, for v 2-13. **B.** That is, *about*; or, *proclaimed by*. **C.** A quote from Mal 3:1 is joined to one from Isa 40:3. Mark only names the better known prophet. **D.** Or, face. **E.** The main sentence is 'Just as it has been written... John came'. **F.** Or, countryside. **G.** Or, openly-admitting, acknowledging. **H.** Or, *in*. **I.** Or, in. **J.** Or, going up, coming up. **K.** Or, split. **L.** Or, on. **M.** Or, am well-pleased. See Mt 3:17. **N.** Or, puts Him out, drives Him out. **O.** Or, serving. **P.** That is, by Herod Antipas, 6:17. **Q.** That is, *from*; or, *about*. **R.** Or, putting in order, restoring. **S.** Or, overwhelmed, amazed, astonished.

was *a* man in their synagogue with^A *an* unclean spirit. And he cried-out, **24** saying "What^B do we have to do with You, Jesus from-Nazareth? Did You come to destroy us? I know You, Who You are— the Holy *One of* God!" **25** And Jesus rebuked him, saying "Be silenced and come out of him". **26** And the unclean spirit, having convulsed^C him and called-out *with a* loud voice, came out of him. **27** And they were all astonished, so that^D *they were* discussing with themselves, saying "What is this? *A* new teaching based-on authority^E! He commands even the unclean spirits and they obey Him!" **28** And the report *about* Him immediately went out everywhere into the whole surrounding-region *of* Galilee.

> *That Evening The Whole City of Capernaum Brings Their Sick To Him For Healing*
> **29** And immediately, having gone out of the synagogue, they came into the house *of* Simon and Andrew, with James and John. **30** Now the mother-in-law *of* Simon was lying-down, being sick-with-fever. And immediately they speak *to* Him concerning her. **31** And having gone to *her*, He raised her, having taken-hold-of *her* hand. And the fever left her and she was serving them. **32** And having become evening, when the sun set^F, they were bringing to Him all the *ones* being ill and the *ones* being demon-possessed. **33** And the whole city was gathered-together at the door. **34** And He cured many being ill *with* various diseases. And He cast-out many demons, and was not permitting the demons to speak, because they knew Him. **35** And having arisen early-in-the-morning^G, very *late* at-night, He went out and went away to *a* desolate^H place, and was praying there. **36** And Simon and the *ones* with him hunted-for Him, **37** and found Him. And they say *to* Him that "Everyone is seeking You". **38** And He says *to* them, "Let us be going elsewhere, into the next towns, in order that I may proclaim there also. For I came-forth for this *purpose*".

Jesus Heals a Leper, Who Spreads The Word of Him. People Come From All Directions
39 And He went proclaiming in their synagogues in all Galilee and casting out the demons. **40** And *a* leper comes to Him, appealing-to Him and kneeling, and saying *to* Him that "If You are willing, You are able to cleanse me". **41** And having felt-deep-feelings [of compassion], having stretched-out His hand, He touched *him.* And He says *to* him, "I am willing^I. Be cleansed". **42** And immediately the leprosy departed from him and he was cleansed. **43** And having sternly-commanded^J him, He immediately sent him out. **44** And He says *to* him, "See *that* you tell no one anything. But go, show yourself *to* the priest^K, and offer for your cleansing *the things* which Moses commanded, for *a* testimony *to* them". **45** But the *one,* having gone forth, began to proclaim greatly and widely-spread the word, so that He *was* no longer able to enter openly into *a* city, but was outside at desolate places. And they were coming to Him from-all-directions.

Jesus Heals a Paralytic To Prove He Has Authority To Forgive Sins
2:1 And having entered again into Capernaum after *some* days, it was heard that He was

---

A. Or, in; that is, in the sphere of, in the power of. **B.** Lit, What *is there for* us and *for* You? **C.** Or, thrown him into convulsions. **D.** That is, with the result that. **E.** Or, *A* new teaching! With authority He commands. **F.** That is, after the Sabbath (v 21) was over. **G.** This word refers to the time between 3 and 6 A.M. **H.** Or, deserted, solitary, lonely. **I.** Jesus alone heals in His own name, without calling on God. **J.** Or, sternly-warned. That is, commanded him with intense emotion. Mark next tells us what Jesus said. **K.** That is, in Jerusalem at the temple.

at home[A]. [2] And many were gathered together, so that *the house was* no longer having-room, not even the *places* at the door. And He was speaking the word *to* them. [3] And they come bringing to Him *a* paralytic being picked-up by four *men*. [4] And not being able to bring *him* to Him because of the crowd, they unroofed the roof where He was. And having dug out *an opening*, they lower the cot on-which the paralytic was lying-down. [5] And Jesus, having seen their faith, says *to* the paralytic, "Child, your sins are forgiven". [6] Now some *of* the scribes were sitting there and reasoning in their hearts, [7] "Why is this *One* speaking in this manner? He is blaspheming. Who is able to forgive sins except One— God?" [8] And immediately Jesus, having known[B] *in* His spirit that they were reasoning in this manner within themselves, says *to* them "Why are you reasoning these *things* in your hearts? [9] Which is easier— to say *to* the paralytic 'Your sins are forgiven', or to say 'Arise, and pick-up your cot and walk'? [10] But in order that you may know that the Son *of* Man has authority to forgive sins on earth"— He says *to* the paralytic, [11] "I say *to* you, arise, pick up your cot and go to your house". [12] And he arose, and immediately having picked-up the cot, went out in front of everyone, so that everyone *was* astonished[C] and glorifying God, saying that "We never saw *anything* like this".

Jesus Calls Levi The Tax Collector And Eats With His Friends: I Came For Sinners
[13] And He went out again beside the sea. And all the multitude[D] was coming to Him. And He was teaching them. [14] And while passing on He saw Levi, the *son of* Alphaeus, sitting at the tax-office[E]. And He says *to* him "Be following Me!" And having stood-up, he followed Him. [15] And it comes about *that* He *was* reclining [to eat] in his[F] house. And many tax-collectors and sinners were reclining-back-with Jesus and His disciples. For there were many, and they were following Him. [16] And the scribes *of* the Pharisees, having seen that He was eating with the sinners and tax collectors, were saying *to* His disciples "*Why is it that*[G] He is eating with the tax collectors and sinners?" [17] And having heard, Jesus says *to* them that "The *ones* being strong have no need *of a* physician, but the *ones* being ill. I did not come to call righteous *ones*, but sinners".

Why Do Your Disciples Not Fast? The Bridegroom Is Here. New Wine Needs New Wineskins
[18] And the disciples *of* John and the Pharisees[H] were fasting. And they come and say *to* Him, "For what reason are the disciples *of* John and the disciples *of* the Pharisees fasting, but **Your** disciples are not fasting?" [19] And Jesus said *to* them, "The sons *of* the wedding-hall[I] cannot **be fasting** while the bridegroom is with them, *can they?* As long *a* time as they have the bridegroom with them, they cannot be fasting. [20] But days will come when the bridegroom is taken-away from them, and then they will fast in that day. [21] No one sews *a* patch *of* unshrunk cloth on *an* old garment. Otherwise the fullness [of the patch] takes from it— the new *from* the old— and *a* worse tear[J] takes place. [22] And no one puts new wine into old wineskins. Otherwise the wine will burst the wineskins, and the wine is lost, and the wineskins. But *one puts* new wine into fresh[K] wineskins".

A. Or, in *the* house. **B.** Or, recognized, understood. **C.** Or, beside-*themselves*. **D.** Or, the whole crowd. **E.** Or, tax-booth. Levi (Matthew) was on the job, collecting taxes for Herod Antipas. **F.** That is, Levi's house, Lk 5:29. **G.** Or, disciples that "He is... sinners!" **H.** On why these two groups may have been fasting, see Mt 9:14. **I.** That is, the attendants of the groom, referring to the disciples. **J.** In other words, Jesus is not a patch on the old Jewish system, sewn on to make repairs. He is a new garment, so His disciples act in a new way. **K.** Jesus cannot be contained within the worn-out Jewish system. A new system is needed.

The Disciples Pluck Grain On The Sabbath. I Am Lord of The Sabbath
23 And it came about *that* He *was* passing through the grainfields on the Sabbath, and His disciples began to make *their* way while pluckingᴬ the heads [of grain]. **24** And the Pharisees were saying *to* Him, "Look! Why are they doing *on* the Sabbath what is not lawful?" **25** And He says *to* them, "Did you never read [in 1 Sam 21:1-6] what David did when he had *a* need and was hungry, he and the *ones* with him— **26** how he entered into the house *of* God in the timeᴮ of Abiathar *the* high-priest and ate the Bread *of* Presentationᶜ which is not lawful *for anyone* to eat but the priests, and he gave *it* also *to* the *ones* being with him?" **27** And He was saying *to* them, "The Sabbath was madeᴰ for the sake of mankind, and not mankind for the sake of the Sabbath. **28** So thenᴱ, the Son *of* Man is **Lord** evenᶠ *of* the Sabbath".

Is It Lawful To Heal On The Sabbath? Jesus Heals a Man, Inflaming The Pharisees
3:1 And He entered again into the synagogue. And there was *a* man there having *his* hand having become-withered. **2** And they were closely-watching Him *to see* if He would cure him *on* the Sabbath, in order that they might accuse Him. **3** And He says *to* the man having the withered hand, "Arise into the middle". **4** And He says *to* them, "Is it lawful *on* the Sabbath to do good or to do-harmᴳ, to save *a* life or to kill?" But the *ones* were being silent. **5** And having looked-around-*at* them with anger, while being deeply-grieved at the hardness *of* their heart, He says *to* the man, "Stretch out the hand". And he stretched *it* out, and his hand was restored. **6** And having gone out, the Pharisees immediately were giving counsel against Him with the Herodiansᴴ so that they might destroy Him.

A Great Multitude Comes To Jesus To Be Healed
7 And Jesus withdrewᴵ to the sea with His disciples, and *a* great multitude from Galilee followed. And from Judea, **8** and from Jerusalem, and from Idumea and beyond the Jordan and around Tyre and Sidon, *a* great multitude hearing all that He was doing came to Him. **9** And He said *to* His disciples that *a* small-boat should be standing-ready-for Him because of the crowd— in order that they might not be pressingᴶ Him. **10** For He cured many, so that *they were* falling-upon Him in order that all who were having scourgesᴷ might touch Him. **11** And the unclean spirits, whenever they were seeing Him, were falling-before Him and crying-out, saying that "**You** are the Son *of* God". **12** And He was sternly rebuking them in order that they might not make Him known.

The Twelve Are Appointed
13 And He goes up on the mountain and summons whom **He** was wanting. And they went to Him. **14** And He appointed twelve, whom He also named apostles, in order that they might be with Him, and in order that He might send them out to proclaim **15** and to have

A. This was permitted under the Law, Deut 23:25. The Pharisees object because it was the Sabbath. **B.** This event indeed took place in the time of this pivotal high priest in the life of David. But Abiathar's father Ahimelech was actually still high priest when David ate this bread. **C.** That is, the bread 'set before' God, 'presented' to God, consecrated to God; the twelve loaves of showbread, Lev 24:6-9. **D.** Or, came into being, came about. Mankind was not created for the purpose of keeping the Sabbath. Rather, that day was created for the benefit of mankind. In David's case, the more urgent benefit he needed came at the expense of the normal Sabbath rules. **E.** Because Jesus is the Lord of mankind, He is the Lord of mankind's Sabbath. **F.** Or, also. **G.** The answer is that the day makes no difference. It is good to do good and wrong to do harm on all seven days. The Sabbath is a day of rest from one's work, not from doing good. **H.** That is, those politically linked to Herod's family. As a false prophet, being a Sabbath-breaker, Jesus is a religious and political problem for these leaders. **I.** Or, went-back. **J.** Or, crowding, squeezing. **K.** That is, ailments perceived as a scourge from God.

authority to cast out the demons. **16** And He appointed the twelve, even Peter (He put *the* name on Simon), **17** and James, the *son of* Zebedee, and John, the brother *of* James (and He put on them *the* name Boanerges, which means "sons *of* thunder"), **18** and Andrew, and Philip, and Bartholomew, and Matthew, and Thomas, and James, the *son of* Alphaeus, and Thaddaeus, and Simon, the Cananaean^A, **19** and Judas Iscariot, who also handed Him over.

Scribes Say Jesus Uses Satan's Power. Such Blasphemy of The Spirit Will Not Be Forgiven
20 And He goes into *a* house^B. And the crowd comes-together again, so that they *were* not even able to eat bread. **21** And having heard-*of it*, the ones^C from Him went-forth to take-hold-of^D Him. For they were saying^E that "He lost-*His*-senses". **22** And the scribes having come down from Jerusalem were saying that "He has Beelzebul", and that "He is casting-out the demons by^F the ruler *of* the demons". **23** And having summoned them, He was speaking *to* them in parables: "How is Satan able to be casting-out Satan? **24** And if *a* kingdom is divided against itself, that kingdom is not able to stand; **25** and if *a* house is divided against itself, that house will not be able to stand. **26** And if Satan stood-up against himself and was divided, he is not able to stand, but he has *an* end^G. **27** But no one, having entered into the house *of* the strong *man,* can plunder his things unless he first binds the strong *man.* And then he will plunder^H his house. **28** Truly I say *to* you that all sins and blasphemies will be forgiven *to* the sons *of* humans^I, whatever they may blaspheme. **29** But whoever blasphemes against the Holy Spirit does not have forgiveness forever, but is guilty *of an* eternal sin"— **30** because^J they were saying "He has *an* unclean spirit".

Whoever Does The Will of God Is My Family
31 And His mother and His brothers come. And while standing outside, they sent-forth *a message* to Him, calling Him. **32** And *a* crowd was sitting around Him. And they say *to* Him, "Behold— Your mother and Your brothers and Your sisters are outside seeking You". **33** And having responded *to* them, He says "Who is My mother and My brothers?" **34** And having looked-around-*at* the *ones* sitting *in a* circle around Him, He says "Look— My mother and My brothers! **35** For whoever does the will *of* God— this *one* is My brother and sister and mother".

Jesus Teaches The Multitudes In Parables
4:1 And again He began to teach beside the sea. And *a* very large crowd is gathered-together with Him so that He, having gotten into *a* boat, sits-*down* in the sea [to teach]. And all the multitude were near^K the sea on the land. **2** And He was teaching them many *things* in parables.

A. That is, the zealot. **B.** Mark may mean '*His* house', connecting this with the coming of His family in v 31. **C.** That is, the relatives of Jesus, who arrive in v 31; or, the friends or associates of Jesus. These people heard of the problem and went forth to solve it. **D.** Or, take charge of, seize, take custody of. **E.** This could be the statement of a well-intentioned mother or disciple who felt the need to rescue Jesus (Have some sense! Come and eat!); or, the misinformed statement of brothers who did not understand His mission or believe in Him (Jn 7:5); or, an impersonal statement meaning 'people were saying'. **F.** Or, in union with. **G.** That is, he is finished; he is defeated. **H.** Jesus is binding Satan by casting out demons, and will plunder his house. **I.** That is, the human race. **J.** This is Mark's explanation of why Jesus said this, and what Jesus meant by it. If Jesus does a miracle which you fully acknowledge but attribute to Satan, what more can be done? You have called the Spirit of God Satan. You have cut yourself off from God. **K.** Or, [facing] toward; at, before.

The Sower's Seed Falls On Different Kinds of Soil. Only The Good Soil Produces Fruit
And He was saying *to* them in His teaching, ³ "Listen! Behold— the *one* sowing
went out to sow. ⁴ And it came about during the sowing *that* some *seed* fell along
the road. And the birds came and ate it up. ⁵ And other[A] *seed* fell on the rocky[B] *place*
where it was not having much soil. And immediately it sprang-up because of not
having *a* depth *of* soil. ⁶ And when the sun rose, it was scorched. And because of not
having *a* root, it was dried-up. ⁷ And other *seed* fell into the thorns. And the thorns
came-up and choked it, and it did not give fruit. ⁸ And others[C] fell into the good soil,
and were giving fruit while coming up and growing. And they were bearing thirty
fold[D] and sixty fold and *a* hundred fold". ⁹ And He was saying, "He who has ears to
hear, let him hear".

Jesus Tells The Disciples The Purpose of Parables
¹⁰ And when He came-to-be alone, the *ones* around Him with the twelve were
questioning Him *as to* the parables. ¹¹ And He was saying *to* them, "The mystery[E] *of*
the kingdom *of* God has been given *to* you. But all *things* come in parables *to* those
outside ¹² in order that[F] while seeing, they may be seeing and not perceive, and while
hearing, they may be hearing and not understanding, that they may not ever turn-
back and it be forgiven them".

Jesus Explains The Parable of The Sower
¹³ And He says *to* them, "Do you not know this parable? And how will you
understand all the parables? ¹⁴ The *one* sowing sows the word[G]. ¹⁵ Now these
people are the *ones* along the road, where the word is sown. And when they hear,
immediately Satan comes and takes away the word having been sown into them.
¹⁶ And these *people* are the *ones* being sown *the seed* on the rocky *places*— who,
when they hear the word, immediately are receiving it with joy. ¹⁷ And they do
not have *a* root in themselves, but are temporary[H]. Then affliction or persecution
having come about because of the word, immediately they are caused-to-fall.
¹⁸ And other *people* are the *ones* being sown *the seed* into the thorns. These are
the *ones* having heard the word— ¹⁹ and coming-in, the anxieties[I] *of* the age[J] and
the deceitfulness[K] *of* riches and the desires with respect to the other *things* are
choking the word, and it becomes unfruitful[L]. ²⁰ And those *people* are the *ones*
having been sown[M] *the seed* on the good soil, who are hearing[N] the word and
accepting *it* and bearing-fruit— thirty fold and sixty fold and *a* hundred fold".

The Lamp Comes To Shine, Not To Be Hidden
²¹ And He was saying *to* them, "The lamp does not come in order that it may be put

---

A. That is, another portion of seed, viewed as a group. **B.** That is, bedrock, or a rocky outcropping. **C.** That
is, other seeds viewed as individuals. **D.** Or, one, thirty; and one, sixty; and one, a hundred. Likewise in v 20.
E. That is, the hidden truth about the kingdom of God now being revealed by Jesus. **F.** Jesus here gives the
purpose of His speaking in parables. It was in order that the people might remain spiritually blind. In Mt 13:13
it is because the people willfully choose to be blind. **G.** Or, message. **H.** Or, transitory. **I.** Or, worries, cares,
concerns. **J.** Or, world. **K.** Or, deception. **L.** Fruitbearing is the evidence of life. **M.** That is, who have been
sown the seed. Note the change in tense. The second two soils are 'being sown'; they are in the process of being
sown in hopes that a fruitful crop can be grown. This soil has been sown and is bearing fruit. **N.** That is, listening
to, in the sense of 'obeying'. Note the change of tense that stresses continuous action here (are hearing), in
contrast to the first three soils.

under the basket or under the bed, *does it*? Is it not in order that it may be put on the lampstand? **22** For it is not hidden, except in order that it may be made-visibleᴬ. Nor did it become hidden-away, but in order that it may come into visibility. **23** If anyone has ears to hear, let him hear".

With The Measure You Use It Will Be Measured To You
24 And He was saying *to* them, "Be watching what you listen-toᴮ. With what measure you measureᶜ, it will be measured *to* you— and it will be added *to* you. **25** For he who has— it will be given *to* him. And he who does not have— even what he has will be taken-away from him".

The Kingdom of God Is Like Seed That Grows From Within Itself To Maturity
26 And He was saying, "The kingdom *of* God is like this: as-*if a* person would throw the seed upon the soil, **27** and would be sleeping and arising night and day, and the seed would be budding and growing-long— how, **he** does notᴰ know. **28** The soil bears-fruit by-itselfᴱ— first grass, then *a* head, then *a* full grain in the head. **29** And whenever the fruit permitsᶠ, immediately heᴳ sends-forth the sickle because the harvest has comeᴴ".

The Kingdom of God Is Like a Mustard Seed. It Starts Small And Grows Large
30 And He was saying, "How should we liken the kingdom *of* God, or with what parable may we present it?— **31** as *a* seed *of a* mustard-plant, which when it is sown upon the soil *is* being smaller *than* allᴵ the seeds upon the soil. **32** And when it is sown, it goes-up and becomes larger *than* all the garden-plants. And it makes large branches so that the birds *of* the heaven are able to be nesting under the shade *of* it".

Jesus Spoke To The Crowd In Parables And Explained Everything To His Disciples
33 And *with* many such parables He was speaking the word *to* them, as they were able to hear *it*. **34** And He was not speaking *to* them apart from *a* parable. But He was explainingᴶ everything privately *to His* own disciples.

Jesus Calms The Wind And Sea. The Disciples Say, Who Is This Man?
35 And on that day, having become evening, He says *to* them, "Let us go to the other side". **36** And having left the crowd, they take Him along as He wasᴷ, in the boat. And other boats were with Him. **37** And *a* great storm *of* wind takes place. And the waves were throwing-

A. Or, revealed. One would only hide a lamp for the purpose of shining it at the proper time. The lamp may be Jesus, who came to light the world, but is hidden from Israel until the proper time; or, the truth Jesus brings, which is now hidden in parables in order that it may come into visibility at the proper time. Or, the lamp may refer to the word of God which believers hide in their hearts in order that it may shine at the opportune time. **B.** Or, hear. That is, in the sense of 'obey'. **C.** The measure you use reflects your spiritual capacity, and your ability to receive. If you listen to the traditions of the Pharisees, it will limit your ability to receive spiritual truth. **D.** The seed has life in it, and grows without the assistance or understanding of the sower. The sower sows. God causes the growth in ways the sower does not understand. Then the person harvests the fruit. **E.** Or, on-its-own. **F.** Lit, hands-*itself*-over. That is, when it has ripened itself. **G.** That is, the person who sowed the seed. **H.** Or, is here. **I.** That is, all the seed people in that day sowed in their gardens. The point is that it has a small and insignificant beginning, but grows larger than all. **J.** Or, interpreting. **K.** This may be describing the condition of Jesus— straight from His speaking without any rest, explaining why He slept; or, His location— still in the boat (v 1).

over into the boat so that the boat *was* already being filled. **38** And **He** was in the stern on the cushion, sleeping. And they wake Him and say *to* Him, "Teacher, do You not care[A] that we are perishing?" **39** And having awakened, He rebuked the wind, and said *to* the sea "Be still, be silenced[B]". And the wind stopped. And there was *a* great calm. **40** And He said *to* them, "Why are you afraid[C]? Do you not yet have faith?" **41** And they feared *a* great fear[D]. And they were saying to one another, "Who then is this *One*, that[E] even[F] the wind and the sea obey Him?"

Jesus Casts Demons Out of a Man Into a Herd of Pigs. The Locals Beg Him To Leave
5:1 And they came to the other side *of* the sea, to the country *of* the Gerasenes. **2** And He having gone out of the boat, immediately *a* man with[G] *an* unclean spirit met Him, out of the tombs— **3** who was having *his* dwelling-place in the tombs. And no one was able to bind him any-more, not even *with a* chain, **4** because he often *had* been bound *with* shackles[H] and chains and the chains *had* been torn-apart by him, and the shackles broken. And no one was strong-*enough* to subdue him. **5** And continually, *by* night and *by* day, in the tombs and in the mountains, he was crying-out and cutting himself *with* stones. **6** And having seen Jesus from *a* distance, he ran and prostrated-*himself before* Him. **7** And having cried-out *with a* loud voice, he says "What[I] do I have to do with You, Jesus, Son *of* the Most-High God? I make You swear[J] *by* God, do not torment me". **8** For He was saying *to* him, "Come out of the man, unclean spirit". **9** And He was asking him, "What *is the* name *for* you?" And he says *to* Him, "*The* name *for* me *is* Legion[K], because we are many". **10** And he was begging Him greatly that He not send them outside *of* the country. **11** Now there was *a* large herd *of* pigs feeding there at the mountain. **12** And they begged Him, saying "Send us to the pigs, in order that we may enter into them". **13** And He permitted them. And the unclean spirits, having come out, entered into the pigs. And the herd, about two-thousand, rushed down the steep-bank into the sea. And they were drowning in the sea. **14** And the *ones* feeding[L] them fled and reported *it* in the city and in the fields. And they came to see what the *thing* having happened was. **15** And they come to Jesus, and see the *one* being demon-possessed sitting, having been clothed and being sound-minded— the *one* having had the "legion". And they became afraid. **16** And the *ones* having seen *it* related *to* them how it happened *to* the *one* being demon-possessed, and about the pigs. **17** And they began to beg Him to depart[M] from their districts. **18** And while He *was* getting into the boat, the *one* having been demon-possessed was begging Him that he might be with Him. **19** And He did not permit him, but says *to* him, "Go to your house, to your *people*, and report *to* them all-that the Lord has done *for* you, and *that* He had mercy on you". **20** And he departed and began to proclaim in Decapolis[N] all-that Jesus did *for* him. And they all were marveling.

A Synagogue Official Comes To Jesus About His Dying Daughter. Jesus Goes With Him
21 And Jesus having crossed-over again in the boat to the other side, *a* large crowd was gathered to Him. And He was beside the sea. **22** And one *of* the synagogue-officials

---

A. Lit, is it not *a* concern *to* You? **B.** The tense is unusual for a command. It implies, be silenced and stay silent. **C.** Or, cowardly, fearful. **D.** That is, they were extremely afraid. **E.** Or, because. **F.** Or, both. **G.** Or, in. See 1:23. **H.** That is, bindings for the feet. **I.** Lit, What *is there for* me and *for* You. **J.** Or, I put You on oath. **K.** A Roman legion had about 6000 soldiers, plus horsemen and auxiliaries. **L.** Or, tending, grazing, driving to pasture. **M.** The people accept what happened as an 'act of God', but they do not want anything more to happen to them, so they ask Jesus to leave. **N.** That is, the region of 'ten cities' east of Galilee and the Jordan River.

comes, Jairus *by* name. And having seen Him, he falls at His feet **23** and begs Him greatly, saying that "My little-daughter is at the point of death. *I beg* that having come, You lay *Your* hands on her in order that she may be restored^A and live". **24** And He departed with him. And *a* large crowd was following Him, and they were pressing-upon Him.

On The Way, a Woman Touches His Garment And Is Healed Because of Her Faith
25 And *a* woman^B— being in *a* flow *of* blood *for* twelve years, **26** and having suffered many *things* by many physicians, and having spent everything of hers^C and not having been benefitted at all, but rather having come to the worse, **27** having heard about Jesus, having come in the crowd from behind— touched His garment. **28** For she was saying that "If I touch even His garments, I will be restored". **29** And immediately the fountain^D *of* her blood was dried-up, and she knew *in her* body that she had been healed from the scourge. **30** And immediately Jesus— having known in Himself the power^E having gone forth from Him, having turned around in the crowd— was saying "Who touched My garments?" **31** And His disciples were saying *to* Him, "You see the crowd pressing-upon You and You say 'Who touched Me?' " **32** And He was looking around to see the *one* having done this. **33** And the woman— having become afraid, and while trembling, knowing what had happened *to* her— came and fell-before Him and told Him the whole truth. **34** And the *One* said *to* her, "Daughter, your faith has restored you. Go in peace and be^F healthy from your scourge".

The Daughter Dies Before Jesus Arrives. He Raises Her From The Dead
35 While He *is* still speaking, they come from [the house of] the synagogue-official, saying that "Your daughter died. Why are you troubling^G the Teacher further?" **36** But Jesus, having ignored^H the statement being spoken, says *to* the synagogue-official, "Do not be fearing, only be believing^I". **37** And He did not permit anyone to follow with Him except Peter and James and John (the brother *of* James). **38** And they come to the house *of* the synagogue official, and He sees *a* commotion^J and *ones* weeping and wailing loudly. **39** And having gone in, He says *to* them, "Why are you being thrown-into-a-commotion, and weeping? The child did not die, but is sleeping". **40** And they were laughing-scornfully *at* Him. But **He**, having put everyone out, takes along the father *of* the child and the mother and the *ones* with Him, and proceeds in where the child was. **41** And having taken hold of the hand *of* the child, He says *to* her, "Talitha koum" (which being translated is "Little-girl, I say *to* you, arise"). **42** And immediately the little girl stood-up and was walking around (for she was twelve years *old*). And immediately they were astonished *with* great astonishment. **43** And He gave-orders *to* them strictly that no one should know this. And He said *that something should* be given *to* her to eat. **6:1** And He went out from there.

Jesus Teaches In His Hometown Synagogue. They Are Astounded But Unbelieving
And He comes into His hometown^K. And His disciples are following Him. **2** And having

---

A. Or, saved (from this illness). **B:** And *a* woman... touched His garment. The two halves of the main sentence are separated by all the phrases in between, which set the circumstances. **C.** Lit, all the *things* from her; that is, all her resources. **D.** Or, spring. The source of her blood. **E.** Or, miracle. **F.** That is, continue to be. **G.** Or, bothering, annoying. **H.** Or, overheard. **I.** That is, continue believing. **J.** That is, the funeral crowd expressing itself in the customary way. **K.** That is, Nazareth.

become Sabbath, He began to teach in the synagogue. And while listening, many were astounded, saying "From where *did* these *things come to* this *One*? And what *is* the wisdom having been given *to* this *One*? And such miracles taking place by His hands! ³ Is this *One* not the carpenter, the son *of* Mary, and brother *of* James and Joses and Jude^A and Simon? And are not His sisters here with us?" And they were taking-offense^B at Him. ⁴ And Jesus was saying *to* them that "*A* prophet is not without-honor except in his hometown and among his relatives and in his house". ⁵ And He was not able to do any miracle there— except, having laid *His* hands on *a* few sick *ones*, He cured *them*. ⁶ And He was marveling because of their unbelief.

The Twelve Are Sent Out Two By Two To Proclaim Repentance And Heal The Sick
And He was going-around the villages *in a* circle, teaching. ⁷ And He summons the twelve, and began to send them out two *by* two. And He was giving them authority *over* the unclean spirits. ⁸ And He instructed them that they should be taking nothing for *the* journey except *a* staff^C only— no bread, no [traveler's] bag, no money^D for the [money] belt— ⁹ but *should go* having [merely] tied-on sandals. "And do not put on two tunics^E". ¹⁰ And He was saying *to* them, "Wherever you enter into *a* house, be staying there until you go forth from-that-place^F. ¹¹ And whatever place does not welcome you, nor do they listen-to you— while proceeding out from-that-place, shake-out the dirt under your feet for *a* testimony *against* them". ¹² And having gone forth, they proclaimed that they should repent. ¹³ And they were casting out many demons. And they were anointing^G many sick *ones with* oil and curing *them*.

Herod Hears of Jesus And Thinks John The Baptist Arose From The Dead
¹⁴ And King Herod^H heard [of Him], for His name became known. And they^I were saying that "John, the *one* baptizing, has arisen from *the* dead. And for this reason the *miraculous-powers*^J are at-work in Him". ¹⁵ And others were saying that "He is Elijah". And others were saying that "*He is a* prophet like one *of* the [former] prophets". ¹⁶ But having heard, Herod was saying, "John whom **I** beheaded— this *one* arose".

For Herod Had Beheaded John The Baptist
¹⁷ For Herod himself, having sent out *men*, seized John and bound^K him in prison because of Herodias^L, the wife *of* Philip his brother— because he married her. ¹⁸ For John was saying *to* Herod that "It is not lawful *for* you to have the wife *of* your brother". ¹⁹ And Herodias was hostile^M to him and wanting to kill him, and was not being able. ²⁰ For Herod was fearing John, knowing *that* he *was a* righteous and holy man. And he was protecting him. And having heard him, he was greatly perplexed, and-*yet* he was listening-to him with-pleasure. ²¹ And *an* opportune^N day having come about when Herod, *for* his birthday-celebrations, made *a* banquet *for*

A. Or, Judas, Judah. **B.** Or, being caused to fall. **C.** Or, walking stick. **D.** Or, copper [money], as in Mt 10:9. Take no change in your pocket. **E.** That is, an extra undershirt. Take no supplies for the journey, nor the means to carry or acquire them. Just get up and go with what you have on. **F.** That is, from that city. **G.** Or, putting on oil, rubbing on oil. The purpose of the oil may be symbolic of God's Spirit or power, or it may be medicinal as in Lk 10:34. **H.** That is, Herod Antipas. See Mt 14:1. **I.** That is, the ones making Jesus known, or the ones repeating it to Herod. **J.** Or, the Powers; that is, the supernatural beings who were the source of these miracles in Herod's mind. **K.** This took place in Mk 1:14. **L.** See Mt 14:3 on Herodias and Philip. **M.** Lit, was having *it* in *for* him. She was holding in her anger and retaliation until she could destroy John. **N.** That is, for Herodias.

his princes[A] and the commanders[B] and the leading[C] *ones of* Galilee, **22** and his[D] daughter Herodias[E] having come in and danced— she pleased Herod, and the *ones* reclining-back-with *him* [to eat]. The king said *to* the girl[F], "Ask me whatever you wish and I will give *it to* you". **23** And he swore-with-an-oath *to* her solemnly, "Whatever thing you ask me, I will give *it to* you— up to half *of* my kingdom". **24** And having gone out, she said *to* her mother, "What should I ask-*for*?" And the *one* said, "The head *of* John, the *one* baptizing". **25** And having immediately gone in with haste to the king, she asked, saying "I want you to give me at-once on *a* platter the head *of* John the Baptist". **26** And the king, having become deeply-grieved, did not want to reject her because of the oaths and the *ones* reclining-back [to eat]. **27** And immediately having sent-out *an* executioner[G], the king commanded *him* to bring his head. And having gone, he beheaded him in the prison. **28** And he brought his head on *a* platter and gave it *to* the girl. And the girl gave it *to* her mother. **29** And his disciples, having heard-*of it*, came and took away his corpse and laid it in *a* tomb.

Jesus Multiplies Five Loaves And Two Fish To Feed 5000 Men

30 And the apostles are gathered-together with Jesus. And they reported *to* Him all that they did and that they taught. **31** And He says *to* them, "Come, you yourselves privately, to *a* desolate[H] place, and rest *a* little". For the *ones* coming and the *ones* going were many, and they were not even finding-an-opportunity[I] to eat. **32** And they went away privately in the boat to *a* desolate place. **33** And they[J] saw them going, and many knew[K] *where*. And they ran there together *on* foot from all the cities. And they came-ahead-of[L] them. **34** And having gone[M] out, He saw *a* large crowd and felt-deep-feelings [of compassion] toward them because they were like sheep not having *a* shepherd. And He began to teach them many *things*. **35** And already having become *a* late hour, having come to Him, His disciples were saying that "*This* place is desolate, and *it is* already *a* late hour. **36** Send them away in order that having gone away into the surrounding farms and villages, they may buy themselves what they may eat". **37** But the *One*, having responded, said *to* them, "**You** give them *something* to eat". And they say *to* Him, "Should we, having gone away, buy loaves *worth* two-hundred denarii[N] and give them *something* to eat?" **38** And the *One* says *to* them, "How many loaves do you have? Go, see!" And having come-to-know, they say "Five, and two fish". **39** And He commanded them to make everyone lie-back party *by* party on the green[O] grass. **40** And they fell-back grouping *by* grouping, by hundreds and by fifties. **41** And having taken the five loaves and the two fish, having looked up to heaven, He blessed *them*[P], and broke the loaves in pieces, and was giving *them to* His disciples in order that they might be setting *it* before them. And He divided the two fish *to* everyone.

A. That is, Herod's government officials. **B.** That is, the Roman officers. **C.** That is, prominent local citizens and dignitaries. **D.** That is, by virtue of his marriage to Herodias. Philip was her physical father. **E.** Josephus calls her Salome, but she may have also been known as Herodias. This family dynasty took on the name Herod almost like a title. Some manuscripts say 'the daughter *of* Herodias herself'. **F.** Or, maiden, young-woman (of marriageable age). She was about 13-15 years old. **G.** Or, courier, bodyguard. **H.** Or, deserted, lonely. **I.** Or, having-a-favorable-time. **J:** they saw... and many knew. Or, many saw... and knew. **K.** Or, learned *where*, found-out *where*; or, recognized *them*. **L.** That is, the people arrived at the boat landing before the boat; or, the people who knew them 'went before, went ahead of' the people from the cities, leading them to Jesus. **M.** Or, come out. That is, from the boat; or, from the private place to which they had gone. **N.** One denarius was a day's wage for a laborer. **O.** This was a springtime event, near Passover, Jn 6:4. **P.** That is, the bread and fish. Or, blessed *God*.

⁴² And they all ate and were filled-to-satisfaction. ⁴³ And they picked up fragments— *the* fillings *of* twelve baskets, and from the fish. ⁴⁴ And the *ones* having eaten the loaves were five-thousand menᴬ.

Jesus Walks Across The Raging Sea
⁴⁵ And immediately, He compelledᴮ His disciples to get into the boat, and to be going ahead to the other side, towardᶜ Bethsaida, while **He** sends-away the crowd. ⁴⁶ And having said-good-bye *to* themᴰ, He went away on the mountain to pray. ⁴⁷ And having become evening, the boat was in *the* middle *of* the sea and He *was* alone on the land. ⁴⁸ And having seen them being tormentedᴱ in the rowing— for the wind was contrary *to* them— He comes to them around *the* fourth watchᶠ *of* the night, walking on the sea. And He was intendingᴳ to pass-by them. ⁴⁹ But the *ones,* having seen Him walking on the sea, thought that "It is *a* phantomᴴ", and cried-out. ⁵⁰ For they all saw Him and were frightened. But immediately the *One* spoke with them. And He says *to* them, "Take-courage, I amᴵ *the One.* Do not be afraidᴶ". ⁵¹ And He went up with them in the boat. And the wind stopped. And they were very exceedingly astonished in themselves. ⁵² For they did not understandᴷ on the basis of the loaves-of-bread, but their heart had been hardened.

In Gennesaret The People Recognize Him And Bring All Their Sick To Him For Healing
⁵³ And having crossed-over, they came on land in Gennesaret and moored. ⁵⁴ And they having gone out of the boat— immediately having recognized Him, ⁵⁵ *the people* ran around that whole region. And they began to carry around the *ones* being ill on *their* cots *to*-where they were hearing that He was. ⁵⁶ And wherever He was entering— into villages, or into cities, or into fields— they were laying the *ones* being sick in the marketplaces, and were begging Him that they might touch evenᴸ the tassel *of* His garment. And all who touched it were being restoredᴹ.

Pharisees Object To Eating With Unwashed Hands. Jesus Condemns Their Traditions
7:1 And the Pharisees and some *of* the scribes are gathered-together with Him, having come from Jerusalem. ² And having seen some *of* His disciples, that they are eating *their* bread *with* defiledᴺ hands, that is, unwashedᴼ— ³ for the Pharisees and all the Jews do not eat unless they wash *their* hands *with a* fistᴾ, holding-on-to the tradition *of* the elders. ⁴ And they do not eat [when they return]ᑫ from *the* marketplace unless they cleanseᴿ [themselves]. And there are many other *traditions* which they received to hold-on-to— *the* cleansing *of* cups and pitchers and copper-pots and couchesˢ. ⁵ And the Pharisees and the scribes ask Him, "For what reason are Your disciples not walking according to the

---

A. This word means males. **B.** Jn 6:15 explains why. **C.** Or, to. **D.** That is, the crowd. **E.** Or, being harassed, tortured. Or, tormenting *themselves* at the rowing. **F.** That is, between 3 and 6 A.M. **G.** Or, wishing, wanting. **H.** Or, ghost. **I:** I am *the One.* That is, It is I. **J.** That is, Stop being afraid. **K.** They did not understand who Jesus was based on the feeding of the 5000. They thought He was just a prophet. Now they understand He is God's Son, Mt 14:33. **L.** Or, at least. **M.** Or, saved (from their disease). **N.** Or, unclean; that is, not ritually purified from contact with unclean things or people, according to their traditions. **O.** Mark breaks off his sentence here and explains this to his readers, then begins again in v 5. **P.** There are different opinions about the exact procedure in view here. In any case it is a ceremonial washing for which the water is seen in Jn 2:6. Some manuscripts have a different word meaning 'often' or 'thoroughly'. **Q:** [when they return]...cleanse [themselves]. Or, [food]...cleanse [it]. **R.** This refers to a ritual cleansing, as does the related word in the next verse. **S.** That is, the dining couches on which people of that day reclined to eat.

tradition *of* the elders, but are eating *their* bread *with* defiled hands?" **6** And the *One* said *to* them, "Isaiah prophesied rightly concerning you hypocrites, as it has been written [in Isa 29:13], that 'This people honors Me *with their* lips, but their heart is far distant from Me. **7** But they are worshiping Me in-vain^A, teaching *as* teachings^B *the* commandments *of* humans'. **8** Having neglected the commandment *of* God, you are holding on to the tradition *of* humans!" **9** And He was saying *to* them, "You are nicely^C setting-aside^D the commandment *of* God in order that you may establish^E your tradition! **10** For Moses said [in Ex 20:12], 'Be honoring your father and your mother', and [in Ex 21:17], 'Let the *one* speaking-evil-of father or mother come-to-an-end^F *by a* death'. **11** But **you** say if *a* person says *to his* father or mother, 'Whatever you might be benefitted from me *is* Corban (which means "Gift")', **12** you no longer permit him to do anything^G *for his* father or mother— **13** nullifying^H the word *of* God *by* your tradition which you handed-down. And you are doing many similar such *things*". **14** And having summoned the crowd again, He was saying *to* them, "Everyone listen-to Me and understand— **15** there is nothing outside *of* the person proceeding into him which is able to defile him. But the *things* proceeding out of the person are the *things* defiling the person.   **16** ‖

What Goes Into The Body Does Not Defile, But What Comes Out of The Heart

17 And when He entered into *a* house away-from the crowd, His disciples were questioning Him *as to* the parable. **18** And He says *to* them, "So are even **you** without-understanding? Do you not perceive that everything outside proceeding into the person is not able to defile^J him **19** because it does not proceed into his heart, but into *his* stomach, and it proceeds out into the latrine?" (*He was* making all foods clean^K.) **20** And He was saying that "The *thing* proceeding out of the person— that defiles the person. **21** For from within, out of the heart *of* people, proceed the evil thoughts, sexual-immoralities, thefts, murders, **22** adulteries, greeds, evils, deceit, sensuality, *an* evil eye^L, blasphemy, arrogance, foolishness. **23** All these evil *things* proceed-out from within, and defile the person".

A Gentile Woman Begs For Crumbs From The Master's Table

24 And having arisen, He went from there to the districts *of* Tyre. And having entered into *a* house, He was wanting^M no one to know^N it. And-*yet* He was not able to escape-notice. **25** But immediately, *a* woman having heard about Him— *of* whom her little daughter was having *an* unclean spirit— having come, fell at His feet. **26** Now the woman was *a* Greek^O, *a* Syro-Phoenician^P *by* nationality. And she was asking Him that He cast out the demon from her daughter. **27** And He was saying *to* her, "First allow the children to be filled-to-

---

A. Or, to no end, pointlessly, futilely. **B.** Or, doctrines. **C.** Or, splendidly, beautifully (used sarcastically). **D.** Or, rejecting. **E.** Or, make your tradition stand. Some manuscripts say 'keep your tradition'. **F.** That is, die. On this phrase, see Mt 15:4. **G.** In other words, if you vow to give your estate as an offering to God when you die, you must no longer honor any request from your parents to benefit from it. **H.** Or, voiding, annulling, invalidating. **I.** Some manuscripts add here 'If anyone has ears to hear, let him hear'. **J.** Or, make him unclean or impure. It is disobedience to God's Law that defiles a person. Their traditions are not God's laws. **K:** making... clean. Or, declaring... clean, treating... clean. These words may be Mark's comment, as in 3:30; 7:3-4. If these are still the words of Jesus, punctuate this 'latrine, cleansing all foods' (the latrine proves they are clean because they pass through the body without affecting the heart); or, 'latrine, purging all foods' (simply completing the physical description). **L.** This refers to envy in Mt 20:15. **M.** Or, intending, wishing. **N.** Or, learn. **O.** That is, a Gentile. **P.** That is, from Phoenicia, a region of the Roman province of Syria, in which Tyre was one city.

satisfaction. For it is not good to take the bread *of* the children and throw *it to* the little-dogs^A". **28** But the *one* responded and says *to* Him, "Master, even the little dogs under the table eat from the crumbs *of* the children!" **29** And He said *to* her, "Because of this statement, go— the demon has gone out of your daughter". **30** And having gone to her house, she found the child having been put^B on the bed, and the demon having gone out.

Jesus Heals a Deaf-Mute
31 And again having gone out of the districts *of* Tyre, He went through Sidon to the Sea *of* Galilee in the midst *of* the districts *of* Decapolis. **32** And they bring *to* Him *a* deaf and speech-impaired *one,* and are begging Him that He lay *His* hand on him. **33** And having taken him away from the crowd privately, He put His fingers into his^C ears. And having spit^D, He touched his^E tongue. **34** And having looked up to heaven, He sighed. And He says *to* him "Ephphatha", which means "Be opened". **35** And immediately his ears were opened and the binding^F *of* his tongue was released and he was speaking correctly. **36** And He gave-orders *to* them that they should be telling no one. But as much as He was giving orders *to* them, **they** even more abundantly were proclaiming *it.* **37** And they were being super-abundantly astounded, saying "He has done all *things* well. He even makes the deaf to hear and the mute to speak".

Jesus Again Multiplies Loaves And Fish To Feed 4000
8:1 In those days, *there* again being *a* large crowd, and *they* not having anything they might eat— having summoned the disciples, He says *to* them **2** "I feel-deep-feelings [of compassion] toward the crowd because *it is* already three days they are remaining-with Me, and they do not have anything they may eat. **3** And if I send them away to their house hungry, they will become-exhausted^G on the way. And some *of* them have come from *a* distance". **4** And His disciples responded *to* Him that "From where will anyone be able to fill these *ones* to satisfaction *with* bread here in *a* desolate-place?" **5** And He was asking them, "How many loaves do you have?" And the *ones* said "Seven". **6** And He orders the crowd to fall-back on the ground [to eat]. And having taken the seven loaves, having given-thanks, He broke *them,* and was giving *them to* His disciples in order that they might be setting *them* before *them.* And they set *them* before the crowd. **7** And they had *a* few small-fish. And having blessed them, He said to be setting these also before *them.* **8** And they ate and were filled-to-satisfaction. And they picked up *the* leftovers *of* fragments— seven large-baskets. **9** And there were about four-thousand *men.* And He sent them away.

The Pharisees Ask For a Sign. No Sign Will Be Given To This Generation
10 And immediately, having gotten into the boat with His disciples, He went to the regions *of* Dalmanutha. **11** And the Pharisees came out and began to debate^H *with* Him, seeking from Him *a* sign from heaven, testing Him. **12** And having sighed-deeply in His spirit, He says "Why is this generation seeking *a* sign? Truly I say *to* you, *a* sign will *never*^I be given *to* this generation".

A. Or, lap-dogs, house-dogs. Jesus answers with a proverbial-type statement, then she responds with the same type of statement. **B:** having been put. And therefore, lying. **C.** Or, His. The significance of this action is not clear. Some think it was a kind of sign language by which Jesus was telling the man or the onlookers what He was going to heal. **D.** Mark does not tell us where Jesus spit. **E.** Or, His. **F.** That is, the binding which held the man's tongue and impeded his speaking. **G.** Or, faint, give out. **H.** Or, discuss, dispute, argue. **I:** *a sign will never*

Jesus Warns The Disciples To Beware of The Leaven of The Pharisees

13 And having left them, having again gotten *into the boat*, He went to the other side. **14** And they forgot to take bread. And except one loaf, they were not having *any* with them in the boat. **15** And He was giving orders *to* them, saying "Watch out! Beware of the leaven *of* the Pharisees, and the leaven *of* Herod". **16** And they were discussing with one another that they did not have bread. **17** And having known *it*, He says *to* them "Why are you discussing that you do not have bread? Do you not yet perceive nor understand? Do you have your heart hardened? **18** Having eyes, are you not seeing? And having ears, are you not hearing? And do you not remember?— **19** When I broke the five loaves for the five-thousand, how many full baskets *of* fragments did you pick up?" They say *to* Him, "Twelve". **20** "When *I broke* the seven *loaves* for the four-thousand, *the* fillings *of* how many large-baskets *of* fragments did you pick up?" And they say *to* Him, "Seven". **21** And He was saying *to* them, "Do you not yet understand?"

Jesus Heals a Blind Man In Two Stages

22 And they come to Bethsaida. And they bring Him *a* blind *man,* and are begging Him that He touch him. **23** And having taken-hold-of the hand *of* the blind *man,* He brought him outside *of* the village. And having spit in his eyes, having laid *His* hands on him, He was asking him "Do you see anything?" **24** And having looked-up, he was saying "I am seeing people, because I am looking-at *something* like trees walking around". **25** Then again He laid *His* hands on his eyes, and looked-intently, and restored^A *them*. And he was seeing everything clearly. **26** And He sent him away to his house, saying "Do not even enter into the village".

Who Do You Disciples Say That I Am? Peter Says, You Are The Messiah

27 And Jesus and His disciples went forth into the villages *of* Philip's^B Caesarea. And on the way, He was questioning His disciples, saying *to* them "Who do people say *that* I am?" **28** And the *ones* spoke *to* Him, saying "That *You are* John the Baptist. And others, Elijah. But others, that *You are* one *of* the prophets". **29** And **He** was questioning them, "But who do **you** say *that* I am?" Having responded, Peter says *to* Him "**You** are the Christ". **30** And He warned them that they should be telling no one about Him.

Jesus Began To Teach Them That He Must Die And Be Raised. Peter Rebukes Him

31 And He began to teach them that the Son *of* Man must suffer many *things,* and be rejected by the elders and the chief priests and the scribes, and be killed, and rise-up after three days. **32** And He was stating the matter *with* openness. And Peter, having taken Him aside, began to rebuke Him. **33** But the *One,* having turned around, and having looked-at^C His disciples, rebuked Peter. And He says "Get behind Me, Satan— because you are not thinking the *things of* God, but the *things of* humans".

---

be given. Lit, if *a* sign will be given. This is the conclusion of a Hebrew oath, such as 'May [?] happen to Me if a sign will be given'. **A.** Since '*them*' is not expressed in the Greek, some take this verb to mean simply 'he restored'; that is, 'he changed back', 'he recovered'. In this case, these verbs refer to the man instead of Jesus, 'on his eyes. And he looked-intently and recovered, and was seeing everything clearly'. **B.** That is, the capital city of Herod Philip II (see Lk 3:1), north of the Sea of Galilee (as opposed to the Caesarea on the coast). **C.** Or, having seen.

Deny Yourself, Take Up Your Cross, And Follow Me. Some Here Will See My Kingdom
34 And having summoned the crowd with His disciples, He said *to* them, "If anyone wants to be following after Me, let him deny himself[A] and take up his cross[B], and be following Me. **35** For whoever wants to save[C] his life[D] will lose it. But whoever will lose his life for the sake *of* Me and the good-news will save it. **36** For what does it profit *a* person to gain the whole world, and forfeit[E] his life[F]? **37** For what might *a* person give in-exchange-for his life? **38** For whoever *is* ashamed-of Me and My words in this adulterous[G] and sinful generation, the Son *of* Man will also be ashamed of him when He comes in the glory *of* His Father with the holy angels". **9:1** And[H] He was saying *to* them, "Truly I say *to* you that there are some *of* the *ones* standing here who will by-no-means taste death until[I] they see the kingdom *of* God having come in power".

Three Disciples See Jesus Transformed, And Hear God Tell Them To Listen To Jesus
2 And after six days, Jesus takes along Peter and James and John, and brings them up on *a* high mountain privately, alone. And He was transfigured[J] in front of them. **3** And His garments became shining[K], very white, such as *a* bleacher[L] on earth is not able to make so white. **4** And Elijah appeared *to* them, with Moses. And they were talking-with Jesus. **5** And having responded, Peter says *to* Jesus, "Rabbi, it is good *that* we are here. And let us make three dwellings[M]— one *for* You and one *for* Moses and one *for* Elijah". **6** For he did not know what he should respond, for they became terrified. **7** And there came-to-be *a* cloud overshadowing[N] them. And *a* voice came out of the cloud: "This is My beloved Son. Be listening-to Him". **8** And suddenly, having looked around, they no longer saw anyone with themselves but Jesus alone.

The Disciples Ask, Wasn't Elijah Supposed To Come Before The Messiah?
9 And while they *were* coming down from the mountain, He gave orders *to* them that they should relate *to* no one *the things* which they saw, except when the Son *of* Man rises-up from *the* dead. **10** And they held[O] the matter to themselves, discussing what the 'rising-up from *the* dead' meant. **11** And they were questioning Him, saying "*Why is it* that the scribes say that Elijah must come first[P]?" **12** And the *One* said *to* them, "Elijah, having come first, restores all *things*— and-*yet* how has it been written for[Q] the Son *of* Man that He *would* suffer many *things* and be treated-with-contempt[R]? **13** But I say *to* you that Elijah indeed has come[S], and they did *to* him whatever they were wanting, just as it has been written for him".

A. That is, disown and refuse to follow the impulses of self. **B.** That is, the instrument of his or her death to self. **C.** That is, by avoiding his or her cross; refusing to deny himself for Christ. **D.** That is, life in an earthly sense. **E.** Or, suffer loss of. **F.** That is, life in an eternal sense. **G.** That is, spiritually unfaithful to God. **H.** In contrast to the shame of His death, which led to the words of v 33-38, Jesus now speaks of His power. **I.** See Mt 16:28. **J.** Or, transformed. **K.** Or, glistening, gleaming, radiant. **L.** Or, fuller, cloth refiner. **M.** Or, tents. **N.** Or, covering, hovering over. **O:** they held the matter to themselves discussing what. Or, they seized the statement, discussing with themselves what. **P.** Since You are the Messiah, where is Elijah. Mal 4:5 says he comes before You. **Q.** That is, as destined to occur to. **R.** Or, despised. If Elijah restores all things and Messiah comes in glory, how can this be true also? **S.** Jesus may mean Elijah is coming in the future, but already came in John the Baptist; there are two comings of Elijah, just as with the Messiah. Or, He may mean Elijah is coming as the scribes correctly teach, but in fact has already come in John; Elijah came in an unexpected manner, just as the Messiah did. Compare Mt 17:11.

A Father Pleads With Jesus To Heal His Son Whom The Disciples Could Not Heal
14 And having come to the disciples, they saw *a* large crowd around them, and scribes debating[A] with them. **15** And immediately all the multitude, having seen Him, were struck-with-wonder. And running-up, they were greeting Him. **16** And He asked them, "What are you debating with them?" **17** And one from the crowd answered Him, "Teacher, I brought my son having *a* mute spirit to You. **18** And wherever it overcomes[B] him, it throws-him-to-the-ground, and he foams-at-the-mouth and grinds *his* teeth and becomes-stiff. And I spoke[C] *to* Your disciples in order that they might cast it out, and they were not strong-enough[D]". **19** And the *One*, having responded *to* them, says "O unbelieving[E] generation, how long will I be with you? How long will I bear-with you? Bring him to Me". **20** And they brought him to Him. And having seen Him, the spirit immediately convulsed him. And having fallen on the ground, he was rolling-*himself* while foaming-at-the-mouth. **21** And He asked his father, "How long is it since this has happened *to* him?" And the *one* said, "From childhood. **22** And it often threw him even into fire and into waters in order that it might destroy him. But if You are able *to do* anything, help[F] us, having felt-deep-feelings [of pity] toward us". **23** And Jesus said *to* him, " 'If You are able?' All *things are* possible *for* the *one* believing". **24** Immediately, having cried-out, the father *of* the child was saying, "I believe. Help my unbelief ". **25** And Jesus, having seen that *a* crowd is running-together-upon *them*, rebuked the unclean spirit, saying *to* it "Mute and deaf spirit, **I** command you— come out of him and enter into him no longer". **26** And having cried-out, and having convulsed *him* greatly, it came out. And he became as if dead, so that the majority *were* saying that "He died". **27** But Jesus, having taken hold of his hand, raised him. And he stood-up. **28** And He having entered into *a* house, His disciples were questioning Him privately, "*Why is it* that **we** were not able to cast it out?" **29** And He said *to* them, "This kind can come out by nothing except by prayer".

Jesus Again Teaches His Disciples That He Must Die And Be Raised
30 And having gone forth from there, they were passing through Galilee. And He was not wanting anyone to know *it*. **31** For He was teaching His disciples, and saying *to* them that "The Son *of* Man is being handed-over into *the* hands *of* men. And they will kill Him. And having been killed, He will rise-up after three days". **32** But the *ones* were not-understanding the statement, and they were fearing to question Him.

The Disciples Argue About Who Is The Greatest. Jesus Says, To Be First You Must Be Last
33 And they came to Capernaum. And having come-to-be in the house, He was questioning them, "What were you discussing on the way?" **34** But the *ones* were being silent. For on the way they argued with one another who *was* greater[G]. **35** And having sat-*down*, He called the twelve. And He says *to* them, "If anyone wants to be first, he shall[H] be last *of* all, and servant *of* all".

Whoever Welcomes a Child In My Name Welcomes Me
36 And having taken *a* child, He stood him[I] in *the* middle *of* them. And having taken him in *His* arms, He said *to* them, **37** "Whoever welcomes one such-as-these children[J]

A. Or, arguing, discussing. **B.** Or, seizes. **C:** spoke... cast. Or, told Your disciples to cast. **D.** Or, able. **E.** Or, faithless. **F.** Or, come to our aid. **G.** Or, greatest. **H.** That is, must be, a kind of command. Or, will be, a statement of fact. **I.** Or, her. Lit, it (the child). **J.** See Mt 18:5.

on the basis of My name, welcomes Me. And whoever welcomes Me does not [merely] welcome Me, but the *One* having sent Me forth".

John Recalls an Instance When The Disciples Did Not Welcome Someone
[38] John said *to* Him, "Teacher, we saw someone casting-out demons in Your name. And we were forbidding him because he was not following us". [39] But Jesus said, "Do not be forbidding him. For there is no one who will do *a* miracle on the basis of My name, and soon be able to speak-evil-of Me. [40] For he who is not against[A] us is for us. [41] For whoever gives you *a* cup *of* water to drink in *the* name that you are Christ's— truly I say *to* you that he will by no means lose his reward.

Whoever Causes One of These Little Ones To Fall Would Be Better Off Dead
[42] "And whoever causes one *of* these little *ones* believing in Me to fall— it *would* be better *for* him if instead *a* donkey's millstone[B] were lying around his neck, and he had[C] been thrown into the sea.

Better To Remove Whatever Causes You To Fall Than To Go Into Hell
[43] And if your hand should be causing you to fall, cut[D] it off. It is better *that* you enter into life crippled than go into Gehenna[E] having two hands— into the inextinguishable[F] fire. [44 G] [45] And if your foot should be causing you to fall, cut it off. It is better *that* you enter into life lame than be thrown into Gehenna having two feet. [46 G] [47] And if your eye should be causing you to fall, throw it out. It is better *that* you enter into the kingdom *of* God one-eyed than be thrown into Gehenna having two eyes— [48] where their worm[H] does not come-to-an-end, and the fire is not quenched. [49] For everyone will be salted *with* fire.

Have Salt In Yourselves, And Live In Peace
[50] "Salt *is* good. But if the salt should become unsalty, with what will you season it? Be having salt[I] in yourselves, and be living-in-peace with one another".

Jesus Goes Into Judea. The Crowds Come To Him And He Teaches Them
10:1 And having arisen, He goes from there into the districts[J] *of* Judea and beyond the Jordan. And crowds again are coming-together to Him. And as He was accustomed, He again was teaching them.

Pharisees Test Jesus With a Question About Divorce. Divorce Is Not God's Plan
[2] And Pharisees having come to *Him* were asking Him if it is lawful *for a* husband to send-away[K] *a* wife— testing Him. [3] And the *One*, having responded, said *to* them, "What did Moses command you?" [4] And the *ones* said, "Moses permitted *us* to write *a* certificate[L]

A. That is, actively opposing us. **B.** That is, a large millstone turned by a donkey. **C.** That is, he would be better off to have been violently killed before committing this sin than to face the consequences of it. **D.** That is, take whatever measures are necessary to eliminate causes of falling in your life. **E.** That is, hell. **F.** Or, unquenchable. **G.** 9:44 and 46 are added by some manuscripts, "where their worm does not come to an end and the fire is not quenched", as in v 48. **H.** That is, the maggots eating their flesh never die. Jesus is quoting Is 66:24. **I.** Returning to the main point, be salt to those around you by being servants of all. Don't lose your saltiness by focusing on who is greater. **J.** Or, boundaries. **K.** That is, divorce. **L.** This certificate was to protect the woman and allow her to remarry.

of divorce and send *her* away". ⁵ But Jesus said *to* them, "He wrote this commandment *to* you because-of your hardness-of-heart. ⁶ But from *the* beginning *of* creation, 'He made them male and female' [Gen 1:27]. ⁷ 'For this^A reason, *a* man will leave-behind his father and mother and will be joined^B to his wife. ⁸ And the two will be one flesh' [Gen 2:24]. So then, they are no longer two, but one flesh. ⁹ Therefore what God paired-together^C, let *a* person^D not separate". ¹⁰ And the disciples were questioning Him again about this in the house, ¹¹ and He says *to* them, "Whoever sends-away his wife and marries another is committing-adultery against her. ¹² And if she, having sent-away her husband, marries another, she is committing-adultery".

Jesus Blesses The Children. Of Such Is The Kingdom of God
¹³ And they were bringing children to Him in order that He might touch them. But the disciples rebuked them^E. ¹⁴ But Jesus, having seen *it*, was indignant and said *to* them, "Permit the children to be coming to Me. Do not be forbidding them. For the kingdom *of* God is *of*^F such ones. ¹⁵ Truly I say *to* you, whoever does not receive the kingdom *of* God like *a* child will never^G enter into it". ¹⁶ And having taken them in *His* arms, He was blessing^H *them*, while laying *His* hands on them.

A Rich Man Asks What To Do To Enter Heaven. Sell Everything And Follow Me
¹⁷ And while He *was* proceeding out on *the* road^I, one having run up and knelt-before Him was asking Him, "Good Teacher, what should I do in order that I may inherit eternal life?" ¹⁸ And Jesus said *to* him, "Why do you call Me good? No one *is* good except One— God. ¹⁹ You know the commandments: 'Do not murder, do not commit-adultery, do not steal, do not give-false-testimony, do not defraud, be honoring your father and mother' " ²⁰ And the *one* said *to* Him, "Teacher, I kept these all from my youth". ²¹ And Jesus, having looked at him, loved him. And He said *to* him, "One *thing* is lacking *as to* you: Go, sell all-that you have and give *it to* the poor, and you will have treasure in heaven. And come, be following Me". ²² But the *one*, having become downcast at *His* word, went away grieving. For he was having many properties.

It Is Hard For The Rich To Enter. But All Who Leave Anything Will Inherit More
²³ And having looked around, Jesus says *to* His disciples, "How difficultly the *ones* having wealth^J will enter into the kingdom *of* God". ²⁴ And the disciples were astonished at His words. But Jesus, having responded again, says *to* them, "Children, how difficult it is to enter into the kingdom *of* God. ²⁵ It is easier *that a* camel go through the hole *of* the needle^K than^L *that a* rich *one* enter into the kingdom *of* God". ²⁶ And the *ones* were even more astounded, saying to themselves, "Who indeed can be saved?" ²⁷ Having looked at them, Jesus says, "With humans *it is* impossible, but not with God. For all *things are* possible with God". ²⁸ Peter began to say *to* Him, "Behold— **we** left everything, and have followed You". ²⁹ Jesus said, "Truly I say *to* you, there is no one who left house or brothers or sisters or mother or father or

---

A. That is, because God made them to be a complimentary pair. **B.** Or, united, adhered, glued. **C.** Or, yoked-together, joined as a pair. **D.** Or, *a* human, man (generically speaking). The wife is included in v 12. **E.** That is, the ones bringing the children. **F.** That is, made up of. **G.** Or, by no means. **H.** Or, calling-down-blessing-on. **I.** Or, journey. **J.** Or, money. This was a shocking statement, since wealth was often viewed as a sign of God's blessing. **K.** Lit, perforation *of* the sewing-needle. **L.** In other words, it is impossible, as Jesus says next. Another shocking statement.

children or fields for the sake *of* Me and for the sake *of* the good-news [30] except he receive[A] *a* hundred-fold now in this time— houses and brothers and sisters and mothers and children and fields, along-with persecutions— and in the coming age, eternal life. [31] But many first *ones* will be last, and the last *ones*, first".

Jesus Predicts His Death And Resurrection For The Third Time
[32] And they were on the road going up to Jerusalem, and Jesus was going-ahead-of them. And they were astonished. And the *ones* following were fearing. And having again taken aside the twelve, He began to tell them the *things* going-to happen *to* Him, [33] that "Behold— we are going up to Jerusalem. And the Son *of* Man will be handed-over *to* the chief priests and the scribes. And they will condemn Him *to* death, and will hand Him over *to* the Gentiles. [34] And they will mock Him and spit-on Him and whip Him and kill *Him*. And after three days, He will rise-up".

Two Disciples Jockey For Position In The Kingdom. He Says, It Is Not Mine To Give
[35] And James and John, the sons *of* Zebedee, approach Him, saying *to* Him, "Teacher, we want You to do *for* us whatever we ask You". [36] And the *One* said *to* them, "What do you want Me to do *for* you?" [37] And the *ones* said *to* Him, "Grant *to* us that we may sit one on Your right *side* and one on *the* left *side* in Your glory". [38] But Jesus said *to* them, "You do not know what you are asking. Are you able to drink the cup which I drink, or to be baptized the baptism which I am baptized?" [39] And the *ones* said *to* Him, "We are able". And Jesus said *to* them, "You will drink the cup which I drink. And you will be baptized the baptism which I am baptized. [40] But the sitting on My right *side* or on *the* left *side* is not Mine to give, but *it is for* whom it has been prepared".

Whoever Wants To Be First Shall Be Your Slave. Even I Came To Serve
[41] And having heard-*of it*, the ten began to be indignant about James and John. [42] And having summoned them, Jesus says *to* them, "You know that the *ones* having-the-reputation-of [B] being rulers *of* the Gentiles are lording-over[C] them, and their great *ones* are exercising-authority-over[D] them. [43] But it is not so among you. But whoever wants to become great among you shall be your servant, [44] and whoever wants to be first among you shall be slave *of* all. [45] For even the Son *of* Man did not come to be served, but to serve, and to give His life *as a* ransom for many".

Blind Bartimaeus Calls Upon The Messiah To Heal Him
[46] And they come to Jericho. And while He and His disciples and *a* considerable crowd *are* proceeding-out from Jericho, Bartimaeus, the son *of* Timaeus, *a* blind beggar, was sitting beside the road. [47] And having heard that it was Jesus from-Nazareth, he began to cry-out and say, "Son *of* David, Jesus, have-mercy-on me". [48] And many were rebuking him in order that he might keep-silent. But the *one* was crying-out *by* much more, "Son *of* David, have mercy on me". [49] And having stopped, Jesus said, "Call him". And they call the blind *one*, saying *to* him, "Take-courage, arise, He is calling you!" [50] And the *one*, having thrown-off his cloak, having jumped-up, came to Jesus. [51] And having responded *to* him, Jesus said, "What do you want Me to do *for* you?" And the blind *one* said *to* Him,

---

A. That is, who will not receive. **B.** Or, being-recognized-as. **C.** Or, domineering-over, ruling as masters over. **D.** That is, they lead by authority.

"Rabboni^A— that I may see-again!" **52** And Jesus said *to* him, "Go. Your faith has restored^B you". And immediately he saw-again. And he was following Him on the road.

Jesus Rides Into Jerusalem On a Donkey To Shouts of Hosanna

11:1 And when they draw-near to Jerusalem— to Bethphage and Bethany, near the Mount *of* Olives— He sends-forth two *of* His disciples, **2** and says *to* them, "Go to the village before you. And immediately while proceeding into it, you will find *a* colt having been tied, on which none *of* mankind^C yet sat. Untie it, and be bringing *it*. **3** And if someone says *to* you, 'Why are you doing this?', say, 'The Lord has need *of* it, and^D immediately He sends^E it back here^F' ". **4** And they went and found *a* colt having been tied at *a* door, outside on the street. And they untie it. **5** And some *of* the *ones* standing there were saying *to* them, "What are you doing untying the colt?" **6** But the *ones* spoke *to* them just as Jesus spoke, and they permitted them. And they bring the colt to Jesus. **7** And they throw their cloaks on it, and He sat on it. **8** And many spread their cloaks on the road. And others *spread* leafy-branches, having cut *them* from the fields. **9** And the *ones* going ahead and the *ones* following were crying-out "Hosanna! Blessed *is* the *One* coming in *the* name *of the* Lord. **10** Blessed *is* the coming kingdom *of* our father David. Hosanna in the highest [heavens]!"

Jesus Enters Jerusalem

11 And He entered into Jerusalem, into the temple. And having looked-around-*at* everything, the hour being already late, He went out to Bethany with the twelve.

Jesus Curses a Fruitless Fig Tree

12 And *on* the next day, they having departed from Bethany, He was hungry. **13** And having seen from *a* distance *a* fig-tree having leaves, He went *to see* if perhaps He would find anything on it. And having come to it, He found nothing except leaves^G— for it was not the season *for* figs. **14** And having responded, He said *to* it, "May no one eat fruit from you any longer— forever!" And His disciples were listening.

Jesus Cleanses The Temple of Merchandisers. The Priests Seek To Destroy Him

15 And they come into Jerusalem. And having entered into the temple, He began to throw-out the *ones* selling and the *ones* buying in the temple. And He overturned the tables *of* the money-changers^H, and the seats *of* the *ones* selling doves^I. **16** And He was not permitting that anyone carry *an* object^J through the temple. **17** And He was teaching and saying *to* them, "Has it not been written [in Isa 56:7] that 'My house will be called *a* house *of* prayer *for* all the nations'? But **you** have made it *a* den *of* robbers^K". **18** And the chief priests and the scribes heard *it*. And they were seeking how they might destroy Him. For they were fearing Him, for the whole crowd was astounded at His teaching. **19** And when it became evening, they were going outside *of* the city.

A. That is, my rabbi, my teacher. **B.** Or, saved (from this ailment). **C.** That is, no human. **D.** Or, say 'The Lord has need *of* it', and immediately he sends it back here" (that is, to Jesus where He is). **E.** That is, is going to send. **F.** That is, to where the donkey is tied. **G.** This is a parable of Israel. They had the appearance of life, but no fruit. They are not ready, not ripe, not in season. Jesus curses them. **H.** They changed foreign currency into Jewish currency for use in the temple. **I.** That is, doves used in the sacrifices commanded by God. **J.** Or, vessel, dish, merchandise. **K.** Or, bandits, plunderers.

Lessons From The Fig Tree

20 And while passing by early-in-the-morning, they saw the fig tree having dried-up from *the* roots. **21** And having remembered, Peter says *to* Him, "Rabbi, look! The fig tree which You cursed has dried-up". **22** And having responded, Jesus says *to* them, "Be having faith *in* God. **23** Truly I say *to* you that whoever says *to* this mountain, 'Be taken up and be thrown into the sea', and does not doubt in his heart, but is believing that what he is speaking is coming-about, it will happen *for* him. **24** For this reason I say *to* you, be believing that you received all that you are praying and asking, and it will happen *for* you. **25** And whenever you stand praying, forgive— if you have anything against anyone— in order that your Father in the heavens also may forgive you your trespasses". **26** A

Priests Ask, By What Authority Do You Do This? From Where Was John's Authority?

27 And they come again into Jerusalem. And while He *is* walking around in the temple, the chief priests and the scribes and the elders come to Him. **28** And they were saying *to* Him, "By what-kind-of^B authority are You doing these *things,* or who gave You this authority that you may be doing these *things*?" **29** And Jesus said *to* them, "I will ask you one thing, and you answer Me, and I will tell you by what kind of authority I am doing these *things*: **30** Was the baptism *of* John from heaven or from humans? Answer Me!" **31** And they were discussing *it* with themselves, saying, "If we say 'From heaven', He will say 'Then for what reason did you not believe him?' **32** But should we say 'From humans'?" They were fearing the crowd, for they all were holding *as to* John that he **really** was *a* prophet. **33** And having responded *to* Jesus, they say "We do not know". And Jesus says *to* them, "Nor am **I** telling you by what kind of authority I am doing these *things*".

You Priests Are Like Farmers Who Killed The Owner's Messengers And His Son

12:1 And He began to speak *to* them in parables: "*A* man planted *a* vineyard and put *a* fence around *it* and dug *a* pit [for a wine press] and built *a* tower. And he rented it *to* farmers and went-on-a-journey. **2** And he sent forth *a* slave to the farmers *at* the *harvest* time in order that he might receive from the fruits *of* the vineyard from the farmers. **3** And having taken him, they beat *him,* and sent *him* away empty-*handed*.**4** And again he sent-forth another slave to them. And that *one* they struck-on-the-head, and dishonored. **5** And he sent forth another— and that *one* they killed— and many others, *they* beating some and killing others. **6** He was still having one *to send*: *a* beloved son. He sent him forth to them last, saying that 'They will have-regard-for my son'. **7** But those farmers said to themselves that 'This *one* is the heir. Come, let us kill him, and the inheritance will be ours'. **8** And having taken *him,* they killed him and threw him outside *of* the vineyard. **9** Therefore what will the owner *of* the vineyard do? He will come and destroy the farmers, and give the vineyard *to* others.

But As The Psalm Says, The Stone The Builders Rejected Became The Cornerstone

10 Did you not even read this Scripture [in Ps 118:22-23]: '*The* stone which the *ones* building rejected, this became *the* head *of the* corner^C. **11** This came about from *the* Lord, and it is marvelous in our eyes'?" **12** And they were seeking to

---

A. Some manuscripts add, 'But if you do not forgive, neither will your Father in the heavens forgive your trespasses'. **B.** Or, what authority. That is, a prophet's authority? Messiah's? **C.** That is, the cornerstone of the foundation; or, the capstone of the arch.

seize Him. And[A] they feared the crowd. For they[B] knew that He spoke the parable against them. And having left Him, they went away.

The Pharisees Try To Snare Jesus: Shall We Pay Taxes To Caesar?
[13] And they send forth some *of* the Pharisees and the Herodians[C] to Him in order that they might catch Him *in a* statement. [14] And having come, they say *to* Him, "Teacher, we know that You are truthful. And You are not concerned about [pleasing] anyone[D], for You do not look[E] at *the* face *of* people, but You teach the way *of* God in accordance with truth. Is it lawful to give *a* poll-tax[F] *to* Caesar, or not? Should we give *it,* or should we not give *it*?" [15] But the *One,* knowing their hypocrisy, said *to* them, "Why are you testing Me? Bring Me *a* denarius[G] in order that I may see *it*". [16] And the *ones* brought *it.* And He says *to* them, "Whose *is* this image[H] and inscription?" And the *ones* said *to* Him, "Caesar's". [17] And Jesus said *to* them, "Give back[I] the *things of*[J] Caesar *to* Caesar, and the *things of* God *to* God". And they were marveling-greatly at Him.

Sadducees Question Jesus About The Resurrection of a Wife With Seven Husbands
[18] And Sadducees come to Him, who say *that* there is not *a* resurrection. And they were questioning Him, saying [19] "Teacher, Moses wrote *to* us [in Deut 25:5] that if *a* brother *of* someone dies and leaves-behind *a* wife and does not leave *a* child, that his brother should take the wife, and raise-up-from *her a* seed[K] *for* his brother. [20] There were seven brothers. And the first took *a* wife, and dying, did not leave *a* seed. [21] And the second took her, and died, not having left-behind *a* seed. And the third similarly. [22] And the seven did not leave *a* seed. Last *of* all, the woman also died. [23] In the resurrection when they rise up, *of* which *of* them will she be *the* wife? For the seven had her *as* wife". [24] Jesus said *to* them, "Are you not mistaken[L] because of this— not knowing the Scriptures, nor the power *of* God? [25] For when they rise-up from *the* dead, they neither marry nor are they given-in-marriage, but they are like angels[M] in the heavens. [26] And concerning the dead, that they are raised, did you not read in the book *of* Moses at the [place about the burning] bush, how God spoke *to* him, saying [in Ex 3:15] 'I *am* the God *of* Abraham, and the God *of* Isaac, and the God *of* Jacob'? [27] He is not God *of* dead *ones*, but *of* living *ones.* You are greatly mistaken".

A Scribe Asks, Which Is The Foremost Commandment?
[28] And having come to *Him,* one *of* the scribes— having heard them debating, having seen that He answered them well— asked Him, "Which is *the* foremost[N] commandment *of* all?" [29] Jesus answered that "Foremost is: 'Hear, Israel. *The* Lord our God is one Lord. [30] And you shall love *the* Lord your God from your whole heart, and from your whole soul, and from your whole mind, and from your whole strength' [Deut 6:4-5]. [31] Second *is* this: 'You shall love your neighbor as yourself' [Lev 19:18]. There is not another commandment greater *than* these". [32] And the scribe said *to* Him, "Well *said,* Teacher! In accordance with

A: seize Him. And. Or, seize Him, and-*yet.* **B:** crowd. For they knew. That is, for the chief priests and elders knew. Or, crowd, for they knew. That is, the crowd knew. **C.** That is, ones politically linked to Herod's family. **D.** That is, any constituency or individual. **E.** That is, You do not show partiality to anyone. **F.** That is, a tax based on a census and paid to Rome. Is it lawful to pay taxes to a foreign king? **G.** This Roman silver coin was a day's wage for a laborer. **H.** Or, likeness. **I.** Or, Render, Pay. **J.** That is, belonging to. **K.** That is, offspring, and thus, a posterity. **L.** Or, deceived, going-astray; deceiving *yourselves.* **M.** That is, not subject to death (and so not needing to marry and procreate), and members of God's family, not separate families. See Lk 20:36. **N.** Or, first.

[God's] truth, You said[A] that He is one. And there is not another except Him. [33] And the *statement* 'to love Him from the whole heart, and from the whole understanding, and from the whole strength', and the *statement* 'to love the neighbor as himself', are more [important] *than* all the whole-burnt-offerings and sacrifices". [34] And Jesus, having looked-at him because he responded thoughtfully, said *to* him, "You are not far from the kingdom *of* God".

Jesus Asks How The Messiah Can Be The Son of David Since David Calls Him His Lord
And no one was daring to question Him any more. [35] And having responded, Jesus was saying while teaching in the temple, "How *is it that* the scribes say that the Christ is *the* son *of* David? [36] David himself said by the Holy Spirit [in Ps 110:1], '*The* Lord said *to* my Lord, "Be sitting on My right *side* until I put Your enemies under Your feet" '. [37] David himself calls Him 'Lord'. And in what[B] way is He his son?"

Jesus Warns The Crowds To Beware of The Scribes
And the large crowd was listening-to Him with-pleasure. [38] And in His teaching He was saying, "Beware of the scribes— the *ones* delighting to walk around in robes, and *to receive* greetings in the marketplaces, [39] and seats-of-honor in the synagogues, and places-of-honor at the banquets. [40] *They are* the *ones* devouring[C] the houses *of* the widows, and praying long *for a* pretense[D]. These *ones* will receive greater condemnation".

Jesus Uses The Widow's Offering To Illustrate True Giving
[41] And having sat-*down* opposite the treasury[E], He was observing how the crowd throws money into the treasury. And many rich *ones* were throwing much *money.* [42] And one poor widow having come threw two leptos[F], which is *a* quadrans[G]. [43] And having summoned His disciples, He said *to* them, "Truly I say *to* you that this poor widow threw more *than* all the *ones* throwing into the treasury. [44] For they all threw out of the *money* abounding[H] *to* them. But this *one*, out of her need[I], threw all that she was having— her whole living[J]".

Jesus Tells The Disciples That The Temple Will Be Destroyed. They Ask, When?
13:1 And while He *is* proceeding out of the temple, one *of* His disciples says *to* Him, "Teacher, look! What stones and what buildings!" [2] And Jesus said *to* him, "Do you see these great buildings? *A* stone upon *a* stone will by no means be left here which will by-any-means not be torn-down[K]". [3] And while He *was* sitting on the Mount *of* Olives opposite the temple, Peter and James and John and Andrew were questioning Him privately, [4] "Tell us— when will these[L] *things* happen? And what *will be* the sign when all these *things* are about to be accomplished[M]?" [5] And Jesus began to say *to* them:

A: truth, You said that. Or, truth You spoke, because. **B.** If Messiah is David's own Lord, how can He be his distant physical descendant? **C.** That is, taking financial advantage based on spiritual pretexts. **D.** That is, a falsely alleged motive. **E.** That is, the temple treasury in general; or, specifically the trumpet shaped receptacles in which the offerings were placed. **F.** That is, copper Jewish coins. This is the smallest denomination of Jewish coin, 1/128th of a denarius. **G.** This is the smallest denomination of Roman coin. **H.** Or, overflowing, being left over. They gave out of their excess. **I.** Or, lack, want. She gave out of what was already not enough. **J.** That is, means of living. **K.** Or, destroyed, demolished, done-away-with. **L:** these *things* happen... all these *things* are about to be accomplished. That is, when will this prophecy in v 2 happen... and all the events surrounding that event be accomplished. Or, when will this prophecy in v 2 happen... and all these buildings be brought-to-an-end. **M.** Or, carried out, fulfilled, completed, finished, concluded, brought to an end.

There Will Be Birthpangs, So Watch Out. The Gospel Must First Reach All The Nations
"Be watching out *that* no one may deceive you. **6** Many will come on the basis of My name, saying that 'I am^A *the One*'. And they will deceive many. **7** And whenever you hear-*of* wars and rumors *of* wars, do not be alarmed. *They* must take place, but *it is* not yet the end. **8** For nation will arise against nation, and kingdom against kingdom. There will be earthquakes in various places. There will be famines. These *things are*^B *a* beginning *of* birth-pains. **9** But you— be watching yourselves. They will hand you over to councils^C. And you will be beaten in synagogues. And you will be stood before governors and kings for My sake, for *a* testimony *to* them. **10** And the good-news must first be proclaimed to all the nations. **11** And whenever they lead you while handing *you* over, do not be anxious-beforehand *as to* what you should speak. But whatever is given *to* you in that hour, speak this. For **you** are not the *ones* speaking, but the Holy Spirit. **12** And brother will hand-over brother to death, and *a* father *his* child. And children will rise-up-in-rebellion^D against parents, and they will put them to death. **13** And you will be being hated by all because of My name. But the *one* having endured to *the* end^E— this *one* will be saved.

When You See The Abomination of Desolation, Flee. For a Great Affliction Will Occur
14 "But when you see the abomination^F *of* desolation standing where *he*^G should not (let the *one* reading understand), then^H let the *ones* in Judea be fleeing to the mountains. **15** And let the *one* upon the housetop not go down nor go in to take anything out of his house. **16** And let the *one* in the field not turn-back to the *things* behind to take his cloak. **17** And woe *to* the *ones* having *a child* in *the* womb, and *to* the *ones* nursing in those days. **18** And be praying that it may not take place *in* winter. **19** For those days will be *an* affliction^I such-as has not taken place such-as-this since *the* beginning *of the* creation which God created until now, and never will take place [again]. **20** And if *the* Lord had not shortened^J the days, no flesh^K would have been saved. But He shortened the days for the sake of the chosen *ones* whom He chose. **21** And then^L if someone says *to* you, 'Look— here *is* the Christ', 'Look— there *He is*', do not be believing *it*. **22** For false-christs and false-prophets will arise, and will give signs and wonders so-as to be leading-astray^M, if possible, the chosen *ones*. **23** But **you** be watching out. I have told you everything beforehand.

After That Affliction, The Powers Will Be Shaken. Then I Will Come In Glory
24 "But in those days after that affliction, the sun^N will be darkened, and the moon will not give its glow, **25** and the stars will be falling from the heaven, and the powers in the heavens will be shaken. **26** And then they will see the Son *of* Man coming in *the* clouds with great power and glory. **27** And at that time He will send out the angels, and He will gather together His chosen *ones* from the four winds, from *the* end *of the* earth to *the* end *of the* heaven.

A: I am *the One*. Or, I am *He*. That is, the Christ. **B.** Or, *will be*. See Mt 24:5. **C.** That is, local Jewish courts, as in Mt 10:17. **D.** Or, stand-up-against. **E.** That is, the end of his life or the coming of Christ, whichever comes first. **F.** See Mt 24:15. **G.** Or, *it*. **H.** Or, at that time. See Mt 29:9 on this word. **I.** Or, distress, trouble, tribulation. **J.** Or, curtailed, cut short. **K:** no flesh would have. Lit, all flesh would not have. Some think all flesh means all humanity; others, all those in Judea, v 14. **L.** Or, at that time, as in v 14. **M.** Or, misleading. **N:** sun... moon... stars...powers. See Mt 24:29.

The Parable of The Fig Tree: When You See These Things, You Know I Am Near

28 "Now learn the parable from the fig[A] tree: when its branch already becomes tender and grows-out *its* leaves, you know that the summer is near. **29** So also you— when you see these[B] *things* taking place, you know[C] that He[D] is near, at *the* doors. **30** Truly I say *to* you that this generation[E] will by no means pass away until which *time* these *things* all take place. **31** Heaven and earth will pass away, but My words will by-no-means pass away.

But No One Knows The Day Or Hour, So Keep Watching

32 "But no one knows about that day or the hour— not even the angels in heaven, nor the Son— except the Father. **33** Be watching out, be keeping-alert, for you do not know when the time is. **34** *It is* like *a* man away-on-a-journey. Having left his house and having given authority *to* his slaves— to each[F] *as to* his work— he also commanded the doorkeeper that he should be keeping-watch. **35** Therefore, keep watching— for you do not know when the master *of* the house is coming, whether evening[G] or midnight or rooster-crowing or early-morning— **36** *that* having come suddenly, he may not find you sleeping. **37** And what I say *to* you I say *to* everyone: 'Keep watching' ".

The Priests Plot To Seize And Kill Jesus

14:1 Now the Passover [Feast] and the *Feast of* Unleavened-Bread was after two days. And the chief priests and the scribes were seeking how, having seized Him by deceit[H], they might kill *Him*. **2** For they were saying, "Not during the Feast, so that there will not perhaps be *an* uproar *of* the people".

Jesus Is Anointed With Oil In Preparation For His Burial

3 And He being in Bethany at the house *of* Simon the leper, while He *is* reclining [to eat], *a* woman came having *an* alabaster-jar *of* very-precious genuine[I] nard[J] perfume[K]. Having broken the alabaster-jar, she poured *it* down *over* His head. **4** But some were being indignant to themselves— "For what *purpose* has this waste *of* perfume taken place? **5** For this perfume could have been sold *for* over three-hundred[L] denarii and given *to* the poor". And they were sternly-scolding her. **6** But Jesus said, "Leave her *alone*. Why are you causing troubles *for* her? She worked *a* good work[M] in[N] Me. **7** For you **always** have the poor with you. And whenever you want, you are able to do good *for* them. But you do not always have **Me**. **8** She did what she had[O]. She anticipated to perfume My body for *its* preparation-for-burial. **9** And truly I say *to* you, wherever the good-news is proclaimed in the whole world, what this *one* did will also be spoken for *a* memorial *of* her".

Judas Betrays Jesus To The Priests

10 And Judas Iscariot, the one *from* the twelve, went to the chief priests in order that he

---

A. See Mt 24:32. **B.** That is, v 5 or 14 to v 23 or 25. **C.** Or, know that (a command). **D.** Or, it; Christ's coming. **E.** See Mt 24:34. **F.** Or, [and] *to* each *one* his work. **G:** evening... early-morning. These are the names of the four three-hour watches of the night, from 6 P.M. to 6 A.M. **H.** Or, treachery, cunning. **I.** Or, pure. **J.** Or, spikenard. **K.** Or, fragrant oil. **L.** That is, nearly a year's wages for a laborer. Some think this was a family heirloom. **M.** Or, did a good deed. **N.** That is, in connection with Me; or, in My case. **O.** That is, she took action with what was available to her.

might hand Him over *to* them. **¹¹** And the *ones,* having heard, rejoiced and promised to give him money. And he was seeking how he might conveniently[A] hand Him over.

Jesus Celebrates Passover With The Twelve

¹² And *on* the first day *of* the *Feast of* Unleavened-Bread, when they were[B] sacrificing the Passover [lamb], His disciples say *to* Him, "Where do You want us, having gone, to prepare in order that You may eat the Passover [meal]?" **¹³** And He sends-forth two of His disciples. And He says *to* them, "Go into the city, and *a* man will meet you carrying *a* jar[C] *of* water. Follow him. **¹⁴** And wherever he enters, say *to* the house-master that 'The Teacher says, "Where is My guest-room where I may eat the Passover [meal] with My disciples?" ' **¹⁵** And **he** will show you *a* large upstairs room having been spread [with furnishings], prepared. And prepare *for* us there". **¹⁶** And the disciples went forth and came to the city, and found *it* just as He told them. And they prepared the Passover [meal]. **¹⁷** And having become evening, He comes with the twelve.

Judas Is Exposed

¹⁸ And while they *were* reclining-back and eating, Jesus said, "Truly I say *to* you that one of you will hand Me over— the *one* eating[D] with Me!" **¹⁹** They began to be grieved, and to say *to* Him one by one, "*It is* not I, *is it* ?" **²⁰** And the *One* said *to* them, "*It is* one *of* the twelve, the *one* dipping with Me into the bowl. **²¹** Because the Son *of* Man is going just as it has been written about Him— but woe *to* that man by whom the Son *of* Man is being handed-over! *It would have been* better *for* him if that man had not been born".

The Bread And The Wine Are Given a New Meaning

²² And while they *were* eating, having taken bread, having blessed *it*[E], He broke *it* and gave *it to* them and said, "Take *it*. This is My body". **²³** And having taken *a* cup, having given-thanks, He gave *it to* them. And they all drank from it. **²⁴** And He said *to* them, "This is My blood *of*[F] the covenant— the *blood* being poured-out for many. **²⁵** Truly I say *to* you that I will no longer by any means drink of the fruit *of* the grapevine until that day when I drink it new in the kingdom *of* God".

You Will All Be Scattered In Fulfillment of Zechariah. Peter's Denial Is Predicted

²⁶ And having sung-a-hymn, they went out to the Mount *of* Olives. **²⁷** And Jesus says *to* them that "You will all be caused-to-fall, because it has been written [in Zech 13:7]: 'I will strike the Shepherd and the sheep will be scattered'. **²⁸** But after I am raised, I will go ahead of you to Galilee". **²⁹** But Peter said *to* Him, "Even[G] though all will be caused to fall, nevertheless, I *will* not". **³⁰** And Jesus says *to* him, "Truly I say *to* you, that you, today, *on* this night, before *a* rooster crows twice— you will deny Me three-times". **³¹** But the *one* was saying emphatically[H], "If I have-to-die-with You, I will never deny You". And they all were also speaking similarly.

A. Or, opportunely. **B.** That is, were actually sacrificing (placing this after 3 P.M.); or, were customarily sacrificing (placing this any time on that day). **C.** These were normally carried by women, so this is unusual. **D.** That is, one of the very ones eating with Me! **E.** Or, blessed *God.* **F.** That is, inaugurating the new covenant. **G.** That is, assuming that even all. **H.** Or, insistently.

Jesus Waits And Prays In The Garden of Gethsemane

32 And they come to *a* place *of* which the name *is* Gethsemane. And He says *to* His disciples, "Sit here while^A I pray". **33** And He takes along Peter and James and John with Him. And He began to be alarmed^B and distressed. **34** And He says *to* them, "My soul is deeply-grieved, to the point of death. Stay here and keep-watching". **35** And having gone ahead *a* little, He was falling on the ground, and praying that if it is possible, the hour might pass from Him. **36** And He was saying, "Abba^C! Father! All *things are* possible *for* You. Remove this cup from Me. But not what **I** want^D, but what You *want* ". **37** And He comes and finds them sleeping. And He says *to* Peter, "Simon, are you sleeping? Were you^E not strong-*enough*^F to keep watch *for* one hour? **38** Keep watching, and be praying that^G you may not come into temptation^H. The spirit *is* willing^I, but the flesh *is* weak". **39** And having gone away again, He prayed, having spoken the same thing^J. **40** And again having come, He found them sleeping. For their eyes were being very-weighed-down. And they did not know what they should answer Him. **41** And He comes the third-*time*, and says *to* them, "Are you sleeping^K and resting from now on? It is enough. The hour came. Behold— the Son *of* Man is being handed-over into the hands *of* the sinners. **42** Arise, let us be going. Behold— the *one* handing Me over has drawn-near".

Jesus Is Betrayed With a Kiss And Arrested

43 And immediately, while He *is* still speaking, Judas, one *of* the twelve, arrives. And with him *is a* crowd from the chief priests and the scribes and the elders with swords and clubs. **44** Now the *one* handing Him over had given *a* signal *to* them, saying, "Whomever I kiss is He. Seize Him, and lead *Him* away securely^L". **45** And having come, having immediately gone to Him, he says "Rabbi". And he kissed Him. **46** And the *ones* put *their* hands on Him and seized Him. **47** And *a* certain one *of* the *ones* standing near, having drawn *his* sword, hit the slave *of* the high priest and took-off his ear. **48** And having responded, Jesus said *to* them, "Did you come out to arrest Me with swords and clubs as-*if* against *a* robber? **49** Daily I was with you in the temple teaching, and you did not seize Me. But *this is* in order that the Scriptures might be fulfilled". **50** And having left^M Him, they all fled. **51** And *a* certain young-man^N was following Him, having put-on *a* linen-cloth over *his* naked *body*. And they seize him. **52** But the *one*, having left-behind the linen-cloth, fled naked.

Jesus Is Led Before The High Priest And The Sanhedrin. Peter Follows

53 And they led Jesus away to the high priest. And all the chief priests and the elders and the scribes come together. **54** And Peter followed Him at *a* distance, as far as inside in the courtyard *of* the high priest. And he was sitting-together with the officers^O, and warming *himself* toward the light [of the fire].

Jesus Says, I Am The Son of God. They Condemn Him To Death

55 Now the chief priests and the whole Sanhedrin were seeking testimony against Jesus, so that *they might* put Him to death. And they were not finding *it.* **56** For many

---

A. Or, until. **B.** Or, anxious, troubled. **C.** This is a transliterated Aramaic word whose meaning Mark gives next. **D.** Or, wish, will. **E.** This word is singular. **F.** Or, able. **G:** Keep watching, and be praying that. Or, Keep watching and praying, in order that. **H.** That is, the temptation to deny Jesus as He predicted; or, to sleep. **I.** See Mt 26:41. **J.** Or, statement, word *of prayer*. That is, the same request. **K.** On this response, see Mt 26:45. **L.** Or, safely. **M.** Or, abandoned. **N.** Mark may be referring to himself. **O.** That is, temple guards.

were giving-false-testimony against Him. And the testimonies were not identical. [57] And some, having stood up, were giving false testimony against Him, saying [58] that "**We** heard Him saying that 'I will tear down this temple made-by-*human*-hands, and in three days I will build another not-made-by-*human*-hands' ". [59] And not even thus[A] was their testimony identical. [60] And the high priest, having stood up into *the* middle, questioned Jesus, saying "Are You not answering anything? What[B] *is it* these *ones* are testifying against You?" [61] But the *One* was being silent. And He did not answer anything. Again the high priest was questioning Him. And he says *to* Him, "Are **You** the Christ, the Son *of* the Blessed *One*?" [62] And Jesus said, "**I** am[C]. And you will see the Son *of* Man sitting on *the* right *side of* the Power[D], and coming with the clouds *of* heaven". [63] And the high priest, having torn his clothes, says "What further need do we have *of* witnesses? [64] You heard the blasphemy. What appears *right to* you?" And the *ones* all condemned Him to be subject-to[E] death. [65] And some began to spit-on Him, and to cover His face and beat Him and say *to* Him, "Prophesy!" And the officers received Him *with* slaps.

Peter Denies Jesus Three Times
[66] And Peter being below in the courtyard, one *of* the servant-girls *of* the high priest comes. [67] And having seen Peter warming *himself,* having looked at him, she says "**You** also were with the *One* from-Nazareth, Jesus". [68] But the *one* denied *it,* saying "I neither know nor understand what **you** are saying". And he went outside to the entryway[F]. And *a* rooster crowed. [69] And the[G] servant-girl having seen him began again[H] to say *to* the *ones* standing near that "This *one* is *one* of them". [70] But the *one* was again denying *it.* And after *a* little *while*, again the *ones* standing near were saying *to* Peter, "Truly you are *one* of them, for you also are *a* Galilean". [71] But the *one* began to curse[I], and to swear-with-an-oath[J] that "I do not know this man Whom you are saying". [72] And immediately *a* rooster crowed for *a* second-*time*. And Peter remembered the word, how Jesus said *to* him that "Before *a* rooster crows twice, you will deny Me three-times". And having put *his mind* upon[K] *it*, he was weeping.

Jesus Is Led Before Pilate, Who Orders Him Crucified To Please The Crowd
15:1 And immediately, early-in-the-morning, the chief priests (with the elders and scribes) and the whole Sanhedrin having made *a* consultation[L], having bound Jesus, took *Him* away and handed *Him* over *to* Pilate. [2] And Pilate questioned Him, "Are **You** the King *of* the Jews?" And the *One*, having responded *to* him, says "**You** are saying[M] *it* ". [3] And the chief priests were accusing Him *as to* many *things*. [4] And Pilate again was questioning Him, saying "Are You not answering anything? Look how many *things* they are accusing You". [5] But Jesus no longer answered anything, so that Pilate *was* marveling. [6] Now at *the* Feast, he was [in the habit of] releasing *for* them one prisoner whom they were requesting. [7] And

---

A. Or, in this manner. That is, with such testimony as this. **B:** anything? What *is it* these. Or, anything *as to* what these. **C.** Compare Mt 26:64. **D.** That is, God. Or, *of* power; God's power. Jesus is claiming to be the fulfillment of Ps 110:1 and Dan 7:13. **E.** Or, liable to, deserving of. **F.** Or, gateway, forecourt. **G.** That is, the one there; or, the one previously mentioned. **H.** That is, for a second time, as in v 70 it means for a third time. **I.** That is, to bind himself under a curse, such as, May I be cursed if I know Him. **J.** For example, By heaven, I do not know Him. **K.** Or, having put *his hands* on *his face*; having thrown *himself* over. The exact nuance of this phrase is not certain. **L.** Or, plan. That is, having held a council meeting; or, having passed a resolution at such a meeting. **M.** See Mt 27:11.

the *one* being called Barabbas had been bound with the rebels[A] who had committed murder in the rebellion[B]. **8** And having come up, the crowd began to ask *him to do* as he was [in the habit of] doing *for* them. **9** And Pilate responded *to* them, saying "Do you want me to release the King *of* the Jews *for* you?" **10** For he knew that the chief priests had handed Him over because of envy[C]. **11** But the chief priests stirred-up the crowd in order that he might release Barabbas *for* them instead. **12** And Pilate, again having responded, was saying *to* them "Then what do you want me to do *as to the One* whom you call the King *of* the Jews?" **13** And the *ones* cried-out again[D], "Crucify Him!" **14** But Pilate was saying *to* them, "What indeed[E] did He do wrong?" But the *ones* cried out even more, "Crucify Him!" **15** And Pilate, wanting to do enough[F] *for* the crowd, released Barabbas *for* them, and handed-over Jesus, having flogged[G] *Him*, in order that He might be crucified.

Jesus Is Mocked, Beaten, Spit On, And Crucified
16 And the soldiers led Him away inside the palace (that is, *the* Praetorium[H]). And they call together the whole [Roman] cohort[I]. **17** And they dress Him in *a* purple[J] *cloak*. And having woven *a* crown made-of-thorns, they set *it* on Him. **18** And they began to greet Him, "Hail[K], King *of* the Jews!" **19** And they were striking His head *with a* staff, and spitting-on Him. And while putting-*down their* knees, they were paying-homage *to* Him. **20** And when they mocked Him, they stripped the purple *cloak* off Him and put His garments on Him. And they lead Him out in order that they might crucify Him. **21** And they press-into-service *a* certain *one* passing by, coming from *the* country— Simon, *a* Cyrenian[L], the father *of* Alexander and Rufus— in order that he might take up His cross. **22** And they bring Him to the Golgotha[M] place, which being translated is "*The* Place *of a* Skull". **23** And they were giving wine[N] having been mixed-with-myrrh *to* Him, but *the* One did not take *it*. **24** And they crucify Him, and divide His garments among *themselves*, casting *a* lot for them *to decide* who should take what. **25** And it was *the* third[O] hour, and they crucified Him. **26** And the inscription *of* His charge had been inscribed "The King *of* the Jews". **27** And they crucify two robbers[P] with Him— one on *the* right *side* and one on His left *side*. **28** [Q]

The King of Israel Is Mocked While Hanging On The Cross
29 And the *ones* passing by were blaspheming Him while shaking their heads and saying, "Ha! The *One* tearing-down the temple and building *it* in three days— **30** save Yourself, having come down from the cross". **31** Likewise also the chief priests, mocking *Him* to one another with the scribes, were saying, "He saved others— Himself He is not able to save! **32** Let the Christ, the King *of* Israel, come down now from the cross that we may see and believe". And the *ones* having been crucified with Him were reproaching Him.

A. Or, revolutionaries, insurrectionists, rioters. **B.** Or, insurrection, revolt, riot, uprising. **C.** Or, jealousy. **D.** This means the first cry is implied in v 11. Or, cried back. **E.** Or, Why? What did He do wrong? Pilate is incredulous. **F.** That is, to do what is sufficient to placate the crowd. **G.** Or, scourged. That is, whipped with a whip. This was common Roman practice before a crucifixion. **H.** See Mt 27:27. **I.** See Mt 27:27. **J.** That is, a Roman soldier's cloak. **K.** Or, Greetings, Farewell. This was a common greeting. **L.** That is, from the city of Cyrene west of Egypt on the coast of Africa. **M.** See Mt 27:33. **N:** wine... -with-myrrh. This was to dull the senses. **O.** That is, 9 A.M. **P.** Or, insurrectionists. **Q.** Some manuscripts add here, And the Scripture saying 'And He was counted with the lawless *ones*' was fulfilled.

Jesus Dies

33 And having become *the* sixth hour, *a* darkness came over the whole land[A] until *the* ninth hour. **34** And *at* the ninth hour Jesus shouted *with a* loud voice, "Eloi, Eloi, lema sabachthani?", which being translated is "My God, My God, for what *purpose* did You forsake[B] Me?" **35** And some *of* the *ones* standing near, having heard, were saying "Look— He is calling Elijah". **36** And someone— having run, and having filled *a* sponge *of* sour-wine[C], having put *it* on *a* stick[D]— was giving-a-drink *to* Him, saying "Leave *Him* alone. Let us see if Elijah comes to take Him down". **37** And Jesus, having let-go *a* loud shout[E], expired[F].

The Curtain of The Temple Is Torn In Two

38 And the curtain *of* the temple was torn[G] in two from top to bottom. **39** And the centurion standing-by from opposite Him, having seen that He expired in this manner, said "Truly this man was God's Son[H]!"

Many Women Followers Watch At a Distance

40 And women were also watching at *a* distance, among whom *were* both Mary the Magdalene[I] and Mary the mother *of* James the little[J] and Joses, and Salome[K]— **41** who, when He was in Galilee, were following Him and serving Him— and many other *women* having come up with Him to Jerusalem.

Joseph of Arimathea Lays Jesus In a Rock Tomb, With The Women Watching

42 And having already become evening[L], because it was Preparation[M] *day* (that is, the-day-before-the-Sabbath), **43** Joseph from Arimathea having come (*a* prominent council-member[N] who also himself was waiting-for the kingdom *of* God), having become daring[O], went in to Pilate and asked-*for* the body *of* Jesus. **44** But Pilate wondered whether He was dead by-this-time. And having summoned the centurion, he asked him whether He died already. **45** And having come-to-know *it* from the centurion, he granted the corpse *to* Joseph. **46** And having bought linen-cloth, having taken Him down, he wrapped *Him* in the linen cloth, and laid Him in *a* tomb which had been hewn out of rock. And he rolled *a* stone against[P] the door *of* the tomb. **47** And Mary the Magdalene and Mary the *mother of* Joses were observing where He had been laid.

Jesus Rises From The Dead. The Women Find The Tomb Empty

16:1 And the Sabbath having passed[Q], Mary the Magdalene, and Mary the *mother of* James, and Salome bought spices in order that having come, they might anoint Him. **2** And very early-in-the-morning *on* the first *day of* the week, they come to the tomb— the sun having risen. **3** And they were saying to themselves, "Who will roll-away the stone from the door *of* the tomb *for* us?" **4** And having looked-up, they see that the stone has been rolled-away. For it was extremely large. **5** And having entered into the tomb, they saw *a* young-man sitting at the right, having

---

A. Or, earth. **B.** Or, abandon, desert. Jesus is quoting Ps 22:1. **C.** Or, wine-vinegar (watered down). This was a favorite beverage of the soldiers and common people. **D.** Or, rod, staff, reed, branch. **E.** The words Jesus shouted are recorded in Lk 23:46 and Jn 19:30. **F.** Or, breathed-out *His last*. **G.** See Mt 27:51. **H.** See Mt 27:54. **I.** That is, the one from Magdala, on the Sea of Galilee. **J.** That is, small; or, young. **K.** This may be the mother of James and John. See Mt 27:56. **L.** That is, between 3 and 6 P.M., before the Sabbath began at dark. **M.** That is, Friday. **N.** That is, member of the Sanhedrin. **O.** Or, courageous, bold. **P.** Or, to, over, across, upon. **Q.** That is, after sunset on Saturday night (as we call it).

been clothed-with *a* white robe. And they were alarmed. **6** But the *one* says *to* them, "Do not be alarmed. You are seeking Jesus from-Nazareth, the *One* having been crucified. He arose, He is not here. Look— the place where they laid Him! **7** But go, tell His disciples and Peter that 'He is going-ahead-of you to Galilee. You will see Him there, just as He told you' ". **8** And having gone out, they fled from the tomb. For trembling and astonishment was holding them. And they said nothing *to* anyone, for they were fearing.

[Most Greek manuscripts have this "Long^A Ending" after verse 8, but two of the oldest omit it].

Jesus Appears To Mary, Then To Two In The Country, Then To The Eleven
9 And [Jesus] having risen-up early-in-the-morning *on the* first *day of the* week, He appeared first *to* Mary the Magdalene, from whom He had cast-out seven demons. **10** That *one,* having gone, reported *it to* the ones having been with Him, while *they were* mourning and weeping. **11** And-those-*ones,* having heard that He was alive and was seen by her, did not-believe^B *her.* **12** And after these *things,* He appeared in *a* different form *to* two of them walking, while *they were* proceeding into *the* country. **13** And those *ones,* having gone, reported *it to* the rest. They did not even believe those *ones.* **14** And later He appeared *to* the eleven themselves while *they were* reclining-back [to eat]. And He reproached^C their unbelief and hardness-of-heart because they did not believe the *ones* having seen Him arisen.

Jesus Commissions His Followers To Proclaim The Gospel To All Creation
15 And He said *to* them, "Having gone into all the world, proclaim the good-news *to*^D all creation. **16** The *one* having believed and having been baptized will be saved. But the *one* having not-believed will be condemned. **17** And these signs will accompany^E the *ones* having believed: in My name they will cast-out demons, they will speak *in*^F new tongues^G, **18** and they will pick up snakes^H with *their* hands. And if they drink any deadly *thing,* it will by-no-means^I hurt^J them. They will lay hands on sick *ones,* and they will be well".

Jesus Is Taken Up Into Heaven
19 So indeed the Lord Jesus, after *He* spoke *to* them, was taken-up into heaven and sat-*down* on *the* right *side of* God. **20** And those *ones,* having gone-forth, proclaimed *it* everywhere, the Lord working-with *them* and confirming^K the word by the signs following-after^L *them.*

[A few Greek manuscripts have this "Short^M Ending" after verse 8, followed by the "long ending" above]

And they promptly reported all the *things* having been commanded *them to* the *ones* around Peter. And after these *things,* Jesus Himself also sent-forth the sacred and imperishable proclamation *of* eternal salvation through them, from *the* east and as-far-as *the* west. Amen.

A. Some think Mark wrote this ending; others think another wrote it, perhaps at Mark's direction, after the last page of the manuscript was lost. **B.** Or, refused to believe. **C.** Or, reprimanded. **D.** Or, *in.* **E.** Or, closely follow, follow beside. **F.** Or, *with.* **G.** Or, languages. **H.** Compare Lk 10:19, Acts 28:3-6. **I.** Or, never. **J.** Or, harm, injure. **K.** Or, establishing, strengthening, making firm. **L.** Or, authenticating, confirming. **M.** None consider this an original part of Mark's gospel.

Luke

Introduction 1:1-4

A. In the days of Herod, king of Judea, there was a priest, Zechariah, and his wife, Elizabeth 1:5

 1. Zechariah was told by an angel that Elizabeth would bear a son— John 1:5-25
 2. Mary was told by an angel that she would bear a Son by the Holy Spirit— Jesus 1:26-38
 3. Mary went to Elizabeth and stayed three months. They both praised God 1:39-56
 4. Elizabeth gave birth. Zechariah praised God. John lived in the desolate places 1:57-80
 5. Mary gave birth in Bethlehem. Shepherds rejoiced. Jesus was circumcised 2:1-21
 6. They brought Jesus to Jerusalem. Simeon and Anna praised God. They returned to 2:22-40
  Nazareth. The Child was growing and becoming strong. God's grace was upon Him

B. When He was twelve, they found Jesus in His Father's temple, listening and questioning 2:41-52
C. In the fifteenth year of Tiberius, John began to preach and baptize. Jesus was baptized 3:1-22
D. Jesus was about thirty when He began His ministry. His genealogy and temptation 3:23-4:13
E. Jesus returned to Galilee in the power of the Spirit and began teaching in their synagogues 4:14-15

 1. At Nazareth, He read Isaiah and said, Today this Scripture is fulfilled, enraging them 4:16-30
 2. Jesus went to Capernaum and cast out a demon. At Simon's house, He healed many 4:31-43
 3. At the lake of Gennesaret, He taught from a boat, and led Simon to a great catch 4:44-5:11
 4. In one of the cities, Jesus healed a leper. News spread more. Large crowds came 5:12-16
 5. On one day He healed and forgave a paralytic. Pharisees objected. Which is easier? 5:17-26
 6. Jesus called Levi, a tax collector, and ate at his house. Pharisees objected. New wine 5:27-39
 7. Passing through grainfields, His disciples violated a Sabbath rule of the Pharisees 6:1-5
 8. On a Sabbath, He healed a man. Pharisees were enraged, and discussed what to do 6:6-11
 9. Jesus spent the night in prayer, then chose the twelve, healed and taught 6:12-49
 10. After He finished, He entered Capernaum and healed a centurion's slave 7:1-10
 11. Afterward, He proceeded to Nain and raised a widow's son from his coffin 7:11-17
 12. John the Baptist asked, Are You the One? Tell him what you see. Jesus spoke of John 7:18-35
 13. While eating with some Pharisees, a sinful woman anointed Him. They objected 7:36-50
 14. Then He traveled from city to city. He spoke of the sower. His mother and brother 8:1-21
 15. Crossing the sea, Jesus calmed the winds and the water 8:22-25
 16. In the country of the Gerasenes, Jesus cast demons into a herd of pigs 8:26-39
 17. Returning, Jesus raised Jairus's daughter, healing a woman along the way 8:40-56
 18. He empowered and sent out the twelve. Herod hears. On their return, He fed 5000 9:1-17
 19. Who do the crowds say I am? Who do you say? Take up your cross and follow Me 9:18-27
 20. Eight days later, on a mountain with Peter, John, and James, He was transfigured 9:28-36
 21. On the next day, Jesus cast out a demon the disciples could not 9:37-43
 22. Jesus said to His disciples that He must be killed and raised. They did not understand 9:43-45
 23. His disciples argued over who was greatest. He said, the one who is least among you 9:46-50

F. While the days were being fulfilled for His ascension, Jesus set His face to go to Jerusalem 9:51

 1. Jesus sent ahead messengers, who were not welcomed by a village in Samaria 9:52-56
 2. While they were proceeding, Jesus responded to some wanting to follow Him 9:57-62
 3. The Lord appoints and sends out 72 others, two by two 10:1

  a. First Jesus empowers and instructs them 10:2-16
  b. The 72 return rejoicing in their power. Jesus says, rejoice in your salvation instead 10:17-20
  c. Jesus thanks God for revealing these things to children. Jesus reveals the Father 10:21-24

 4. A Law-expert said, What must I do to inherit eternal life? The good Samaritan parable 10:25-37

5.   Jesus stayed with Martha. Mary preferred to sit and listen, the good part   10:38-42

6.   After He prayed, the disciples asked Jesus how to pray. He instructed them   11:1-13

7.   Some said He cast out demons by Beelzebul. Others asked for a sign. He responds   11:14-36

8.   At lunch, Jesus did not wash. They objected. He rebuked the Pharisees and lawyers   11:37-52

9.   They plotted against Jesus, and myriads flocked to Him, in which circumstances   11:53-12:1

      a.   He taught His disciples. Beware of the Pharisees. Do not fear them. Confess Me   12:1-12

      b.   One said to settle a dispute. Who made Me your judge? Be rich toward God   12:13-21

      c.   Do not be anxious about life. Seek God's kingdom. Be ready   12:22-53

      d.   He said to the crowds, Judge the right thing for yourselves. Repent or perish   12:54-13:9

10.   Jesus healed a woman on the Sabbath. The official objected. Jesus rebuked him   13:10-21

11.   One asked, Are there few being saved? He said, Strive to enter by the narrow door   13:22-30

12.   Some Pharisees said, Herod wants to kill You. Jesus mourned the fate of Jerusalem   13:31-35

13.   Jesus healed a man on the Sabbath at a Pharisee's house   14:1-6

      a.   Jesus says to the invited, Humble yourselves, and wait on the one who invited you   14:7-11

      b.   Jesus says to the host, Serve those who cannot repay   14:12-14

      c.   When the invited refuse to attend God's banquet, the outcasts are welcomed   14:15-24

14.   Jesus said to the crowds, Whoever does not carry his own cross cannot be My disciple   14:25-35

15.   Tax collectors and sinners drew near to hear, and Pharisees grumbled about them   15:1-2

      a.   Jesus told them of the lost sheep and coin. God seeks the lost, rejoices in repentance   15:3-10

      b.   The parable of the two sons— the wild living son and his unloving brother   15:11-32

      c.   Jesus spoke to the disciples about money. Invest it in your eternal dwellings   16:1-13

      d.   The Pharisees sneered at all this. Jesus told them the parable of Lazarus   16:14-31

      e.   Jesus warned about causes of falling. Rebuke and forgive your brother   17:1-4

      f.   The apostles ask for more faith. Jesus said the smallest amount is enough   17:5-10

16.   While proceeding, Jesus healed ten lepers. One came back to thank Him   17:11-19

17.   Jesus is asked when the kingdom of God is coming. The kingdom is within you   17:20-21

      a.   You will desire to see that day, and you will not. It will come like lightning   17:22-25

      b.   It will be like the days of Noah and Lot: life will be going on as usual   17:26-37

      c.   So pray and do not lose heart. God will avenge His people   18:1-8

18.   Jesus told a parable for ones trusting in themselves— the Pharisee and the tax collector   18:9-14

19.   They also were bringing Him babies. You must receive the kingdom like a child   18:15-17

20.   A rich ruler said, What shall I do to inherit eternal life? Sell all, be following Me   18:18-30

21.   Jesus said to the twelve, I will be killed and raised again. They did not understand   18:31-34

22.   Drawing near to Jericho, Jesus healed a blind man   18:35-43

23.   Jesus stayed in Jericho with Zacchaeus. Because they supposed the kingdom would   19:1-27
come immediately, He told a parable about servants investing the master's resources

G.   Having said these things, Jesus was proceeding ahead, going up to Jerusalem   19:28

1.   The disciples get Jesus a colt. The crowds said, Blessed is the King. The Pharisees   19:29-44
objected. Jesus wept over Jerusalem. You did not recognize your time of visitation

2.   Jesus entered the temple and drove out the sellers. And He was teaching daily   19:45-48

3.   On one day, the priests asked, By what authority do you do these things? The parable of   20:1-19
the vine-growers who killed the owner's son. The vineyard will be taken away

4.   They sent spies to try to trap Him. Is it lawful to pay tributes to Caesar?   20:20-26

5.   Some Sadducees questioned Him. In the resurrection, whose wife is she?   20:27-40

6.   Jesus said to them, How is it that they say the Christ is David's son?   20:41-44

7. While all were listening, Jesus warned His disciples to beware of the scribes   20:45-47
8. Jesus saw a widow giving her offering. She gave more than all   21:1-4
9. Jesus says the temple will be destroyed. When will it happen? And what will be the sign?   21:5-7

   a. Don't be deceived by false Christs or frightened by disturbances   21:8-9
   b. Then He said, There will be wars and disasters, and great signs from heaven   21:10-11
   c. But before all this, you will be persecuted for My name   21:12-19
   d. When You see Jerusalem surrounded, flee. These are days of vengeance   21:20-24
   e. There will be signs in heaven and on earth. Then I will come in great glory   21:25-28
   f. The parable of the fig tree: When it puts forth leaves, summer is near   21:29-33
   g. It will come suddenly. Keep alert, and pray that you may be able to escape   21:34-36

10. Jesus taught during the day, but would go out at night to the Mount of Olives   21:37-38

H. Now Passover was drawing near. And the priests sought how to kill Him   22:1-2

1. Satan entered Judas, and he plotted with the priests to betray Jesus   22:3-6
2. Jesus sends Peter and John to find the place where they will eat the Passover   22:7-13

   a. During the Passover meal, Jesus gives the bread and cup a new meaning   22:14-23
   b. The disciples argue over who is greater. Jesus predicts Peter's denial   22:24-34
   c. Jesus tells the disciples to prepare for changed circumstances   22:35-38

3. They went to the Mount of Olives. Jesus prayed. Judas kissed Him. He is arrested   22:39-53
4. They led Him to the house of the high priest. Peter followed, and denied Him   22:54-65
5. When it became day, the elders assembled and condemned Him   22:66-71
6. They all led Him before Pilate, who found no guilt in Him. He sent Him to Herod   23:1-7
7. Herod questioned Him, but He did not answer. He mocked Him and returned Him   22:8-12
8. Pilate tried to release Him three times, and then handed Him over to their will   22:13-25
9. They led Him away and crucified Him. They mocked Him. Jesus expired   23:26-49
10. Joseph of Arimathea asked for the body, and placed it in a tomb   23:50-54

I. Having closely followed, the women looked at the tomb and how His body was laid. And   23:55-24:8
they rested on the Sabbath, but then went to the tomb. Angels said He was raised

1. They reported these things to the eleven. They did not believe. Peter ran to see   24:9-12
2. That day, two were on the road to Emmaus. Jesus spoke with them and revealed Himself   24:13-32
3. That night, the two returned to the eleven in Jerusalem. The Lord appeared to them all 24:33-45
4. Jesus said, You are witnesses. Wait in Jerusalem for power   24:46-49
5. Jesus led them outside near Bethany. He blessed them, and went up into heaven   24:50-53

1:1 In-as-much-as many undertook[A] to compile *a* narrative about the things having been fulfilled[B] among us, **²** just as the eyewitnesses from *the* first[C] and *ones* having become servants *of* the word handed-down *to* us, **³** it seemed *good to* me also, having closely-followed[D] everything carefully from-the-beginning[E], to write *it for* you in-order, most-excellent Theophilus, **⁴** in order that you may fully-know the certainty *of the* things about which you were instructed.

The Birth of John And Jesus
⁵ In the days *of* Herod[F], king *of* Judea:

There Was a Priest Named Zechariah Whose Wife Elizabeth Was Barren
There was *a* certain priest— Zechariah *by* name, from *the* division *of* Abijah— and *a* wife *for* him from the daughters *of* Aaron. And her name *was* Elizabeth. **⁶** And they were both righteous *ones* in the sight of God, walking in all the commandments and regulations *of* the Lord *as* blameless[G] *ones.* **⁷** And there was not *a* child *for* them, because Elizabeth was barren. And they were both advanced in their days.

During His Temple Service, an Angel Tells Him Elizabeth Will Bear a Son
⁸ And it came about during his serving-as-priest before God in the order *of* his division, **⁹** *that* according to the custom[H] *of* the priestly-office, he obtained-by-lot *that he might* offer-incense[I], [after] having entered into the temple *of* the Lord. **¹⁰** And *the* whole assembly *of* the people was praying outside *at* the hour *of* the *offering of* incense. **¹¹** And *an* angel *of the* Lord appeared *to* him, standing on *the* right *side of* the altar *of* incense. **¹²** And having seen *him,* Zechariah was frightened, and fear fell upon him. **¹³** But the angel said to him, "Do not be fearing, Zechariah, because your prayer was heard. And your wife Elizabeth will bear you *a* son, and you shall call his name John. **¹⁴** And there will be joy and gladness *for* you. And many will rejoice over his birth. **¹⁵** For he will be great in the sight of the Lord, and he will never drink wine and fermented-drink[J], and he will be filled *with the* Holy Spirit *while* still of[K] his mother's womb, **¹⁶** and he will turn-back many *of* the sons *of* Israel to *the* Lord their God. **¹⁷** And **he** will go-ahead before Him in *the* spirit and power *of* Elijah to turn-back[L] *the* hearts *of* fathers to *their* children, and *to turn back* disobedient *ones* with[M] *the* understanding[N] *of* righteous *ones,* to prepare *a* people having been made-ready *for the* Lord". **¹⁸** And Zechariah said to the angel, "Based-on what shall I know this? For **I** am *an* old-man, and my wife *is* advanced in her days". **¹⁹** And having responded, the angel said *to* him, "**I** am Gabriel, the *one* standing in the presence of God. And I was sent forth to speak to you, and to announce these *things* as-good-news *to* you. **²⁰** And behold— you shall be silent and not able to speak until which day these *things* take place, because you did not believe my words, which will be fulfilled in their proper-time". **²¹** And the people were waiting for Zechariah. And they were wondering during his delaying in the temple. **²²** And having come out, he was not

---

A. Or, set-*their*-hand. **B.** Or, accomplished. **C.** That is, the beginning of Christ's ministry. **D.** Or, accurately-traced. **E.** That is, from before John's birth. **F.** See Mt 2:1. **G.** Or, faultless. **H.** That is, the custom of casting lots to see who would perform this duty. **I.** That is, offer it inside the Holy Place, a once in a lifetime event for a priest. **J.** That is, alcoholic beverages made from things other than grapes. **K.** Or, from. That is, still in the womb; or, still a newborn baby. **L:** turn back *the* hearts... children. See Mal 4:5-6. **M.** Or, by means of. **N.** Or, way-of-thinking.

able to speak *to* them. And they realized that he had seen *a* vision in the temple. And **he** was motioning *to* them and continuing *to be* mute.

Elizabeth Conceives And Hides It For Five Months

23 And it came about *that* when the days *of* his service were fulfilled, he went to his house. **24** And after these days, Elizabeth his wife conceived. And she was concealing herself *for* five months, saying **25** that "Thus *the* Lord has done *for* me in *the* days *in* which He looked-upon *me* to take-away my reproach among people".

In The Sixth Month, an Angel Appears To Mary, a Virgin Promised In Marriage To Joseph

26 Now in the sixth month, the angel Gabriel was sent-forth from God to *a* city *of* Galilee *for* which *the* name *was* Nazareth, **27** to *a* virgin having been promised-in-marriage[A] to *a* man *for* whom *the* name *was* Joseph, from *the* house *of* David. And the name *of* the virgin *was* Mary. **28** And having come-in to[B] her, he said, "Greetings, favored *one*! The Lord *is* with you". **29** But the *one* was very-troubled at the statement, and was pondering what-kind-of greeting this might be.

The Angel Tells Mary She Will Give Birth To a Son— Jesus, The Son of God

30 And the angel said *to* her, "Do not be fearing, Mary. For you found favor[C] with God. **31** And behold— you will conceive in *your* womb and give-birth to *a* son. And you shall call His name Jesus. **32** This *One* will be great, and will be called 'Son *of the* Most-High'. And *the* Lord God will give Him the throne *of* David, His father. **33** And He will reign[D] over the house *of* Jacob forever. And there will not be *an* end *of* His kingdom". **34** And Mary said to the angel, "How will this happen, since I am not knowing[E] *a* man?" **35** And having responded, the angel said *to* her, "*The* Holy Spirit will come upon you, and *the* power *of the* Most-High will overshadow you. For this reason[F] also the Holy *Child* being born will be called God's Son. **36** And behold— Elizabeth your relative also herself has conceived *a* son in her old age. And this is *the* sixth month *for* her, the *one* being called barren, **37** because no word[G] from God will be impossible". **38** And Mary said, "Behold the slave *of the* Lord. May it be done *to* me according to your word". And the angel departed from her.

Mary Goes To See Elizabeth

39 And having arisen during these days, Mary proceeded to the hill country with haste, to *a* city *of* Judah, **40** and entered into the house *of* Zechariah, and greeted Elizabeth. **41** And it came about *that* when Elizabeth heard the greeting *of* Mary, the baby leaped[H] in her womb.

Elizabeth Recognizes Mary As The Mother of Her Lord

And Elizabeth was filled[I] *with the* Holy Spirit, **42** and exclaimed *with a* loud shout and said, "You *are* blessed[J] among women, and blessed *is* the fruit *of* your womb. **43** And why[K] *has* this *happened to* me— that the mother *of* my Lord should come to me? **44** For behold— when the sound *of* your greeting came-to-be in my ears, the baby

---

A. That is, by her parents, according to the custom of that day. **B.** That is, come into her house. **C.** Or, grace. **D.** Or, be king. **E.** That is, having sexual relations with. **F.** That is, because God will be the child's father. **G.** Or, no thing. **H.** Or, leaped-for-joy. **I.** This is how Elizabeth knew the things she says next. **J.** That is, blessed by God. **K.** Or, from where, how.

leaped with gladness in my womb. **45** And blessed[A] *is she* having believed that[B] there will be *a* fulfillment *to* the *things* having been spoken *to* her from *the* Lord".

Mary Rejoices Over God Her Savior

46 And Mary said, "My soul magnifies[C] the Lord, **47** and my spirit rejoiced-greatly over God my Savior. **48** Because He looked-upon[D] the lowliness[E] *of* His slave, for behold— from now *on*, all generations will consider me blessed[F], **49** because the Powerful *One* did great *things for* me. And His name *is* holy. **50** And His mercy to generations and generations *is on* the *ones* fearing Him. **51** He did *a* mighty-deed[G] with His arm. He scattered *ones* proud[H] *in the* thought[I] *of* their heart. **52** He brought-down rulers from *their* thrones, and lifted-up lowly *ones*. **53** He filled *ones* being hungry with good *things,* and sent *ones* being rich away empty. **54** He helped Israel His servant *so that He might* remember[J] mercy, **55** just as He spoke to our fathers— *to* Abraham, and *to* his seed forever". **56** And Mary stayed with her about three months, and returned to her house.

Elizabeth Bears a Son, Who Is Named John. People Wonder What This Child Will Be

57 Now *for* Elizabeth, the time was fulfilled *that* she *might* give-birth, and she bore *a* son. **58** And the neighbors and her relatives heard that *the* Lord magnified His mercy with her, and they were rejoicing-with her. **59** And it came about *that* on the eighth day they came to circumcise the child. And they[K] were calling[L] him Zechariah, on the basis of the name *of* his father. **60** And having responded, his mother said, "No! Instead he will be called John". **61** And they said to her that "There is no one from your relatives who is called *by* this name". **62** And they were motioning *to* his father *as to* what he would wish him to be called. **63** And having asked-*for a* tablet, he wrote, saying "John is his name". And they all marveled. **64** And at-once his mouth **was opened**, and his tongue *loosed*. And he was speaking, blessing God. **65** And awe came over all the *ones* living around them. And all these things were being talked-over in the whole hill country *of* Judea. **66** And all the *ones* having heard *it* put *these matters* in their heart, saying, "What then will this child be?" For[M] indeed, *the* hand *of the* Lord was with him.

Zechariah Prophesies That John Will Prepare The Way For The Messiah

67 And Zechariah, his father, was filled *with the* Holy Spirit and prophesied, saying **68** "Blessed *be the* Lord God[N] *of* Israel, because He visited *us* and accomplished[O] redemption *for* His people, **69** and raised-up *a* horn *of* salvation *for* us in *the* house *of* David His servant (**70** just as He spoke through *the* mouth *of* His holy prophets from *the past* age[P]), **71** *a* salvation from our enemies and from *the* hand *of* all the *ones* hating us, **72** *so as* to show mercy to[Q] our fathers and remember[R] His holy covenant (**73** *the*

A. Or, fortunate, happy. **B.** Or, because. **C.** In Latin, this word is *Magnificat*, which has become a name for this 'magnification' of God by Mary. **D.** That is, with favor. **E.** That is, humble status. **F.** Or, fortunate. That is, a most fortunate recipient of God's favor. **G.** Or, showed strength, defined by what follows. **H.** Or, arrogant, haughty. **I.** Or, way of thinking. **J.** Or, keep-in-mind. **K.** That is, the people at the ceremony. **L.** Or, were *going to* call. **M.** This may be part of the quote, and refer to the circumstances of John's birth. Or, this may be Luke's comment. **N.** Or, *the* Lord, the God *of* Israel. **O.** Or, brought about. Zechariah is speaking prophetically. **P.** Or, from long-ago, from *of* old. **Q.** That is, by at last carrying out His promises to them. **R.** That is, be mindful of the covenant He swore to them. In Gen 22:16-18 God swore that all nations of the earth would be blessed in Abraham.

oath which He swore to Abraham our father)— *that He might* grant *to* us *that* [74] having been delivered from *the* hand *of our* enemies, *we might* be serving[A] Him **fearlessly** [75] in holiness and righteousness before Him *for* all our days. [76] And indeed **you**, child, will be called *a* prophet *of the* Most-High. For you will go before *the* Lord *so as* to prepare His ways[B], [77] *that you might* give[C] His people *the* knowledge *of* salvation by *the* forgiveness *of* their sins [78] because of *the* deep-feelings-*of* mercy *of* our God, with which[D] *the* rising[E] *Sun* from on-high will visit us [79] *so as* to shine-upon the *ones* sitting in darkness and *a* shadow *of* death, *that He might* direct[F] our feet into *the* way *of* peace".

John Remains In Seclusion Until His Public Appearance To Israel
[80] And the child was growing and becoming-strong *in* spirit. And he was in the desolate *places* until *the* day *of* his public-appearance[G] to Israel.

Mary Gives Birth In Bethlehem, Where She And Joseph Went Because of The Roman Census
2:1 Now it came about during those days *that a* decree went out from Caesar Augustus[H] *that* all the world *should* be registered[I]. [2] This first[J] registration took place while Quirinius *was* being-governor *of* Syria. [3] And they were all going to register-*themselves*[K]— each *one* to his *own* city[L]. [4] And Joseph also went up from Galilee, out of *the* city *of* Nazareth, to Judea, to *the* city *of* David, which is called Bethlehem— because of his being from *the* house and family *of* David— [5] *so as* to register *himself* with Mary, the *one* having been promised-in-marriage *to* him, being pregnant. [6] And it came about during their being there *that* the days were fulfilled *that* she *might* give-birth. [7] And she gave birth to her firstborn son. And she wrapped Him in swaddling-cloths[M], and laid Him in *a* manger[N], because there was not *a* place *for* them in the inn.

Angels Announce The Birth of The Savior To Shepherds In The Field
[8] And shepherds were in the same region, living-in-the-fields and watching over their flock *for* watches *of* the night. [9] And *an* angel *of the* Lord stood near them, and *the* glory *of the* Lord shined around them, and they feared *a* great fear. [10] And the angel said *to* them, "Do not be fearing. For behold— I am announcing-as-good-news *to* you *a* great joy which will be *for* all the people, [11] because[O] *a* Savior was born *for* you today in *the* city *of* David, Who is Christ *the* Lord. [12] And this *will be* the sign *for* you: you will find *a* baby having been wrapped in swaddling cloths and lying in *a* manger". [13] And suddenly *a* multitude *of the* heavenly host was with the angel, praising God and saying, [14] "Glory *to* God in *the* highest [heavens]. And peace on earth among people *of*[P] [His] good-will[Q]". [15] And it came about *that* when the angels

A. Or, worshiping. **B.** Or, paths. **C.** That is, through the One coming after you. **D.** This is plural, referring either to deep-feelings of mercy, or to salvation, forgiveness, and deep-feelings of mercy. **E.** Or, *the* rising *Star*; or, *the* Dawn. That is, the Messiah, alluding to Mal 4:2. **F.** Or, lead, guide. **G.** Or, manifestation. **H.** This Roman emperor, also known as Octavian, ruled from 27 B.C to A.D. 14. **I.** Or, enrolled, listed *on a census roll.* **J.** Or, This was *the* first registration while. This was in about 4 B.C. A second, or a finishing of this first one, took place in A.D. 6, and is mentioned in Act 5:37. **K.** Or, be registered. **L.** This indicates Herod was conducting the census according to Jewish customs. **M.** That is, bands of cloth. **N.** That is, an animal feeding trough in a stall or stable, as in 13:15. **O.** Or, that. **P.** That is, people who are recipients or objects of His good-will, people with whom He is pleased; or, people characterized by good-will toward God. Some manuscripts say 'earth, good-will among people'. **Q.** Or, good-pleasure, favor.

departed from them into heaven, the shepherds were saying to one another, "Let us go now to Bethlehem and see this thing having taken place which the Lord made-known *to* us". **16** And they came, having hurried, and found both Mary and Joseph, and the baby lying in the manger. **17** And having seen *Him*, they made-known about the thing having been spoken *to* them about this Child. **18** And all the *ones* having heard *it* marveled about the *things* having been spoken to them by the shepherds. **19** But Mary was preserving^A all these things, pondering *them* in her heart. **20** And the shepherds returned, glorifying and praising God for everything which they heard and saw, just as it was spoken to them.

His Name Is Called Jesus
21 And when eight days were fulfilled *that they might* circumcise Him, His name was indeed called Jesus— the *name* having been named by the angel before^B He was conceived in the womb.

The Parents Bring Jesus To The Temple To Redeem Him Before The Lord
22 And when the days *of* their purification according to the Law *of* Moses were fulfilled^C, they brought Him up to Jerusalem *so as* to present *Him* to the Lord **23** just as it has been written in *the* Law *of the* Lord [in Ex 13:2], that "every male opening *the* womb shall be called holy *to* the Lord"; **24** and *that she might* give *a* sacrifice in accordance with the *thing* having been said in the Law *of the* Lord [in Lev 12:8]: "*a* pair *of* turtledoves or two young ones *of* pigeons".

Simeon Recognizes The Child As The Messiah, But a Sword Will Pierce Mary's Soul
25 And behold— *a* man was in Jerusalem *for* whom *the* name *was* Simeon. And this man *was* righteous and reverent^D, waiting-for *the* consolation *of* Israel. And *the* Holy Spirit was upon him. **26** And it had been revealed *to* him by the Holy Spirit *that he would* not see death before he would see the Christ *of the* Lord. **27** And he came in the Spirit into the temple. And at the parents bringing-in the child Jesus *that* they *might* do for Him according to the *thing*^E having become-a-custom *from* the Law, **28** **he** also took Him into *his* arms. And he blessed God, and said, **29** "Now You are releasing Your slave in peace in accordance with Your word, Master, **30** because my eyes saw Your salvation **31** which You prepared in the presence *of* all the peoples— **32** *the* light for *the* revelation *of the* Gentiles, and *the* glory *of* Your people Israel". **33** And His father and mother were marveling at the *things* being spoken about Him. **34** And Simeon blessed them, and said to Mary His mother, "Behold— this *One* is appointed^F for^G *the* falling and rising *of* many in Israel, and for^H *a* sign being spoken-against^I— **35** and indeed *a* sword will pierce the soul *of* you yourself— so that *the* thoughts of many hearts may be revealed".

Anna The Prophet Thanks God For the Child
36 And there was Anna— *a* prophet, *a* daughter *of* Phanuel, from *the* tribe *of* Asher.

A. Or, treasuring-up, holding *in memory*. **B.** In other words, the Child's Father chose His name. **C.** That is, after 33 more days, Lev 12:1-8. **D.** Or, God-fearing, devout. **E.** Luke is referring to the practice in v 23. **F.** Or, destined. **G.** That is, for the purpose of causing a fall. **H.** That is, for the purpose of becoming a sign. **I.** Or, opposed, contradicted.

This *one was* advanced in *her* many days, having lived with *a* husband seven years from her virginity, **37** and herself *being a* widow up-to^A eighty four years, who was not departing *from* the temple, serving^B night and day *with* fastings and prayers. **38** And having come-upon *them at* the very hour, she was returning-thanks *to* God, and was speaking about Him *to* all the *ones* waiting for *the* redemption *of* Jerusalem.

The Family Returns To Nazareth In Galilee
39 And when they finished all the *things* according to the Law *of the* Lord, they returned to Galilee— to their *own* city, Nazareth. **40** And the Child was growing and becoming strong, while being filled *with* wisdom. And *the* grace *of* God was upon Him.

In Jerusalem At Age Twelve, Jesus Stays Behind When His Parents Leave For Home
41 And His parents were going to Jerusalem yearly *for* the Feast *of* the Passover. **42** And when He became twelve years *old*— they going up in accordance with the custom *of* the Feast, **43** and having completed the days— during their returning, the boy Jesus stayed-behind in Jerusalem. And His parents did not know *it,* **44** but having thought *that* He was in the caravan^C, they went *a* day's journey. And they were searching-for Him among the relatives and the acquaintances. **45** And not having found *Him*, they returned to Jerusalem, searching-for Him.

Jesus Is Found In The Temple Listening To And Questioning The Teachers
46 And it came about after three days *that* they found Him in the temple, sitting in *the* midst *of* the teachers, both listening-to them and questioning them. **47** And all the *ones* listening-to Him were astonished at *His* understanding and His answers. **48** And having seen Him, they were astounded. And His mother said to Him, "Child, why did you do^D us like this? Behold— Your father and I were looking-*for* You, while suffering-pain". **49** And He said to them, "Why *is it* that you were looking-*for* Me? Did you not know that I must be in^E the *things of* My^F Father'? **50** And **they** did not understand the thing which He spoke *to* them. **51** And He went down with them, and came to Nazareth, and was being subject *to* them. And His mother was keeping all *these* things in her heart. **52** And Jesus was advancing in wisdom and stature, and *in* favor with God and people.

In The Fifteenth Year of Tiberius, John Is Sent Out By God
3:1 Now in *the* fifteenth^G year *of* the government *of* Tiberius^H Caesar— Pontius Pilate^I being-governor *of* Judea, and Herod^J being-tetrarch^K *of* Galilee, and Philip^L his brother being tetrarch *of* the region *of* Ituraea and Trachonitis, and Lysanias being tetrarch *of* Abilene, **2** in-the-time-of *the* high priest Annas and Caiaphas— *the* word *of* God came to^M John, the son *of* Zechariah, in the wilderness.

John Proclaims a Baptism of Repentance, In Fulfillment of Isaiah
3 And he went into all the surrounding-region *of* the Jordan, proclaiming *a* baptism *of*

A. Or, until. That is, until her 84th year; or, for 84 years after becoming a widow. **B.** Or, worshiping. **C.** Or, travel-group. **D.** Or, act *toward* us. **E.** That is, engaged in the interests or business of My Father (answering the stated 'Why' question); or, located in the possessions or house of My Father (answering the implied 'Where' question). **F.** Note the contrast with 'your father' in v 48. **G.** This points to a year between A.D. 26 and 29. **H.** He was the Roman emperor from A.D. 14 to 37. **I.** He was the fifth Roman prefect (a military officer put in charge of a district to maintain order) of Judea, serving from A.D. 26 to 36. **J.** That is, Herod Antipas. See Mt 14:1. **K.** That is, being-governor, appointed by Rome. **L.** This Philip II was a half-brother of Herod Antipas. His capital was Philip's Caesarea (seen in Mt 16:13). He reigned from 4 B.C. to A.D. 34. **M.** Or, upon.

repentance for *the* forgiveness *of* sins, **⁴** as it has been written in *the* book *of the* words *of* Isaiah the prophet [in Isa 40:3-5], "*A* voice *of one* shouting in the wilderness: 'Prepare the way *of the* Lord; be making His paths straight. **⁵** Every valley will be filled and every mountain and hill will be made-low. And the crooked *paths* will become straight, and the rough *will become* smooth paths. **⁶** And all flesh will see the salvation *of* God' ". **⁷** Therefore he was saying *to* the crowds coming out to be baptized by him, "Brood *of* vipers— who showed^A you to flee from the coming wrath? **⁸** Therefore produce fruits worthy *of* repentance. And do not begin to say within^B yourselves, 'We have Abraham *as our* father'. For I say *to* you that God is able to raise-up children *for* Abraham from these stones! **⁹** And indeed the axe is **already** lying^C at the root *of* the trees. Therefore every tree not producing good fruit is cut down and thrown into *the* fire".

The People Ask John What They Should Do To Produce Fruit Worthy of Repentance
¹⁰ And the crowds were questioning him, saying, "What then should we do?" **¹¹** And having responded, he was saying *to* them, "Let the *one* having two tunics^D give *to* the *one* not having, and let the *one* having food be doing likewise". **¹²** And tax collectors also came to be baptized. And they said to him, "Teacher, what should we do?" **¹³** And the *one* said to them, "Be collecting nothing more than the *amount* having been commanded". **¹⁴** And *ones* serving-as-soldiers also were questioning him, saying, "And us, what should we do?" And he said *to* them, "Do not violently-extort^E anyone, nor extort-with-false-charges. And be content *with* your wages^F".

John Says One More Powerful Is Coming, Who Will Baptize With The Spirit And Fire
¹⁵ And while the populace *was* waiting-in-expectation and all *were* pondering in their hearts about John— if perhaps **he** might be the Christ— **¹⁶** John responded, saying *to* everyone, "**I** am baptizing you *with*^G water, but the One more powerful *than* me is coming, *of* Whom I am not fit to untie the strap *of* His sandals. **He** will baptize you with^H *the* Holy Spirit and fire^I— **¹⁷** Whose winnowing-tool *is* in His hand *so as* to clean-out^J His threshing floor and gather the wheat into His barn; but He will burn up the chaff *with an* inextinguishable fire". **¹⁸** So indeed, while also exhorting many other *things*, he was announcing-good-news-to the people.

Herod Locked Up John In Prison
¹⁹ But Herod the tetrarch— while being rebuked^K by him concerning Herodias^L, the wife *of* his brother, and concerning all *the* evil *things* which Herod did— **²⁰** also added this to everything: he also locked-up John in prison.

Jesus Was Baptized When All The People Were Baptized
²¹ And it came about when^M all the people were baptized, Jesus also having been baptized and praying, *that* the heaven was opened **²²** and the Holy Spirit descended upon Him *in a* bodily form like^N *a* dove, and *a* voice came from heaven: "**You** are My beloved Son. With You I was^O well-pleased".

A. Or, indicated to, warned. **B.** Or, among. **C.** Or, being laid. **D.** That is, undergarments. **E.** That is, threaten or use violence to get money from citizens. **F.** Or, rations. **G.** Or, in. **H.** Or, in. **I.** See Mt 3:11. **J.** That is, by separating the threshings into wheat and chaff, and taking each to their destinations. **K.** Or, exposed. **L.** See Mt 14:3. **M.** That is, at the period of time when all the people were baptized. **N.** That is, having a body with an outward appearance similar to a dove. **O.** Or, am well pleased. See Mt 3:17.

At About Age Thirty, Jesus Begins His Ministry
²³ And Jesus Himself was, [when] beginning *His ministry,* about thirty years *old,* being *a* son, as it was being supposed, *of* Joseph, the *son of* Heli, ²⁴ the *son of* Matthat, the *son of* Levi, the *son of* Melchi, the *son of* Jannai, the *son of* Joseph, ²⁵ the *son of* Mattathias, the *son of* Amos, the *son of* Nahum, the *son of* Hesli, the *son of* Naggai, ²⁶ the *son of* Maath, the *son of* Mattathias, the *son of* Semein, the *son of* Josech, the *son of* Joda, ²⁷ the *son of* Joanan, the *son of* Rhesa, the *son of* Zerubbabel, the *son of* Shealtiel, the *son of* Neri, ²⁸ the *son of* Melchi, the *son of* Addi, the *son of* Cosam, the *son of* Elmadam, the *son of* Er, ²⁹ the *son of* Joshua, the *son of* Eliezer, the *son of* Jorim, the *son of* Matthat, the *son of* Levi, ³⁰ the *son of* Simeon, the *son of* Judah, the *son of* Joseph, the *son of* Jonam, the *son of* Eliakim, ³¹ the *son of* Melea, the *son of* Menna, the *son of* Mattatha, the *son of* Nathan, the *son of* David, ³² the *son of* Jesse, the *son of* Obed, the *son of* Boaz, the *son of* Sala, the *son of* Nahshon, ³³ the *son of* Aminadab, the *son of* Admin, the *son of* Arni, the *son of* Hezron, the *son of* Perez, the *son of* Judah, ³⁴ the *son of* Jacob, the *son of* Isaac, the *son of* Abraham, the *son of* Terah, the *son of* Nahor, ³⁵ the *son of* Serug, the *son of* Reu, the *son of* Peleg, the *son of* Heber, the *son of* Shelah, ³⁶ the *son of* Cainan, the *son of* Arphaxad, the *son of* Shem, the *son of* Noah, the *son of* Lamech, ³⁷ the *son of* Methuselah, the *son of* Enoch, the *son of* Jared, the *son of* Mahalaleel, the *son of* Cainan, ³⁸ the *son of* Enosh, the *son of* Seth, the *son of* Adam, the *son of* God.

In The Wilderness, Jesus Is Tempted By Satan To Act Contrary To His Father's Will
4:1 And Jesus, full *of the* Holy Spirit, returned from the Jordan. And He was being led in the Spirit in the wilderness ² *for* forty days while being tempted by the devil. And He did not eat anything during those days. And they having been completed, He was hungry. ³ And the devil said *to* Him, "If You are^A God's **Son**, say^B *to* this stone that it should become bread". ⁴ And Jesus responded to him, "It has been written [in Deut 8:3] that 'Mankind^C shall not live on bread alone' ". ⁵ And having led Him up, he showed Him all the kingdoms *of* the world in *a* moment *of* time. ⁶ And the devil said *to* Him, "I will give You all this authority and their glory, because it has been handed-over *to* me, and I give it *to* whomever I wish. ⁷ Therefore if **You** worship before me, it will all be Yours". ⁸ And having responded, Jesus said *to* him "It has been written [in Deut 6:13], 'You shall worship *the* Lord your God, and serve Him only' ". ⁹ And he led Him into Jerusalem and stood *Him* on the pinnacle *of* the temple. And he said *to* Him, "If You are God's **Son**, throw Yourself down from here. ¹⁰ For it has been written [in Ps 91:11] that 'He will command His angels concerning You *that they might* protect You', ¹¹ and [in Ps 91:12] that 'They will lift You up on *their* hands that You may not ever strike Your foot against *a* stone' ". ¹² And having responded, Jesus said *to* him that "It has been said [in Deut 6:16], 'You shall not put *the* Lord your God to the test' ". ¹³ And having completed every temptation, the devil departed from Him until *an* opportune-time.

Jesus Returns To Galilee And Begins Teaching In Their Synagogues
¹⁴ And Jesus returned to Galilee in the power *of* the Spirit. And news about Him went out throughout the whole surrounding-region. ¹⁵ And **He** was teaching in their synagogues, while being glorified by all.

A. That is, Assuming You are, as God said in 3:22. **B.** That is, prove it by exercising Your creative power. **C.** Or, The man, The person, Man, Humankind.

Jesus Comes To Nazareth And Reads Isaiah 61:1-2 In The Synagogue

16 And He came to Nazareth, where He had been brought-up. And in accordance with the *thing* having become-a-custom *with* him, He entered into the synagogue on the day *of* the Sabbath, and stood up to read. **17** And *the* scroll *of* the prophet Isaiah was given *to* Him. And having unrolled the scroll, He found the place where it had been written [in Isa 61:1-2]: **18** "*The* Spirit *of the* Lord *is* upon Me, because of which He anointed Me to announce-good-news *to* poor *ones*. He has sent me out to proclaim *a* release *to* captives and recovery-of-sight *to* blind *ones*, to send-out with *a* release *ones* having been broken[A], **19** to proclaim *the* acceptable[B] year *of the* Lord". **20** And having rolled up the scroll, having given *it* back *to* the attendant, He sat-*down*[C]. And the eyes *of* everyone in the synagogue were looking-intently *at* Him.

Jesus Says: Today This Scripture Is Fulfilled In Your Ears. They Drive Him Out

21 And He began to say *to* them that "Today this Scripture has been fulfilled in your ears". **22** And they all were[D] testifying *concerning* Him, and marveling at the words *of*[E] grace proceeding from His mouth. And they were saying, "Is not this *One* Joseph's son?" **23** And He said to them, "You will surely speak this proverb *to* Me: 'Physician, cure yourself'. Do also here in your hometown all-that we heard having taken place in Capernaum". **24** But He said, "Truly I say *to* you that no prophet is acceptable[F] in his hometown. **25** And I say *to* you in accordance with [God's] truth—there were many widows in Israel in the days *of* Elijah when the heaven was shut for three years and six months, when *a* great famine took place over all the land. **26** And Elijah was sent to none[G] *of* them, except to [the village of] Zarephath of-Sidon, to *a* widow woman. **27** And there were many lepers in Israel in the time of Elisha the prophet. And none *of* them was cleansed, except Naaman the Syrian". **28** And they were all filled *with* fury in the synagogue while hearing these *things*. **29** And having arisen, they drove Him outside *of* the city, and led Him up to *the* brow *of* the hill on which their city had been built so as to throw Him down the cliff. **30** But **He**, having gone through *the* middle *of* them, was proceeding.

Jesus Goes To Capernaum And Teaches. They Are Astounded At His Authority

31 And He went down to Capernaum, *a* city *of* Galilee. And He was teaching them on the Sabbath. **32** And they were astounded at His teaching, because His message was with authority.

Jesus Orders a Demon To Leave a Man. They Are Astonished At His Power

33 And in the synagogue there was *a* man having *a* spirit *of an* unclean demon. And he cried-out *with a* loud voice, **34** "Let-*us*-alone[H]! What[I] do we have to do with You, Jesus from-Nazareth? Did You come to destroy us? I know You, Who You are: the Holy *One of* God!" **35** And Jesus rebuked him, saying, "Be silenced and come out from him". And the demon, having thrown him down into *their* midst, came out from

---

A. Or, shattered, whether in spirit or body; and thus, oppressed. **B.** Or, favorable, welcome. It is the Lord's favored year at last! **C.** That is, sat down facing them from the front. In that day, teachers stood to read and sat to teach. **D.** That is, up until this speech. **E.** That is, characterized by grace; gracious words. **F.** Or, welcome. **G.** Elijah and Elisha did not do the miracle for Israel. Jesus is putting His hometown people in the same class as unbelieving Israel in the days of Elijah and Elisha. **H.** Or, Ah! (a scream). **I.** Lit, What [is there] *for* us and *for* You?

him, not having hurt him at all. **36** And astonishment came over everyone. And they were talking-with one another, saying, "What *is* this message? Because He commands the unclean spirits with authority and power, and they come out!" **37** And *the* news about Him was going out into every place *of* the surrounding-region.

In Simon's Home That Night, Many Are Healed

38 And having arisen from the synagogue, He entered into the house *of* Simon. Now *the* mother-in-law *of* Simon was being gripped^A *with a* high fever. And they asked Him concerning her. **39** And having stood over her, He rebuked the fever, and it left her. And having stood up at-once, she was serving them. **40** And while the sun *was* setting^B, all who were having *ones* being sick *with* various diseases brought them to Him. And the *One*, laying *His* hands on each one *of* them, was curing them. **41** And demons also were coming out from many, shouting, and saying that "**You** are the Son *of* God!" And rebuking *them,* He was not allowing them to speak, because they knew *that* He was the Christ.

Jesus Proceeds On To Announce The Kingdom of God To Other Cities

42 And having become day, having gone out, He went to *a* desolate^C place. And the crowds were seeking-for Him. And they came to Him and were holding^D Him back *that He might* not proceed from them. **43** And the *One* said to them that "I must **also** announce the kingdom *of* God as good news *to* the other cities, because I was sent-forth for this *purpose*".

While Jesus Teaches The Crowds By The Lake of Gennesaret, He Uses Simon's Boat

44 And He was proclaiming in the synagogues *of* Judea. **5:1** And it came about during the crowd's pressing-upon Him and listening-to the word *of* God that **He** was standing beside the lake *of* Gennesaret^E. **2** And He saw two boats standing beside the lake. And the fishermen, having gotten-out of them, were washing *their* nets. **3** And having gotten into one *of* the boats, which was Simon's, He asked him to put-out *a* little from the land. And having sat-*down*, He was teaching the crowds from the boat.

Jesus Brings Simon a Great Catch of Fish. Now You Will Be Catching People

4 And when He ceased speaking, He said to Simon, "Put-out into the deep [water] and lower^F your nets for *a* catch". **5** And having responded, Simon said, "Master, having labored through *the* whole night, we took nothing. But at^G Your word, I will lower the nets. **6** And having done this, they enclosed *a* large number *of* fish. And their nets were being torn. **7** And they signaled *to their* companions in the other boat *that* having come, *they might* help them. And they came. And they filled both the boats so that they *were* sinking. **8** And having seen *it,* Simon Peter fell at the knees *of* Jesus, saying, "Depart from me, because I am *a* sinful man, Master". **9** For astonishment at the catch *of* fish which they took seized him, and all the *ones* with him. **10** And likewise also James and John, sons *of* Zebedee, who were partners *with* Simon. And Jesus said to Simon, "Do not be fearing. From now *on* you will be catching^H people!" **11** And having brought *their* boats on land, having left everything, they followed Him.

A. Or, held; and thus, afflicted. **B.** That is, after the sun went down, ending the Sabbath, but before dark. **C.** Or, deserted, solitary, lonely. **D.** Or, detaining Him. **E.** That is, the Sea of Galilee. **F.** This command is plural, referring to Simon and his crew. **G.** Or, upon. **H.** Or, capturing. That is, catching-alive.

Jesus Heals a Man Full of Leprosy. Word of Jesus Spread Even More

12 And it came about during His being in one *of* the cities that behold— *there was a* man full *of* leprosy. And having seen Jesus, having fallen on *his* face, he begged Him, saying, "Master, if You are willing, You are able to cleanse me". **13** And having stretched-out *His* hand, He touched him, saying, "I am willing^A. Be cleansed". And immediately the leprosy departed from him. **14** And **He** ordered him to tell no one, "But having gone, show yourself *to* the priest^B and offer *the things* for your cleansing just as Moses commanded, for *a* testimony *to* them". **15** But the word about Him was spreading more, and large crowds were coming together to hear, and to be cured from their infirmities. **16** But **He** was retreating within the desolate *places* and praying.

Jesus Heals a Paralyzed Man To Prove He Has The Authority To Forgive Sins

17 And it came about on one *of* the days, that **He** was teaching. And Pharisees and Law-teachers were sitting *there* who had come from every village *of* Galilee and Judea and Jerusalem. And *the* power *of the* Lord was *present* that He *might* be healing. **18** And behold— men bringing on *a* bed *a* man who had been paralyzed. And they were seeking to bring him in, and to place him before Him. **19** And not having found by what *way* they might bring him in because of the crowd, having gone up on the housetop, they let him down through the tiles with the little-bed into *their* midst, in front of Jesus. **20** And having seen their faith, He said, "Man, your sins have been forgiven you". **21** And the scribes and the Pharisees began to reason, saying, "Who is this *One* Who is speaking blasphemies? Who is able to forgive sins except God alone?" **22** But Jesus, having known their reasonings, having responded, said to them, "Why are you reasoning in your hearts? **23** Which is easier: to say, 'Your sins have been forgiven you', or to say, 'Arise and walk'? **24** But in order that you may know that the Son *of* Man has authority on earth to forgive sins"— He said *to* the *one* having been paralyzed, "I say *to* you, arise, and having picked up your little-bed, proceed to your house". **25** And having stood-up at once in their presence, having picked up *the thing* upon which he was lying-down, he went to his house glorifying God. **26** And astonishment seized everyone. And they were glorifying God. And they were filled *with* awe, saying that "We saw incredible *things* today".

Jesus Calls Levi The Tax Collector And Eats With His Friends. I Came For Sinners

27 And after these *things*, He went out and saw *a* tax-collector, Levi *by* name, sitting at the tax-office^C. And He said *to* him, "Be following Me!" **28** And having left-behind everything, having stood up, he was following Him. **29** And Levi made *a* great reception^D *for* Him in his house. And there was *a* large crowd *of* tax collectors and others who were reclining [to eat] with them. **30** And the Pharisees and their scribes were grumbling to His disciples, saying, "For what reason are you eating and drinking with the tax collectors and sinners^E?" **31** And having responded, Jesus said to them, "The *ones* being healthy have no need *of a* physician, but the *ones* being ill. **32** I have not come to call righteous *ones* to repentance, but sinners".

Why Do Your Disciples Not Fast? The Bridegroom Is Here. New Wineskins

33 And the *ones* said to Him, "The disciples *of* John are fasting^F frequently and making

---

A. Only Jesus heals in His own name, without calling upon God. **B.** That is, in Jerusalem. **C.** Or, tax-booth. Levi (Matthew) was on the job, collecting taxes for Herod Antipas. **D.** Or, banquet. **E.** That is, irreligious people living outside of God's Law. **F.** On why these two groups may have been fasting, see Mt 9:14.

prayers. Likewise also the *ones of* the Pharisees. But **Yours** are eating and drinking". **34** And Jesus said to them, "You cannot make the sons[A] *of* the wedding-hall **fast** while the bridegroom is with them, *can you*? **35** But days will come. And when the bridegroom is taken-away from them, then they will fast in those days". **36** And He was also speaking *a* parable to them, that "No one having torn *a* patch from *a* new garment puts *it* on *an* old garment. Otherwise indeed he[B] will both tear the new, and the patch from the new will not agree[C] *with* the old. **37** And no one puts new[D] wine into old wineskins. Otherwise indeed the new wine will burst the wineskins, and **it** will spill-out, and the wineskins will be ruined. **38** But new wine must-be-put into fresh wineskins. **39** And no one having drunk old *wine* desires[E] new. For he says, 'The old is good' ".

The Pharisees Object To Plucking Grain On The Sabbath. I Am Lord of The Sabbath
6:1 And it came about on *a* Sabbath *that* He *was* proceeding through grainfields. And His disciples were plucking[F] and eating the heads [of grain], rubbing *them in their* hands. **2** And some *of* the Pharisees said, "Why are you[G] doing what is not lawful *on* the Sabbath?" **3** And having responded to them, Jesus said, "Did you not even read [in 1 Sam 21:1-6] this which David did when he was hungry, he and the *ones* being with him?— **4** how he entered into the house *of* God, and having taken the Bread[H] *of* Presentation, he ate *it* and gave *it to* the *ones* with him, which is not lawful *for anyone* to eat but the priests alone? **5** And He was saying *to* them, "The Son *of* Man is **Lord** *of* the Sabbath".

Is It Lawful To Heal On The Sabbath? Jesus Heals a Man, Enraging The Pharisees
6 And it came about on another Sabbath *that* He entered into the synagogue and *was* teaching. And there was *a* man there, and his right hand was withered. **7** And the scribes and the Pharisees were closely-watching Him *to see* if He cured on the Sabbath, in order that they might find *a reason* to be accusing Him. **8** But **He** knew their reasonings. And He said *to* the man having the withered hand, "Arise, and stand into the middle". And having stood-up, he stood *there*. **9** And Jesus said *to* them, "I am asking you[I] if it is lawful[J] *on* the Sabbath to do-good or to do-harm, to save *a* life or to destroy *it*?" **10** And having looked-around *at* them all, He said *to* him, "Stretch-out your hand". And the *one* did *it*, and his hand was restored. **11** And **they** were filled *with* rage[K], and were talking-over with one another what they might do *to* Jesus.

After Choosing The Twelve, Jesus Stands Before a Huge Crowd To Teach Them
12 And it came about during these days *that* He went out to the mountain to pray. And He was spending the night in prayer *to* God. **13** And when it became day, He called to His disciples. And having chosen twelve from them, whom He also named apostles— **14** Simon, whom He also named Peter, and Andrew, his brother, and James, and John, and Philip, and Bartholomew, **15** and Matthew, and Thomas, and James, *the son of* Alphaeus, and

A. That is, the attendants of the groom; the groomsmen. **B.** Or, it; such an action as just described. **C.** Or, fit, match. Jesus is not a patch on the old Jewish system. He is a new garment, so His disciples behave in a new way. **D.** Jesus, the new and fresh, cannot be contained in the old Jewish system. **E.** Those in the old Jewish system are comfortable with it, and not naturally inclined to drink the new wine Jesus brings. **F.** The Law permitted this, Deut 23:25. **G.** This is plural. **H.** That is, the bread 'set before' or 'presented to' God; the twelve loaves of showbread, Lev 24:6-9. **I.** This is plural, referring to the scribes and Pharisees. **J.** The answer is that is makes no difference. It is good to do good and wrong to do harm on all seven days. The Sabbath is a rest from one's work, not from doing good. **K.** Or, senseless anger.

Simon, the *one* being called *a* Zealot, [16] and Judas, *the son of* James, and Judas Iscariot, who became *a* traitor— [17] and having come down with them, He stood on *a* level place. And *there was a* large crowd *of* His disciples, and *a* great multitude *of* the people from all Judea and Jerusalem and the coastal-region *of* Tyre and Sidon, [18] who came to hear Him and to be healed from their diseases. And the *ones* being troubled by unclean spirits were being cured. [19] And all the multitude were seeking to touch Him because power was going forth from Him and healing everyone.

These Are The Ones God Considers Blessed And In Danger

[20] And **He**, having lifted-up His eyes toward His disciples, was saying— "Blessed[A] *are* the poor *ones*, because the kingdom *of* God is yours. [21] Blessed *are* the *ones* hungering now, because you will be filled-to-satisfaction. Blessed *are* the *ones* weeping now, because you will laugh. [22] You are blessed whenever people hate you, and whenever they separate[B] you, and reproach *you*, and throw-out your name as evil because-of[C] the Son *of* Man. [23] Rejoice on that day and leap-for-joy, for behold— your reward *is* great in heaven. For their fathers were doing *it* in the same *way to* the prophets. [24] But woe *to* you rich *ones*, because you are receiving your comfort in full. [25] Woe *to* you, the *ones* having been filled now, because you will hunger. Woe— the *ones* laughing now, because you will mourn and weep. [26] Woe— when all people speak well *of* you. For their fathers were doing *it* in the same *way to* the false-prophets.

Love Your Enemies. Be Compassionate And Do Good To All

[27] "But I say *to* you, the *ones* hearing[D]— Be loving your enemies. Be acting commendably *to* the *ones* hating you. [28] Be blessing[E] the *ones* cursing you. Be praying for the *ones* mistreating you. [29] *To* the *one* striking you on the cheek, be offering also the other. And from the *one* taking away your cloak, also do not withhold[F] the tunic[G]. [30] *To* everyone asking you, be giving. And from the *one* taking away your *things*, do not be demanding *them* back. [31] And just as you want people to be doing *to* you, be doing *to* them likewise. [32] If indeed you are loving the *ones* loving you, what-kind-of credit is it *to* you? For even the sinners are loving the *ones* loving them. [33] For if indeed you are doing-good-*to* the *ones* doing-good-*to* you, what kind of credit is it *to* you? Even the sinners are doing the same. [34] And if you lend-*to* ones from whom you are expecting[H] to receive, what kind of credit is it *to* you? Even sinners are lending *to* sinners to receive-back the equal[I] *amounts*. [35] But be loving your enemies, and be doing good, and be lending, expecting-back[J] nothing, and your reward will be great. And you will be sons[K] *of the* Most-High, because **He** is good to the ungrateful and evil *ones*. [36] Be compassionate, just-as[L] your Father also is compassionate.

Do Not Judge Or Condemn Others. Pardon And Give To Them

[37] "And do not be judging[M], and you will never be judged. And do not be

---

A. Or, Fortunate, Happy, from God's point of view. **B.** That is, exclude. **C.** That is, from the persecutor's point of view; or, for the sake of, from the believer's point of view. **D.** That is, hearing and obeying, taking My word to heart. **E.** That is, giving a blessing to, or calling down God's blessings on. **F.** Or, forbid *him*. **G.** That is, the undergarment. **H.** Or, hoping. **I.** That is, repayment in full. **J.** Or, despairing nothing. That is, not despairing about getting it back. **K.** That is, ones of like nature to; ones like your Father in heaven in character and action. **L.** That is, in the same manner as. **M.** That is, in the sense of finding fault with, criticizing, passing judgment on.

condemning, and you will never be condemned. Be pardoning, and you will be pardoned. **38** Be giving, and it will be given *to* you. They[A] will give *a* good measure— having been pressed down, having been shaken, running over— into your fold[B] [of the garment]. For *with* what measure you measure, it will be measured-back *to* you".

The Blind Cannot Guide The Blind. Correct Yourself First

39 And He also spoke *a* parable *to* them— "*A* blind *one* is not able to guide *a* blind one, *is he*? Will they not both fall into *a* pit? **40** *A* disciple is not above the teacher. But everyone having been fully-trained will be like his teacher. **41** And why do you look-*at* the speck in the eye *of* your brother, but do not consider[C] the log in *your* own eye? **42** How can you say *to* your brother, 'Brother, permit me to take-out the speck in your eye', while yourself not seeing *the* log in your eye? Hypocrite! First take out the log from your eye. And then you will see-clearly to take out the speck in the eye *of* your brother.

A Tree Is Known By Its Fruit. The Mouth Speaks From The Heart

43 "For there is no good[D] tree producing bad fruit; nor again, *a* bad tree producing good fruit. **44** For each tree is known[E] by *its* own fruit. For they do not collect figs from thorns, nor do they gather *a* grape-bunch from *a* bramble-bush. **45** The good person brings forth the good *thing* out of the good treasure[F] *of his* heart. And the evil *person* brings forth the evil *thing* out of *his* evil *treasure*. For his mouth speaks out of *the* abundance *of the* heart.

Don't Just Call Me Lord. Be a Doer of My Words

46 "And why are you calling Me 'Lord, Lord[G]', and you are not doing *the things* which I say? **47** Everyone coming to Me and hearing My words and doing them— I will show you *to* whom he is like. **48** He is like *a* man building *a* house who dug, and went down deep, and laid *a* foundation on the bed-rock. And *a* flood[H] having come about, the river broke-against[I] that house. And it was not strong-*enough* to shake it, because it *had* been built well. **49** But the *one* having heard and not having done *My words* is like *a* man having built *a* house on the ground without *a* foundation, which the river broke-against. And immediately it collapsed, and the breakage *of* that house became great".

Jesus Heals a Centurion's Servant From Afar By Speaking The Word

7:1 After He completed all His words in the hearing *of* the people, He entered into Capernaum. **2** And *a* certain centurion's[J] slave, who was precious[K] *to* him, being ill, was about to come-to-an-end[L]. **3** But having heard about Jesus, he sent-forth elders *of* the Jews to Him, asking Him so that having come, He might restore his slave. **4** And the *ones* having come to Jesus were appealing-*to* Him earnestly, saying that "He *for* whom You will grant this is worthy. **5** For he loves our nation, and **he** built the synagogue *for* us". **6** Now Jesus was proceeding with them. And He already being not far distant from the house, the

---

A. That is, God's agents for disbursing His rewards. **B.** That is, into your garment or apron pulled up at the waist to form a pocket. **C.** Or, notice, perceive. **D:** good tree... bad fruit. See Mt 7:17. **E.** Or, recognized. **F.** Or, treasure-house, treasury. **G.** Or, Master, Master. **H.** Or, high-water. **I.** Or, burst-against. **J.** That is, a Roman commander of a hundred soldiers. **K.** Or, esteemed *by*. **L.** That is, die.

centurion sent friends, saying *to* Him, "Master, do not be troubling *Yourself.* For I am not fit that You should come in under my roof. **7** For this reason I did not even consider myself worthy to come to You. But speak *it in a* word^A, and let my servant be healed. **8** For **I** also am *a* man being placed under authority, having soldiers under myself. And I say *to* this *one*, 'Go!', and he goes; and *to* another, 'Come!', and he comes; and *to* my slave, 'Do this!', and he does *it*". **9** And having heard these *things*, Jesus marveled-*at* him. And having turned *to* the crowd following Him, He said, "I say *to* you, not even in Israel did I find so great *a* faith". **10** And having returned to the house, the *ones* having been sent found the slave being healthy.

Jesus Raises a Woman's Only Son From The Dead
11 And it came about afterwards^B *that* He proceeded to *a* city being called Nain. And His disciples and *a* large crowd were proceeding-with Him. **12** Now when He drew-near *to* the gate *of* the city, and behold— *one* having died was being carried out, *an* only-born son *to* his mother. And she was *a* widow. And *a* considerable crowd *from* the city was with her. **13** And having seen her, the Lord felt-deep-feelings [of compassion] for her. And He said *to* her, "Do not be weeping". **14** And having come to *it*, He touched the funeral-bed. And the *ones* bearing *it* stopped. And He said, "Young-man, I say *to* you, arise!" **15** And the dead *one* sat up and began to speak. And He gave him *to* his mother. **16** And awe seized everyone. And they were glorifying God, saying that "*A* great prophet arose among us", and that "God visited His people". **17** And this statement concerning Him went out in all Judea and *in* all the surrounding-region.

John The Baptist Asks, Are You The One? Jesus Points Him To His Miraculous Works
18 And his disciples reported *to* John about all these *things.* And having summoned *a* certain two *of* his disciples, John **19** sent *them* to the Lord, saying, "Are **You** the *One* coming, or should we be looking-for another *one*?" **20** And having come to Him, the men said, "John the Baptist sent us forth to You, saying, 'Are **You** the *One* coming^C, or should we be looking for another *one*?' " **21** At that hour, He cured many from diseases and scourges and evil spirits. And He granted seeing *to* many blind *ones*. **22** And having responded, He said *to* them, "Having gone, report *to* John *the things* which you saw^D and heard— blind *ones* are seeing-again, lame *ones* are walking, lepers are being cleansed. And deaf *ones* are hearing, dead *ones* are being raised, poor *ones* are having-good-news-announced^E *to them*. **23** And blessed is whoever does not take-offense^F in Me".

John Is The One Preparing The Way For The Messiah In Fulfillment of Malachi
24 And the messengers *of* John having departed, He began to speak to the crowds about John. "What^G did you go out into the wilderness to look-*at*? *A* reed being shaken by *the* wind? **25** But what did you go out to see? *A* man having been dressed in soft garments? Behold— the *ones* being^H in glorious^I clothing and luxury are in the royal *palaces*! **26** But what did you go out to see? *A* prophet? Yes, I say *to* you, and more *than a* prophet. **27** This *one* is about whom it has been written [in Mal 3:1]:

A. That is, a word of command. **B.** Or, next. **C.** Or, the Coming *One*; the Messiah. **D.** The works of Jesus answer the question. **E.** Or, are being-told-good-news, are being-evangelized. **F.** Or, is not caused-to-fall by. **G.** Or, Why, with different punctuation of the questions. See Mt 11:7. **H.** Or, existing, and thus, living. **I.** Or, splendid, distinguished.

'Behold— I am sending forth My messenger ahead *of* Your presence[A], who will make Your way ready in front of You'. **28** I say *to* you— no one is greater[B] among *ones* born *of* women *than* John. But the least *one* in the kingdom *of* God is greater *than* he. **29** And all the people having heard *him*[C], even the tax collectors, vindicated[D] God, having been baptized *with* the baptism *of* John. **30** But the Pharisees and the Law-experts rejected the purpose *of* God for themselves, not having been baptized by him.

But This Generation Rejects Both The One Preparing And He Who Came
31 "*To* what then will I liken the people *of* this generation, and *to* what are they like? **32** They are like children sitting in *the* marketplace and calling to one another, who say 'We played the flute *for* you and you did not dance. We lamented[E] and you did not weep'. **33** For John the Baptist has come not eating bread nor drinking wine, and you say 'He has *a* demon'. **34** The Son *of* Man has come eating and drinking, and you say 'Behold— *a* man w*ho is a* glutton and drunkard[F], *a* friend *of* tax-collectors and sinners'. **35** And wisdom was vindicated[G] by all her children".

Jesus Is Anointed By a Sinful Woman. A Pharisee Objects
36 And one *of* the Pharisees was asking Him to eat with him. And having entered into the house *of* the Pharisee, He laid-down [to eat]. **37** And behold— *there was a* woman in the city who was *a* sinner. And having learned that He is reclining [to eat] at the house *of* the Pharisee, having brought *an* alabaster-jar *of* perfume[H], **38** and having stood behind *Him* at His feet weeping— she began to wet His feet *with* the tears, and was wiping *them with* the hair *of* her head. And she was kissing His feet, and anointing *them with* the perfume. **39** And having seen *it*, the Pharisee having invited Him spoke within himself, saying, "If **this** One were *a* prophet, He would know who and what-kind-of *person* the woman *is* who is touching Him— that she is *a* sinner".

The One Forgiven Much Loves Much. Jesus Forgives Her Sins
40 And having responded, Jesus said to him, "Simon, I have something to speak *to* you". And the *one* says, "Teacher, speak". **41** "There were two debtors *to a* certain lender. The one was owing five-hundred denarii[I], and the other, fifty. **42** They not having *the means* to pay, he forgave both. So which *of* them will love him more?" **43** And having responded, Simon said, "I assume that *it is to* whom he forgave the more". And the *One* said *to* him, "You judged correctly". **44** And having turned toward the woman, He said *to* Simon, "Do you see this woman? I entered into your house— You did not give Me water for *My* feet. But this *one* wet My feet *with her* tears and wiped *them with* her hair. **45** You did not give Me *a* kiss. But this *one* did not stop kissing My feet from which *hour* I came-in. **46** You did not anoint My head *with* oil. But this *one* anointed My feet *with* perfume. **47** For which reason I say *to* you— her many sins have been forgiven, because she loved much. But he *to* whom little is forgiven, loves little". **48** And He said *to* her, "Your sins have been forgiven". **49** And the *ones*

---

reclining-back-with *Him* [to eat] began to say among themselves, "Who is this *One*, Who even forgives sins?" **50** And He said to the woman, "Your faith has saved you. Go in peace".

Jesus Speaks To The Crowd With a Parable
8:1 And it came about during the successive *days* that **He** was traveling-through according to city and village, proclaiming and announcing the kingdom *of* God as good news. And the twelve *were* with Him, **2** and some women who had been cured from evil spirits and infirmities— Mary, the *one* being called Magdalene^A, from whom seven demons had come out, **3** and Joanna, *the* wife *of* Chuza, Herod's steward^B, and Susanna, and many others, who were serving them out of their possessions. **4** And while *a* large crowd *was* gathering, and the *ones* from every city *were* coming to Him, He spoke with *a* parable—

The Sower's Seed Falls On Different Kinds of Soil. Only The Good Soil Produces Fruit
5 "The *one* sowing went out *that he might* sow his seed. And during his sowing some *seed* fell along the road. And it was trampled-underfoot. And the birds *of* the heaven ate it up. **6** And other *seed* fell-down on the bed-rock. And having grown, it was dried-up because of not having moisture. **7** And other *seed* fell in *the* middle *of* the thorns. And the thorns, having grown-with *it,* choked it. **8** And other *seed* fell into the fertile soil. And having grown, it produced fruit, *a* hundred-fold". While saying these *things*, He was calling, "Let the *one* having ears to hear, hear".

Jesus Explains The Purpose of Parables And The Meaning of The Sower
9 And His disciples were asking Him what this parable might mean. **10** And the *One* said— "It has been given *to* you to know^C the mysteries *of* the kingdom *of* God. But *I speak* in parables *to* the others in order that while seeing they may not be seeing, and while hearing, they may not be understanding. **11** Now the parable means this: the seed is the word *of* God. **12** And the *people* along the road are the *ones* having heard. Then the devil comes and takes away the word from their heart in order that they may not be saved, having believed. **13** And the *people* on the bed-rock *are ones* who are welcoming the word with joy when they hear *it.* And these do not have *a* root— *they are ones* who are believing for *a* time, and are departing^D in *a* time *of* testing^E. **14** And the *seed* having fallen into the thorns— these *people* are the *ones* having heard, and while proceeding are being choked by *the* anxieties^F and riches and pleasures *of* life. And they are not bringing-*fruit*-to-maturity. **15** And the *seed* in the good soil— these *people* are *ones* who, having heard the word in *a* good and fertile heart, are holding-on-to *it* and bearing-fruit with endurance.

Lamps Are To Give Light And Reveal What Is Hidden
16 "And no one having lit *a* lamp covers it *with a* container or puts *it* under *a* bed. But he puts *it* on *a* lampstand^G in order that the *ones* coming in may see the light. **17** For there is not *a* hidden *thing* which will not become visible, nor *a* hidden-away *thing* which will never be known and come into visibility.

A. That is, from Magdala, on the Sea of Galilee. **B.** Or, manager, administrator. **C.** Or, understand. **D.** Or, withdrawing. **E.** Or, trial. **F.** Or, concerns, cares. **G.** The light from God which Jesus brings shines on all, and will expose the hearts of all. See Mk 4:21.

Watch How You Listen

18 "Therefore be watching how you listen. For whoever has— it will be given *to* him. And whoever does not have— even what he thinks[A] *that he* has will be taken-away from him".

Those Who Do The Word of God Are My Family

19 And His mother and brothers came to Him, and they were not able to meet *with* Him because of the crowd. **20** And it was reported *to* Him, "Your mother and Your brothers are standing outside, wishing to see You". **21** But the *One*, having responded, said to them, "My mother and My brothers are these— the *ones* hearing and doing the word *of* God".

Jesus Calms The Sea. Who Is This Man? Even The Winds And Sea Obey Him!

22 And it came about on one *of* the days that **He** got into *a* boat, and His disciples. And He said to them, "Let us go to the other side *of* the lake[B]". And they put-to-sea. **23** Now while they *were* sailing, He fell-asleep. And *a* storm *of* wind came down on the lake, and they were being filled-with *water* and were being-in-danger. **24** And having gone to *Him*, they woke Him up, saying, "Master, Master, we are perishing!" And the *One*, having awakened, rebuked the wind and the surge *of* the water. And they ceased, and there was calm. **25** And He said *to* them, "Where *is* your faith?" But having feared, they marveled, saying to one another, "Who then is this *One*, that[C] He commands even[D] the winds and the water, and they obey Him?"

Jesus Casts Demons Out of a Man Into a Herd of Pigs. The Locals Beg Him To Leave

26 And they sailed-down to the country *of* the Gerasenes, which is opposite Galilee. **27** And He having gone out on the land, *a* certain man from the city met *Him,* having demons. And *for a* considerable time he did not put-on *a* garment, and was not staying in *a* house, but in the tombs. **28** And having seen Jesus, having cried out, he fell before Him and said *with a* loud voice, "What do[E] I have to do with you, Jesus, Son *of* the Most-High God? I beg You, do not torment me". **29** For He ordered the unclean spirit to come out from the man. For it had seized him many times. And he was being bound *with* chains and shackles[F], while being guarded. And tearing the bonds, he was being driven by the demon into the desolate *places.* **30** And Jesus asked him, "What is *the* name *for* you?" And the *one* said, "Legion[G]", because many demons entered into him. **31** And they were begging Him that He not command them to go into the abyss. **32** Now there was *a* herd *of* many pigs there feeding on the mountain. And they begged Him that He permit them to enter into those *pigs.* And He permitted them. **33** And the demons, having come out from the man, entered into the pigs. And the herd rushed down the steep-bank into the lake, and was drowned. **34** And the *ones* feeding[H] *them,* having seen the *thing* having happened, fled and reported *it* in the city and in the fields. **35** And they came out to see the *thing* having happened. And they came to Jesus and found the man from whom the demons went out sitting— having been clothed, and being sound-minded— at the feet *of* Jesus. And they became afraid. **36** And the *ones* having seen reported *to* them how the *one* having been

---

A. Or, seems to have. **B.** That is, the Sea of Galilee. **C.** Or, because. **D.** Or, both. **E.** Lit, What [is there] *for* me and *for* You. **F.** That is, bindings for the feet. **G.** A Roman legion had about 6000 soldiers, plus horsemen and auxiliaries. **H.** Or, tending, grazing.

demon-possessed was restored. ³⁷ And the whole crowd *from* the surrounding-region *of* the Gerasenes asked Him to depart from them because they were being gripped^A *with* great fear. And **He**, having gotten into *a* boat, returned. ³⁸ But the man from whom the demons had gone out was begging Him to be *with* Him. But He sent him away, saying, ³⁹ "Return to your house and be relating^B all-that God did *for* you". And he departed, proclaiming throughout the whole city all-that Jesus did *for* him.

Jairus, a Synagogue Official, Comes To Jesus About His Dying Daughter
⁴⁰ And during Jesus' returning, the crowd welcomed Him, for they were all expecting Him. ⁴¹ And behold— *a* man came, *for* whom *the* name *was* Jairus. And this *one* was *an* official^C *of* the synagogue. And having fallen at^D the feet *of* Jesus, he was begging Him to enter into his house, ⁴² because there was *an* only-born daughter *to* him, about twelve years *old*, and **she** was dying.

On The Way, a Woman Touches The Garment of Jesus And Is Healed
Now during His going, the crowds were thronging^E Him. ⁴³ And *a* woman being in *a* flow *of* blood for twelve years— who, having expended *her* whole living *on* physicians, was not able to be cured by anyone— ⁴⁴ having approached from behind, touched the tassel *of* His garment. And at once her flow *of* blood stopped. ⁴⁵ And Jesus said, "Who *is* the *one* having touched Me?" And while all *were* denying *it*, Peter said, "Master, the crowds are enclosing You and pressing-against *You*". ⁴⁶ But Jesus said, "Someone touched Me, for **I** recognized^F power^G having gone forth from Me". ⁴⁷ And the woman, having seen that she did not escape-notice, came trembling. And having fallen before Him, she declared in the presence of all the people for what reason she touched Him, and how she was healed at-once. ⁴⁸ And the *One* said *to* her, "Daughter, your faith has restored^H you. Go in peace".

The Daughter Dies Before Jesus Arrives. He Raises Her From The Dead
⁴⁹ While He *is* still speaking, someone comes from [the house of] the synagogue-official, saying that "Your daughter is dead. Be troubling the Teacher no longer". ⁵⁰ But Jesus, having heard, responded *to* him, "Do not be fearing. Only believe, and she will be restored". ⁵¹ And having come to the house, He did not permit anyone to go in with Him except Peter and John and James, and the father *of* the child, and the mother. ⁵² Now they^I were all weeping and beating-their-breasts *for* her. But the *One* said, "Do not be weeping, for she did not die, but she is sleeping". ⁵³ And they were laughing-scornfully *at* Him, knowing that she died. ⁵⁴ But **He**, having taken hold of her hand, called, saying, "Child, arise!" ⁵⁵ And her spirit returned, and she stood up at-once. And He directed *that something should* be given *to* her to eat. ⁵⁶ And her parents were astonished. And the *One* ordered them to tell no one the *thing* having taken place.

Jesus Sends Out The Twelve To Proclaim The Kingdom And Heal The Sick
9:1 Now having called together the twelve, He gave them power and authority over all the demons, and to cure diseases. ² And He sent them out to proclaim the kingdom *of*

A. Or, held under the control *of*. **B.** Or, narrating, describing. **C.** Or, leader. **D.** Or, near. **E.** Or, pressing, crowding. **F.** Or, perceived. **G.** Or, *a* miracle. **H.** Or, saved (from this disease). **I.** That is, the ones in the house when Jesus and the others entered.

God, and to heal the sick *ones.* [3] And He said to them, "Be taking nothing for the journey— neither *a* staff, nor *a* [traveler's] bag, nor bread, nor money, nor *are you* to have two tunics[A] each. [4] And into whatever house you enter, be staying there, and going forth from there. [5] And all who do not welcome you— while going out from that city, be shaking-off the dust from your feet for *a* testimony against them". [6] And going forth, they were going from village-to-village announcing-the-good-news and curing everywhere.

Herod Hears of What Jesus Is Doing And Seeks To See Him
[7] And Herod[B] the tetrarch heard-*of* all the *things* taking place. And he was greatly-perplexed because of *it* being said by some that John arose from *the* dead, [8] and by some that Elijah appeared, and *by* others that some prophet *of* the ancients[C] rose-up. [9] And Herod said, "**I** beheaded John. But who is this *One* about Whom I am hearing such *things?*" And he was seeking to see Him.

The Twelve Return. Jesus Multiplies Bread And Fish To Feed 5000 Men
[10] And having returned, the apostles related *to* Him all that they did. And having taken them along, He retreated privately toward *a* city being called Bethsaida. [11] But the crowds, having known[D] *it*, followed Him. And having welcomed them, He was speaking *to* them about the kingdom *of* God and healing the *ones* having *a* need *of a* cure. [12] And the day began to decline. And having come to *Him*, the twelve said *to* Him, "Send-away the crowd in order that having gone into the surrounding villages and farms, they may take-up-lodging and find provisions, because here we are in *a* desolate place". [13] But He said to them, "**You** give them *something* to eat". And the *ones* said, "There are not more than five loaves and two fish *with* us— unless perhaps, having gone, **we** should buy food for this whole *group-of*-people!". [14] For there were about five-thousand men. And He said to His disciples, "Make them lie-down [to eat] *in* eating-groups— about fifty each". [15] And they did so, and made everyone lie down. [16] And having taken the five loaves and the two fish, having looked up to heaven, He blessed them, and broke *them* in pieces, and was giving *them to* the disciples to set-before the crowd. [17] And they ate and were all filled-to-satisfaction. And the *amount of* fragments left-over *by* them was picked up— twelve baskets.

Who Do You Say That I Am? Peter Says, You Are The Christ of God
[18] And it came about during His being alone praying *that* the disciples were with Him. And He questioned them, saying, "Who do the crowds say *that* I am?" [19] And the *ones*, having responded, said, "John the Baptist; and others, Elijah; and others, that some prophet *of* the ancients rose-up". [20] And He said *to* them, "But who do **you** say *that* I am?" And Peter, having responded, said, "The Christ *of* God". [21] But the *One*, having warned them, ordered *them* to be telling this *to* no one— [22] having said that "The Son *of* Man must suffer many *things,* and be rejected by the elders and chief priests and scribes, and be killed, and be raised *on* the third day".

Deny Yourself, Take Up Your Cross, Follow Me. Some Here Will See My Kingdom
[23] And He was saying to everyone, "If anyone wants to be coming after Me, let him

---

A. That is, undergarments. Take no provisions for the journey; just go. **B.** See Mt 14:1. **C.** That is, ancient *ones*; or, ancient *times.* **D.** Or, learned, recognized.

deny[A] himself, and let him take up his cross[B] daily, and let him be following Me. [24] For whoever wants to save[C] his life will lose it. But whoever loses his life for My sake— this *one* will save it. [25] For what is *a* person profited— having gained the whole world, but having lost or having forfeited himself? [26] For whoever *is* ashamed-of Me and My words, the Son *of* Man will be ashamed-of **this one** when He comes in the glory *of* Himself and the Father and the holy angels. [27] And I say *to* you truly, there are some[D] *of* the *ones* standing here who will by-no-means taste death until they see the kingdom *of* God".

Three Disciples See Jesus Transformed, And Hear God Tell Them To Listen To Jesus
[28] And it came about, about eight days after these words, that having taken-along Peter and John and James, He went up on the mountain to pray. [29] And during His praying the appearance *of* His face became different, and His clothing *became* white, while gleaming-out. [30] And behold, two men were talking-with Him, who were Moses and Elijah— [31] who, having appeared in glory, were speaking *of* His departure which He was about to bring-to-fulfillment[E] in Jerusalem. [32] Now Peter and the *ones* with him had been weighed-down *with* sleep. But having fully-awakened, they saw His glory and the two men standing-with Him. [33] And it came about during their parting from Him, *that* Peter said to Jesus, "Master, it is good *that* we are here. And let us make three dwellings[F]; one *for* You, and one *for* Moses, and one *for* Elijah"— not knowing what he was saying. [34] And while he *was* saying these *things*, there came-to-be *a* cloud. And it was overshadowing[G] them. And they became afraid at their entering into the cloud. [35] And *a* voice came out of the cloud, saying, "This is My chosen Son. Be listening-to Him". [36] And at the voice coming, Jesus was found alone. And **they** kept-silent, and reported *to* no one during those days anything *of the things* which they had seen.

Jesus Heals a Boy His Disciples Could Not Heal
[37] And it came about *on* the next day, they having come down from the mountain, *that a* large crowd met Him. [38] And behold— *a* man from the crowd shouted, saying, "Teacher, I beg You to look upon my son, because he is *an* only-born *son to* me. [39] And behold— *a* spirit seizes him and he suddenly cries-out. And it convulses him, along with foam [at the mouth]. And it departs from him with difficulty, while bruising[H] him. [40] And I begged Your disciples to cast it out, and they were not able". [41] And having responded, Jesus said, "O unbelieving[I] and perverted generation, how long will I be with you, and bear-with you? Bring your son to *Me* here". [42] And while he *was* still approaching, the demon threw him to the ground and convulsed *him.* And Jesus rebuked the unclean spirit, and healed the boy, and gave him back *to* his father. [43] And they were all astounded at the majesty *of* God.

Jesus Predicts His Death
But while all *were* marveling at everything which He was doing, He said to His disciples, [44] "**You** put these words into your ears— for the Son *of* Man is going to be handed-over

---

A. That is, disown and refuse to follow the impulses of self. **B.** That is, the instrument of his death to self. **C.** That is, by avoiding his cross. **D.** See Mt 16:28. **E.** This views the death as something prophesied for the Christ in the OT, Lk 24:44. Or, complete, finish; viewing the death as a task yet to be accomplished by Jesus. **F.** Or, tents, tabernacles. **G.** Or, covering, hovering over. **H.** That is, physically. Or, crushing (emotionally). **I.** Or, faithless.

into *the* hands *of* men". **45** But the *ones* were not understanding this statement. And it had been concealed from them, so that they did not perceive it. And they were fearing to ask Him about this statement.

The Disciples Argue Over Who Is The Greatest. Jesus Says The Least Is The Greatest
46 And *an* argument came-in among them *as to* which *of* them might be greater^A. **47** But Jesus, knowing the reasoning *of* their heart, having taken-hold-of *a* child, stood him^B beside Himself, **48** and said *to* them, "Whoever welcomes this child on the basis of My name, welcomes Me. And whoever welcomes Me, welcomes the *One* having sent Me forth. For the *one* being least among you all, this *one* is great^C". **49** And having responded, John said, "Master, we saw someone casting-out demons in Your name. And we were forbidding him because he is not following with us". **50** And Jesus said to him, "Do not be forbidding^D *him*. For he who is not against you is for you".

Jesus Sets His Course For Jerusalem
51 Now it came about during the days *of*^E His ascension being fulfilled, that **He** set *His* face^F *that He might* proceed to Jerusalem.

Jesus Sends Messengers Ahead To Samaria. They Are Not Welcomed
52 And He sent out messengers ahead *of* His presence. And having gone, they entered into *a* village *of* Samaritans so-as to prepare *for* Him. **53** And they did not welcome Him, because His face was going toward Jerusalem. **54** And the disciples having seen *it*, James and John said, "Lord, do You want us to call fire to come down from heaven and consume them?" **55** But having turned, He rebuked them. **56** And they proceeded to another village.

Jesus Says Follow Me Now, Unbound By Earthly Concerns
57 And while they *were* proceeding on the road, someone said to Him, "I will follow You wherever You go". **58** And Jesus said to him, "The foxes have holes, and the birds *of* the heaven *have* nests, but the Son *of* Man does not have *a place* where He may lay *His* head". **59** And He said to another, "Be following Me". But the *one* said, "Master, permit me, having gone, to first bury^G my father". **60** But He said *to* him, "Allow the dead to bury their *own* dead. But **you**, having gone, be proclaiming the kingdom *of* God". **61** And another also said, "I will follow You, Master. But first permit me to say-good-bye *to* the *ones* in my house". **62** But Jesus said to him, "No one having put *his* hand on *the* plow and looking to the *things* behind^H is fit^I *for* the kingdom *of* God".

Jesus Sends Seventy-Two To The Cities Ahead of Him
10:1 And after these *things*, the Lord appointed seventy two^J others, and sent them out ahead *of* His presence two by two, to every city and place where He Himself was going to go.

Jesus Empowers Them And Instructs Them On How To Conduct Themselves
2 And He was saying to them "The harvest *is* great, but the workers *are* few! Therefore

---

A. Or, greatest. **B.** Or, her. Lit, it (the child). **C.** Or, greatest. **D:** forbidding... you... you. These words are plural. Jesus addresses them all through John. **E.** That is, leading to the event named next. **F.** That is, firmly established His purpose and direction. **G.** This man's father may have just died; or, he may mean 'Let me fulfill my duties to my father. When he dies, I will follow you'. **H.** Or, looking back. **I.** Or, useful, suitable. **J.** Some manuscripts omit this word here and in v 17.

ask the Lord *of* the harvest that He send-out workers into His harvest. **3** Go! Behold— I am sending you out as lambs in *the* midst *of* wolves. **4** Do not be carrying *a* money-bag^A; not *a* [traveler's] bag, not sandals. And greet^B no one along the road. **5** And into whatever house you enter, first say 'Peace *on* this house'. **6** And if *a* son *of*^C peace is there, your peace will rest on him. Otherwise indeed, it will return to you. **7** And be staying in the very house, eating and drinking the *things* from them. For the worker *is* worthy *of* his wages. Do not be passing from house to house. **8** And into whatever city you enter and they welcome you, be eating the *things* being set-before you. **9** And be curing the sick *ones* in it. And be saying *to* them, 'The kingdom *of* God has drawn-near to you'. **10** But into whatever city you enter and they do not welcome you, having gone out into its wide-roads, say **11** 'We are wiping-off *against* you even the dust having clung *to* us from your city— to *our* feet. Nevertheless know this: that the kingdom *of* God has drawn near'. **12** I say *to* you that it will be more-tolerable^D on that day *for* Sodom than *for* that city! **13** Woe *to* you, Chorazin! Woe *to* you, Bethsaida! Because if the miracles having taken place in you had been done in Tyre and Sidon, they would have repented long-ago, sitting in sackcloth and ashes. **14** Nevertheless^E it will be more tolerable *for* Tyre and Sidon at the judgment than *for* you. **15** And you, Capernaum, will you be exalted up to heaven? You will go-down as far as Hades. **16** The *one* listening-to you is listening-to Me. And the *one* rejecting you is rejecting Me. And the *one* rejecting Me is rejecting the *One* having sent Me forth".

The Seventy-Two Return Rejoicing In Their Power. Rejoice In Your Salvation Instead
17 And the seventy two returned with joy, saying, "Lord, even the demons are subject *to* us in Your name". **18** And He said *to* them, "I was seeing^F Satan having fallen like^G lightning from heaven. **19** Behold— I have given you the authority to trample^H on snakes and scorpions, and over all the power *of* the enemy. And nothing will by-any-means^I harm you. **20** Nevertheless, do not be rejoicing in this— that the spirits are subject *to* you. But be rejoicing that your names have been recorded in the heavens".

It Pleases God To Hide The Kingdom From The Wise And Reveal It To The Childlike
21 At the very hour, He rejoiced-greatly in the Holy Spirit and said, "I praise You, Father, Lord *of* heaven and earth, that^J You hid these *things* from wise *ones* and intelligent *ones*, and You revealed them *to* children^K. Yes, Father, because^L in this manner it became well-pleasing in Your sight. **22** All *things* were handed-over *to* Me by My Father. And no one knows^M Who the Son is except the Father, and Who the Father is except the Son— and *anyone to* whom^N the Son wills^O to reveal *Him*". **23** And having turned to the disciples, He said privately, "Blessed^P *are* the eyes seeing *the things* which you are seeing. **24** For I say *to* you that many prophets and kings wanted to experience^Q *the things* which **you** are seeing, and they did not experience *them*; and to hear *the things* which you are hearing, and they did not hear *them*".

A: money-bag... sandals. That is, take no provisions, nor the means to buy or carry them. Go as you are. **B.** That is, move quickly from city to city. **C.** That is, characterized by peace toward you. **D.** Or, more-endurable, more-bearable. **E.** See Mt 11:22. **F.** Or, observing, perceiving. **G.** That is, clearly and unmistakably; or, suddenly and repeatedly. **H.** Or, tread. **I.** Or, ever. Nothing can stop them from completing the mission Jesus has given them. **J.** Or, because. **K.** Or, childlike *ones*. **L.** Or, that; Yes Father, *I praise You* that. **M.** Or, understands, recognizes, acknowledges. **N.** Or, and *to* whomever. **O.** Or, desires, wants, wishes. **P.** Or, Fortunate. **Q.** Or, see, but not the same word as next.

What Shall I Do To Inherit Life? Love God And Your Neighbor. Who Is My Neighbor?
25 And behold— *a* certain Law-expert stood up, putting Him to the test, saying, "Teacher, [by] having done what shall I inherit eternal life?" **26** And the *One* said to him, "What has been written in the Law? How do you read *it*?" **27** And the *one*, having responded, said, "You shall love *the* Lord your God from your whole heart, and with your whole soul, and with your whole strength, and with your whole mind, and your neighbor as yourself ". **28** And He said *to* him, "You answered correctly. Be doing this and you will live". **29** But the *one*, wanting to vindicate^A himself, said to Jesus, "And who is my neighbor?"

The Parable of The Good Samaritan: Be a Neighbor To Everyone
30 Having taken-up *the question*, Jesus said, "A certain man was going down from Jerusalem to Jericho. And he fell-into^B robbers, who, both having stripped him and having laid-on blows, went away— having left *him* half-dead. **31** And by coincidence, *a* certain priest was going down on that road. And having seen him, he passed-by-on-the-other-side. **32** And likewise also *a* Levite having come-to-be upon the place, having come and having seen, passed by on the other side. **33** But *a* certain Samaritan, while traveling, came upon him. And having seen, he felt-deep-feelings [of compassion]. **34** And having gone to *him*, he bound his wounds, pouring on oil and wine. And having put him on *his* own mount, he brought him to *an* inn and took-care-of him. **35** And on the next day, having taken out two denarii^C, he gave *them to* the innkeeper and said, 'Take-care-of him. And whatever thing you spend-further **I** will give-back *to* you during my returning'. **36** Which *of* these three seems *to* you to have become^D *a* neighbor *of* the *one* having fallen into the robbers?" **37** And the *one* said, "The *one* having shown mercy to him". And Jesus said *to* him, "Go, and **you** be doing likewise".

Mary Chooses The Good Part: Listening To The Word of Jesus
38 And during their proceeding, **He** entered into *a* certain village. And *a* certain woman, Martha *by* name, received^E Him. **39** And *to* this *one* there was *a* sister being called Mary, who also was listening-to His word, having sat near to the feet *of* the Lord. **40** But Martha was being distracted^F with much service. And having stood-near, she said "Lord, do You not care that my sister left me to be serving alone? Tell her then that she should help me". **41** But having responded, the Lord said *to* her, "Martha, Martha, you are anxious and troubled about many *things.* **42** But there is *a* need *of* one *thing*. For Mary chose the good^G part, which will not be taken-away *from* her".

Jesus Teaches His Disciples To Pray
11:1 And it came about during His being in *a* certain place praying, *that* when He ceased, *a* certain *one of* His disciples said to Him, "Lord, teach us to pray, just as John also taught his disciples". **2** And He said *to* them, "Whenever you pray, say, 'Father— let^H Your name be treated-as-holy. Let Your kingdom come. **3** Be giving us each day our daily bread. **4** And forgive us our sins, for **we** also are forgiving everyone being indebted *to* us. And do not bring us into *a* temptation^I' ".

A. Or, justify. **B.** Or, encountered. **C.** That is, two day's wages for a laborer. **D.** Or, proved-to-be. **E.** That is, into her house as a guest. **F.** Or, pulled-away, diverted, drawn-off. **G.** Or, better, best, based on the context. **H.** That is, make it a reality that Your name is treated as holy. These five requests are in the form of a command (as usual), with a change of grammar on the third request. 'Let' does not mean 'allow'. **I.** That is, a situation in which we will be tempted by the evil one. Or, *a* testing, *a* trial.

Keep Asking And You Will Receive

5 And He said to them, "Which of you will have *a* friend, and will go to him *at* midnight and say *to* him, 'Friend, lend me three loaves-of-bread, **6** because my friend came to me from *a* journey and I do not have what I will set-before him'; **7** and that *one,* having responded from inside says 'Do not be causing me troubles. The door has already been locked, and my children are with me in bed. I am not able, having arisen, to give *it to* you'? **8** I say *to* you: even though he will not, having arisen, give *to* him because of being his friend, yet because of his shamelessness^A he will, having been raised^B, give *to* him as much as he needs. **9** And **I** say *to* you: be asking, and it will be given *to* you. Be seeking, and you will find. Be knocking, and it will be opened *to* you. **10** For everyone asking receives. And the *one* seeking finds. And *to* the *one* knocking, it will be opened.

God Knows How To Give Good Answers To Your Prayers

11 "And what father from-*among* you will *his* son ask-*for a* fish, and he will give him *a* snake^C instead of *a* fish? **12** Or indeed he will ask-*for an* egg— will he give him *a* scorpion? **13** Therefore if **you**, being evil, know-*how* to give good gifts *to* your children, how much more will *your* Father from heaven give *the* Holy Spirit *to* the *ones* asking Him!"

Some Say Jesus Casts Out Demons By Satan's Power

14 And He was casting-out *a* demon, and **it** was mute. And it came about, the demon having gone out, *that* the mute *man* spoke. And the crowds marveled. **15** But some of them said, "He is casting out the demons by^D Beelzebul, the ruler *of* the demons". **16** And others, testing *Him*, were seeking from Him *a* sign out of heaven.

A Kingdom Divided Cannot Stand. Watch Out Or You Will Be Worse Off

17 But **He**, knowing their thoughts, said *to* them— "Every kingdom having been divided against itself is desolated, and *a* house *divided* against *a* house falls; **18** and if indeed Satan was divided against himself, how will his kingdom stand?— because you are saying *that* I *am* casting out the demons by Beelzebul. **19** And if **I** am casting out the demons by Beelzebul, by whom^E are **your sons** casting *them* out? For this reason, **they** will be your judges; **20** but if **I** am casting out the demons by *the* finger *of* God, then the kingdom *of* God came^F upon you. **21** Whenever the strong *man* having fully-armed-*himself*^G is guarding his *own* courtyard, his possessions are in peace. **22** But when *one* stronger *than* he, having come against *him*, overcomes him— he takes away his full-armor upon which he trusted, and distributes his spoils. **23** The *one* not being with Me is against Me. And the *one* not gathering with Me is scattering. **24** When the unclean spirit departs from the person, it goes-through waterless places seeking rest^H. And not finding *it,* then it says, 'I will return to my house from where I came out'. **25** And having come, it finds *it* having been swept and put-in-order^I. **26** Then

---

A. That is, his shameless (from the friend's point of view) persistence (from the asker's point of view). **B:** having arisen... having been raised. That is, having voluntarily gotten up... having been forced to get up by the persistent asking. **C.** That is, something harmful. **D.** Or, in union with. **E.** The reasoning required to prove that the Jews were not using the power of Satan to cast out demons will also prove it in the case of Jesus. **F.** Or, arrived. **G.** Or, being fully-armed. **H.** Or, *a* resting place. **I.** Or, adorned, decorated.

it proceeds, and takes along **seven** other spirits more evil *than* itself. And having gone in, they dwell there. And the last *state of* that person becomes worse *than* the first".

Blessed Are Those Hearing And Keeping The Word of God
[27] And it came about during His saying these *things that a* certain woman from the crowd, having raised *her* voice, said *to* Him, "Blessed *is* the womb having carried You, and *the* breasts which You sucked". [28] But **He** said, "More-than-that, blessed *are* the *ones* hearing the word *of* God and keeping *it*".

This Is an Evil Generation. No Sign Will Be Given Except The Sign of Jonah
[29] And while the crowds *were* assembling-more, He began to say "This generation is *an* evil generation. It is seeking *a* sign. And *a* sign will not be given *to* it except the sign *of* Jonah. [30] For as Jonah became *a* sign *to* the Ninevites, so the Son *of* Man also will be *to* this generation. [31] *The* Queen *of the* South will be raised at the judgment with the men *of* this generation, and she will condemn them. Because she came from the ends *of* the earth to hear the wisdom *of* Solomon, and behold— *a* greater *thing than* Solomon *is* here. [32] Ninevite men will rise-up at the judgment with this generation, and they will condemn it. Because they repented at the proclamation *of* Jonah, and behold— *a* greater *thing than* Jonah *is* here.

The Lamp Shines So People Can See. Watch Out That Your Eye Can Receive The Light
[33] "No one having lit *a* lamp puts *it* in *a* crypt[A], nor under the basket, but on the lampstand, in order that the *ones* coming in may see the light. [34] The lamp[B] *of* the body is your eye. When your eye is single[C], your whole body is also full-of-light. But when it is bad, your body *is* also full-of-darkness. [35] So be watching-out *that* the light in[D] you is not darkness! [36] Therefore if your whole body *is* full-of-light, not having any part full-of-darkness, [then] *the* whole *body* will be full-of-light as when the lamp gives-light-to you *with its* bright-light".

Woe To You Pharisees
[37] Now at the speaking, *a* Pharisee asks Him so that He might eat-the-morning-meal with him. And having gone in, He fell-back [to eat]. [38] And the Pharisee, having seen *it*, marveled that He was not first cleansed[E] before the morning-meal. [39] But the Lord said to him, "Now[F] **you** Pharisees cleanse the outside *of* the cup and the platter, but the inside *of* you is full *of* plundering and evilness. [40] Foolish *ones*— did not the *One* having made the outside also make the inside? [41] But give the *things* being-within *as* alms, and behold— all *things* are clean *for* you. [42] But woe *to* you Pharisees, because you are giving-a-tenth-of the mint and the rue and every garden-plant, and are disregarding[G] the justice and the love *of* God. But *you* ought-to-have done these *things,* and not be slackening[H] those *things*. [43] Woe *to* you Pharisees, because you love the seat-of-honor in the synagogues and the greetings in the marketplaces. [44] Woe *to* you, because you are like unmarked[I] graves, and the people walking over *them* do not know *it* ".

A. Or, vault, hidden place. The lamp is on the lampstand shining for all to see. No further sign is needed for any whose eye is not bad. **B.** That is, the source of light. **C.** Or, sincere, simple. That is, single-focused on God; or, spiritually-healthy. **D.** That is, allowed into your heart by your spiritual eye. **E.** Compare Mk 7:2-4. **F.** That is, Right-now; or, As-it-is. **G.** Or, passing-by. **H.** Or, relaxing. **I.** That is, people who come into contact with you become defiled and polluted, and don't even know it.

Woe To You Law-Experts

45 And having responded, one *of* the Law-experts says to Him, "Teacher, while saying these *things* You also are insulting us". **46** And the *One* said, "Woe *to* you Law-experts also, because you burden people *with* hard-to-bear burdens[A], and **you** do not touch[B] the burdens *with* one *of* your fingers. **47** Woe *to* you, because you build the tombs *of* the prophets, and your fathers killed them! **48** Therefore you are witnesses and are giving-approval *to* the works *of* your fathers, because **they** killed them— and **you** build *their tombs*. **49** For this reason the wisdom *of* God also said, 'I will send-forth prophets and apostles to them, and *some* of them they will kill and persecute, **50** in order that the blood *of* all the prophets having been shed since *the* foundation *of the* world may be required[C] from this generation— **51** from *the* blood *of* Abel up to *the* blood *of* Zechariah[D], the *one* having perished between the altar and the house [of God]. Yes, I say *to* you, it shall be required from this generation'. **52** Woe *to* you Law-experts, because you took away the key *of* knowledge. **You** did not enter, and you hindered the *ones* entering".

With His Enemies Lying In Wait To Destroy Him, Myriads Gather To Hear Jesus

53 And He having gone out from there, the scribes and the Pharisees began to be terribly[E] hostile[F], and to question[G] Him concerning more *things* **54** while lying-in-wait-for Him to catch something from His mouth— **12:1** in which *circumstances*, the myriads *of* the crowd having been gathered-together so that *they were* trampling one another:

Watch Out For The Leaven of The Pharisees, But Do Not Fear Them

He began to speak to His disciples first, "Take heed to yourselves because of the leaven *of* the Pharisees, which is hypocrisy. **2** But nothing has been covered-up[H] which will not be revealed, and *is* secret which will not be known. **3** Because whatever you said in the darkness will be heard in the light. And what you spoke to the ear in the inner-rooms will be proclaimed on the housetops. **4** And I say *to* you My friends, do not fear *anything* from[I] the *ones* killing the body, and after these *things* not having anything more to do. **5** But I will show you Whom you should fear— fear the *One* having *the* authority to throw into Gehenna[J] after the killing. Yes, I say *to* you, fear this *One*. **6** Are not five sparrows sold *for* two assarion[K]? And one of them has not been forgotten before God. **7** Yet even the hairs *of* your head have all been numbered. Do not be fearing; you are more valuable *than* many sparrows. **8** And I say *to* you, everyone who confesses Me in front of people, the Son *of* Man also will confess him in front of the angels *of* God. **9** But the *one* having denied Me before people will be denied before the angels *of* God. **10** And everyone who shall speak *a* word against the Son *of* Man— it will be forgiven *to* him. But *to* the *one* having blasphemed against the Holy Spirit— it will not be forgiven. **11** And whenever they bring you in before the synagogues and the rulers and the authorities, do not be anxious-*about* how or

---

A. Jesus is referring to their traditions, their man-made rules of conduct. **B.** That is, to carry them yourselves. Many rules that burdened the common working person addressed issues that never arose in the life of a priest. **C.** That is, so that the blood-guilt of your fathers may be avenged on you as you repeat their crimes on those I will send to you. **D.** That is, the first and last murder recorded in the OT in the Hebrew order of books. **E.** Or, fearfully, fiercely. **F.** That is, internally hostile and plotting. **G.** That is, to ask calculated questions; to bait Him with questions. **H.** Or, concealed. **I.** Or, be-afraid of. **J.** That is, hell. **K.** One assarion was one sixteenth of a denarius (a day's wage for a laborer).

what you should speak-in-defense, or what you should say. **12** For the Holy Spirit will teach you at the very hour *the things* which *you* ought-to say".

Life Is Not In What Abounds To You From Your Possessions. Be Rich Toward God
13 And someone from the crowd said *to* Him, "Teacher, tell my brother to divide the inheritance with me". **14** But the *One* said *to* him, "Man, who appointed Me judge or arbitrator over you?" **15** And He said to them, "Watch out and guard *yourselves* from all greed, because one's life is not in *what* abounds *to* him out of his possessions". **16** And He spoke *a* parable to them, saying, "The land *of a* certain rich man was productive. **17** And he was reasoning within himself, saying, 'What should I do, because I do not have *a place* where I will gather my fruits?' **18** And he said, 'I will do this— I will tear-down my barns and build larger *ones*, and there I will gather all my grain and good *things.* **19** And I will say *to* my soul, "Soul, you have many good *things* lying-*in-store* for many years. Be resting. Eat, drink. Be enjoying-yourself" '. **20** But God said *to* him, 'Foolish *one*! *On* this night they^A are demanding your life^B from you. And *the things* which you prepared— *for* whom will they be?' **21** So *is* the *one* storing-up *for* himself, and not being rich toward God".

Do Not Worry About The Necessities of This Life; Seek God's Kingdom
22 And He said to His disciples, "For this reason^C, I say *to* you, do not be anxious *for your* life *as to* what you may eat, nor *for your* body *as to* what you may put-on. **23** For life is more *than* food, and the body *is more than* clothing. **24** Consider the ravens— that they do not sow nor reap, *for* which there is not *a* storeroom nor *a* barn. And God feeds them. How much more are **you** worth *than* the birds! **25** And which of you while being anxious is able to add *a* cubit^D upon his life-span? **26** If then you are not even able *to do a* very little *thing*, why are you anxious about the rest? **27** Consider the lilies, how they grow. They do not labor nor spin, but I say *to* you— not even Solomon in all his glory clothed *himself* like one *of* these! **28** But if God dresses in this manner the grass in *a* field existing today and being thrown into *an* oven tomorrow, how much more *will He care for* you— *ones*-of-little-faith? **29** And don't **you** be seeking what you may eat and what you may drink. And do not be unsettled^E. **30** For the nations *of* the world are seeking-after all these *things.* And your Father knows that you have need *of* these *things.* **31** But be seeking His kingdom, and these *things* will be added *to* you.

Do Not Fear. Sell Your Possessions For a Heavenly Return
32 "Do not be fearing, little flock, because your Father was well-pleased to give you the kingdom. **33** Sell your possessions, and give *it as* alms^F. Make yourselves money-bags not becoming-old— *an* unfailing^G treasure in the heavens, where *a* thief does not draw-near, nor does *a* moth destroy. **34** For where your treasure is, there also your heart will be.

Keep Watch For Your Master's Return. Be Prepared
35 Let your waists be girded^H and *your* lamps burning, **36** and you *be* like people

---

A. That is, the angels sent by God for this purpose. **B.** Or, soul. **C.** That is, the true source of life. **D.** That is, 18 inches; one step. **E.** That is, worried, in suspense, up in the air about things. **F.** That is, charitable giving to the poor. **G.** Or, inexhaustible. That is, treasure that will never run out. **H.** That is, tied with your belt, in a state of readiness.

waiting-for their master when he departs from the wedding-celebrations— in order that *he* having come and having knocked, they may immediately open [the door] *for* him. **37** Blessed *are* those slaves whom the master, having come, will find keeping-watch. Truly I say *to* you that he will gird *himself*, and have them lie back [to eat]. And having come-to *the table*, he will serve them. **38** Even if in the second^A, even if he comes in the third watch and finds *them* so, blessed are those *ones*. **39** And you know^B this *saying*— that if the house-master had known *at* which hour the thief was coming, he would not have permitted his house to be broken-into. **40 You** also be^C prepared *ones*, because the Son *of* Man is coming *at an* hour which you do not expect".

Wise Servants Found Working When The Master Returns Will Be Rewarded
41 And Peter said, "Lord, are You speaking this parable to us, or also to everyone?" **42** And the Lord said, "Who then^D is the faithful, wise steward^E whom *his* master will put-in-charge over his body-of-servants, *that he might* be giving *them their* food-allowance at *the* proper-time? **43** Blessed *is* that slave whom his master, having come, will find so doing. **44** Truly I say *to* you that he will put him in charge over all his possessions. **45** But if that slave says in his heart, 'My master is delaying to come', and he begins to strike the male-servants and the female-servants, and to eat and drink and get-drunk— **46** the master *of* that slave will come on *a* day which he does not expect, and at *an* hour which he does not know. And he will cut him in two, and assign *him* his part^F with the unbelievers^G. **47** But that slave having known the will *of* his master, and not having prepared or acted in accordance with his will, will be beaten many *blows*. **48** But the *one* not having known, and having done *things* worthy *of* blows, will be beaten *a few blows*. And *to* everyone whom much was given, much will be sought from him. And *to* whom they entrusted much, they will ask him even more.

I Came To Cause Division On Earth, Not To Bring It Peace
49 "I came to cast **fire** upon the earth; and how I wish that it were already kindled! **50** But I have *a* **baptism** to be baptized; and how I am held^H *by it* until it is accomplished! **51** Do you think that I came^I to grant peace on earth? No, I say *to* you, but rather division! **52** For from now *on*, there^J will be five in one house having been divided— three against two, and two against three. **53** They will be divided— father against son and son against father, mother against daughter and daughter against mother, mother-in-law against her daughter-in-law and daughter-in-law against mother-in-law".

Read The Signs of The Times. Judge For Yourselves
54 And He was also saying *to* the crowds, "Whenever you see the cloud rising in *the* west, immediately you say that '*A* rainstorm is coming', and so it happens. **55** And

---

A. That is, the second watch, 9 P.M. to midnight. The third watch is midnight to 3 A.M. **B.** Or, know (a command); And know this. **C.** Or, prove-to-be. **D.** In view of the sudden nature of Christ's return, who is the wise steward among those left to lead when the master left? The wise one is the one still doing his will when he returns. **E.** That is, household manager. **F.** Or, share, place. **G.** Or, unfaithful *ones*, faithless *ones*. **H.** Or, gripped, occupied, under the control of. Or taking it negatively, distressed. **I.** Or, appeared, arrived. **J.** Or, five in one house will have been divided.

whenever *a* south *wind is* blowing, you say that 'There will be burning-heat', and it happens. **⁵⁶** Hypocrites! You know-*how* to test the appearance *of* the earth and the heaven, but how *is it* you do not know-*how* to test this time? **⁵⁷** And why also are you not judging the right *thing* from yourselves? **⁵⁸** For as you are going with your adversary to the magistrate, make *an* effort on the way to be released from him, so that he may not perhaps drag you before the judge, and the judge will hand you over *to* the bailiff, and the bailiff will throw you into prison. **⁵⁹** I say *to* you, you will by no means come out from there until you pay even the last leptosᴬ".

Unless You Repent, You Will Perish

13:1 And some were present at the very time, reporting *to* Him about the Galileans whose blood Pilate mixed with their sacrifices. **²** And having responded, He said *to* them, "Do you think that these Galileans were sinners more than all the Galileans, because they have suffered these *things*? **³** No, I say *to* you. But unless you repent, you will all likewise perish. **⁴** Or those eighteen on whom the tower in Siloam fell and killed them— do you think that **they** were debtorsᴮ more than all the people dwelling in Jerusalem? **⁵** No, I say *to* you. But unless you repent, you will all similarly perish".

If The Tree Does Not Bear Fruit, It Will Be Cut Down

⁶ And He was telling this parable— "*A* certain *one* had *a* fig tree having been planted in his vineyard. And he came seeking fruit on it, and did not find *it.* **⁷** And he said to the vine-keeper, 'Behold— *it is* three years from which *time* I am coming seeking fruit on this fig tree, and I am not finding *it.* Therefore, cut it down! Why is it even using-upᶜ the soil?' **⁸** But the *one*, having responded, says *to* him, 'Master, leave it also this year, until I dig around it and throw manure. **⁹** And if it produces fruit in the future— otherwise indeed, cut it down' ".

Jesus Heals a Woman On The Sabbath. The Synagogue Official Objects

¹⁰ Now He was teaching in one *of* the synagogues on the Sabbath, **¹¹** and behold— *there was a* woman having *a* spirit *of*ᴰ infirmity eighteen years. And she was bending-over, and not being able to bend-up completely. **¹²** And having seen her, Jesus called to *her* and said *to* her, "Woman, you have been released *from* your infirmity". **¹³** And He laid *His* hands on her. And at-once she was made-straight. And she was glorifying God. **¹⁴** But having responded, the synagogue official— being indignant because Jesus cured *on* the Sabbath— was saying *to* the crowd that "There are six days on which *one* ought-to work. So be cured while coming on **them**, and not *on* the day *of* the Sabbath". **¹⁵** But the Lord responded *to* him and said, "Hypocrites! Does not each *of* you *on* the Sabbath release his ox or donkey from the mangerᴱ, and having led *it* away, water *it*? **¹⁶** But this *one, being a* daughter *of* Abraham whom Satan bound *for* behold, ten and eight years— ought *she* not to have been released from this bond *on* the day *of* the Sabbath?" **¹⁷** And while He *was* saying these *things*, all the *ones* being opposed *to* Him were being put-to-shame.

A. This is the smallest Jewish coin, 1/128th of a denarius. **B.** That is, to God. Sin produces a debt owed to God which must be paid. **C.** Or, wasting. **D.** That is, causing. **E.** That is, feeding-trough.

The Crowd Rejoices Over What Jesus Did. He Says, The Kingdom of God Starts Small
And the whole crowd was rejoicing over all the glorious *things* being done by Him. **18** Therefore, He was saying, "*To* what is the kingdom *of* God like, and *to* what shall I liken it? **19** It is like *a* seed *of a* mustard-plant which, having taken, *a* man threw into his *own* garden. And it grew and became *a* tree. And the birds *of* the heaven nested in its branches". **20** And again He said, "*To* what shall I liken the kingdom *of* God? **21** It is like leaven, which having taken, *a* woman concealedᴬ into three measures *of* wheat-flour until which *time the* whole *thing* was leavened".

Enter Through The Narrow Door Before It Is Too Late
22 And He was journeying-through according to cities and villages, teaching and making *the* journey to Jerusalem. **23** And someone said *to* Him, "Master, *are* the *ones* being saved few?" And the *One* said to them, **24** "Be striving to enter through the narrow door, because many, I say *to* you, will seek to enter, and will not be able. **25** From whatever *time* the house-master arises and shuts the door, and you begin to stand outside and to be knocking on the door saying 'Master, open *for* us', and having responded, he will say *to* you, 'I do not know you, where you are from'— **26** then you will begin to say, 'We ate and drank in your presence, and you taught on our wide-roads'. **27** And he will speak, saying *to* you, 'I do not know you— where you are from. Depart from me, all *you* workers *of* unrighteousness'. **28** In that place, there will be the weeping and the grinding *of* teeth when you shall see Abraham and Isaac and Jacob and all the prophets in the kingdom *of* God, but you being thrown outside. **29** And they will come from east and west, and from north and south, and lie back [to eat] in the kingdom *of* God. **30** And behold— there are last *ones* who will be first, and there are first *ones* who will be last".

Jesus Proceeds Away From Herod, Because a Prophet Cannot Perish Outside Jerusalem
31 At the very hour, some Pharisees came to *Him*, saying *to* Him, "Go out, and proceed from here, because Herodᴮ wants to kill You". **32** And He said *to* them, "Having gone, tell this fox, 'Behold— I am casting-out demons and performingᶜ healings today and tomorrow, and *on* the third *day* I come-to-the-endᴰ'. **33** Nevertheless, I must proceed today and tomorrow and the next *day*, because it cannot-be *that a* prophet *should* perish outside *of* Jerusalem. **34** Jerusalem, Jerusalem, the *one* killing the prophets and stoning the *ones* having been sent to her. How often I wanted to gather-together your children the way *a* hen *does* her *own* brood under *her* wings, and you did not want *it*. **35** Behold— your house is being left *to* you. And I say *to* you, you will by no means see Me untilᴱ *the time* will come when you say, 'Blessed *is* the *One* coming in *the* name *of the* Lord' ".

At The House of a Pharisee, Jesus Heals a Man With Dropsy On The Sabbath
14:1 And it came about at His going into *the* house *of* one *of* the leaders *of* the Pharisees *on a* Sabbath to eat bread, that **they** were closely-watching Him. **2** And behold— *a* certain man in front of Him was suffering-from-dropsy. **3** And having responded, Jesus spoke to the Law-experts and Pharisees, saying, "Is it lawful to cure *on* the Sabbath, or not?" **4** But

---

A. Or, hid in. See Mt 13:33. **B.** That is, Herod Antipas. See Mt 14:1. **C.** Or, finishing. **D.** That is, come to the completion of My work. I will finish My work here and leave. Jesus will not alter His divine schedule based on Herod's threats. Or, come to the end of My life, be perfected. In this case the three days refers to the brief time before Jesus dies. Or, come to My goal, reach My goal. **E.** See 19:38.

the *ones* were quiet. And having taken-hold-of *him*, He healed him, and sent *him* away.
5 And He said to them, "Whose son or ox *of* yours will fall into *a* well, and he will not immediately pull him up on *the* day *of* the Sabbath?" **6** And they were not able to answer-back to these *things*.

Jesus Says To The Ones Invited, Humble Yourself. Wait On The One Who Invited You
7 And He was speaking *a* parable[A] to the *ones* having been invited, fixing-*His*-attention-on[B] how they were choosing the places-of-honor, saying to them— **8** "Whenever you are invited by someone to wedding-celebrations, do not lie down [to eat] in the place-of-honor lest *a* more distinguished *one than* you may have been invited by him, **9** and having come, the *one* having invited you and him will say *to* you, 'Give *your* place *to* this *one*', and then you will begin to hold the last place with shame. **10** But whenever you are invited, having gone, fall back [to eat] in the last place, so that when the *one* having invited you comes, he will say *to* you, 'Friend, move up higher'. Then there will be glory *for* you in the presence of all the *ones* reclining back with you [to eat]. **11** Because everyone exalting himself will be humbled. And the *one* humbling himself will be exalted".

Jesus Says To The One Who Invited Him, Serve Those Who Cannot Repay
12 And He was also saying to the *one* having invited Him, "Whenever you make *a* morning-meal[C] or *a* dinner, do not be calling your friends, nor your brothers, nor your relatives, nor rich neighbors— that **they** also might not perhaps invite you in return, and it become *a* repayment[D] *to* you. **13** But whenever you make *a* reception, be inviting poor *ones*, crippled *ones*, lame *ones*, blind *ones*, **14** and you will be blessed because they do not have *the means* to repay you. For it will be repaid *to* you at the resurrection *of* the righteous".

When The Invited Are Not Willing To Come, The Uninvited Will Be Welcomed
15 And one *of* the *ones* reclining back with *Him* [to eat], having heard these *things,* said *to* Him, "Blessed *is* whoever will eat bread in the kingdom *of* God!" **16** But the *One* said *to* him— "*A* certain man was making *a* great dinner, and he invited many. **17** And he sent-out his slave *at* the hour *of* the dinner to say *to* the *ones* having been invited, 'Come, because it is already prepared'. **18** And they all alike began to excuse-*themselves.* The first said *to* him, 'I bought *a* field. And I have *a* necessity, having gone out, to see it. I ask you, have me excused'. **19** And another said, 'I bought five pair[E] *of* oxen, and I am proceeding to test them. I ask you, have me excused'. **20** And another said, 'I married *a* woman, and for this reason I am not able to come'. **21** And having come, the slave reported these *things to* his master. Then, having become-angry[F], the house-master said *to* his slave, 'Go out quickly into the wide-roads[G] and lanes[H] *of* the city, and bring in here the poor *ones* and crippled *ones* and blind *ones* and lame *ones*'. **22** And the slave said, 'Master, what you commanded has been done, and there is still room'. **23** And the master said to the slave, 'Go out to the roads[I] and

---

A. Note that what follows is a parable aimed at the Pharisees, not a lesson on manners. **B.** Or more mildly, 'noting'. **C.** Or, luncheon. **D.** In such a case, you have your reward in full. **E.** Or, yoke, team. **F.** Or, become-wrathful. **G.** Or, main streets, broad ways. **H.** Or, narrow streets, alleys. **I.** Or, paths.

fences, and compel[A] *them* to come in, in order that my house may be filled. **24** For I say *to* you[B] *all* that none *of* those men having been invited will taste my dinner' ".

Carry Your Own Cross And Follow Me. Calculate The Cost First

25 And large crowds were proceeding-with Him. And having turned, He said to them, **26** "If anyone comes to Me and does not hate his *own* father and mother and wife and children and brothers and sisters, and furthermore, even his *own* life, he cannot be My disciple. **27** Whoever is not carrying his *own* cross[C] and coming after Me, cannot be My disciple. **28** For which of you wanting to build *a* tower does not first, having sat-*down*, calculate the cost *to see* whether he has *enough* for *the* completion?— **29** in order that he having laid *a* foundation and not being able to finish *it* out, all the *ones* observing may not perhaps begin to mock him, **30** saying that 'This man began to build and was not able to finish *it* out!' **31** Or what king going to engage another king in battle will not, having sat-*down* first, deliberate whether he is able with ten thousand *men* to meet[D] the *one* coming against him with twenty thousand? **32** Otherwise indeed, *the one coming* still being far away— *the king*, having sent-forth *a* delegation, asks the *things* for peace. **33** So therefore, any of you who is not saying-goodbye[E] *to* all his possessions cannot be My disciple. **34** Therefore, salt *is* good. But if indeed the salt should become-tasteless, with what will it be seasoned? **35** It is fit neither for soil nor for *the* manure-pile. They throw it outside. Let the *one* having ears to hear, hear".

Parables For Sinners And Pharisees

15:1 Now all the tax-collectors and the sinners were drawing-near *to* Him to hear Him. **2** And both the Pharisees and the scribes were grumbling, saying that "This *One* is welcoming sinners and eating with them".

The Lost Sheep And Lost Coin: Heaven Rejoices When a Sinner Repents

3 And He spoke this parable to them, saying **4** "What man from-*among* you having *a* hundred sheep and having lost one of them, does not leave-behind the ninety nine in the wilderness and proceed after the *one* having become-lost until he finds it? **5** And having found *it*, he puts *it* on his shoulders, rejoicing. **6** And having come to the house, he calls-together *his* friends and neighbors, saying *to* them, 'Rejoice-with me, because I found my lost sheep!' **7** I say *to* you that in this manner there will be joy in heaven over one sinner repenting *more*-than[F] over ninety nine righteous *ones* who have no need *of* repentance. **8** Or what woman having ten drachmas[G], if she loses one drachma, does not light *a* lamp and sweep the house and seek carefully until which *time* she finds *it*? **9** And having found *it*, she calls together *her women* friends and neighbors, saying, 'Rejoice-with me, because I found the drachma which I lost!' **10** In this manner, I say *to* you, joy comes-about in the presence of the angels *of* God over one sinner repenting".

A. Persuade them it is a serious offer. **B.** This word is plural. **C.** That is, the instrument of his own death, symbolizing his death to self and this world. **D.** That is, successfully engage. **E.** Or, bidding-farewell. The disciple's habit of life must be one of separating himself or herself from possessions to take hold of real life (1 Tim 6:19). **F.** Or, *rather*-than. **G.** A drachma is a Greek coin equivalent to the Roman denarius. It is one day's wage for a laborer.

The Prodigal Son: The Father Rejoices When His Lost Son Returns

11 And He said, "*A* certain man had two sons. **12** And the younger *of* them said *to his* father, 'Father, give me the part *of your* substance^A falling to *me*'. And the *one* distributed^B *his* property *to* them. **13** And after not many days, having gathered together everything, the younger son went-on-a-journey to *a* distant country. And there he squandered his substance living wildly. **14** And he having spent everything, *a* severe famine came about in relation to that country, and **he** began to be-in-need. **15** And having gone, he joined *himself to* one *of* the citizens *of* that country. And he sent him into his fields to feed pigs. **16** And he was desiring to be filled-to-satisfaction with the carob-pods which the pigs were eating. And no one was giving *anything to* him. **17** But having come to himself, he said, 'How many hired-workers *of* my father *are* abounding^C *with* bread, but **I** am perishing^D here *in a* famine! **18** Having arisen, I will proceed to my father and say *to* him, "Father, I sinned against heaven and in your sight. **19** I am no longer worthy to be called your son. Make me as one *of* your hired-workers"'. **20** And having arisen, he went to his father. But he still being far distant, his father saw him and felt-deep-feelings [of love]. And having run, he fell upon his neck and kissed him. **21** And the son said *to* him, 'Father, I sinned against heaven and in your sight. I am no longer worthy to be called your son'. **22** But the father said to his slaves, 'Quickly, bring-out the best robe and put *it* on him. And give *him a* ring for his hand and sandals for the feet. **23** And bring the fatted calf. Slaughter *it*. And having eaten, let us celebrate! **24** Because **this** son *of* mine was dead, and he became-alive-again. He had become-lost, and he was found'. And they began to celebrate.

The Older Brother Is Angered By His Father's Joy

25 "Now his older son was in *the* field. And when while coming he drew-near *to* the house, he heard music and dancing. **26** And having summoned one *of* the servants, he was inquiring *as to* what these *things* might be. **27** And the *one* said *to* him that 'Your brother has come. And your father slaughtered the fatted calf because he received him back being healthy'. **28** And he became-angry, and was not willing to go in. And his father, having come out, was appealing-to him. **29** But the *one*, having responded, said *to* his father, 'Behold— I am slaving *for* you *for* so many years, and I never disregarded your command. And you never gave **me** *a* goat in order that I might celebrate with my friends. **30** But when this **son** *of* **yours** came— the *one* having devoured your property with prostitutes— you slaughtered the fatted calf *for* him!' **31** And the *one* said *to* him, 'Child, **you** are always with me, and all my *things* are yours. **32** But it-was-necessary to celebrate and rejoice, because this **brother** *of* **yours** was dead, and he became-alive. And *he had* become-lost, and he was found'".

The Unrighteous Steward: Use Earthly Money For Heavenly Gain

16:1 And He was also saying to the disciples, "There was *a* certain rich man who had *a* steward^E. And this *one* was accused *to* him as squandering his possessions. **2** And having called him, he said *to* him, 'What *is* this I am hearing about you? Render the

---

A. Or, property, estate. **B.** Or, divided. One third went to the younger son; two thirds to the older, Deut 21:17. **C.** Or, having leftovers *of*. **D.** Or, losing-*myself*. This is another form of the key word 'lost' found in all three parables in chapter 15. **E.** Or, household manager, administrator.

account *of* your stewardship, for you can no longer be steward'. **³** And the steward said within himself, 'What should I do, because my master is taking-away the stewardship^A from me? I am not strong-*enough* to dig. I am ashamed to beg. **⁴** I know what I will do so that they will welcome me into their houses when I am removed from the stewardship'. **⁵** And having summoned each one *of* the debtors *of* his master, he was saying *to* the first, 'How much do you owe *to* my master?' **⁶** And the *one* said, '*A* hundred baths^B *of* olive-oil'. And the *one* said *to* him, 'Take your writings^C, and having sat-*down* quickly, write fifty'. **⁷** Then he said *to* another, 'And you, how much do you owe?' And the *one* said, '*A* hundred cor^D *of* wheat'. He says *to* him, 'Take your writings, and write eighty'. **⁸** And the master praised the unrighteous steward because he acted shrewdly^E. Because the sons *of*^F this age are more shrewd in-relation-to their *own* kind than the sons *of* the light. **⁹** And **I** say *to* you— make friends *for* yourselves by means of unrighteous wealth, so that when it fails^G they^H will welcome you into the eternal dwellings. **¹⁰** The *one* trustworthy^I in *a* very-little *thing* is also trustworthy in much. And the *one* unrighteous in *a* very little *thing* is also unrighteous in much. **¹¹** Therefore if you did not prove-to-be trustworthy with unrighteous wealth, who will entrust the true^J *thing to* you? **¹²** And if you did not prove-to-be trustworthy with the *thing* belonging to another^K, who will give you your *own thing*? **¹³** No household-servant can be serving^L two masters. For either he will hate^M the one and love the other, or he will be devoted to one and disregard the other. You cannot be serving God and wealth^N".

Jesus Rebukes The Pharisees: The Thing You Highly Value Is Worthless To God
¹⁴ Now the Pharisees, being money-lovers, were listening-to all these *things,* and they were sneering-at^O Him. **¹⁵** And He said *to* them, "**You** are the *ones* declaring yourselves righteous in the sight of people, but God knows your hearts— because the highly-*valued thing* among people *is an* abomination^P in the sight of God. **¹⁶** The Law and the Prophets *were* until John. From that time *on*, the kingdom *of* God is being announced-as-good-news, and everyone is forcing-*himself*^Q into it. **¹⁷** But it is easier *that* the heaven and the earth *should* pass away than *that* one stroke^R *of* the Law *should* fail. **¹⁸** Everyone sending-away^S his wife and marrying another is committing-adultery. And the *one* marrying *one* having been sent-away from *her* husband is committing-adultery.

The Rich Man And Lazarus: What God Values Is What Matters
¹⁹ "Now there was *a* certain rich man. And he was dressing *himself* in purple and fine-linen, radiantly enjoying-himself daily. **²⁰** And *a* certain poor *man,* Lazarus

---

A. That is, position of management responsibility. **B.** A bath was a liquid measure ranging from 5 to 10 gallons (21-39 liters). **C.** Or more specifically, records, receipts, accounts. **D.** This dry measure ranged from 6 to 11 bushels (50-90 gallons; 220-393 liters). **E.** The point is that he used the resources his master entrusted to him to create a new life for himself. We are to do likewise with regard to our coming heavenly life, v 9. **F.** That is, belonging to. **G.** Or, gives-out, comes-to-an-end. **H.** That is, the ones affected by your generosity who have passed on before you; or, God's angels. **I.** Or, faithful. **J.** Or, genuine, real. **K.** That is, God. Our present things are God's resources entrusted to us. **L.** That is, be serving-as-slave to. **M:** hate... disregard. See Mt 6:24. **N.** Or, property, money. **O.** The idea of spending now to build up treasures then always seems foolish to those outside God's family. **P.** Or, detestable. **Q.** That is, trying to force his way into it, whether on God's terms or not. **R.** See Mt 5:18. **S.** That is, divorcing. This is an example of the difference in values mentioned in v 15, and a law that will not fail in v 17.

by name, had been put at his gate— having been covered-with-sores, [21] and desiring to be filled-to-satisfaction by the *things* falling from the table *of* the rich *man*. Even[A] indeed the dogs coming were licking his sores. [22] And it came about *that* the poor *man* died and he was carried-away by the angels to the bosom *of* Abraham. And the rich *man* also died and was buried. [23] And having lifted-up his eyes in Hades while being in torments, he sees Abraham from a-distance, and Lazarus in his bosom[B]. [24] And **he**, having called, said, 'Father Abraham, have-mercy-on me and send Lazarus in order that he may dip the tip *of* his finger *in* water and cool-off my tongue, because I am suffering-pain in this flame'. [25] But Abraham said, 'Child, remember that during your life you received your good *things*, and likewise Lazarus the bad *things*. But now, here, he is being comforted and **you** are suffering-pain. [26] And in all these *regions*, *a* great chasm has been fixed[C] between us and you[D], so that the *ones* wanting to cross from here to you are not able, nor may they cross-over from there to us'. [27] And he said, 'Then I ask you, father, that you send him to the house *of* my father— [28] for I have five brothers— so that he may solemnly-warn them in order that **they** also might not come to this place *of* torment'. [29] But Abraham says, 'They have Moses and the Prophets. Let them listen-to them'. [30] But the *one* said, 'No, father Abraham. But if someone goes to them from *the* dead, they will repent'. [31] But he said *to* him, 'If they do not listen-to Moses and the Prophets, neither will they be persuaded if someone rises-up from *the* dead' ".

Woe To The One Who Causes Others To Fall. Rebuke Sin In Your Brother. Forgive
17:1 And He said to His disciples, "It is impossible *that* the causes-of-falling *should* not[E] come. Nevertheless, woe *to the one* through whom they come. [2] It *would* be better *for* him if *a* mill's stone were lying-around his neck and he had been[F] thrown-off into the sea, than that he should cause one *of* these[G] little *ones* to fall. [3] Take heed to yourselves— If your brother sins, rebuke him. And if he repents, forgive him. [4] And if he sins against you seven times *in* the day, and returns to you seven times saying 'I repent', forgive him".

The Apostles Ask For More Faith. The Smallest Amount Is Enough
[5] The apostles said *to* the Lord, "Increase faith *for* us". [6] And the Lord said, "If you have faith like *a* seed[H] *of a* mustard-plant, you would say *to* this mulberry-tree, 'Be uprooted and be planted in the sea', and it would have obeyed you. [7] And who from-among you *is there* who, having *a* slave plowing or shepherding, will say *to* him having come in from the field, 'Immediately having come-to *the table*, fall back [to eat]!'? [8] But will he not say *to* him, 'Prepare something I may have-for-dinner. And

---

A. That is, Lazarus received help only from passers-by, even the dogs cleaning his sores. Or, But even. That is, Lazarus desired to be filled, but even the dogs tormented him. **B.** Same word as earlier, but plural. That is, at his side; or, in his folds (of the garment, as in 6:38), in his lap. This is a reference either to a loving expression of comfort (v 25) and welcome, or to a place of honor. **C.** Or, set, established. **D.** This word is plural. **E.** This is stated positively in Mt 18:7. **F.** Better to be once and for all dead at the bottom of the sea than to do this and face the eternal consequences. **G.** That is, such insignificant ones as Lazarus and the sinners and tax collectors in the audience (15:1) disdained by the Pharisees, assuming 15:1 to 17:10 was spoken on a single occasion; otherwise, those confronted by the causes of falling mentioned in v 1. **H.** That is, the tiniest amount of faith is enough because God does the work, not you.

having girded-*yourself*, be serving me until I eat and drink. And after these *things*, **you** will eat and drink'? **9** He does not have gratitude^A *for* the slave because he did the *things* having been commanded, *does he*? **10** So also you, when you do all the *things* having been commanded *to* you, be saying that 'We are unprofitable^B slaves. We have done what we were obligated to do' ".

Jesus Heals Ten Lepers. One Returns To Give Thanks

11 And it came about during the proceeding to Jerusalem that **He** was going through *the* midst *of* Samaria and Galilee. **12** And while He *was* entering into *a* certain village, ten leprous men met Him, who stood at-a-distance. **13** And **they** lifted *their* voice, saying, "Jesus, Master, have-mercy-on us!" **14** And having seen *them*, He said *to* them, "Having gone, show yourselves *to* the priests". And it came about during their going *that* they were cleansed. **15** And one of them, having seen that he was healed, returned glorifying God with *a* loud voice. **16** And he fell on *his* face at His feet while giving-thanks *to* Him. And **he** was *a* Samaritan. **17** And having responded, Jesus said, "*Were* not ten cleansed? But where *are* the nine? **18** Were none found having returned to give glory *to* God except this foreigner?" **19** And He said *to* him, "Having arisen, go. Your faith has restored you".

Jesus Is Asked When The Kingdom Is Coming. The Kingdom Is Within You

20 And having been asked by the Pharisees when the kingdom *of* God is coming, He responded *to* them and said, "The kingdom *of* God is not coming with observation^C, **21** nor will they say, 'Behold— here *it is*', or, 'There *it is*'. For behold— the kingdom *of* God is within^D you".

The Coming of The Son Will Be Like Lightning

22 And He said to the disciples, "Days will come when you will desire to see one *of* the days *of* the Son *of* Man, and you will not see *it*. **23** And they will say *to* you, 'Behold— there *He is*', or, 'Behold— here *He is*'. Do not go, nor pursue *them*. **24** For just like the lightning flashing out of the *one part* under heaven shines^E to the *other part* under heaven, so will the Son *of* Man be in His day. **25** But first He must suffer many *things* and be rejected by this generation.

The Coming of The Son Will Be Like The Days of Noah And Lot

26 "And as it happened in the days *of* Noah [in Gen 6-7], so it will be also in the days *of* the Son *of* Man— **27** they were eating, drinking, marrying, being given-in-marriage, until which day^F Noah entered into the ark and the flood came and destroyed everyone. **28** Likewise, just as it happened in the days *of* Lot [in Gen 19]— they were eating, drinking, buying, selling, planting, building. **29** But *on* the day Lot departed from Sodom, it rained fire and sulphur from heaven and destroyed everyone. **30** It will be^G the same *way* on the day the Son *of* Man is revealed. **31** On that day, let he who will be on the housetop and his things in the house not go down to take them. And

---

A. Or, thankfulness. **B.** No matter how far our faith in action extends, we are unable to bring our Master any gain exceeding His investment in us. **C.** Or, close-watching. That is, with physically observable changes to this world. Later Jesus will say 'My kingdom is not of this world'. **D.** Or, inside. This may have an individual sense (in your hearts) or a national sense (among you, in your midst). **E.** That is, it will be visible to everyone. **F.** That is, life was going on as normal, and God suddenly and unexpectedly intervened into human history. **G.** Or, happen.

let the *one* in *a* field likewise not turn-back to the *things* behind. ³² Remember Lot's
wife. ³³ Whoever seeks to preserve his life will lose it. But whoever loses *it* will keep
it alive. ³⁴ I say *to* you, *on* this night there will be two *people*ᴬ on one bed— the one
will be takenᴮ, and the other will be left. ³⁵ There will be two *women* grinding at the
same *place*— the one will be taken, and the other will be left. ³⁶ ᶜ   ³⁷ And having
responded, they say *to* Him, "Where, Lord?" And the *One* said *to* them, "Whereᴰ the
body *is*, there alsoᴱ the vultures will be gathered-together".

Pray And Don't Lose Heart: God Will Avenge His People
18:1 And He was speaking *a* parable *to* them with-regard-toᶠ *it* being necessary *that*
they always be praying and not losing-heart, ² saying, "There was in *a* certain city *a*
certain judge not fearing God and not having-regard-forᴳ *the* person. ³ And there was
a widow in that city. And she was coming to him, saying, 'Avengeᴴ me from my
adversary'. ⁴ And he was not willing for *a* time. But after these *things*, he said within
himself, 'Even though I do not fear God nor have regard for *the* person, ⁵ yet because
of this widow's causing me trouble, I will avenge her— in order that she, while
continuallyᴵ coming, may not be wearing me out' ". ⁶ And the Lord said, "Listen-to
what the unrighteous judge is sayingᴶ. ⁷ And shall not God execute vengeanceᴷ *for*
His chosen *ones*— the *ones* crying-out *to* Him by day and by night and He is being
patientᴸ with them? ⁸ I say *to* you that He will execute vengeance *for* them quickly.
However, the Son *of* Man having come, will He find faithᴹ on the earth?"

Two Men In Prayer: One Exalts Himself, The Other Begs For Mercy
⁹ And He also spoke this parable to some putting-confidence upon themselves that they
were righteous, and treating the rest with contempt— ¹⁰ "Two men went up to the temple
to pray: the one *a* Pharisee, and the other *a* tax-collector. ¹¹ The Pharisee, having stoodᴺ,
was praying these *things* toᴼ himself: 'God, I thank You that I am not just-like the rest *of*
the people— swindlers, unrighteous *ones*, adulterers, or even like this tax collector. ¹² I fast
twice *a* week. I give-a-tenth-of all that I get'. ¹³ But the tax collector, standing at-a-distance,
was not willing even to lift-up *his* eyes to heaven, but was striking his chest, saying, 'God,
be mercifulᴾ *to* me, the sinner!' ¹⁴ I say *to* you, this *one* went-downᑫ to his house having
been declared-righteous, rather-than that *one*. Because everyone exalting himself will be
humbled, but the *one* humbling himself will be exalted".

A. Jesus is referring to a nighttime scene here, and a daytime scene next. Or, *men*, if Jesus is also referring to
men here and women next. **B:** taken... left. See Mt 24:41. **C.** Some manuscripts add 'Two men *will be* in *a*
field— one will be taken and the other will be left'. **D.** See Mt 24:28. **E.** Or, indeed. **F.** Or, so-as *to show them
that* they must always. **G.** Or, respecting. This judge followed his own mind. **H.** Or, Grant me justice. Depending
on the issue, this widow could mean 'Punish him for his crime', 'Protect me from his attack', or, 'Make him
fulfill his contract'. **I.** Or, while coming she may not be completely (or, eventually) wearing me out. **J.** The
judge is saying he will answer because of her continual coming and persistent asking. **K.** Or, punishment.
L. Unlike the unrighteous judge who only answered out of impatience, God is patient with those crying out to
Him. Or, and He is delaying [to act] for them? (from their point of view). Or, night? And is He delaying over
them? **M.** Or, faithfulness. Lit, the faith. That is, the faith spoken of in this parable, which prays and does not
lose heart; or more broadly, a true faith in God that would act in this way. No answer is implied by the grammar
of the question. **N.** Or, stood by himself, was praying these *things*. **O.** Or, with-reference-to. **P.** Lit, be propitiated
to me. That is, turn away your wrath from me, and thus, be merciful to me, forgive me, pardon me. **Q.** The
temple was 'up', v 10.

Permit The Children To Come, For of Such Is The Kingdom of God

15 And they were also[A] bringing babies[B] to Him in order that He might touch them. But having seen *it*, the disciples were rebuking them[C]. **16** But Jesus summoned them[D], saying, "Permit the children to be coming to Me, and do not be forbidding them. For the kingdom *of* God is *of* [E] such *ones*. **17** Truly I say *to* you, whoever does not receive the kingdom *of* God like *a* child will never enter into it".

A Rich Ruler Asks What To Do To Inherit Life. Sell All You Have And Follow Me

18 And *a* certain ruler questioned Him, saying, "Good Teacher, [by] having done what shall I inherit eternal life?" **19** And Jesus said *to* him, "Why do you call Me good? No one *is* good except One— God. **20** You know the commandments: 'Do not commit-adultery, do not murder, do not steal, do not give-false-testimony, be honoring your father and mother' ". **21** And the *one* said, "I kept these all from *my* youth". **22** And having heard *it*, Jesus said *to* him, "One *thing* is still lacking *for* you— Sell all that you have and distribute *it to* poor *ones*, and you will have treasure in the heavens. And come, be following Me". **23** But the *one*, having heard these *things*, became deeply-grieved. For he was extremely rich. **24** And having seen him having become deeply grieved, Jesus said, "How difficultly the *ones* having wealth come into the kingdom *of* God. **25** For it is easier *that a* camel enter through *an* opening *of a* needle than[F] *that a* rich *one* enter into the kingdom *of* God".

All Who Leave Behind Anything For Me Will Receive Back Many Times As Much

26 And the *ones* having heard *it* said, "Who indeed can be saved?" **27** And the *One* said, "The *things* impossible with humans are possible with God". **28** And Peter said, "Behold— **we**, having left *our* own *things,* followed You". **29** And the *One* said *to* them, "Truly I say *to* you[G] *all* that there is no one who left house or wife or brothers or parents or children for the sake *of* the kingdom *of* God, **30** who will by any means not receive back many-times-as-much in this time, and in the coming age— eternal life".

Jesus Predicts His Death And Resurrection

31 And having taken aside the twelve, He said to them, "Behold— we are going up to Jerusalem. And all the *things* having been written by the prophets *for* the Son *of* Man will be fulfilled. **32** For He will be handed-over *to* the Gentiles. And He will be mocked and mistreated and spit-on. **33** And having whipped *Him*, they will kill Him. And *on* the third day, He will rise-up". **34** And **they** understood none *of* these *things*. Indeed this statement had been hidden from them, and they were not coming-to-know[H] the *things* being said.

A Blind Man Begs Mercy From The Messiah, And Receives His Sight

35 And it came about during His drawing-near to Jericho, *that a* certain blind *one* was sitting beside the road, begging. **36** And having heard *a* crowd proceeding through, he was inquiring *as to* what this might be. **37** And they reported *to* him that "Jesus the Nazarene is passing by". **38** And he shouted, saying, "Jesus, Son *of* David, have-mercy-on me!" **39** And the *ones* preceding *Him* were rebuking him in order that he might be silent. But **he** was crying out *by* much more, "Son *of* David, have mercy on me!" **40** And

---

A. Or, even. **B.** Or, infants. **C.** That is, the ones bringing the babies. **D.** That is, the babies. **E.** That is, made up of; or, belonging to. **F.** That is, it is impossible apart from God, as Jesus says next. **G.** This word is plural. **H.** Or, understanding.

having stood [still], Jesus ordered *that* he be brought to Him. And he having drawn near, He asked him, **41** "What do you want Me to do *for* you?" **42** And the *one* said, "Master— that I may see-again!" And Jesus said *to* him, "See-again! Your faith has restored you". **43** And at once he saw-again. And he was following Him, glorifying God. And all the people, having seen *it,* gave praise *to* God.

Salvation Comes To a Rich Tax Collector Named Zacchaeus

19:1 And having entered, he was going through Jericho. **2** And behold— *there was a* man being called *by the* name Zacchaeus. And **he** was *a* chief-tax-collector. And **he** *was* rich. **3** And he was seeking to see Who Jesus was. And he was not able because of the crowd, because he was short *in* stature. **4** And having run ahead to the *place* in front, he went up on *a* sycamore-tree in order that he might see Him, because He was going to come through that *way.* **5** And when He came upon the place, having looked-up, Jesus said to him, "Zacchaeus, having hurried, come down. For today I must stay at your house". **6** And having hurried, he came down and received[A] Him, rejoicing. **7** And having seen *it,* they all were grumbling, saying that "He went in to take-up-lodging with *a* sinful man". **8** And having stood[B], Zacchaeus said to the Lord, "Behold, Master— I am giving **half** *of* **my possessions** *to* the poor. And if I extorted anything *from* anyone, I am giving *it* back fourfold". **9** And Jesus said with-regard-to[C] him that "Today salvation came[D] *to* this house, because even[E] **he** is *a* son *of* Abraham. **10** For the Son *of* Man came to seek and to save the lost".

The Parable of The Minas: Do Business With The Resources I Have Given You

11 And while they *were* listening-to these *things,* having proceeded [to speak further], He spoke *a* parable because of His being near Jerusalem and their thinking[F] that the kingdom *of* God was about to appear[G] at-once. **12** Therefore He said, "*A* certain well-born[H] man traveled to *a* distant country to receive *a* kingdom *for* himself, and to return. **13** And having called ten *of* his *own* slaves, he gave them ten minas[I] and said to them,'Do business while I am coming'. **14** But his citizens were hating him, and they sent-forth *a* delegation after him, saying, 'We do not want this *one* to be-king over us'. **15** And it came about at his return, having received the kingdom, that he said *that* these slaves *to* whom he had given the money *should* be called *to* him in order that he might come-to-know what they gained-through-doing-business. **16** And the first *one* arrived, saying, 'Master, your mina earned ten minas'. **17** And he said *to* him, 'Very-well *done,* good slave. Because you proved-to-be faithful[J] in *a* very-little *thing*— be having authority over ten cities'. **18** And the second *one* came, saying, 'Your mina, master, made five minas'. **19** And he said also *to* this *one,* 'And **you**— be over five cities'. **20** And the other *one* came, saying, 'Master, behold your mina, which I was holding, laying-away in *a* handkerchief. **21** For I was fearing you, because you are *a* harsh[K] man. You take-up[L] what you did not lay-*down,* and you reap what you did not sow'. **22** He says *to* him, 'I will judge you out of your *own* mouth, evil slave. You

---

A. That is, as a guest in his house. **B.** That is, in his house, perhaps at the meal. Or, having stopped, if the setting for this is on the road after leaving the house. **C.** Or, to him; that is, to Zacchaeus, but addressing all present. **D.** Or, came-about *in.* **E.** Or, he also. **F.** Or, supposing, presuming. **G.** Or, come-into-sight. **H.** Or, noble, socially important. **I.** A mina is equivalent to 100 denarii (100 days' wages for a laborer). **J.** Or, trustworthy. **K.** Or, strict, exacting. The slave blames his inaction on the master. Because of the way you are, I did nothing. **L.** In a banking sense, this means you withdraw what you did not deposit. You expect a return beyond your investment!

knew that **I** am *a* harsh man, taking up what I did not lay-*down* and reaping what I did not sow[A]! **²³** And for what reason did you not give my money *to be* on *a* [banker's] table, and **I**, having come, would have collected it with interest?' **²⁴** And he said *to* the *ones* standing-near, 'Take the mina away from him and give *it to* the *one* having the ten minas'. **²⁵** And they said *to* him, 'Master, he has ten minas [already]'. **²⁶** I say *to* you that *to* everyone having, it will be given. But from the *one* not having, even what he has will be taken away. **²⁷** However, bring here these enemies *of* mine— the *ones* not having wanted me to be king over them— and slay them in front of me".

Jesus Goes Up To Jerusalem
²⁸ And having said these *things*, He was proceeding ahead, going up to Jerusalem.

He Enters Jerusalem Riding a Colt, To The Praise of The People. He Weeps Over The City
²⁹ And it came about when He drew-near to Bethphage and Bethany— near the mountain being called '*of* Olives'— *that* He sent-forth two *of* the disciples, **³⁰** saying, "Go to the village before *you,* in which while proceeding you will find *a* colt having been tied on which none[B] *of* mankind ever sat. And having untied it, bring *it.* **³¹** And if someone asks you, 'For what reason are you untying *it*?', thus you shall say— that[C] 'The Lord has need *of* it' ". **³²** And having gone, the *ones* having been sent-forth found *it* just as He said *to* them. **³³** And while they *were* untying the colt, its owners said to them, "Why are you untying the colt?" **³⁴** And the *ones* said that "The Lord has need *of* it". **³⁵** And they brought it to Jesus. And having cast their cloaks upon the colt, they put Jesus on *it.* **³⁶** And while He *was* proceeding, they were spreading their cloaks under *Him* in the road. **³⁷** And while He *was* drawing-near now[D], at the descent *of* the Mount *of* Olives, the whole crowd *of* the disciples began to praise God, rejoicing *with a* loud voice for all *the* miracles which they saw, **³⁸** saying, "Blessed *is* the King coming in *the* name *of the* Lord. Peace in heaven and glory in *the* highest [heavens]!" **³⁹** And some *of* the Pharisees from the crowd said to Him, "Teacher, rebuke Your disciples". **⁴⁰** And having responded, He said, "I say *to* you, if these will be silent, the stones will cry out!" **⁴¹** And when He drew-near, having seen the city, He wept over it, **⁴²** saying that "If you, even you, had known on this day the *things* for peace! But now[E] they were hidden from your eyes. **⁴³** Because days will come upon you— and your enemies will throw-up *a* palisade[F] *against* you, and encircle you, and confine you from all sides. **⁴⁴** And they will dash[G] you to the ground, and your children within you. And they will not leave *a* stone upon *a* stone within you, because you did not recognize the time *of* your visitation".

Jesus Throws The Merchandisers Out of The Temple. The Priests Seek To Destroy Him
⁴⁵ And having entered into the temple, He began to throw-out the *ones* selling, **⁴⁶** saying *to* them, "It has been written [in Isa 56:7]: 'And My house shall be *a* house *of* prayer'. But **you** made it *a* den *of* robbers[H]". **⁴⁷** And He was teaching daily in the temple. And the chief priests and the scribes and the leading *ones of* the people were seeking to destroy Him. **⁴⁸** And they were not finding what they might do, for all the people hung-on[I] Him, listening.

A. Or, sow? **B.** That is, no human. **C.** 'That' introduces the quotation, and would usually be omitted in English. Or, 'Because the Lord'. Same in v 34. **D.** Or, drawing-near, now at. **E.** Or, But as-it-is. **F.** Or, siege-work. This verse describes the centuries-old military strategy for attacking a walled city. Jesus is predicting Jerusalem would be attacked. Next He predicts the outcome. **G.** Or, raze. The reference is to buildings and people. **H.** Or, plunderers, bandits. **I.** Or, hung-on, listening-to Him.

The Priests Ask By What Authority He Does This. From Where Was John's Authority?
20:1 And it came about on one *of* the days while He *was* teaching the people in the temple and announcing-the-good-news, *that* the chief priests and the scribes with the elders stood-near. **2** And they spoke, saying to Him, "Tell us, by what-kind-of^A authority are You doing these *things*, or who is the *one* having given You this authority?" **3** And having responded, He said to them, "I also will ask you *a* thing, and you tell Me— **4** was the baptism *of* John from heaven, or from humans?" **5** And the *ones* reasoned with themselves, saying that "If we say, 'From heaven', He will say, 'For what reason did you not believe him?' **6** But if we say, 'From humans', all the people will stone us to death. For they are convinced *that* John is *a* prophet". **7** And they answered *that they did* not know from where *it was*. **8** And Jesus said *to* them, "Nor am **I** telling you by what-kind-of authority I am doing these *things*".

You Priests Are Like Farmers Who Killed The Owner's Messengers And His Son
9 And He began to tell this parable to the people: "*A* certain man planted *a* vineyard and rented it *to* farmers, and went-on-a-journey *for* considerable periods-of-time. **10** And *at harvest* time, he sent-forth *a* slave to the farmers so that they would give *to* him from the fruit *of* the vineyard. But the farmers sent him out empty-*handed*, having beaten *him*. **11** And he proceeded to send another slave. But the *ones,* having beaten and dishonored that *one* also, sent *him* out empty-*handed*. **12** And he proceeded to send *a* third. But the *ones* also threw out this *one*, having wounded *him*. **13** And the owner *of* the vineyard said, 'What shall I do? I will send my beloved son. Perhaps they will have-regard-for this *one*'. **14** But having seen him, the farmers were reasoning with one another, saying, 'This *one* is the heir. Let us kill him in order that the inheritance may become ours'. **15** And having thrown him outside *of* the vineyard, they killed *him*. Therefore, what will the owner *of* the vineyard do *to* them? **16** He will come and destroy these farmers, and give the vineyard *to* others". And having heard *it*, they said, "May it never be!"

But As It Is Written, The Stone The Builders Rejected Became The Cornerstone
17 But the *One*, having looked-at them, said, "Then what is this having been written [in Ps 118:22]: '*The* stone which the *ones* building rejected, this became *the* head^B *of the* corner'? **18** Everyone having fallen upon that stone will be broken-to-pieces. And^C upon whomever it may fall, it will crush^D him". **19** And the scribes and the chief priests sought to put *their* hands on Him at the very hour. And^E they feared the people. For they^F knew that He spoke this parable against them.

The Priests Try To Snare Jesus: Shall We Pay Taxes To Caesar?
20 And having closely-watched *Him*, they sent forth spies pretending themselves to be righteous, in order that they might take-hold-of *a* statement *of* His, so as to hand Him over *to* the rule and the authority *of* the governor. **21** And they questioned Him, saying, "Teacher, we know that You speak and teach correctly. And You do not receive^G the face, but You teach the way *of* God in accordance with truth. **22** Is it lawful *that* we *should* give *a* tribute^H *to* **Caesar**, or not?" **23** But having perceived their craftiness, He said to them, **24** "Show Me

---

A. Or, by what. That is, a prophet's authority? Messiah's? A teacher's? **B.** That is, the cornerstone of the foundation; or, the capstone of the arch. **C.** Or, But. **D.** See Mt 21:44. **E.** Or, And-*yet*. **F.** That is, the priests; or, the people. **G.** That is, show partiality. **H.** That is, a tax paid to a foreign state. Should we pay our Roman taxes?

a denarius^A. *Of* whom does it have *an* image^B and inscription?" And the *ones* said, "*Of* Caesar". **25** And the *One* said to them, "Well-then^C give-back^D the *things of* Caesar *to* Caesar, and the *things of* God *to* God". **26** And they were not able to take-hold-of *a* word *of* His in the presence *of* the people. And having marveled at His answer, they became silent.

Sadducees Question Jesus About The Resurrection of a Wife With Seven Husbands
27 And having come to *Him*, some *of* the Sadducees— the *ones* denying *that there* is *a* resurrection— questioned Him, **28** saying, "Teacher, Moses wrote *to* us [in Deut 25:5] *that* if *a* brother *of* someone dies having *a* wife, and this^E *one* is childless, that his brother should take the wife and raise-up-from *her a* seed^F *for* his brother. **29** So there were seven brothers. And the first, having taken *a* wife, died childless. **30** And the second. **31** And the third took her. And similarly, the seven also did not leave-behind children, and died. **32** Last, the woman also died. **33** The woman, therefore, at the resurrection— *of* which *of* them does she become *the* wife? For the seven had her *as* wife". **34** And Jesus said *to* them, "The sons *of*^G this age marry and are given-in-marriage. **35** But the *ones* having been considered-worthy to attain^H that age and the resurrection from *the* dead neither marry, nor are they given-in-marriage. **36** For they are not even still able to die, for they are angel-like^I. And they are sons^J *of* God, being sons *of*^K the resurrection. **37** But that the dead are raised, even Moses showed^L at the bush [in Ex 3:16]— when he calls *the* Lord the 'God *of* Abraham and God *of* Isaac and God *of* Jacob'. **38** Now He is not God *of* dead *ones*, but *of* living *ones*. For *to* Him all are alive". **39** And having responded, some *of* the scribes said, "Teacher, You spoke well". **40** For they were no longer daring to ask Him anything.

Jesus Asks How The Messiah Can Be The Son of David Since David Calls Him His Lord
41 And He said to them, "How *is it that* they say *that* the Christ is David's son? **42** For David himself says in *the* book *of* Psalms [110:1], '*The* Lord said *to* my Lord, "Be sitting on My right *side* **43** until I put Your enemies *as a* footstool *of* Your feet" '. **44** Therefore David calls Him 'Lord'. And how^M is He his son?"

Jesus Warns The Disciples To Beware of The Scribes
45 And while all the people *were* listening, He said *to* His disciples, **46** "Beware of the scribes— the *ones* delighting to walk around in robes, and loving greetings in the marketplaces and seats-of-honor in the synagogues and places-of-honor at the banquets; **47** who are devouring^N the houses *of* the widows, and praying long *for a* pretense. These *ones* will receive greater condemnation".

Jesus Uses The Widow's Offering To Illustrate True Giving
21:1 And having looked-up, He saw the rich *ones* throwing their gifts into the treasury^O. **2** And He saw *a* certain needy widow throwing two leptos^P there. **3** And He said, "Truly I say *to* you that this poor widow threw more *than* all. **4** For all these *ones* threw into the

---

A. This was a Roman silver coin, worth a day's wage for a laborer. **B.** Or, likeness. **C.** Or, So-indeed, Therefore. **D.** Or, render, pay. **E.** That is, the dead brother. **F.** Or, posterity. **G.** That is, belonging to. **H.** Or, obtain, gain, find, reach. **I.** That is, in the sense just stated. See Mt 22:30. **J.** That is, members of His family, not separate families. **K.** That is, originating in or proceeding from the resurrection to life. **L.** Or, indicated, made-known. **M.** If Messiah is David's own Lord, how can He be his distant physical descendant? **N.** That is, taking financial advantage. **O.** See Mk 12:41. **P.** This copper coin was the smallest denomination of Jewish coins, 1/128th of a denarius.

gifts out of the *money* abounding^A *to* them. But this *one*, out of her lack^B, threw all the living^C which she was having.

Jesus Says The Temple Will Be Destroyed. The Disciples Ask, When?
^5 And while some *were* talking about the temple— that it has been adorned *with* beautiful stones and gifts-dedicated-to-God— He said, ^6 "*As to* these *things* which you are observing, days will come during which *a* stone on *a* stone will not be left which will not be torn-down^D". ^7 And they questioned Him, saying, "Teacher, when therefore will these *things* happen? And what *will be* the sign when these *things* are about to take place?"

Do Not Be Deceived By False Christs Or Frightened By Wars And Disturbances
^8 And the *One* said, "Be watching-out *that* you may not be deceived. For many will come on the basis of My name, saying 'I am^E *the One*', and 'The time has drawn-near'. Do not go after them. ^9 And whenever you hear-*of* wars and disturbances^F, do not be frightened. For these *things* must take place first, but *it is* not immediately the end".

There Will Be Disasters On Earth And Great Signs From Heaven
^10 Then He was saying *to* them, "Nation will arise against nation, and kingdom against kingdom. ^11 There will be both great earthquakes, and famines and plagues in various places. There will be both fearful^G *things* and great signs from heaven.

But Before All This, You Will Be Imprisoned
^12 "But before all these *things,* they will put their hands on you and persecute *you— they* handing *you* over to the synagogues and prisons, *you* being led-away before kings and governors for-the-sake-of ^H My name. ^13 It will turn-out *for* you *to be* for *a* testimony. ^14 So put in your hearts not to prepare-beforehand to speak-a-defense. ^15 For I will give you *a* mouth, and wisdom which all the *ones* being opposed *to* you will not be able to resist or to speak-against^I. ^16 And you will be handed-over even by parents and brothers and relatives and friends. And they will put *some* of you to death. ^17 And you will be being hated by all because of My name. ^18 And *a* hair of your head will by no means be^J lost. ^19 Gain^K your souls^L by your endurance.

And You Will See Days of Vengeance And Wrath Against This People
^20 "But when you see Jerusalem being surrounded by army-encampments, then recognize that her desolation has drawn-near. ^21 Then^M let the *ones* in Judea be fleeing to the mountains. And let the *ones* in *the* midst *of* her^N be going-out. And let the *ones* in the fields not be entering into her. ^22 Because these are days *of* vengeance, *that* all the *things* having been written *may* be fulfilled. ^23 Woe *to* the *ones* having *a child* in *the* womb, and *to* the *ones* nursing in those days. For there will be *a* great distress^O upon the land, and wrath *against* this people. ^24 And they will fall *by the* edge *of the*

A. Or, overflowing, being left over. **B.** Or, shortcoming, deficiency. That is, out of what was already not enough. **C.** That is, means-of-living. **D.** Or, destroyed, demolished, done-away-with. **E.** Or, I am *He.* That is, I am the Messiah. **F.** Or, insurrections, instabilities. **G.** Or, terrors, horrors. That is, fearful sights or events. **H.** That is, from your point of view. Or, because-of, from the persecutor's point of view. **I.** Or, contradict. **J.** Or, perish. That is, eternally; or, without God's permission. **K.** Or, Acquire, Obtain, Get. **L.** Or, lives. That is, your eternal lives with God. **M.** Or, At that time. See Mt 24:9. **N.** That is, Jerusalem. **O.** Or, calamity, trouble.

sword. And they will be taken-captive to all the nations. And Jerusalem will be being trampled[A] by *the* Gentiles[B] until which *time the* times *of the* Gentiles are fulfilled.

Then They Will See The Son Coming On The Clouds With Great Glory

25 "And there will be signs in *the* sun and moon and stars, and on earth *the* anguish *of* nations in perplexity *about the* roar *of the* sea and *wave*-tossing— **26** people fainting[C] from fear and *the* expectation *of* the *things* coming-upon the world. For the powers *of* the heavens will be shaken. **27** And then[D] they will see the Son *of* Man coming in *a* cloud with power and great glory. **28** Now [when] these *things* [are] beginning to take place, straighten-up and lift-up your heads, because your redemption is drawing-near".

The Parable of The Fig Tree: When You See This You Know The Kingdom Is Near

29 And He spoke *a* parable *to* them: "Look at the fig-tree, and all the trees. **30** When they already put-forth *leaves*, seeing *it*, you know from[E] yourselves that summer is already near. **31** So also you— when you see these *things* taking place, you know[F] that the kingdom *of* God is near. **32** Truly I say *to* you that this generation[G] will by no means pass away until all *things* take place. **33** Heaven and earth will pass away, but My words will by-no-means pass away.

Be Prepared And Keep Alert

34 "But take heed to yourselves that your hearts may not at any time be weighed-down with carousing and drunkenness and anxieties[H] pertaining-to-life, and that unexpected[I] day suddenly-come-upon[J] you **35** like *a* snare. For it will come-in-upon all the *ones* sitting on *the* face *of* all the earth. **36** And be keeping-alert[K] in every season, praying that you may have strength to escape[L] all these *things* being about to take place, and to stand before the Son *of* Man".

Jesus Spends His Days In The Temple and His Nights On The Mount of Olives

37 Now *as to* the days, He was teaching in the temple. But *as to* the nights, going out [of Jerusalem], He was spending-the-night on the mountain being called 'of Olives'. **38** And all the people were arising-very-early[M] *to come* to Him in the temple to hear Him.

The Priests Plot How To Kill Jesus

22:1 Now the Feast *of* Unleavened-Bread, the *one* being called Passover, was drawing-near. **2** And the chief priests and the scribes were seeking *as to* how they might kill[N] Him, for they were fearing the people.

Judas Betrays Jesus To The Priests

3 And Satan entered into Judas, the *one* being called "Iscariot", being *one* of the number *of* the twelve. **4** And having gone, he talked-with the chief priests and [temple] captains *as to* how he might hand Him over *to* them. **5** And they rejoiced[O] and agreed to give him

---

A. Or, tread-on. **B.** Or, nations. **C.** Or, expiring (dying). **D.** Or, at that time. **E.** That is, from your own knowledge and experience. **F.** Or, know that (a command). **G.** See Mt 24:34. **H.** Or, worries, cares. **I.** Or, unforeseen, sudden. **J.** Or, spring-upon. **K.** Or, keeping-alert, praying in every season. **L.** Or, flee-from. **M.** That is, before dawn. **N.** Or, execute, do away with. **O.** Or, were delighted.

money. **6** And he consented, and was seeking *a* favorable-opportunity *that he might* hand Him over without^A *a* crowd *with* them.

Jesus Celebrates Passover With The Twelve
7 And the [first] day *of* the *Feast of* Unleavened-Bread came— on which it-was-necessary *that* the Passover [lamb] be sacrificed. **8** And He sent-forth Peter and John, having said, "Having gone, prepare the Passover [meal] *for* us in order that we may eat *it* ". **9** And the *ones* said *to* Him, "Where do You want us to prepare *it*?" **10** And the *One* said *to* them, "Behold— you having entered into the city, *a* man will meet you carrying *a* jar *of* water. Follow him to the house into which he proceeds. **11** And you will say *to* the master *of* the house, 'The Teacher says *to* you, "Where is the guest-room where I may eat the Passover [meal] with My disciples?" ' **12** And that *one* will show you *a* large upstairs-room having been spread [with furnishings]. Prepare *it* there". **13** And having gone, they found *it* just as He had told them. And they prepared the Passover [meal].

The Bread And The Wine Are Given a New Meaning
14 And when the hour came, He fell back [to eat], and the apostles with Him. **15** And He said to them, "I greatly desired to eat this Passover [meal] with you before I suffer. **16** For I say *to* you that I will by no means eat it until it is fulfilled in the kingdom *of* God". **17** And having taken *a* cup^B, having given-thanks, He said "Take this and distribute *it* to yourselves. **18** For I say *to* you that I will by no means drink from the fruit *of* the grapevine from now *on* until which *time* the kingdom *of* God comes". **19** And having taken bread, having given-thanks, He broke *it* and gave *it* *to* them, saying "This is My body, the *one* being given for you. Be doing this for My remembrance". **20** And similarly the cup after the dining, saying "This cup *is* the new covenant in My blood— the *blood* being poured-out for you. **21** Yet behold— the hand *of* the *one* handing Me over *is* with Mine on the table! **22** Because the Son *of* Man is proceeding according-to the *thing* having been determined^C— nevertheless, woe *to* that man by whom He is being handed-over!" **23** And **they** began to discuss with themselves *as to* which of them then the *one* going to do this *thing* might be.

The Disciples Argue Over Who Is Greatest. The Greatest Is The Servant of All
24 And *a* contention also took place among them *as to* which *of* them seems^D to be greater^E. **25** And the *One* said *to* them, "The kings *of* the Gentiles are lording-over^F them. And the *ones* having-authority *over* them are calling-*themselves* 'Benefactors^G'. **26** But you *shall* not *be* so. But let the greater^H *one* among you be like the younger *one*; and the *one* leading like the *one* serving. **27** For who *is* greater, the *one* reclining-back [to eat] or the *one* serving? Is it not the *one* reclining-back? But **I** am in your midst as the *One* serving! **28** But **you** are the *ones* having continued with Me in My trials. **29** And **I** am conferring^I you *a* kingdom, just as My Father conferred Me **30** so that you may eat and drink at My table in My kingdom. And you will sit on thrones judging^J the twelve tribes *of* Israel.

A. Or, over *to* them without *a* crowd. **B.** This is either in preparation for v 20, or it is the first cup of the Passover meal and this verse is equivalent to 'while they were eating' in Mt 26:26. **C.** Or, designated. That is, by God. **D.** Or, is reputed. **E.** Or in this context, greatest. **F.** That is, reigning as masters over their subjects. **G.** That is, ones who view themselves as exercising their authority for the public good. **H.** Or in this context, older. **I.** Or, ordaining, assigning, covenanting. **J.** That is, administering justice to.

Peter Will Deny Jesus

[31] "Simon, Simon. Behold— Satan asked-for[A] you[B] *all that he might* sift[C] *you* like wheat. [32] But **I** prayed for you[D], that your faith may not fail. And when **you** *have* turned-back, establish[E] your brothers". [33] But the *one* said *to* Him, "Lord, I am prepared to go **with You** even[F] to prison and to death!" [34] And the *One* said, "I say *to* you, Peter, *a* rooster will not crow today until you deny three-times *that you* know Me".

Jesus Tells The Disciples To Prepare For a New Assignment

[35] And He said *to* them, "When I sent you out without money-bag and [traveler's] bag and sandals, you did not lack anything, *did you*?" And the *ones* said, "Nothing". [36] And He said *to* them, "But now[G] let the *one* having *a* money-bag take *it*. Likewise also *a* [traveler's] bag. And let the *one* not having *one* sell his cloak and buy *a* sword. [37] For I say *to* you that this [saying] having been written [in Isa 53:12] must be fulfilled in Me: 'And He was counted[H] with lawless *ones*'. For indeed the *thing* concerning Me has *a* fulfillment[I]". [38] And the *ones* said, "Lord, behold— here *are* two swords". And the *One* said *to* them, "It is enough".

Jesus Waits And Prays On The Mount of Olives

[39] And having gone out, He went in accordance with *His* custom to the Mount *of* Olives. And the disciples also, they followed Him. [40] And having come-to-be at the place, He said *to* them, "Be praying *that you may* not enter into temptation". [41] And **He** withdrew from them about *a* stone's throw. And having put *down His* knees, He was praying, [42] saying "Father, if You are willing, remove this cup from Me. Yet let not My will, but Yours be done". [43] And[J] *an* angel from heaven appeared *to* Him, strengthening Him. [44] And having come-to-be in agony, He was praying more-fervently. And His sweat became like[K] drops *of* blood going down upon the ground. [45] And having arisen from prayer, having come to the disciples, He found them being asleep because of grief. [46] And He said *to* them, "Why are you sleeping? Having stood-up, be praying that[L] you may not enter into temptation".

Jesus Is Betrayed With a Kiss, And Arrested

[47] While He *was* still speaking, behold— *a* crowd. And the *one* being called Judas, one *of* the twelve, was preceding[M] them. And he drew-near *to* Jesus to kiss Him. [48] And Jesus said *to* him, "Judas, are you handing-over the Son *of* Man **with a kiss**?" [49] And the *ones* around Him, having seen the *thing which* will happen, said "Lord, shall we strike with *a* sword?" [50] And *a* certain one of them struck the slave *of* the high priest and took-off his right ear. [51] But having responded, Jesus said, "Allow[N] up to this". And having touched *his* ear, He healed him. [52] And Jesus said to *the* chief priests and captains *of* the temple and elders having come against Him, "Did you come out with

---

A. Or, demanded. **B.** This word is plural. **C.** Or, winnow. **D.** This is singular, referring to Simon. **E.** Or, stabilize, support. **F.** Or, both. **G.** Now the situation is changed. You must prudently plan and make provisions for your lives and ministries. **H.** That is, classed. **I.** The prophecy will be fulfilled. Or, *an* end, meaning that My life is coming to an end. **J.** Some manuscripts omit verses 43-44. **K.** Or, as-if. The similarity in view here may be in the quantity (dripping like blood from an open wound), or the color (a sweat containing some blood). **L.** Or, be praying, in order that. **M.** Or, going before. **N.** Or, Permit, Leave-off. If addressed to the crowd, this means Allow up to this action by Peter or this touch by Jesus next. Addressed to the disciples it would mean Leave off what you have done up to this point!; Stop it!; No more of this!

swords and clubs as-*if* against *a* robber? [53] Daily while I *was* being with you in the temple, you did not stretch-out *your* hands against Me. But this is your hour, and the authority *of* darkness".

Jesus Is Led Into The House of The High Priest; Peter Denies Him Three Times

[54] And having arrested Him, they led *Him,* and brought *Him* into the house *of* the high priest. And Peter was following at-a-distance. [55] And *they* having kindled *a* fire in *the* middle *of* the courtyard, and having sat-down-together, Peter was sitting amidst them. [56] And *a* certain servant-girl, having seen him sitting toward the light, and having looked-intently *at* him, said "This *one* also was with Him". [57] But the *one* denied *it,* saying "I do not know Him, woman". [58] And after *a* short *time,* another *man* having seen him said, "**You** also are *one* of them". But Peter said, "Man, I am not!" [59] And about one hour having passed[A], *a* certain other *man* was insisting, saying "In accordance with truth, this *one* also was with Him, for he also is *a* Galilean". [60] But Peter said, "Man, I do not know what you are saying". And at-once, while he *was* still speaking, *a* rooster crowed. [61] And having turned, the Lord looked-at Peter. And Peter was reminded *of* the word *of* the Lord— how He said *to* him that "Before *a* rooster crows today, you will deny Me three-times". [62] And having gone outside, he wept bitterly. [63] And the men holding Him were mocking Him while beating *Him.* [64] And having covered Him, they were asking *Him,* saying "Prophesy— who is the *one* having hit You?" [65] And blaspheming, they were saying many other *things* against Him.

Jesus Is Led Before The Sanhedrin. He Tells Them He Is The Son of God

[66] And when it became day, the Council-of-elders *of* the people was gathered together— both chief priests and scribes. And they led Him away to their council[B] [chamber], [67] saying "If **You** are the Christ, tell us". But He said *to* them, "If I tell you, you will by no means believe. [68] And if I question *you,* you will by no means answer. [69] But from now *on,* the Son *of* Man will be sitting[C] on *the* right *side of* the power *of* God". [70] And they all said, "Are **You** then the Son *of* God?" And the *One* said to them, "**You** are saying[D] that **I** am". [71] And the *ones* said, "What further need do we have *of* testimony? For we ourselves heard *it* from His mouth".

Jesus Is Led Before Pilate. He Tells Him He Is The King of The Jews

23:1 And having arisen, the whole assembly *of* them led Him before Pilate. [2] And they began to accuse Him, saying "We found this *One* perverting our nation, and forbidding to give tributes[E] *to* Caesar, and saying *that* He is Christ, *a* King". [3] And Pilate asked Him, saying "Are **You** the King *of* the Jews?" And the *One,* having responded *to* him, said "**You** are saying[F] *it* ". [4] And Pilate said to the chief priests and the crowds, "I find no guilt[G] in this man". [5] But the *ones* were insisting[H], saying that "He is stirring-up the people, teaching throughout all Judea— having indeed begun from Galilee, as far as here". [6] And Pilate, having heard *it,* asked if the man was *a* Galilean. [7] And having learned that He was from the authority *of* Herod[I], he sent Him up to Herod— he also being in Jerusalem during these days.

A. Or, intervened. **B.** Or, Sanhedrin, naming this judicial body for the reader. **C.** Jesus is claiming to be the fulfillment of Ps 110:1. **D.** That is, you are [rightly] saying, as seen by the next verse. See Mt 26:64. **E.** See 20:22. **F.** See Mt 27:11. **G.** Or, cause, source, basis for accusation. **H.** Or, growing emphatic, urgent. **I.** That is, Herod Antipas, governor over Galilee. See Mt 14:1 on him.

Before Herod, Jesus Says Nothing

8 Now Herod, having seen Jesus, rejoiced greatly. For he was wanting to see Him for considerable periods-of-time because of hearing about Him. And he was hoping to see some sign being done by Him. **9** And he was questioning Him with many words, but **He** answered him nothing. **10** And the chief priests and the scribes were standing *there*, accusing Him vigorously[A]. **11** And Herod also— with his troops— having treated Him with contempt, and having mocked *Him*, having clothed *Him* with shining clothing, sent Him back *to* Pilate. **12** Now both Herod and Pilate became friends with one another on the very day. For they were-previously existing with hostility[B] toward them.

Pilate Offers To Release Jesus. The Crowd Demands He Be Crucified

13 Now Pilate, having called-together the chief priests and the rulers and the people, **14** said to them, "You brought me this man as *One* turning-away[C] the people. And behold— **I**, having examined *Him* in your presence, found **no** guilt in this man *of the things* which you are accusing against Him. **15** But neither *did* Herod, for he sent Him back to us. And behold— nothing worthy *of* death has been committed *by* Him. **16** Therefore, having disciplined Him, I will release *Him*". **17** [D] **18** But they cried-out all-together, saying, "Take away this *One*, and release Barabbas *for* us"— **19** who had been thrown in prison because of *a* certain rebellion[E] having taken place in the city, and murder. **20** And again Pilate addressed them, wanting to release Jesus. **21** But the *ones* were calling-out, saying "Crucify, crucify Him!" **22** And *a* third *time* the *one* said to them, "What indeed[F] did this *One* do wrong? I found no guilt *worthy of* death in Him. Therefore, having disciplined Him, I will release *Him*". **23** But the *ones* were pressing-upon *him with* loud voices, asking *that* He be crucified. And their voices were prevailing. **24** And Pilate decided[G] *that* their request *should* be done. **25** And he released the *one* having been thrown into prison because of rebellion and murder, whom they were asking-*for*. And he handed-over Jesus *to* their will.

Jesus Is Crucified

26 And when they led Him away, having taken-hold-of *a* certain Simon, *a* Cyrenian[H] coming from *the* country, they laid the cross on him to carry behind Jesus. **27** And *a* large crowd *of* the people, and *of* women who were beating-their-breasts and lamenting Him, was following Him. **28** But having turned to them, Jesus said, "Daughters *of* Jerusalem, do not be weeping for Me. But weep for yourselves and for your children. **29** Because behold— days are coming during which they will say, 'Blessed[I] *are* the barren, and[J] the wombs which did not bear and breasts which did not feed[K]'. **30** At-that-time they will begin to say *to* the mountains, 'Fall on us', and *to* the hills, 'Cover us'. **31** Because if they are doing these *things* in-the-case-of the wet wood[L], what will happen in-the-case-of the dry[M]?" **32** And two other[N] criminals were also being led to be executed with Him. **33** And

---

A. Or, vehemently, forcefully. **B.** That is, each feeling the other was hostile to him. **C.** That is, from their duties toward Rome. **D.** Some manuscripts add 'Now he was having *an* obligation to release one [prisoner] *to* them at the feast'. **E.** Or, insurrection, revolt, riot, uprising. **F.** Or, Why? What evil did this *One* do? Pilate is incredulous. **G.** Or, adjudged, determined. He rendered his judicial decision. **H.** That is, from Cyrene, a city on the coast of Africa. **I.** Or, Fortunate. **J.** Or, even. **K.** Or, nourish. **L.** Or, green tree. That is, Jesus. **M.** That is, unbelieving Israel. If the Innocent One is made to die, what will happen to guilty Israel? The answer came in A.D. 70 when the Romans destroyed Jerusalem. **N.** That is, others of a different kind. Luke may be stating it this way in fulfillment of 22:37. Or, this may be punctuated to avoid classing Jesus as a criminal, 'And others were also being led, two criminals, to be executed with Him'.

when they came to the place being called "*The* Skull^A^", there they crucified Him and the criminals— one on *the* right *side*, and the other on *the* left *side*. ^34^ But^B^ Jesus was saying, "Father, forgive them, for they do not know what they are doing". And they cast lots, dividing His garments among *themselves.*

The King of The Jews Is Mocked While Hanging On The Cross

^35^ And the people were standing *there* watching. And the rulers were also sneering- at *Him*, saying "He saved others. Let Him save Himself if this *One* is the Christ *of* God, the Chosen *One*". ^36^ And the soldiers also mocked Him, coming to *Him*, offering Him sour-wine^C^, ^37^ and saying "If **You** are the King *of* the Jews, save Yourself". ^38^ And there was also *an* inscription over Him— "This *is* the King *of* the Jews". ^39^ And one *of* the criminals having been hung was blaspheming Him, saying "Are **You** not the Christ? Save Yourself and us". ^40^ But having responded, the other, rebuking him, said "Do **you** not even fear God? Because you are under the same condemnation^D^! ^41^ And we *are suffering* justly, for we are receiving-back *things* worthy *of the things* which we did— but this *One* did nothing out-of-place^E^". ^42^ And he was saying, "Jesus, remember me when You come into Your kingdom". ^43^ And He said *to* him, "Truly I say *to* you, you will be with Me **today** in paradise".

Darkness Comes Over the Land And The Temple Curtain Is Torn. Jesus Dies

^44^ And it was now about *the* sixth^F^ hour. And *a* darkness came over the whole land^G^ until *the* ninth hour, ^45^ the sun having failed. And the curtain *of* the temple was torn^H^ in-the-middle. ^46^ And having called-out *with a* loud voice, Jesus said, "Father, I commend^I^ My spirit into Your hands". And having said this, He expired. ^47^ And having seen the *thing* having taken place, the centurion was glorifying God, saying "This man **really** was righteous". ^48^ And all the crowds having come together for this sight, having watched the *things* having taken place, were returning striking *their* chests. ^49^ But all His acquaintances and the women accompanying Him from Galilee were standing at *a* distance while seeing these *things*.

Jesus Is Buried In a Tomb On Friday Afternoon Before Sunset

^50^ And behold, *there was a* man, Joseph *by* name— being *a* council-member and *a* good and righteous man (^51^ this *one* had not consented *to* the plan^J^ and their action)— from Arimathea, *a* city *of* the Jews, who was waiting-for the kingdom *of* God. ^52^ This *one,* having gone to Pilate, asked-*for* the body *of* Jesus. ^53^ And having taken *it* down, he wrapped it in linen-cloth, and laid Him in *a* tomb cut-in-the-rock where **no one** was yet lying. ^54^ And it was *the* day *of* Preparation^K^, and *the* Sabbath was dawning^L^.

On Sunday Morning, The Women Go To The Tomb And Discover That Jesus Is Risen

^55^ Now having closely-followed, the women who had come-with Him from Galilee saw the tomb and how His body was laid. ^56^ And having returned, they prepared spices and perfumes.

A. That is, Golgotha. See Mt 27:33. **B.** Some manuscripts omit this sentence. **C.** Or, wine-vinegar (watered down). This was a favorite beverage of the soldiers and the common people. **D.** That is, the same sentence of death. **E.** That is, morally wrong. **F:** sixth hour... ninth hour. That is, noon... 3 P.M. **G.** Or, earth. **H.** Or, split. See Mt 27:51. **I.** Or, entrust, deposit. **J.** Or, resolution, plot. **K.** That is, Friday, the day of preparation for the Sabbath. **L.** That is, the sun was going down. The Sabbath day began at sundown.

And *on* the Sabbath they rested in-accordance-with the commandment— **24:1** but *on* the first *day of* the week *at* deep dawn, they went to the tomb bringing *the* spices which they prepared. [2] And they found the stone having been rolled-away from the tomb. [3] But having gone in, they did not find the body *of* the Lord Jesus. [4] And it came about during their being perplexed about this, that behold— two men[A] stood-near them in gleaming[B] clothing. [5] And they[C] having become terrified and bowing *their* faces to the ground, they[D] said to them, "Why are you seeking the Living *One* among the dead? [6] He is not here, but He arose. Remember how He spoke *to* you while still being in Galilee, [7] saying *as to* the Son *of* Man that *He* must be handed-over into *the* hands *of* sinful men, and be crucified, and rise-up *on* the third day". [8] And they remembered His words.

The Women Report To The Others. Peter Runs To See

[9] And having returned from the tomb, they reported all these *things to* the eleven and *to* all the rest. [10] Now *the women* were the Magdalene[E] Mary, and Joanna, and Mary the *mother of* James, and the other *women* with them. They were saying these *things* to the apostles. [11] And these words appeared in their sight as if nonsense[F], and they were not-believing[G] them. [12] But Peter, having arisen, ran to the tomb. And having stooped-to-look, he sees the linen-cloths only[H]. And he went away marveling[I] to himself *as to* the *thing* having taken place.

Jesus Meets Two Disciples On The Way To Emmaus And Explains The Scriptures

[13] And behold— two of them[J] were going on the very day to *a* village being sixty stades[K] distant from Jerusalem, *for* which *the* name *was* Emmaus. [14] And **they** were conversing with one another about all these *things* having happened. [15] And it came about during their conversing and discussing, that Jesus Himself, having drawn-near, was going with them. [16] But their eyes were being held-back *that they might* not[L] recognize Him. [17] And He said to them, "What *are* these words which you are exchanging with one another while walking?" And they stood [still], sad-faced. [18] And having responded, one— Cleopas *by* name— said to Him, "Are **You** alone[M] staying *in* Jerusalem and did not know the *things* having taken place in it in these days?" [19] And He said *to* them, "What *things*?" And the *ones* said *to* Him, "The *things* concerning Jesus from-Nazareth, Who became *a* man *who was a* prophet, powerful in deed and word before God and all the people; [20] and how the chief priests and our rulers handed Him over for condemnation *to* death, and they crucified Him. [21] But **we** were hoping that **He** was the *One* going to redeem Israel. Yet indeed also in-addition-to[N] all these *things*, it is the third day from which *time* these *things* took place. [22] Yet some women from-*among* us also astonished us. Having come-to-be at the tomb very-early, [23] and not having found His body, they came saying also to have seen *a* vision *of* angels who say *that* He *is* alive. [24] And some *of* the *ones* with us went to the tomb and found *it* so— just as the women indeed said. But they did not see Him". [25] And **He** said to them, "O foolish *ones,* and slow *in* the heart to be putting-faith upon all that the prophets spoke! [26] Did not the Christ have-to suffer these *things,* and enter into His glory?"

A. That is, angels, v 23, in the form of men. **B.** Or, brightly-shining. **C.** That is, the women. **D.** That is, the two men. **E.** She is referred to in this way only here. She was from Magdala on the Sea of Galilee. **F.** Or, idle talk, delirious talk, raving. **G.** Or, refusing-to-believe. **H.** Or, alone. That is, without the body. **I.** Or, wondering. **J.** That is, two of 'the rest' in v 9. **K.** That is, about 7 miles or 11 kilometers. **L.** Or, *so that they* did not. **M.** That is, are You the only one. **N.** Or, besides.

²⁷ And beginning from Moses and from all the prophets, He interpreted^A *to* them the *things* concerning Himself in all the Scriptures. ²⁸ And they drew-near to the village where they were going. And **He** made-as-if to be proceeding farther. ²⁹ And they strongly-urged Him, saying "Stay with us, because it is toward evening, and the day has already declined". And He went in *that He might* stay with them. ³⁰ And it came about at His lying down [to eat] with them *that* having taken the bread, He blessed *it*^B. And having broken *it*, He was giving *it to* them. ³¹ And their eyes were opened, and they recognized Him. And **He** became invisible from them. ³² And they said to one another, "Was not our heart burning within us as He was speaking *to* us on the road, as He was opening the Scriptures *to* us?"

Jesus Appears To The Eleven And Helps Them Understand The Scriptures

³³ And having arisen *at* the very hour, they returned to Jerusalem. And they found the eleven^C and the *ones* with them having been assembled, ³⁴ saying that "The Lord really arose! And He appeared *to* Simon". ³⁵ And **they** were describing^D the *things* on the road, and how He was recognized *by* them in^E the breaking *of* the bread. ³⁶ And while they *were* speaking these *things*, He Himself stood in *the* midst *of* them. And He says *to* them, "Peace *to* you". ³⁷ But having been frightened and having become terrified, they were thinking *that* they *were* seeing *a* spirit. ³⁸ And He said *to* them, "Why are you troubled? And for what reason are doubts coming-up in your heart? ³⁹ Look at My hands and My feet, that **I** am Myself. Touch^F Me and see, because *a* spirit does not have flesh and bones as you observe Me having". ⁴⁰ And having said this, He showed them *His* hands and *His* feet. ⁴¹ But while they *were* still not-believing *it* because of the joy, and marveling, He said *to* them, "Do you have something edible here?" ⁴² And the *ones* gave Him *a* part *of a* broiled fish. ⁴³ And having taken *it*, He ate *it* in their presence. ⁴⁴ And He said to them, "These *are* My words which I spoke to you while still being with you— that all the *things* having been written about Me in the Law *of* Moses and the Prophets and *the* Psalms must be fulfilled". ⁴⁵ Then He opened their mind *that they might* understand the Scriptures.

The Christ Had To Suffer And Rise Up, And The Message Go Forth. You Are Witnesses

⁴⁶ And^G He said *to* them that "Thus it has been written— *that* the Christ suffers and rises-up from *the* dead *on* the third day, ⁴⁷ and *that* repentance for *the* forgiveness *of* sins is proclaimed on the basis of His name to all the nations, beginning from Jerusalem. ⁴⁸ You *are* witnesses *of* these *things*. ⁴⁹ And behold— **I** am sending-forth the promise^H *of* My Father upon you. But **you** sit in the city^I until which *time* you put-on^J power from on-high".

Jesus Ascends Into Heaven

⁵⁰ And He led them outside^K until near Bethany. And having lifted-up His hands, He blessed them. ⁵¹ And it came about during His blessing them *that* He separated^L from them, and was being carried-up^M into heaven. ⁵² And **they**, having worshiped Him, returned to Jerusalem with great joy. ⁵³ And they were continually in the temple blessing God.

A. Or, explained. **B.** Or, *God*. **C.** This is used here as a title, not a count. Thomas was not with them, so only ten were present. **D.** Or, expounding. **E.** That is, in connection with. **F.** Or, Handle. **G.** The break from the first Sunday may occur here, in v 44, or in v 50 (which is forty days later). **H.** That is, the Holy Spirit. **I.** That is, Jerusalem. **J.** Or, clothe-*yourselves*-with. **K.** That is, outside the city, v 49. **L.** Or, parted. **M.** Or, taken-up.

John

A. The Word was with God and was God. The Word became flesh and we beheld His glory. John 1:1-18
testifies to Him. We all received of His fullness. He expounded God to us
B. And this is the testimony of John— Jesus is the Lamb of God, the Son of God   1:19-34
C. Two of John's disciples follow Jesus, Who makes the water wine. They go to Capernaum   1:35-2:12
D. At Passover, Jesus went to Jerusalem. He drove out the sellers. He spoke to Nicodemus   2:13-3:21
E. Jesus went into Judea. John the Baptist said, He must grow, I must diminish   3:22-36
F. Jesus spoke to a Samaritan woman at a well. In Galilee, He healed the son of a royal one   4:1-54
G. Jesus went up to Jerusalem. At a pool, Jesus healed a man sick for 38 years on the Sabbath   5:1-9

    1. The Jews objected. Since Jesus claimed equality with God, they wanted to kill Him   5:9-19

        a. The Son does what He sees the Father doing. He will give life and judge   5:19-30
        b. The Father testifies about the Son— in His works, His voice, and the Scriptures   5:31-47

H. Jesus went to the other side of the Sea of Galilee, where He fed the 5000   6:1-15

    1. That evening, His disciples left by boat for Capernaum. Jesus walked on the water   6:16-21
    2. The next day, the crowd went to Capernaum seeking Jesus   6:22-24

        a. Jesus said to them, Work for food remaining for eternal life. I am the Bread of life   6:25-40
        b The Jews grumbled at this. He said, The bread I give for the world is My flesh   6:41-51
        c. The Jews fought over this. Eat My flesh and drink My blood for eternal life   6:52-59
        d. Many disciples said, This statement is hard. Jesus said, My words are spirit and life   6:60-65
        e. From this time, many withdrew. The twelve said, You have the words of eternal life   6:66-71

    3. After these things, Jesus was in Galilee, for the Jews in Judea were seeking to kill Him   7:1

I. The Tent-pitching Feast of the Jews was near. Jesus went up to the temple and was teaching   7:2-13

    1. In the middle of the feast, Jesus was teaching   7:14

        a. My teaching is not Mine, but His Who sent Me. Why do you want to kill Me?   7:15-24
        b. You know Me, but I have not come of Myself. I know Him who sent Me forth   7:25-30
        c. Many from the crowd believed in Jesus and said, Will the Christ do more signs?   7:31-36

    2. On the last day, Jesus said, If any one is thirsting, let him come to Me and drink   7:37-8:1
    3. They brought Jesus a woman caught in adultery. Let the sinless one throw first   8:2-11
    4. Jesus said, I am the light of the world. My testimony is true. My Father is testifying   8:12-20
    5. Jesus said, I am going, and unless you believe that I am the One, you will die in your sin   8:21-30
    6. Many believed. Jesus said, If you remain in My word, the truth will set you free   8:31-32

        a. They said, We are the seed of Abraham, and not slaves. Jesus said, You are slaves of   8:33-59
        sin. Your father is the devil. Before Abraham came into being, I am

    7. While passing on, Jesus saw a man blind from birth. Jesus healed him   9:1-12

        a. They bring him to the Pharisees, who object because it was the Sabbath   9:13-34
        b. Jesus finds him and says, Do you believe in the Son of Man? I am He. I came that   9:35-39
        the ones not seeing may see, and the ones seeing may become blind
        c. Some Pharisees said, We are not blind ones, are we? Jesus said, Your sin remains.   9:40-10:6
        You are thieves and robbers in the fold. The sheep will follow Me out
        d. I am the door to life, the good shepherd who lays down his life for the sheep   10:7-18
        e. A division occurred among them because of these words   10:19-21

J.   The Feast of Dedication took place. Are You the Christ? Jesus said, I told you. The works   10:22-42
      testify. I and the Father are One. They tried to stone Him because He made Himself God
K.   Mary and Martha send to Him. Jesus came and raised Lazarus. Many believed in Him   11:1-54
L.   Now the Passover was near. Many were wondering if Jesus would come to the feast at all   11:55-57

      1.   Jesus came to Bethany, and Mary anointed Him with perfume. He said, for My burial   12:1-11
      2.   The next day, the crowd laid palm branches before Him and shouted Hosanna   12:12-19
      3.   Some Greeks came to see Him. Jesus said, The Light is with you a little longer   12:20-36
      4.   He having done so many signs, they did not believe, that Scripture might be fulfilled   12:37-43
      5.   Jesus said, He who believes in Me, believes in Him who sent Me. I am the Light. My   12:44-50
            words will judge those who reject Me. I speak the Father's words

M.   Jesus loved His own to the end   13:1

      1.   At dinner Jesus washed the disciples' feet, then explained it to them. Follow My example   13:2-20
      2.   Jesus was troubled in spirit and said, One of you will hand Me over. Judas leaves   13:21-30
      3.   Jesus says, Now the Son of Man was glorified. God will glorify Him   13:31-32

            a.   Little children, I am going, you cannot come. Love one another as I loved you   13:33-38
            b.   Do not be troubled. I am going to prepare a place for you in My Father's house   14:1-11
            c.   The one believing will do greater works, because I am going to the Father   14:12-17
            d.   I will not leave you as orphans. I am coming to you. I will reveal Myself to you   14:18-26
            e.   I leave you peace, My peace. Do not be troubled or afraid   14:27-31

      4.   Let us be going from here. I am the true vine. Abide in Me and bear much fruit   14:31-15:17
      5.   If the world hates you, it hated Me first, without a cause. The Helper will testify   15:18-16:4
      6.   It is better that I go, for I will send you the Helper. He will convict the world, guide you   16:4-15
            into all truth, disclose the future, and glorifyMe
      7.   I am leaving the world, going to the Father. I will see you again, you will rejoice   16:16-33
      8.   Jesus lifted up His eyes and said, Father, the hour has come. Glorify Your Son   17:1-5

            a.   I revealed Your name to the men You gave Me. Keep them in Your name   17:6-13
            b.   I gave them Your word. Keep them from the evil one. Set them apart in truth   17:14-19
            c.   I ask also for those believing through their word, that they may be one in Us   17:20-23
            d.   Father, I desire that they be with Me where I am, and see My glory   17:24
            e.   Father, these men knew You sent Me. I will make You known to them   17:25-26

N.   Having said these things, they went to the garden. Judas came. Whom are you seeking?   18:1-11

      1.   They arrested Jesus and took Him to Annas and Caiaphas. Peter denied Him   18:12-27
      2.   They led Him to Pilate, who found no fault in Him, but condemned Him   18:28-19:16
      3.   Pilate handed Him over to be crucified. Jesus said, It has been accomplished   19:16-30
      4.   The Jews asked that His legs be broken. But He was already dead   19:31-37
      5.   Joseph asked for His body and with Nicodemus, placed it in his tomb   19:38-42

O.   On the first day of the week, Mary came to the tomb and saw the stone rolled away   20:1-10

      1.   Mary was weeping by the tomb. Jesus appeared to her. She told the disciples   20:11-18
      2.   Jesus appeared to the disciples in a room and sends them. Thomas was not there   20:19-23
      3.   After eight days, Jesus appeared again with Thomas present. My Lord and My God   20:24-29
      4.   Jesus did many other signs not written here. These are written that you may believe   20:30-31
      5.   After these things, Jesus manifested Himself to them in Galilee. Feed My sheep   21:1-24

Conclusion   21:25

The Word Was With God, And The Word Was God. He Is The Light Shining In The Darkness
1:1 In *the* beginning was the Word, and the Word was with God, and the Word was God. **²** This *One* was in *the* beginning with God. **³** All *things* came-into-being[A] through Him, and apart from Him not even one *thing* came into being which[B] has come-into-being. **⁴** In Him was life, and the life was the light *of* mankind. **⁵** And the light is shining in the darkness, and the darkness did not overcome[C] it.

John Was Sent By God To Bear Witness To The Light In Order That All Might Believe
⁶ There came-to-be[D] *a* man, having been sent-forth from God. *The* name *for* him *was* John. **⁷** This *one* came for *a* testimony— in order that he might testify concerning the Light, in order that all might believe through him. **⁸** That *one* was not the Light, but *came* in order that he might testify concerning the Light— **⁹** the true[E] Light which gives-light-to[F] every person was coming into the world.

The World Did Not Accept The Light, But All Who Did Became Children of God
¹⁰ He was in the world, and the world came-into-being through Him, and the world did not know[G] Him. **¹¹** He came to *His* own *things*, and *His* own *ones* did not accept Him. **¹²** But all who did receive Him, He gave them— the *ones* believing in His name— *the* right[H] to become children *of* God, **¹³** who **were born** not of bloods[I], nor of *the* will *of the* flesh, nor of *the* will *of a* husband, but of God[J].

The Word Became Flesh And We Saw His Unique Glory. John Bore Witness To Him
¹⁴ And the Word became flesh and dwelt[K] among us, and we saw His glory— glory as *of the* only-born[L] from *the* Father, full *of* grace and truth. **¹⁵** John testifies concerning Him, and has cried-out saying, "This *One* was *the One of* Whom I said, 'The *One* coming after me has become ahead of me, because He was before me' ".

We All Received From The Fullness of Grace And Truth He Brought
¹⁶ Because **we** all received from His fullness— even grace upon grace. **¹⁷** Because the Law was given through Moses; grace and truth came through Jesus Christ.

The Only-Born God Revealed The Father To Us
¹⁸ No one has ever seen God; *the* only-born[M] God, the *One* being[N] in the bosom *of the* Father— that *One* expounded[O] *Him.*

John Came Baptizing To Make Straight The Way of The Lord, As Isaiah Prophesied
¹⁹ And this is the testimony *of* John, when the Jews from Jerusalem sent-out priests and Levites to him in order that they might ask him, "Who are **you**?", **²⁰** and he confessed and did not deny.

A. Or, became existent, were made. **B:** being which has. Or, being. What has come-into-being in Him was life. **C.** Or, overtake, overpower. All the forces of darkness did not overcome the Light. Or, grasp, comprehend. The darkness (unbelieving people) did not understand the Light. **D.** Or, arose. **E:** Light— the true Light. Or, Light. There was the true Light which, coming into the world, gives-light-to every person. **F.** Or, illuminates. **G.** Or, recognize, acknowledge. **H.** Or, authority, capability. **I.** That is, bloodlines, human parents. **J.** That is, in a second birth. **K.** Or, lived. **L.** Or, one-and-only, one-of-his-kind, unique *one*. He had a unique glory. The emphasis may be on His glory as God's eternal Son, or as God's incarnate Son. **M.** That is, the unique, one-of-a-kind Deity, the Word who was God (v 1) who became flesh (v 14), the only God-man, expounded the Father to us. The emphasis is on His self-identity. 'Only-born Son' (3:16, 18) emphasizes His unique relationship to His Father. Or, '*the* unique *One,* [Himself] God.' **N.** That is, presently; or, eternally. **O.** Or, described, explained.

And he confessed that "**I** am not the Christ", **21** and they asked him, "What then? Are **you** Elijah?" And he says, "I am not". "Are **you** the^A Prophet?" And he answered, "No". **22** Then they said *to* him, "Who are you, in order that we may give *an* answer *to* the *ones* having sent us? What do you say about yourself ?" **23** He said, "I *am the* 'voice *of one* shouting in the wilderness: "Make-straight the way *of the* Lord" ', just as Isaiah the prophet said [in Isa 40:3]". **24** And they^B had been sent-out from the Pharisees. **25** And they asked him, and said *to* him, "Why then are you baptizing if **you** are not the Christ, nor Elijah, nor the Prophet?" **26** John responded *to* them saying, "I am baptizing with^C water. Amidst you stands *One* Whom **you** do not know— **27** the *One* coming after me, *of* Whom **I** am not worthy that I may untie the strap *of* **His** sandal". **28** These *things* took place in Bethany beyond the Jordan, where John was baptizing.

John Identifies Jesus As The Son of God Sent To Take Away The Sin of The World
29 *On* the next day he sees Jesus coming toward him. And he says, "Look— the Lamb *of* God, the *One* taking-away the sin *of* the world. **30** This *One* is *the One* about Whom **I** said, '*A* man is coming after me Who has become ahead of me, because He was before me'. **31** And **I** did not know Him. But **I** came baptizing with water for this reason— that He might be revealed *to* Israel". **32** And John testified, saying that "I have seen the Spirit descending like *a* dove out of heaven. And He remained upon Him. **33** And **I** did not know Him. But the *One* having sent me to baptize with water, that *One* said *to* me, 'Upon whomever you see the Spirit descending and remaining upon Him— this *One* is the *One* baptizing with^D *the* Holy Spirit'. **34** And **I** have seen, and have testified that this *One* is the Son *of* God".

John Points His Disciples To The Lamb of God. Andrew And Peter Find The Messiah
35 *On* the next day John was again standing *there*, and two of his disciples. **36** And having looked at Jesus walking, he says, "Look— the Lamb *of* God". **37** And the two disciples heard him speaking, and followed Jesus. **38** And Jesus, having turned and seen them following, says *to* them, "What are you seeking?" And the *ones* said *to* Him, "Rabbi (which being translated means "Teacher"), where are You staying?" **39** He says *to* them, "Come, and you will see". So they went, and saw where He was staying, and stayed with Him that day. *The* hour was about *the* tenth^E. **40** Andrew, the brother *of* Simon Peter, was one of the two having heard *it* from John, and having followed Him. **41** This *one* first finds *his* own brother Simon, and says *to* him, "We have found the Messiah" (which being translated is "Christ"). **42** He brought him to Jesus. Having looked-at him, Jesus said, "**You** are Simon, the son *of* John. **You** will be called Cephas^F" (which is translated "Peter").

Jesus Finds Philip, Who Finds Nathanael. They Follow The Son of God, The King of Israel
43 *On* the next day He wanted^G to go forth to Galilee. And He finds Philip. And Jesus says *to* him, "Be following Me". **44** Now Philip was from Bethsaida, of the city *of* Andrew and Peter. **45** Philip finds Nathanael and says *to* him, "We have found *the One of* whom Moses wrote in the Law, and the Prophets *wrote*— Jesus, son *of* Joseph, from Nazareth". **46** And Nathanael said *to* him, "Is anything good able to be **out of Nazareth**?" Philip says *to* him, "Come and see". **47** Jesus saw Nathanael coming to Him, and says about him, "Look— truly *an* Israelite in whom there is no deceit". **48** Nathanael says *to* Him, "From where do

A. That is, the one like Moses, Deut 18:15-19. **B.** Or, *some*. **C.** Or, in. **D.** Or, in. **E.** That is, 4 P.M. Jewish time; or, 10 A.M. Roman time. **F.** This Aramaic name means 'rock', as does the Greek name 'Peter'. **G.** Or, intended.

You know me?" Jesus responded and said *to* him, "Before Philip called you, while being[A] under the fig tree, I saw you". **⁴⁹** Nathanael responded *to* Him, "Rabbi, **You** are the Son *of* God. **You** are *the* King *of* Israel". **⁵⁰** Jesus responded and said *to* him, "Do[B] you believe because I said *to* you that I saw you under the fig tree? You will see greater *things than* these!" **⁵¹** And He says *to* him, "Truly, truly, I say *to* you[C] *all*, you will see heaven opened and the angels *of* God ascending and descending upon the Son *of* Man".

They All Visit a Wedding, Where Jesus Reveals His Glory By Turning Water Into Wine
2:1 And *on* the third[D] day a wedding took place in Cana *of* Galilee. And the mother *of* Jesus was there. **²** And both Jesus and His disciples were invited to the wedding-celebration. **³** And *it* having come-short-of wine, the mother *of* Jesus says to Him, "They do not have wine". **⁴** And Jesus says *to* her, "What[E] do I have to do with you, woman[F]? My hour has not yet come". **⁵** His mother says *to* the servants, "Do[G] whatever thing He says *to* you". **⁶** Now six stone waterpots were setting there for the purification[H] [rite] *of* the Jews, each having-room-for two or three measures[I]. **⁷** Jesus says *to* them, "Fill the waterpots *with* water". And they filled them up to *the* top. **⁸** And He says *to* them, "Draw *some* now, and carry *it to* the headwaiter[J]". And the *ones* carried *it*. **⁹** And when the headwaiter tasted the water having become wine— and he did not know where it was from, but the servants having drawn the water knew— the headwaiter calls the bridegroom, **¹⁰** and says *to* him, "Every person first puts *out* the fine wine, and when they get-drunk[K], the lesser. **You** have kept the fine wine until now". **¹¹** Jesus did this beginning[L] *of* signs in Cana *of* Galilee, and revealed His glory. And His disciples believed in Him. **¹²** After this He went down to Capernaum— He and His mother and His brothers and His disciples. And they stayed there not many days.

At The Passover, Consumed By Zeal For God's House, Jesus Cleanses The Temple
¹³ And the Passover [Feast] *of* the Jews was near, and Jesus went up to Jerusalem. **¹⁴** And in the temple, He found the *ones* selling oxen and sheep and doves, and the changers-of-money sitting [at their tables]. **¹⁵** And having made *a* lash[M] from ropes, He drove *them* all out of the temple, and[N] the sheep and the oxen. And He poured-out the coin *of* the money-changers. And He overturned the tables. **¹⁶** And He said *to* the *ones* selling the doves, "Take these *things* from here. Do not be making the house *of* My Father a house *of a* market". **¹⁷** His disciples remembered that it has been written [in Ps 69:9], "Zeal *for* Your house will consume Me". **¹⁸** Then the Jews responded and said *to* Him, "What sign do You show us, that you are doing these *things*?" **¹⁹** Jesus responded and said *to* them, "Destroy this temple, and in three days I will raise it". **²⁰** Then the Jews said, "This temple was built *for* forty and six years, and **You** will raise it in three days?" **²¹** But that *One* was speaking about the temple *of* His body. **²²** So when He was raised from *the* dead, His disciples remembered that He was saying this, and believed the Scripture, and the word which Jesus spoke.

A. That is, while you (Nathanael) were. **B.** Or, You believe... tree! **C.** This word is plural. **D.** That is, the third day of their travels since 1:43. **E.** Lit, What [is there] *for* Me and *for* you? What business do I share with you in this matter? **F.** Jesus distances Himself from His mother, using this term one would use to address any woman. His ministry has begun, during which He no longer relates to her in a family, mother-son way, fulfilling her requests. **G.** Mary takes Jesus to mean He will answer her on His own terms, not hers. He chooses a miracle as the Son of God rather than an errand as the son of Mary. **H.** See Mk 7:3. **I.** That is, 20-30 gallons or 80-120 liters. **J.** Or, master-of-ceremonies. **K.** This whole proverbial-type comment is about the quality of the wine, not the state or intention of these guests. **L.** Or, this *as a* beginning. **M.** Or, whip. **N.** Or, both.

Many Believed, But Jesus Did Not Entrust Himself To Them
23 Now while He was in Jerusalem at the Passover during the Feast, many believed in His name, seeing His signs which He was doing. **24** But Jesus Himself was not entrusting Himself *to* them— because of His knowing all *people*; **25** and because He was having no need that someone should testify about the person, for He Himself was knowing what was in the person.

Nicodemus, a Ruler of The Jews, Comes To Jesus, And Is Told He Must Be Born Again
3:1 Now there was *a* man from the Pharisees— the name *for* him *was* Nicodemus— *a* ruler *of* the Jews. **2** This *one* came to Him *by* night and said *to* Him, "Rabbi, we know that You have come from God *as a* teacher. For no one is able to be doing these signs which **You** are doing unless God is with him". **3** Jesus responded and said *to* him, "Truly, truly, I say *to* you— unless one is born again^A, he is not able to see the kingdom *of* God". **4** Nicodemus says to Him, "How is *a* person able to be born while being *an* old-man? He is not able to enter *a* second *time* into the womb *of* his mother and be born, *is he*?" **5** Jesus responded, "Truly, truly, I say *to* you, unless one is born of water^B and *the* Spirit, he is not able to enter into the kingdom *of* God. **6** The *thing* having been born of the flesh is flesh, and the *thing* having been born of the Spirit is spirit. **7** Do not marvel that I said *to* you, 'You^C all must be born again'— **8** the wind blows where it wants, and you hear the sound *of* it, but you do not know from where it comes, and where it is going. So^D is everyone having been born of the Spirit". **9** Nicodemus responded and said *to* Him, "How are these^E *things* able to happen?" **10** Jesus responded and said *to* him, "Are **you** the teacher *of* Israel and you do not understand these *things*? **11** Truly, truly, I say *to* you that we are speaking what we know, and we are testifying what we have seen, and you^F *people* are not receiving our testimony. **12** If I told you *people* earthly *things* and you do not believe, how will you believe if I tell you heavenly *things*? **13** And no one has gone up into heaven except the *One* having come down from heaven— the Son *of* Man. **14** And just as Moses lifted-up the serpent in the wilderness, so the Son *of* Man must be lifted up **15** in order that everyone putting-faith in Him may have^G eternal life.

God Sent His Son Into The World That All Believing In Him May Have Eternal Life
16 "For^H God so^I loved the world that He gave *His* only-born Son, in order that everyone believing in Him may not perish, but may have eternal life. **17** For God did not send-forth the Son into the world in order that He might judge^J the world, but in order that the world might be saved through Him. **18** The *one* believing in Him is not judged. But the *one* not believing has been judged already, because he has not believed in the name *of* the only-born Son *of* God. **19** And this is the judgment^K: that the Light has come into the world, and people loved the darkness rather than the Light, for their

A. Or, from-above. **B.** Jesus may be detailing the idea of being born again in v 3, in which case the water refers to the visible aspect of it, that is, baptism; or, Jesus may explain His meaning by the illustration in v 6, water referring to 'of the flesh', that is, human birth. **C.** This word is plural. **D.** We do not understand the 'how' (v 4) of wind; we only see its effects. So it is with the spiritual wind of birth from God (spirit and wind are the same word in Greek). **E.** That is, this being born again from God. **F.** This word is plural. **G.** After the chastisement of v 10-12, and stating the authority for His answer in v 13, Jesus here answers the question of v 9, and then explains it in what follows. **H.** Jesus may continue speaking in v 16-21; or, these may be John's words of explanation for us. **I.** That is, in this manner; or, to such an extent. **J.** That is, pass judgment upon, execute judgment upon. **K.** That is, this is God's present judgment with regard to unbelievers.

works were evil. **20** For everyone practicing bad *things* hates the Light, and does not come to the Light in order that his works may not be exposed. **21** But the *one* doing the truth comes to the Light in order that his works may become-visible— that[A] they have been worked **in**[B] **God**".

Jesus Goes To Judea. John The Baptist Declares Himself The Friend of The Bridegroom
22 After these *things* Jesus and His disciples went into the Judean land, and there He was spending-time with them and baptizing. **23** Now John also was baptizing in Aenon near Salim, because there were many waters[C] there. And they were coming and being baptized. **24** For John had not yet been thrown into prison. **25** Then *a* debate[D] arose from the disciples *of* John with *a* Jew about purification. **26** And they came to John and said *to* him, "Rabbi, He who was with you beyond the Jordan, *concerning* Whom **you** have testified, look— this *One* is baptizing, and all are going to Him!" **27** John responded and said "*A* person cannot receive even one *thing* unless it has been given *to* him from heaven. **28** **You** yourselves are testifying *concerning* me that I said that 'I am not the Christ', but that 'I am *one* having been sent-forth ahead of that *One*'. **29** The *one* having the bride is *the* bridegroom. And the friend *of* the bridegroom, the *one* standing *there* and hearing him, rejoices *with* joy[E] because of the voice *of* the bridegroom. So this[F], my joy, has been made-full. **30** It-is-necessary *for* that *One* to grow, and *for* me to diminish.

Jesus Has Come From Heaven With The Words of God. He Is Above All
31 "The[G] *One* coming from-above is above[H] all. The *one* being from the earth is from the earth and is speaking from the earth. The *One* coming from heaven is above all. **32** What He has seen and did hear— this He is testifying. And no one is receiving His testimony. **33** The *one* having received His testimony certified[I] that God is truthful, **34** for He Whom God sent forth is speaking the words *of* God. For He does not give *Him* the Spirit from *a* measure[J]. **35** The Father loves the Son, and has given all *things* in His hand. **36** The *one* believing in the Son has eternal life. But the *one* disobeying[K] the Son will not see life, but the wrath *of* God remains on him".

Jesus Goes To Galilee
4:1 So when Jesus knew[L] that the Pharisees heard that Jesus was making and baptizing more disciples than John **2** (although Jesus Himself was not baptizing, but His disciples), **3** He left Judea and went again[M] toward Galilee. **4** And He had-to go through Samaria.

On The Way, Jesus Stops At a Well In Samaria
5 So He comes into *a* city *of* Samaria being called Sychar, near the place which Jacob gave *to* his son Joseph. **6** Now *a* spring *of* Jacob was there. So Jesus, having become weary from the journey, was sitting thus[N] at the spring. *The* hour was about *the* sixth[O].

He Talks With a Woman At The Well, And Tells Her He Is The Awaited Messiah
7 *A* woman of Samaria comes to draw water. Jesus says *to* her, "Give Me *water* to

---

A. Or, because. **B.** That is, in union with. **C.** That is, many streams or springs of water. **D.** Or, controversy. **E.** That is, rejoices greatly. **F.** That is, this friend-of-the-bridegroom kind of joy. **G.** Verses 31-36 may continue to be the Baptist's words; or, they may be the apostle John's comment. **H.** Or, over. **I.** Or, attested, set his seal. **J.** God does not give Jesus a measured manifestation of the Spirit, as He does with all other prophets. **K.** Or, refusing-to-believe. **L.** Or, learned. **M.** Or, back. **N.** That is, wearied. **O.** That is, noon Jewish time; or, 6 P.M. Roman time.

drink". **8** For His disciples had gone into the city in order that they might buy food. **9** So the Samaritan woman says *to* Him, "How *is it* **You**, being *a* Jew, are asking *something* to drink from me, being *a* Samaritan woman?" For Jews do not use-*things*-together-with^A Samaritans. **10** Jesus responded and said *to* her, "If you knew the gift *of* God, and Who the *One* saying *to* you 'Give Me *water* to drink' is— **you** would have asked Him, and He would have given you living water". **11** The woman says *to* Him, "Sir, You have no bucket and the well is deep. From where then do You have the living water? **12 You** are not greater *than* our father Jacob, *are You*, who gave us the well, and himself drank from it, and his sons, and his animals?" **13** Jesus responded and said *to* her, "Everyone drinking from this water will thirst again. **14** But whoever should drink from the water which **I** will give him— he will never thirst, ever. On the contrary, the water which I will give him will become *a* spring *of* water in him, bubbling-up to eternal life". **15** The woman says to Him, "Sir, give me this water in order that I may not be thirsting, nor coming here to draw *it*". **16** He says *to* her, "Go, call your husband and come here". **17** The woman responded and said *to* Him, "I do **not** have *a* husband". Jesus says *to* her, "You said rightly that 'I do not have *a* **husband**'. **18** For you had five husbands. And now he whom you have is not your husband. You have spoken this *as a* true *thing*". **19** The woman says *to* Him, "Sir, I perceive that **You** are *a* prophet. **20** Our fathers worshiped on this^B mountain, and **you**^C *Jews* say that the place where one must worship is in Jerusalem". **21** Jesus says *to* her, "Believe Me, woman, that *an* hour is coming when you^D *Samaritans* will give-worship *to* the Father neither on this mountain nor in Jerusalem. **22 You** *Samaritans* worship what you do not know. **We** *Jews* worship what we know, because salvation is from the Jews. **23** But *an* hour is coming, and now is, when the true worshipers will give-worship *to* the Father in spirit and truth. For indeed the Father is seeking such *ones to be* the *ones* worshiping Him. **24** God *is* spirit, and the *ones* worshiping Him must worship in spirit and truth". **25** The woman says *to* Him, "I know that Messiah is coming— the *One* being called Christ. When that *One* comes, He will declare all *things to* us". **26** Jesus says *to* her, "**I**, the *One* speaking *to* you, am *He*".

The Disciples Marvel That He Was Speaking With a Woman
27 And at this *point* His disciples came, and they were marveling that He was speaking with *a* woman. Yet no one said, "What are you seeking?" or, "Why are You speaking with her?" **28** So the woman left her waterpot, and went into the city. And she says *to* the people, **29** "Come, see *a* man Who told me everything that I did. This *One* is not the Christ, *is He*?" **30** They went out of the city, and were coming to Him.

Jesus Explains: I Came To Do God's Will. The Harvest Is Ripe
31 In the meantime the disciples were asking Him, saying, "Rabbi, eat". **32** But the *One* said *to* them, "**I** have food to eat that **you** do not know *about*". **33** So the disciples were saying to one another, "Someone did not bring Him *something* to eat, *did he*?" **34** Jesus says *to* them, "My food is that I may do the will *of* the *One* having sent Me, and accomplish His work. **35** Do **you** not say that 'There are still^E four months, and the

---

A. Or, make-use-of-*vessels*-with; or more broadly, *socially*-associate-with. **B.** This well was at the foot of Mount Gerizim, where the Samaritans worshiped. **C.** This word is plural. **D.** This word is plural. **E.** That is, do you not expect a delay between sowing and harvesting?

harvest comes'? Behold, I say *to* you— lift-up your eyes and look-*at* the fields, that[A] they are white for harvest[B]. Already [36] the *one* reaping is receiving wages, and is gathering fruit for life eternal, so that the *one* sowing and the *one* reaping may rejoice together. [37] For in this *case* the saying is true, that 'One is the *one* sowing and another[C] is the *one* reaping. [38] I sent you out to be reaping what **you** have not[D] labored-*for.* Others have labored, and **you** have entered into their labor".

Many Samaritans Believe His Message After Hearing His Words
[39] And many *of* the Samaritans from that city believed in Him because of the word *of* the woman testifying that "He told me everything which I did". [40] Therefore when the Samaritans came to Him, they were asking Him to stay with them. And He stayed there *for* two days. [41] And many more believed because of His word. [42] And they were saying *to* the woman that "We are no longer believing because of your speaking. For we ourselves have heard, and we know that this *One* is truly the Savior *of* the world". [43] And after the two days, He went forth from there to Galilee. [44] For Jesus Himself testified that *a* prophet does not have honor in *his* own homeland.

Arriving In Galilee, a Royal Jew Believes After Jesus Heals His Son
[45] So when He came to Galilee, the Galileans welcomed Him, having seen all that He did in Jerusalem at the Feast. For **they** also went to the Feast. [46] So He came again to Cana *of* Galilee, where He made the water wine. And there was *a* certain royal *one* whose son was sick in Capernaum. [47] This *one*, having heard that Jesus had come from Judea to Galilee, went to Him, and was asking that He come down and heal his son. For he was about to die. [48] So Jesus said to him, "Unless you[E] *people* see signs and wonders, you will by no means believe". [49] The royal *one* says to Him, "Master, come down before my child dies". [50] Jesus says *to* him, "Go, your son lives". The man believed the word which Jesus spoke *to* him, and was going. [51] Now while he *was* already going down, his slaves met him, saying that his boy lives. [52] So he inquired from them the hour at which he got better. So they said *to* him that "The fever left him yesterday *at the* seventh[F] hour". [53] Then the father knew that *it was* at that hour at which Jesus said *to* him, "Your son lives". And he believed[G], he and his whole household. [54] Now this again *was a* second[H] sign Jesus did, having come from Judea to Galilee.

Jesus Goes To Jerusalem For a Feast, And Heals a Man On The Sabbath
5:1 After these *things* there was *a* Feast *of* the Jews, and Jesus went up to Jerusalem. [2] Now in Jerusalem near the Sheep *gate*, there is *a* pool— the *one* being called Bethzatha *in* Hebrew, having five porticos[I]. [3] In these *porticos*, a multitude *of* the ones being sick were lying-down— blind *ones*, lame *ones*, withered *ones*. [4][J] [5] And there was *a* certain man there having thirty and

---

A. Or, because. **B:** white for harvest. Already the *one*. Or, already white for harvest. The *one*. **C.** Jesus and the woman are both reaping. They entered into a harvest prepared by others. **D.** Jews and those connected with them throughout the world were already prepared for reaping, anticipating the Messiah. **E.** This word is plural. **F.** That is, 1 P.M. Jewish time, meaning these slaves met the official that evening after sundown (which begins the next day); or, 7 P.M. Roman time, meaning the official spent the night due to the late hour and met these slaves the next day. **G.** Note how this proves what Jesus said in v 48, and stands in contrast to v 41-42. **H.** That is, second in Galilee or Cana; or, second manifesting His glory, due to the special nature of both (see 2:11); or, second of the seven John records in this book. **I.** That is, covered colonnades where people gathered. **J.** Some manuscripts add as verse 4, For *an* angel in due season was going down in the pool and stirring up the water.

eight years in his sickness. **⁶** Jesus— having seen this *one* lying down, and having known^A that he already had *a* long time [in his sickness]— says *to* him, "Do you want to become healthy?" **⁷** The *one* being sick answered Him, "Sir, I do not have *a* man to put me into the pool when the water is stirred-up. But while **I** am going, another goes down before me". **⁸** Jesus says *to* him, "Arise, pick up your cot and walk!" **⁹** And immediately the man became healthy, and picked up his cot and was walking.

They Want To Kill Jesus Because He Breaks The Sabbath And Makes Himself Equal To God
Now it was *a* Sabbath on that day. **¹⁰** So the Jews were saying *to* the *one* having been cured, "It is *the* Sabbath, and it is not lawful *for* you to pick up your cot". **¹¹** But the *one* answered them, "The *One* having made me healthy, that *One* said *to* me, 'Pick up your cot and walk' ". **¹²** They asked him, "Who is the man having said *to* you, 'Pick up and walk'?" **¹³** But the *one* having been healed did not know who He was. For Jesus withdrew, *a* crowd being in the place. **¹⁴** After these *things*, Jesus finds him in the temple. And He said *to* him, "See— you have become healthy! Do not be sinning any longer in order that something worse may not happen *to* you". **¹⁵** The man went away and reported *to* the Jews that Jesus was the *One* having made him healthy. **¹⁶** And for this reason, the Jews were persecuting Jesus— because He was doing these *things* on *a* Sabbath. **¹⁷** But Jesus answered them, "My Father is working until now, and^B **I** am working". **¹⁸** Therefore, for this reason the Jews were seeking more to kill Him: because He was not only breaking^C the Sabbath, but He was also calling God *His* own Father, making Himself equal^D *to* God! **¹⁹** Therefore Jesus responded and was saying *to* them—

Jesus Responds Regarding His Work: The Son Does Only What The Father Does
"Truly, truly, I say *to* you— the Son can do nothing from Himself except^E something He sees the Father doing. For whatever *things* that *One* is doing, these *things* the Son is also likewise doing. **²⁰** For the Father loves the Son, and shows Him all *things* that He Himself is doing. And He will show Him **greater** works *than* these, in order that **you** may marvel.

The Son Raises And Judges The Dead, And Thus Is Due Equal Honor With God
²¹ "For^F just as the Father raises the dead and gives-life-to *them*, so also the Son gives-life-to *the ones* whom He wishes^G. **²²** For the Father does not even judge anyone, but He has given all judgment *to* the Son, **²³** in order that all may honor the Son just-as^H they are honoring the Father. The *one* not honoring the Son is not honoring the Father having sent Him. **²⁴** Truly, truly, I say *to* you that the *one* hearing My word and believing the *One* having sent Me has eternal life. And he does not come into judgment, but has passed from death to life.

Then the *one* first having stepped in after the stirring up *of* the water was becoming healthy *for* whatever disease he was indeed being afflicted. **A.** Or, learned. **B.** Jesus places His working on the Sabbath on an equal plane with God's doing so. **C.** That is, annulling the authority of the Sabbath over how people should live. **D.** If God is His own Father, then Jesus has the same nature and essence as God, as do all fathers and sons, and thus is Himself God. Jesus was killed for claiming this, 19:7. **E.** That is, the Son does only and always what the Father does, explaining v 17. They are in perfect harmony. **F.** Jesus gives the ultimate example of 'whatever things' the Father is doing. **G.** Or, wills, wants, desires. **H.** Or, in the same manner. Only one claiming to be equal to God would say such a thing.

The Son Has Life In Himself And Gives Life To The Spiritually Dead
25 "Truly, truly, I say *to* you that *an* hour is coming, and now is, when the dead will hear the voice *of* the Son *of* God, and the *ones* having heard will live. **26** For just as the Father has life in Himself, so also He gave *to* the Son to have life in Himself. **27** And He gave Him authority to execute judgment, because He is *a* son[A] *of* man.

The Son Will Give Life To The Physically Dead
28 Do not be marveling-*at* this, because *an* hour is coming in which all the *ones* in the graves will hear His voice, **29** and will come out— the *ones* having done the good *things* to *a* resurrection *of* life; the *ones* having practiced the bad *things* to *a* resurrection *of* judgment.

I Am Doing The Will of The One Who Sent Me
30 "**I** can do nothing from Myself. Just as I am hearing[B], I am judging. And **My** judgment is righteous, because I am not seeking **My** will, but the will *of* the One having sent Me.

Jesus Responds Regarding His Identity: Others Testify About Him
31 "If **I** am[C] testifying about Myself, My testimony is not true. **32** There is Another— the *One* testifying about Me— and I know that the testimony which He is testifying about Me is true.

John The Baptist Testified
33 "**You** have sent out *messengers* to John, and he has testified *to* the truth[D]. **34** But **I** do not receive[E] testimony from *a* human. Nevertheless, I am saying these *things* in order that **you** may be saved. **35** That *one* was the burning and shining lamp, and **you** were willing to be overjoyed in his light for *an* hour.

Three Greater Witnesses Testify: My Works, The Father, And-The Scriptures
36 "But **I** have testimony greater *than* John's. For the works which the Father has given *to* Me that I should accomplish them— the works themselves which I am doing are testifying about Me, that the Father has sent Me forth. **37** And the Father having sent Me— that *One* has testified about Me. Neither His voice have you ever heard, nor His form have you seen. **38** And you do not have His word abiding in you, because *the One* Whom that *One* sent-forth— this *One* **you** are not believing! **39** You[F] search the Scriptures because **you** think *that* in them *you* have eternal life— and those *Scriptures* are the *ones* testifying about Me! **40** And you are not willing to come to Me in order that you may have life.

But You Are Not Receiving Me Because You Do Not Love God
41 "I do not receive glory from people, **42** but I know you— that you do not have the love *of* God in yourselves. **43** **I** have come in the name *of* My Father, and you

---

A. That is, a human. Or, *the* Son *of* Man, the one mentioned in Dan 7:13. **B.** That is, hearing from the Father, complementing the seeing in v 19. **C.** That is, If I alone am, apart from God. **D.** See 1:34. **E.** That is, do not merely receive. **F.** Or, this may be a command, Search.

are not receiving Me. If another comes in *his* own name, you will receive that *one*. **44** How are **you** able to believe while receiving glory from one another, and you are not seeking the glory from the only God?

Moses Will Be Your Accuser. For If You Believed Him, You Would Believe Me
45 Do not be thinking that **I** will accuse you before the Father. The *one* accusing you is Moses, in whom **you** have put-hope. **46** For if you were believing Moses, you would be believing Me, for that *one* wrote about Me. **47** But if you do not believe the writings *of* that *one*, how will you believe My words?"

Jesus Returns To Galilee And Feeds The 5000
6:1 After these *things,* Jesus went away to the other side *of* the Sea *of* Galilee— *of* Tiberias[A]. **2** And *a* large crowd was following Him, because they were seeing the signs which He was doing on the *ones* being sick. **3** And Jesus went up on the mountain, and was sitting there with His disciples. **4** And the Passover, the Feast *of* the Jews, was near. **5** Then Jesus, having lifted-up *His* eyes and seen that *a* large crowd was coming to Him, says to Philip, "From where may we buy bread in order that these *ones* may eat?" **6** Now He was saying this testing him. For He Himself knew what He was going to do. **7** Philip answered Him, "Loaves *worth* two-hundred denarii[B] are not enough *for* them, in order that each *one* may receive *a* little bit". **8** One of His disciples— Andrew, the brother *of* Simon Peter— says *to* Him, **9** "There is *a* boy here who has five barley loaves and two fish, but what are these for so many?" **10** Jesus said, "Make the people fall-back [to eat]". And there was much grass in the place. So the men— about five-thousand *as to* the number— fell back [to eat]. **11** Then Jesus took the loaves. And having given-thanks, He distributed *them to* the *ones* reclining-back [to eat]— likewise also from the fish— as much as they were wanting. **12** And when they were filled, He says *to* His disciples, "Gather the left-over fragments so that nothing may be lost". **13** So they gathered, and filled twelve baskets *of* fragments from the five barley loaves, which were left over *by* the *ones* having eaten. **14** Therefore the people, having seen *the* sign which He did, were saying that "This *One* is truly the Prophet[C] coming into the world". **15** Then Jesus, having known that they were about to come and take Him away-by-force in order that they might make Him king, withdrew again to the mountain, Himself alone.

Jesus Walks On Water To Capernaum
16 Now when it became evening, His disciples went down to the sea. **17** And having gotten into *a* boat, they were going to the other side *of* the sea, to Capernaum. And darkness already had come, and Jesus had not-yet come to them. **18** And the sea was becoming aroused *from a* great wind blowing. **19** So having rowed about twenty five or thirty stades[D], they see Jesus walking on the sea and becoming near the boat. And they became afraid. **20** But the *One* says *to* them, "**I** am[E] *the One*. Do not be afraid". **21** So they were willing to take Him into the boat. And immediately the boat came-to-be at the land to which they were going.

The Crowd Follows Him There
22 *On* the next day the crowd standing on the other side *of* the sea saw that there had not

---

A. This is the Roman name for this Sea. **B.** One denarius was a day's wage for a laborer. **C.** See 1:21. **D.** That is, 2.9 to 3.5 miles or 4.6 to 5.6 kilometers; about half way across. **E.** That is, It is I.

been another small boat there except [the] one, and that Jesus had not entered into the boat with His disciples, but His disciples had gone away alone. **23** Other^A small-boats came from Tiberias near the place where they ate the bread, the Lord having given-thanks. **24** So when the crowd saw that Jesus was not there, nor His disciples, **they** got into the small boats, and went to Capernaum seeking Jesus.

Jesus Says, Work For The Food Leading To Eternal Life, Which The Son Will Give You
25 And having found Him on the other side *of* the sea, they said *to* Him, "Rabbi, when have You come here?" **26** Jesus responded *to* them and said, "Truly, truly, I say *to* you— you are seeking Me not because you saw signs^B, but because you ate of the loaves-of-bread and were filled-to-satisfaction. **27** Do not be working *for* the food *which is* perishing, but *for* the food *which is* remaining to^C eternal life— which the Son *of* Man will give *to* you. For God the Father certified^D this *One*".

The Work God Requires of You Is To Believe In The One Sent Forth By God
28 So they said to Him, "What may we be doing in order that we may be working the works *of* God?" **29** Jesus responded and said *to* them, "This is the work *of* God: that you be believing in *the One* Whom that *One* sent-forth".

My Father Is Giving You The True Bread From Heaven, Which Came To Give Life
30 So they said *to* Him, "What then do **You** do *as a* sign, in order that we may see *it* and believe You? What *thing* do you work? **31** Our fathers ate the manna in the wilderness, just as it has been written [in Ps 78:24]: 'He gave them bread from heaven to eat' ". **32** So Jesus said *to* them, "Truly, truly, I say *to* you, Moses has not given you the bread from heaven, but My Father is giving you the true Bread from heaven. **33** For the bread *of* God is the *One* coming^E down from heaven and giving life *to* the world".

I Am The Bread of Life Come From Heaven. He Who Believes In Me Has Eternal Life
34 So they said to Him, "Master, give us this bread always". **35** Jesus said *to* them, "**I** am the bread *of* life. The *one* coming to Me will never hunger, and the *one* believing in Me will never ever^F thirst. **36** But I said *to* you that you have indeed seen Me^G, and you are not believing. **37** All that the Father gives *to* Me will come to Me, and I will never^H throw outside the *one* coming to Me. **38** Because I have come down from heaven not in order that I may be doing **My** will, but the will of the *One* having sent Me. **39** And this is the will *of* the *One* having sent Me: that *as to* all that He has given *to* Me, I will not lose *anything* from it, but I will raise it up on the last day. **40** For this is the will *of* My Father: that everyone seeing the Son and believing in Him may have eternal life, and **I** will raise him up on the last day".

I Am The Living Bread From Heaven: Eat And Live Forever. The Bread Is My Flesh
41 Then the Jews were grumbling about Him because He said, "I am the bread having come down from heaven". **42** And they were saying, "Is this *One* not Jesus, the son

---

A. Or, However, small-boats. **B.** That is, saw signs and want to know what they signify. They merely want the earthly benefit. **C.** Or, into, for. **D.** Or, attested, set His seal on. This is the meaning of the signs. **E.** Jesus is referring to Himself. But grammatically this can also mean 'the *bread* coming', which is how the hearers took it, as seen next. **F.** Or, at-any-time. **G.** That is, seen Me in action, seen God certify Me by signs, v 27. **H.** Or, by-no-means.

of Joseph, whose father and mother **we** know? How does He now say that 'I have come down from heaven'?" **43** Jesus responded and said *to* them, "Do not be grumbling with one another. **44** No one is able to come to Me unless the Father having sent Me draws him. And **I** will raise him up on the last day. **45** It has been written in the prophets [in Isa 54:13]: 'and they shall all be taught *ones of* God'. Everyone having heard from the Father and having learned, comes to Me— **46** not that anyone has seen the Father, except the *One* being from God; this *One* has seen the Father. **47** Truly, truly, I say *to* you— the *one* believing has eternal life. **48** I am the bread *of* life. **49** Your fathers ate the manna in the wilderness and died. **50** This is the bread coming down from heaven in order that anyone may eat of it and not die. **51** I am the living bread having come down from heaven. If anyone eats of this bread, he will live forever. And indeed the bread which **I** will give for the life *of* the world is My flesh".

My Flesh Is True Food; My Blood Is True Drink. Partake And Live Forever
52 Then the Jews were fighting with one another, saying, "How can this *One* give us His flesh to eat?" **53** So Jesus said *to* them, "Truly, truly, I say *to* you, unless^A you eat the flesh *of* the Son *of* Man and drink His blood, you do not have life in yourselves. **54** The *one* eating My flesh and drinking My blood has eternal life, and **I** will raise him up *on* the last day. **55** For My flesh is true^B food, and My blood is true drink. **56** The *one* eating My flesh and drinking My blood abides in Me, and I in him. **57** Just as the living Father sent Me forth, and **I** live because of the Father, indeed the *one* eating Me— that *one* also will live because of Me. **58** This is the bread having come down from heaven; not as *the manna* the fathers ate and died. The *one* eating this bread will live forever". **59** He said these *things* in *a* synagogue while teaching in Capernaum.

These Words Are Spirit And Life. But Some of You Disciples Do Not Believe
60 Then many of His disciples, having heard, said, "This statement is hard^C. Who can hear^D it?" **61** But Jesus, knowing in Himself that His disciples are grumbling about this, said *to* them, "Does this offend you? **62** Then *what* if you see the Son *of* Man going up where He was formerly? **63** The Spirit is the *One* giving-life. The flesh profits nothing. The words which **I** have spoken *to* you are spirit, and are life. **64** But there are some of you who do not believe". For Jesus knew from *the* beginning who the *ones* not believing were, and who the *one who* will hand Him over was. **65** And He was saying, "For this reason I have said *to* you that no one is able to come to Me unless it has been granted *to* him from the Father".

From This Time, Many of His Disciples No Longer Followed Him
66 From this *time*, many of His disciples went back, and were no longer walking with Him. **67** So Jesus said *to* the twelve, "**You** also are not wanting to go-away, *are you*?" **68** Simon Peter answered Him, "Lord, to whom shall we go? You have *the* words *of* eternal life. **69** And **we** have believed, and have come-to-know that **You** are the Holy *One of* God". **70** Jesus answered them, "Did **I** not choose you, the twelve, and one of

A. Rather than soften or explain v 51b, Jesus emboldens it. He makes no attempt to resolve their fighting, but inflames it even more. A more shocking, repugnant, and Law-violating phrase for a Jew can hardly be imagined. In response to their desire to force Him to be king (v 15), Jesus is forcing them to a decision concerning His true nature and mission. **B.** Or, genuine, real. It produces true life. **C.** Not hard to understand, but hard to accept, offensive, harsh, objectionable. **D.** That is, accept and obey.

you is *the* devil?" **71** Now He was speaking-*of* Judas, *son of* Simon Iscariot. For this *one*, one of the twelve, was going to hand Him over.

Jesus Remained In Galilee Because They Were Seeking To Kill Him In Judea
7:1 And after these *things* Jesus was walking in Galilee. For He was not willing to be walking in Judea, because the Jews were seeking to kill Him.

Jesus Goes To Jerusalem For The Feast of Tabernacles
2 Now the Tent-pitching^A Feast *of* the Jews was near. **3** So His brothers said to Him, "Pass-on from here and go to Judea, so that Your disciples [there] also will see Your works which You are doing. **4** For no one does something in secret and himself seeks to be in public. If You are doing these *things*, make Yourself known^B *to* the world". **5** (For not even His brothers were believing in Him). **6** So Jesus says *to* them, "**My** time^C is not yet here, but your time is always ready. **7** The world cannot hate you, but it is hating Me because **I** am testifying about it that its works are evil. **8** **You** go up to the Feast. I am not going up to this Feast, because My time has not yet been fulfilled". **9** And having said these *things,* **He** remained in Galilee. **10** But when His brothers went up to the Feast, then **He** also went up— not openly, but as in secret. **11** Then the Jews were seeking-*for* Him at the Feast, and saying "Where is that *One*?" **12** And there was much grumbling about Him among the crowds. Some were saying that "He is good". But others were saying, "No, but He is deceiving the crowd". **13** Yet no one was speaking *with* openness^D about Him because of fear *of* the Jews.

In The Middle of The Feast, Jesus Began Teaching In The Temple:
14 Now the Feast already being-at-the-middle, Jesus went up to the temple, and was teaching.

My Teaching Is From God And For His Glory. Why Do You Want To Kill Me?
15 Then the Jews were marveling, saying, "How does this *One* know writings^E, not having learned?" **16** So Jesus responded *to* them and said "My teaching is not Mine, but the *One's* having sent Me. **17** If anyone is willing^F to be doing His will, he will know about the teaching— whether it is from God, or **I** am speaking from Myself. **18** The *one* speaking from himself is seeking *his* own glory. But the *One* seeking the glory *of* the *One* having sent Him— this *One* is true, and there is no unrighteousness in Him. **19** Has not Moses given you the Law? And none of you is doing the Law! Why are you seeking to kill Me?"

Do Not Judge According To Appearance
20 The crowd answered, "You have *a* demon! Who is seeking to kill You?" **21** Jesus responded and said *to* them, "I did one^G work, and you all marvel! **22** For this reason^H Moses has given you circumcision (not that it is from Moses, but *it is* from the fathers), and you circumcise *a* man **on** *a* **Sabbath**. **23** If *a* man receives **circumcision** on *a* Sabbath in order that the Law *of* Moses may not be broken,

---

A. Or, Booth-building. That is, the Feast of Tents (Tabernacles) in October. **B.** Or, reveal Yourself. **C.** Or, favorable-time, right-time. That is, My time to go up openly (v 10) and reveal Myself (v 4). **D.** Or, in public. **E.** Or, learning. That is, how can Jesus be educated in these matters, not having learned it in our schools? **F.** Or, wanting, resolving. **G.** That is, one work of healing, referring to 5:9. **H.** That is, for healing, for 'making sound' one member, setting up the comparison in v 23; or, as an example of work on the Sabbath.

are you angry[A] *at* Me because I made *an* **entire man** sound[B] on *a* Sabbath? **24** Do not be judging according to appearance, but be judging the righteous judgment".

The God Whom You Do Not Know Sent Me To You

25 Then some of the people-of-Jerusalem were saying, "Is not this *the One* Whom they are seeking to kill? **26** And look— He is speaking *in* public, and they are saying nothing *to* Him. The rulers did not perhaps really know[C] that this *One* is the Christ, *did they*? **27** However, we know where this *One* is from. But when the Christ is coming, no one knows where He is from". **28** So Jesus cried-out while teaching in the temple and saying, "You both know Me and You know where I am from. And[D] I have not come of Myself. However, the *One* having sent Me is true— Whom **you** do not know. **29** I know Him, because I am from Him. And that *One* sent Me forth". **30** Therefore they were seeking to seize Him. And no one put *his* hand on Him, because His hour had not yet come.

I Will Be With You a Short Time Longer, Then I Am Returning To God

31 But many from the crowd believed in Him. And they were saying, "When the Christ comes, He will not do more[E] signs *than the ones* which this *One* did, *will He*?" **32** The Pharisees heard the crowd murmuring these *things* about Him. And the chief priests and the Pharisees sent out officers in order that they might seize Him. **33** So Jesus said, "I am with you *a* short time longer, and [then] I am going to the *One* having sent Me. **34** You will seek Me, and will not find Me. And where **I** am, **you** are not able to come". **35** Then the Jews said to themselves, "Where is this *One* going to go that **we** will not find Him? He is not going to go to the Dispersion *of* the Greeks and teach the Greeks, *is He*? **36** What is this statement that He said: 'You will seek Me and will not find Me. And where **I** am, **you** are not able to come'?"

On The Last Day Jesus Said, Come To Me. The Crowd Remained Divided Over Him

37 Now on the last day, the great *day of* the Feast, Jesus was standing *there*. And He cried-out, saying, "If anyone is thirsting, let him come to Me and drink. **38** The *one* believing in Me, just as the Scripture said— Rivers *of* living water will flow from his[F] belly". **39** Now He said this concerning the Spirit, Whom the *ones* having believed in Him were going to receive. For *the* Spirit was not yet *given*, because Jesus was not yet glorified. **40** Then *some* from the crowd, having heard these words, were saying "This *One* is truly the Prophet[G]". **41** Others were saying "This *One* is the Christ". But the[H] *ones* were saying "The Christ is not indeed[I] coming from Galilee, *is He*? **42** Did not the Scripture say that the Christ comes from the seed *of* David, and from Bethlehem, the village where David was?" **43** So *a* division took place in the crowd because of Him. **44** And some of them were wanting to seize Him, but no one put *his* hands on Him.

Most of The Jewish Rulers And Pharisees Did Not Believe In Him

45 Then the officers went to the chief priests and Pharisees. And those *ones* said *to*

A. Or, galled, bitterly-angry. **B.** Or, healthy. If the Law requires the making sound of this one member on the Sabbath, surely the making sound of the entire man is permitted. **C.** Or, learn, recognize. **D.** Or, And-*yet*. **E.** Or, greater. **F.** Or, let him come to Me. And let the *one* believing in Me drink. Just as the Scripture said, rivers *of* living water will flow from His (Christ's) belly. **G.** See 1:21. **H.** That is, the group in v 40. Or, But others, referring to a third group. **I.** This question has an incredulous tone, as in Mt 27:23.

them, "For what reason did you not bring Him?" **46** The officers answered, "Never did *a* man speak in this manner". **47** Then the Pharisees responded *to* them, "**You** also have not been deceived, *have you*? **48** Someone from the rulers did not believe in Him, *did he,* or from the Pharisees? **49** But this crowd not knowing the Law— they are accursed *ones*". **50** Nicodemus— the *one* having come to Him formerly, being one of them— says to them, **51** "Our Law does not judge the person unless it first hears from him, and knows what he is doing, *does it*?" **52** They responded and said *to* him, "**You** also are not from Galilee, *are you*? Search and see that *a* prophet does not arise from Galilee". **53** And^A each *one* went to his house, **8:1** but Jesus went to the Mount *of* Olives.

The Pharisees Bring Jesus a Woman Caught In Adultery

2 Now *at* dawn, He again arrived in the temple. And all the people were coming to Him. And having sat-*down*, He was teaching them. **3** And the scribes and the Pharisees bring *a* woman having been caught in adultery. And having stood her in *the* middle, **4** they say *to* Him, "Teacher, this woman has been caught in the-act, while committing-adultery. **5** Now in the Law, Moses commanded us to be stoning such *women*^B. What then do **You** say?" **6** Now they were saying this testing Him, in order that they might have *grounds* to be accusing Him. But Jesus, having stooped down, was writing in the ground *with His* finger. **7** But as they were continuing-on asking Him, He straightened-up and said *to* them, "Let the sinless *one among* you throw *a* stone at her first". **8** And again having stooped-down, He was writing in the ground. **9** And the *ones,* having heard *it,* were going out one by one, beginning from the older *ones*. And He was left-behind alone, and the woman being in *the* middle. **10** And Jesus, having straightened up, said *to* her, "Woman, where are they? Did no one condemn you?" **11** And the *one* said, "No one, Sir". And Jesus said, "Neither do **I** condemn^C you. Go. And from now *on,* do not be sinning any longer".

I Am The Light of The World, To Which I And My Father Are Testifying

12 Then Jesus again spoke *to* them, saying, "I am the light *of* the world. The *one* following Me will never walk in the darkness, but will have the light *of*^D life". **13** So the Pharisees said *to* Him, "**You** are testifying about Yourself— Your testimony is not true". **14** Jesus responded and said *to* them, "Even if **I** am testifying about Myself, My testimony is true, because I know from where I came, and where I am going. But **you** do not know from where I come, or where I am going. **15** **You** are judging according to the flesh. I am not judging anyone. **16** But even if **I** am judging, My judgment is true, because I am not alone— but *it is* I and the Father having sent Me. **17** But even in your Law, it has been written that the testimony *of* two people is true. **18** **I** am the *One* testifying about Myself. And the **Father** having sent Me is testifying about Me". **19** So they were saying *to* Him, "Where is Your Father?" Jesus answered, "You know neither Me nor My Father. If you knew Me, you would also know My Father". **20** These words He spoke in the treasury, while teaching in the temple. And no one seized Him, because His hour had not yet come.

I Am Going Away. Unless You Believe That I Am The One, You Will Die In Your Sins

21 Then He said again *to* them, "I am going away. And you will seek Me. And you will

---

A. Some manuscripts omit 7:53-8:11; others have it in a different place. **B.** Actually, Deut 22:22-24 and Lev 20:10 say both should be stoned. **C.** That is, execute sentence upon you at this time. **D.** That is, proceeding from; or, leading to.

die **in your sin**. Where **I** am going, **you** are not able to come". [22] So the Jews were saying, "He will not kill Himself, *will He*— because He says, 'Where **I** am going, **you** are not able to come'?" [23] And He was saying *to* them, "**You** are from below, **I** am from above. **You** are from **this** world, **I** am not from this world. [24] Therefore I said *to* you that you will die in your sins. For unless you believe that **I** am[A] *the One*, you will die in your sins".

I Am What I Have Been Saying I Am From The Beginning

[25] So they were saying *to* Him, "Who[B] are **You**?" Jesus said *to* them, "What[C] thing *from* the beginning I am indeed telling you! [26] I have many *things* to speak and to judge concerning you. However, the *One* having sent Me is true. And what *things* I heard from Him— these *things* I am speaking to the world". [27] They did not know that He was speaking *to* them *about* the Father.

When You Lift Up The Son of Man, You Will Know I Am The One

[28] Then Jesus said *to* them, "When you lift-up[D] the Son *of* Man, then you will know that **I** am *the One*, and I am doing nothing from Myself, but I am speaking these *things* just as the Father taught Me. [29] And the *One* having sent Me is with Me. He did not leave Me alone, because **I** am always doing the *things* pleasing *to* Him". [30] While He *was* speaking these *things,* many believed in Him.

If You Remain In My Word, Then You Are Truly My Disciples And The Truth Will Set You Free

[31] Then Jesus was saying to the Jews having believed Him, "If **you** remain[E] in My word, you are truly My disciples, [32] and you will know the truth, and the truth will set you free".

You Are Slaves of Sin. If The Son Sets You Free, You Will Truly Be Free

[33] They responded to Him, "We are *the* seed *of* Abraham, and *to* no one have we ever been slaves[F]. How *is it* **You** say that 'You will become free'?" [34] Jesus answered them, "Truly, truly, I say *to* you that everyone doing[G] sin is *a* slave *of* sin. [35] Now the slave does not remain in the house forever. The son remains forever. [36] Therefore if the Son sets you free, you will really[H] be free. [37] I know that you are *the* seed *of* Abraham. But you are seeking to kill Me, because My word is not advancing[I] in you. [38] I am speaking *the things* which **I** have seen with *My*[J] Father. And **you** therefore are doing[K] *the things* which you heard from *your* father".

You Are Doing The Works of Your Father, Not Abraham

[39] They responded and said *to* Him, "Our father is Abraham". Jesus says *to* them, "If you are children *of* Abraham, you *would* be doing the works *of* Abraham. [40] But now[L] you are seeking to kill Me— *a* man Who has told you the truth, which I heard from God. Abraham did not do this. [41] **You** are doing the works *of* your father".

If God Were Your Father, You Would Be Loving Me. Your Father Is The Devil
So they said *to* Him, "**We** have not been born out of sexuality-immorality; we have one father— God". **⁴²** Jesus said *to* them, "If God were your Father, you would be loving Me, for **I** came-forth and am-here from God. For I have not even come of Myself, but that *One* sent Me forth. **⁴³** For what reason are you not understanding My speaking? *It is* because you are not able to hear My word. **⁴⁴** **You** are of *your* father the devil. And you are wanting^A to do the desires *of* your father. That *one* was *a* murderer from *the* beginning, and was not standing^B in the truth, because there is no truth in him. Whenever he speaks the lie^C, he speaks from *his* own *things,* because he is *a* liar, and the father *of* it. **⁴⁵** And because **I** am speaking the truth, you are not believing Me. **⁴⁶** Which of you convicts Me concerning sin? If I am speaking truth, for what reason are **you** not believing Me? **⁴⁷** The *one* being of ^D God hears the words *of* God. For this reason **you** are not hearing— because you are not of God".

I Am Honoring My Father. If You Keep My Word, You Will Never See Death
⁴⁸ The Jews responded and said *to* Him, "Do **we** not rightly say that **You** are *a* Samaritan^E and have *a* demon?" **⁴⁹** Jesus answered, "**I** do not have *a* demon, but I am honoring My Father, and **you** are dishonoring Me. **⁵⁰** But **I** am not seeking My glory. There is the *One* seeking *it,* and judging. **⁵¹** Truly, truly, I say *to* you— if anyone keeps My word, he will never^F see death, ever".

You Do Not Know God, But I Do. And Abraham Was Glad When He Saw My Day
⁵² So the Jews said *to* Him, "Now we have come-to-know that You have *a* demon. Abraham died, and the prophets! And **You** say, 'If anyone keeps My word, he will never taste death, ever!' **⁵³** **You** are not greater *than* our father Abraham who died, *are you*? The prophets died also. Whom do You make Yourself?" **⁵⁴** Jesus answered, "If **I** glorify Myself, My glory is nothing. The *One* glorifying Me is My Father— Whom **you** say that 'He is our God'. **⁵⁵** And you have not come-to-know Him, but **I** know Him. And if I say that I do not know Him, I will be *a* liar like you. But I know Him, and I am keeping His word. **⁵⁶** Abraham your father rejoiced-greatly to see My day. And he saw *it,* and was glad".

Before Abraham Was, I Am. Hearing This, They Picked Up Stones To Kill Jesus
⁵⁷ So the Jews said to Him, "You do not yet have fifty years, and You have seen Abraham?" **⁵⁸** Jesus said *to* them, "Truly, truly, I say *to* you— before Abraham came-into-being^G, **I** am^H". **⁵⁹** Therefore they picked up stones in order that they might throw *them* at Him. But Jesus was hidden^I, and went out of the temple.

While Passing On, Jesus Heals a Man Born Blind
9:1 And while passing on, He saw *a* man blind from birth. **²** And His disciples asked Him, saying "Rabbi, who sinned— this *one* or his parents, that he should be born blind?" **³** Jesus answered, "Neither this *one* sinned nor his parents, but *it was* in order that the works *of*

A. Or, intending. **B.** Or, does not stand. **C.** Or, falsehood. **D.** That is, belonging to God. **E.** That is, you are making up your own religion. **F.** Or, by no means. **G.** Or, came-to-be, and in this sense 'was' or 'was born'. **H.** Jesus is claiming to preexist Abraham, and therefore unlike v 24 and 28, His meaning is clear to them: He is claiming to be God, as in Ex 3:14; Isa 41:4; 43:10; 48:12, etc. **I.** That is, was hidden from them amidst the crowds as He went out of the temple. They could not find Him to stone Him. Or, hid *Himself.*

God might be made-visible in him. **4** We must be working the works *of* the *One* having sent Me while it is day. Night is coming, when no one can work. **5** When I am in the world, I am *the* light *of* the world". **6** Having said these *things*, He spat on the ground and made mud from the saliva, and smeared its mud on the eyes, **7** and said *to* him, "Go, wash in the pool *of* Siloam" (which is translated "Sent"ᴬ). So he went away and washed, and cameᴮ [back] seeing. **8** Then the neighbors, and the *ones* seeing him formerly— becauseᶜ he was *a* beggar— were saying "Is not this the *one* sitting and begging?" **9** Others were saying that "This is he". Others were saying, "No, but he is like him". That *one* was saying that "**I** am *he*". **10** So they were saying *to* him, "How then were your eyes opened?" **11** That *one* answered, "The man being called Jesus made mud and smeared *it* on my eyes, and said *to* me 'Go to Siloam and wash'. So having gone away and washed, I received-sight". **12** And they said *to* him, "Where is that *One*?" He says, "I do not know".

The Pharisees Were Divided Over This Sign, Because It Was Done On a Sabbath
13 They bring him to the Pharisees— the formerly blind *one*. **14** Now it was *a* Sabbath on the day Jesus made the mud and opened his eyes. **15** Therefore the Pharisees also were asking him again how he received-sight. And the *one* said *to* them, "He put mud on my eyes, and I washed, and I see". **16** Then some of the Pharisees were saying, "This man is not from God, because He does not keep the Sabbath". But others were saying, "How is *a* sinful man able to do such signs?" And there was *a* division among them. **17** So they say *to* the blind *one* again, "What do **you** say about Him, *seeing*-that He opened your eyes?" And the *one* said that "He is *a* prophet".

The Pharisees Question Whether He Was Blind, And Call In The Parents
18 Then the Jews did not believe concerning him that he was blind and received-sight— until they called the parents *of* him having received-sight. **19** And they asked them, saying "Is this your son whom **you** are saying that he was born blind? How then does he see now?" **20** So his parents responded and said, "We know that this is our son, and that he was born blind. **21** But how he now sees— we do not know. Or who opened his eyes— **we** do not know. Ask him. He has *a* mature-age. **He** will speak about himself". **22** His parents said these *things* because they were fearing the Jews. For the Jews already had agreed that if anyone confessed Him *as the* Christ, he should become put-out-of-the-synagogue. **23** For this reason his parents said that "He has *a* mature-age, question him".

They Don't Want To Believe Jesus Did It, So They Question The Man Again
24 Then they called for *a* second *time* the man who was blind, and said *to* him, "Give glory *to* God. **We** know that this man is *a* sinner". **25** So that *one* responded, "Whether He is *a* sinner, I do not know. I know one *thing*— that being *a* blind *one*, now I see". **26** So they said *to* him, "What did He do *to* you? How did He open your eyes?" **27** He answered them, "I told you already and you did not listen. Why do you want to hear *it* again? **You** also do not want to become His disciples, *do you*?" **28** And they reviled him and said, "**You** are *a* disciple *of* that *One*, but **we** are disciples *of* Moses. **29** **We** know that God has spoken *to* Moses. But we do

---

A. The water was 'sent' to this pool from a spring outside the wall through an underground tunnel built by King Hezekiah. **B.** Or, went [home]. **C.** Or, that.

not know where **this *One*** is from". [30] The man responded and said *to* them, "Why, in this is[A] the marvel[B]— that **you** do not know where He is from, and He opened my eyes! [31] We know that God does not hear[C] sinners. But if anyone is *a* God-fearing *one,* and is doing His will— He hears this *one.* [32] It was not ever heard that someone opened *the* eyes *of one* having been born blind. [33] If this *One* were not from God, He *would* be able to do nothing". [34] They responded and said *to* him, "**You** were born entirely in sins, and **you** are teaching us?" And they threw him outside[D].

Jesus Tells The Man, I Came So The Blind May See And The Seeing May Become Blind
[35] Jesus heard that they threw him outside, and having found him, said "Do **you** believe in the Son *of* Man?" [36] That *one* responded and said, "Who indeed is He, Sir, in order that I may believe in Him?" [37] Jesus said *to* him, "You have both seen Him, and that *One* is the *One* speaking with you". [38] And the *one* said, "Master, I believe", and prostrated-*himself* [E] *before* Him. [39] And Jesus said, "**I** came into this world for judgment— so that the *ones* not seeing[F] may be seeing, and the *ones* seeing may become blind".

You Pharisees Are Thieves, Not Shepherds, So God's Sheep Do Not Follow You
[40] *Some* of the Pharisees heard these *things*— the *ones* being with him— and said *to* Him, "**We** indeed are not blind *ones, are* we?" [41] Jesus said *to* them, "If you were blind[G] *ones,* you would not have[H] sin. But you are saying now that 'We see'— your sin remains. **10:1** Truly, truly, I say *to* you, the *one* not entering into the fold *of* the sheep through the door, but going-up from-another-place— that *one* is *a* thief and *a* robber. [2] But the *One* entering through the door is *the* shepherd *of* the sheep. [3] The doorkeeper opens *to* this *One.* And the sheep hear[I] His voice. And He calls *His* own sheep by name, and leads them out. [4] When He brings out all *His* own, He proceeds in front of them. And the sheep are following Him, because they know His voice. [5] But they will never follow *a* stranger, but will flee from him, because they do not know the voice *of* strangers". [6] Jesus spoke this figure-of-speech *to* them, but those *ones* did not understand what *the things* were which He was speaking *to* them.

I Am The Door of The Sheep. All Who Enter Through Me Will Be Saved
[7] Then Jesus said again, "Truly, truly, I say *to* you that **I** am the door *of* [J] the sheep. [8] All who came before Me are thieves and robbers, but the sheep did not listen-to them. [9] **I** am the door. If anyone enters **through Me**, he will be saved. And he will go in and go out, and he will find pasture. [10] The thief does not come except that he may steal and kill and destroy. **I** came that they may have life, and have abundance[K].

A. Or, In this is indeed the. The man is incredulous. **B.** Or, the amazing *thing.* **C.** That is, listen to and answer. **D.** That is, physically out of the temple; or, out of the synagogue, v 22. **E.** Or, gave-worship *to.* **F.** That is, the ones not having spiritual sight versus the ones claiming to have spiritual sight. **G.** That is, not having spiritual sight. **H.** That is, be guilty of sin against Me. **I.** That is, listen to and obey. The blind man is the specific example in view, v 38. **J.** That is, to; or, for. **K.** Or, excess, overflow, surplus. That is, have an overflowing spiritual life abounding to others (as in 7:38), not mere existence. Jesus is referring to an abundance of 'real' life, 1 Tim 6:19.

I Am The Good Shepherd. All My Sheep Know Me. I Give My Life For Them
11 "**I** am the good shepherd. The good shepherd lays-*down* His life for the sheep.
12 The *one* being *a* hired *one* and not *a* shepherd, *of* whom the sheep are not *his*
own— he sees the wolf coming and leaves[A] the sheep and flees, and the wolf
snatches them and scatters *them*, **13** because he is *a* hired *one,* and he is not
concerned about the sheep. **14** I am the good shepherd. And I know My *sheep,* and
My *sheep* know Me— **15** just as the Father knows Me, and **I** know the Father. And
I lay-*down* My life for the sheep. **16** And I have other sheep, which are not of this
fold[B]. I must bring those also. And they[C] will hear My voice. And they will
become one flock, [with] one Shepherd. **17** For this reason the Father loves Me—
because **I** lay *down* My life so that I may take it *up* again. **18** No one takes it away
from Me, but **I** lay it *down* of Myself. I have authority to lay it *down,* and I have
authority to take it *up* again. I received this commandment from My Father".

The Pharisees Remain Divided
19 *A* division again[D] took place among the Jews because of these words. **20** And many
of them were saying, "He has *a* demon, and He is mad. Why are you listening-to
Him?" **21** Others[E] were saying, "These words are not *from one* being demon-
possessed. *A* demon is not able to open *the* eyes *of* blind *ones, is he*?"

During The Festival of Hanukkah, Jesus Says He And The Father Are One
22 Then the Festival-of-Dedication[F] took place in Jerusalem. It was winter. **23** And Jesus was
walking in the temple, in the portico *of* Solomon. **24** Then the Jews surrounded Him. And they
were saying *to* Him, "How long are You keeping us in suspense[G]? If **You** are the Christ, tell us
with plainness". **25** Jesus answered them, "I told you, and you do not believe. The works which
I am doing in the name *of* My Father— these are testifying about Me. **26** However, **you** do not
believe, because you are not of My sheep. **27** My sheep hear My voice. And **I** know them, and
they follow Me. **28** And **I** give them eternal life, and they will never perish, ever. And someone
will not snatch them out of My hand. **29** What[H] My Father has given *to* Me is greater *than* all.
And no one is able to snatch *them* out of the hand *of* the Father. **30** I and the Father are one[I]".

The Jewish Leaders Want To Kill Jesus For Blasphemy Because He Is Making Himself God
31 The Jews again carried stones in order that they might stone Him. **32** Jesus responded *to*
them, "I showed you many good works from the Father. For which work *of* them do you
stone Me?" **33** The Jews answered Him, "We do not stone You for *a* good work, but for
blasphemy— even because **You**, being *a* human, are making Yourself God".

A. Or more strongly, abandons. **B.** Jesus may mean the Jewish fold, making the ones in view the Gentiles; or,
the nation-of-Israel fold, making the ones in view the 'children of God scattered' outside Israel, Jews and
Gentiles, 11:52. **C.** That is, all My sheep from both folds. **D.** See 9:16. **E.** So the case of the man born blind
(9:1-10:21) comes down to this: Is Jesus empowered by God or Satan? **F.** That is, Hanukkah, the Feast of Lights,
commemorating the rededication of the temple by Judas Maccabaeus in 165 B.C. after it had been desecrated
by Antiochus Epiphanes. **G:** keeping us in suspense. Lit, lifting-up our soul [in suspense or anticipation]. **H.** Or,
That-which. Jesus may be referring to the flock itself viewed as an abstract whole; or, to His 'authority over all
flesh to give eternal life' (17:2), making what follows 'snatch *it*'. In either case, both the Father and the Son
ensure the safety of the flock. **I.** That is, one in will and action. Jesus is claiming a oneness He shares with God
because He is His Son (v 36) and therefore shares the essence or substance of His Father. Jesus is claiming to
be acting as God and thus to be God, to which His listeners respond next.

Jesus Responds: Saying "I Am God's Son" Is Not Blasphemy If I Am Doing God's Works
34 Jesus responded *to* them, "Has it not been written in your Law that '**I** said, you are
gods^A^'? **35** If He^B^ called those *ones* to whom the word *of* God came gods— and the
Scripture cannot be broken— **36** do **you**^C^ say *as to the One* Whom the Father set-apart and
sent-forth into the world that 'You are blaspheming' because I said, 'I am God's Son'?
37 If I am not doing the works *of* My Father, do not be believing Me. **38** But if I am doing
them— even if you do not believe Me, be believing the works, in order that you may come-
to-know and be understanding^D^ that the Father *is* in Me, and I in the Father". **39** Then they
were seeking again to seize Him, and He went out of their hand.

Jesus Leaves Judea
40 And He went away again beyond the Jordan, to the place where John was first baptizing.
And He was staying there. **41** And many came to Him, and were saying that "John did no
sign— but all that John said about this *One* was true". **42** And many believed in Him there.

Jesus Hears That Lazarus Is Sick
11:1 Now there was *a* certain *one* being sick— Lazarus, from Bethany, of the village *of* Mary
and Martha, her sister. **2** And it was Mary, the *one* having anointed^E^ the Lord *with* perfume
and having wiped His feet *with* her hair, whose brother Lazarus was sick. **3** So the sisters sent
out *a message* to Him, saying, "Lord, look— *the one* whom You love is sick". **4** And having
heard, Jesus said "This sickness is not *leading* to death, but for the glory *of* God, in order that
the Son *of* God may be glorified through it".

Jesus Returns To Judea To Raise Lazarus From The Dead
5 Now Jesus was loving Martha, and her sister, and Lazarus. **6** So when He heard that he
was sick, at that time He remained *for* two days in which place He was— **7** then after this,
says *to* the disciples, "Let us be going to Judea again". **8** The disciples say *to* Him, "Rabbi,
the Jews were *just*-now seeking to stone You, and You are going there again?" **9** Jesus
answered, "Are there not twelve hours *of* the day? If one walks during the day, he does
not stumble, because he sees the light *of* this world. **10** But if one walks during the night,
he stumbles, because the light is not in him". **11** He said these *things,* and after this He
says *to* them, "Our friend Lazarus has fallen-asleep, but I am going in order that I may
awaken him". **12** So the disciples said *to* Him, "Lord, if he has fallen asleep, he will be
restored". **13** Now Jesus had spoken concerning his death, but those *ones* thought that He
was speaking concerning the sleep *of* slumber^F^. **14** So at-that-time Jesus said *to* them *with*
plainness, "Lazarus died. **15** And I am glad for your sakes that I was not there, so that you
may believe. But let us be going to him". **16** Then Thomas, the *one* being called Didymus^G^,
said *to his* fellow-disciples, "Let **us** indeed be going, so that we may die with Him^H^".

Jesus Says, I Am The Resurrection And The Life. The One Believing In Me Will Live
17 So having come, Jesus found him already having four days in the tomb. **18** Now Bethany

---

A. Jesus is quoting Ps 82:6, where the psalmist calls the judges of Israel gods (in authority over the people)
because they carried out divine justice. **B.** Or, he (the psalmist); or, it (the Scripture). **C.** If God in Scripture
called those judges gods, does this term not even more apply to Me, based on My works alone? Jesus is arguing
from the lesser to the greater. **D.** Or, acknowledging. **E.** That is, in 12:3. **F.** That is, *consisting of* physical sleep.
G. Thomas is a Greek rendering of the Aramaic word for 'twin'. Didymus is the Greek word meaning 'twin'.
H. Or, him (Lazarus).

was near Jerusalem, about fifteen stades[A] away. **19** And many of the Jews had come to Martha and Mary in order that they might console them concerning *their* brother. **20** So Martha, when she heard that Jesus was coming, met Him. But Mary was sitting in the house. **21** Then Martha said to Jesus, "Lord, if You had been here, my brother would not have died. **22** But even now I know that whatever You ask God, God will give You". **23** Jesus says *to* her, "Your brother will rise-up". **24** Martha says *to* Him, "I know that he will rise-up in the resurrection at the last day". **25** Jesus said *to* her, "**I** am the resurrection and the life. The *one* believing in Me— even though he dies, he will live. **26** And everyone living and believing in Me will never die, ever. Do you believe this?" **27** She says *to* Him, "Yes, Lord. **I** have believed that **You** are the Christ, the Son *of* God, the *One* coming into the world". **28** And having said this, she went away and called Mary her sister secretly, having said, "The Teacher is here and is calling you". **29** And that *one,* when she heard, arose quickly and was going to Him. **30** Now Jesus had not yet come into the village, but was still in the place where Martha met Him. **31** So the Jews— the *ones* being with her in the house and consoling her—having seen that **Mary** stood up quickly and went out, followed her, having supposed that she was going to the tomb in order that she might weep there. **32** Then Mary— when she came where Jesus was, having seen Him— fell at His feet, saying *to* Him, "Lord, if You had been here, my brother would not have died". **33** Then Jesus— when He saw her weeping, and the Jews having come with her weeping— was deeply-moved[B] in *His* spirit, and troubled[C] Himself. **34** And He said, "Where have you laid him?" They say *to* Him, "Lord, come and see". **35** Jesus wept. **36** So the Jews were saying, "Look— how He was loving him!" **37** And[D] some of them said, "Was not this *One*— the *One* having opened the eyes *of* the blind *one*— able to cause that this *one* also should not die?"

Jesus Calls Lazarus Out of The Tomb. Many Believe In Him
38 Then Jesus, again being deeply-moved in Himself, comes to the tomb. Now it was *a* cave, and *a* stone was lying upon[E] it. **39** Jesus says, "Take away the stone". Martha, the sister *of* the one having come-to-an-end[F], says *to* Him, "Lord, he already stinks, for it is *the* fourth-day". **40** Jesus says *to* her, "Did I not say *to* you that if you believe, you will see the glory *of* God?" **41** So they took away the stone. And Jesus lifted *His* eyes upward, and said, "Father, I thank You that You heard Me. **42** Now **I** knew that You always hear Me. But I said *this* for the sake of the crowd having stood around— in order that they may believe that **You** sent Me forth". **43** And having said these *things,* He shouted *with a* loud voice, "Lazarus, come outside!" **44** The *one* having died came out, having been bound *as to* the feet and the hands *with* grave-cloths. And his face had been bound-around *with a* face-cloth. Jesus says *to* them, "Unbind him, and allow him to go". **45** Therefore many of the Jews— the *ones* having come to Mary, and having seen *the things* which He did— believed in Him.

Some Told The Pharisees. Caiaphas Prophesies, Better For One To Die For The People
46 But some[G] of them went to the Pharisees and told them *the things* which Jesus did. **47** So the chief priests and the Pharisees gathered together *a* council[H]. And they were

---

A. That is, 1.7 miles or 2.8 kilometers. **B.** The emotion in view must be determined from the context. Some think Jesus shared their bereaved perspective, culminating in the weeping in v 35; others think anger at death is in view. If this intense emotion was expressed, this may be rendered 'groaned'. **C.** Or, stirred, agitated. **D.** Or, But. **E.** Or, against, over. **F.** That is, died. **G.** That is, some Jews who did not believe; or, some of the many who believed, to present proof of who Jesus was. **H.** That is, an informal meeting of some of the leaders. Or, *the*

saying, "What are we doing? Because this man is doing many signs! [48] If we tolerate Him in this manner, everyone will believe in Him, and the Romans will come and take away both **our** place[A] and nation". [49] But *a* certain one of them, Caiaphas, being *the* high priest *of* that year, said *to* them, "**You** do not know anything— [50] nor do you consider that it is better *for* you that one Man die for the people, and the whole nation not perish". [51] Now he did not say this from himself, but being *the* high priest *of* that year, he prophesied that Jesus was going to die for the nation. [52] And not for the nation only, but in order that He might also gather together into one the children *of* God having been scattered [in the world]. [53] Therefore from that day, they planned to kill Him.

Jesus Withdraws From The Public

[54] Therefore Jesus was no longer walking *in* public among the Jews, but went away from there to the region near the wilderness, to *a* city being called Ephraim. And He stayed there with the disciples.

At The Passover, Everyone Was Looking For Jesus

[55] Now the Passover [Feast] *of* the Jews was near. And many went up to Jerusalem from the country[B] before the Passover [Feast], in order that they might purify themselves. [56] So they were seeking Jesus, and saying, standing with one another in the temple, "What seems *right to* you— that He will by no means come to the Feast?" [57] And the chief priests and the Pharisees had given commands that if anyone came-to-know where He was, he should disclose *it*— so that they might seize Him.

In Bethany At a Dinner For Jesus And Lazarus, Mary Anoints Jesus

12:1 Therefore Jesus, six days before the Passover [Feast], came to Bethany where Lazarus was, *the one* whom Jesus raised from *the* dead. [2] So they made *a* dinner *for* Him there. And Martha was serving. And Lazarus was one of the *ones* reclining-back [to eat] with Him. [3] Then Mary, having taken *a* pound *of* very-valuable genuine[C] nard perfume, anointed the feet *of* Jesus, and wiped His feet *with* her hair. And the house was filled from the aroma *of* the perfume. [4] But Judas the Iscariot— one of His disciples, the *one* going to hand Him over— says, [5] "For what reason was this perfume not sold *for* three-hundred denarii[D] and given *to* poor *ones*?" [6] Now he said this, not because he was concerned about the poor, but because he was *a* thief. And having the *money*-box, he was carrying[E] the *things* being put *there*. [7] So Jesus said, "Leave her *alone*. It was[F] in order that she might keep it for the day *of* My preparation-for-burial. [8] For you always have **the poor** with you, but you do not always have **Me**". [9] Then the large crowd[G] of the Jews came-to-know that He was there. And they came— not because of Jesus only, but in order that they might also see Lazarus, whom He raised from *the* dead. [10] And the chief priests planned to kill Lazarus also, [11] because many *of* the Jews were going-away and were believing in Jesus because of him.

Sanhedrin, the whole council of elders. **A.** That is, our position; or, our Holy Place, our temple. **B.** That is, the land of Judea. Passover could only be celebrated inside Jerusalem. **C.** See Mk 14:3. **D.** One denarius was one day's wage for a laborer. **E.** Or, pilfering. **F.** Or, *alone. She had it.* This implies she had it for this purpose, and poured it all out on this occasion. Or, *alone,* in order that. This implies she did not pour it all out, and was to keep the remainder until after the death of Jesus. **G.** That is, the crowd that was at the funeral, 11:19, 45; the friends of Mary, Martha, and Lazarus; the 'Lazarus crowd'.

Jesus The King Enters Jerusalem On a Donkey, As Predicted By Zechariah
12 *On* the next day the large crowd[A]— the *one* having come to the Feast— having heard[B] that Jesus was coming to Jerusalem, **13** took the branches *of* palm-trees and came out to meet Him. And they were shouting, "Hosanna! Blessed *is* the *One* coming in *the* name *of the* Lord, even the King *of* Israel". **14** And Jesus, having found *a* young-donkey, sat on it, just as it has been written [in Zech 9:9]: **15** "Do not be fearing, daughter *of* Zion. Behold— your King is coming, sitting on *a* colt *of a* donkey". **16** His disciples did not understand these *things at* first. But when Jesus was glorified, then they remembered that these *things* had been written for[C] Him, and *that* they did these *things to* Him. **17** Then the crowd[D] was testifying— the *one* being with Him when He called Lazarus out of the tomb and raised him from *the* dead. **18** For this reason also the crowd[E] met Him— because they heard *that* He had done **this** sign. **19** Then the Pharisees said to themselves, "You see that you are profiting nothing! Look— the world went after Him!"

Jesus Says The Hour For Which He Came Has Come. A Seed Must Die To Bear Fruit
20 Now some of the *ones* going up in order that they might worship at the Feast were Greeks[F]. **21** So these *ones* came to Philip, the *one* from Bethsaida *of* Galilee, and were asking him, saying, "Sir, we wish to see Jesus". **22** Philip comes and tells Andrew. Andrew and Philip come, and they tell Jesus. **23** And Jesus responds *to* them, saying, "The hour has come for[G] the Son *of* Man to be glorified. **24** Truly, truly, I say *to* you, unless the seed *of* wheat having fallen to the earth dies, **it** remains alone. But if it dies, it bears much fruit. **25** The *one* loving his life loses it, and the *one* hating his life in this world will keep[H] it for eternal life. **26** If anyone serves **Me**, let him be following Me. And where **I** am, there also My servant will be. If **anyone** serves Me, the Father will honor him. **27** Now My soul has been troubled. And what should I say— 'Father, save Me from this hour'? But for this reason I came to this hour! **28** Father, glorify Your name!"

Now Is The Judgment of This World. If I Am Lifted Up, I Will Draw All People To Myself
Then *a* voice came from heaven: "I both glorified *it*, and will again glorify *it*". **29** Then the crowd, the *one* standing *there* and having heard, was saying *that* thunder had taken place. Others were saying, "*An* angel has spoken *to* Him". **30** Jesus responded and said, "This voice has taken place not for My sake, but for your sakes. **31** Now is *the* judgment *of* this world! Now the ruler *of* this world will be cast out! **32** And if **I** am lifted-up[I] from the earth, I will draw all *people* to Myself". **33** Now He was saying this signifying *by* what-kind-of death He was going to die.

Believe In The Light While You Have The Light, That You May Become Sons of Light
34 Then the crowd responded *to* Him, "**We** heard from the Law that the Christ remains forever. How indeed do **You** say that 'The Son *of* Man must be lifted-up[J]'? Who is this Son *of* Man?" **35** Then Jesus said *to* them, "The Light is among you *for a* short time

A. That is, the crowd of those who had come to the Passover; the crowd of 11:55-56; the 'Feast crowd'. **B.** How did they hear? Probably from the Lazarus crowd. **C.** That is, as something destined for Him to fulfill. **D.** That is, the Lazarus crowd. **E.** That is, the Feast crowd. **F.** That is, Gentiles who were Jewish proselytes or God-fearers. **G.** That is, having this as its purpose in the plan of God. **H.** Or, preserve. **I.** See 18:32. Or, exalted, as in 3:14; 8:28; and next in v 34. **J.** If the Messiah remains as King on earth forever, how can He be exalted to heaven? Are You talking about someone other than the Messiah? Jesus doesn't answer because they cannot now understand that by 'lifted-up' He means 'crucified'. He exhorts them to act on what they know.

longer. Be walking while you have the Light, in order that darkness may not overtake you. Indeed the *one* walking in the darkness does not know where he is going. [36] While you have the Light, be believing in the Light, in order that you may become sons *of* Light". Jesus spoke these *things*, and having gone away, was hidden from them.

Isaiah Is Fulfilled: God Blinded Their Eyes And Hardened Their Hearts
[37] Now He having done so-many[A] signs in front of them[B]— they were not believing in Him, [38] in order that the word *of* Isaiah the prophet might be fulfilled which he spoke [in Isa 53:1]: "Lord, who believed our report? And *to* whom was the arm *of the* Lord revealed?" [39] For this reason[C] they were not able to believe: because again Isaiah said [in Isa 6:10] [40] "He has blinded their eyes, and He hardened their heart, in order that they might not see *with their* eyes, and comprehend *in their* heart, and be turned, and I shall heal them". [41] Isaiah said these *things* because he saw His glory and spoke about Him. [42] Yet indeed, even many of the rulers believed in Him. But because of the Pharisees, they were not confessing *it* in order that they might not become put-out-of-the-synagogue. [43] For they loved the glory *of* people more[D] than the glory *of* God.

I Came To Save The World, And I Spoke The Father's Words. My Words Are Eternal Life
[44] And[E] Jesus cried-out and said "The *one* believing in Me is not believing in Me, but in the *One* having sent Me. [45] And the *one* seeing Me is seeing the *One* having sent Me. [46] I have come into the world *as a* **light**, so that everyone believing in Me should not remain in the darkness. [47] And if anyone hears My words and does not keep *them*, I do not judge him. For I did not come in order that I might judge the world, but in order that I might save the world. [48] The *one* rejecting Me and not receiving My words has *that which* judges him— the word which I spoke, that will judge him at the last day. [49] Because I did not speak out of Myself, but the Father having sent Me— **He** has given Me *a* commandment *as to* what I should say and what I should speak. [50] And I know that His commandment is eternal life. Therefore *the things* which I speak— just as the Father has told Me, so I speak".

Jesus Loves His Own To The End
13:1 Now before the Feast *of* the Passover, Jesus— knowing[F] that His hour came for Him to pass from this world to the Father— having loved *His* own *ones* in the world, loved them to *the* end[G].

At Dinner, Jesus Washes The Feet of The Twelve As an Example For Them To Follow
[2] And dinner taking-place[H], the devil having already put into *his* heart that Judas, *son of* Simon Iscariot, should hand Him over— [3] *Jesus*, knowing[I] that the Father gave Him all *things* into *His* hands, and that He came forth from God and is going to God, [4] arises from the dinner and lays-*down His* [outer] garments. And having taken *a* towel, He tied *it* around Himself. [5] Then He puts water into the wash-basin. And He began to wash the feet *of* the disciples, and to wipe *them with* the towel which had been tied-around *Himself.* [6] Then He comes to Simon Peter. He says *to* Him, "Lord, do **You** wash my feet?" [7] Jesus

---

A. Or, such-great. **B.** That is, Israel. **C.** That is, the fulfillment of prophecy. **D.** Or, rather. **E.** John does not give the occasion for these words, but chooses to close Christ's public ministry with them. **F.** John may mean although He knew; or, because He knew. **G.** Or, to *the* uttermost. **H.** Or, coming-about. **I.** John may mean although He knew; or, because He knew.

responded and said *to* him, "**You** do not know what **I** am doing now, but you will understand after these *things*". **8** Peter says *to* Him, "You will never wash my feet, ever!" Jesus responded *to* him, "If I do not wash you, you have no part^A with Me". **9** Simon Peter says *to* Him, "Lord, *wash* not my feet only, but also the hands and the head!" **10** Jesus says *to* him, "The *one* having bathed has no need except to wash *his* feet, but is entirely clean. And **you**^B are clean— but not all *of you*". **11** For He knew the *one* handing Him over. For this reason He said that "You are not all clean". **12** Then when He washed their feet, and took His garments, and fell back again [to eat], He said *to* them, "Do you understand what I have done *for* you? **13** **You** call Me 'Teacher' and 'Lord'— and you speak rightly, for I am. **14** Therefore if **I**, the Lord and the Teacher, washed your feet, **you** also ought to be washing the feet *of* one another. **15** For I gave you *an* example, in order that **you** also should be doing just as **I** did *for* you. **16** Truly, truly, I say *to* you, *a* slave is not greater *than* his master, nor *is a* messenger greater *than* the *one* having sent him. **17** If you know these *things,* you are blessed if you are doing them. **18** I am not speaking with-reference-to all *of* you. I know *the ones* whom I chose. But *it is taking place* in order that the Scripture [in Ps 41:9] might be fulfilled: 'The *one* eating My bread lifted-up his heel against Me'. **19** From now *on,* I am telling you ahead *of it* taking place, in order that when it takes place you may believe that I am *the One.* **20** Truly, truly, I say *to* you, the *one* receiving whomever I send is receiving Me. And the *one* receiving Me is receiving the *One* having sent Me".

Judas Is Identified As The Betrayer, And Leaves The Room
21 Having said these *things*, Jesus was troubled *in His* spirit. And He testified and said "Truly, truly, I say *to* you that one of you will hand Me over". **22** The disciples were looking at one another, being perplexed about whom He was speaking. **23** One of His disciples was reclining-back at the bosom *of* Jesus— *the one* whom Jesus was loving. **24** So Simon Peter nods^C *to* this *one* to inquire *as to* who it might be about whom He is speaking. **25** So that *one,* having leaned back thus on the chest *of* Jesus, says *to* Him, "Lord, who is it?" **26** Jesus answers, "It is that *one for* whom **I** will dip the piece-of-bread and give *it to* him". Then having dipped the piece-of-bread, He takes and gives *it to* Judas, *son of* Simon Iscariot. **27** And after the piece-of-bread, at that time Satan entered into that *one.* Then Jesus says *to* him, "What you are doing, do quicker^D". **28** Now none *of* the *ones* reclining-back [to eat] understood this— for what *purpose* He said *it to* him. **29** For some were thinking, since Judas had the *money*-box, that Jesus was telling him, "Buy *the things of* which we have *a* need for the Feast", or that he should give something *to* the poor. **30** So having received the piece-of-bread, that *one* went out immediately. And it was night.

Then Jesus Says, Now God Was Glorified In Me. And He Will Yet Glorify Me
31 Then when he went out, Jesus says, "Now^E the Son *of* Man was glorified^F, and God was glorified in Him. **32** If God was^G glorified in Him, God will also glorify Him in Himself— and will glorify Him immediately.

Where I Am Going You Cannot Come. Love One Another As I Have Loved You
33 "Little-children, I am with you *a* little longer. You will seek Me, and just as I told

A. Or, share. **B.** This word is plural. **C.** Or, gestures. **D.** Or, sooner. Or, quickly. **E.** In sending out Judas, Jesus has set in motion the hour of His death. He speaks as if it were already all finished. **F.** That is, in voluntarily entering His hour of death; or, prophetically, in His death. **G:** was glorified... will glorify. That is, in His life... in His death; or prophetically, in His death... in His resurrection.

the Jews that where **I** am going, **you** are not able to come, I also tell you now. [34] I am giving you *a* new commandment— that you be loving one another; just as I loved you, that **you** also be loving one another. [35] By this everyone will know that you are disciples *to* Me: if you are having love in-the-case-of[A] one another".

Peter Asks Why He Can't Come. You Will Follow Later, But Deny Me Tonight

[36] Simon Peter says *to* Him, "Lord, where are You going?" Jesus answered him, "Where I am going, you are not able to follow Me now. But you will follow later". [37] Peter says *to* Him, "Lord, for what reason am I not able to follow You right-now? I will lay-*down* my life for You". [38] Jesus responds, "Will you lay-*down* your life for Me? Truly, truly, I say *to* you, *a* rooster will by no means crow until which *time* you deny Me three-times!

I Go To Prepare a Place For You So That You May Be With Me. And You Know The Way

14:1 "Do not let your[B] heart be troubled. Be believing[C] in God. Be believing also **in Me**. [2] There are many places-to-stay[D] in the house *of* My Father— otherwise, I would have told you. [3] For I am going to prepare *a* place *for* you. And if I go and prepare *a* place *for* you, I am coming back[E]. And I will take[F] you to Myself— in order that where **I** am, **you** also may be. [4] And you know the way where **I** am going".

I Am The Way, The Truth, And The Life. And You Have Seen The Father

[5] Thomas says *to* Him, "Lord, we do not know where You are going. How are we able to know the way?" [6] Jesus says *to* him, "**I** am the way, and the truth, and the life. No one comes to the Father except through[G] Me. [7] If you[H] have known Me, you will know[I] My Father also. And from now *on,* you know Him, and you have seen Him".

He Who Has Seen Me Has Seen The Father

[8] Philip says *to* Him, "Lord, show us the Father, and it is enough *for* us". [9] Jesus says *to* him, "Am I with you[J] all *for* so long *a* time, and you[K] have not known[L] Me, Philip?— the *one* having seen Me has seen the Father. How *is it* **you** say, 'Show us the Father'? [10] Do you not believe that **I** *am* in the Father, and the Father is in Me? I am not speaking the words which **I** am saying *to* you[M] from Myself, but the Father abiding in Me is doing His works. [11] Be believing Me— that **I** *am* in the Father and the Father *is* in Me. Otherwise, be believing because of the works themselves.

You Will Do Greater Works Than I. The Father Will Send You The Helper

[12] "Truly, truly, I say *to* you— the *one* believing in Me, that *one* also will do the works which **I** am doing. And he will do greater[N] *works than* these, because **I** am going to the Father. [13] And whatever thing you ask in My name, this I will do, in order that the

---

A. Or, among; in-connection-with. **B.** This word is plural. Jesus resumes addressing them all. **C.** Or, this may be a statement, You are believing. **D.** Or, abodes, dwellings, rooms, homes. **E.** Or, again. **F.** Or, receive. **G.** Or, by-means-of. **H.** This is plural. Jesus addresses them all through Thomas. **I.** This is a promise. Some manuscripts have this as a rebuke, If you had known Me, you would have known. **J.** This word is plural, referring to them all. **K.** This word is singular. **L.** Or, come-to-know. **M.** This word is plural again. **N.** That is, works producing greater (more extensive) results than the miracles of Jesus.

Father may be glorified in the Son. **14** If you ask Me anything in My name, **I** will do *it*. **15** If you love Me, you will keep My commandments. **16** And **I** will request the Father, and He will give you another Helper^A to be with^B you forever— **17** the Spirit *of* truth, Whom the world is not able to receive because it does not see nor know Him. **You** know Him because He abides with^C you, and will be in^D you.

You Will See Me Again. And I Will Reveal Myself To Those Who Love Me
18 "I will not leave you *as* orphans. I am *going to* come to you. **19** *A* little longer, and the world is no longer *going to* see Me, but **you** are *going to* see Me. Because **I** live, **you** also will live. **20** On that day, **you** will know that I *am* in My Father, and you *are* in Me, and I *am* in you. **21** The *one* having My commandments and keeping them— that *one* is the *one* loving^E Me. And the *one* loving Me will be loved by My Father. And **I** will love him and reveal Myself *to* him".

The Father And I Will Abide With Those Who Love Me And Keep My Word
22 Judas (not the Iscariot) says *to* Him, "Lord, what indeed has taken place that You are going to reveal Yourself *to* **us** and not *to* the world^F?" **23** Jesus responded and said *to* him, "If anyone loves Me, he will keep My word. And My Father will love him. And We will come to him. And We will make *a* place-to-stay with him. **24** The *one* not loving Me does not keep My words. And the word which you^G are hearing is not Mine, but the Father's having sent Me.

The Holy Spirit Whom The Father Will Send In My Name Will Teach You All Things
25 "I have spoken these *things to* you while staying^H with you. **26** But the Helper— the Holy Spirit, Whom the Father will send in My name— that *One* will teach you all *things,* and remind you of everything which **I** said *to* you.

I Leave You My Peace. Do Not Be Troubled. I Am Returning To The Father
27 "I leave you peace. I give you My peace. **I** do not give *to* you as the world gives. Do not let your heart be troubled, nor let it be afraid^I. **28** You heard that **I** said *to* you, 'I am going, and I am coming to you'. If you were loving^J Me, you would have rejoiced that I am going to the Father, because^K the Father is greater *than* Me. **29** And now I have told you before *it* takes place, in order that when it takes place, you may believe.

I Love The Father And Am Doing Just What He Commanded Me To Do
30 "I will no longer speak many *things* with you, for the ruler *of* the world is coming. And he does not have anything^L in Me, **31** but *it is taking place* in order that the world may know that I love^M the Father, and *that* just as the Father commanded Me, so I am doing.

A. Or, Comforter, Counselor. **B.** Or, in your midst. **C.** Or, among, beside. **D.** Or, within. **E.** Jesus broadens His promise in this verse from 'you' to all the ones loving Him. **F.** The Jews expected Messiah to reveal Himself to the world and reign from Jerusalem. Jesus answers by reiterating His statement. **G.** This is plural. Jesus may mean 'you apostles', emphasizing the authority of His words; or, 'you people on earth' in general, emphasizing the gravity of not keeping them. **H.** Or, remaining, abiding. **I.** Or, cowardly, timid. That is, afraid to act. **J.** That is, able to be expressing your love for Me right now. **K.** That is, because I am returning to the greatness and glory I share with the Father, having accomplished what I came to do, 17:4-5. **L.** Satan has no claim on Jesus, no point under his authority or rule. What Jesus does, He does voluntarily. **M.** This love is seen in Christ's obedience to the Father's will for Him (as it is with us, v 15, 21).

I Am The Vine. Abide In Me And Bear Much Fruit. Abide In My Love
"Arise, let us be going from here. **15:1** I am the true grapevine, and My Father is the farmer. **²** Every branch in Me not bearing fruit— He takes it away^A. And every *branch* bearing fruit— He cleans^B it in order that it may bear more fruit. **³ You** are already clean, because of the word which I have spoken *to* you. **⁴** Abide^C in Me, and I in you. Just as the branch is not able to bear fruit from itself unless it is abiding in the grapevine, so neither *are* you *able* unless you are abiding in Me. **⁵** I am the grapevine, you *are* the branches. The *one* abiding^D in Me and I in him— this *one* bears much fruit. Because apart from Me, you can do nothing. **⁶** If anyone is not abiding in Me— he was thrown^E outside like the branch, and was dried-up. And they gather them together, and throw *them* into the fire. And they are burned. **⁷** If you abide in Me, and My words abide in you, ask whatever you want, and it will be done *for* you. **⁸** By this My Father is glorified— that you be bearing much fruit, and be^F disciples *to* Me. **⁹** Just as the Father loved Me, I also loved you. Abide^G in My love. **¹⁰** If you keep My commandments, you will abide in My love— just as I have kept the commandments *of* My Father and am abiding in **His** love.

You Are My Friends. I Chose You And Appointed You To Bear Much Fruit
¹¹ "I have spoken these *things to* you in order that My joy may be in you, and your joy may be made full. **¹²** This is My commandment: that you be loving one another just as I loved you. **¹³** No one has greater love *than* this: that one lay-*down* his life for his friends. **¹⁴ You** are My friends if you are doing *the things* which **I** command you. **¹⁵** I no longer call you slaves, because the slave does not know what his master is doing. But I have called you friends, because I made-known *to* you everything which I heard from My Father. **¹⁶ You** did not choose Me, but **I** chose you and appointed you, in order that **you** may go and bear fruit and your fruit may remain, in order that He may give you whatever thing you ask the Father in My name. **¹⁷** I am commanding these *things to* you so-that you will love one another.

The World Will Hate You As It Hated Me, Because You Will Be Testifying of Me
¹⁸ "If the world hates you, you know^H that it has hated Me before you. **¹⁹** If you were of the world, the world would be loving *its* own. But because you are not of the world, but **I** chose you out of the world— for this reason the world hates you. **²⁰** Remember^I the word that **I** said *to* you, '*A* slave is not greater *than* his master'. If they persecuted Me, they will also persecute you. If they kept My word, they will also keep yours. **²¹** But they will do all these *things* to you because of My name, because they do not know the *One* having sent Me. **²²** If I had not come and spoken *to* them, they *would* not be having sin. But now they do not have *an* excuse for their sin. **²³** The *one* hating **Me** is also hating My Father. **²⁴** If I had not done among them the works which no other one did, they *would* not be

---

A. That is, He cuts it off and it eventually burns it up, v 6. Or, He lifts it up. That is, He lifts it up to the trellis in the spring, training and tending it so that it bears fruit next season. **B:** cleans... clean. Or, prunes... pruned. The agricultural metaphor and the human application are intertwined here, using the same root word in a play on words. The branches are pruned (the suckers are pruned off to allow the branch to bear more fruit), the apostles are clean (morally and spiritually purified). **C.** Or, Remain, Continue, Stay. **D:** abiding in Me and I in him. That is, having a living reciprocal relationship with Jesus. **E.** Jesus sums up the final state of the branch. He is found to be thrown out and dried up, as always with such branches. **F.** Or, prove-to-be. **G:** Abide... keep. Jesus plainly states the main point of the vine illustration: Abide in My love by doing as I command. **H.** Or, this may be a command: know that, recognize that. **I:** Remember... master. Or, Do you remember... master?

having sin. But now they have both seen and have hated both Me and My Father. **²⁵** But *it has taken place* in order that the word having been written in their Law [in Ps 69:4] might be fulfilled— that 'They hated Me without-a-reason'. **²⁶** When the Helper comes Whom I will send *to* you from the Father— the Spirit *of* truth, Who proceeds from the Father— that *One* will testify about Me. **²⁷** And **you** also are *going to be* testifying, because you are [the ones] with Me from *the* beginning.

I Have Told You In Advance So That You May Not Fall

16:1 "I have spoken these *things to* you in order that you may not be caused-to-fall. **²** They will make you put-out-of-the-synagogue *ones*. Indeed, *an* hour is coming for everyone having killed you to think *that he* is offering serviceᴬ *to* God. **³** And they will do these *things* because they did not know the Father nor Me. **⁴** But I have spoken these *things to* you so that when their hour comes, you may remember that **I** told you *of* **them.**

It Is Better That I Go Away, For I Will Send You The Helper To Convict The World

"Now I did not say these *things to* you from *the* beginning, because I was with you. **⁵** But now I am going to the *One* having sent Me. And none of you is asking Me, 'Where are You going?', **⁶** but grief has filled your heart because I have spoken these *things to* you. **⁷** But I tell you the truth— it is betterᴮ *for* you that **I** go away. For if I do not go away, the Helper will not come to you. But if I go, I will send Him to you. **⁸** And having come, that *One* will convict the world concerning sin, and concerning righteousness, and concerning judgment— **⁹** concerning sin, becauseᶜ they are not believing in Me; **¹⁰** and concerning righteousness, becauseᴰ I am going to the Father and you are no longer *going to* see Me; **¹¹** and concerning judgment, because the ruler *of* this world has been judged.

When The Helper Comes, He Will Guide You Into All Truth

¹² "I still have many *things* to say *to* you, but you are not able to bear *them* now. **¹³** But when that *One,* the Spirit *of* truth, comes— He will guide you in all the truth. For He will not speak from Himself, but He will speak whatever He will hear. And He will declare *to* you the *things* coming. **¹⁴** That *One* will glorify Me, because He will take from *what is* Mine and declare *it to* you. **¹⁵** Allᴱ that the Father has is Mine. For this reason I said that He takes from *what is* Mine and will declare *it to* you.

A Little While Longer And I Will Be Gone. A Little While Longer And You Will See Me

¹⁶ "*A* little *while* and you are no-longer *going to* see Me. And again *a* little *while*, and you will see Me". **¹⁷** Then *some* of His disciples said to one another, "What is this which He is saying *to* us— '*A* little *while*, and you are not *going to* see Me. And again *a* little *while*, and you will see Me'. And— 'Because I am going to the Father'?" **¹⁸** Then they were saying, "What is this which He is saying— '*A* little *while*'? We do not know what He is speaking *about.*

A. Or, worship. **B.** Or, profitable, advantageous. **C.** Or, that, in-that. Likewise in v 10 and 11. **D.** One who understands why Jesus returned to the Father will also understand what true righteousness is and how it can be obtained. **E.** Only One making Himself equal to God (5:18) could make such a statement. No finite being could say this. See 17:10.

You Will Weep, Then You Will Rejoice When I See You Again

¹⁹ Jesus knew that they were wanting to question Him, and He said *to* them, "Are you seeking with one another concerning this, that I said, '*A* little *while*, and you are not *going to* see Me. And again *a* little *while*, and you will see Me'? ²⁰ Truly, truly, I say *to* you that **you** will weep and lament, but the world will rejoice. **You** will be grieved, but your grief will become joy. ²¹ The woman has grief when she gives-birth, because her hour came. But when she bears the child, she no longer remembers the affliction because of the joy that *a* person was born into the world. ²² **You** then also now have grief— but I will see you again, and your heart will rejoice. And no one is *going to* take away your joy from you. ²³ And in that day you will not question Me *as to* anything. Truly, truly, I say *to* you, if you ask the Father anything in My name, He will give *it to* you. ²⁴ Until now you did not ask anything in My name. Be asking and you will receive, in order that your joy may be full.

Then I Will Speak To You Plainly About The Father

²⁵ "I have spoken these *things to* you in figures-of-speech. *An* hour is coming when I will no longer speak *to* you in figures-of-speech, but I will tell you about the Father *with* plainness. ²⁶ In that day you will ask in My name. And I am not saying *to* you that **I** will request the Father onᴬ your behalf. ²⁷ For the Father Himself loves you, because **you** have loved Me, and have believed that **I** came forth from God. ²⁸ I came forth from the Father, and I have come into the world. Againᴮ, I am leaving the world and going to the Father".

But Soon You Will Be Scattered

²⁹ His disciples say, "Look— now You are speaking with plainness, and You are speaking no figure-of-speech. ³⁰ Now we know that You know all *things*, and You have no need that anyone question You. By this we believe that You came forth from God". ³¹ Jesus responded *to* them, "Nowᶜ you believe! ³² Behold, *an* hour is coming, and has come, for you to be scattered— each to *his* own *things*— and leave Me alone. And-*yet* I am not alone, because the Father is with Me.

Take Courage, I Have Overcome The World

³³ "I have spoken these *things to* you in order that you may have peace in Me. You have affliction in the world, but take-courage— **I** have overcome the world".

Jesus Prays: Father, Glorify Your Son

17:1 Jesus spoke these *things,* and having lifted-up His eyes to heaven, said, "Father, the hour has come. Glorify Your Son, so that the Son may glorify You— ² just as You gave Him authority *over* all flesh in order that *as to* all thatᴰ You have given Him, He may give eternal life *to* them. ³ And this is eternal life: that they may be knowing You, the only true God, and Jesus Christ Whom You sent-forth. ⁴ I glorified You on the earth, having accomplished the work which You have given *to* Me that I should do. ⁵ And now Father, **You** glorify Me with Yourself *with* the glory which I was having with You before the world was.

A. Or, for you. You will directly ask the Father in My name. **B.** That is, Again [I say], I am... going to; or, I am leaving...and going **again** to. **C.** Or, Do you now believe? **D:** all that. This views all believers as an abstract whole.

I Have Revealed Your Name To The Men You Gave Me. Keep Them In Your Name
6 "I revealed Your name *to* the men whom You gave *to* Me out of the world. They were Yours, and You gave them *to* Me. And they have kept Your word. **7** They have now come-to-know that all^A *things* that You have given *to* Me are from You— **8** because I have given them the words which You gave *to* Me, and **they** received *them,* and truly understood that I came forth from You, and believed that **You** sent Me forth. **9** I am praying^B for them. I am not praying for the world, but for *the ones* whom You have given *to* Me— because they are Yours; **10** indeed all^C My *things* are Yours, and Yours, Mine^D. And I have been glorified in them. **11** And I am^E no longer in the world, and **they** are in the world, and I am coming to You. Holy Father, keep^F them in^G Your name which You have given *to* Me, in order that they may be one, just as We *are.* **12** When I was with them, I was keeping them in Your name which You have given *to* Me. And I guarded *them,* and none of them perished— except the son *of* ^H destruction, in order that the Scripture might be fulfilled. **13** But now I am coming to You. And I am speaking these *things* in the world so that they may have My joy made-full in themselves.

I Have Given Them Your Word. Set Them Apart In The Truth, Which Is Your Word
14 "**I** have given them Your word, and the world hated them— because they are not of the world, just as **I** am not of the world. **15** I am not praying that You take them out of the world, but that You keep them from the^I evil *one.* **16** They are not of the world, just as **I** am not of the world—**17** set them apart^J in^K the truth. Your word is truth. **18** Just as You sent Me forth into the world, **I** also sent them forth into the world. **19** And **I** am setting apart Myself for them, in order that **they** may also be set apart in truth.

May These And The Ones Believing Through Them All Be One
20 "And I am not praying for these *ones* only, but also for the *ones* believing in Me through their word, **21** that^L they may all be^M one^N— just as You, Father, *are* in Me and I *am* in You, that^O **they** also may be in Us— in order that the world may be believing that **You** sent Me forth. **22** And **I** have given them the glory^P which You have given *to* Me in order that they may be one just as We *are* one, **23** I in them and You in Me; in order that they may be perfected into one— in order that the world may be knowing that **You** sent Me forth, and loved them just as You loved Me.

A. That is, all the words and works. **B.** Or, asking on-behalf-of; asking with-reference-to. **C.** Or, all *that is* Mine is Yours. **D:** And Yours, Mine. Only One equal to God (5:18) could say this. A lesser being could at best say 'Most of what is Yours is mine'. **E:** I am no longer in... and I am coming to. That is, My public ministry is done... and I am coming back to You; or, I am coming back to You... and I am coming to You now in prayer. **F.** Or, preserve, protect, guard. **G.** Or, by. That is, in the sphere of all Your name means, includes, and stands for. Preserve them in their living relationship with You. Or, by means of. Protect them from evil and the evil one by the power of Your name. **H.** That is, destined for; or, belonging to this destiny. **I.** Or, from evil. **J.** That is, make them holy; or, set them apart for service, for the mission on which I sent them, v 18. **K.** That is, in the sphere of; or, by means of. **L.** This gives the content of this prayer, that they may all be one. Or, in order that, giving the purpose of it. I do not pray 'Keep them' and 'Set them apart' for them alone, but for all, in order that they may all be one. **M.** That is, be continuing to be; or, keep on being; not 'get to be'. **N.** That is, one with Us (as defined by what follows, and equivalent to 'may all abide in Us and Us in them'); or, one with each other (linking it to the command to love one another). **O.** Or, in order that. **P.** That is, the glory of Your name and word revealed through Me; or, the glory of My working through them, 14:13-14; or, the glory of humbly taking up their cross and serving You as I did; or, the glory of I in them (v 23), of the divine nature indwelling them (2 Pet 1:4).

Father, I Want Them To Be With Me And See The Glory You Have Given Me

²⁴ "Father, *as to* what^A You have given *to* Me, I desire that those *ones* also may be with Me where **I** am, in order that they may be seeing My glory which You have given *to* Me because You loved Me before *the* foundation *of the* world.

Father, I Made You Known To Them In Order That Your Love May Be In Them

²⁵ "Righteous Father, indeed the world did not know You— but **I** knew You. And these *ones* knew that **You** sent Me forth. ²⁶ And I made Your name known *to* them, and will make *it* known, in order that the love *with* which You loved Me may be in^B them, and I *may be* in them".

Jesus Is Handed Over To The Authorities

18:1 Having said these *things*, Jesus went-out with His disciples to the other side *of* the ravine^C *of* Kidron where there was *a* garden, into which He entered, He and His disciples. ² Now Judas, the *one* handing Him over, also knew the place, because Jesus often was gathered there with His disciples. ³ So Judas— having received^D the [Roman] cohort^E, and officers from the chief priests and from the Pharisees— comes there with lanterns and torches and weapons. ⁴ Then Jesus, knowing all the *things* coming upon Him, went forth. And He says *to* them, "Whom are you seeking?" ⁵ They answered Him, "Jesus the Nazarene". He says *to* them, "I am *He*". Now Judas, the *one* handing Him over, was also standing *there* with them. ⁶ So when He said *to* them, "I am *He*", they^F went back, and fell on the ground. ⁷ Then He again asked them, "Whom are you seeking?" And the *ones* said, "Jesus the Nazarene". ⁸ Jesus responded, "I told you that **I** am *He*. If then you are seeking Me, permit these *ones* to go"— ⁹ in order that the word which He spoke^G might be fulfilled, that "*The ones* whom You have given Me— I did not lose any of them". ¹⁰ Then Simon Peter, having *a* sword, drew it and hit the slave *of* the high priest, and cut-off his right ear. And *the* name *for* the slave was Malchus. ¹¹ Then Jesus said *to* Peter, "Put the sword into the sheath. The cup which the Father has given Me— shall not I drink it?"

Jesus Stands Before Annas And Caiaphas

¹² Then the [Roman] cohort and *its* commander^H, and the officers *of* the Jews, arrested Jesus, and bound Him. ¹³ And they led *Him* to Annas first. For he was *the* father-in-law *of* Caiaphas, who was *the* high priest *of* that year. ¹⁴ And Caiaphas was the *one* having counseled^I the Jews that it was better *that* one Man die for the people.

Peter Denies Jesus

¹⁵ Now Simon Peter and another disciple^J were following Jesus. And that disciple was known *to* the high priest, and he entered with Jesus into the courtyard *of* the high priest. ¹⁶ But Peter was standing at the door outside. So the other disciple, the *one* known *by* the high priest, went out and spoke *to* the doorkeeper, and brought in Peter. ¹⁷ Then the doorkeeper servant-girl says *to* Peter, "**You** are not also *one* of the disciples *of* this man, *are you*?" That *one* says, "I am not". ¹⁸ And the slaves and the officers,

A. This views the totality of believers as an abstract whole. **B.** That is, within; or, among. **C.** Or, brook (the winter stream that flowed in the ravine). **D.** Or, taken. **E.** See Mt 27:27. The size of this detachment is not known. **F.** Perhaps John means the priests began to step back to let the soldiers and officers take Jesus, and fell down. **G.** That is, in 17:12. **H.** Or, tribune, the Roman commander of a thousand men, equivalent to a major or colonel. Centurions (commanders of a hundred) reported to him. **I.** See 11:50. **J.** John may be referring to himself; or, to a non-apostle.

having made *a* charcoal-fire because it was cold, were standing *there* and warming *themselves*. And Peter was also with them, standing *there* and warming *himself*.

Jesus Says To Annas, Question Those Who Heard Me. He Is Led Out to Caiaphas
19 So the high priest questioned Jesus about His disciples, and about His teaching. **20** Jesus answered him, "**I** have spoken *in* public *to* the world. **I** always taught at synagogue, and in the temple, where all the Jews come together. And I spoke nothing in secret. **21** Why are you questioning Me? Question the *ones* having heard what I spoke *to* them. Look, these *ones* know *the things* which **I** said". **22** And He having said these *things*, one *of* the officers standing near gave Jesus *a* slapᴬ, having said, "In this manner do you answer the high priest?" **23** Jesus answered him, "If I spoke wrongly, testify about the *thing* wrong. But if *I spoke* rightly, why do you beat Me?" **24** Then Annas sent Him forth, having been bound, to Caiaphas the high priest.

Peter Denies Jesus a Second And Third Time
25 And Simon Peter is standing *there* and warming *himself*. So they said *to* him, "**You** are not also *one* of His disciples, *are you*?" That *one* denied *it* and said, "I am not". **26** One of the slaves *of* the high priest, being *a* relative *of the one of* whom Peter cut-off the ear, says, "Did **I** not see you in the garden with Him?" **27** Then again Peter denied *it*. And immediately *a* rooster crowed.

Jesus Stands Before Pilate
28 Then they lead Jesus from Caiaphas to the Praetoriumᴮ. And it was early-morning. And they themselves did not enter into the Praetorium in order that they might not be defiled, but might eat the Passover [Feast]ᶜ.

The Jewish Rulers Tell Pilate They Want Jesus Executed
29 So Pilate went outside to them. And he says, "What accusation do you bring against this man?" **30** They responded and said *to* him, "If this *One* were not doing wrongᴰ, we would not have handed Him over *to* you". **31** So Pilate said *to* them, "**You** take Him and judge Him according to your Law". The Jews said *to* him, "It is not lawfulᴱ *for* **us** to execute anyone"— **32** in order that the word *of* Jesus might be fulfilled which He spoke signifyingᶠ *by* what kind of death He was going to die.

Jesus Says To Pilate, My Kingdom Is Not of This World
33 So Pilate entered again into the Praetorium, and called Jesus. And he said *to* Him, "Are **You** the King *of* the Jews?" **34** Jesus answered, "Are **you** saying this from yourself, or did others tell you about Me?" **35** Pilate answered, "**I** am not *a* Jew, *am I*? **Your** nationᴳ and the chief priests handed You over *to* me. What did You do?" **36** Jesus answered, "My kingdom is not of this world. If My kingdom were of this world, My servants would be fighting in order that I might not be handed-over *to* the Jews. But

A. That is, with the hand. Or, a blow, using a rod or club. **B.** That is, the Roman palace or fortress, Pilate's residence while in Jerusalem. **C.** Or, [meal]. That is, participate in the eight-day Feast of Unleavened Bread, also called Passover (as in Lk 22:1); or, eat the Passover meal itself, implying they had not yet eaten it. **D.** That is, a civil, criminal wrong. **E.** That is, under Roman law. **F.** See 12:33. 'Lifted up' points to a Roman crucifixion, not a Jewish stoning. **G.** In other words, Pilate is repeating the Jews' accusation that Jesus is rebelling against Rome. So Jesus affirms that His kingdom is not earthly or political.

as-it-is^A, My kingdom is not from here". ^37 Therefore Pilate said *to* Him, "So-then **You** are *a* king?" Jesus answered, "**You** are saying^B that^C I am *a* king. **I** have been born for this. And I have come into the world for this: that I might testify *to* the truth. Everyone being of the truth hears^D My voice". ^38 Pilate says *to* Him, "What is truth?"

Pilate Finds No Charge Against Jesus, But Has Him Whipped
And having said this, he again went out to the Jews. And he says *to* them, "**I** find **no** charge^E in^F Him. ^39 But it is *a* custom *for* you that I release one *prisoner for* you at the Passover [Feast]. So do you wish me to release the King *of* the Jews *for* you?" ^40 Then they shouted back^G, saying, "Not this *One*, but Barabbas!" Now Barabbas was *a* robber^H. **19:1** So at that time Pilate took Jesus and whipped *Him*. ^2 And the soldiers, having woven *a* crown out of thorns, put *it* on His head. And they clothed Him with *a* purple garment. ^3 And they were coming to Him and saying, "Hail^I, King *of* the Jews!" And they were giving Him slaps.

The Jews Shout, Crucify Him, Because He Made Himself To Be God's Son!
^4 And Pilate again went outside. And he says *to* them, "Look— I am bringing Him outside *to* you in order that you may know that I find no charge in Him". ^5 Then Jesus came outside, wearing the crown made-of-thorns and the purple garment. And he says *to* them, "Behold, the man!" ^6 Then when they saw Him, the chief priests and the officers shouted, saying, "Crucify, crucify!" Pilate says *to* them, "**You** take Him and crucify *Him*, for **I** do not find *a* charge in Him". ^7 The Jews responded *to* him, "**We** have *a* law. And according to the law He ought to die, because He made Himself *to be* God's Son".

Pilate Asks Jesus, Where Are You From? Jesus Does Not Answer
^8 Then when Pilate heard this statement, he became more afraid. ^9 And he entered into the Praetorium again. And he says *to* Jesus, "Where are **You** from?" But Jesus did not give him *an* answer. ^10 So Pilate says *to* Him, "You do not speak *to* me? Do **You** not know that I have authority to release You, and I have authority to crucify You?" ^11 Jesus answered him, "You *would* not have any authority against^J Me unless it^K had been given *to* you from above. For this reason the *one* having handed Me over *to* you has *a* greater sin".

Pilate Tries To Release Jesus, But The Jewish Leaders Stop Him
^12 From this *time*^L, Pilate was seeking to release Him, but the Jews shouted saying, "If you release this *One*, you are not *a* friend *of* Caesar. Everyone making himself the king is speaking-against Caesar".

Pilate Hesitates Again, But Condemns Jesus
^13 Therefore Pilate, having heard these words, brought Jesus outside, and sat on *a*

A. Or, now, at-the-present-time. **B.** That is, you are saying [correctly], as seen by what follows. See Mt 27:11. **C.** Or, saying *it*, because. **D.** That is, listens to and obeys. **E.** Or, guilt, blame, ground of accusation (from the Roman law point of view. He sees the case as religious, not criminal). **F.** That is, in His case; or, in-connection-with Him. **G.** Or, again. **H.** Or, insurrectionist. **I.** Or, Greetings, Welcome. This was a common greeting. **J.** Or, in-relation-to. **K.** This does not refer back to 'authority', but to something more abstract: this handing over of Me to you; or, your exercising power over Me. **L.** Or, *statement*.

judgment-seat in *a* place being called '*The* Pavement' (but *in* Hebrew, 'Gabbatha'). **14** Now it was Preparation^A *day of* the Passover [Feast]^B. *The* hour was about *the* sixth^C. And he says *to* the Jews, "Look— your King!" **15** Then those *ones* shouted, "Take *Him* away, take *Him* away, crucify Him!" Pilate says *to* them, "Shall I crucify your King?" The chief priests answered, "We do not have *a* king except Caesar". **16** So at that time he handed Him over *to* them^D in order that He might be crucified.

The King of The Jews Is Crucified
So they took Jesus. **17** And bearing the cross *for* Himself, He went out to the *place* being called *"The* Place *of a* Skull" (which is called *in* Hebrew, "Golgotha"), **18** where they crucified Him and two others with Him— on this *side* and on this *side*, and Jesus in the middle. **19** And Pilate also wrote *a* title^E and put *it* on the cross. And it had been written, "Jesus the Nazarene, the King *of* the Jews". **20** Therefore many *of* the Jews read this title, because the place where Jesus was crucified was near the city. And it had been written *in* Hebrew, Latin, Greek. **21** So the chief priests *of* the Jews were saying *to* Pilate, "Do not write, 'The King *of* the Jews', but that that *One* said, 'I am King *of* the Jews' ". **22** Pilate responded, "What I have written, I have written".

The Soldiers Take His Garments, Fulfilling Psalm 22
23 Then the soldiers, when they crucified Jesus, took His garments and made four parts— *a* part *for* each soldier— and the tunic^F. Now the tunic was seamless, woven from the top through *the* whole. **24** So they said to one another, "Let us not tear it, but let us cast-lots for it *to decide* whose it will be"— in order that the Scripture [in Ps 22:18] might be fulfilled, the *one* saying, "They divided My garments among themselves, and they cast *a* lot for My clothing". So indeed, the soldiers did these *things*.

John Takes Mary Into His Household
25 Now His mother, and the sister *of* His mother, Mary the *wife of* Clopas, and Mary the Magdalene, were standing beside the cross *of* Jesus. **26** So Jesus, having seen *His* mother and the disciple^G whom He was loving standing near, says *to His* mother, "Woman, look— your son!" **27** Then He says *to* the disciple, "Look— your mother!" And from that hour the disciple took her into^H *his* own *things*.

Jesus Dies
28 After this, Jesus— knowing that all *things* have already^I been finished, in order that the Scripture [in Ps 69:21] might be accomplished— says, "I am thirsty". **29** *A* jar full *of* sour-wine was setting *there*. So having put *a* sponge full *of* the sour wine on *a* hyssop *branch*, they brought *it* to His mouth. **30** Then when He received the sour wine, Jesus said, "It has been finished!" And having bowed *His* head, He gave-over^J *His* spirit.

Jesus Is Pierced With a Spear, But a Bone Is Not Broken, Fulfilling The Prophecies
31 Then the Jews— because it was Preparation *day*, in order that the bodies might not

---

A. That is, preparation for the Sabbath. It was Friday. **B.** Or, [meal]. **C.** That is, noon, Jewish time; or, 6 A.M. Roman time. **D.** That is, to the priests' will, as in Lk 23:25; or, to the Roman soldiers. **E.** Or, notice. **F.** That is, the undergarment. Jesus was naked. **G.** That is, John himself. **H.** That is, under his care. **I.** Or, now. **J.** Or, handed-over, delivered.

remain on the cross during the Sabbath (for the day *of* that Sabbath was *a* great[A] *day*)— asked Pilate that their legs be broken, and they be taken away. [32] So the soldiers came and broke the legs *of* the first *one,* and *of* the other *one* having been crucified-with Him. [33] But having come to Jesus, when they saw Him already dead, they did not break His legs. [34] But one *of* the soldiers stabbed His side *with a* spear, and immediately blood and water came out. [35] And the one[B] having seen *it* has testified, and his testimony is true. And that *one*[C] knows that he is speaking true *things,* so that **you** also may believe. [36] For these *things* took place in order that the Scripture [in Ex 12:46] might be fulfilled: "*A* bone *of* His will not be broken". [37] And again another Scripture [Zech 12:10] says, "They will look at *the One* Whom they pierced".

Joseph Lays Jesus In a Tomb
[38] Now after these *things* Joseph from Arimathea— being *a* disciple *of* Jesus, but having been hidden[D] because of the fear *of* the Jews— asked Pilate in order that he might take away the body *of* Jesus. And Pilate permitted *it.* So he came and took away His body. [39] And Nicodemus also came— the *one* having first come to Him *by* night— bringing *a* mixture *of* myrrh and aloes, about *a* hundred pounds[E]. [40] So they took the body *of* Jesus and bound it *in* linen-cloths with the spices, as is *the* custom *for* the Jews to prepare-for-burial. [41] Now there was *a* garden in the place where He was crucified. And in the garden *was a* new tomb in which no one yet had been laid. [42] So there— because of the Preparation *day of* the Jews, because the tomb was near— they laid Jesus.

On The First Day of the Week, Jesus Is Not Found In The Tomb
20:1 Now *on* the first *day of* the week, Mary the Magdalene goes to the tomb early-in-the-morning— *there* still being darkness— and sees the stone having been taken away from the tomb. [2] So she runs and comes to Simon Peter, and to the other disciple[F] whom Jesus was loving. And she says *to* them, "They took the Lord out of the tomb, and we do not know where they put Him". [3] So Peter and the other disciple went forth, and were going to the tomb. [4] And the two were running together. And the other disciple ran ahead faster *than* Peter, and came to the tomb first. [5] And having stooped-to-look, he sees the linen-cloths lying *there*, but he did not enter. [6] Then Simon Peter also comes, following him. And he entered into the tomb. And he sees the linen-cloths lying *there*, [7] and the face-cloth which was on His head— not lying with the linen-cloths, but apart-from *them*, having been wrapped-up[G] in one place. [8] So at that time the other disciple also entered— the *one* having come to the tomb first— and saw and believed[H]. [9] For they did not yet understand the Scripture— that He must rise-up from *the* dead. [10] Then the disciples went away again to them[I].

Jesus Meets Mary The Magdalene And Tells Her To Announce His Resurrection
[11] Now Mary was standing outside at the tomb, weeping. Then as she was weeping, she stooped-to-look into the tomb. [12] And she sees two angels in white, sitting— one at the

A. That is, it was a special Sabbath; the Sabbath during Passover week. **B.** John seems to be referring again to himself. **C.** That is, the witness, John. Or, that *One.* That is, God. **D.** Or, concealed, secret. **E.** That is, Roman pounds (11.5 ounces or 327 grams). Thus, about 72 sixteen-ounce pounds or 33 kilograms. This is an amount fitting for a king. **F.** That is, John himself. **G.** Or, rolled-up, folded-up. The point of all this detail is that the graveclothes were not missing or strewn about, as would be the case if the body had been stolen. **H.** That is, believed Jesus returned to the Father, as He had said in 13:33; 14:3; 16:28. But he did not yet understand that Jesus would walk with them again. **I.** That is, the other disciples; or, their homes.

head and one at the feet where the body *of* Jesus was lying. ¹³ And those *ones* say *to* her, "Woman, why are you weeping?" She says *to* them, "Because^A they took my Lord, and I do not know where they put Him". ¹⁴ Having said these *things*, she turned back, and sees Jesus standing *there*. And she did not know that it was Jesus. ¹⁵ Jesus says *to* her, "Woman, why are you weeping? Whom are you seeking?" That *one*, thinking that He is the gardener, says *to* Him, "Sir, if **you** carried Him away, tell me where you put Him, and **I** will take Him". ¹⁶ Jesus says *to* her, "Mary". That *one*, having turned, says *to* Him *in* Hebrew, "Rabboni!" (which means, Teacher). ¹⁷ Jesus says *to* her, "Do not be clinging-to^B Me, for I have not^C yet gone-up to the Father. But go to My brothers and say *to* them, 'I am going-up^D to My Father and your Father, and My God and your God' ". ¹⁸ Mary the Magdalene comes, announcing *to* the disciples that "I have seen the Lord", and *that* He said these *things to* her.

That Evening, Jesus Meets Ten of The Disciples And Says, Receive The Holy Spirit
¹⁹ Then— being evening *on* that first^E day *of* the week, and the doors having been locked where the disciples were because of the fear *of* the Jews— Jesus came and stood in *their* midst. And He says *to* them, "Peace *to* you". ²⁰ And having said this, He showed them *His* hands and *His* side. Then the disciples rejoiced, having seen the Lord. ²¹ Then Jesus said *to* them again, "Peace *to* you. Just as the Father has sent Me forth, **I** also am sending you". ²² And having said this, He breathed-on^F *them*. And He says *to* them, "Receive *the* Holy Spirit. ²³ If you forgive the sins *of* any, they have been forgiven *for* them. If you retain^G *the* sins *of* any, they have been retained".

After Eight Days, Jesus Meets Thomas, Who Says, My Lord And My God!
²⁴ Now Thomas, one of the twelve, the *one* being called Didymus^H, was not with them when Jesus came. ²⁵ So the other disciples were saying *to* him, "We have seen the Lord!" But the *one* said *to* them, "Unless I see the mark^I *of* the nails in His hands, and put my finger into the mark *of* the nails, and put my hand into His side, I will by no means believe". ²⁶ And after eight days, His disciples were again inside, and Thomas *was* with them. Jesus comes— the doors having been locked. And He stood in *their* midst and said, "Peace *to* you". ²⁷ Then He says *to* Thomas, "Bring your finger here and see My hands. And bring your hand and put *it* into My side. And do not be unbelieving, but believing". ²⁸ Thomas responded and said *to* Him^J, "My Lord and my God!" ²⁹ Jesus says *to* him, "You have believed because you have seen Me. Blessed *are* the *ones* not having seen and having believed".

A. Or, this word may simply introduce the quote: *to* them, "They took. **B.** Or, holding-on-to. Mary needs to stop clinging, and be going. **C.** Jesus may mean He must first ascend to the Father (for reasons of which we are ignorant); or, that there is no need to cling to Him now because He is not yet returning to the Father. She will see Him again (over the next forty days). **D.** Jesus may mean ascending now, first; or, *going to* go-up. He is beginning the process of going up, but has not done so yet. **E.** That is, Sunday night. This is the Roman way of speaking. For the Jews, Saturday night (as we call it) was the evening of the first day. **F.** Or, blew-on. This visibly connects the giving of the Spirit to Jesus. **G.** Or, hold firm; hold fast. On forgiving and retaining sins, compare Mt 16:19; 18:18. Some think that Jesus is giving authority to His ministers to absolve sins; others, that He is giving His authority to all believers to speak regarding God's response to sin and repentance. **H.** See 11:16. **I.** Or, imprint. **J.** Note that these words are spoken to Jesus, not as a mere exclamation. Thomas here honors the Son even as the Father, 5:23. He addresses Jesus as God.

Jesus Did Many Other Signs

30 Then indeed Jesus also did many other signs^A in the presence of His disciples, which have not been written in this book. **31** But these *things* have been written so that you may believe that Jesus is the Christ, the Son *of* God, and so that believing, you may have life in His name.

Later, Jesus Meets The Disciples By The Sea of Galilee

21:1 After these *things* Jesus manifested Himself again *to* the disciples at the Sea *of* Tiberias^B. And He manifested *Himself* as follows: **2** Simon Peter, and Thomas (the *one* being called Didymus), and Nathanael (the *one* from Cana *of* Galilee), and the *sons of* Zebedee, and two other of His disciples were together. **3** Simon Peter says *to* them, "I am going to fish". They say *to* him, "**We** are also coming with you". They went out and got into the boat. And during that night they caught nothing. **4** Now having already become early-morning, Jesus stood at the shore. But the disciples did not know that it was Jesus. **5** So Jesus says *to* them, "Children^C, you do not have any fish-to-eat, *do you*?" They answered Him, "No". **6** And the *One* said *to* them, "Cast the net to the right side *of* the boat and you will find *them*". So they cast *it*, and they were no longer strong-*enough* to draw it [into the boat] because *of* the multitude *of* the fish. **7** Then that disciple whom Jesus was loving says *to* Peter, "It is the Lord". So Simon Peter, having heard that it was the Lord, tied *his* outer-garment around *himself* (for he was naked^D), and threw himself into the sea. **8** But the other disciples came in the small-boat (for they were not far from the land, but about two-hundred cubits^E away)— dragging the net *of* fish. **9** Then when they got out to the land, they see *a* charcoal-fire lying *there*, and fish lying upon *it*, and bread. **10** Jesus says *to* them, "Bring from the fish which you now caught". **11** So Simon Peter went up and drew the net to land, full *of* large fish— *a* hundred fifty three. And *though* being so many, the net was not torn. **12** Jesus says *to* them, "Come, eat-breakfast". And none *of* the disciples was daring to question Him, "Who are **You**?", knowing that it was the Lord. **13** Jesus comes and takes the bread and gives *it to* them, and the fish likewise. **14** This *is* now *the* third^F *time* Jesus was manifested *to* the disciples *after* having arisen from *the* dead.

At Breakfast, Jesus Restores Peter. Do You Love Me? Feed My Sheep

15 Then when they ate-breakfast, Jesus says *to* Simon Peter, "Simon, *son of* John, do you *devotedly*-love^G Me more *than* these^H?" He says *to* Him, "Yes, Lord. **You** know that I *affectionately*-love You". He says *to* him, "Be feeding My lambs". **16** He says *to* him again *a* second *time*, "Simon, *son of* John, do you *devotedly*-love Me?" He says *to* Him, "Yes, Lord. **You** know that I *affectionately*-love You". He says *to* him, "Be shepherding My sheep". **17** He says *to* him the third *time*, "Simon, *son of* John, do you *affectionately*-love Me?" Peter was grieved because^I He said *to* him the third

---

A. This may be taken narrowly of signs regarding the resurrection (such as eating broiled fish, Lk 24:43), making this the conclusion of the resurrection event. Or, this may be taken broadly, making this the conclusion of the book, to which John adds additional information next. **B.** That is, of Galilee. This is the Roman name for it. **C.** Or, Boys, Lads. **D.** That is, stripped for work, stripped down to his undergarment. **E.** That is, 100 yards or 92 meters. **F.** That is, the third mentioned by John, the others being in 20:19 and 26. **G:** *devotedly*-love... *affectionately*-love. Or, simply 'love' in both cases, if no distinction is intended between the two words (*agapao* and *phileo*). **H.** That is, these other disciples, since Peter had said 'Though all fall, I will not' (Mt 26:33; Mk 14:29); or, these fish; your former life. **I.** John may mean because Jesus asked a third time; or, because on this third time He used the same word Peter himself had been using.

time, "Do you *affectionately*-love Me?". And he says *to* Him, "Lord, **You** know all *things.* **You** recognizeᴬ that I *affectionately*-love You". Jesus says *to* him, "Be feeding My sheep. **¹⁸** Truly, truly, I say *to* you, when you were younger you were girdingᴮ yourself and walking where you were wanting *to go*. But when you become-oldᶜ, you will stretch-out your hands and another will gird you andᴰ bring *you* where you are not wanting *to go*". **¹⁹** Now this He said signifying *by* what kindᴱ of death he will glorify God. And having said this, He says *to* him, "Be following Me!"

Peter Asks Jesus About John
²⁰ Peter, having turned around, sees the discipleᶠ following *them* whom Jesus was loving— *the one* who also leaned back on His chest during dinner and said, "Lord, who is the *one* handing You over?" **²¹** So Peter, having looked-at this *one*, says *to* Jesus, "Lord, and what *of* this *one*? **²²** Jesus says *to* him, "If I want him to remain until I come, what *is it* to you? **You** be following Me!" **²³** Therefore this statement went out to the brothers, that "that disciple does not die". But Jesus did not say *to* him that he does not die, but "If I want him to remain until I come, what *is it* to you?"

John Concludes The Book
²⁴ Thisᴳ *one* is the disciple testifying about these *things,* andᴴ the *one* having written these *things*, and we know that his testimony is true. **²⁵** And there are also many other *things* which Jesus did, which if they should be written individually, I suppose *that* not even the world itself *would* have-room-for the books being written.

A. Or, know, understand. **B.** That is, tying on your belt. **C.** Or, grow-aged. **D.** That is, others will have control over you and lead you away to death. You will be executed. **E.** That is, a martyr's death; or, a crucifixion. **F.** That is, John. **G.** That is, this one referred to in v 20-23. With the reference to himself still in mind, John transitions to the conclusion of the book. **H.** Or, even.

Acts

A. Jesus commanded the apostles to wait for the promise of the Father, and was lifted up   1:1-14

B. During these days, the brothers chose Matthias to take Judas's place   1:15-26

C. On the day of Pentecost, they began to speak in other tongues. The Jews marveled   2:1-13

   1. Peter said, God raised Jesus whom you killed, and He has poured forth what you see.   2:14-36
Know for certain, God made Him both Lord and Christ— this Jesus whom you crucified

   2. And they said, What shall we do? Peter said, repent and be saved from this generation   2:37-41

D. They were devoting themselves to teaching, fellowship, breaking bread, and prayer. Signs and   2:42-47
wonders were taking place through the apostles. They were sharing with one another

E. Peter and John were going up to the temple at the hour of prayer. Peter healed a lame man   3:1-10

   1. Peter said, God glorified Jesus, whom you denied. On the basis of faith in His name, this   3:11-26
man was healed. And now, repent and return

   2. While they were speaking, the priests came upon them and jailed them   4:1-4

   3. Peter says it was by the name of Jesus whom you crucified that this man was healed   4:5-22

   4. Having been released, they all praised God, and prayed to speak with boldness   4:23-31

F. The heart and soul of the believers was one. They sold their belongings to help those in need.   4:32-5:11
Ananias did so deceitfully and died. Great fear came upon all among them

G. Signs and wonders were taking place through the apostles. Many were coming to them. The   5:12-42
priests, filled with jealousy, arrested them. Peter said, We must obey God, not man

H. A complaint arose over the serving of food. They selected seven men to put in charge of it   6:1-7

I. Stephen was doing great wonders and signs among the people. Some argued with him, but they   6:8-7:1
were unable to resist his wisdom. They dragged him before the Sanhedrin

   1. Stephen said, Your fathers killed the Prophets who announced the Messiah, whom you   7:2-53
also betrayed and murdered. You received the Law, but do not keep it

   2. They were infuriated in their hearts, grinding their teeth at him. They stoned him   7:54-8:1

   3. A great persecution arose. They were dispersed to the regions of Judea and Samaria   8:1-4

J. Now Philip, having gone to Samaria, was proclaiming Christ to them. They were baptized   8:5-13

   1. The apostles in Jerusalem, having heard, sent Peter and John, who prayed so that they   8:14-25
might receive the Spirit. Simon tried to buy this power,and was rebuked by Peter

   2. An angel directed Philip to an Ethiopian court official reading Isa 53. He was saved   8:26-39

   3. And Philip was evangelizing all the cities from Azotus to Caesarea   8:40

K. Saul requested letters to Damascus authorizing him to imprison any belonging to the Way.   9:1-9
Drawing near Damascus, Jesus appeared to him and said, Why are you persecuting Me?

   1. Ananias was sent to him. Saul regained his sight and was baptized   9:10-19

   2. Saul proclaimed Jesus in Damascus. They plotted against him, but he escaped   9:19-25

   3. Having arrived in Jerusalem, Barnabas led him to the apostles   9:26-30

   4. So indeed the church in Judea, Galilee and Samaria was having peace and increasing   9:31

L. Peter, passing through all the regions, came down to Lydda and healed a man   9:32-35

   1. Called to Joppa, Peter raised Tabitha (Dorcas). He stayed with Simon, the tanner   9:36-43

   2. God told Cornelius to call for Peter. He believed and God poured out the Spirit on him   10:1-48

   3. Those in Jerusalem objected to this at first, but then perceived it as the work of God   11:1-18

M. Those dispersed to Antioch saw many Gentiles turn to the Lord. The church at Jerusalem sent   11:19-26
Barnabas. He got Saul, and they taught there for a year

   1.   Agabus predicted a famine. The church sent Barnabas and Saul with an offering   11:27-30
   2.   Herod had James put to death and imprisoned Peter, but the Lord freed him   12:1-23
   3.   The Word was growing. Barnabas and Saul returned   12:24-25

N. The Spirit spoke through prophets in the church at Antioch, sending out Barnabas and Saul   13:1-3

   1.   So indeed, having sailed to Cyprus, Paul blinded Elymas. The proconsul believed   13:4-12
   2.   Mark leaves. In Pisidian Antioch, Paul and Barnabas enter the synagogue   13:13-15

      a.   Paul said God had sent a Savior for Israel, Jesus, whom John had announced   13:16-25

         i.   Fulfilling the Scriptures, the rulers killed Him, but God raised Him from the   13:26-37
            dead. He appeared to His people for many days, and we are now His witnesses
         ii.   Through Him, forgiveness of sins is proclaimed. Don't be scoffers   13:38-41

      b.   Paul speaks again on the next Sabbath, and many believe. The Jews dispute   13:42-48
      c.   The Jews incite the city against Paul and Barnabas, and they are driven out   13:49-52

   3.   In Iconium, the same thing occurred   14:1-7
   4.   In Lystra, Paul was declared to be a god. After Jews came, he was stoned   14:8-20
   5.   In Derbe, Paul proclaimed the gospel. Then he returned, strengthening the churches   14:20-27

O. In Antioch, some came saying Gentile Christians must be circumcised. After no small   14:28-15:5
dispute, the church sent Paul and Barnabas to Jerusalem to resolve the issue

   1.   Peter said both Jews and Gentiles are saved by faith. Don't lay the Law on their necks   15:6-11
   2.   James said the Prophets agree, having predicted that Gentiles would turn to God   15:12-21
   3.   A letter is sent to Antioch to clear up the matter, accompanied by Silas   15:22-34

P. After spending some days in Antioch, Paul wanted to return with Barnabas to the cities.   15:35-39
Barnabas was wanting to take John Mark. Paul disagreed, and they split up

   1.   Paul chose Silas and went through Syria, Cilicia, Derbe and Lystra   15:40-16:5
   2.   They passed through to Troas, where in a vision, God called them to Macedonia   16:6-10
   3.   In Philippi, Paul meets Lydia, who turns to the Lord   16:11-15

      a.   Paul casts a demon out of a profitable fortune-telling servant girl   16:16-18
      b.   The girl's masters have Paul and Silas beaten and imprisoned   16:19-24
      c.   An earthquake frees the prisoners, and the jailer is saved   16:25-34
      d.   The Magistrates release Paul and Silas after learning they are Roman citizens   16:35-40

   4.   In Thessalonica, the Jews dragged Jason before the authorities and forced Paul to leave   17:1-9
   5.   In Berea, they searched the Scriptures. The Jews from Thessalonica came to agitate   17:10-14
   6.   In Athens, Paul spoke in the synagogues, the market, and the Areopagus   17:15-21

      a.   Paul proclaimed the Creator-God, and Jesus as His Judge raised from the dead   17:22-31
      b.   At the mention of a resurrection, some scoffed. Some joined Paul and believed   17:32-34

   7.   In Corinth, Paul found Aquila and Priscilla. Paul taught there for 18 months   18:1-17
   8.   Paul sailed off to Syria. He stopped in Ephesus, and promised to return, leaving Priscilla   18:18-22
      and Aquila there. From Caesarea, he went up to the church, then back to Antioch

Q. After some time, Paul departed, passing through Galatia and Phrygia, strengthening the 18:23-28
disciples. Apollos was instructed by Priscilla and Aquila in Ephesus, and went to Corinth

1. Paul came to Ephesus. He laid hands on some to receive the Spirit 19:1-7
2. Paul spoke in the synagogue, then in the school of Tyrannus for two years 19:8-20

R. When these things were completed, Paul put in his spirit to go to Jerusalem, and then Rome 19:21-22

1. At this time in Ephesus, Demetrius caused no small disturbance concerning the Way 19:23-41
2. After the uproar ceased, Paul went to Macedonia, then to Greece, then to Philippi, then 20:1-12
sailed to Troas, where Eutychus fell from the window
3. In Miletus, Paul summoned the elders from Ephesus, and exhorted them 20:13-38
4. In Tyre, the disciples were telling Paul not to go to Jerusalem 21:1-6
5. In Caesarea, at the house of Philip, Agabus said Paul would be bound in Jerusalem 21:7-14
6. In Jerusalem, Paul was welcomed by the brothers 21:15-17

   a. On the following day, James suggested a plan to quiet the Jews 21:18-25
   b. Paul was going to the temple, carrying out this plan. But Jews from Asia saw him 21:26-30
   and stirred up the crowd, and dragged him out
   c. The Roman commander rescued him, chained him, and was taking him in 21:31-36
   d. Paul asked permission to speak to the crowd 21:37-22:2

      i. I am a Jewish man trained by Gamaliel, and was persecuting the church 22:2-5
      ii. On the way to Damascus, Jesus appeared to me, and I was blinded 22:6-11
      iii. Ananias restored my sight and said God appointed me to be a witness of Jesus 22:12-16
      iv. In a vision in the temple Jerusalem, Jesus sent me to the Gentiles 22:17-21

   e. They were listening until he spoke of going to the Gentiles. The commander jailed 22:22-29
   Paul, and discovered he was a Roman
   f. On the next day, the commander took Paul before the Sanhedrin 22:30-23:10
   g. That night the Lord said, Take courage. You must witness also in Rome 23:11
   h. The commander discovered a plot to kill Paul, and sent him to Caesarea 23:12-30

7. The soldiers delivered Paul and the commander's letter to Felix in Caesarea. Felix 23:31-35
ordered Paul held until the Jews arrived

   a. After five days, the Jews came to accuse him before Felix, and Paul responded 24:1-23
   b. After some days, Paul spoke to Felix and Drusilla about the gospel 24:24-26
   c. After two years, they accused Paul before Festus. Paul appealed to Caesar 24:27-25:12
   d. Some days later, Paul defended himself before King Agrippa and Bernice 25:13-26:32

8. Paul was sent to Rome by ship. After days of hard sailing, they sail around Crete 27:1-12

   a. A storm seizes the ship and drives it toward Africa Paul predicts what will happen 27:13-26
   b. On the fourteenth night, Paul says God told him none would perish 27:27-38
   c. They shipwreck, and all are brought safely to land 27:39-44
   d. While stranded on Malta, Paul heals the sick 28:1-10
   e. After three months, they board another ship and sail for Rome 28:11-15

9. In Rome, Paul was kept under house arrest with a soldier guarding him for two years. 28:16-31
And he was preaching the kingdom of God and teaching about Jesus Christ

1:1 I made the **first** account about everything, O Theophilus, which Jesus began both to do and teach ² until which day He was taken-up [after] having given-commands through *the* Holy Spirit *to* the apostles whom He chose— ³ *to* whom He indeed presented Himself alive after His suffering by many convincing-proofs, appearing[A] *to* them during forty days, and speaking the *things* concerning the kingdom *of* God.

Jesus Ascends After Directing His Apostles To Be His Witnesses By The Spirit's Power
⁴ And being assembled-with[B] *them,* He ordered them not to depart from Jerusalem, but to wait-for the promise *of* the Father "which you heard *from* Me. ⁵ Because John baptized *with*[C] water, but **you** will be baptized with[D] *the* Holy **Spirit** after these not many days!" ⁶ So indeed the *ones* having come together were asking Him, saying "Lord, are You restoring[E] the kingdom *to* Israel at this time?". ⁷ And He said to them, "It is not yours to know *the* times or seasons which the Father appointed[F] by *His* own authority. ⁸ But you will receive power, the Holy Spirit having come upon you. And you will be My witnesses— both in Jerusalem and in all Judea and Samaria, and as far as *the* last *place of* the earth". ⁹ And having said these *things*, while they *were* looking He was lifted-up. And *a* cloud received[G] Him from their eyes. ¹⁰ And as they were looking-intently into heaven, while He *was* going— and behold, two men in white clothing were standing near them, ¹¹ who also said, "Galilean men, why do you stand looking into heaven? This Jesus having been taken-up from you into heaven will come in this manner— the way you saw Him going into heaven".

The Apostles Return to Jerusalem And Await The Holy Spirit In Prayer
¹² Then they returned to Jerusalem from *the* mountain being called '*of* Olives', which is near Jerusalem (having *a* Sabbath's *day* journey[H]). ¹³ And when they went in *the city*, they went up to the upper-room where they were staying— both Peter and John, and James and Andrew, Philip and Thomas, Bartholomew and Matthew, James *the son of* Alphaeus, and Simon the Zealot, and Judas *the son of* James. ¹⁴ These all were devoting-themselves with-one-accord *to* prayer, along with women, and Mary the mother *of* Jesus, and His brothers.

Peter Suggests That According To Scripture, Judas Should Be Replaced
¹⁵ And during these days, Peter, having stood up in *the* midst *of* the brothers (and *the* crowd *of* names at the same *place* was about one-hundred twenty), said, ¹⁶ "Men, brothers, the Scripture had-to be fulfilled which the Holy Spirit spoke-beforehand through *the* mouth *of* David concerning Judas, the *one* having become *a* guide *for* the *ones* having arrested Jesus, ¹⁷ because[I] he was numbered among us, and received *his* share *of* this ministry". (¹⁸ Now indeed this *one* acquired *a* field with *the* wages *of* unrighteousness[J]. And having become prostrate[K], he burst-open in the middle and all his inward-parts spilled-out. ¹⁹ And it became known *to* all the *ones* dwelling-in Jerusalem, so that that field was called 'Hakeldama' *in* their own language, that is, 'Field *of* Blood'). ²⁰ "For it has been written in *the* book *of* Psalms, 'Let his residence become desolate[L], and let there not be the *one* dwelling in it' [Ps 69:25], and 'let another take his office'

A. Or, being-seen *by*. **B.** Or, And coming-together; or, And while eating-with *them*; or, And while staying-with *them*. **C.** Or, *in*. **D.** Or, in. **E.** Compare Mt 21:43. **F.** Or, fixed, set. **G.** Or, took Him up. **H.** The Rabbi's taught that 2000 cubits or 5 stades (about 1000 yards or 914 meters) was the maximum journey permitted on a Sabbath. **I.** Judas was counted as one of the twelve because the prophecies concerning him (v 20) had to be fulfilled. **J.** That is, unrighteous wages; or, wages *received for his* unrighteousness. **K.** Or, prone. That is, flat on his face. **L.** Or, deserted.

[Ps 109:8]. **²¹** Therefore, *from* the men having accompanied us during all *the* time that the Lord Jesus went in and went out among us, **²²** beginning from the baptism *of* John until the day that He was taken-up from us— **one *of* these must** become *a* witness *of* His resurrection with us".

Matthias Is Chosen

²³ And they put-*forward* two: Joseph (the *one* being called Barsabbas, who was called Justus), and Matthias. **²⁴** And having prayed, they said, "**You**, Lord, heart-knower *of* all— appoint^A *the* one whom You chose from these two **²⁵** to take the place *of* this ministry and apostleship from which Judas turned-aside to go to *his* own place". **²⁶** And they gave lots *for* them. And the lot fell upon Matthias, and he was added with the eleven apostles.

On Pentecost The Spirit Empowers Them To Speak To The Crowd In Their Native Languages

2:1 And during the day *of* Pentecost being fulfilled, they were all together at the same *place*. **²** And suddenly *a* noise from heaven like *of a* violent rushing wind took place, and filled the whole house where they were sitting. **³** And dividing^B tongues as-if *of* fire appeared *to* them. And it sat on each one *of* them. **⁴** And they were all filled *with the* Holy Spirit, and began to speak *in* other tongues^C as the Spirit was giving^D *the* uttering^E *to* them. **⁵** Now there were Jews dwelling in Jerusalem, reverent men from every nation under heaven. **⁶** And this sound having taken place, the crowd came together and was confounded^F because they were each one hearing them speaking *in his* own language! **⁷** And they were astonished, and were marveling, saying "Behold, are not all these *ones* speaking Galileans? **⁸** And how *is it* **we** are each *one* hearing *in* our own language in which we were born?— **⁹** Parthians and Medes and Elamites; and the *ones* dwelling-in Mesopotamia, and Judea and Cappadocia, Pontus and Asia, **¹⁰** and Phrygia and Pamphylia, Egypt and the regions *of* Libya toward Cyrene; and the Romans residing *here*; **¹¹** both Jews and proselytes, Cretans and Arabs; we are hearing them speaking the great^G *things of* God *in* our *own* tongues". **¹²** And they were all astonished and greatly-perplexed, saying one to another, "What does this mean?" **¹³** But others, while scoffing^H, were saying that "They have been filled *with* sweet-new-wine".

Peter Declares To The Crowd That This Event Is God Pouring Out His Promised Spirit

¹⁴ And Peter, having stood with the eleven, raised his voice and declared^I *to* them, "Men, Jews, and all the *ones* dwelling-in Jerusalem: let this be known *to* you, and pay-attention-to my words. **¹⁵** For these *ones* are not drunk, as **you** are assuming^J. For it is *the* third^K hour *of* the day. **¹⁶** But this is the *thing* having been spoken through the prophet Joel [in Joel 2:28-32]: **¹⁷** 'And it shall be in the last days, God says, *that* I will pour-out from^L My Spirit upon all flesh; and your sons and your daughters will prophesy, and your young men will see visions, and your older men will dream *with* dreams. **¹⁸** And^M indeed upon My *male*-slaves and upon My *female*-slaves I will pour-out from My Spirit in those days, and they will prophesy. **¹⁹** And I will give wonders in the heaven above, and signs on the earth below— blood, and fire and *a* vapor *of* smoke. **²⁰** The sun will be changed into darkness, and the moon into blood, before the great and glorious^N day *of the* Lord comes. **²¹** And it shall be *that* everyone who calls-upon the name *of the* Lord will be saved'.

A. Or, show-forth, reveal. **B.** That is, dividing up to the people; or, divided, split, cloven, in appearance. **C.** That is, other languages than Hebrew (Aramaic), as described next. **D.** Or, giving *it to* them to be uttering. **E.** Or, speaking out, declaring. **F.** Or, bewildered. **G.** Or, magnificent, mighty, grand. **H.** Or, sneering, mocking. **I.** Or, uttered, as in v 4. **J.** Or, supposing. **K.** That is, 9 A.M. **L.** That is, *manifestations* from, as described next. **M.** Or, Even. **N.** Or, remarkable, notable, renowned, famous.

Listen Everyone: You Killed Jesus The Nazarene, But God Raised Him From The Dead
22 "Men, Israelites, listen-to these words: *As to* Jesus the Nazarene, *a* man having been attested by God to you *with*[A] miracles and wonders and signs which God did through Him in your midst, just as you yourselves know— **23** this *One,* given-over[B] *by* the determined[C] purpose[D] and foreknowledge *of* God, you killed, having fastened[E] *Him to a cross* by *the* hand *of* Lawless *ones,* **24** Whom God raised-up, having put-an-end-to[F] the pains[G] *of* death, because it was not possible *that* He be held-on-to by it.

David Predicted This. And Jesus Poured Out What You Both See And Hear
25 "For David says with reference to Him [in Ps 16:8-11], 'I was seeing the Lord in my presence continually, because He is on my right *side* so that I may not be shaken. **26** For this reason my heart was cheered and my tongue rejoiced-greatly. And furthermore, my flesh will also dwell in hope, **27** because You will not abandon my soul to Hades, nor give[H] Your holy *One* to see[I] decay. **28** You made *the* ways *of* life known *to* me. You will make me full *of* gladness with Your presence'.
29 Men, brothers, *it is* proper to say to you with confidence about the patriarch David that he both came-to-an-end[J] and was buried. And his tomb is with us to this day. **30** Therefore, being *a* prophet, and knowing that God swore *to* him *with an* oath to seat *One* from *the* fruit *of* his loins upon his throne, **31** having foreseen *it,* he spoke concerning the resurrection *of* the Christ— that He was neither abandoned to Hades, nor did His flesh see decay. **32** God raised up this Jesus, *of* which **we** are all witnesses. **33** Therefore having been exalted *to* the right *hand of* God, and having received the promise *of* the Holy Spirit from the Father, He poured-out this which **you** are both seeing and hearing. **34** For David did not go up into the heavens, but he himself says [in Ps 110:1], 'The Lord said *to* my Lord, "Be sitting on My right *side* **35** until I put Your enemies *as a* footstool *of* Your feet" '.

Therefore, Let All Israel Know That God Made Jesus Both Lord And Messiah
36 "Therefore let all *the* house *of* Israel know with-certainty that God made Him both Lord and Christ— this Jesus Whom **you** crucified".

Peter Urges The Crowd To Repent And Be Baptized. About 3,000 Respond
37 And having heard *it,* they were pierced *in* the heart, and said to Peter and the other apostles, "Men, brothers, what should we do?" **38** And Peter says to them, "Repent, and let each *of* you be baptized on-the-basis-of[K] the name *of* Jesus Christ for *the* forgiveness *of* your sins, and you will receive the gift *of* the Holy Spirit. **39** For the promise is *for* you, and *for* your children, and *for* all the *ones* far-away— all-whom *the* Lord our God will call-to *Himself*". **40** And he solemnly-testified *with* many other words, and was exhorting them, saying, "Be saved from this crooked generation". **41** So indeed, the *ones* having welcomed[L] his word were baptized. And about three-thousand souls were added on that day.

Life In The First Church: The Apostles Teach and Do Miracles, Believers Learn And Love
42 Now they were devoting-themselves[M] *to* the teaching *of* the apostles and *to* fellowship, *to*

A. Or, *by.* **B.** Or, delivered-up. **C.** Or, decided, appointed. **D.** Or, plan. **E.** Or, affixed. **F.** Or, annulled, brought to an end, broken (the authority of). **G.** Or, birth-pains. **H.** That is, permit. **I.** That is, experience. **J.** That is, died. **K.** Or, in-reference-to, by-use-of, for. **L.** Or, received, accepted. **M.** Or, continuing *in,* busying-themselves *with,* attending *to.*

the breaking[A] *of* the bread and *to* prayers. [43] And awe was taking place *in* every soul. And many wonders and signs were taking place through the apostles. [44] And all the *ones* believing were at the same[B] *place*, and were having all *things* common. [45] And they were selling properties and possessions, and distributing them *to* all— as anyone was having *a* need. [46] And while continuing daily with-one-accord in the temple and breaking bread[C] house by house, they were sharing-in food with gladness and simplicity *of* heart, [47] while praising God and having favor with the whole people. And the Lord was adding the *ones* being saved daily at-the-same-*place*.

Peter Heals a Man Lame From Birth In The Name of Jesus Christ The Nazarene
3:1 Now Peter and John were going up to the temple at the hour *of* prayer, the ninth[D] *hour.* [2] And *a* certain man being lame from his mother's womb was being carried, whom they were putting daily at the gate *of* the temple being called "Beautiful", *that he might* be asking-*for* alms[E] from the *ones* coming into the temple— [3] who, having seen Peter and John being about to go into the temple, was asking to receive alms. [4] And Peter, along with John, having looked-intently at him, said, "Look at us!" [5] And the *one* was fixing-*his*-attention-on them, expecting to receive something from them. [6] And Peter said, "There is no silver and gold *with* me. But what I have, this I give *to* you— in the name *of* Jesus Christ the Nazarene, arise and walk". [7] And having seized him *by* the right hand, he raised him. And at once his feet and ankles were made-strong[F]. [8] And leaping-up, he stood and was walking-around. And he entered with them into the temple, walking and leaping and praising God. [9] And all the people saw him walking and praising God. [10] And they were recognizing him— that **he** was the *one* sitting for alms at the Beautiful Gate *of* the temple. And they were filled *with* wonder and astonishment at the *thing* having happened *to* him.

A Crowd Comes Together, And Peter Speaks To Them:
[11] And while he *was* holding-on-to Peter and John, all the people ran-together to them at the portico being called "Solomon's", struck-with-wonder. [12] And having seen *it*, Peter responded to the people—

God Raised Jesus, The One You Denied And Killed. And Jesus Healed This Man
"Men, Israelites, why are you marveling at this? Or why are you looking-intently *at* **us** as-*if we* caused him to walk *by our* own power or godliness? [13] The God *of* Abraham and the God *of* Isaac and the God *of* Jacob, the God *of* our fathers— He glorified His servant Jesus, Whom **you** indeed handed-over and denied in the presence *of* Pilate, that *one* having determined[G] to release *Him.* [14] But **you** denied the Holy and Righteous *One,* and asked *that a* man *who was a* murderer be granted *to* you. [15] And you killed the Author[H] *of* life, Whom God raised from *the* dead— *of* which **we** are witnesses. [16] And on-the-basis-of [our] faith *in* His name, His name made this *one* strong whom you see and know. And the faith *that comes* through Him gave him this wholeness in front of all *of* you.

The Prophets Said The Christ Would Suffer, Which God Now Fulfilled. Therefore Repent
[17] "And now, brothers, I know that you acted in-accordance-with[I] ignorance, just as

---

A. That is, eating together; or, the Lord's Supper. **B.** Or, were together. **C.** That is, sharing meals, as defined next; or, eating the Lord's Supper, in addition to that defined next. **D.** That is, 3 P.M. **E.** That is, charitable giving. **F.** Or, made-firm. **G.** Or, judged, resolved. That is, made a judicial decision. **H.** Or, Originator, Pioneer, Leader. **I.** Or, based-on.

also your rulers. **¹⁸** But God fulfilled in this manner *the things* which He announced-beforehand through *the* mouth *of* all the prophets— *that* His Christ *would* suffer. **¹⁹** Therefore repent and turn-back so that your sins *may* be wiped-outᴬ, **²⁰** so that times *of* refreshing may come from *the* presence *of* the Lord, and He may send-forth the Christᴮ having been appointedᶜ *for* you— Jesus, **²¹** Whom it-is-necessaryᴰ *that* **heaven** receive until *the* times *of* restoration *of* all *things, of* which God spoke through *the* mouth *of* His holy prophets from *the past* age.

> *Moses And The Prophets Announced This Day. God Has Sent Jesus To You First*
> **²²** "Moses said [in Deut 18:15-19] that '*The* Lord your God will raise-up *a* prophet *for* you from your brothers like me. You shall listen-toᴱ Him in relation to all that He says to you. **²³** And it will be *that* every soul who does not listen-to that prophet will be utterly-destroyed out of the people'. **²⁴** Andᶠ indeed all the prophets from Samuel and *his* successors who spoke also announced these days. **²⁵ You** are the sons *of* the prophets, and *of* the covenant which God covenanted with your fathers, saying to Abraham [in Gen 22:18], 'And all the families *of* the earth will be blessed in your seed'. **²⁶** God, having raised-up His Servant, sent Him forth *to* **you first**— blessing you inᴳ turning-away each *of you* from your evil-*ways*".

The Jewish Leaders Jail Peter And John For Proclaiming The Resurrection
4:1 And while they *were* speaking to the people, the priests and the captain *of* the temple [guard] and the Sadducees suddenly-came-upon them, **²** being greatly-disturbed because of their teaching the people and proclaiming the resurrection from *the* dead **in**ᴴ **Jesus**. **³** And they put *their* hands on them, and put *them* in jailᴵ until the next day. For it was already evening. **⁴** But many of the *ones* having heard the word believed. And the number *of* the men became about five thousand.

Peter Responds: Jesus, Whom You Crucified And God Raised, Healed This Man
⁵ And it came about on the next *day that* their rulers and elders and scribes were gathered together in Jerusalem— **⁶** and Annas the high priest, and Caiaphas, and John, and Alexander, and all who were of *the* high-priestly family. **⁷** And having stood them in the middle, they were inquiring, "By what power or by what name did **you** do this?" **⁸** Then Peter, having been filled *with the* Holy Spirit, said to them, "Rulers *of* the people, and elders: **⁹** If **we** are being examined today for *a* good-deed *to a* weakᴶ man, by what *means*ᴷ this *one* has been restored, **¹⁰** let it be known *to* you all and *to* all the people *of* Israel that by the name *of* Jesus Christ the Nazarene— Whom **you** crucified, Whom God raised from *the* dead— by this Oneᴸ this *one* stands before you healthy. **¹¹** This *One* is the stone— the *One* having been treated-with-contemptᴹ by you, the builders; the *One* having become *the* headᴺ *of the* corner. **¹²** And there is no salvation inᴼ any other, for neither is there another name under heaven having been given among people by which we must be saved".

A. Or, rubbed-out, wiped-away. **B.** Or, the *One* having been appointed *for* you— Christ Jesus. **C.** Or, selected, chosen. **D.** Or, Whom **heaven** must receive. **E.** That is, obey. **F:** And indeed... also announced. Or, And all the prophets also, from Samuel and *his* successors— as many as spoke also announced. **G.** Or, by. **H.** That is, by-means-of Jesus; or, in-the-case-of Jesus. **I.** Or, custody. **J.** Or, feeble. **K.** Or, *name*. 'Means' includes the power and the name. **L.** Or, *name*. **M.** Or, despised. **N.** That is, the cornerstone of the foundation; or, the capstone of the arch. Peter is quoting Ps 118:22. **O.** Or, by-means-of.

The Jewish Leaders Ponder What To Do In View of This Undeniable Miracle
13 Now observing the boldness *of* Peter and John, and having understood that they were uneducated and untrained men, they were marveling. And they were recognizing them, that they had been with Jesus. **14** And seeing the man standing *there* with them, the *one* having been cured, they were having nothing to speak-against *it*. **15** But having ordered them to go outside *of* the council [chamber], they were conferring with one another, **16** saying, "What should we do *with* these men? For that *a* known sign has taken place through them *is* evident *to* all the *ones* dwelling-in Jerusalem, and we cannot deny *it*— **17** but in order that it may not spread further to the people, let us threaten them to no longer be speaking on the basis of this name *to* any *of* mankind".

They Command Peter And John Not To Speak Or Teach About Jesus. But They Refuse
18 And having called them, they commanded *them* not to be speaking[A] nor teaching at all on the basis of the name *of* Jesus. **19** But having responded, Peter and John said to them, "Whether it is right in the sight of God to listen-to you rather than God, you judge. **20** For **we** are not able to not be speaking *the things* which we saw and heard".
21 And the *ones*, having threatened further, released them, finding nothing *as to* how they might punish them, because of the people— because they were all glorifying God for the *thing* having taken place. **22** For the man was more *than* forty years *old* upon whom this sign *of* healing had taken place.

Peter And John Are Released. The Believers Rejoice And Ask God For More Boldness
23 And having been released, they went to *their* own *people* and reported all-that the chief priests and the elders said to them. **24** And the *ones* having heard *it* lifted *their* voice to God with-one-accord and said, "Master, **You** *are* the One having made the heaven and the earth and the sea and all the *things* in them; **25** the *One* having said by *the* Holy Spirit *from the* mouth *of* our father David, Your servant [in Ps 2:1-2], 'Why did *the* Gentiles[B] rage[C], and *the* peoples plot futile *things*? **26** The kings *of* the earth took-their-stand, and the rulers were gathered-together at the same[D] *place* against the Lord, and against His Anointed-One'. **27** For in accordance with [Your] truth, both Herod and Pontius Pilate together with *the* Gentiles and *the* peoples *of* Israel were gathered-together in this city against Your holy servant Jesus Whom You anointed, **28** to do all-that Your hand and Your purpose predestined to take place. **29** And *as to* the *things* now, Lord— look-upon[E] their threats. And grant *to* Your slaves to speak Your word with all boldness **30** while[F] You *are* stretching-out Your hand for healing, and signs[G] and wonders *are* taking place through the name *of* Your holy servant Jesus". **31** And they having prayed, the place in which they had been gathered-together was shaken. And they were all filled *with* the Holy Spirit. And they were speaking the word *of* God with boldness.

The Believers Sell Property To Help Any In Need Among Them
32 Now *the* heart and soul *of* the multitude *of* the *ones* having believed was one. And not even one *of them* was saying *that* any *of* the *things* belonging *to* him were *his* own, but all *things* were common[H] *to* them. **33** And *with* great power, the apostles were rendering[I] *their* testimony

---

A. Or, uttering-a-word, producing-a-sound. **B.** Or, nations. **C.** Or, behave arrogantly, act haughtily. **D:** at the same *place*. This corresponds to 'in this city' in v 27. **E.** That is, concern Yourself with. **F.** That is, during Your stretching-out; or, by Your stretching-out. **G.** Or, and *that* signs and wonders *might be*. **H.** Or, shared. **I.** Or, duly-giving.

of the resurrection *of* the Lord Jesus. And great grace was upon them all— **34** for there was not even someone in-need among them. For all-who were owners *of* lands or houses, selling *them,* were bringing the proceeds *of* the *things* being sold **35** and laying *it* at the feet *of* the apostles. And it was being distributed *to* each *one* as anyone was having *a* need.

Barnabas Sells a Field And Brings The Money To The Apostles

36 Now Joseph— the *one* having been called Barnabas by the apostles (which being translated is "son *of* [A] encouragement[B]"), *a* Levite, *a* Cyprian *by* nationality, **37** *a* field belonging *to* him— having made-a-sale, brought the money and laid *it* at the feet *of* the apostles.

Ananias And Sapphira Sell a Property, But Deceive The Church About Their Generosity

5:1 But *a* certain man, Ananias *by* name, along with his wife Sapphira, sold property. **2** And he kept-back[C] *some* of the proceeds, *his* wife also having shared-the-knowledge. And having brought *a* certain part *of it,* he laid *it* at the feet *of* the apostles. **3** But Peter said, "Ananias, for what reason did Satan fill your heart *that* you *should* lie-to the Holy Spirit and keep-back *some* of the proceeds *of* the land? **4** While remaining *unsold,* was it not remaining yours? And having been sold, was it *not* within your authority? Why *is it* that you put this thing in your heart? You did not lie *to* people, but *to* God". **5** And Ananias, hearing these words, having fallen-*down,* expired. And great fear came upon all the *ones* hearing *it.* **6** And having arisen, the younger *men* wrapped him up. And having carried *him* out, they buried *him.* **7** Now *an* interval *of* about three hours took place, and his wife came in— not knowing the *thing* having happened. **8** And Peter responded to her, "Tell me whether you[D] *two* sold the land *for* so much?" And the *one* said, "Yes, *for* so much". **9** And Peter *said* to her, "Why *is it* that it was agreed *by* you *two* to test the Spirit *of the* Lord? Behold— the feet *of* the *ones* having buried your husband *are* at the door. And they will carry you out". **10** And she fell at-once at his feet, and expired. And having come in, the young-men found her dead. And having carried *her* out, they buried *her* with her husband. **11** And great fear came upon the whole church, and upon all the *ones* hearing-*of* these *things.*

The Apostles Continue To Speak And Do Miracles. Multitudes Believe. Many Are Healed

12 Now many signs and wonders were taking place through the hands *of* the apostles among the people. And they were all with-one-accord in the portico[E] *of* Solomon. **13** But none *of* the rest[F] was daring to join[G] them, yet the people were magnifying them. **14** And more *people* believing *in* the Lord[H] were being added— multitudes *of* both men and women, **15** so that *they were* even bringing-out the sick into the wide-roads and putting *them* on little-beds and cots, in order that while Peter *was* coming, if-even[I] *his* shadow might overshadow one *of* them. **16** And the multitude *from* the cities around Jerusalem was also coming-together, bringing sick *ones* and *ones* being troubled by unclean spirits, who all were being cured.

A. That is, characterized by. **B.** Or, exhortation. **C.** Or, removed *for himself;* pilfered (from the donation he had announced). **D.** This word is plural. **E.** That is, the covered colonnade in the temple where people gathered. In other words, the apostles were publicly violating the command in 4:18. **F.** Or, the others. That is, the rest of the people not coming for the signs and wonders; or, the other believers, who did not dare to publicly defy the Jewish leaders in this way. **G.** Or, associate *with.* **H.** Or, believing were being added *to* the Lord. **I.** This expresses the people's hope of being healed.

The Jewish Leaders Jail The Apostles Again, But an Angel Lets Them Out

17 And having arisen, the high priest and all the *ones* with him— the sect[A] *of* the Sadducees existing *there*— were filled *with* jealousy. **18** And they put *their* hands on the apostles and put them in *the* public jail. **19** But *an* angel *of the* Lord— having opened the doors *of* the prison during *the* night, and having led them out— said, **20** "Go! And having stood, be speaking in the temple *to* the people all the words *of* this life". **21** And having heard, they entered into the temple at dawn[B] and were teaching.

The Apostles Are Found In The Temple, And Are Brought Before The Sanhedrin

And having arrived, the high priest and the *ones* with him called together the Sanhedrin— even the whole council-of-elders *of* the sons *of* Israel. And they sent-out *officers* to the jailhouse *that* they *might* be brought. **22** But having arrived, the officers did not find them in the prison. And having returned, they reported, **23** saying that "We found the jailhouse having been locked with all security, and the guards standing at the doors. But having opened, we found no one inside". **24** And when both the captain *of* the temple [guard] and the chief priests heard these words, they were greatly-perplexed about them *as to* what this would become. **25** But having arrived, someone reported *to* them that "Behold— the men whom you put in the prison are standing in the temple and teaching the people". **26** Then the captain, having gone away with the officers, was bringing them— not with violence (for they were fearing the people, that they might be stoned).

Peter Responds: God Raised Jesus As The Savior of Israel. We Are Witnesses

27 And having brought them, they stood *them* in the council[C] [chamber]. And the high priest questioned them, **28** saying, "Did we not command you *with a* command not to be teaching on the basis of this name? And behold— you have filled Jerusalem *with* your teaching. And you intend[D] to bring the blood *of* this man upon us". **29** But having responded, Peter and the apostles said, "It-is-necessary to obey God rather than people. **30** The God *of* our fathers raised Jesus— Whom **you** murdered, having hung *Him* on *a* cross. **31** God exalted this *One to* His right *hand as* Leader[E] and Savior, *that He might* grant repentance *to* Israel and forgiveness *of* sins. **32** And **we** are witnesses *of* these things. And *so is* the Holy Spirit, Whom God gave *to* the *ones* obeying Him". **33** And the *ones* having heard *it* were infuriated, and were intending to kill them.

Gamaliel Advises a Wait-And-See Approach. The Apostles Are Beaten And Released

34 But having stood up, *a* certain Pharisee in the Sanhedrin— Gamaliel *by* name, *a* Law-teacher honored *by* all the people— gave-orders to make the men be outside *for a* little *while*. **35** And he said to them, "Men, Israelites, take heed to yourselves *as to* what you are about to do to these men. **36** For before these days, Theudas arose saying *that* he was somebody, *with* whom *a* number *of* men joined-up (about four-hundred)— who was killed. And all who were being persuaded[F] *by* him were dispersed, and they became nothing. **37** After this *one*, Judas the Galilean arose in the days *of* the registration[G] and drew-away *a group-of*-people after him. That *one* also perished, and all who were being persuaded *by* him were scattered. **38** And *as to the things* now, I say *to* you, draw-away from these men and leave them *alone.* Because if this plan or this work should be from humans, it will be overthrown^A; **39** but if it is from God, you will not be able to overthrow them— that you indeed may not perhaps be found *to be* fighting-against-God". And they were persuaded *by* him. **40** And having summoned the apostles, having beaten *them*, they commanded *them* not to be speaking on the basis of the name *of* Jesus, and released *them*.

The Apostles Rejoice In Their Mistreatment, And Continue Proclaiming Jesus As Messiah
41 So indeed the *ones* were going from *the* presence *of* the Sanhedrin rejoicing that they were considered-worthy to be dishonored for the^B Name. **42** And every day, in the temple and house by house, they were not ceasing teaching and announcing-the-good-news *as to* Jesus, the Christ^C.

When Problems Arise In Serving The Needy In The Church, Deacons Are Chosen To Oversee It
6:1 Now during these days, while the disciples *were* multiplying, grumbling arose *from* the Hellenists against the Hebrews^D because their widows were being overlooked^E in the daily ministry [of food]. **2** And the twelve, having summoned the multitude *of* the disciples, said, "It is not pleasing^F *that* we, having left-behind the word *of* God, *should* be serving tables^G. **3** But brothers, look-for^H seven men from-*among* you being attested, full *of the* Spirit and wisdom, whom we will put-in-charge^I over this need^J. **4** And **we** will devote-ourselves *to* prayer and the ministry *of* the word". **5** And the statement was pleasing in the sight of the whole multitude. And they chose Stephen (*a* man full *of* faith and *of the* Holy Spirit), and Philip, and Prochorus, and Nicanor, and Timon, and Parmenas, and Nicolas (*a* proselyte *from* Antioch), **6** whom they stood before the apostles. And having prayed, they laid *their* hands on them. **7** And the word *of* God was growing. And the number *of* the disciples in Jerusalem was being multiplied greatly. And *a* large crowd *of* the priests were obeying the faith.

Stephen Is Seized While Doing Miracles And Proclaiming Christ With Irresistible Wisdom
8 Now Stephen, full *of* grace and power, was doing great wonders and signs among the people. **9** But some *of* the *ones* from the synagogue being called "*of* Freedmen^K"— both^L Cyrenians and Alexandrians, and the *ones* from Cilicia and Asia— rose-up, debating^M *with* Stephen. **10** And they were not able to resist the wisdom and the Spirit *with* which he was speaking. **11** Then they secretly-induced^N men [to begin] saying that "We have heard him speaking blasphemous words against Moses and God". **12** And they stirred-up the people and the elders and the scribes. And having suddenly-come-upon *him*, they seized him and brought *him* to the Sanhedrin. **13** And they put-*forward* false witnesses, saying, "This man does not cease speaking words against this holy place and the Law. **14** For we have heard him saying that this Jesus the Nazarene will tear-down this place, and change the customs which Moses handed-down *to* us". **15** And having

A. Since Jesus has been killed, like Theudas and Judas, His followers will soon be scattered as theirs were. **B.** Or, *His*. **C.** Or, *as to* Christ Jesus; or, *of* Jesus *as* the Christ. **D:** Hellenists... Hebrews. That is, the Greek-speaking Jewish Christians... the Judean Hebrew Jewish Christians. **E.** Or, neglected. **F.** Or, not *a* pleasing *thing*. **G.** That is, food tables, dispersing food; or, money tables, dispersing money for food. **H.** Or, look-at, examine; and thus, select. **I.** Or, appoint, set. **J.** Or, function, task, business. **K.** That is, Hellenistic Jewish slaves who were freed and then returned to Israel. **L.** Or, and. Luke may be naming five, two, or one synagogue. **M.** Or, disputing. **N.** Or, suborned.

looked-intently at him, all the *ones* sitting in the council [chamber] saw his face *was* like *a* face *of an* angel. **7:1** And the high priest said, "Do these *things* hold so?"

Stephen Defends Himself Before The Sanhedrin:
2 And the *one* said, "Men, brothers, and fathers, listen—

God Promised Abraham's Descendants Would Inherit The Land
"The God *of* ᴬ glory appeared *to* our father Abraham while being in Mesopotamia, before he dwelled in Haran, **3** and said to him [in Gen 12:1], 'Go out from your land and from your relatives, and come to the land which I will show you'. **4** Then having gone out from *the* land *of the* Chaldeans, he dwelled in Haran. And from there, after his father died, He removedᴮ him to this land in which **you** are now dwelling. **5** And He did not give him *an* inheritance in it, not even *the* step *of a* foot. And He promised to give it *to* him for *a* possession, and *to* his seed after him— *there* not being *a* child *for* him! **6** But God spoke as follows [in Gen 15:13-14]: that his seed 'will be *a* foreigner in *a* land belonging-to-another. And they will enslave itᶜ and mistreat *it for* four-hundred years. **7** And **I** will judge the nation *in* whichever they will serve-as-slaves', said God. 'And after these *things*, they will come out and worship Me' in this place. **8** And He gave him *the* covenant *of* circumcision.

Abraham's Children Moved To Egypt During a Famine
"And so he fathered Isaac, and circumcised him *on* the eighth day; and Isaac, Jacob; and Jacob, the twelve patriarchs. **9** And the patriarchs, having become-jealous-of Joseph, sold *him* into Egypt. And God was with him, **10** and rescued him from all his afflictions, and gave him favor and wisdom in the sight of Pharaoh, king *of* Egypt. And he appointed him *to be* ruling over Egypt, and over his whole house. **11** And *a* famine came over all Egypt and Canaan, and *a* great affliction. And our fathers were not finding food. **12** But Jacob, having heard-*of* grain being in Egypt, sent-forth our fathers first. **13** And during the second *visit*, Joseph was made-known-again *to* his brothers, and the family *of* Joseph became known *to* Pharaoh. **14** And having sent-forth *his brothers*, Joseph summoned Jacob his father and all *his* relatives, amounting-to seventy fiveᴰ souls. **15** And Jacob went down to Egypt. And **he** came-to-an-endᴱ, and our fathers. **16** And they were transferred to Shechem, and placed in the tomb which Abraham bought *for a* price *of* silver from the sons *of* Hamor in Shechem.

When The Time Came, God Raised Up Moses, Whom The People Rejected
17 "Now as the time *of* the promise which God declared *to* Abraham was drawing-near, *our* people grew and were multiplied in Egypt, **18** until which *time* another king arose over Egypt who did not know Joseph. **19** This *one,* having dealt-shrewdly-with our nationᶠ, mistreated our fathers, *so that he*ᴳ caused their babies *to be* exposedᴴ that *they might* not be kept-alive; **20** at which time Moses was born— and he was beautiful *to* God— who was brought-up *for* three months in the house *of his* father. **21** And he having been exposed, the daughter *of* Pharaoh took him up, and brought

---

A. That is, characterized by. The glorious God. **B.** Or, resettled. **C.** That is, Abraham's seed (descendants), viewed as a collective whole. **D.** Stephen is quoting from the Septuagint. **E.** That is, died. **F.** Or, people, race. **G.** Or, *they*. **H.** Or, put-out, abandoned.

him up *for* herself for *a* son. **²²** And Moses was trained in all *the* wisdom *of the* Egyptians. And he was powerful in his words and deeds. **²³** And as *a* forty-year period was being fulfilled *for* him, it came-up^A on his heart to visit^B his brothers, the sons *of* Israel. **²⁴** And having seen someone being wronged^C, he defended *him,* and executed vengeance *for* the *one* being oppressed, having struck the Egyptian. **²⁵** Now he was thinking *that* his brothers *were* understanding that God was granting them deliverance by his hand. But the *ones* did not understand. **²⁶** And *on* the following day, he appeared *to* them while *they were* fighting. And he was reconciling^D them to peace, having said, 'Men, you are brothers. Why are you wronging one another?' [Ex 2:13]. **²⁷** But the *one* wronging *his* neighbor rejected him, having said, 'Who appointed **you** ruler and judge over us? **²⁸ You** do not intend to kill me the way you killed the Egyptian yesterday, *do you?'* [Ex 2:14]. **²⁹** And Moses fled at this word. And he became *a* foreigner in *the* land *of* Midian, where he fathered two sons. **³⁰** And forty years having been fulfilled, *an* angel appeared *to* him in the wilderness *of* Mount Sinai, in *the* flame *of* fire *of a* bush. **³¹** And having seen *it,* Moses was marveling-*at* the sight. And while he *was* approaching to look-closely, *the* voice *of the* Lord came: **³²** 'I *am* the God *of* your fathers, the God *of* Abraham and Isaac and Jacob'. And having become trembling, Moses was not daring to look-closely. **³³** And the Lord said *to* him, 'Untie the sandal *from* your feet, for the place upon which you stand is holy ground. **³⁴** Having seen, I saw^E the mistreatment *of* My people in Egypt, and I heard their groaning, and I came down to rescue them. And now, come, I will^F send you forth to Egypt'.

This Moses Whom Israel Denied, God Sent To Be Both Ruler And Deliverer
³⁵ "This Moses whom they denied, having said, 'Who appointed **you** ruler and judge?' [Ex 2:14]— this *one* God has sent-forth *to be* both ruler and deliverer^G, with^H *the* hand *of the* angel having appeared *to* him in the bush. **³⁶** This *one* led them out, having done wonders and signs in Egypt land, and in *the* Red Sea, and in the wilderness *for* forty years.

This Moses Said That God Would Raise Up a Prophet Like Him
³⁷ "This *one* is the Moses having said *to* the sons *of* Israel, 'God will raise-up *a* prophet like me *for* you from your brothers' [Deut 18:15].

This Moses Brought Israel God's Word, Which They Rejected
³⁸ "This *one* is the *one* having been in the congregation in the wilderness, with the angel speaking *to* him at Mount Sinai, and *with* our fathers, who received living oracles^I to give *to* us— **³⁹** *to* whom our fathers were not willing to become obedient, but they rejected *him* and turned-*away* in their hearts to Egypt, **⁴⁰** having said to Aaron, 'Make gods *for* us who will go before us. For this Moses who led us out of *the* land *of* Egypt, we do not know what happened *to* him' [Ex 32:1]. **⁴¹** And they made-a-calf in those days, and brought-up *a* sacrifice *to* the idol. And they were celebrating in the works *of* their hands.

A. Or, arose. **B.** Or, look-after. **C.** Or, harmed, injured. **D.** That is, was *trying to* reconcile. **E:** Having seen, I saw. This is a Hebrew way of speaking, meaning, I have surely seen. **F.** Lit, Let Me, a command spoken to Himself, an expression of His own resolve. God is not asking permission from Moses. **G.** Or, redeemer. **H.** Or, together-with, accompanied-by. **I.** Or, sayings, declarations.

So God Turned Away From Them And Handed Them Over To Idolatry
42 "And God turned-*away*, and handed them over to worship the host *of* heaven, just as it has been written in *the* book *of* the prophets [in Amos 5:25-27]: 'House *of* Israel, you did not offer victims^A and sacrifices *to* Me *for* forty years in the wilderness, *did you*? **43** Indeed you took-up the tabernacle *of* Moloch^B and the star *of* your god Rephan^C— the images which you made to give-worship *to* them. Indeed I will remove^D you beyond Babylon!'

The Fathers Had The Tabernacle And The Temple. But God Does Not Dwell In Either
44 "The tabernacle *of* testimony was *with* our fathers in the wilderness, just as the *One* speaking *to* Moses directed *him* to make it according to the pattern which he had seen; **45** which our fathers, having received-*it*-in-succession, also brought in with Joshua during the taking-possession *of* the nations whom God drove-out from *the* presence *of* our fathers— until the days *of* David, **46** who found favor before God. And he asked *that he might* find *a* dwelling-place^E *for* the house *of* Jacob, **47** but Solomon built *a* house *for* Him. **48** But the Most-High does not dwell in *things* made-by-*human*-hands, just as the prophet says [in Isa 66:1-2]: **49** 'The heaven *is a* throne *for* Me, and the earth *is a* footstool *of* My feet. What kind of house will you build *for* Me?' says *the* Lord, 'or what *will be the* place *of* My rest? **50** Did not My hand make all these *things*?'

You Always Resist God! Your Fathers Killed The Prophets, And You The Messiah
51 "Stiff-necked *ones*, and uncircumcised *in your* hearts and ears— **you** are always resisting^F the Holy Spirit. As your fathers *did*, you also^G *are doing*. **52** Which *of* the prophets did your fathers not persecute? And they killed the *ones* having announced-beforehand about the coming *of* the righteous *One, of* Whom **you** now became^H betrayers^I and murderers— **53** you who received the Law by *the* directions^J *of*^K angels and did not keep *it*!"

Stephen Reports Seeing Jesus At The Right Hand of God. The Jews Stone Him To Death
54 And hearing these *things*, they were infuriated *in* their hearts, and were grinding *their* teeth at him. **55** But being full *of the* Holy Spirit, having looked-intently into heaven, he saw *the* glory *of* God, and Jesus standing on *the* right *side of* God. **56** And he said, "Behold— I see the heavens opened, and the Son *of* Man standing on *the* right *side of* God!" **57** And having cried-out *with a* loud voice, they held-shut their ears, and rushed against him with-one-accord. **58** And having driven *him* outside *of* the city, they were stoning *him*. And the witnesses laid-aside their garments at the feet *of a* young-man being called Saul. **59** And they were stoning Stephen while *he was* calling-upon *Jesus* and saying, "Lord Jesus, receive my spirit". **60** And having put *down his* knees, he cried-out *with a* loud voice, "Lord, do not set this sin *against* them". And having said this, he fell-asleep. **8:1** And Saul was giving-approval *to* his killing.

A. That is, slaughtered animals. **B.** A Canaanite god. **C.** Some manuscripts spell this Rompha or Remphan. **D.** Or, deport, resettle. **E.** That is, a permanent temple for the people of Israel. **F.** Or, opposing. **G.** Both rejected God's appointed messenger and put an improper value on a man-made temple. **H.** Or, proved-to-be. **I.** Or, traitors. **J.** Or, decrees, ordinances. **K.** That is, *given to*; or, *given by*.

The Church Is Persecuted And Driven Out of Jerusalem
And *a* great persecution came about on that day against the church in Jerusalem, and they were all dispersed[A] throughout the regions *of* Judea and Samaria, except the apostles. **2** And reverent men carried-in Stephen [for burial], and made *a* loud lamentation over him. **3** And Saul was destroying[B] the church. Entering from house to house, dragging-away both men and women, he was handing *them* over to prison. **4** So indeed, the *ones* having been dispersed went about announcing the word as good news.

Philip Proclaims Christ And Does Miracles In Samaria. Many Are Baptized, Including Simon
5 Now Philip, having gone down to the city[C] *of* Samaria, was proclaiming the Christ *to* them. **6** And the crowds were with-one-accord paying-attention-to[D] the *things* being said by Philip, during their hearing and seeing the signs which he was doing. **7** For many *of* the *ones* having unclean spirits— they were coming out while shouting *with a* loud voice. And many paralyzed *ones* and lame *ones* were cured. **8** And there was great joy in that city. **9** Now *a* certain man, Simon *by* name, was-previously in the city practicing-magic and astonishing the nation *of* Samaria, saying *that* he was someone great, **10** *to* whom they all, from *the* small up to *the* great, were paying attention, saying, "This *one* is the Power[E] *of* God being called 'Great' ". **11** And they were paying attention to him because *he had* astonished them *for a* considerable time *with* the magic-arts. **12** And when they believed Philip announcing-the-good-news about the kingdom *of* God and the name *of* Jesus Christ, they were being baptized— both men and women. **13** Now Simon himself also believed. And having been baptized, he was attaching-himself *to* Philip. He was astonished, seeing both signs and great miracles taking place.

Peter and John Come So The Samaritans Might Receive The Holy Spirit
14 And the apostles in Jerusalem, having heard that "Samaria has accepted the word *of* God", sent-forth Peter and John to them— **15** who, having come down, prayed for them so that they might receive *the* Holy Spirit. **16** For He had not yet fallen upon any *of* them, but they had only been baptized in the name *of* the Lord Jesus. **17** Then they were laying *their* hands on them, and they were receiving *the* Holy Spirit. **18** Now Simon, having seen that the Spirit was given through the laying-on *of* the hands *of* the apostles, offered them money, **19** saying, "Give this authority *to* me also, so-that *on* whomever I lay on *my* hands, he may receive *the* Holy Spirit". **20** But Peter said to him, "May your silver be with you for destruction, because you thought to acquire the gift *of* God with money. **21** There is no part nor share *for* you in this matter. For your heart is not straight before God. **22** Therefore repent from this evilness *of* yours, and pray *to* the Lord, if perhaps[F] the intention *of* your heart will be forgiven you. **23** For I see you being in *the* gall[G] *of*[H] bitterness and *the* bond[I] *of*[J] unrighteousness". **24** And having responded, Simon said, "You[K] *two* pray to the Lord for me, so that nothing *of the things* which you have spoken may come upon me". **25** So indeed the *ones*— having solemnly-testified, and having spoken the word *of* the Lord— were returning to Jerusalem and announcing-the-good-news-to many villages *of* the Samaritans.

A. Or, scattered. **B.** Or, inflicting outrages upon, inflicting personal injuries upon. **C.** That is, the main city (Sebaste, known as Samaria in the OT, and called such here to link this to 1:8); or, the main religious city (Neapolis, known as Shechem in the OT). **D.** Or, giving-heed-to. **E.** That is, the supernatural spirit-being from God. **F.** That is, in the hope that. Peter expresses some uncertainty about whether this will happen, for which he gives his reason in v 23, on which compare Deut 29:18-19. **G.** Or, poison, venom. **H.** That is, characterized by; a bitter gall, a bitter poison. **I.** That is, binding, fetter, chain. **J.** That is, proceeding from or belonging to. **K.** This word is plural, referring to Peter and John.

An Angel Sends Philip Down The Road To an Ethiopian Eunuch Reading Isaiah

26 Now *an* angel *of the* Lord spoke to Philip saying, "Arise and go toward *the* south^A on the road going down from Jerusalem to Gaza". This^B is *a* wilderness [road]. **27** And having arisen, he proceeded. And behold— *there was* an Ethiopian man, *a* eunuch^C, *a* court-official *of* Candace^D (queen *of the* Ethiopians), who was over all her treasury, who had come to Jerusalem *to* worship, **28** and was returning, and sitting on his chariot^E. And he was reading the prophet Isaiah. **29** And the Spirit said *to* Philip, "Approach and join this chariot". **30** And having run up, Philip heard him reading Isaiah the prophet, and said, "Do you indeed understand *the things* which you are reading?" **31** And the *one* said, "How indeed might I be able, unless someone will guide me?" And he invited Philip to sit with him, having come up.

Philip Explains That Isaiah 53 Refers To Jesus

32 Now the passage *of* Scripture which he was reading was this: "He was led like *a* sheep to slaughter. And as *a* lamb before the *one* having sheared it *is* silent, so He does not open His mouth. **33** In His humiliation, His justice^F was taken-away. Who will describe^G His generation^H? Because His life is taken-away from the earth" [Isa 53:7-8]. **34** And having responded, the eunuch said *to* Philip, "I ask you, about whom is the prophet saying this— about himself or about some other?" **35** And Philip— having opened his mouth, and beginning from this Scripture— announced Jesus as good news *to* him.

The Man Believes And Is Baptized, And Continues Home Rejoicing

36 And as they were proceeding along the road, they came upon some water. And the eunuch says, "Behold— water. What is preventing me from being baptized?" **37** ı **38** And he ordered the chariot to stop. And they both went down into^J the water, both Philip and the eunuch, and he baptized him. **39** And when they came up out-of^K the water, *the* Spirit *of the* Lord snatched Philip away. And the eunuch did not see him any longer, for he was going his way rejoicing.

Philip Continues Announcing The Good News In Other Cities

40 And Philip was found at Azotus. And while going through, he was announcing-the-good-news-to all the cities until he came to Caesarea.

While Saul Is Going To Damascus To Persecute Believers, Jesus Appears To Him

9:1 Now Saul, still breathing threat and murder against the disciples *of* the Lord, having gone to the high priest, **2** asked-*for* letters from him to the synagogues at Damascus so that if he found any being *of* the Way, both men and women, he might bring *them* bound to Jerusalem. **3** And during the proceeding, it came about *that* he *was* drawing-near *to* Damascus. And suddenly *a* light from heaven flashed-around him. **4** And having fallen on the ground, he heard *a* voice saying *to* him, "Saul, Saul, why are you persecuting Me?" **5** And he said, "Who are You, sir^L?"

A: toward *the* south. Or, at mid-day. **B.** Or, this explanation may continue as part of the angel's words. **C.** That is, a castrated male. **D.** This is a title, like Pharaoh, not a name. **E.** That is, traveling chariot or carriage. Not a war or racing chariot. **F.** Or, judgment. That is, the justice due Him. **G.** Or, tell-of-in-detail. **H.** That is, His contemporaries who did this. Or, descendants; His posterity. Or, family; His origin. **I.** Some manuscripts add here, And Philip said *to* him, 'If you believe from your whole heart, it is permitted'. And having responded, he said, 'I believe *that* Jesus Christ is the Son *of* God'. **J.** Or, to. **K.** Or, from. **L.** Or, lord, as in 10:4; Rev 7:14.

And the *One said*, "**I** am Jesus Whom **you** are persecuting. ⁶ But arise and enter into the city, and it will be told you what thing you must do". ⁷ And the men traveling-with him were standing speechlessᴬ, hearing the voiceᴮ but seeing no one. ⁸ And Saul was raisedᶜ from the ground. And his eyes having been opened, he was seeing nothing. And hand-leading him, they brought *him* into Damascus. ⁹ And he was not seeing *for* three days. And he did not eat nor drink.

God Tells Ananias To Go Give Saul His Sight, For He Is God's Chosen Instrument
¹⁰ Now *a* certain disciple was in Damascus— Ananias *by* name. And the Lord said to him in *a* vision, "Ananias". And the *one* said, "Behold, I *am here*, Lord". ¹¹ And the Lord *said* to him, "Having arisen, go on the lane being called 'Straight', and seek *one*-from-Tarsus, Saul *by* name, in *the* house *of* Judas. For behold— he is praying. ¹² And he saw *a* man in *a* vision, Ananias *by* name, having come in and laid hands on him so that he might see-again". ¹³ And Ananias responded, "Lord, I heard about this man from many— how many bad *things* he did *to* Your saints in Jerusalem. ¹⁴ And here he has authority from the chief priests to bind all the *ones* calling-upon Your name". ¹⁵ And the Lord said to him, "Go, because this *one* is *a* chosen instrumentᴰ *for* Me— *that he might* carry My name before both Gentiles and kings, and sons *of* Israel. ¹⁶ For **I** will show him how-many *things* he must suffer for My name". ¹⁷ And Ananias departed, and entered into the house. And having laid *his* hands on him, he said, "Brother Saul, the Lord has sent me forth— Jesus, the *One* having appeared *to* you on the road *on* which you were coming— so that you may see-again and be filled *with the* Holy Spirit". ¹⁸ And immediately *something* like scalesᴱ fell from his eyes. And he saw-againᶠ, and having arisen, was baptized. ¹⁹ And having taken food, he strengthened.

Saul Begins Proclaiming Christ In Damascus. He Escapes a Plot To Kill Him
Now he came-to-be with the disciples in Damascus *for* some days. ²⁰ And immediately he was proclaiming Jesus in the synagogues— that this *One* is the Son *of* God. ²¹ And all the *ones* hearing were astonished, and were saying, "Is not this the *one* having destroyed in Jerusalem the *ones* calling-upon this name? And he had come here for this— that he might bring them bound to the chief priests!" ²² And Saul was becoming more strong. And he was confoundingᴳ the Jews dwelling in Damascus, proving that this *One* is the Christ. ²³ And when considerable days were being fulfilled, the Jews plotted to kill him. ²⁴ But their plot was known *by* Saul. And they were even closely-watching the gates both *by* day and *by* night so that they might kill him. ²⁵ But his disciples, having taken *him by* night, let him down through the wall, having loweredᴴ *him* in *a* large-basket.

Saul Joins The Disciples In Jerusalem. Due To a Plot To Kill Him, He Is Sent To Tarsus
²⁶ And having arrived in Jerusalem, he was trying to join the disciples. And they all were fearing him, not believing that he was *a* disciple. ²⁷ But Barnabas, having taken-hold-of *him*, brought him to the apostles and related *to* them how he saw the Lord on the road, and that ᴵ He spoke *to* him; and how in Damascus he spoke-boldly in the name *of* Jesus. ²⁸ And he was with them, going in and going out in Jerusalem, speaking-boldly in the name *of* the Lord. ²⁹ And he was speaking and debating with the Hellenists, but the *ones* were

---

A. Or, dumbfounded. **B.** Or, sound. **C.** Or, arose. **D.** Or, vessel, tool. **E.** That is, scales of a fish. Or, 'flakes' of skin. **F.** Or, received sight. **G.** Or, throwing-into-confusion. **H.** On this incident, compare 2 Cor 11:32-33. **I.** Or, and what thing He spoke *to* him.

attempting[A] to kill him. [30] But the brothers, having learned *it*, brought him down to Caesarea and sent him away to Tarsus.

The Church Enjoys Peace And Growth
[31] So indeed the church throughout all Judea and Galilee and Samaria was having peace, while being built-up. And it was being multiplied while walking *in* the fear *of* the Lord and *in* the comfort[B] *of* the Holy Spirit.

Peter Goes Through The Regions Healing And Proclaiming Christ. He Heals Aeneas in Lydda
[32] Now it came about *that* Peter, while going through all *the* regions[C], came down also to the saints dwelling-in Lydda. [33] And he found there *a* certain man, Aeneas *by* name, who had been paralyzed, lying down on *a* cot for eight years. [34] And Peter said *to* him, "Aeneas, Jesus Christ heals you. Arise and make your bed *for* yourself". And immediately he arose. [35] And all the *ones* dwelling-in Lydda and Sharon saw him— who[D] [then] turned to the Lord.

Peter Raises Dorcas From The Dead In Joppa
[36] Now in Joppa, there was *a* certain disciple, Tabitha *by* name (which being interpreted[E] means "Dorcas"). This *one* was full *of* good works and acts-of-almsgiving[F] which she was doing. [37] And it came about in those days *that* having become sick, she died. And having washed *her*, they laid her in *an* upper-room. [38] Now Lydda being near Joppa, the disciples, having heard that Peter was in it, sent-out two men to him urging, "Do not delay to come to us". [39] And having arisen, Peter went with them— whom[G], having arrived, they brought up into the upper room. And all the widows stood near him, weeping and showing *him* tunics[H] and garments— all-that Dorcas was making while being with them. [40] And Peter— having put everyone outside, and having put *down his* knees— prayed. And having turned to the body, he said, "Tabitha, rise-up". And the *one* opened her eyes! And having seen Peter, she sat up. [41] And having given her *his* hand, he raised her up. And having called the saints and the widows, he presented her alive. [42] And it became known throughout all Joppa, and many put-faith upon the Lord. [43] And it came about *that* he stayed considerable days in Joppa with *a* certain Simon, *a* tanner.

After a Vision, a Gentile Named Cornelius Sends Men To Joppa To Get Peter
10:1 Now *a* certain man in Caesarea, Cornelius *by* name— *a* centurion[I] from *the* cohort[J] being called "Italian[K]", [2] *a* devout *one,* and *one* fearing God with all his household, doing many acts-of-almsgiving *to* the [Jewish] people, and praying *to* God continually— [3] saw in *a* vision[L] clearly[M], as-if[N] *it were* around *the* ninth[O] hour *of* the day, *an* angel *of* God having come-in[P] to him, and having said *to* him, "Cornelius!" [4] And the *one*— having looked-intently *at* him, and having become terrified— said, "What is it, sir[Q]?" And he said *to* him, "Your prayers and your acts-of-almsgiving went up for *a* memorial before God. [5] And now, send men to Joppa, and send-for *a* certain Simon who is called Peter.

A. Or, undertaking, taking-in-hand. **B.** Or, encouragement. **C.** Or, *districts*, *places*. **D.** This word is plural. **E.** Or, translated. Dorcas means gazelle. **F.** That is, charity to the poor. **G.** That is, Peter. **H.** That is, undergarments. **I.** That is, commander of 100 soldiers. **J.** That is, battalion of Roman soldiers, one tenth of a legion, and thus about 600 soldiers. **K.** This may mean it was made up of native Italians. Cornelius may have volunteered for this duty in order to come to Israel. **L.** Or, sight. **M.** Or, distinctly, plainly. **N.** That is, as if it were broad daylight inside his house. Some manuscripts simply say 'about'. **O.** That is, 3 P.M. **P.** That is, come into his house. **Q.** Or, lord, as in Rev 7:14.

⁶ This *one* is lodging with *a* certain Simon, *a* tanner, whose house is beside *the* sea". **⁷** And when the angel speaking *to* him departed, having called two of *his* household-servants and *a* devout soldier *from* the *ones* attaching-themselves^A *to* him, **⁸** and having described everything *to* them, he sent them forth to Joppa.

Before They Arrive, Peter Has a Vision To Treat As Clean What God Has Made Clean
⁹ Now *on* the next day, while those *ones were* journeying and drawing-near *to* the city, Peter went up on the housetop around *the* sixth^B hour to pray. **¹⁰** And he became hungry and was wanting to eat. And while they *were* preparing *it, a* trance came upon him. **¹¹** And he sees the heaven having been opened and *a* certain object like *a* large sheet coming down, being let down *by* four corners on the ground— **¹²** in which were all the four-footed-animals and reptiles *of* the earth, and birds *of* the heaven. **¹³** And *a* voice came to him, "Having arisen, Peter, slaughter and eat!" **¹⁴** But Peter said, "By no means, Lord, because I never ate anything defiled and unclean". **¹⁵** And *a* voice again *came* to him for *a* second *time*, "*The things* which God made-clean^C, don't **you** be making-defiled^D". **¹⁶** And this^E took place three-times, and immediately the object was taken-up into heaven.

The Spirit Tells Peter He Has Sent Three Men, And He Is To Go With Them
¹⁷ Now while Peter was being greatly-perplexed within himself *as to* what the vision which he saw might mean, behold— the men having been sent-forth by Cornelius, having asked-repeatedly *as to* the house *of* Simon, stood at the gate. **¹⁸** And having called, they were inquiring, "Is Simon, the *one* being called Peter, lodging here?" **¹⁹** And while Peter *was* pondering about the vision, the Spirit said *to* him, "Behold— three men *are* seeking you. **²⁰** But^F having arisen, go down and proceed with them not doubting^G at all, because **I** have sent them forth". **²¹** And Peter, having gone down to the men, said, "Behold— **I** am *the one* whom you are seeking. What *is* the reason for which you are-here?" **²²** And the *ones* said, "Cornelius— *a* centurion, *a* righteous man, and *one* fearing God, and *one* being attested by the whole nation *of* the Jews— was directed by *a* holy angel to summon you to his house and to listen-to words from you". **²³** Then having invited them in, he gave-*them*-lodging.

Peter Goes To Cornelius. Peter Now Understands That His Vision Pertained To Gentiles
And *on* the next day, having arisen, he went forth with them. And some *of* the brothers from Joppa went with him. **²⁴** And *on* the next day, he entered into Caesarea. And Cornelius was expecting them, having called together his relatives and close friends. **²⁵** And when Peter's entering *the house* came about, Cornelius— having met him, having fallen at *his* feet— paid-homage. **²⁶** But Peter raised him, saying, "Stand up. **I** myself also am *a* man". **²⁷** And while conversing-with him, he went in and finds many having come-together. **²⁸** And he said to them, "**You** know how it is unlawful *for a* Jewish man to be joining^H or coming-to^I *a* foreigner. And-*yet* God showed me

---

A. Or, devoting-themselves *to* him. That is, not ones merely 'attached to' his regiment, but ones attaching-themselves to him personally; friends; fellow God-fearers. **B.** That is, noon. **C.** Or, declared-clean, treated-as-clean. **D.** Or, declaring-defiled, treating-as-defiled. Note the change in tense. **E.** That is, this conversation. **F.** That is, in contrast to what your conscience will tell you. **G.** Or, hesitating, wavering. **H.** Or, associating *with*, keeping-company *with*. **I.** That is, coming to his home.

that I should be calling **no** person defiled or unclean. [29] Therefore, having been sent-for, I indeed came without-objection. So I ask, *for* what reason did you send-for me?" [30] And Cornelius said, "Four days ago at this hour, I was praying in my house *at* the ninth[A] *hour*, and behold— *a* man stood before me in shining clothing. [31] And he says, 'Cornelius, your prayer was heard, and your acts-of-almsgiving were remembered before God. [32] Therefore send to Joppa, and summon Simon, who is called Peter. This *one* is lodging in *the* house *of* Simon, *a* tanner, beside *the* sea'. [33] Therefore I sent to you at-once, and **you** did[B] well, having come. So now **we** are all here before God to hear all the *things* having been commanded you by the Lord".

Peter Begins Proclaiming The Gospel To Cornelius
[34] And Peter, having opened *his* mouth, said, "I understand, in accordance with [God's] truth, that God is not *a* respecter-of-persons, [35] but in every nation, the *one* fearing Him and working righteousness is acceptable[C] *to* Him. [36] *As to* the message which He sent-forth *to* the sons *of* Israel announcing-the-good-news-of peace through Jesus Christ, this *One* is Lord *of* all[D]. [37] **You** know the matter[E] having taken place throughout all Judea, beginning from Galilee after the baptism which John proclaimed[F], [38] *as to* Jesus from Nazareth— how God anointed Him *with the* Holy Spirit and *with* power; Who went about doing-good and healing all the *ones* being oppressed by the devil, because God was with Him. [39] And we *are* witnesses *of* everything which He did both in the country *of* the Jews and in Jerusalem; Whom indeed they killed, having hung *Him* on *a* cross. [40] God raised this *One* on the third day, and granted *that* He become visible— [41] not *to* all the people, but *to* witnesses having been chosen-beforehand by God; *to* us, who ate with and drank with Him after He rose-up from *the* dead. [42] And He commanded us to proclaim *to* the people, and to solemnly-warn that this *One* is the *One* having been designated[G] by God *as* judge *of the* living and *the* dead. [43] All the prophets testify *concerning*[H] this *One*, *that* everyone believing in Him receives forgiveness *of* sins through His name".

While Peter Is Speaking, The Spirit Falls On These Gentiles Just Like At Pentecost
[44] While Peter *was* still speaking these words, the Holy Spirit fell upon all the *ones* hearing the message. [45] And the believers of *the* circumcision— all-who came with Peter— were astonished that the gift *of* the Holy Spirit had been poured-out also on the Gentiles! [46] For they were hearing them speaking *in* tongues and magnifying God. Then Peter responded, [47] "No one is able to forbid[I] the water *so that* these *may* not be baptized, *is he?*— who received the Holy Spirit as also we *did*. [48] And he commanded *that* they be baptized in the name *of* Jesus Christ. Then they asked him to stay some days.

Back In Jerusalem, Peter Explains How God Gave The Identical Gift To The Gentiles
11:1 Now the apostles and the brothers being throughout Judea heard that the Gentiles also accepted the word *of* God. [2] But when Peter went up to Jerusalem, the *ones* of *the*

A. That is, at my 3 o'clock prayers. **B.** Or, acted commendably. **C.** Or, welcome. That is, even non-Jews fearing and obeying the true God are welcome to Him. They do not have to become Jews first, a revolutionary idea to Peter. **D.** That is, Jews and Gentiles. **E.** Or, thing. **F.** Or, proclaimed: how God anointed Him— Jesus from Nazareth— *with*. **G.** Or, ordained, appointed. **H.** Or, *to* this. **I.** Or, withhold.

circumcision were disputing with him, ³ saying that "You went in to men having uncircumcision, and you ate with them". ⁴ But having begun, Peter was explaining *it to* them in-order, saying, ⁵ "I was in *the* city *of* Joppa praying. And in *a* trance, I saw *a* vision— *a* certain object like *a* large sheet coming down, being let down *by* four corners from heaven. And it came to me, ⁶ into which having looked-intently, I was observing. And I saw the four-footed-animals *of* the earth, and the wild-beasts, and the reptiles, and the birds *of* the heaven. ⁷ And I also heard *a* voice saying *to* me, 'Having arisen, Peter, slaughter and eat!' ⁸ But I said, 'By no means, Lord, because *a* defiled or unclean *thing* never entered into my mouth'. ⁹ But *a* voice responded for *a* second *time* from heaven, '*The things* which God made-clean, don't **you** be making-defiled'. ¹⁰ And this took place three times, and everything was pulled-up again into heaven. ¹¹ And behold— three men immediately stood at the house in which we were *staying*, having been sent forth from Caesarea to me. ¹² And the Spirit told me to go-with them, having made no distinction. And these six brothers also went with me. And we entered into the house *of* the man. ¹³ And he reported *to* us how he saw the angel having stood in his house, and having said, 'Send-forth to Joppa, and send-for Simon, the *one* being called Peter, ¹⁴ who will speak words to you by which you will be saved— you and all your household'. ¹⁵ And at my beginning to speak, the Holy Spirit fell upon them just as also upon us at *the* beginning. ¹⁶ And I remembered the word *of* the Lord, how He was saying, 'John baptized *with* water— but **you** will be baptized with *the* Holy Spirit!' ¹⁷ Therefore if God gave the **identical gift** *to* them as also *to* us— [we both] having put faith upon the Lord Jesus Christ— who was I *to be* able to forbid God?" ¹⁸ And having heard these *things*, they were quiet. And they glorified God, saying, "Then God granted the repentance leading-to life *to* the Gentiles also!"

Many Gentiles Believe In Antioch. Barnabas And Saul Teach These Christians
¹⁹ Now indeed the *ones* having been dispersed because of the affliction having taken place over Stephen went as far as Phoenicia and Cyprus and Antioch, speaking the word *to* no one except Jews only. ²⁰ But there were some of them— Cyprian and Cyrenian men— who, having come to Antioch, were speaking also to the Hellenists^A, announcing-as-good-news the Lord Jesus. ²¹ And *the* hand *of the* Lord was with them. And *a* large number, having believed, turned to the Lord. ²² And the word about them was heard in the ears *of* the church existing in Jerusalem. And they sent out Barnabas to go to Antioch— ²³ who, having arrived and having seen the grace *of* God, rejoiced. And he was encouraging^B everyone to be continuing-in the Lord *with*^C purpose^D *of* heart, ²⁴ because he was *a* good man, and full *of the* Holy Spirit and *of* faith. And *a* considerable crowd was added *to* the Lord. ²⁵ And he went forth to Tarsus to search-for Saul. ²⁶ And having found *him*, he brought *him* to Antioch. And it came about *for* them that^E *for a* whole year *they* were gathered-together^F in the church and taught *a* considerable crowd; and *that* the disciples *were* first called Christians in Antioch.

Agabas Comes And Predicts A Famine; Barnabas And Saul Take Relief To Judea
²⁷ And during these days, prophets came down from Jerusalem to Antioch. ²⁸ And having stood up, one of them, Agabus *by* name, signified through the Spirit *that* there would-certainly be *a* great famine over the whole world— which took place in-the-time-of

---

A. Here, this must mean 'Gentiles' in contrast to 'Jews only' in v 19. **B.** Or, exhorting. **C.** That is, to be continuing... with purpose of heart; or, he was encouraging... with purpose of heart. **D.** Or, resolution. **E.** Or, *that for* indeed *a* whole year. **F.** That is, brought together for a joint ministry. Or, brought-in by. Or, *the disciples* were gathered-together in the church, and *Barnabas and Saul* taught.

Claudius^A. **29** And as any *of* the disciples was prospering, each *of* them determined to send *money* for *a* ministry *to* the brothers dwelling in Judea— **30** which they also did, having sent *it* forth to the elders by *the* hand *of* Barnabas and Saul.

During This Time, King Herod Kills The Apostle James And Imprisons Peter

12:1 And about that time, Herod^B the king put hands on some *of* the *ones* from the church to mistreat *them*. **2** And he killed James^C, the brother *of* John, *with a* sword. **3** And having seen that it was pleasing *to* the Jews, he proceeded to arrest Peter also (now the days *of* the *Feast of* Unleavened-Bread were *taking place*)— **4** whom indeed having seized, he put into prison, having handed *him* over *to* four squads^D *of* soldiers to guard him, intending to bring him up *to* the people after the Passover [Feast]. **5** So indeed Peter was being kept in the prison. And prayer was fervently being made by the church to God for him.

An Angel Releases Peter

6 And when Herod was about to bring him forth, *on* that night Peter was sleeping between two soldiers, having been bound *with* two chains. And guards in front of the door were keeping-watch-over the prison. **7** And behold— *an* angel *of the* Lord stood near, and light^E shined in the cell. And having struck the side *of* Peter, he woke him, saying, "Arise quickly". And his chains fell off of *his* hands. **8** And the angel said to him, "Gird-*yourself*^F and tie-on your sandals". And he did so. And he says *to* him, "Put-on your cloak and be following me". **9** And having gone forth, he was following. And he did not know that the *thing* taking place by-means-of the angel was real, but he was thinking *that he was* seeing *a* vision. **10** And having gone through *a* first guard-post^G and *a* second, they came to the iron gate leading into the city, which by-itself was opened *for* them. And having gone out, they went ahead one lane^H, and immediately the angel departed from him.

Peter Goes To The House of The Mother of John Mark, Where They Were Praying

11 And Peter, having become within^I himself, said, "Now I know truly that the Lord sent-out His angel and rescued me from *the* hand *of* Herod, and *from* all the expectation *of* the people *of* the Jews". **12** And having become-aware^J, he went to the house *of* Mary, the mother *of* John (the *one* being called Mark), where there were many assembled-together and praying. **13** And he having knocked-on the door *of* the gate, *a* servant-girl went to *it* to answer— Rhoda *by* name. **14** And having recognized the voice *of* Peter, because of *her* joy she did not open the gate, but having run in, she reported *that* Peter was standing in front of the gate. **15** But the *ones* said to her, "You are mad^K". But the *one* was insisting *that it was* holding so. But the *ones* were saying, "It is his angel". **16** But Peter was continuing-on knocking. And having opened, they saw him and were astonished. **17** And having motioned *to* them *with his* hand to be silent, he related *to* them how the Lord led him out of the prison. And he said, "Report

---

A. He was Roman emperor in A.D. 41-54. **B.** That is, Herod Agrippa I, the last king of Israel. His death, mentioned in verse 23, occurred in A.D. 44. **C.** That is, the apostle James. **D.** Or, quaternians. That is, four four-man squads working three-hour watches overnight, two men inside chained to the prisoner and two outside at the door. This was the Roman custom. **E.** Or, *a* light. **F.** That is, put on your belt, which was worn over the tunic (undergarment) and under the cloak. **G.** Or, prison-ward. **H.** Or, alley. **I.** That is, having collected himself and seen that it was real. **J.** That is, of where he was. **K.** Or, out-of-your-mind.

these *things to* James[A] and the brothers". And having gone out, he proceeded to another place.

When Peter Can't Be Found, The Guards Are Executed. Herod Dies In Caesarea
18 Now having become day, there was no small disturbance[B] among the soldiers *as to* what then became *of* Peter. **19** And Herod, having searched-for him and not having found *him,* having examined the guards, ordered *that they* be led[C] away. And having gone down from Judea to Caesarea, he was spending-time *there.* **20** Now he was being very-angry *with the* Tyrians and Sidonians. And they were coming to him with-one-accord. And having won-over[D] Blastus, the *one* over the bedroom[E] *of* the king, they were asking-*for* peace, because of their country being provided-for[F] from the royal *land.* **21** And *on an* appointed day, Herod— having put on *the* royal clothing, and having sat on the judgment-seat— was giving-a-public-address to them. **22** And the public-assembly was calling-out, "*The* voice *of a* god and not *of a* man!" **23** And at once *an* angel *of the* Lord struck him because he did not give the glory *to* God. And having become eaten-by-worms, he expired[G].

Barnabas And Saul Return To Antioch From Judea, With John Mark
24 But the word *of* God was growing and being multiplied. **25** And Barnabas and Saul returned, having fulfilled the ministry to Jerusalem, having taken along John[H] with *them* (the *one* having been called Mark).

While Teaching In Antioch, The Spirit Sends Saul And Barnabas On a Missionary Journey
13:1 Now there were prophets and teachers at Antioch in[I] the church existing *there*— Barnabas and Simeon (the *one* being called Niger[J]) and Lucius the Cyrenian, and Manaen (*one* brought-up-with[K] Herod the tetrarch) and Saul. **2** And while they *were* ministering[L] to[M] the Lord and fasting, the Holy Spirit said, "Separate now Barnabas and Saul *for* Me, for the work which I have called them to". **3** Then, having fasted and prayed and laid *their* hands on them, they sent[N] *them* away.

On Cyprus, Bar-Jesus The Magician Is Blinded, Sergius Paulus The Proconsul Believes
4 So indeed, having been sent-out by the Holy Spirit, **they** went down to Seleucia, and from there sailed-away to Cyprus. **5** And having come-to-be in Salamis, they were proclaiming the word *of* God in the synagogues *of* the Jews. And they also were having John *as an* assistant[O]. **6** And having gone through the whole island as far as Paphos, they found *a* certain man *who was a* magician, *a* Jewish false-prophet *for* whom *the* name *was* Bar-Jesus[P]— **7** who was with the proconsul[Q], Sergius Paulus, *an* intelligent man. This *one,* having summoned Barnabas and Saul, sought to hear the word *of* God. **8** But the magician Elymas[R] (for so his name is translated) was opposing them, seeking to turn away the

---

A. That is, the brother of the Lord, and leader of the Jerusalem church. **B.** Or, commotion. **C.** That is, to execution, the Roman custom. **D.** Or, persuaded, convinced. **E.** That is, the chamberlain, a trusted attendant. **F.** Or, providing-for *itself.* In either case, the port cities of Tyre and Sidon, which were not part of Herod's kingdom, were economically dependent on his land, and so sought peace with him. **G.** Josephus, who also speaks of this, adds that Herod died five days later. **H.** John-Mark is the cousin of Barnabas, Col 4:10. **I.** Or, throughout. **J.** This is a Latin name, meaning 'black'. **K.** Or, *a* childhood-companion *of.* **L.** Or, rendering-priestly-service. **M.** That is, praying or worshiping. Or, *for.* That is, teaching or prophesying. **N.** Or, let *them* go. **O.** Or, helper. **P.** Or, Bar-Joshua. Bar means 'son of '. **Q.** That is, the Roman governor of the province. **R.** This is not a translation of Bar-Jesus, nor it is a Greek word otherwise known to us. Luke's intent is currently unclear to us.

proconsul from the faith. ⁹ But Saul (the *one* also *called* Paul), having been filled *with the* Holy Spirit, having looked-intently at him, ¹⁰ said "O son *of the* devil full *of* all deceit and all villainyᴬ, enemy *of* all righteousness, will you not cease pervertingᴮ the straight ways *of* the Lord? ¹¹ And now, behold— *the* hand *of the* Lord *is* upon you and you shall be blind, not seeing the sun for *a* time". And at-once mistiness and darkness fell upon him. And going around, he was seeking *ones*-leading-by-the-handᶜ. ¹² Then the proconsul, having seen the *thing* having taken place, believed, being astounded at the teaching *of* the Lord.

In Perga John Mark Leaves. Paul And Barnabas Go On To Pisidian Antioch
¹³ And having put-to-sea from Paphos, the *ones* aroundᴰ Paul came to Perga *of* Pamphylia. But John, having departedᴱ from them, returned to Jerusalem. ¹⁴ But **they**, having gone throughᶠ from Perga, arrived at Pisidian Antioch. And having entered into the synagogue *on* the day *of* the Sabbath, they sat-*down.* ¹⁵ And after the reading *of* the Law and the Prophets, the synagogue-officials sent forth *a message* to them, saying, "Men, brothers, if there is any word *of* exhortationᴳ among you for the people, speak".

Paul Proclaims That John Announced The Coming of The Davidic Savior, Jesus
¹⁶ And Paul, having stood up, and having motioned *with his* hand, said "Men, Israelites, and the *ones* fearing God: listen. ¹⁷ The God *of* this people Israel chose our fathers. And He lifted-up the people during the stay in *the* land *of* Egypt, and with *an* uplifted arm led them out of it. ¹⁸ And *for* about *a* forty year period He put-up-withᴴ them in the wilderness. ¹⁹ And having brought-down sevenᴵ nations in *the* land *of* Canaan, He gave *them* their land as-an-inheritance ²⁰ aboutᴶ *in* [a total of] four-hundred and fifty years. And after these *things* He gave *them* judges until Samuel the prophet. ²¹ And from there they asked-*for a* king. And God gave them Saul— *the* son *of* Kish, *a* man from *the* tribe *of* Benjamin— *for* forty years. ²² And having removed him, He raised-up David *for* them for *a* king— *concerning* whom also having testified, He said, 'I found David the *son of* Jesse, *a* man in-accordance-withᴷ My heart, who will do all My desires'. ²³ From the seed *of* **this** one, in accordance with *the* promise, God brought *a* Savior *for*ᴸ Israel, Jesus— ²⁴ John having publicly-proclaimed *a* baptism *of* repentance *for* all the people *of* Israel before *the* presence *of* His coming. ²⁵ And as John was completing *his* course, he was saying, 'What do you suppose *that* I am? **I** am not *the* One. But behold— He is coming after me, *of* Whom I am not worthy to untie the sandal *of* His feet'.

Fulfilling The Scriptures, The Rulers Killed Jesus And God Raised Him Up
²⁶ "Men, brothers, sons *of the* family *of* Abraham, and the *ones* among you fearing God: the message *of* this salvation was sent-out **to us.** ²⁷ For the *ones* dwelling in Jerusalem and their rulers, not having known this *One* and the voices *of* the prophets being read every Sabbath— having condemned *Him*, fulfilled

---

A. Or, fraud. **B.** Or, making-crooked. **C.** Or, hand-leaders, guides. **D.** That is, around Paul as their leader. **E.** Or, gone-away, left, withdrawn. Or more strongly (based on one's understanding of this event), abandoned, deserted. Compare 15:38. **F.** That is, gone through the Taurus mountain range. **G.** Or, encouragement. **H.** Some manuscripts say 'carried', meaning 'cared-for', as in the Hebrew of Deut 1:31, where this same variation occurs in the Greek manuscripts. **I.** See Deut 7:1. **J.** That is, about 450 years after they left the land for Egypt. Some manuscripts instead have this phrase in the next sentence, He gave them judges *for* about 450 years. **K.** Or, in-harmony-with. **L.** Or, *to.*

them. **28** And having found no charge *worthy of* death, they asked Pilate *that* He
be executed. **29** And when they fulfilled all the *things* having been written about
Him, having taken *Him* down from the cross, they laid *Him* in *a* tomb. **30** But God
raised Him from *the* dead— **31** Who appeared for many days *to* the *ones* having
come up with Him from Galilee to Jerusalem, who now are His witnesses to the
people. **32** And **we** are announcing-as-good-news-to you the promise having been
made to the fathers— **33** that God has fulfilled **this** *promise for* us their children,
having raised-up^A Jesus, as it has also been written in the second Psalm: 'You
are My Son. Today I have fathered You' [Ps 2:7]. **34** And that^B He raised Him up
from *the* dead *as One* no longer going to return to decay, He has spoken in this
manner [in Isa 55:3]: that 'I will give You the holy, trustworthy^C *things of* ^D
David'. **35** Therefore^E also in another *place* it says, 'You will not give^F Your holy
One to see^G decay' [Ps 16:10]. **36** For David, having served the purpose^H *of* God
in his own generation, fell asleep and was put-with^I his fathers, and saw decay.
37 But He Whom God raised did not see decay.

Forgiveness Is Now Being Proclaimed To You. Don't Be Scoffers
38 "Therefore let it be known *to* you, men, brothers, that through this *One*
forgiveness *of* sins is being proclaimed *to* you. And from all *things from* which
you could not be declared-righteous by *the* Law *of* Moses— **39** by^J this *One*
everyone believing is declared-righteous. **40** Therefore be watching-out *that* the
thing having been spoken in the Prophets [in Hab 1:5] may not come upon *you*:
41 'Look, scoffers, and marvel and perish. Because I am working *a* work in your
days, *a* work which you will never believe if someone tells you in detail' ".

At The Next Sabbath Meeting, The Jews Contradict Paul. He Turns To The Gentiles
42 And while they *were* going out, they were begging *that* these words *might* be spoken
to them on the next Sabbath. **43** And the gathering^K having been released^L, many *of*
the Jews and *of* the worshiping proselytes followed Paul and Barnabas— who,
speaking to them, were persuading them to continue-in the grace *of* God. **44** Now *on*
the coming Sabbath, almost the whole city was gathered together to hear the word
of the Lord. **45** But the Jews, having seen the crowds, were filled *with* jealousy. And
they were contradicting^M the *things* being spoken by Paul, blaspheming. **46** And Paul
and Barnabas, having spoken-boldly, said, "It was necessary *that* the word *of* God be
spoken **to you** first. Since you are rejecting it and judging yourselves not worthy *of*
eternal life, behold— we are turning to the Gentiles. **47** For thus the Lord has
commanded us [in Isa 49:6]: 'I have placed you for^N *a* light *to the* Gentiles, *that* you
may be *a* light for salvation as far as *the* last *place of* the earth'". **48** And the Gentiles,

---

A. That is, brought to Israel, as this word is used in 3:22; or, raised from the dead, as this word is used next
in v 34. **B.** That is, And as to the fact that. **C.** Or, faithful, sure, dependable. **D.** That is, promised to. **E.** If
Messiah permanently fulfills what was promised to David, He cannot decay in the grave as David did. This
is why Ps 16 says He will not see decay. **F.** That is, permit. **G.** That is, experience. **H.** Or, plan. **I.** Or, added-
to. **J.** That is, by means of this One, in contrast with 'not... by *the* Law'. Or, in, so that it says 'Moses—
everyone believing in this *One* is declared-righteous'. **K.** Or, synagogue, congregation, meeting. **L.** Or,
dismissed. **M.** Or, speaking against. **N.** That is, to be a light.

having heard *it,* were rejoicing and glorifying the word *of* the Lord. And all who had been appointed^A to eternal life believed.

The Jews Drive Paul And Barnabas Out of Their Districts

49 And the word *of* the Lord was being carried^B through the whole region^C. **50** But the Jews incited the prominent worshiping women and the leading *men of* the city, and aroused *a* persecution against Paul and Barnabas, and drove them out from their districts. **51** But the *ones,* having shaken-out the dust *from their* feet against them, went to Iconium. **52** And the disciples were being filled *with* joy and *with the* Holy Spirit.

In Iconium, Paul And Barnabas Again Proclaim, And Then Flee a Plot To Kill Them

14:1 Now it came about in Iconium *that* according to the same *plan,* they entered into the synagogue *of* the Jews and spoke in this manner, so that *a* large number *of* both Jews and Greeks believed. **2** But the Jews having disobeyed^D aroused and embittered^E the souls *of* the Gentiles against the brothers. **3** So indeed they spent *a* considerable time speaking-boldly for the Lord, *Who was* testifying to the word *of* His grace, granting^F *that* signs and wonders be taking place by their hands. **4** And the multitude *of* the city was divided— indeed some were with the Jews; and others with the apostles. **5** But when *an* attempt^G came about *by* both the Gentiles and Jews together with their rulers to mistreat and to stone them, **6** having become-aware, they fled^H to the cities *of* Lycaonia^I— Lystra and Derbe, and the surrounding-region. **7** And there they were announcing-the-good-news.

In Lystra, Paul Heals a Man And Is Declared a God, Then Is Stoned

8 And in Lystra, *a* certain man powerless in the feet was sitting— *a* lame *one* from his mother's womb, who never walked. **9** This *one* heard Paul speaking— who, having looked-intently *at* him, and having seen that he had faith *that he might* be restored, **10** said *with a l*oud voice, "Stand up straight on your feet". And he leaped and was walking. **11** And the crowds, having seen what Paul did, raised their voice, saying in Lycaonian, "The gods came down to us, having become-like men!" **12** And they were calling Barnabas "Zeus^J", and Paul "Hermes^K", since **he** was the *one* leading the speaking. **13** And the priest *of* the *temple of* Zeus being before^L the city, having brought bulls and garlands to the gates, was intending to offer-sacrifice with the crowds. **14** But the apostles, Barnabas and Paul— having heard-*of it,* having torn their garments— leaped-out into the crowd, crying-out **15** and saying, "Men, why are you doing these *things*? **We** also are men of-like-nature *to* you, announcing-the-good-news to turn you from these worthless^M *things* to *the* living God, Who made the heaven and the earth and the sea and all the *things* in them, **16** Who allowed all the nations to be going their ways in the generations having gone-by. **17** And yet He did not leave Himself without-witness^N: doing-good, giving you rains from heaven

---

A. Or, assigned, arrayed, arranged. That is, predestined by God to believe; or, providentially arranged for eternal life that day as ripe fruit ready for harvest. **B.** Or, spread. **C.** That is, the region of Phrygia, in which Pisidian Antioch (v 14) was located. This region is in the Roman province of Galatia. **D.** Or, refused-to-believe. **E.** Lit, made-evil. **F.** This explains how the Lord was testifying. **G.** Or, impulse, onset, start. **H.** Or, fled-for-refuge. **I.** This is the district. Lystra and Derbe are cities in this district, which is still in the Roman province of Galatia. **J.** This is the Greek name of the chief god, the god of the sky, known as Jupiter to the Romans. **K.** This is the son of Zeus, the messenger of the gods, known as Mercury to the Romans. Thus Paul is seen as the spokesman for Barnabas. **L.** The temple was on the road before one entered the city. **M.** Or, futile, pointless. **N.** God's works bear testimony to Him.

and fruitful[A] seasons, filling your hearts *with* food and gladness". **18** And saying these *things*, with-difficulty they restrained[B] the crowds, *that they might* not offer-sacrifice *to* them. **19** But Jews came-over from Antioch and Iconium. And having won-over[C] the crowds, and having stoned Paul, they were dragging *him* outside *of* the city, thinking[D] *that* he was dead[E]. **20** But the disciples having surrounded him— having stood-up, he entered into the city.

In Derbe They Make Disciples, Then Return Home, Strengthening The Churches
And *on* the next day he went forth with Barnabas to Derbe. **21** And having announced-the-good-news-to that city, and having made many disciples, they returned to Lystra and to Iconium and to Antioch, **22** strengthening the souls *of* the disciples, encouraging[F] *them* to continue-in[G] the faith, and that "It-is-necessary *that* we enter into the kingdom *of* God through many afflictions". **23** And having appointed elders *for* them in each church, having prayed with fastings, they commended[H] them *to* the Lord in Whom they had believed. **24** And having gone through Pisidia, they came to Pamphylia. **25** And having spoken the word in Perga, they went down to Attalia. **26** And from there they sailed-away to Antioch— from where they had been handed-over *to* the grace *of* God for the work which they completed. **27** And having arrived, and having gathered together the church, they were reporting all that God did with them, and that He opened *a* door *of* faith *to* the Gentiles.

A Controversy Erupts: Do Gentile Christians Have To Follow Jewish Laws To Be Saved?
28 Now they were spending not *a* little time[I] with the disciples. **15:1** And certain *ones* having come down from Judea were teaching the brothers that "Unless you are circumcised *by* the custom *of* Moses, you cannot be saved". **2** And no small dispute and debate *by* Paul and Barnabas with them having taken place, they[J] appointed[K] Paul and Barnabas and some others of them to go up to the apostles and elders in Jerusalem concerning this issue. **3** So indeed the *ones*, having been sent-forward by the church, were going through both Phoenicia and Samaria describing-in-detail the conversion[L] *of* the Gentiles. And they were producing great joy *in* all the brothers. **4** And having arrived in Jerusalem, they were welcomed by the church and the apostles and the elders. And they reported all-that God did with them. **5** But some *of* the *ones* from the sect *of* the Pharisees having believed[M] stood-up-out-of *the assembly*, saying that "It-is-necessary to circumcise them and to command *them* to keep the Law *of* Moses".

Peter Says That Both Jews And Gentiles Are Saved By Grace And Faith, Not By The Law
6 And the apostles and the elders were gathered together to see about this matter. **7** And much debate having taken place, Peter, having stood up, said to them, "Men, brothers, **you** know that from *the* old[N] days God made-a-choice among you *that* by my mouth the Gentiles *should* hear the message *of* the good-news and believe. **8** And God, the heart-knower, testified[O]— having given the Holy Spirit *to* them, just as also *to* us. **9** And He made no distinction between both us and them, having cleansed their hearts *by* faith.

A. Or, fruitbearing. **B.** Or, brought-to-rest. **C.** Or, persuaded, convinced. **D.** Or, supposing. **E.** Or, had died. **F.** Or, exhorting. **G.** Or, remain-in, be-true-to. **H.** Or, entrusted. **I.** That is, a long time. Some think this is when Galatians was written (or, in 18:5 or 19:10 or 20:3) to the churches just founded in 13:14-14:23 (the South-Galatia theory). Others think it was written in Acts 18:5 or 19:10 or 20:3 to the unnamed churches visited in 16:6 or 18:23 (the North-Galatia theory). **J.** That is, the brothers in Antioch, v 1. **K.** Or, assigned. **L.** Or, turning. **M.** That is, some believers who were formerly Pharisees. **N.** That is, the days of Acts 10, now some ten years in the past. **O.** That is, testified that Cornelius was truly and fully saved.

[10] Therefore[A] why are you now testing God *by* laying *a* yoke on the neck *of* the disciples which neither our fathers nor **we** were able to bear? [11] Rather, we believe *that we* are saved through the grace *of* the Lord Jesus in accordance with the way those also *are saved*".

James Quotes The Prophets To Show That It Is God's Plan To Save The Gentiles

[12] And the whole assembly was silent. And they were listening-to Barnabas and Paul describing all the signs and wonders that God did through them among the Gentiles. [13] And after they *were* silent, James responded, saying, "Men, brothers, listen-to me. [14] Simeon[B] described how God first visited to take *a* people *for* His name from *the* Gentiles. [15] And the words *of* the prophets agree *with* this, just as it has been written [in Amos 9:11- 12]: [16] 'After these *things* I will return and I will rebuild the fallen tent *of* David. And I will rebuild its *things* having been torn-down. And I will restore it [17] so that the rest *of* mankind may seek-out the Lord— even all the Gentiles upon whom My name has been called-upon them[C]', says *the* Lord doing these *things* [18] known from *the past* age. [19] Therefore **I** judge *that we* not be troubling the *ones* from the Gentiles turning to God, [20] but *that we* write to them *that they should* be abstaining *from* the contaminated[D] *things of* idols, and sexual-immorality, and the strangled[E] *thing,* and blood. [21] For from ancient generations, Moses has the *ones* proclaiming him in each city— being read in the synagogues every Sabbath".

A Letter Is Sent To Clear Up The Issue And Encourage The Gentile Believers

[22] Then it seemed *good to* the apostles and the elders, along with the whole church, *that* having chosen men from-*among* them *they should* send *them* to Antioch with Paul and Barnabas— Judas (the *one* being called Barsabbas) and Silas, leading men among the brothers, [23] having written by their hand:

"The apostles and the elders, *your* brothers, *to* the brothers from *the* Gentiles throughout Antioch and Syria and Cilicia: Greetings. [24] Because we heard that some having gone out from us disturbed you *with* words, unsettling your souls— *to* whom we did not give-orders— [25] it seemed *good to* us, having become of-one-accord, having chosen men, *that we should* send *them* to you with our beloved Barnabas and Paul— [26] men[F] having handed-over their lives for the name *of* our Lord Jesus Christ. [27] Therefore we have sent-forth Judas and Silas; they also *will be* declaring the same *things* by *spoken* word. [28] For it seemed *good to* the Holy Spirit and *to* us to be laying-on you no greater burden except these essentials[G]: [29] *that you* be abstaining *from* foods-sacrificed-to-idols, and blood, and strangled *things,* and sexual immorality; keeping yourselves from which *things,* you will do well. Farewell".

[30] So indeed the *ones,* having been sent-away, went down to Antioch. And having gathered together the multitude, they delivered the letter. [31] And having read *it,* they rejoiced over the encouragement. [32] Both Judas and Silas, also themselves being prophets, encouraged and strengthened the brothers with *a* long[H] message. [33] And having

---

A. The believers in Antioch are a continuation of what God started to do back in Acts 10. These former Pharisees are rejecting the testimony God gave in Acts 10, and seeking to lay on these Gentiles things they themselves could not keep. **B.** That is, Peter, v 7. This is the Aramaic form of 'Simon'. **C.** That is, upon whom God has placed His name. **D.** Or, polluted, defiled. That is, the foods (v 29) contaminated by their association with idol-worship. **E.** That is, meat from strangled animals, because the blood remained in it, violating a command that goes back to Noah's time, Gen 9:4. **F.** This refers specifically to Barnabas and Paul. **G.** Or, necessities. **H.** Or, *a* great message. That is, long in duration; or great in quality. If Luke is referring to multiple occasions rather than one speaking event, then this means 'much speaking', as in 20:2.

done time *there*, they were sent-away with *greetings of* peace from the brothers to the *ones* having sent them out. **34** A

Paul And Barnabas Plan a Second Missionary Journey From Antioch, But Split Over John Mark
35 Now Paul and Barnabas were spending-time in Antioch, teaching and announcing-as-good-news the word *of* the Lord, along with many others also. **36** And after some days, Paul said to Barnabas, "Having returned, let us now visit the brothers in every city in which we proclaimed the word *of* the Lord *to see* how they are having[B] *things*". **37** And Barnabas was wanting to also take along John with *them*, the *one* being called Mark. **38** But Paul was considering-*it*-fitting *that they* not be taking-along-with *them* this *one* having withdrawn[C] from them since Pamphylia, and not having gone with them to the work. **39** And *a* disagreement took-place, so that they were separated from one another. And Barnabas, having taken along Mark, sailed-off to Cyprus[D].

Paul And Silas Revisit The Churches From Paul's First Journey. Timothy Joins Them
40 And Paul, having chosen[E] Silas[F], went forth, having been handed-over *to* the grace *of* the Lord by the brothers. **41** And he was going[G] through Syria and Cilicia, strengthening the churches. **16:1** And he came also to Derbe and to Lystra. And behold, *a* certain disciple was there— Timothy *by* name, *the* son *of a* believing Jewish woman[H], but *of a* Greek father— **2** who was being attested by the brothers in Lystra and Iconium. **3** Paul wanted this *one* to go forth with him. And having taken *him*, he circumcised him because of the Jews being in those places, for they all knew that his father was *a* Greek. **4** And as they were proceeding through the cities, they were delivering[I] *to* them the decrees[J] to be keeping[K] having been determined[L] by the apostles and elders in Jerusalem. **5** So indeed the churches were being made-firm *in* the faith and were abounding *in* number daily.

Paul Sees a Vision of a Macedonian Asking For His Help, And Makes Plans To Go
6 And they went through the Phrygian[M] and Galatian region, having been forbidden[N] by the Holy Spirit to speak the word in Asia. **7** And having come opposite Mysia, they were trying to proceed into Bithynia and the Spirit *of*[O] Jesus did not allow them. **8** And having passed-by[P] Mysia, they came down to Troas. **9** And *a* vision appeared *to* Paul during the night— *a* certain Macedonian man[Q] was standing and appealing-to him, and saying, "Having crossed to Macedonia, help us". **10** And when he saw the vision, immediately we[R] sought to go forth to Macedonia, concluding that God had called us to announce-the-good-news-to them.

In Philippi, Paul Meets Lydia And She Becomes a Believer
11 And having put-to-sea from Troas, we ran-a-straight-course to Samothrace, and *on* the following *day* to Neapolis. **12** And from there *we went* to Philippi, which is *a* city *of the*

A. Some manuscripts add here, But it seemed *good* to Silas to remain there. Note v 40. **B.** That is, how things are going. **C.** Or, more strongly (based on one's understanding of this event), abandoned, deserted. This word is not related to 'departed' in 13:13. **D.** Barnabas and Mark return to the cities they had visited with Paul in chapter 13. Cyprus is the native country of Barnabas, 4:36. Paul and Silas visit the churches he and Barnabas had founded. **E.** Or, selected, called-upon. **F.** He is called Silvanus in 1 Thes 1:1. **G.** This time, Paul goes by land. **H.** Her name was Eunice, 2 Tim 1:5. **I.** Or, passing-on, handing-down. **J.** Or, decisions, commands. **K.** Or, *that they should* be keeping the decrees. **L.** Or, decided. **M.** Or, Phrygia and *the* Galatian region (meaning North Galatia). See 14:28. **N.** Or, prevented... from speaking. **O.** That is, given by. **P.** That is, in terms of ministry. **Q.** Some think this was Luke, who joins Paul in v 10. **R.** This is the first time Luke includes himself in Paul's group.

first^A district *of* Macedonia, *a* colony^B. And we were spending some days in this city. ^13 And *on* the day *of* the Sabbath, we went outside the gate beside *a* river where we were supposing *that* there was *a* place of prayer^C. And having sat-*down*, we were speaking *to* the women having come together. ^14 And a certain woman worshiping God— Lydia *by* name, *a* purple-fabric-dealer *from the* city *of* Thyatira— was listening, whose heart the Lord opened to pay-attention-to the *things* being spoken by Paul. ^15 And when she and her household were baptized, she urged *us*, saying, "If you have judged me to be *a* believer^D *in* the Lord, *then* having entered into my house, be staying *with me*". And she prevailed-upon us.

Paul Casts a Demon Out of a Fortune-Telling Servant-Girl
^16 And it came about while we *were* going to the *place of* prayer *that a* certain servant-girl having *a* soothsaying^E spirit met us, who was bringing-about *a* large profit *to* her masters telling-fortunes. ^17 This *one*, while closely-following Paul and us^F, was crying-out, saying, "These men are slaves *of* the Most-High God^G, who are proclaiming *to* you *a* way^H *of* salvation". ^18 And she was doing this for many days. And Paul, having been greatly-annoyed, and having turned *to* the spirit, said, "I command you in *the* name *of* Jesus Christ to depart from her!" And it went out *at* the very hour.

The Girl's Masters Have Paul And Silas Beaten And Imprisoned
^19 And her masters, having seen that their hope *of* profit went-out, having taken-hold-of Paul and Silas, dragged *them* into the marketplace^I before the rulers. ^20 And having brought them to the magistrates^J, they said, "These men are throwing our city into confusion, being Jews. ^21 And they are proclaiming customs which it is not lawful *for* us to be accepting nor to be doing, being Romans".^22 And the crowd rose up together against them. And the magistrates, having torn-off their^K garments, were giving-orders to beat *them* with rods^L. ^23 And having laid many blows on them, they threw *them* into prison, having commanded the jailer to keep them securely— ^24 who, having received such *a* command, threw them into the inner prison and secured their feet to the wood^M.

After an Earthquake Opens The Jail, The Jailer Believes And Is Baptized
^25 And about midnight Paul and Silas were singing-praise-to God while praying. And the prisoners were listening-to^N them. ^26 And suddenly *a* great earthquake took place, so that the foundations *of* the jailhouse were shaken. And at-once all the doors were opened, and the bonds^O *of* everyone were unfastened^P. ^27 And the jailer— having become awakened, and having seen the doors *of* the prison having been opened, having drawn *his* sword— was about to kill himself, supposing *that* the prisoners had escaped. ^28 But Paul called-out *with a* loud voice, saying, "Do no harm *to*

A. Or, *a* leading city *of* the district. **B.** That is, a Roman colony, with its special privileges. **C.** There were apparently not enough Jews in this Roman colony to have a synagogue (ten men were required). **D.** Or, faithful *to*, trustworthy *in*. **E.** Or, divination. **F.** This is the last time Luke includes himself with Paul until 20:5, again in Philippi. **G.** Or, god. She may mean the highest of the gods she worships; or, the true God. **H.** Or, *the* way. The hearers probably understood her to mean *a* way, not the only way. **I.** That is, the public square where the rulers and courts were also found. **J.** That is, the two Roman governors of the colony. **K.** That is, those of Paul and Silas. **L.** This was a Roman method of punishment, carried out by the officers in v 35. **M.** That is, the beam, log, or post, with chains. Or, in the stocks. **N.** Or, overhearing. **O.** Or, bindings, fetters, chains. **P.** Or, loosened, let go.

yourself, for we are all here". [29] And having asked-*for* lights, he rushed-in. And having become trembling, he fell before Paul and Silas. [30] And having brought them outside, he said, "Sirs, what must I do in order that I may be saved?" [31] And the *ones* said, "Put faith upon the Lord Jesus and you will be saved— you and your household". [32] And they spoke the word *of* the Lord *to* him, along with all the *ones* in his house. [33] And having taken them at that hour *of* the night, he washed off *their* wounds. And he was baptized at-once— he and all his *household.* [34] And having led them up to *his* house, he set *a* table before *them* and rejoiced-greatly— having believed *in* God with-*his*-whole-household.

The Magistrates Release Paul And Silas After Learning They Are Roman Citizens
[35] And having become day, the magistrates sent forth *their* officers[A], saying, "Release those men". [36] And the jailer reported these words to Paul, that "The magistrates have sent forth in order that you may be released. Now therefore having come out, proceed in peace". [37] But Paul said to them, "Having beaten us *in* public— uncondemned[B] men being Romans[C]— they threw *us* into prison. And now they are throwing us out secretly? No indeed! But having come themselves, let them lead us out!" [38] And the officers reported these words *to* the magistrates. And having heard that they were Romans, they became afraid. [39] And having come, they appealed-to them. And having led *them* out, they were asking *them* to depart from the city. [40] And having gone forth from the prison, they went-in[D] to Lydia. And having seen the brothers[E], they encouraged *them*, and went forth.

In Thessalonica Paul Reasons From The Scriptures That The Christ Had To Suffer
17:1 Now having traveled-through Amphipolis and Apollonia, they came to Thessalonica, where there was *a* synagogue *of* the Jews. [2] And in accordance with the *thing* having become-a-custom *with* Paul, he went-in to them. And on three Sabbaths he reasoned *with* them from the Scriptures, [3] opening *them,* and putting-before *them* that the Christ had-to suffer and rise-up from *the* dead, and that "This *One* is the Christ— the Jesus Whom **I** am proclaiming *to* you". [4] And some of them were persuaded and were allotted-to[F] Paul and Silas— both *a* large number *of* the worshiping Greeks, and not *a* few *of the* leading women. [5] But the Jews— having become-jealous, and having taking along some evil men *from* the marketplace, and having formed-a-crowd— were throwing the city into-a-commotion. And having suddenly-come-upon the house *of* Jason, they were seeking them[G] to bring *them* forth to the public-assembly. [6] But not having found them, they were dragging Jason and some brothers before the city-authorities[H], shouting that "The *ones* having upset the world— these *ones* are also present here, [7] whom Jason has received[I]. And these *ones* all are acting contrary to the decrees *of* Caesar, saying *that* Jesus is another **king**". [8] And they stirred-up the crowd and the city-authorities hearing these *things.* [9] And having received the bond[J] from Jason and the others, they released them.

A. Or, lictors, rod-bearers. **B.** That is, by a proper trial. It was illegal to do this to a Roman citizen. **C.** That is, Roman citizens. **D.** That is, went into her house. **E.** That is, fellow-believers, including Lydia. **F.** Or, assigned-to, attached-to. That is, by God. Related to the concept of 'lots' in 1 Pet 5:3. **G.** That is, Paul and Silas. **H.** Or, politarchs. This is the title for the five or six member city council in Thessalonica. **I.** That is, received as guests. **J.** Or, the sufficient-amount-of *money.* The city authorities got a pledge from Jason that he would sent away Paul and Silas, and took a large enough bond to ensure he did so. Because of this quick and effective expulsion, whereby Paul was 'orphaned' (1 Thes 2:17) from them, we have Paul's two letters to the Thessalonians.

In Berea, The People Examine The Scriptures With Paul And Silas
10 And the brothers immediately sent-away both Paul and Silas during *the* night to Berea— who, having arrived, were going into the synagogue *of* the Jews. **11** Now these *ones* were more-noble^A *than* the *ones* in Thessalonica— who^B received the word with all eagerness, examining the Scriptures daily *to see* if these *things* might hold so. **12** So indeed many of them believed— and not *a* few *of* the prominent Greek women and men. **13** But when the Jews from Thessalonica came-to-know that the word *of* God was proclaimed by Paul in Berea also, they came there also, shaking^C and stirring-up the crowds. **14** And at that time the brothers immediately sent Paul away, *that he might* go as-far-as to the sea. And both Silas and Timothy remained there.

In Athens, Paul Reasons With The Philosophers In The Marketplace
15 Now the *ones* conducting Paul brought *him* as far as Athens. And having received *a* command for Silas and Timothy that they should come to him as soon as *they could*, they were going away [to them]. **16** And while Paul *was* waiting-for them in Athens, his spirit was being provoked^D within him while observing the city being full-of-idols. **17** So indeed he was reasoning in the synagogue *with* the Jews and the *ones* worshiping, and in the marketplace every day with the *ones* happening-to-be-there. **18** And some *of* the Epicurean and Stoic philosophers also were conversing *with* him. And some were saying, "What would this scavenger^E be intending to say?" And others, "He seems to be *a* proclaimer *of* strange deities^F"— because he was announcing-the-good-news *as to* Jesus and the resurrection. **19** And having taken-hold-of him, they brought *him* to the Areopagus^G, saying, "Can we know what this new teaching being spoken by you *is*? **20** For you are bringing-in some *things* being strange to our ears. So we want to know what these *things* mean". **21** Now all Athenians and the strangers residing *there* were finding-an-opportunity^H for nothing other than to say something or to hear something newer.

Paul Proclaims To Them The Creator-God And What He Wants From Mankind
22 And Paul, having been stood in *the* midst *of* the Areopagus, said, "Men, Athenians, I see how you *are* very-religious in all *respects*. **23** For while going-about and looking-carefully-at^I your objects-of-worship, I also found *an* altar in which it had been inscribed, 'To *a* not-known god'. Therefore what you are worshiping while not-knowing, this **I** am proclaiming *to* you: **24** God, the *One* having made the world and all the *things* in it— this *One*, being Lord *of* heaven and earth, does not dwell in temples made-by-*human*-hands. **25** Nor is He served by human hands, [as if] being-in-need *of* something^J— He Himself giving life and breath and all *things to* all *people*. **26** And He made from one *man* every nation *of* mankind, *that they should* dwell upon all *the* face *of* the earth, having determined *the* times^K having been appointed^L *for* them and the boundaries *of* their dwelling-places^M; **27** *that they should* seek God— if

---

A. That is, more spiritually noble-minded, as seen in their willingness to examine the Scriptures. **B.** This refers to the Bereans. **C.** Or, agitating. **D.** Or, stimulated. **E.** This rendering ridicules Paul as a gatherer of random tidbits of truth, like a bird in the marketplace. Or, babbler. This rendering ridicules him as an unsophisticated proclaimer of such tidbits. **F.** Or, gods, divinities, as the pagans used this term. To Jews and Christians this word meant 'demons'. **G.** That is, the city's governing council, which met on the 'hill of Ares' (the Greek god of war, whom the Romans called 'Mars'). **H.** Or, finding-the-time, having leisure, spending-the-time. **I.** Or, examining, considering. **J.** Or, someone. **K.** That is, periods of ascendancy. **L.** Or, commanded, fixed, assigned. **M.** Or, settlements, colonies.

perhaps indeed they might grope-for[A] Him and find *Him,* though indeed *He* being not far from each one *of* us. **28** For in Him we live and move and exist, as also some *of* your poets[B] have said— 'For we are indeed the *One's* offspring[C]'. **29** Being then offspring *of* God, we ought not to think *that* the divine *being* is like gold or silver or stone— *a* work *of* human craft and thought. **30** So indeed, having overlooked[D] the times *of* ignorance, God, *as to* the present *things,* is commanding people *that* everyone everywhere *should* repent. **31** Because He set *a* day on which He is going to judge the world in righteousness by *a* Man Whom He designated, having granted[E] *a* proof[F] *to* everyone— having raised Him up from *the* dead".

At The Mention of a Resurrection From The Dead, Some Scoffed

32 Now having heard-*of a* resurrection *of the* dead, some were scoffing, but others said, "We will indeed again hear you concerning this". **33** So Paul went out of their midst. **34** And some men having joined him believed, among whom also *were* Dionysius the Areopagite[G]; and *a* woman— Damaris *by* name; and others with them.

In Corinth Paul Teaches The Gentiles For 18 Months

18:1 After these *things,* having departed from Athens, he went to Corinth. **2** And having found *a* certain Jew— Aquila *by* name, *a* Pontian *by* nationality, having recently come from Italy because Claudius[H] *had* ordered all the Jews to depart from Rome— and Priscilla his wife, he went to them. **3** And because of being the same-trade, he was staying with them and working— for they were tent-makers *by* trade. **4** And he was reasoning in the synagogue every Sabbath, and persuading Jews and Greeks. **5** But when both Silas and Timothy came[I] down from Macedonia, Paul was occupying-*himself with* the word[J], solemnly-testifying *to* the Jews *that* the Christ is Jesus. **6** But while they *were* opposing and blaspheming, he said to them, having shaken-out *his* garments, "Your blood *be* upon your head; I *am* clean. From now *on* I will go to the Gentiles". **7** And having passed on from there, he entered into *the* house *of a* certain *one* worshiping God—Titius Justus *by* name— whose house was bordering[K] *on* the synagogue. **8** And Crispus, the synagogue-official, believed *in* the Lord with his whole household. And many *of* the Corinthians hearing were believing and being baptized. **9** And the Lord said *to* Paul during *the* night through *a* vision, "Do not be afraid, but be speaking and do not be silent— **10** because I am with you, and no one will set-upon you to harm you; because there is *a* large people *for* Me in this city". **11** And he sat *for a* year and six months[L], teaching the word *of* God among them.

Paul Is Brought Before The Proconsul By The Jews. Gallio Refuses To Intervene

12 Now while Gallio[M] *was* being proconsul *of* Achaia, the Jews with-one-accord rose-up-against Paul and brought him before the judgment-seat, **13** saying that "This *one* is persuading[N] people to worship God **contrary to the Law**". **14** And Paul being about

---

A. Or, feel-about-for. **B.** Paul quotes from Aratus (270 B.C.) or Cleanthes (220 B.C.). **C.** Or, family, people. **D.** Or, disregarded, looked-beyond. **E.** Or, shown, presented. **F.** Or, *a* pledge, assurance [of this]. **G.** That is, a member of the council that just heard Paul. **H.** He was Roman emperor from A.D. 41-54. The event named here may refer to an incident in A.D. 49. **I.** At this point Paul wrote 1 Thessalonians (1Thes 3:6). Some think he wrote Galatians during this stay in Corinth (see 14:28). **J.** Some manuscripts instead say 'Paul was compelled *by* the Spirit'. **K.** Or, adjacent *to.* **L.** During this period between Paul wrote 2 Thessalonians. **M.** Junius Gallio, the brother of Seneca the philosopher, was the Roman proconsul (governor) of Achaia in A.D. 51-52. **N.** Or more negatively, inducing.

to open *his* mouth, Gallio said to the Jews, "If it were some crime or evil villainy, O Jews, I would have borne-with you in accordance with reason— **15** but since it is issues about talk[A] and names[B] and your Law, see *to it* yourselves. **I** am not willing to be *a* judge *of* these *things*". **16** And he drove them away from the judgment-seat. **17** And having all taken-hold-of Sosthenes, the synagogue-official, they were striking *him* in front of the judgment seat. And none *of* these[C] *things* was-a-concern *to* Gallio.

In Ephesus, Paul Prepares Them For a Future Visit And Then Returns Home To Antioch
18 And Paul, having stayed-on considerable days longer, having said-good-bye *to* the brothers, was sailing-off to Syria— and Priscilla and Aquila with him— having sheared *his* head in Cenchrea, for he had *a* vow[D]. **19** And they came to Ephesus. And those[E] *ones* he left-behind there[F]. And he himself, having entered into the synagogue, reasoned *with* the Jews. **20** And while they *were* asking *him* to stay for more time, he did not consent. **21** But having said-goodbye, and having said, "I will return again to you, God willing", he put-to-sea from Ephesus. **22** And having come down to Caesarea, having gone up and greeted the church, he went down to Antioch[G].

Paul Embarks On a Third Journey. Priscilla And Aquila Update Apollos
23 And having done some time *there*, he went forth[H], going successively through the Galatian region[I] and Phrygia, strengthening all the disciples. **24** Now *a* certain Jew— Apollos *by* name, *an* Alexandrian *by* nationality, *an* eloquent man— came to Ephesus, being powerful in the Scriptures. **25** This *one* had been instructed *as to* the way *of* the Lord. And boiling *in* spirit, he was speaking and teaching accurately the *things* concerning Jesus, knowing-about only the baptism *of* John. **26** And this *one* began to speak-boldly in the synagogue. And having heard him, Priscilla and Aquila took him aside and explained the way *of* God *to* him more-accurately. **27** And he wanting to go to Achaia, the brothers, having urged *him* forward, wrote *to* the disciples to welcome him; who, having arrived, greatly helped the *ones* having believed through grace. **28** For he was vigorously[J] refuting the Jews *in* public, showing through the Scriptures *that* the Christ is Jesus.

Paul Arrives In Ephesus. He Baptizes Some Disciples of Apollos
19:1 And it came about during Apollos's being in Corinth *that* Paul, having gone through the upper regions, came down to Ephesus and found some disciples. **2** And he said to them, "Did you receive *the* Holy Spirit, having believed?" And the *ones said* to him, "But we did not even hear if[K] *the* Holy Spirit is *given*". **3** And he said, "Into what then were you baptized?" And the *ones* said, "Into John's baptism". **4** And Paul said, "John baptized *a* baptism *of* repentance, saying *to* the people that they should believe in the *One* coming after him, that is, in Jesus". **5** And having heard *it*, they were baptized in the name *of* the

---

A. That is, as opposed to deeds. Or, *a* word, *a* message. **B.** Perhaps Gallio means whether 'Jesus' is also 'Christ'. **C.** That is, the matters raised by the Jews; or, the beating of Sosthenes; or, both. **D.** Or, prayer. As a result of an answered prayer or vow, probably with regard to his just completed work in Corinth, Paul cut off his hair, a Jewish custom. **E.** That is, Priscilla and Aquila. **F.** That is, in Ephesus, to prepare for Paul's planned return, mentioned next. **G.** Thus Paul completes this second journey on which this church had sent him back in 15:40. **H.** Note that the church is not mentioned this time. Paul is returning to the base of operations in Ephesus in Asia which he has already chosen and prepared in v 19. **I.** Or, the Galatian and Phrygian region, referring to one region instead of two, as in 16:6. **J.** Or, forcefully. **K.** Or, whether there is [yet] *a* Holy Spirit. They had not heard that John's prediction had come to pass, Mt 3:11.

Lord Jesus. **6** And Paul having laid *his* hands on them, the Holy Spirit came upon them, and they were speaking *in* tongues and prophesying. **7** And all the men were [totaling] about twelve.

Paul Ministers In Ephesus For Over Two Years, Teaching And Doing Miracles
8 And having entered into the synagogue, he was speaking-boldly for three months, reasoning and persuading *as to* the *things* concerning the kingdom *of* God. **9** But when some were becoming-hardened, and were disobeying, speaking-evil-of the Way before the assembly— having departed from them, he separated the disciples, reasoning daily in the school^A *of* Tyrannus. **10** And this took place for two^B years, so that all the *ones* dwelling-in Asia heard the word *of* the Lord— both Jews and Greeks. **11** And God was doing not the ordinary^C miracles by the hands *of* Paul— **12** so that handkerchiefs or aprons^D *were* even being carried-forth^E from his skin to the *ones* being sick, and the diseases *were* being released from them, and the evil spirits *were* going out.

Even Some Non-Believing Priests Tried To Utilize Paul's Power
13 And even some *of* the Jewish exorcists^F going-around attempted to name the name *of* the Lord Jesus over the *ones* having the evil spirits, saying, "I make you swear^G *by* the Jesus Whom Paul is proclaiming". **14** Now there were seven sons *of a* certain Sceva^H, *a* Jewish chief priest, doing this. **15** But having responded, the evil spirit said *to* them, "I know Jesus and know-about Paul, but who are **you**?" **16** And the man in whom was the evil spirit— having leaped on them, having subdued^I all^J *of them*— prevailed against them, so that *they* fled out of that house naked and having been wounded. **17** And this became known *to* all the *ones* dwelling-in Ephesus— both Jews and Greeks. And fear fell upon them all.

Jesus Was Being Magnified And The Word of The Lord Was Prevailing
18 And the name *of* the Lord Jesus was being magnified. And many *of* the *ones* having believed were coming, confessing-out^K and declaring^L their [evil] practices. **19** And many *of* the *ones* having practiced sorceries, having brought-together *their* books, were burning *them* up in the presence of everyone. And they calculated-up the prices *of* them, and found *it to be* fifty thousand silver-coins^M. **20** Thus in accordance with *the* might^N *of* the Lord, the word was growing and prevailing.

Paul Decides To Return To Jerusalem And Then Go To Rome. He Sends Timothy Ahead
21 Now when these^O *things* were completed, Paul put^P in *his* spirit *that*, having gone through Macedonia and Achaia, *he should* be going to Jerusalem, having said that "After I come-to-be there, I must also see Rome". **22** And having sent-out two *of* the *ones* ministering *with* him to Macedonia— Timothy and Erastus— he himself held-on in Asia *for a* time.

A. That is, school building. **B.** During this time, Paul wrote 1 Corinthians, and perhaps Galatians (see 14:28). **C.** In other words, unusual, uncommon. **D.** That is, such as a worker would wear. **E.** Or, brought, taken. **F.** These men cast out demons using magical formulas and oaths. They tried using the sentence that follows as part of their ritual. **G.** This seems to be intended to force the demon to leave rather than swear allegiance to Christ. **H.** This is the man's name. **I.** Or, overpowered. **J.** Or, both, if only two were active participants in this case. **K.** Or, confessing-openly. That is, confessing Jesus; or, confessing their practices. **L.** Or, disclosing. **M.** This probably refers to the drachma, which is equivalent to a denarius, one day's wage for a laborer. Thus, this is a considerable sum of money. **N.** Or, *His* might, the word *of the Lord* (the emphasis being upon 'of the Lord'). **O.** That is, Paul's work in Asia, based in Ephesus, 19:1-20. **P.** Or, resolved in *the* Spirit. Note 20:22.

There Is a Big Uproar In Ephesus Over a Decline In The Sale of Idols Due To Paul
23 Now about that time, no small disturbance took place concerning the Way. **24** For *a* certain Demetrius *by* name, *a* silversmith making silver shrines[A] *of* Artemis[B], was bringing-about no small business *for* the craftsmen— **25** whom having assembled-together, and the workers with respect to such *things,* he said, "Men, you know that prosperity *for* us is from this business. **26** And you are seeing and hearing that this Paul— having persuaded *people* not only *from* Ephesus, but *from* almost all Asia— turned-away *a* considerable crowd, saying that the *gods* being made with hands are not gods. **27** But not only is-there-a-danger *for* us *that* **this**[C] part *may* come into disrepute, but also *that* the temple *of* the great goddess Artemis *may* be counted for nothing, and *that she* whom all Asia and the world worships *may* even be about to be torn-down[D] *from* her majesty".

Amid The City-Wide Confusion, Friends of Paul Are Seized
28 And having heard *it,* and having become full *of* rage, they were crying-out, saying, "Great *is* Artemis *of the* Ephesians!" **29** And the city was filled *with* confusion. And they rushed with-one-accord into the theater, having seized Gaius and Aristarchus— Macedonian fellow-travelers *of* Paul. **30** And while Paul *was* wanting to enter into the public-assembly, the disciples were not letting him. **31** And even some *of* the Asian-officials[E]— being friends *with* him, having sent to him— were urging *him* not to give himself to the theater. **32** Then indeed, other *ones* were crying-out another[F] thing. For the assembly was confused, and the majority did not know for **what** reason they had come together. **33** And *some* from the crowd gave-instructions-to[G] Alexander— the Jews having put him forward. And Alexander, having waved *his* hand, was intending to speak-a-defense *to* the public-assembly. **34** But having recognized that he was *a* Jew, one voice came[H] from everyone— crying-out for about two hours, "Great *is* Artemis *of the* Ephesians!"

The Town Mayor Calms And Dismisses The Crowd
35 And the town-mayor[I], having calmed the crowd, says, "Men, Ephesians, who indeed is there *of* mankind who does not know the city *of the* Ephesians *as* being temple-keeper[J] *of* the great Artemis, and *of the image* fallen-from-heaven[K]? **36** These *things* then being undeniable, you must *continue*-being calmed[L] and doing nothing reckless— **37** for you brought *here* these men *being* neither temple-robbers nor *ones* blaspheming our goddess. **38** So indeed if Demetrius and the craftsmen with him have *a* complaint against anyone, courts are being led[M], and there are proconsuls. Let them bring-a-charge *against* one another. **39** Now if you are seeking-for anything further[N], it will be settled in the lawful assembly. **40** For indeed we are in-danger-of being charged *with a* riot because of today— *there* being no cause[O] *for it*— in relation to

---

A. That is, miniature replicas of this world-famous temple, which was considered one of the wonders of the world. **B.** She was a many-breasted goddess of fertility, and perhaps is the same goddess known to the Romans as Diana. **C.** That is, their personal line of work. **D.** Or, thrown-down. **E.** Or, Asiarchs, high officials of the province. **F.** That is, something different than Demetrius. Perhaps it was something anti-Jewish, causing them to put forth Alexander to defend themselves. **G.** Or, concluded *it was.* **H.** Or, arose. **I.** Or, town-secretary. This man was the chief executive of the city, and answered to the proconsul. **J.** Or, temple-guardian. **K.** The Ephesians claimed that the statue of this goddess fell from heaven. **L.** Or, restrained, quiet. **M.** That is, are in session. **N.** That is, beyond what can be settled in a private court action, and thus requiring a town meeting. **O.** No crime or guilty person can be pointed to as the cause of this gathering.

which^A we will not be able to render *an* account for this gathering". **41** And having said these *things*, he dismissed the assembly.

After The Uproar, Paul Departs For Jerusalem Through Macedonia And Greece
20:1 And after the uproar ceased, Paul— having sent for the disciples and having encouraged *them*, having said-farewell— went forth to proceed^B to Macedonia. **2** And having gone^C through those regions, and having encouraged them *with* much speaking, he came to Greece^D. **3** And having done three^E months *there*, *a* plot having been made *against* him by the Jews while *he was* about to put-to-sea for Syria— he became *of a* mind *that he should* be returning through Macedonia^F. **4** And Sopater, *son of* Pyrrhus, *a* Berean, was accompanying him; and Aristarchus and Secundus *of the* Thessalonians; and Gaius, *a* Derbean; and Timothy; and Tychicus and Trophimus, Asians. **5** But these^G, having gone ahead, were awaiting us^H in Troas. **6** And **we** sailed-off from Philippi after the days *of* the *Feast of* Unleavened-Bread, and came to them at Troas within five days, where we spent seven days.

While Paul Is Speaking In Troas, Eutychus Falls To His Death, And Is Raised
7 And on the first *day of* the week, we having been gathered together to break bread, Paul was speaking *to* them, being about to go away *on* the next day. And he was extending the message until midnight. **8** And there were many lamps in the upper-room where we had been gathered-together. **9** And *a* certain young-man, Eutychus *by* name, sitting on the window [sill], *was* being carried-away *by a* deep sleep while Paul *was* speaking further. Having been carried-away by the sleep, he fell down from the third floor, and was picked-up dead. **10** But having gone down, Paul fell upon him, and having embraced *him*, said, "Do not be thrown-into-a-commotion, for his life is in him!" **11** And *Paul*^I having gone up, and having broken the bread and eaten and having conversed for *a* considerable *time*, until daybreak— in this manner he departed. **12** And they brought the boy [along]^J alive. And they were not moderately comforted.

In His Hurry To Reach Jerusalem By Pentecost, Paul Sails By Ephesus To Miletus
13 And **we**, having gone ahead to the ship, put-to-sea for Assos, intending from there to pick-up Paul. For thus having arranged *it*, **he** was intending to go-on-foot^K. **14** And as he was meeting us in Assos, having picked him up, we came to Mitylene. **15** And having sailed-away from there *on* the following *day,* we arrived opposite Chios. And *on* another *day* we crossed-over to Samos. And *on* the next *day*, we came to Miletus. **16** For Paul had determined to sail-by Ephesus so that it might not happen *to* him *that he* lose-time in Asia. For he was hurrying to be in Jerusalem— if it might be possible *for* him— the day *of* Pentecost.

A. That is, a charge of rioting. **B.** That is, according to his plan in 19:21. **C.** On this trip, Paul met Titus (2 Cor 7:5-7) and wrote 2 Corinthians. **D.** Specifically, the city of Corinth. **E.** During this period in Corinth Paul wrote Romans to prepare his way there according to his plan in 19:21. He may also have written Galatians (see 14:28). **F.** That is, by land, up to Philippi. **G.** The men mentioned in v 4 are the delegates carrying the offering from the churches of Macedonia, Galatia, and Asia to the poor believers in Jerusalem, mentioned in 1 Cor 16:1-4; 2 Cor 8-9; Rom 15:26. **H.** Luke reappears. See 16:17. **I.** The following verbs are singular, referring to Paul. **J.** That is, to the ship. Or, [home], after the meeting. **K.** Or, go-by-land. Assos was about 20 miles or 32 kilometers south of Troas.

Paul Exhorts Elders From Ephesus: You Know How I Served The Lord Among You
17 But having sent from Miletus^A to Ephesus, he summoned the elders *of* the church.
18 And when they came to him, he said *to* them, "**You** know, from *the* first day from which I set-foot in Asia, how I **was**^B with you the whole time— **19** serving the Lord with all humblemindedness and tears and trials (the *ones* having happened *to* me by the plots *of* the Jews); **20** how^C I in no way drew-back *from* the *things* being profitable^D *so as* not to declare *them to* you and teach you *in* public and from house-to-house, **21** while solemnly-testifying both *to* Jews and *to* Greeks *as to* the repentance toward God and faith in our Lord Jesus. **22** And now, behold— having been bound *in my* spirit^E, I am going to Jerusalem, not knowing the *things that* will meet^F me in it, **23** except that the Holy Spirit is solemnly-warning me in each city, saying that imprisonment and afflictions are awaiting me. **24** But I am making *my* life *of* no account^G *as to* value *to* myself so-as to finish my course and the ministry which I received from the Lord Jesus— to solemnly-testify *to* the good-news *about* the grace *of* God.

Take Heed To Yourselves And To Shepherd The Flock. For Wolves Are Coming
25 "And now, behold— **I** know that **you all,** among whom I went-about proclaiming the kingdom, will no longer see^H my face. **26** Therefore, I am bearing-witness *to* you on this very day that I am clean of the blood *of* everyone. **27** For I did not draw back *so as* not to declare the whole purpose^I *of* God *to* you. **28** Take heed to yourselves, and *to* all the flock among which the Holy Spirit placed^J **you** *as* overseers— to shepherd the church *of* God which He obtained with *His* own^K blood. **29** I know that after my departure savage wolves will come in among you, not sparing the flock. **30** And men will rise-up from you yourselves, speaking *things* having been perverted, *that they might* be drawing-away the disciples after them. **31** Therefore keep-watching, remembering that night and day *for* three years I did not cease admonishing each one *of you* with tears. **32** And *as to* the *things* now, I commend you *to* God, and *to* the word *of* His grace being able to build *you* up and to give *you* the inheritance among all the *ones* having been sanctified.

I Did Not Serve You For Money
33 "I coveted *the* silver or gold or clothing *of* no one. **34** **You** know that **these hands** served my *own* needs, and the *people* being with me. **35** *In* all *respects,* I showed you that laboring in this manner, it-is-necessary^L to help the *ones* being weak and remember the words *of* the Lord Jesus— that He Himself said, 'It is more blessed to be giving than to be receiving' ".

Paul Departs Amid Prayer And Weeping
36 And having said these *things,* having put-*down* his knees with them all, he prayed.

A. This was about 30 miles or 48 kilometers south of Ephesus. **B.** Or, became, proved-to-be. That is, how I conducted myself. **C.** Or, that. **D.** Or, beneficial, helpful. **E.** Or, *by the* Spirit. Note that because of Paul's determination to proceed with the plan of 19:21, we have Romans, Ephesians, Philippians, Colossians, Philemon, Luke, and Acts. **F.** Or, befall, happen *to.* **G.** Continuing to live on this earth is not even a factor Paul considers as he focuses on finishing his course for Jesus. **H.** This is because Paul plans to go from Jerusalem to Rome (19:21) and beyond (Rom 15:28). **I.** Or, plan, counsel. **J.** Or, set, appointed. **K.** Or, the blood *of His* own *Son.* **L.** Or, *you* must help.

³⁷ And there was much weeping *from* everyone. And having fallen upon the neck *of* Paul, they were kissing him, ³⁸ suffering-pain especially over the statement which he had spoken— that they were no longer going see his face. And they were accompanying him to the ship.

Paul Travels By Ship To Tyre, Where He Is Again Warned Not To Go To Jerusalem
21:1 And when it came about *that* having withdrawn^A from them we put-to-sea, having run-a-straight-course we came to Cos, and *on* the next *day* to Rhodes, and from there to Patara. ² And having found *a* ship crossing-over to Phoenicia, having boarded, we put-to-sea. ³ And having sighted Cyprus, and having left it behind on the left, we were sailing to Syria. And we came down to Tyre, for there the ship was unloading *its* cargo. ⁴ And having found the disciples, we stayed there seven days— who were telling Paul through the Spirit not to be setting-foot in Jerusalem. ⁵ But when it came about *that* we finished the days, having gone out, we were proceeding—everyone accompanying us, with wives and children, as far as outside the city. And having put *down our* knees on the beach, having prayed, ⁶ we said-farewell to one another. And we went-up into the ship, and those *ones* returned to *their* own *things.*

When Paul Arrives In Caesarea, Agabas The Prophet Foretells Imprisonment
⁷ And **we,** having completed^B the voyage from Tyre, arrived in Ptolemais. And having greeted the brothers, we stayed with them one day. ⁸ And having gone-out *on* the next day, we came to Caesarea. And having entered into the house *of* Philip the evangelist (being *one* of the seven^C), we stayed with him ⁹ (and this *one* had four virgin daughters prophesying!). ¹⁰ And while *we were* staying-on *for* more days, *a* certain prophet from Judea, Agabus *by* name, came down. ¹¹ And having come to us, and having taken Paul's belt, having bound his *own* feet and hands, he said, "These *things* says the Holy Spirit: 'In this manner the Jews in Jerusalem will bind the man whose belt this is, and hand *him* over into *the* hands *of the* Gentiles' ". ¹² And when we heard these *things*, both we and the local-residents were begging *that* he not be going up to Jerusalem. ¹³ Then Paul responded, "What are you doing, weeping and breaking my heart? For **I** am ready not only to be bound, but even to die in Jerusalem for the name *of* the Lord Jesus". ¹⁴ And he not being persuaded, we were quiet, having said, "Let the Lord's will be done".

Paul Arrives In Jerusalem
¹⁵ And after these days, having made-preparations, we were going up to Jerusalem. ¹⁶ And *some of* the disciples from Caesarea also came with us, bringing^D *us to* Mnason— *a* certain Cyprian, *an* old disciple, with whom we might lodge. ¹⁷ And we having come-to-be in Jerusalem, the brothers welcomed us gladly.

Paul Meets James. They Formulate a Plan For His Acceptance Among The Jews
¹⁸ And *on* the following *day* Paul was going in with us to James, and all the elders were present. ¹⁹ And having greeted them, he was describing individually each *of the things* which God did among the Gentiles through his ministry. ²⁰ And the *ones,* having heard *it,* were glorifying God. And they said *to* him, "You see, brother, how many myriads *of* the *ones* having believed there are among the Jews! And they are all

---

A. Or, been parted. **B.** Or, continued. **C.** That is, the seven chosen in 6:5. **D.** Or, bringing Mnason *with them.*

zealots[A] *for* the Law. **21** And they were informed about you— that you are teaching all the Jews[B] throughout the nations **apostasy** from Moses, saying *that* they *should* not be circumcising *their* children, nor walking in *their* customs. **22** What, then, is *to be done*? They will surely hear that you have come. **23** Therefore do this which we tell you: There are four men *with* us having *a* vow upon themselves. **24** Having taken along these *men*, be purified together-with them. And spend[C] *money* for them, so that they will shave[D] the head. And everyone will know that there is nothing *true of the things* which they have been informed about you, but even you yourself are walking-in-line[E], keeping the Law. **25** But concerning the Gentiles having believed— **we** wrote-to *them,* having determined *that* they *should* guard-*themselves as to* food-sacrificed-to-an-idol and blood and *the* strangled *thing* and sexual immorality".

While Executing The Plan, Paul Is Recognized By Ephesian Jews And Attacked
26 Then Paul— having taken along the men *on* the next *day*, having been purified together-with them— was going into the temple, giving-notice *as to* the completion *of* the days *of* purification, until which *time* the offering was offered for each one *of* them. **27** But as the seven days were about to be completed, the Jews from Asia[F], having seen him in the temple, were stirring-up the whole crowd. And they put *their* hands on him, **28** crying-out, "Men, Israelites, help! This is the man teaching everyone everywhere against *our* people and the Law and this place. And furthermore, he also brought Greeks into the temple, and has defiled this holy place". **29** For they had previously-seen Trophimus the Ephesian in the city with him, whom they were supposing that Paul brought into the temple. **30** And the whole city was set-in-motion, and *a* running-together *of* the people took place. And having taken-hold-of Paul, they were dragging him outside *of* the temple. And immediately the doors were shut.

The Romans Swoop Down And Take Paul Into Custody
31 And while *they were* seeking to kill him, *a* report went up *to* the commander[G] *of* the [Roman] cohort[H] that all Jerusalem was stirred-up— **32** who at-once, having taken along soldiers and centurions[I], ran down upon them. And the *ones*, having seen the commander and the soldiers, ceased striking Paul. **33** Then having drawn-near, the commander took-hold-of him. And he ordered *that he* be bound *with* two chains. And he was inquiring *as to* who he might be and what he has done. **34** But other[J] *ones* in the crowd were calling-out another thing. And he not being able to know the certainty *of it* because of the uproar— he ordered *that* he be brought into the barracks. **35** But when he[K] came-to-be on the stairs, it happened *that* he was carried by the soldiers because of the violence *of* the crowd— **36** for the multitude *of* the people were following, crying-out, "Take him away".

A. That is, these Jewish believers are zealously holding on to their Jewish way of life derived from the Law. **B.** That is, the Jewish believers to whom Paul had ministered. These in Jerusalem did not object to Paul teaching the Gentile believers in the manner described next, but to his teaching the Jewish believers to abandon their Jewish customs. **C.** That is, pay their expenses. This was perceived as a good deed for a Jew. **D.** These four would cut off their hair upon completion of their vow, as Paul did in 18:18. **E.** That is, with his Jewish heritage. **F.** The plan may have worked with the local Jewish Christians, but when these Jews from Asia (Ephesus) aroused the Jews against Paul, the believers could do nothing. **G.** Or, tribune, a commander of 600-1000 men, to whom centurions reported. He reported to the procurator, who for this man was Felix (23:24). **H.** See Mt 27:27. **I.** That is, commanders of 100 men. **J.** The one with whom the commander was inquiring was saying one thing, but others in the crowd were shouting different things. **K.** That is, Paul.

Paul Asks To Speak To The Mob
37 And being about to be brought into the barracks, Paul says *to* the commander, "Is it permissible *for* me to say something to you?" And the *one* said, "You know Greek? **38** Then are **you** not the Egyptian— the *one* before these days having caused-an-upset^A and led out into the wilderness the four-thousand men *of* the Assassins^B?" **39** And Paul said, "**I** am *a* Jewish man from-Tarsus^C *of* Cilicia, *a* citizen *of* no insignificant city— and I beg you, permit me to speak to the people". **40** And he having permitted *it*, Paul, standing on the stairs, motioned *with his* hand *to* the people. And *a* great silence having come about, he addressed *them in* the Hebrew language, saying: **22:1** "Men, brothers, and fathers, hear my defense to you now". **2** And having heard that he was addressing them *in* the Hebrew language, they granted more quietness.

I Am a Jew Trained By Gamaliel, And Was Zealously Persecuting The Church
And he says, **3** "**I** am *a* Jewish man, having been born in Tarsus *of* Cilicia, but having been brought-up in this city; having been trained at the feet *of* Gamaliel^D in accordance with *the* strictness^E *of* the Law *of* ^F *my* ancestor^G; being *a* zealot *for* God just as **you** all are today— **4** who persecuted this Way to the point *of* death, binding and handing-over both men and women to prisons, **5** as indeed the high priest testifies *concerning* me, and the whole Council-of-elders, from whom also having received letters to the brothers, I was proceeding to Damascus *to* bring bound to Jerusalem even the *ones* being there, in order that they might be punished.

On The Way To Damascus For This Purpose, Jesus Spoke To Me And Blinded Me
6 "But it came about *in* my proceeding and drawing-near *to* Damascus about mid-day, *that* suddenly *a* great light from heaven flashed around me. **7** And I fell to the ground, and heard *a* voice saying *to* me, 'Saul, Saul, why are you persecuting Me?' **8** And **I** answered, 'Who are You, sir^H?' And He said to me, '**I** am Jesus the Nazarene, Whom **you** are persecuting'. **9** And the *ones* being with me saw the light, but did not hear^I the voice *of* the One speaking *to* me. **10** And I said, 'What shall I do, Lord?' And the Lord said to me, 'Having arisen, proceed into Damascus. And there it will be told you concerning everything which has been assigned^J *to* you to do'. **11** But since I was not seeing because of the glory *of* that light, I came into Damascus being hand-led by the *ones* being with me.

Ananias Restored My Sight And Said God Appointed Me To Be His Witness
12 "And *a* certain Ananias— *a* reverent man in-relation-to the Law, being attested by all the Jews dwelling *there*, **13** having come to me and having stood near— said *to* me, 'Brother Saul, see again'. And **I** looked-up at him *at* the very hour. **14** And the *one* said, the God *of* our fathers appointed^K you to know His will, and to see the Righteous *One* and hear *a* voice from His mouth, **15** because you will be *a* witness *for* Him to all people *of the things* which you have seen and *which*

A. Or, caused-a-revolt. **B.** Or, the Sicarii. This was a Jewish nationalist group that used assassination against their political opponents. **C.** Tarsus was the capital city of the province of Cilicia. **D.** This was a famous and respected rabbi, mentioned also in 5:34. **E.** Or, exactness, accurateness. **F.** That is, handed down from. **G.** Paul's father was a Pharisee, 23:6. **H.** See 9:5. **I.** That is, understand. **J.** Or, appointed. **K.** Or, selected, chose.

you heard. **16** And now, why are you delaying? Having arisen, be baptized, and wash-away your sins, having called-upon His name'.

In a Vision At The Temple, God Said He Was Sending Me To The Gentiles
17 "And it came about *at* my having returned to Jerusalem, and while I *was* praying in the temple, *that* I came-to-be in *a* trance **18** and saw Him saying *to* me, 'Hurry, and go out from Jerusalem quickly, because they will not accept your testimony about Me'. **19** And I said, 'Lord, they themselves know that throughout the synagogues I was imprisoning and beating the *ones* putting-faith upon You. **20** And when the blood *of* Stephen Your witness was being shed, I myself also was standing-near and giving-approval and guarding the garments *of* the *ones* killing him'. **21** And He said to me, 'Be going, because I will send you out far away to *the* Gentiles' ".

At The Mention of Gentiles, The Mob Erupts. The Romans Take Paul Away
22 And they were listening-to him up to this statement. And they raised their voice, saying, "Take away such *a one* from the earth, for it was^A not proper *that* he *continue-living*". **23** And while they *were* shouting and throwing-off *their* cloaks and throwing dust into the air, **24** the commander ordered *that* he be brought into the barracks—having said *that* he *should* be interrogated with whips in order that he might learn for what reason they were calling-out *against* him in this manner. **25** But when they stretched him out *with*^B the straps^C, Paul said to the centurion standing *there*, "Is it lawful^D *for* you to whip *a* man *who is a* Roman and uncondemned?" **26** And having heard *it*, the centurion, having gone to the commander, reported, saying, "What are you about to do? For this man is *a* Roman". **27** And having gone to *him*, the commander said *to* him, "Tell me, are **you** *a* Roman?" And the *one* said, "Yes". **28** And the commander responded, "**I** acquired this citizenship *with a* large sum [of money]". And Paul said, "But **I** indeed have been born *one*". **29** So the *ones* being about to interrogate him **immediately** withdrew from him. And the commander also became afraid, having learned that he was *a* Roman, and because he had bound him.

The Romans Take Paul Before The Sanhedrin
30 And *on* the next day, wanting to know the certainty *as to* why he was being accused by the Jews, he released^E him and ordered the chief priests and the whole Sanhedrin to come together. And having brought Paul down, he stood *him* before them. **23:1** And Paul, having looked-intently *at* the Sanhedrin, said, "Men, brothers, I have conducted-*myself*^F *with* all good conscience *before* God up to this day". **2** And the high priest Ananias^G commanded the *ones* standing near him to strike his mouth. **3** Then Paul said to him, "God is going to **strike** you— whitewashed wall! Do **You** indeed sit *there* judging me according to the Law, and violating-the-Law, order *that* I be struck?" **4** And the *ones* standing near said, "Are you reviling the high priest *of* God?" **5** And Paul said, "I did not know, brothers, that he was high priest. For it has been written [in Ex 22:28] that 'You shall not speak badly *of a* ruler *of* your people' ".

A. In other words, he should have been killed when he first turned to Christ. **B.** Or, *for*. **C.** This word could refer to the bindings or to the whip. **D.** It was not lawful to treat a Roman citizen in this way. **E.** Or, unbound. **F.** Or, conducted-*my*-citizenship. **G.** He was high priest from A.D. 47-58.

Paul Divides The Assembly Over The Question of The Resurrection
6 And Paul, having known that the one part *of them* was *of* Sadducees and the other *of* Pharisees, was crying-out in the Sanhedrin, "Men, brothers, I am *a* Pharisee, *a* son *of* Pharisees. I am being judged concerning *the* hope^A and resurrection *of the* dead". **7** And he having said this, *a* dispute *between* the Pharisees and Sadducees took place, and the assembly was divided. **8** For Sadducees say *that* there is not *a* resurrection, nor *an* angel, nor *a* spirit— but Pharisees confess all^B *three.* **9** And *a* great clamor took place. And having stood up, some *of* the scribes *of* the Pharisees' part were battling, saying, "We are finding no evil in this man. And *what* if *a* spirit did speak *to* him, or *an* angel?"

The Romans Take Paul Away
10 And while *a* great dispute *was* taking place, the commander— having feared that Paul might be torn-to-pieces by them— ordered the troop^C, having gone down, to snatch him out of *the* midst *of* them and bring *him* to the barracks.

That Night The Lord Appears To Paul And Says He Will Also Testify In Rome
11 And *on* the following^D night, the Lord, having stood near him, said, "Take-courage. For as you solemnly-testified in Jerusalem *as to* the *things* concerning Me, so you must also testify in Rome".

The Next Day, Over 40 Jews Swear an Oath To Kill Paul, And Hatch a Plot
12 And having become day, the Jews, having held *a* gathering, bound themselves under-a-curse, saying *that they would* neither eat nor drink until which *time* they killed Paul. **13** Now there were more *than* forty having made^E this sworn-pact— **14** who, having gone to the chief priests and the elders, said, "*With a* curse^F, we bound ourselves under-a-curse to eat nothing until which *time* we kill Paul. **15** Now therefore, **you,** along with the Sanhedrin, notify the commander so that he may bring him down to you, as-*though you are* intending to determine the *things* concerning him more accurately. And **we** are prepared *that we might* kill him before he draws-near".

Paul's Nephew Hears of The Plot, And Informs The Roman Commander
16 But the son *of* the sister *of* Paul— having heard-*of* the ambush, having come and entered into the barracks— reported *it to* Paul. **17** And Paul, having summoned one *of* the centurions, said, "Lead this young-man away to the commander, for he has something to report *to* him". **18** So indeed the *one,* having taken him along, led *him* to the commander. And he says, "Paul the prisoner, having summoned me, asked *that I* lead this young man to you— *he* having something to tell you". **19** And the commander— having taken-hold-of his hand, and having withdrawn privately— was asking, "What is it that you have to report *to* me?" **20** And he said that "The Jews agreed to ask you so that tomorrow you might bring Paul down to the Sanhedrin, as-*though* intending to inquire

---

A. That is, the hope for and resurrection of the dead. Or, *our* hope— even *the* resurrection. **B.** Or, both, if 'nor *an* angel nor *a* spirit' is viewed as one thing. **C.** Or, squad, detachment. **D.** In other words, that night; the night following the day mentioned in 22:30. **E.** Or, formed this conspiracy. **F:** *With a* curse... under-a-curse. This a a Hebrew way of speaking, meaning 'We bound ourselves under a solemn curse'. They said 'May God curse us if we eat before we kill Paul'.

something more accurately concerning him. **21** So don't **you** be persuaded *by* them. For more *than* forty men from-*among* them are lying-in-wait-for him who bound themselves under-a-curse neither to eat nor drink until which *time* they kill him. And now they are prepared, waiting-for the promise^A from you".

The Roman Commander Makes Arrangements To Send Paul To Caesarea
22 Then indeed the commander sent away the young-man, having commanded *him* to tell no one "that you revealed^B these *things* to me". **23** And having summoned *a* certain two *of* the centurions, he said, "Prepare two-hundred soldiers and seventy horsemen and two-hundred spearmen^C so that they may proceed to Caesarea at *the* third^D hour *of* the night"; **24** and *that they should* provide mounts in order that having put-on Paul, they might bring *him* safely through to Felix^E the governor, **25** *he* having written *a* letter having this form:
     26 "Claudius Lysias, *to* the most-excellent governor Felix: Greetings. **27** I rescued this man having been seized by the Jews and being about to be killed by them, having come-suddenly-upon *them* with the troop— having learned that he was *a* Roman^F. **28** And wanting to know the reason for which they were accusing him, I brought *him* down to their Sanhedrin— **29** whom I found being accused about issues *of* their Law, but having no accusation^G worthy *of* death or imprisonment. **30** And *a* plot having been disclosed *to* me *that* would be against the man, I sent *him* to you at once, having also ordered *his* accusers to speak the *things* against him before you".

Roman Soldiers Take Paul To Caesarea, Where He Awaits The Arrival of His Accusers
31 So indeed the soldiers, in accordance with the *thing* having been commanded them, having picked-up Paul, brought *him* during *the* night to Antipatris. **32** And *on* the next day, they^H returned to the barracks, having let the horsemen depart with him— **33** who, having entered into Caesarea, and having delivered the letter *to* the governor, presented Paul *to* him also. **34** And having read *it*, and having asked from what province he was, and having learned that *he was* from Cilicia, **35** he said, "I will give you a hearing whenever your accusers also arrive"— having ordered *that* he be guarded in the Praetorium^I *of* Herod.

Paul Is Accused Before Felix The Roman Governor By The High Priest And Others
24:1 And after five days, the high priest Ananias came down with some elders and *an* attorney^J, *a* certain Tertullus— who^K brought-charges against Paul *to* the governor. **2** And he^L having been called, Tertullus began to accuse *him*, saying, "Attaining much^M peace through you, and reforms taking place *for* this nation through your foresight **3** both^N in every way and everywhere— we welcome *it*, most-excellent

---

A. That is, the promise to bring Paul at a certain time. **B.** Or, gave-notice-of. **C.** Or, slingers, bowmen. The precise meaning of this military term is not certain. **D.** That is, 9 P.M. **E.** After the death of King Herod Agrippa I (Act 12:1), the Roman emperor Claudius (Act 18:2) put Judea under the control of a Roman procurator (similar to the prefects like Pilate). Felix was the fourth, and ruled from A.D. 52-59. **F.** Lysias gives himself the higher motive (rescuing a Roman citizen) rather than his actual motive (maintaining order; doing his duty), omitting the messy details. **G.** Or, charge. **H.** That is, the walking soldiers; the bulk of the detachment. **I.** That is, governor's headquarters or palace in Caesarea. **J.** Or, advocate. That is, a lawyer in the Roman sense who could skillfully argue their case. **K.** This word is plural, referring to them all. **L.** That is, Paul. **M.** Or, *a* long. **N.** Punctuated this way, Tertullus is exaggerating Felix's accomplishments. Or, foresight. We welcome *it* both in every way and everywhere, most. This exaggerates the Jews' submission to and appreciation of Felix.

Felix, with all thankfulness. **4** But in order that I may not hinder you further, I beg you to hear us briefly, *by* your kindness. **5** For having found this man *to be a* plague^A, and setting-in-motion disputes^B *among* all the Jews throughout the world, and *a* ringleader *of* the sect *of* the Nazarenes, **6** who even tried to profane^C the temple, whom also we seized—^D ^7 ^E **8** from whom you yourself, having examined *him*, will be able to learn about all these *things of* which **we** are accusing him". **9** And the Jews also joined-in-the-attack, asserting *that* these *things* hold so.

Paul Defends Himself Against Their Charges
10 And Paul responded, the governor having nodded *to* him to speak, "Knowing-about you being *a* judge^F *to* this nation for many years, I cheerfully speak-a-defense *as to* the *things* concerning myself— **11** you being able to learn that it is not more than twelve days from which *day* I went up to Jerusalem *to* worship. **12** And neither in the temple did they find me arguing with anyone or causing *an* onset *of a* crowd— nor in the synagogues, nor throughout the city! **13** Nor are they able to prove *to* you *the things* concerning which they now are accusing me. **14** But I confess this *to* you— that according to the Way which they call *a* sect, thus I am worshiping^G the God *of my* ancestor^H, believing all the *things* in accordance with the Law, and the *things* having been written in the Prophets, **15** having *a* hope in God which these *ones* themselves also are waiting-for^I— that there will-certainly be *a* resurrection *of* both righteous *ones* and unrighteous *ones*. **16** In this^J indeed **I** am striving to have *a* blameless conscience toward God and people continually. **17** Now after many years I came *to* do acts-of-almsgiving^K for my nation, and offerings, **18** during which they found me in the temple, having been purified^L— not with *a* crowd, nor with *a* commotion. **19** But *there were* some Jews from Asia— who ought-to-have been present before you and accusing *me*, if they have something against me. **20** Or let these *ones* themselves say what crime they found, I having stood before the Sanhedrin— **21** other-than concerning this one shout which I cried-out while standing among them, that 'I am being judged before you today concerning *the* resurrection *of the* dead' ".

Felix Adjourns The Hearing, But Keeps Paul In Relaxed Custody
22 And Felix adjourned^M them, knowing more-accurately the *things* concerning the Way, having said, "Whenever Lysias the commander comes down, I will determine^N the *things* concerning you^O *people*", **23** having given-orders *to* the centurion *that* he be kept [in custody] and *that he* have *a* relaxation^P [of custody] and *that they* forbid none *of* his own *people* to serve him.

A. That is, a public menace, a diseased one threatening our society. **B.** Or more strongly, riots. **C.** Tertullus is referring to 21:28-29. If he could prove this, Felix would execute Paul. **D.** Tertullus stops short of expressing their demand, leaving it to Felix to determine the penalty for himself. **E.** Some manuscripts say 'seized. And we wanted to judge *him* according to our Law. But having arrived, Lysias the commander led *him* away from our hands with much violence, having commanded his accusers to come before you, from whom'. **F.** That is, one administering justice. **G.** Or, serving. **H.** Paul is linking himself and the Way to historic Judaism, which had the protection of Roman law. **I.** Or, accepting. **J.** That is, this way of worshiping and serving. **K.** That is, acts of charity. This may refer to the gift brought from the Gentile churches, Rom 15:26. **L.** That is, in obedience to its laws, not in violation of them. **M.** Or, deferred, postponed. **N.** Or, decide. **O.** This word is plural. **P.** Or, loosening, abatement. That is, that Paul have a measure of freedom within his confinement, in deference to his Roman citizenship.

Paul Frequently Speaks To Felix, Who Hopes To Get Money From Paul

24 And after some days, Felix, having arrived with Drusilla[A] *his* own wife (*she* being *a* Jew), sent for Paul and listened-to him concerning faith in Christ Jesus. **25** But while he *was* speaking about righteousness, self-control and the coming judgment, Felix, having become afraid, responded, "*As to* the present, go. And having received *an* opportunity, I will summon you"— **26** at the same time also hoping that money would be given *to* him by Paul. Therefore indeed, sending for him very-frequently, he was conversing *with* him.

Two Years Later, Paul Is Accused Before The New Governor, Festus

27 Now two years[B] having been fulfilled, Felix received *a* successor— Porcius Festus[C]. And wishing to gain[D] favor *with* the Jews, Felix left Paul bound. **25:1** So Festus, having set-foot *in* the province, went up after three days to Jerusalem from Caesarea. **2** And the chief priests and the leading *ones of the* Jews brought-charges *to* him against Paul. And they were appealing-to him, **3** asking-*for a* favor against him, so that he might summon him to Jerusalem— while making *an* ambush to kill him along the way. **4** Then indeed Festus responded *that* Paul *was* being kept in Caesarea, and *that he* himself *was* about to be proceeding-out [of Jerusalem] shortly. **5** "So", he says, "the powerful *ones* among you having gone-down-with *me*— if there is something out-of-place in the man, let them be accusing him *there*". **6** And having spent days among them (not more *than* eight or ten), having come down to Caesarea, having sat on the judgment-seat *on* the next day, he ordered *that* Paul be brought.

When Festus Suggests a Trial In Jerusalem, Paul Appeals To Caesar

7 And he having arrived, the Jews having come down from Jerusalem stood around him bringing many and weighty charges against *him,* which they were not able to prove— **8** Paul speaking-in-defense that "Neither against the Law *of* the Jews, nor against the temple, nor against Caesar, did I sin anything". **9** But Festus, wishing to gain favor *with* the Jews, having responded *to* Paul, said, "Are you willing, having gone up to Jerusalem, to be judged there before me concerning these *things*?" **10** And Paul said, "I am standing *here* before the judgment-seat *of* Caesar, where I ought-to be judged. I did *the* Jews no wrong, as **you** also are knowing very well. **11** So if I am doing wrong[E] and have committed something worthy *of* death, I am not refusing to die. But if *the things of* which these *ones* are accusing me are nothing, no one is able[F] to freely-give me *to* them. I appeal-to Caesar[G]". **12** Then Festus, having talked-with *his* council, responded, "You have appealed-to Caesar— you will go before Caesar".

A. She was the daughter of Agrippa I (12:1), and sister of Agrippa II and Bernice (25:13). **B.** During this period, Luke gathered the information to write (and may have written) Luke and much of Acts. See also 28:30. **C.** He was the fifth procurator of Judea, serving from A.D. 59-62. He was appointed by the emperor Nero. **D.** Or, grant *a* favor *to*. Having been recalled to Rome regarding another incident, Felix wanted no further problems following him there, as might have happened if he had released Paul. **E.** That is, against Roman law. Paul is being held for political, not legal purposes. **F.** That is, under Roman law. **G.** This was the right of every Roman citizen in a capital case. The Caesar in view here is Nero, who was emperor from A.D. 54-68.

King Agrippa Arrives In Caesarea And Asks To Hear From Paul
13 Now some days having passed, Agrippa^A the king and Bernice^B arrived in Caesarea, having greeted^C Festus. **14** And while they were spending more days there, Festus laid-before the king the *things* concerning Paul, saying, "*A* certain man has been left-behind by Felix *as a* prisoner, **15** concerning whom— I having come-to-be in Jerusalem— the chief priests and the elders *of* the Jews brought-charges, asking-*for a* sentence-of-condemnation against him, **16** to whom I responded that it is not *a* custom *with* Romans to freely-give any person^D before the *one* being accused should have *his* accusers face-to-face, and should receive *a* place^E *for a* defense concerning the accusation. **17** So they having come-with^F *me* here— *I* having made no delay, having sat on the judgment-seat *on* the next *day*— I ordered *that* the man be brought, **18** concerning whom, the accusers having stood were bringing no charge *of the* evil^G *things* which **I** was supposing^H, **19** but were having certain issues with him concerning *their* own religion and concerning *a* certain Jesus having died, whom Paul was asserting^I to be alive. **20** And **I**, being perplexed *as to* the investigation concerning these *things*, was saying whether he might be willing to go to Jerusalem, and there be judged concerning these *things.* **21** But Paul having appealed *that* he be kept for the decision *of* the Emperor, I ordered *that* he *continue*-being-kept [in custody] until which *time* I might send him up to Caesar". **22** And Agrippa *says* to Festus, "I myself also was wanting^J to hear the man". "Tomorrow", he says, "you will hear him".

Festus Introduces Paul, Hoping To Learn Something To Write To Caesar
23 So *on* the next day, Agrippa and Bernice having come with great pageantry, and having entered into the auditorium with both commanders^K and prominent men *of* the city, and Festus having given-orders— Paul was brought. **24** And Festus says, "King Agrippa, and all the men being present-with us— you see this *one* concerning whom the whole assembly *of* the Jews appealed *to* me, both in Jerusalem and here, shouting *that* he ought not to live any longer, **25** but **I** found-out *that* he had committed nothing worthy *of* death. And this *one* himself having appealed-to the Emperor, I determined to send *him*— **26** concerning whom, I do not have something certain to write *to my* lord. Therefore I brought him before you, and especially before you King Agrippa, so that the examination having taken place, I may have something I may write. **27** For it seems unreasonable *to* me, while sending *a* prisoner, not also to signify the charges against him". **26:1** And Agrippa said to Paul, "It is permitted *to* you to speak concerning yourself ".

Paul Says He Is Being Judged For His View of The Promise All Israel Awaits
Then Paul, having stretched-out *his* hand, was speaking-a-defense: **2** "King Agrippa, I regard myself fortunate— being about to speak-a-defense before you today concerning everything *of* which I am being accused by *the* Jews, **3** especially

A. That is, Agrippa II, son of Herod Agrippa I (12:1). His Roman name was Marcus Julius Agrippa. His capital was Caesarea Philippi, which he renamed Neronias. He ruled much of the territory in the region, but not Judea (although he did appoint the high priests), until about A.D. 100. **B.** She was the sister of Agrippa II and Drusilla (24:24). **C.** Or, greeting. Agrippa probably came from Neronias to Caesarea to welcome Festus to his new post. **D.** That is, Roman person, Roman citizen. **E.** That is, a place in the process; an opportunity. **F.** Or, come-together, assembled. **G.** Or more specifically, crimes. **H.** Or, suspecting. **I.** Or, claiming. **J.** Or, *would* wish to hear. **K.** Or, tribunes. There were five cohorts in Caesarea, each led by a tribune.

you being[A] *an* expert *of* all *of* both the customs and issues in relation to *the* Jews. Therefore I beg *that you* listen-to me patiently. **4** Indeed then, all the Jews know my manner-of-life from youth— *it* having taken place from *the* first in my nation and in Jerusalem, **5** *they* knowing me beforehand[B] from-the-beginning if they are willing to testify— that I lived *as a* Pharisee in accordance with the strictest sect *of* our religion. **6** And now I am standing *here* being judged for *the* hope *of* the promise having been made by God to our fathers, **7** to which our twelve tribes are hoping to attain while worshiping night and day with fervency[C]!— concerning which hope I am being accused by *the* Jews, King. **8** Why is it being judged unbelievable[D] among you[E] *people* if God raises *the* dead?

At First I Persecuted This Name. Then Jesus Spoke To Me and Sent Me
9 "So indeed[F], I thought *to* myself *that I* ought-to do many *things* contrary[G] to the name *of* Jesus the Nazarene— **10** which indeed I did in Jerusalem. And I both locked-up many *of* the saints in prisons, having received the authority from the chief priests, and while they *were* being killed[H], cast *my* vote against *them.* **11** And while punishing them often throughout all the synagogues, I was compelling[I] *them* to blaspheme. And being exceedingly enraged *at* them, I was persecuting *them* as far as even to the outside cities— **12** during which, while proceeding to Damascus with authority and *a* commission *from* the chief priests, **13** *in the* middle *of the* day along the road, King, I saw *a* **light** from heaven beyond the brightness *of* the sun, having shined-around me and the *ones* going with me. **14** And we all having fallen down to the ground, I heard *a* voice saying to me *in* the Hebrew language, 'Saul, Saul, why are you persecuting Me? *It is* hard *for* you to kick[J] against *the* goads'. **15** And I said, 'Who are You, sir?' And the Lord said, '**I** am Jesus Whom **you** are persecuting. **16** But arise and stand on your feet. For I appeared *to* you for this— to appoint you *as a* servant, and *a* witness both *of* which *things* you saw *as to* Me and *of* which *things* I shall be seen *by* you **17** while rescuing you from the [Jewish] people, and from the Gentiles— to whom **I** am sending you forth **18** to open their eyes *that they may* turn from darkness to light and *from* the authority *of* Satan to God, *that* they *may* receive forgiveness *of* sins and *a* share among the *ones* having been sanctified *by* faith in Me'.

So I Proclaimed His Message To The Gentiles, And The Jews Want Me Dead
19 "Hence, King Agrippa, I did not become[K] disobedient *to* the heavenly vision, **20** but was declaring *to* the *ones* both in Damascus first and *in* Jerusalem, and *throughout* all the country *of* Judea, and *to* the Gentiles *that* they *should* repent and turn to God, doing works worthy *of* repentance. **21** For these reasons*,* Jews, having seized me while being in the temple, were trying

---

A. Or, you being especially. **B.** That is, before this incident. **C.** Or, earnestness. **D.** Or, not-believable. **E.** This word is plural, referring to the audience, or meaning 'you *Jews*'. **F.** Having summarized his case in v 6-8, Paul now resumes from v 5 with the details. **G.** Or, opposed, hostile. **H.** That is, in mob actions like Stephen's case, not legal executions through Rome. **I.** That is, *trying to* compel; or, *repeatedly* compelling. **J.** That is, to resist the divine force pricking your heart. Paul tells us what only Saul knew. **K.** Or, prove to be.

to murder *me*. **22** Therefore, having obtained help from God, I stand to this day[A] bearing-witness *to* both small and great, saying nothing outside *of the things* which both the Prophets and Moses spoke *about things* going to take place— **23** whether[B] the Christ *is* subject-to-suffering[C]; whether He first[D] from[E] *a* resurrection *from the* dead is going to proclaim light both *to* the [Jewish] people and *to* the Gentiles".

Festus Says Paul Has Gone Mad. Paul Makes a Personal Appeal To King Agrippa
24 And while he *was* speaking these *things* in *his* defense, Festus says *in a* loud voice, "You are mad[F], Paul. Great[G] learning is turning **you** to madness". **25** But Paul says, "I am not mad, most-excellent Festus, but I am declaring[H] words *of* truth and *of* sound-mindedness. **26** For the king knows about these *things*— to whom indeed I am speaking while speaking-openly. For I am in no way persuaded *that* any *of* these *things* escape-notice-of him, for this has not been done in *a* corner. **27** King Agrippa, do you believe the Prophets? I know that you believe". **28** And Agrippa *says* to Paul, "In *a* short[I] *time*, are you persuading me *so as* to make *me a* Christian?" **29** And Paul *says*, "I would pray *to* God *that* both in *a* short *time* and in *a* long *time*[J], not only you, but also all the *ones* hearing me today *might* become such *ones* of-what-sort **I** also am— except for these[K] bonds". **30** And the king stood up, and the governor; and Bernice and the *ones* sitting with them. **31** And having gone-away, they were speaking to one another, saying that "This man is in no way doing anything worthy *of* death or imprisonment". **32** And Agrippa said *to* Festus, "This man could have been released if he had not appealed-to Caesar".

Paul Is Put On a Ship Under Guard For The Voyage To Rome
27:1 And when it was determined *that* we[L] *should* sail-away to Italy, they were handing-over both Paul and some other prisoners *to a* centurion *of the* Imperial[M] cohort, Julius *by* name. **2** And having boarded *an* Adramyttian[N] ship being about to sail to the places along [the coast of] Asia, we put-to-sea— Aristarchus, *a* Macedonian *of* Thessalonica, being with us. **3** And *on* another *day* we put in at Sidon. And Julius, having treated Paul humanely, permitted *him* to obtain care[O], having gone to *his* friends. **4** And from there, having put-to-sea, we sailed-under-*the-shelter*[P]-*of* Cyprus because of the winds being contrary. **5** And having sailed-through the open-sea along Cilicia and Pamphylia, we came down to Myra *of* Lycia. **6** And there the centurion, having found *an* Alexandrian ship sailing to Italy, put us on board in it. **7** And in many[Q] days, sailing-slowly and with-

---

A. Or, help from God to this day, I stand *here* bearing-witness. **B.** Or, if. Paul presents these two issues as questions to be considered based on the Scripture. These two subjects are the same two mentioned by Jesus in Lk 24:46. **C.** That is, whether the Scripture teaches that Messiah is capable of suffering, as opposed to being a conquering king reigning in glory forever. **D.** That is, first before He comes in glory; or, first before others, whether He, *the* first *One* from. **E.** Or, by. **F.** Or, raving, out of your mind. **G.** Or, Much. **H.** Or, uttering, as in 2:4. **I.** Or, With *a* little *effort*, In *a* little *while*, With *a* brief *speech*. In addition, this may be a question, In [such] *a* short *time*?; or, an exclamation, In *a* short *time* [longer]! **J.** Or, With *a* little *effort* and with *a* great *effort*; with *a* brief *speech* and with *a* long *speech*. **K.** Or, this imprisonment. **L.** Luke was last included in 21:18. **M.** Or, Augustan. That is, the cohort performing duties for the emperor. **N.** That is, from the seaport town of Adramyttium, near Troas. **O.** Or, attention. Medical care, personal refreshment, or spiritual fellowship may be in view. This does not imply Paul was unaccompanied by a guard. **P.** Or, *lee-of*. **Q.** With favorable winds, the trip from Myra to Cnidus would have taken one day.

difficulty, having come-to-be off Cnidus[A]— the wind not permitting us to go farther[B]—
we sailed-under-*the-shelter-of* Crete off Salmone. [8] And sailing-along it[C] with-difficulty,
we came to *a* certain place being called Fair Havens, near *to* which was *the* city Lasea.
[9] And *a* considerable time having passed, and the voyage being already dangerous[D]
because even the Fast[E] *had* passed-by already, Paul was advising, [10] saying *to* them, "Men,
I perceive[F] that the voyage will-certainly be with damage[G] and great loss— not only *of*
the cargo and the ship, but also *of* our lives". [11] But the centurion was being persuaded
more *by* the helmsman and the captain than *by* the *things* being said by Paul. [12] And the
harbor being unsuitable for wintering, the majority made *a* plan[H] to put-to-sea from
there— if somehow they might be able to spend-the-winter having attained to Phoenix[I],
a harbor *of* Crete looking toward *the* southwest and toward *the* northwest.

A Severe Storm Catches The Ship

[13] Now *a* south-*wind* [J] having blown-moderately— having supposed *that they* had
taken-hold-of *their* purpose, having lifted *anchor*, they were sailing-along very-near
Crete. [14] But after not much *time a* violent[K] wind rushed down *from* it[L], the *one* being
called the "Northeaster[M]". [15] And the ship having been seized and not being able to
face-into the wind, we were being carried-along, having given *ourselves* up *to it.*
[16] And having run-under-*the-shelter-of a* certain small-island being called Cauda[N], we
were able with-difficulty to come-to-be in-control *of* the [ship's] boat[O]— [17] having
lifted which, they were using supports[P], undergirding the ship. And fearing that they
might run-aground at Syrtis[Q], having lowered[R] the gear, in this manner they were
being carried-along. [18] And we being violently storm-tossed, *on* the next *day* they
were doing *a* jettison. [19] And *on* the third *day* they threw-off the equipment *of* the
ship with-*their*-own-hands. [20] And neither sun nor stars appearing[S] for many days,
and no small storm lying-upon[T] us, finally all hope *that* we *might* be saved was being
taken-away[U]. [21] And much[V] abstinence-from-food[W] being present, at that time Paul,
having stood in their midst, said, "O men, having obeyed me, *you* indeed should-
have not put-to-sea from Crete and gained[X] this damage and loss. [22] And *as to* the
things now, I advise *that* you cheer-up. For there will be no loss *of* life from-*among*

A. This town is on the southwest extremity of modern Turkey. **B.** That is, farther north and west toward Italy.
Instead they turn south to Crete. **C.** That is, the south side of Crete. **D.** Or, prone-to-fail. **E.** That is, the fast on
the Day of Atonement at the end of September or early October, the only fast commanded by the Law. The
Mediterranean was considered unsafe for sailing between mid-September and mid-November, when sailing
ceased for the winter. The Day of Atonement in view here may have been the one on October 5, 59. **F.** That is,
based on his own experience. He had been shipwrecked at least three times prior to this, 2 Cor 11:25. **G.** Or,
disaster, hardship. **H.** Or, gave counsel. **I.** This more favorable port was 38 miles or 61 kilometers further west.
J. That is, a wind blowing from the south, which would have taken them to Phoenix in a few hours. **K.** Or,
typhonic, tempestuous. **L.** That is, down off the island, blowing them away from the coast. **M.** Or, Euraquilo,
blowing from the northeast. Some manuscripts spell it Euroclydon. **N.** This island is about 30 miles or 50
kilometers south of Crete. **O.** Or, skiff. That is, the small boat towed behind the ship used to go to and from
shore. **P.** Ships carried ropes or cables for such an emergency. They were run under the hull and secured on deck
to help hold the ship together. The straining caused by the heavy mast as the ship was tossed in the sea would
spread the planks of the hull, causing the ship to founder and sink. **Q.** That is, the Gulf of Sidra, off the coast
of modern Libya, a place of shallow and shifting sands. The sailors feared the winds would blow them to certain
destruction off the coast of Africa. **R.** That is, the gear that would turn the ship as much northward as the winds
would allow, and away from Africa. Perhaps it was a floating sea anchor. **S.** This would make it impossible for
the sailors to determine their position. **T.** Or, pressing-upon. **U.** Or, removed. **V.** That is, a long; or, a serious.
W. Or, lack-of-appetite. **X.** Or, incurred. Or, spared-*yourselves.*

you, only *of* the ship. [23] For *an* **angel** stood-before me *on* this night *from* the God Whose **I** am, Whom also I serve, [24] saying, 'Do not be afraid, Paul. You must stand-before Caesar. And behold— God has granted you all the *ones* sailing with you'. [25] Therefore, cheer up, men. For I believe God that it shall happen in this manner— in accordance with the way it has been spoken *to* me. [26] But we must run-aground on *a* certain island".

On The Fourteenth Night, The Sailors Fear Running Aground
[27] Now when *the* fourteenth night came, while we *were* being driven-about in the Adriatic-sea, during *the* middle *of* the night the sailors were suspecting *that* some land *was* approaching them. [28] And having taken-soundings[A], they found *it to be* twenty fathoms[B]. And having set *a* short interval[C], and again having taken-soundings, they found *it to be* fifteen fathoms. [29] And fearing that we might run-aground somewhere against rocky places, having thrown-off four anchors from *the* stern[D], they were praying *that* day *might* come. [30] And while the sailors *were* seeking to flee from the ship, and *had* lowered the [ship's] boat to the sea *on a* pretense as-*though* intending to stretch-out anchors from *the* bow, [31] Paul said *to* the centurion and the soldiers, "Unless these *ones* remain in the ship, **you** cannot be saved". [32] Then the soldiers cut-off the ropes *of* the [ship's] boat, and let it fall-away. [33] And until which *time* day was about to come, Paul was urging everyone to receive food, saying, "While waiting-in-expectation *for a* fourteenth day today, you are continuing without-food, having taken nothing. [34] Therefore I urge you to receive food. For this is for your preservation. For *a* hair from the head *of* none *of* you will be lost[E]". [35] And having said these *things*, and having taken bread, he gave-thanks *to* God in the presence of everyone. And having broken *it*, he began to eat. [36] And everyone having become cheerful, **they** also were taking food. [37] Now we, all the souls in the ship, were two-hundred seventy six. [38] And having been satisfied *with* food, they were lightening[F] the ship— throwing-out the wheat into the sea.

Shipwrecked On an Island, All Make It Safely Ashore
[39] And when it became day, they were not recognizing the land. But they were looking-closely-at *a* certain bay having *a* beach, to which they were deliberating[G] whether they might be able to drive-out the ship. [40] And having cast-off the anchors, they were leaving *them* in the sea. At the same time, having unfastened the ropes *of* the rudders[H], and having raised the sail[I] *to* the blowing [wind], they were holding [course] for the beach. [41] But having fallen-into[J] *a* place between-seas[K], they grounded the vessel. And the bow, having become stuck, remained immovable; but the stern was being broken-up by the force *of* the waves. [42] Now *the* plan *of* the soldiers came-

---

A. Or, heaved-the-lead. That is, having dropped a weighted line to the bottom. **B.** A fathom is the length of a man's outstretched arms, about 6 feet or 1.8 meters. The sailor thus counted the fathoms as he pulled up the line. **C.** That is, interval of time, and thus distance. Based on the geography, this may have been about 30 minutes. Or, separated *a* short *distance*. **D.** That is, the sailors threw four anchors from the rear of the ship to hold it in place pointing in to shore until daylight when they could see to navigate. **E.** Or, will perish. **F.** The sailors wanted to get the ship as close to shore as possible before it ran aground. **G.** Or, were planning (if they could) to drive-out. **H.** Greek ships had two oarlike steering paddles. The sailors unlashed them and put them back in the water so they could steer the ship. **I.** That is, the foresail, near the bow. **J.** Or, encountered. **K.** That is, an underwater reef or sandbar or point of land with deeper sea on both sides.

to-be that they should kill the prisoners, *that* none should escape, having swum-away.
43 But the centurion, wanting to bring Paul safely through, forbid them *from their* intention. And he ordered the *ones* being able to swim, having jumped-overboard[A] first, to go away to the land, **44** and the rest *to follow*— some upon planks, and others on some *of* the *things* from the ship. And so it happened *that* everyone was brought-safely-through to the land.

While Stranded On The Island of Malta, Paul Heals the Sick
28:1 And having been brought-safely-through, then we learned that the island was called Malta. **2** And the natives[B] were showing us not the ordinary humaneness. For having lit *a* fire, they welcomed us all because of the rain having set-upon *us* and because of the cold. **3** And Paul having gathered *a* certain quantity *of* dry-sticks, and having put *them* on the fire— *a* viper having come-out because of the heat fastened-on his hand. **4** And when the natives saw the beast hanging from his hand, they were saying to one another, "Surely this man is *a* murderer whom, having been brought-safely-through from the sea, Justice[C] did not allow to live". **5** Then indeed the *one*, having shaken-off the beast into the fire, suffered no harm. **6** And the *ones* were expecting *that* he *was* about to be swelling-up, or suddenly be falling down dead. But while they for *a* long *time were* waiting-in-expectation and observing nothing out-of-place happening to him— having changed *their* minds, they were saying *that* he was *a* god. **7** Now in the *areas* around that place were lands *belonging to* the leading[D] *official of* the island, Publius *by* name— who, having welcomed us, entertained[E] *us* courteously *for* three days. **8** And it came about *that* the father *of* Publius *was* lying-down, being gripped *with* fevers and dysentery, to whom having gone in and having prayed, having laid *his* hands on him, Paul healed him. **9** And this having taken place, the others on the island having infirmities were also coming to *him* and being cured— **10** who also honored us *with* many honors, and *at our* putting-to-sea provided the *things* for *our* needs.

After Three Winter Months, They Boarded Another Ship And Sailed For Rome
11 And after three[F] months, we put-to-sea in *a* ship having spent the winter at the island[G]— *an* Alexandrian *one* marked *with the* Twin-brothers[H]. **12** And having put-in at Syracuse, we stayed three days— **13** from which, having cast-off, we came to Rhegium. And after one day, *a* south *wind* having come up, we came on the second day to Puteoli— **14** where, having found brothers, we were invited to stay with them *for* seven[I] days. And so[J] we came[K] to Rome. **15** And from there the brothers, having heard the *things* concerning us, came as far as *the* Forum[L] *of* Appius and *the* Three Taverns[M] to meet us— whom having seen, Paul, having given-thanks *to* God, took courage[N].

A. Lit, thrown [themselves] from [the ship]. **B.** That is, the local non-Greek-cultured people. **C.** That is, the goddess by this name; or, justice as an abstract concept. **D.** Or, the first *man*, a title for this official found in inscriptions on Malta. **E.** Or, received *us* as guests, gave *us* lodging. **F.** That is, some time in February of A.D. 60. **G.** It would have been in the port of Valetta. **H.** Or, Dioscuri. That is, the Greek gods Castor and Pollux, twin sons of Zeus and Leda, patron gods of sailors. The mark may refer to a carved figurehead, or to painted emblems on each side of the prow. **I.** During this time, Julius (v 1) would have been making arrangements for the 130 mile or 210 kilometer journey by road to Rome. **J.** Or, in this manner. **K.** Or, went. **L.** This location was 39 miles or 63 kilometers south of Rome. **M.** Or, Inns. This location was 30 miles or 49 kilometers south of Rome. **N.** Paul had written them the book of Romans (in 20:2) about three years earlier, and now takes

In Rome Paul Explains His Circumstance To The Jews, Who Ask To Hear His Message
16 And when we entered into Rome, it was permitted *to* Paul to stay by himself ᴬ, with the soldier guarding him. **17** And it came about after three days *that* he called-together the *ones* being leading *ones of* the Jews. And they having come together, he was saying to them, "**I**, men, brothers, having done nothing contrary *to our* people or *our* ancestors' customs, was handed-over *as a* prisoner from Jerusalem into the hands *of* the Romans— **18** who, having examined me, were wanting to release *me* because of *there* being no charge *worthy of* death in connection with me. **19** But the Jews speaking-against *it*, I was compelled to appeal-to Caesar— not as-*though* having anything to accuse my nation. **20** For this reason therefore, I called-for you, to see and speak to *you*. For I am wearing this chain for the sake of the hope *of* Israel". **21** And the *ones* said to him, "**We** neither received letters from Judea concerning you, nor did any *of* the brothers having arrived report or speak anything evil concerning you. **22** And we consider-*it*-fitting *that we* hear from you *the things* which you think. For indeed concerning this sectᴮ, it is known *to* us that it is being spoken-against everywhere".

Some Believed Paul's Message, Others Rejected. Paul Turns To The Gentiles
23 And having appointed *a* day *for* him, more came to him at *his* lodging— *to* whom he was explaining *it* from early-in-the-morning until evening, solemnly-testifying *as to* the kingdom *of* God, and persuading them concerning Jesus from both the Law *of* Moses and the Prophets. **24** And some were being persuaded *by* the *things* being said, but others were not-believingᶜ. **25** And being not-in-agreement with one another, they were departing, Paul having spoken one statement— that "The Holy Spirit spoke **rightly** through Isaiah the prophet [in Isa 6:9-10] to your fathers, **26** saying, 'Go to this people and say: *In* hearing, you will hear and by no means understand. And while seeing, you will see and by no means perceive. **27** For the heart *of* this people became dullᴰ, and they hardlyᴱ heard *with their* ears, and they closed their eyes, that they might not ever seeᶠ *with their* eyes, and hear *with their* ears, and understand *in their* heart, and turn-back, and I shall healᴳ them'. **28** Therefore let it be known *to* you that this salvation *of* God was sent-forth *to the Gentiles*. **They**ᴴ also will hear *it*". **29** ᴵ

While Two Years Pass, Paul Continues To Proclaim Christ
30 And he stayed twoᴶ whole years in *his* own rented-*quarters*ᴷ. And he was welcoming all the *ones* coming-in to him— **31** proclaiming the kingdom *of* God, and teaching the *things* concerning the Lord Jesus Christ with all boldness, without-hindrance.

---

courage at their concern for him. **A.** That is, in his own rented quarters (v 30), rather than in prison. **B.** That is, Christians. **C.** Or, refusing-to-believe. **D.** Or, thick, fat, insensitive. **E.** That is, with difficulty. They are spiritually hard of hearing. **F.** This expresses the purpose of the people. They closed their eyes to God that they might not ever see what they did not want to see, and never have to change their ways and return to God. **G.** Paul places the blame on these Jews for not entering the process that results in spiritual healing: see and hear, understand, and turn back. **H.** Or, And **they** will listen. **I.** Some manuscripts add 'And he having spoken these *things*, the Jews departed, having *a* great dispute among themselves.' **J.** Thus, closing the book some time in A.D. 62. Some think Paul was then tried and released; others that his case was dismissed because the Jews failed to prosecute it. Some think Paul wrote Ephesians, Philippians, Colossians, and Philemon during this time. Others think these letters were written during the two years in Caesarea (24:27); others, in an imprisonment in Ephesus during Acts 19. **K.** Or, at *his* own expense (in Roman government quarters).

Romans

Introduction   1:1-17

A.   The wrath of God is revealed against all ungodliness of people   1:18

    1.   Because the thing known of God is evident in them, for God made it evident to them   1:19-20
    2.   Because having known God, they did not glorify Him, but became futile in thinking   1:21-32
    3.   Therefore you are without excuse— everyone judging. For in what you judge others, you   2:1-8
        condemn yourself, because you do the same things. You are storing up wrath for yourself
    4.   There will be affliction and distress upon everyone doing evil— the Jew and the Greek.   2:9-13
        For all who sinned will be judged, whether without the Law or through the Law

        a.   For the Gentiles will be judged by the things of the Law written on their hearts   2:14-16
        b.   But do you as a Jew obey the Law? Circumcision will not profit transgressors   2:17-29

    5.   What then is the advantage of the Jew? Much in every way. God keeps His promises   3:1-8
    6.   Therefore what? Are we better than they? No. All are under sin, accountable to God   3:9-20

B.   But now apart from law, the righteousness of God has been revealed   3:21

    1.   And it is the righteousness of God through faith in Jesus Christ to all the ones believing.   3:22-26
        For there is no distinction— all have sinned and are declared righteous as a gift through
        the redemption in Christ, whom God set forth as the satisfaction of His wrath

        a.   Where then is the boasting? It was shut out by faith. God is God of all by faith   3:27-31
        b.   Abraham also believed God, and it was credited for righteousness. This was apart   4:1-25
            from circumcision and Law, so that he might become the father of all believers

    2.   Therefore we have peace with God, and access by faith into this grace in which we stand.   5:1-11
        And we boast in the hope of the glory of God, a hope which does not put to shame
    3.   Because of this, just as sin and death entered the world through one man, so also the gift   5:12-21
        of righteousness and life came through one Man. Grace now reigns over sin and death
    4.   Therefore should we be continuing in sin that grace might increase? No, we died to sin.   6:1-14
        Or do you not know that we were baptized into His death? So do not let sin reign in your
        body, for you are not under the Law, but grace
    5.   Therefore should we commit a sin because we are not under the Law but under grace? No   6:15

        a.   Do you not know you are slaves to whom you obey? Present yourself to God   6:16-23
        b.   Or do you not know that the Law lords over a person only while he lives? You have   7:1-25
            died to the Law and now serve in the newness of the Spirit. But the Law did not
            cause my sin or death. The sin in me used the Law to kill me

    6.   Therefore there is now no condemnation for the ones in Christ. For the law of the Spirit of   8:1-2
        life in Christ Jesus set you free from the law of sin and death

        a.   For what the Law could not do, God did through His own Son for us walking in   8:3-9
            accordance with the Spirit. For you are not in the flesh, but in the Spirit
        b.   And if Christ is in you, the body is dead, but the Spirit is life. God will give life to   8:10-11
            your mortal bodies through the Spirit
        c.   So then, brothers, we are debtors not to live according to the flesh. If you are putting   8:12-13
            to death the practices of the body you will live—

            i.   For all who are being led by the Spirit are sons of God   8:14-16

ii. And if we are children, we are heirs, and fellow heirs with Christ, since we are 8:17-27
suffering with Him in order that we might be glorified with Him

iii. And all things are working together for good for the ones loving God 8:28-30

7. Therefore, what shall we say to these things? If God is for us, who can be against us? 8:31-39

C. I am telling the truth. There is great grief for me and unceasing pain in my heart over Israel. For 9:1-5
I would pray that I might be accursed from Christ on behalf of my kinsmen, the Israelites

1. But it is not such as that the word of God has failed. For all these ones from Israel are not 9:6-29
Israel, nor children of promise. God has mercy and He hardens whom He wants

2. Therefore what shall we say? Gentiles not pursuing righteousness took hold of it by faith. 9:30-33
But Israel, pursuing the Law of righteousness, did not attain it, but stumbled on Christ

3. Brothers, I pray for their salvation, but their zeal is not in accordance with knowledge 10:1-2

a. For being ignorant of God's righteousness, they did not subject themselves to it. For 10:3-17
Christ is the end of the Law for righteousness for everyone believing. For Scripture
says everyone putting faith in Him will be saved. There is no distinction

b. But I say— it is not that they did not hear. The word went out 10:18

c. But I say— it is not that they did not know. Moses and the prophets told them 10:19-21

4. Therefore did God reject His people? No. The remnant was saved, the rest hardened 11:1-10

5. Therefore did they stumble in order to fall? No. By their trespass salvation came to the 11:11-32
Gentiles. How much more will their fullness be! God can regraft them into their tree.
A partial hardening has happened to Israel until the fullness of Gentiles comes in

7. O the depths of God's wisdom and knowledge. To Him be the glory forever, amen 11:33-36

D. Therefore I urge you to present your bodies as a sacrifice to God as your spiritual worship. And 12:1-2
do not be conformed to this age, but be transformed by the renewing of your mind

1. For I say to all of you by the grace given to me— be thinking accurately about yourself 12:3

a. As we have many body parts in one body, so also is Christ's body. Do your part 12:4-8

b. I say to let your love be sincere; to be diligent. Bless your enemies. Be humble 12:9-21

2. Let every soul be subject to superior authorities. They are God's servants for good 13:1-7

3. Owe nothing to anyone except to love one another. Love is the fulfillment of the Law 13:8-10

4. And do this knowing the time. Lay aside darkness and put on the weapons of light 13:11-14

5. Now be accepting the one being weak in faith, but not for disputes about opinions 14:1

a. One has faith to eat, another not. Do not treat with contempt or judge one another 14:2-4

b. One judges a day above another. Let each be assured in his own mind. We live for 14:5-12
the Lord. We will all stand before His judgment seat and give an account

c. Therefore judge this— not to place a cause of stumbling or falling for your brother 14:13-18

d. So then, let us pursue the things of peace and edification 14:19-15:6

e. Therefore be accepting one another as Christ accepted you, for the glory of God 15:7-12

6. Now may the God of hope fill you with joy and peace in believing 15:13

E. Paul explains why he wrote, his commission by God, his present and future plans 15:14-33

Conclusion 16:1-27

1:1 Paul[A], *a* slave *of* Christ Jesus, *a* called apostle[B], having been separated[C] for *the* good-news *of* God **²** which He promised-beforehand through His prophets in *the* Holy Scriptures **³** concerning His Son— the *One* having come from *the* seed *of* David according-to[D] *the* flesh, **⁴** the *One* having been designated[E] *as the* Son *of* God with power according to *the* Spirit[F] *of* holiness by *the* resurrection *from the* dead, Jesus Christ our Lord— **⁵** through Whom we received grace and apostleship for *the* obedience *of* [G] faith among all the Gentiles for the sake of His name, **⁶** among whom **you** also are called ones *of* Jesus Christ, **⁷** *to* all the *ones* being in Rome, beloved *ones of* God, called saints: Grace *to* you and peace from God our Father and *the* Lord Jesus Christ.

⁸ First, I am giving-thanks *to* my God through Jesus Christ for you all because your faith is being proclaimed in the whole world. **⁹** For God is my witness— Whom I am serving in my spirit in[H] the good-news *of* His Son— how unceasingly I am making mention *of* you **¹⁰** always in my prayers, asking if somehow now at last I shall be prospered in the will *of* God to come to you.

¹¹ For I am yearning to see you in order that I may impart some spiritual gift *to* you so that you *may* be established. **¹²** And this is *that I may* be encouraged-together-with *you* among you— through each other's faith, both yours and mine.

¹³ And I do not want you to be-unaware, brothers, that often I planned to come to you— and was prevented until now— in order that I might have some fruit among you also, as indeed among the other Gentiles. **¹⁴** I am *a* debtor both *to* Greeks and barbarians, both *to* wise and foolish. **¹⁵** So for my part, *I am* eager also to announce-the-good-news *to* you, the *ones* in Rome.

¹⁶ For I am not ashamed-of the good-news, for it is *the* power *of* God for salvation *to* everyone believing[I]— both *to the* Jew first and *to the* Greek. **¹⁷** For *the* righteousness *of* [J] God is revealed in it from faith to faith, just as it has been written [in Hab 2:4]: "But the righteous *one* shall live by faith".

God's Wrath Is Upon All Sin
¹⁸ For *the* wrath *of* God is revealed from heaven against all ungodliness[K] and unrighteousness[L] *of* people holding-down[M] the truth in[N] unrighteousness.

Because God Revealed Enough of Himself In Creation For The World To Be Without Excuse
¹⁹ Because the *thing* known *of* God is evident[O] in[P] them, for God made *it* evident *to* them. **²⁰** For His invisible *things*— both His eternal power and divine-nature— are clearly-seen, being understood since *the* creation *of the* world *in* the *things* made, so that they are without-excuse.

A. On when this book was written, see Act 20:3. Paul was in Corinth, Rom 16:23. **B.** Or, called *to be an* apostle. **C.** That is, set apart, appointed. **D.** Or, with respect to. **E.** Or, declared *to be*. **F.** Or, *His* spirit. **G.** That is, *consisting of*; or, *proceeding from*. **H.** That is, in connection with. **I.** Or, exercising faith. Same root word as 'faith' in v 17. **J.** That is, *from* God; or, *belonging to* God; or, the God-*kind of*-righteousness. **K.** That is, lack of reverence toward God; profaneness. **L.** That is, wrongdoing; actions violating God's standards. **M.** Or, suppressing, holding back, restraining. **N.** That is, in connection with; or, by means of. **O.** Or, clear, visible, plainly seen. **P.** Or, among.

And Having Known This Truth About God, The World Did Not Honor Him As God
21 Because having known God, they did not glorify *Him* as God or give-thanks, but became futile in their thoughts, and their senseless heart was darkened.

They Turned From The Glory of The Immortal God To Their Crafted Images of God
22 While claiming to be wise, they became-foolish **23** and exchanged the glory *of* the immortal God for *a* likeness— *an* image *of a* mortal person and *of* birds and *of* four-footed-animals and *of* reptiles. **24** Therefore God handed them over^A in the desires *of* their hearts to impurity *so that*^B their bodies are dishonored among them.

They Turned From The Truth To Worship The Creation Rather Than The Creator
25 Who exchanged the truth *of* God for the lie^C, and worshiped and served the creation^D rather than the *One* having created— Who is blessed forever, amen. **26** For this reason God handed them over to passions *of*^E dishonor. For both their females exchanged the natural [sexual] function for the *one* contrary to nature, **27** and likewise also the males, having left the natural [sexual] function *of* the female, were inflamed by their craving for one another— males with males committing the indecent-act^F and receiving-back in themselves the return^G which was due their error^H.

They Disapproved of Keeping God In Mind
28 And as they did not approve to have^I God in *their* knowledge, God handed them over to *a* disapproved mind, to do the *things* not being proper— **29** having been filled *with* all unrighteousness, evilness, greed, badness; full *of* envy, murder, strife, deceit, malice; whisperers^J, **30** slanderers, God-haters^K, violent, proud, boasters, inventors *of* evils, disobedient *to* parents, **31** senseless, unfaithful^L, unaffectionate^M, unmerciful; **32** who, having known the regulation *of* God that the *ones* practicing such *things* are worthy *of* death, not only are doing them, but are also giving-approval *to* the *ones* practicing *them.*

You Who Know More Truth And Judge Others By It Are Also Without Excuse
2:1 Therefore you are without-excuse, O human— everyone judging. For in what^N you are judging the other *person*, you are condemning yourself; for you, the *one* judging, are practicing the same *things*! **2** And we know that the judgment *of* God is according to truth upon^O the *ones* practicing such *things.*

Do You Think You Will Escape God's Judgment When You Do The Same Things?
3 But are you thinking this, O human— the *one* judging the *ones* practicing such *things* and doing them [yourself]— that **you** will escape the judgment *of* God? **4** Or are you disregarding the riches *of* His goodness and forbearance and patience, not knowing that the good *thing of* God is leading you to repentance? **5** But in-accordance-with your hardness and *your* unrepentant heart, you are storing-up wrath *for* yourself on

---

A. Or, gave them up. **B.** Or 'impurity, the dishonoring *as to* their bodies among themselves'. **C.** That is, the lie of false religion. Or, falsehood. **D.** Or, creature. **E.** That is, *characterized by*; or, *leading to*; or, *proceeding from.* **F.** Or, the shameful-deed. **G.** This is a neutral rendering; negatively it means 'penalty'. **H.** Or, deception, delusion. **I.** Or, hold, retain. **J.** That is, gossips. **K.** Or, God-hated. These may be combined as slandering whisperers, God-hated violent *ones*, proud boasters. **L.** Or, undutiful. **M.** Or, without good feelings for others. **N.** Or, For while. **O.** That is, it is truly upon them.

the day *of* wrath and *the* revelation *of the* righteous-judgment *of* God, **⁶** Who will render *to* each *one* according to his works— **⁷** *to* the *ones* seeking glory and honor and immortality in accordance with endurance *in* good work, *He will render* eternal life; **⁸** but *to* the *ones* indeed disobeying the truth and obeying unrighteousness out of selfish-interstᴬ, *there will be* wrath and fury.

There Is No Respect of Persons With God Regarding Sin And Judgment
⁹ *There will be* affliction and distress upon every soul *of* the personᴮ committing evil— both *of the* Jew first and *of the* Greek. **¹⁰** But *there will be* glory and honor and peace *to* everyone working good— both *to the* Jew first and *to the* Greek. **¹¹** For there is no respect-of-persons with God. **¹²** For all who sinned without-Law will also perish without-Law, and all who sinned underᶜ *the* Law will be judged by *the* Law. **¹³** For not the hearers *of* lawᴰ *are* righteous before God, but the doers *of* law will be declared-righteous.

For Gentiles Will Be Judged By Their Own Standards Insofar As They Agree With God's
¹⁴ For whenever Gentiles, the *ones* not having *the* Law, are doing *by* nature the *things of* the Law, these *ones* not having *the* Law are *a* law *to* themselves, **¹⁵** who are demonstratingᴱ the work *of* the Law written in their hearts— their conscience bearing co-witness and *their* thoughts accusing or even defending between one another **¹⁶** on *the* day when God judges the hidden *things of* people according to my good-news, through Christ Jesus.

And Jews Will Be Judged By The Law They Rely Upon
¹⁷ But if **you** call-*yourself a* Jew, and rely upon *the* Law, and boast in God, **¹⁸** and know *His* will, and approve the *things* matteringᶠ— being instructed out of the Law— **¹⁹** and are confident *as to* yourself *that you* are *a* guide *of* blind *ones, a* light *of* the *ones* in darkness, **²⁰** *a* corrector *of* foolish *ones, a* teacher *of* children, *one* having the embodiment *of* knowledge and truth in the Law, **²¹** then— the *one* teaching another, are you not teaching yourself? The *one* proclaiming not to steal, do you steal? **²²** The *one* saying not to commit-adultery, do you commit-adultery? The *one* detesting idols, do you rob-temples?

Their Transgression of The Law Dishonors God
²³ You who are boasting in *the* Law are dishonoring God through transgression *of* the Law. **²⁴** For "the name *of* God is being blasphemed among the Gentiles because of you", just as it has been written [in Isa 52:5].

Circumcision Will Not Help Transgressors
²⁵ For circumcision profits if you practice *the* Law— but if you are *a* transgressor *of the* Law your circumcision has become uncircumcision. **²⁶** So if the uncircumcised *one* keeps the requirements *of* the Law, will not his uncircumcision be counted for circumcision? **²⁷** And the uncircumcised *one* by nature *who is* fulfilling the Law will judge you, the transgressor *of the* Law with

---

A. Or, self-seeking, selfish-ambition. **B.** That is, every soul belonging to the class defined as 'the person committing evil'; every individual in this category, both Jew and Gentile. **C.** Or, in the sphere of, in the domain of. **D.** This is lowercase because it applies to both groups in v 12 in the different senses Paul defines next. **E.** Or, showing, proving. **F.** Or, being worth more, being more valuable, and thus excellent, superior, essential.

the letter[A] and circumcision! **28** For the *Jew* in the visible *thing* is **not** *a* Jew, nor is the *circumcision* in the visible[B] *thing* in *the* flesh circumcision, **29** but the *Jew* in the hidden *thing is a* Jew, and circumcision *is of the* heart, by[C] *the* Spirit not *the* letter— whose praise *is* not from people, but from God.

So Then What Is The Advantage of The Jew?

3:1 What then *is* the advantage *of* the Jew? Or what *is* the profit *of* circumcision? **2** Much in every way. For first— that they were entrusted the oracles[D] *of* God!

God Will Be Faithful To His Promises To The Jews Even If Some Reject Him

3 What indeed if some[E] were faithless[F]? Their faithlessness[G] will not nullify the faithfulness *of* God, *will it*? **4** May it never be! But let God be [seen to be] true and every person *a* liar, just as it has been written [in Ps 51:4]: "So that You might be declared-righteous[H] in Your words and prevail in Your being judged[I]".

But God Is Not Unrighteous To Inflict Wrath On Jews Who Sin

5 But if our[J] unrighteousness demonstrates[K] *the* righteousness *of* God, what shall we say? God, the *One* inflicting the wrath, is not unrighteous, *is He*? (I am speaking in accordance with human *thinking*[L]). **6** May it never be! Otherwise how will God judge the world?

God Holds Jews Accountable For Their Sin Too

7 But if the truth *of* God abounded in my lie[M] to His glory, why am **I** also still being judged as *a* sinner? **8** Indeed, *why* not *say* "Let us do evil *things* that good *things* may come", as we are blasphemed, and as some affirm us to say— whose condemnation is just[N]!

Scripture Declares All Are Accountable And Guilty Before God. None Are Righteous

9 Therefore what? Are we better[O] [than they]? Not at-all. For we already-charged[P] *that* both Jews and Greeks are all under sin, **10** just as it has been written: "There is not *a* righteous *one*, not even one. **11** There is no *one* understanding. There is no *one* seeking-out God. **12** They all turned-away, together they became useless[Q]. There is no *one* doing goodness. There is not as-many-as one" [Ps 14:1-3]. **13** "Their throat *is an* opened grave. With their tongues they were deceiving" [Ps 5:9]. "*The* poison *of* asps *is* under their lips" [Ps 140:3]. **14** "Whose mouth is full *of* cursing[R] and bitterness" [Ps 10:7]. **15** "Their feet *are* swift to shed blood. **16** Destruction and misery *are* in their ways. **17** And they did not know *the* way *of* peace" [Isa 59:7-8]. **18** "There is no fear *of* God before their eyes" [Ps 36:1]. **19** And we know that whatever the Law says, it speaks *to* the *ones* under the Law— in order that every mouth may be stopped[S] and the whole world may become accountable[T] *to* God. **20** Because by *the* works *of* law[U] no flesh will be declared-righteous in His sight. For through law *comes the* knowledge *of* sin.

A. That is, the written code, the Law. **B.** That is, the outward, open, public things. **C.** Or, in *the* spirit. **D.** That is, the sacred writings, the Scriptures. **E.** Or, What then? If some. Paul now refutes three objections to or false inferences from his teaching. **F.** Or, did not believe, were unfaithful, with reference to the oracles they were given. **G.** Or, unbelief. **H.** Or, vindicated. **I.** Or, in your judging. **J.** That is, Israel's; the some who were faithless, v 3. **K.** Or, exhibits. **L.** Or, with mankind. **M.** Or, falsehood. Note 11:11-12. **N.** Or, deserved. **O.** Or, Do we [Jews] have an advantage? Or, Are we [Jews] excused? **P.** Or, previously-charged. That is, in 1:18-2:29. **Q.** Or, worthless. **R.** That is, calling down evil on someone. **S.** Or, shut. **T.** Or, liable, answerable. **U.** Or, '*of the* Law'.

But Now Righteousness From God Has Been Revealed

21 But now apart from law[A], *the* righteousness *of* God has been revealed, being attested by the Law and the Prophets.

It Comes As an Undeserved Gift Through Faith In Christ, Who Satisfied God's Wrath

22 And *it is the* righteousness *of* God through faith[B] *in* Jesus Christ for all the *ones* believing! For there is no distinction, **23** for all sinned and are coming-short-of the glory *of* God, **24** being declared-righteous as-a-gift[C] *by* His grace through the redemption in Christ Jesus, **25** Whom God set-forth[D] *as* that-which-satisfies[E] [His wrath] through faith, in[F] His blood— for *the* demonstration[G] *of* His righteousness because of the passing-by *of* the sins having previously-taken-place **26** in the forbearance[H] *of* God; for the demonstration *of* His righteousness at the present time, so that He *might* be righteous and declaring-righteous the *one* of [I] faith *in* Jesus.

There Can Be No Boasting In Our Works: It Is By Faith For All!

27 Where then *is* the boasting? It was shut-out[J]. Through what kind of law[K]? *Of* works? No, but through *a* law *of* faith. **28** For we consider *a* person to be declared-righteous *by* faith apart from works *of the* Law. **29** Or *is* He the God *of* Jews only[L]? *Is He* not also *the God of* Gentiles? Yes, *of* Gentiles also, **30** since *there is* one God— Who will declare-righteous *the* circumcised by faith, and *the* uncircumcised through the *same*[M] faith. **31** Do we then nullify *the* Law through the faith? May it never be! On the contrary, we establish *the* Law.

What About Abraham?

4:1 What then shall we say *that* Abraham, our forefather according-to[N] *the* flesh, has found? **2** For if Abraham was declared-righteous by works, he has *a* boast— but not before God.

His Righteousness Came By Faith

3 For what does the Scripture say?— "And Abraham believed God, and it was credited *to* him for righteousness" [Gen 15:6]. **4** Now *to* the *one* working, the wages are not credited *to him* based-on grace, but based on debt. **5** But *to* the *one* not working but putting-faith upon the *One* declaring the ungodly righteous— his faith is credited for righteousness. **6** Just as David also says [in Ps 32:1-2] *as to* the blessedness *of* the person *to* whom God credits righteousness apart from works: **7** "Blessed *are the ones* whose lawless-*deeds* were forgiven and whose sins were covered. **8** Blessed *is the* man whose sin *the* Lord will never count".

A. That is, any kind of law, Jewish or Gentile. Or, Law, the Law of Moses. **B.** Or, through *the* faithfulness *of* Jesus Christ (to what God sent Him to do). **C.** Or, freely, without a cause. **D.** Or, presented, publicly displayed. **E.** Or, that-which-propitiates, the-means-of-satisfaction, the-satisfying-sacrifice. That is, that which satisfies God's wrath and obtains His mercy; the focus being on God. Jesus is the sacrifice that removes or satisfies God's wrath against sin that Paul has just proven is upon all flesh. Or, that-which-expiates, covers, cleanses [our sin]. That is, that which removes our sin and guilt; the focus being on our sin. **F.** Or, by. The satisfaction is both through faith (from our viewpoint) and in or by His blood (from His viewpoint). Or, through faith in His blood. **G.** Or, proof. **H.** Or, holding back, clemency, delay of punishment. **I.** That is, characterized by. **J.** Or, excluded. **K.** Or, principle, system. Or, Law (meaning, through a Law wrongly understood as of works? No, through a Law rightly understood as of faith). **L.** This would be the conclusion if we were saved through a Law of Jewish works. **M.** Lit, 'the faith' just mentioned. **N.** Or, with respect to. Or, our forefather, has found according to *the* flesh (that is, by works)?

This Occurred Prior To Circumcision

9 So *is* this blessedness upon the circumcised, or upon the uncircumcised also? For we say "Faith was credited *to* Abraham for righteousness". **10** How then was it credited— *to one* being in circumcision, or in uncircumcision? Not in circumcision, but in uncircumcision! **11** And he received *the* sign *of* circumcision, *a* seal *of* the righteousness *of* [A] faith *while* in uncircumcision, so that he *might* be[B] *the* father *of* all the *ones* believing through uncircumcision— so that righteousness *might* be credited also *to* them— **12** and *the* father *of the* circumcised *to* the *ones* not of circumcision only, but indeed the *ones* walking-in-line *in* the footsteps *of* the faith *of* our father Abraham *while he was* in uncircumcision.

The Promise Was Not Through The Law But Faith, Making It Firm To All

13 For the promise *to* Abraham or *to* his seed[C] *that* he *should* be the inheritor *of the* world *was* not through *the* Law[D], but through *the* righteousness *of* faith! **14** For if the *ones* of *the* Law *are* inheritors, faith has been made-empty[E] and the promise has been nullified[F]. **15** For the Law brings-about wrath. But where there is no Law, neither *is there* transgression[G]. **16** For this reason *it is* by faith, in order that *it may be* based on grace, so that the promise *might* be firm[H] *to* all the seed— not *to* the *seed* of the Law only[I], but also *to* the *seed* of *the* faith *of* Abraham,

Abraham Is The Father of All Who Believe

... who is *the* father *of* us all— **17** just as it has been written [in Gen 17:5] that "I have made you *a* father *of* many nations"— before God[J] Whom he believed, the *One* giving-life-to the dead and calling the *things* not being as[K] being,

He Believed God's Promise, Contrary To All His Human Circumstances

18 ... who believed contrary-to[L] hope, upon hope, so that he *might* become[M] *the* father *of* many nations in accordance with the *thing* having been spoken [in Gen 15:5]: "So shall your seed be". **19** And not having weakened *in* faith, he considered[N] his *own* body already having become impotent[O], being about *a* hundred years *old,* and the deadness *of* the womb *of* Sarah. **20** But he did not waver *in* unbelief with reference to the promise *of* God, but became-strong *in* faith— having given glory *to* God, **21** and having been fully-convinced that what He had promised He was able also to do.

A. Or, *by* faith; or, *his* faith-righteousness. **B.** That is, from his viewpoint. Or, so that he is (from our viewpoint). **C.** That is, his believing offspring, his spiritual descendants, v 11-12. **D.** Or, law, depending on whether Paul is speaking from the viewpoint of Abraham (who lived before the Law) or his seed (who lived under it). **E.** Or, voided. That is, emptied of any value or place. **F.** The promise of a free gift is nullified, since obedience would be required to obtain it. **G.** Or, violation. There is no law to violate in connection with the promise of a gift, so there can be no transgression and no wrath. **H.** Or, secure, certain. **I.** That is, to people like Paul; believing Jews. **J.** Abraham is the spiritual father of us all before God. **K.** Or, as-*if.* That is, calling the *things* not being [into] being, in an act of creation, as seen in the birth of Isaac. Or, calling/naming the *things* not [yet] being as-*if* being, as if they already existed, as when He calls Abraham the father of many nations when he had no child. **L.** Or, against, beyond. That is, contrary to all human hope could offer, upon the hope God promised. **M.** That is, from his viewpoint. Or, so that he became (from our viewpoint). **N.** Some manuscripts say 'he did not consider'. **O.** Or, dead, as good as dead, lifeless, with regard to procreation.

His Faith Was Credited To Him As Righteousness, And So Is Ours
22 Therefore indeed it was credited *to* him for righteousness. **23** And it was not written for his sake only that it was credited *to* him, **24** but also for our sake *to* whom it is going-to be credited— the *ones* putting-faith upon the *One* having raised Jesus our Lord from *the* dead, **25** Who was handed-over for[A] our trespasses and was raised for[A] our justification.

This Means We Have Peace With God And Access To His Grace Through Jesus Christ
5:1 Therefore, having been declared-righteous by faith, we have peace with God through our Lord Jesus Christ, **2** through Whom also we have the access *by* faith into this grace in which we stand.

And In Spite of Our Afflictions, Our Hope Will Not Disappoint Us, For God Loves Us
And we are boasting over *the* hope *of* the glory *of* God. **3** And not only *this*, but we also are boasting in the afflictions— knowing that the affliction is producing endurance, **4** and the endurance *is producing* approvedness, and the approvedness *is producing* hope, **5** and the hope does not put-to-shame[B] because the love *of* God has been poured-out in our hearts through *the* Holy Spirit having been given *to* us.

For God Shows His Love For Us In That Christ Died To Reconcile And Save Us
6 For while we *were* still being weak, yet at *the* right-time, **Christ** died for ungodly *ones*. **7** For one will rarely[C] die for *a* righteous *person*; for[D] perhaps someone may even dare to die for the good *person*. **8** But God demonstrates[E] His *own* love for us because while we *were* still being sinners, Christ died for us. **9** Therefore *by* much more, having now been declared-righteous by His blood, we shall be saved from the wrath through Him. **10** For if while being enemies we were reconciled *to* God through the death *of* His Son, *by* much more having been reconciled, we shall be saved by His life.

Our Boast Is In God Through Jesus Christ
11 And not only *this*, but *we are* also boasting in God through our Lord Jesus Christ, through Whom we now received the reconciliation.

This Means That Death And Life Each Originated In The Act of One Man
12 Because of this[F], just as[G] through one man sin entered into the world, and death through the sin, and so death went-through[H] to all people because all sinned— **13** for until *the* Law, sin was in *the* world, but sin is not charged-to-the-account, *there* being no law. **14** Nevertheless death reigned from Adam until Moses, even over the *ones* not having sinned in the likeness[I] *of* the transgression *of* Adam, who is *a* pattern[J] *of* the *One* coming.

A. Or, for the sake of, because of. **B.** Or, disappoint. **C.** Or, hardly, scarcely. **D.** Or, though. **E.** Or, shows, exhibits. **F.** That is, summing up 3:21-5:11: Because we have received the reconciliation as a gift by His grace through the sacrifice of Jesus Christ, resulting in righteousness, peace with God, and eternal life. Paul now puts this in broad perspective, comparing Christ's one act bringing life to all His spiritual descendants to Adam's one act bringing death to all his physical descendants. **G.** Paul breaks off this sentence at 'because all sinned' to explain how all sinned; that is, how Adam's one act affected all his progeny. Then he takes this thought up again in v 18 and completes it, giving the 'so also' side. **H.** Or, came through, spread. **I.** Adam violated a requirement of God. Those living until Moses had no such requirement from God, so they did not sin in the same manner. Thus 'all sinned' in v 12 cannot mean 'transgressed God's command'. In some sense death is a consequence upon all humanity of Adam's one act of sin. **J.** Before Paul explains how Adam and Christ are similar (v 18,

One Sin Brought Death To Adam's Many. God's Gift Abounded To Christ's Many
15 But not as *is* the trespass, so also^A *is* the *grace*-gift. For if *by* the trespass *of* the one man the many^B died, *by* much more the grace *of* God and the gift by *the* grace *of* the one man Jesus Christ abounded for the many.

Death Reigned From One Sin. The Gift Brings a Reign In Life To Those Receiving It
16 And not as^C *what resulted* through one *man* having sinned *is* the given-gift. For the judgment *is* from one *trespass*^D, resulting-in *a* verdict-of-condemnation; but the *grace*-gift^E *is* from many trespasses, resulting in *a* verdict-of-righteous^F. **17** For if *by* the trespass *of* the one *man* death reigned through the one, *by* much more the *ones* receiving the abundance *of* the grace and *of* the gift *of* righteousness will reign^G in life through the One, Jesus Christ.

Just As One Act Resulted In Condemnation, So One Act Resulted In Justification
18 So then^H, as *it was* through one^I trespass resulting-in a verdict-of-condemnation for all people, so also *it was* through one righteous-act resulting-in *a* declaring-righteous^J *issuing in*^K life for all people. **19** For just as through the disobedience *of* the one man the many were made^L sinners, so also through the obedience *of* the One the many will be made righteous *ones*.

The Law Increased Sin, But Grace Abounded So As To Reign Through Righteousness
20 And *the* Law^M came-in-beside^N that the trespass might increase. But where sin increased, grace super-abounded, **21** in order that just as sin reigned in death, so also grace might reign through righteousness, resulting-in eternal life through Jesus Christ our Lord.

This Does Not Mean That We Should Keep Sinning Because Salvation Is By Grace
6:1 Therefore, what shall we say? Should we^O be continuing *in* sin in order that grace might increase? **2** May it never be! How shall we who died *to* sin still live in it?

Don't You Know That We Died With Christ In Order To Live a New Life With Him?
3 Or do you not know that all we who were baptized into Christ Jesus were baptized into His death? **4** Therefore we were buried-with Him through baptism into death in

---

as, so also), he first explains how they are not similar, v 15-17. **A:** *not as... so also.* That is, the trespass is not like the gift. The trespass brought a deserved end to life; the undeserved gift abounded in life. **B.** When referring to Adam, 'the many' and 'all' mean all his physical progeny, mankind. When referring to Christ, they mean all His spiritual progeny, those receiving the gift, v 17. **C:** *not as... is.* That is, the result of Adam's act (judgment earned in response to one sin, resulting in condemnation and the reign of death) is not like the gift given (righteousness given in response to many sins, resulting in justification and our reign in life). **D.** Or, *man having sinned.* **E.** That is, gift of the righteousness of God, v 17; 3:21. **F.** Or, justification. **G.** Adam's one act resulted in the reign of death, Christ's in the reign in life for those who receive the gift. **H.** The first half of this verse restates v 12 using the words from v 15-17. **I.** Or, *the* trespass *of* one; and later in the verse, *the* righteous act *of* One. **J.** Or, justification. **K.** Or, *resulting in.* Lit, *of.* **L.** Or, constituted, caused to become. The sin of one resulted in condemnation because we were made sinners. The righteous act of One resulted in justification because those receiving this gift (v17) were made righteous. **M.** Paul now puts the Law into this broad perspective. **N.** Same root word as 'entered' in v 12. Sin 'came in', Law 'came in beside'. **O.** If salvation is all by grace (3:24), and we stand in grace at peace with God (5:1), and where sin increased grace abounded (5:21), then would not God's grace be magnified even more by my continuing in sin?

order that just as Christ arose from *the* dead through the glory *of* the Father, so also **we** might walk in newness *of* life.

For We Share In His Death To Sin And His Life With God

5 For if we have become united-with *Him in* the likeness *of* His death, certainly we shall be also *in the likeness of His* resurrection, **6** knowing this: that our old person was crucified-with *Him* in order that the body *of* sin might be done-away-with[A], *so that* we no longer[B] are-slaves[C] *to* sin. **7** For the *one* having died has been declared-righteous from sin. **8** And if we died with Christ, we believe that we shall also live-with Him, **9** knowing that Christ, having arisen from *the* dead, dies no more. Death lords-over Him no longer. **10** For *the death* that He died, He died *to* sin once-for-all. But *the life* that He is living, He is living *to* God. **11** So also you, be counting yourselves to be dead *to* sin but living *to* God in Christ Jesus.

So Don't Let Sin Reign In You, But Present Yourselves To God As Alive From The Dead

12 Therefore do not let sin be reigning in your mortal body so that *you are* obeying its desires, **13** nor be presenting your body-parts *to* sin *as* instruments[D] *of* unrighteousness. But present yourselves *to* God as-if[E] being alive from *the* dead, and your body-parts *to* God *as* instruments *of* righteousness. **14** For sin shall not lord-over you— for you are not under *the* Law[F], but under grace.

This Does Not Mean We Should Sin Because We Are Not Under Law, But Under Grace

15 Therefore, what? Should we sin[G] because we are not under *the* Law but under grace? May it never be!

You Were Freed From Slavery To Sin. So Present Yourselves As Slaves of Righteousness

16 Do you not know that *to* whom you are presenting yourselves *as* slaves for obedience, you are slaves *to* whom you are obeying— whether *slaves of* sin leading-to[H] death, or *slaves of* obedience leading-to righteousness? **17** But thanks *be to* God that you were slaves *of* sin, but you obeyed from *the* heart *the* form[I] *of* teaching to which you were delivered. **18** And having been set-free from sin, you were enslaved[J] *to* righteousness **19** (I am speaking *in* human *terms* because of the weakness *of* your flesh). For just as you presented your body-parts *as* slaves *to* impurity and lawlessness leading-to lawlessness, so now present your body-parts *as* slaves *to* righteousness leading to holiness.

The Fruit of Sin Is Shame And Death; Righteousness Leads To Holiness And Life

20 For when you were slaves *of* sin, you were free to[K] righteousness. **21** So what fruit were you having at that time? *Things*[L] over which you are now ashamed! For the outcome *of* those *things is* death. **22** But now having been set-free from

---

A. Or, rendered powerless, brought to nothing. **B.** Or, we *might* no longer be-slaves. **C.** Or, are serving as slaves. **D.** Or, tools, weapons, equipment. **E.** That is, as-if presently possessing full resurrection-life like Jesus, v 4. Or, 'as'; that is, as being alive from the spiritually dead. **F.** The escape from the lordship of sin is due to our release from the Law, which occurred when we died to it. Paul explains this in chapter 7. The Law is the power of sin, 1 Cor 15:56. **G.** That is, commit a sin. **H.** Or, resulting in. Same word as in v 19, 22. **I.** Or, pattern. **J.** Or, made slaves. **K.** That is, with regard to. **L.** Paul states the answer. Or, at that time, over which *things* you are now ashamed?, the implied answer being 'None'.

sin and enslaved *to* God, you are having your fruit leading-to holiness. And the outcome *is* eternal life! **23** For the wages *of* sin *is* death, but the gift *of* God *is* eternal life in Christ Jesus our Lord.

But We Are Indeed Not Under The Law, For It Only Has Jurisdiction Over The Living
7:1 Or^A do you not know, brothers (for I am speaking *to ones* knowing *the* Law^B), that the Law lords-over^C the person for as much time as he lives? **2** For the married woman has been bound *by the* Law *to* the living husband; but if the husband dies, she has been released from the law *of*^D the husband. **3** So then, while the husband *is* living, she will be called *an* adulteress if she comes^E *to a* different husband. But if the husband dies, she is free from the law, *so that* she is not *an* adulteress, having come *to a* different husband.

We Have Died To The Law In Christ
4 So-then^F, my brothers, **you** also were put-to-death *with reference to* the Law^G through the body *of* Christ so that you *might* come^H *to a* different *One*— *to* the *One* having arisen from *the* dead— in order that we might bear-fruit *for* God.

Having Died, We Are Released From The Law Through Which Sin Produced Death
5 For when we were in the flesh^I, the passions *of* ^J sins which^K *were* through^L the Law were at-work in our body-parts so as to bear-fruit *for* death. **6** But now we were released^M from the Law, having died *to that* by which we were being held, so that we *are* serving in newness *of the* Spirit^N and not *in* oldness *of the* letter^O.

Not That The Law Is At Fault For My Sin
7 Therefore, what shall we say? *Is* the Law sin^P? May it never be! On-the-contrary, I *would* not *have* known^Q **sin** except through *the* Law.

Sin Used The Law To Produce Sin In Me
For indeed I *would* not *have* known^R coveting^S if the Law were not saying [in Ex 20:17], "You shall not covet". **8** But sin, having taken^T *an* opportunity^U through the commandment, produced^V every^W [kind of] coveting in me. For apart-from^X *the* Law, sin *is* dead^Y.

A. Paul now takes up the other part of 6:14-15, the not being under the Law. **B.** That is, the Law of Moses, God's Law. Or, law, the general principle of law and legal justice.**C.** Or rules over, is the master of. **D.** That is, concerning. **E.** Or, comes-to-be *with*. **F.** Now Paul applies to us the principle of v 1, illustrated by v 2-3, that death ends the authority of the Law. **G.** That is, God's Law as the terms and conditions of which we must be doers (2:13) to have a relationship with Him. Christ did not need to die to release us from our legalism or man's civil law or law in general, but from God's objective standards. **H.** Same word as twice in the illustrations in v 3. It is not the normal word for 'marry', but that is the idea in v 3-4. **I.** That is, before we died with Christ. **J.** That is, *leading to*; or, *belonging to* (sin's passions). **K.** That is, the passions... which. **L.** That is, were increased through the Law, 5:20. Paul explains this next in v 7-8. **M.** Same word as in v 2. **N.** Or, *of* spirit. **O.** That is, the written code of the Law. **P.** If the passions of sins are through the Law, is the Law what makes me a sinner? No. It merely defines the standard against which sin rebels. **Q.** Or, come-to-know sin. That is, known of sin's presence in him as sin (v 7-8) or of its power to kill him in relation to God (v 9-11). Apart from God's Law, sin is merely 'your opinion' or 'my bad choices'. **R.** Or, known-about. **S.** Or, [evil] desire, lust. **T.** Or, received. **U.** Or, occasion, starting point, base of operations. **V.** Or, opportunity, produced... in me through the commandment. **W.** Once aware it was forbidden, sin increased the coveting. This explains how the passions of sins were 'through the Law', v 5. **X.** Or, without *a* law. **Y.** This is stated as a general principle. Sin is present,

And Sin Used The Law To Kill Me

[9] And **I** was once[A] alive apart from *the* Law. But the commandment having come, sin became-alive[B] [10] and **I** died. And the commandment for[C] life— this was found *in* me *to be* for[D] death. [11] For sin, having taken *an* opportunity through the commandment, deceived[E] me, and through it, killed *me.*

So The Law Is Good

[12] So-then the Law *is* holy, and the commandment *is* holy and righteous and good.

Not That The Law Killed Me. Sin Is To Blame For My Death

[13] Therefore did the good *thing* become death[F] *for* me? May it never be! On the contrary, *it was* sin, in order that it might become-visible *as* sin while producing death *in* me through the good *thing,* in order that sin might become extremely[G] sinful through the commandment.

I Agree The Law Is Good, But The Sin In Me Produces Behavior I Hate

[14] For[H] we know that the Law is spiritual. But **I** am made-of-flesh[I], having been sold under sin. [15] For I do not understand[J] what[K] I am producing. For I am not practicing this which I am wanting, but I am doing this which I am hating. [16] But if I am doing this which I am not wanting, I am agreeing-with[L] the Law— that *it is* good. [17] And now **I** am no longer producing it, but the sin[M] dwelling in me *is.*

I Know I Am Not Good, For I Cannot Do The Good I Want To Do

[18] For I know that **good** does not dwell in me, that is, in my flesh. For the wanting is present *in* me, but the producing the good *is* not. [19] For I am not doing *the* good which I am wanting, but I am practicing this evil which I am not wanting. [20] But if I am doing this which **I** am not wanting, **I** am no longer producing it, but the sin[N] dwelling in me *is.*

So The Evil Inside Me Enslaves Me To The Law of Sin And Death In Me

[21] I find then the law[O] *in* me, the *one* wanting to do the good, that the evil is present *in* me. [22] For I am rejoicing-with[P] the Law *of* God according-to[Q] the

---

but inactive until it has a law to transgress. Thus God's Law is the power of sin, 1 Cor 15:56. Or, 'sin *was* dead', stating it as the historical experience of Paul. **A.** Or, formerly. **B.** Or, sprang to life, came back to life. **C.** That is, for the purpose life. **D.** That is, resulting in death. **E.** Or, opportunity, deceived me through the commandment. **F.** If the Law resulted in death, v 5, 10, is God's Law responsible for my death? **G.** Or, supremely, utterly. **H.** The purpose of v14-25 is to prove that sin is responsible for death, not the Law. Paul uses himself as an example, and scholars debate whether he has in view his experience as a Pharisee or a Christian (each view giving a different sense to 'Law' and 'death'). What Paul says in these verses is true of anyone trying to live under law. **I.** That is, carnal, fleshly; or, human, of Adam's race. **J.** Or, 'acknowledge' as representing his true desires. **K.** For example, this coveting, v 7. **L.** Or concurring-with. **M.** When God says not to do it, Paul agrees and does not want to do it, but sin produces it in him anyway. Thus it is sin, not God's Law, that causes his death. The sin in him is against him and against God! How extremely sinful it truly is! This proves v 14b; Paul is under the dominion of sin. **N.** Good is not in him producing good, but sin is in him producing sin, and overcoming his inner desire to obey God's good Law. This proves v 18. **O.** Or, the principle, the law of sin. v 23. **P.** Or, taking pleasure with, delighting in. **Q.** Or with respect to.

inner person. **23** But I am seeing *a* different law in my body-parts waging-war-against[A] the law *of* my mind, and taking me captive[B] under the law *of* sin existing in my body-parts. **24** I *am a* wretched[C] person! Who will deliver me from this[D] body *of* [E] death? **25** But thanks *be to* God through Jesus Christ our Lord! So then, **I** myself am serving *the* Law *of* God *with* the mind, but *the* law *of* sin *with* the flesh.

This Does Mean That There Is Now No Condemnation For Those In Christ Jesus

8:1 Therefore[F], *there is* now no condemnation *for* the *ones* in Christ Jesus. **2** For the law[G] *of* the Spirit *of* life in Christ Jesus set you[H] free from the law *of* sin and death!

For God Did What The Law Could Not Do, For Those Walking In The Spirit

3 For the *thing* impossible[I] *for* the Law, in that it was weak through the flesh, God *did*. Having sent His *own* Son in *the* likeness *of* sinful flesh, and for[J] sin, He condemned sin in the flesh[K], **4** in order that the requirement[L] *of* the Law might be fulfilled in us, the *ones* walking not in-accordance-with[M] *the* flesh, but in accordance with *the* Spirit.

For The Way of The Flesh Is Death. But You Are Not In The Flesh, But In The Spirit

5 For the *ones* being[N] in accordance with *the* flesh are thinking[O] the *things of* [P] the flesh, but the *ones being* in accordance with *the* Spirit, the *things of* the Spirit. **6** For the way-of-thinking *of* the flesh *is* death, but the way-of-thinking *of* the Spirit *is* life and peace. **7** Because the way-of-thinking *of* the flesh *is* hostility toward God; for it is not subject[Q] *to* the Law *of* God, for it is not even able. **8** And the *ones* being in *the* flesh are not able to please God. **9** But **you** are not in *the* flesh, but in *the* Spirit— since[R] *the* Spirit *of* God is dwelling in you. But if anyone does not have *the* Spirit *of* Christ, this *one* is not *of* [S] Him.

And The Spirit Is True Life In Us Now, And Will Give Life To Our Mortal Bodies

10 And if Christ *is* in you, the body *is* dead because of sin, but the Spirit *is* life[T] because of righteousness. **11** And if the Spirit *of* the One having raised Jesus from *the* dead is dwelling in you, the *One* having raised Christ from *the* dead will also give-life-to your mortal bodies through His Spirit dwelling in you.

So We Are Debtors To The Spirit To Put To Death The Deeds of The Flesh And Live

12 So then, brothers, we are debtors— not *to* the flesh, *that we should* be living in accordance with *the* flesh. **13** For if[U] you are living in accordance with *the* flesh, you

---

A. The law of sin's control over Paul's body fights and defeats his inner desires to obey. **B.** Or, making me prisoner. **C.** Or, miserable. **D.** Or, the body *of* this death. **E.** That is, *characterized by*. **F.** Paul now turns from correcting false inferences drawn from salvation by grace (ch 6-7) to again teaching true ones. **G.** That is, the controlling power, the operative power. **H.** This word is singular. Paul makes it personal. **I.** That is, to conquer the death-producing power of sin. **J.** Paul may mean as an offering for sin; or, to deal with sin in all its aspects. **K.** Or, in *His* flesh. **L.** This views the entire Law as a single requirement. **M.** Or, in harmony with, in conformity with. **N.** Or, existing, and thus, living. This is another way of saying 'walking', v 4. **O.** Or, setting their minds on, being intent on. This is the focus of their hearts and minds. **P.** That is, *belonging to; proceeding from*. **Q.** Or, does not subject-*itself*. **R.** Or, if as is the case, if indeed. **S.** That is, does not belong to Him. **T.** That is, the Spirit is true life. Or, the spirit *is* alive, in contrast to the body. **U.** That is, assuming it is true that.

are going-to[A] die. But if *by the* Spirit you are putting-to-death the practices *of* the body, you will live.

For Those Being So Led By The Spirit Are The Adopted Children of God
[14] For[B] all who are being led[C] *by the* Spirit *of* God, these are sons[D] *of* God. [15] For you did not receive *a* spirit[E] *of* slavery again leading-to fear, but you received *a* Spirit[F] *of* adoption by Whom we are crying-out "Abba[G]! Father!" [16] The Spirit Himself bears-witness-with our spirit that we are children *of* God!

This Means We Are Joint-Heirs With Christ, Sharing His Suffering And Glory
[17] And if *we are* children, *we are* heirs also. *We are* heirs *of* God, and fellow-heirs *of* Christ, since[H] we are suffering-with *Him* in order that we may also be glorified-with *Him*. [18] For I consider that the sufferings *of* the present time *are* **not worthy** to the glory destined to be revealed to[I] us.

Creation Itself Groans To Share In Our Glory
[19] For the eager-expectation *of* the creation is awaiting[J] the revelation *of* the sons *of* God. [20] For the creation was subjected *to* futility[K]— not willingly[L], but because of the *One* having subjected *it*— in hope[M] [21] that the creation itself also will be set-free from the slavery *of*[N] decay into the freedom *of*[O] the glory *of* the children *of* God. [22] For we know that the whole creation is groaning-together and suffering-birthpains-together[P] until the present.

We Groan For The Redemption of Our Body
[23] And not only *creation*, but also ourselves having the firstfruit[Q] *of* the Spirit— **we** ourselves also are groaning within ourselves while eagerly-awaiting adoption, the redemption *of* our body. [24] For we were saved *in* hope. But hope being seen is not hope, for who hopes-for what he sees? [25] But since we hope-for what we do not see, we are eagerly-awaiting *it* with endurance.

The Spirit Groans To Help Us In Our Present Weakness
[26] And similarly also[R] the Spirit helps our weakness. For we do not know what we should pray as *we* ought-to, but the Spirit Himself intercedes-for *us with* inexpressible[S] groanings. [27] And the *One* searching *our* hearts knows[T] what the mind *of* the Spirit *is,* because He is interceding for *the* saints in accordance with God.

A. Or, are destined to. **B.** This gives the reason you will live. If you are living by the Spirit, this means you are one of God's children. **C.** This is the broad category of which putting to death the practices of the body is one aspect. **D.** That is, children, family members, as opposed to slaves. **E.** That is, a disposition, a slave kind of spirit. **F.** Or, spirit. **G.** That is, papa, daddy. **H.** That is, if as is the case. **I.** Or, for, in. **J.** Or, eagerly-awaiting. **K.** Or, purposelessness, pointlessness. **L.** Or, not of its own will, again personifying creation. **M.** That is, in the hope granted to it that. This hope results in the eager expectation of v 19. Or, subjected *it* in *the* expectation that the creation. Or, subjected *it* in hope, because the creation (making this the only place in the Bible where 'hope' has God as the subject). **N.** Or, *belonging to, leading to.* **O.** That is, *characterized by*; or, *belonging to.* **P.** That is, for the birth of the new age. **Q.** That is, the initial foretaste of the Spirit, the future fullness of Whom will be the harvest; or, the firstfruit *which is* the Spirit, He being the first installment of all the blessings God will bestow on us. **R.** Or, indeed. **S.** That is, unspoken, wordless; or, unspeakable, inexpressible, too deep for words. **T.** That is, knows in the sense of approves of, recognizes with approval, takes interest in; or, understands.

This Means God Is Working All Things Together Toward Our Glorification
28 And we know that all *things* are[A] working-together[B] for good *for* the *ones* loving God, the *ones* being called *ones* according to *His* purpose[C]. **29** Because whom He foreknew[D], He also predestined[E] *to be* similar-to-the-form *of* the image[F] *of* His Son, so that He *might* be firstborn[G] among many brothers. **30** And whom He predestined, these He also called[H]. And whom He called, these He also declared-righteous. And whom He declared righteous, these He also glorified[I].

So What Shall We Say To All This? If God Is For Us, Who Will Condemn Us?
31 Therefore, what shall we say to these *things*? If[J] God *is* for us, who *is* against us? **32** He Who indeed did not spare *His* own Son but handed Him over for us all, how will He not also with Him freely-give[K] us all *things*? **33** Who will bring-a-charge against *the* chosen[L] *ones of* God? God *is* the *One* declaring-righteous! **34** Who *is* the *one who* will condemn[M]? Christ Jesus *is* the *One* having died, but more, having been raised, Who also is at *the* right *hand of* God, Who also intercedes[N] for us!

Nothing Can Separate Us From Christ's Love; We Are Conquerors Through Him
35 What[O] shall separate us from the love *of* Christ? Affliction, or distress, or persecution, or famine, or nakedness, or danger, or sword? **36** Just as it has been written [in Ps 44:22] that "For your sake we are being put-to-death the whole day. We were considered as sheep *for* slaughter". **37** But in all these *things* we overwhelmingly-conquer[P] through the *One* having loved us. **38** For I am convinced that neither death nor life, nor angels nor rulers, nor *things* present[Q] nor *things* coming, nor powers, **39** nor height nor depth, nor any other creation[R] will be able to separate us from the love *of* God in Christ Jesus our Lord.

My Heart Has Great Grief And Pain Over Israel
9:1 I am telling *the* truth in Christ, I am not lying— my conscience bearing-witness-with me in *the* Holy Spirit— **2** that there is great grief *in* me and unceasing pain *in* my heart. **3** For I *would* pray[S] *that* I myself *might* be **accursed** from Christ for the sake of my brothers, my kinsmen according to *the* flesh— **4** who are Israelites, *of* whom[T] *is* the adoption and the glory[U] and the covenants and the Law-giving and the [temple] service and the promises, **5** *of* whom *are* the fathers, and from whom *is* the Christ according-to[V] *the* flesh, the *One* being[W] over all, God, blessed forever, amen.

A. Or, that He is working all *things* together for good; or, that *in* all *things*, He joins in working for good. **B.** Or, cooperating, helping, assisting. **C.** Or. plan, design, resolve. **D.** Or, knew beforehand, had advance knowledge of. Some think this knowledge is with reference to their actions and choices; others, that He 'knew' them in the sense of 'had regard for, loved, took interest in' them. **E.** Or, preappointed, predesignated. **F.** Or, likeness. **G.** That is, preeminent, first in rank, the supreme One. **H.** Or, summoned. **I.** Paul puts this in the past tense, as something already certain. **J.** That is, If as is the case. **K.** Or, graciously-grant. **L.** Or, elect, selected. **M.** Or, who *is* the *one* condemning? **N.** Or, petitions, appeals. Same word as in v 27. **O.** Or, Who. **P.** Or, completely-victorious. **Q.** Lit, being present; or, having come. **R.** Or creature, created *thing*. **S.** Or, I *would* wish (pray in a non-religious sense). Paul may mean 'I *would* pray' or 'I *could almost* pray', but don't since it is not possible; or, 'I was wishing', meaning he did at one period in his life wish it. **T.** That is, to whom belong. **U.** That is, the glory of God in all its manifestations in their history. **V.** Or, with respect to. **W.** That is, the One Who is the following three things. Or, the *One* being over all, blessed God forever; or, the *One* being God over all, blessed forever.

258

But Not All Abraham's Physical Children Are Children of God

6 But *it is* not such as that the word *of* God has failed— for not all[A] these *ones* from Israel *are* Israel. **7** Nor *are they* all children because they are seed *of* Abraham, but "In Isaac *a* seed will be called *for* you" [Gen 21:12]. **8** That is, these children *of* the flesh *are* not children *of* God, but the children *of*[B] the promise are counted for seed. **9** For the word *of* promise *is* this: "I will come at this time, and there will be *a* son *to* Sarah" [Gen 18:10]. **10** And not only *this,* but *there is* also Rebekah having bed[C] from one *man,* Isaac our father. **11** For *the twins* having not yet been born nor having done anything good or bad— in order that the purpose[D] *of* God according to *His* choosing[E] might continue[F], **12** not of works but of the *One* calling— it was said *to* her [in Gen 25:23] that "the older will serve the younger". **13** Just as it has been written [in Mal 1:2-3]: "I loved Jacob, but I hated Esau".

God Has Mercy On Whom He Wants, And He Hardens Whom He Wants

14 Therefore what shall we say? *There is* not unrighteousness[G] with God, *is there*? May it never be! **15** For He says *to* Moses [in Ex 33:19], "I will have-mercy-on whomever I have-mercy, and I will have-compassion-on whomever I have compassion". **16** So then, *mercy is* not *of*[H] the *one* wanting, nor *of* the *one* running, but *of* the *One* having-mercy[I]— God. **17** For the Scripture says *to* Pharaoh [in Ex 9:16] that "I raised you up for this very *purpose*: so that I might demonstrate My power[J] in you, and so that My name might be proclaimed in all the earth". **18** So then, He has-mercy-on whom He wants, and He hardens[K] whom He wants.

The Creator Is Making Known His Wrath And His Mercy In Humankind

19 Therefore you will say *to* me, "Why then does He still find-fault? For who has resisted[L] His will?" **20** O human, on the contrary, who are **you**, the *one* answering-back *to* God? The *thing* formed will not say *to* the *one* having formed *it*, "Why did you make me like-this?", *will it*? **21** Or does not the potter have **authority** *over* the clay to make from the same lump one vessel for honor and another for dishonor? **22** But *what* if God, wanting[M] to demonstrate *His* wrath and to make-known His power, bore[N] with much patience vessels *of* wrath having been prepared[O] for destruction, **23** and *did so* in order that He might make-known the riches *of* His glory upon vessels *of* mercy which He prepared-beforehand[P] for glory— **24** even us whom He called not only from *the* Jews, but also from *the* Gentiles?

A. All of Abraham's physical descendants are not partakers of God's promises made to him, as seen even in the very first case, Isaac and Ishmael. **B.** That is, *belonging to, originating in, proceeding from* the promise. **C.** That is, having conceived. **D.** Same word as in 8:28. **E.** Or, election, selection. **F.** With Jacob as with Isaac, God chose before their birth, without reference to their works, who would be the promised 'seed' of Abraham. **G.** Is God unjust to choose one over the other without reference to their works? **H.** That is, not dependent on. **I.** God is not unrighteous because mercy is not a matter of justice or debt; it is a matter of undeserved kindness. Gift-giving is the prerogative of the giver. God cannot be faulted for blessing Isaac and Jacob. **J.** That is, My power both to punish (Egypt) and to save (Israel); My wrath and My mercy. **K.** God is not unrighteous to harden because all punishment for sin is earned and deserved. **L.** How can people be held accountable since God has mercy or hardens as He pleases and people cannot resist His will in either direction? Paul's answer is that people are accountable, and the Creator intends to demonstrate both His wrath and mercy on mankind. **M.** Or, willing, wishing, intending. Paul may mean *because of* wanting; or, *although* wanting. **N.** Or, endured, put up with. **O.** By whom? Perhaps God (as in 9:18; 11:7-8; Jn 12:37-40); Satan; or themselves, rendering it 'having prepared-*themselves*'. **P.** Note that God endured the one group, but actively prepared-beforehand the other.

He Is Making Those Not His People His Own Children
25 As[A] He says also in Hosea: "I will call 'Not My people', 'My people'; and 'Not having been loved', 'Having been loved' " [Hos 2:23]. **26** "And it shall be in the place where it was said *to* them 'you *are* not My people', there they will be called sons *of the* living God" [Hos 1:10].

But Only a Remnant of Israel Will Be Saved
27 But[B] Isaiah cries-out concerning Israel: "If the number *of* the sons *of* Israel should be like the sand *of* the sea, the remnant will be saved. **28** For *the* Lord will accomplish[C] *His* word upon the earth, completing[D] and cutting-short[E]" [in Isa 10:22-23]. **29** And just as Isaiah said-before [in Isa 1:9]: "Unless *the* Lord *of* Sabaoth had left-behind *a* seed *for* us, we would have become like Sodom, and we would have been likened[F] as Gomorrah".

Israel Pursued a Righteousness Through The Law, And Did Not Attain It
30 Therefore, what shall we say? That Gentiles, the *ones* not pursuing righteousness, took-hold-of[G] righteousness— but *a* righteousness by faith. **31** But Israel, pursuing *the* Law *of* righteousness, did not attain to *that* Law. **32** For what reason? Because *they pursued it* not by faith, but as-*if it was* by works. They stumbled *on* the Stone *of* stumbling, **33** just as it has been written [in Isa 28:16]: "Behold— I am laying in Zion *a* Stone *of* stumbling and *a* Rock *of* falling. And the *one* putting-faith upon Him will not be put-to-shame".

Israel's Zeal Is Not In Accordance With Knowledge
10:1 Brothers, my heart's desire and petition to God for them *is* for *their* salvation. **2** For I testify *concerning* them that they have *a* zeal *for* God— but not in-accordance-with knowledge.

For They Are Ignorant of The Source of True Righteousness
3 For being-ignorant-of the righteousness *of* God, and seeking to establish *their* own righteousness, they did not subject *themselves to* the righteousness *of* God. **4** For[H] Christ *is the* end[I] *of the* Law for[J] righteousness *for* everyone believing.

The Law Requires Performance; True Righteousness Comes By Faith In Christ
5 For Moses writes [in Lev 18:5] *as to* the righteousness of the Law that "The person having done them will live by them". **6** But the righteousness of faith speaks[K] as follows: "Do not say in your heart, "Who will go up into heaven?", that is, to bring[L] Christ down, **7** or "who will go down into the abyss?", that is, to

---

A. Here Paul proves that those not in a relationship with God would be called to salvation. **B.** Here Paul proves that only a remnant of physical Israel would be saved. **C.** Or more specifically, execute *His* sentence; less specifically, carry-out *the* matter. **D.** That is, completing *the judgment*; or, carrying-out *His word*; or, closing *the account*. **E.** Or, cutting-down, cutting-off. Paul may mean cutting-short the nation, cutting it down to the remnant; or, cutting short the time, 'quickly'. **F.** That is, we would have been used as an illustration of desolation, like Gomorrah. **G.** Or, took possession of, seized. **H.** This sentence summarizes the heart of their ignorance, the relationship between Christ, Law, righteousness, faith, and works. **I.** Or, fulfillment, completion, termination, goal. **J.** Paul may mean 'for purposes *of* righteousness'; or, 'so that *there may be* righteousness'. **K.** In what follows, Paul uses phrases from Deut 30:11-14 to help describe God's saving process, explaining his current application of each. **L.** The righteousness by faith does not ask who will bring the Messiah down from heaven, because He has already come.

bring[A] Christ up from *the* dead. [8] But what does it say? "The word is near you, in your mouth and in your heart", that is, the word *of* [B] faith which we are proclaiming, [9] that[C] if you confess with your mouth Jesus *as* Lord and you believe in your heart that God raised Him from *the* dead, you will be saved. [10] For it is believed *with the* heart resulting-in righteousness, and it is confessed *with the* mouth resulting in salvation.

The Scripture Says Faith Leads To Salvation For Both Jew And Greek
[11] For the Scripture says [in Isa 28:16] "everyone putting-faith upon Him will not be put-to-shame". [12] For there is no distinction *between* both Jew and Greek— for the same Lord *is* Lord *of* all, being rich toward all the *ones* calling-upon Him. [13] For "everyone who calls-upon the name *of the* Lord will be saved" [Joel 2:32].

This Is Why God Sent Forth His Messengers With The Report About Christ
[14] How then[D] may they[E] call-upon *the One* in Whom they did not believe? And how may they believe *the One* Whom[F] they did not hear? And how may they hear without *one* proclaiming? [15] And how may they proclaim if they are not sent-forth?— just as it has been written[G] [in Isa 52:7]: "How beautiful *are* the feet *of* the *ones* announcing-good-news-of good *things*!" [16] But[H] they did not all obey the good-news, for Isaiah says [in Isa 53:1], "Lord, who put-faith-*in* our report?" [17] So[I] the faith[J] *comes* from *a* report-hearing[K], and the report-hearing through *a* word[L] *about*[M] Christ.

But It Is Not As Though Israel Did Not Hear
[18] But I say[N]— *it is* not *that* they did not hear[O], *is it*? On the contrary: "Their voice went-out into all the earth, and their words to the ends *of* the world" [Ps 19:4].

And It Is Not As Though Israel Did Not Know
[19] But I say— *it is* not *that* Israel did not know[P], *is it*? First, Moses says [in Deut 32:21] "**I** will provoke you to jealousy over *what is* not *a* nation. I will provoke you

A. Nor does it ask who will bring Him back from the dead, because He has already been raised. **B.** That is, about, producing, calling for. **C.** This gives the content of the word of faith. Or, because, explaining why the righteousness of faith says this word is near. **D.** Paul now traces out the logical implications of the Scriptures just quoted. They imply that the response of faith is made to a message proclaimed to everyone by ones sent forth from God. **E.** That is, everyone (v 13), Jew and Greek (v 12). Paul carries out his argument in the universal terms of the prophets, which he is here applying to the case of Israel itself. **F.** Or, the *One of* Whom. **G.** Paul quotes Isaiah to prove that God has done His part. He sent forth messengers and they have proclaimed the message. **H.** Isaiah predicted this rejection by Israel as well, further proof of Israel's ignorance. **I.** Paul summarizes the process he has deduced from Scripture. Faith in the hearer comes in response to a report about Christ, and this report comes through a message proclaimed by one sent. **J.** That is, the faith to call upon the Lord and be saved. **K.** This word means both hearing (the act of hearing) and report (the message heard). It is the same word as 'report' in v 16, and is related to 'hear' in v 18, and is rendered this way to show the connection to both. An obedient-hearing is in view here. **L.** Or, message. That is, the word of faith (v 8); the report (v 16); the proclamation (v 15). **M.** Or, *from*, through the word of His messengers. **N.** Paul moves on from describing the content of Israel's ignorance (v 3-17) to their culpability for it. **O.** Israel cannot claim to have not heard the message, for the message was taken from Israel to the whole world. **P.** Or, understand. The prophets do not leave them this excuse. God told them from the beginning that He would go to the Gentiles and Israel would not believe.

to anger over *a* nation without-understanding[A]". [20] And Isaiah is very-bold and says [in Isa 65:1] "I was found by the *ones* not seeking Me. I became visible[B] *to* the *ones* not asking-for Me". [21] But with-regard-to Israel He says [in Isa 65:2], "I held-out[C] My hands the whole day toward *a* disobeying[D] and contradicting[E] people".

But God Did Not Reject His People
11:1 Therefore I say, God did not reject[F] His people, *did He*? May it never be! For **I** also am *an* Israelite, from *the* seed *of* Abraham, *the* tribe *of* Benjamin. [2] God did not reject His people whom He foreknew!

There Is Still a Remnant Chosen By God
Or do you not know what the Scripture says in-connection-with[G] Elijah [in 1 Kings 19:14], how he appeals *to* God against Israel?— [3] "Lord, they killed Your prophets, they tore-down Your altars, and **I** alone was left, and they are seeking my life". [4] But what does the divine-response say *to* him [in 1 Kings 19:18]?— "I left-remaining *for* Myself seven-thousand men[H] who did not bow *a* knee *to* Baal". [5] In this manner then, there has come-to-be *a* remnant[I] also at the present time, according-to *the* choosing *of* grace. [6] And if *it*[J] is *by* grace, *it is* no longer *by* works. Otherwise the grace becomes grace no longer.

But The Rest Were Hardened By God
[7] Therefore what? This[K] which Israel is seeking-for, it did not obtain. But the chosen[L] obtained *it,* and the rest were hardened, [8] just as it has been written: "God gave them *a* spirit *of* stupor [Isa 29:10], eyes *that they may* not see and ears *that they may* not hear, until this very day" [Deut 29:4]. [9] And David says [in Ps 69:22-23], "Let their table become *a* snare and *a* trap and *a* cause-of-falling and *a* retribution *to* them. [10] Let their eyes be darkened *that they may* not see. And bend[M] their back continually".

And Israel Did Not Stumble So As To Fall
[11] Therefore I say, they did not stumble in order that they might fall[N], *did they*? May it never be! On-the-contrary, *by* their trespass[O] salvation *came to* the Gentiles, so as to provoke them to jealousy. [12] But if their trespass *is* riches *for the* world and their defeat[P] *is* riches *for the* Gentiles, how much more *will* their fullness *be*! [13] And I am speaking **to you**, the Gentiles. So indeed to the extent[Q] I am *an* apostle *of the* Gentiles I glorify[R] my ministry— [14] if somehow[S] I might provoke my flesh to jealousy and save some of them. [15] For if their rejection[T] *is* reconciliation *for the* world, what *will their* acceptance[U] *be* if not life from *the* dead?

A. Or, *a* senseless nation, *a* foolish nation. The nation that knows God and has His word and is trained in spiritual matters will be angered by ones with no such expertise. **B.** Or, known. **C.** That is, in an imploring, pleading gesture. **D.** This word means 'refusing to believe'. **E.** Or, speaking-against, opposing. **F.** Or, push aside, push away. **G.** Or, in the case of; or, in *the place about.* **H.** That is, males. **I.** This proves God has not completely rejected Israel. **J.** That is, the choosing. **K.** That is, this righteousness and life; this relationship with God. **L.** Lit, the choosing, an abstract term for the whole group of those chosen. **M.** David may mean in bondage or slavery; or, in fear or grief; or, under their burden. **N.** Or, so that they fell. **O.** Or, false-step, fall. **P.** Or, failure; or, diminishing. **Q.** Or, as long as, as far as, inasmuch as. **R.** That is, I magnify, publicize it. **S.** This is a modestly stated hope that Paul might be part of fulfilling God's plan spoken through Moses. **T.** Or, throwing off, being cast away. That is, by God. **U.** Or, reception.

Their Branches Were Broken Off By Unbelief And You Were Grafted In By Faith

16 But[A] if the firstfruit[B] *is* holy, the lump *is* also. And if the root *is* holy, the branches *are* also. **17** Now if some *of* the branches were broken-off[C] and **you**[D], being *a* wild-olive-tree, were grafted-in among them and became *a* co-partner[E] *of* the root, *of* the fatness[F] *of* the olive tree, **18** do not be vaunting[G] *over* the branches. But if you vaunt, [remember] **you** are not carrying the root, but the root you. **19** You will say then, "Branches were broken off in order that **I** might be grafted-in". **20** Well *said!* They were broken off *by their* unbelief, and **you** stand *by your* faith. Do not be thinking lofty[H] *things*, but be fearing[I]— **21** for if God did not spare the branches in accordance with nature, perhaps[J] neither will He spare you.

They Will Be Re-Grafted If They Believe

22 Therefore behold *the* kindness and severity *of* God— severity upon the *ones* having fallen, but *the* kindness *of* God upon you, if you continue *in His* kindness. Otherwise **you** also will be cut off. **23** But those *ones* also, if they do not continue *in* unbelief, will be grafted-in. For God is able to graft them in again. **24** For if **you** were cut off from the wild-olive-tree according to nature and were grafted-in contrary to nature into *a* cultivated-olive-tree, how much more will these, the *ones* in accordance with nature, be grafted-in *their* own olive tree!

All Israel Will Be Saved

25 For I do not want you to be unaware, brothers, *as to* this mystery[K]— in order that you not be wise among yourselves— that *a* hardness in part[L] has happened *to* Israel until[M] the fullness *of* the Gentiles comes in. **26** And so[N] all Israel[O] will be saved, just as it has been written: "The *One* delivering will come[P] from Zion, He will turn-away ungodliness from Jacob. **27** And this *is* the covenant from Me *with* them, when I take-away their sins" [Isa 59:20-21].

They Are Beloved To God

28 In relation to the good-news *they*[Q] *are* enemies [of God] for your sake— but in relation to the choosing[R] *of* God *they are* beloved *ones* [of God] for the sake of the fathers. **29** For the gifts and the calling *of* God *are* without-regret[S].

A. Paul now turns from Israel's failure, which serves the Gentiles, to their remaining potential for salvation. **B.** That is, the first part offered to God. **C.** That is, unbelieving physical Israel was pruned from spiritual Israel. **D.** In v 17-24 'you' is singular, referring to a single Gentile as a representative. In v 25 'you' is plural again. **E.** Or, joint-sharer, co-participant. **F.** Or, richness, wealth. **G.** Or, gloating. **H.** That is, proud thoughts. **I.** That is, be reverencing God; or, be afraid of unbelief. **J.** Or, nature, *fear* that He will somehow not spare you. **K.** That is, something hidden but now revealed; something known only by revelation from God. **L.** That is, to part of Israel, 'some' of the branches, v 17. **M.** Paul may mean that the hardness in part ends at that future time and the fullness of response comes, a national conversion; or, that it continues until that time, implying Israel's continued existence until Christ returns, but nothing about a national conversion. **N.** Or, in this manner, thus. That is, with the fullness of the Gentiles coming in, and the moving of Israel to jealousy (v 11) so that they believe (v 23) and are regrafted into their tree (v 24). **O.** Paul may mean the nation as a whole, Israel in contrast to the remnant, the emphasis being on 'all' versus 'in part', ending the hardness in part. Or he may mean all individual true spiritual Israelites, the remnant in contrast with Israel, the emphasis being on 'so, in this manner'. Alongside the continuing hardness in part, all true Israelites will believe. **P.** Paul may be referring to the first coming, or to the second. **Q.** That is, the as yet unsaved Jews; or, the Jewish nation as a whole. **R.** That is, God's choosing them as His people. **S.** Or, unregretted, unchanged.

They Will Be Shown Mercy
30 For just as **you** once[A] disobeyed God, but now were shown-mercy *in* the disobedience of these *Jews*, **31** so also these *Jews* now disobeyed *in* the mercy belonging to you, in order that **they** also now may be shown-mercy. **32** For God confined all in disobedience in order that He may show-mercy to all.

O The Depth of God's Wisdom! To Him Be The Glory!
33 O *the* depth *of* riches both[B] *of the* wisdom and *the* knowledge *of* God! How unsearchable *are* His judgments and untraceable[C] His ways! **34** "For who knew *the* mind *of the* Lord? Or who became His counselor?" [Isa 40:13]. **35** "Or who previously-gave[D] *to* Him and it will be repaid *to* him?" [Job 41:11]. **36** Because all *things are* from Him and through Him and for Him. *To* Him *be* the glory forever, amen.

I Urge You To Present Your Bodies To God As a Living Sacrifice, And Renew Your Mind
12:1 Therefore I urge you, brothers, by the compassions[E] *of* God, to present[F] your bodies *as a* living holy sacrifice pleasing *to* God, *as* your spiritual[G] worship[H]. **2** And do not be conformed[I] *to* this age[J], but be transformed *by* the renewing *of your* mind, so that you *may* be approving what[K] *is* the good and pleasing and perfect will *of* God.

Think Sound-Mindedly About Yourself As God Has Apportioned You The Faith
3 For I say *to* everyone being among you through the grace having been given *to* me not to be thinking-highly *of yourself* beyond what *you* ought-to think, but to be thinking so as to be sound-minded, as God apportioned[L] *to* each *a* measure[M] *of* faith.

For We Are One Body In Christ. Use The Gifts And Faith God Has Given You
4 For just as we have many body-parts in one body and all the body-parts do not have the same function, **5** in this manner we the many are one body in Christ, and individually body-parts *of* one another. **6** And having different *grace*-gifts according-to the grace having been given *to* us, *exercise them accordingly*[N]: whether prophecy, in accordance with the proportion[O] *of your* faith[P]; **7** or service[Q], in-the-sphere-of[R] *your* service[S]; or the *one* teaching, in the sphere of *your* teaching[T]; **8** or the *one* exhorting[U], in the sphere of *your* exhortation[V]; the *one* giving, with[W] generosity[X]; the *one* leading[Y], with diligence; the *one* showing-mercy, with cheerfulness.

A. Or, formerly. **B.** Or, and. **C.** Or, inscrutable, incomprehensible. They cannot be traced out. **D.** Or, gave-beforehand, gave in advance. **E.** Or, *acts-of*-compassion. **F.** Or, offer. **G.** Or, reasonable, thoughtful, pertaining to the real (spiritual) nature of things. **H.** Or, service. **I.** Or, molded. **J.** Or, world. **K:** what *is*... God. Or, what *is* the will *of* God— the *thing* good and pleasing and perfect. **L.** Or, divided, distributed. **M.** Or, *a* quantity, *a* measured-portion. **N.** At some point Paul transitions from explanation to exhortation, intending the reader to supply the commands needed. Some add a single command here; others a command after each gift mentioned next. **O.** That is, your measure of faith. Or, the right-relationship *to* the faith. **P.** Or, the faith *given*. **Q.** Or, ministry. **R.** Or, with, by. Both the gift and the sphere or realm in which it is used are gifts from God. **S.** Or, the service *given*. **T.** Or, the teaching *given*. **U.** Or, encouraging, comforting. **V.** Or, the exhortation *given*. **W.** Paul changes from referring to the sphere in which the gift is used to the manner in which it is used. **X.** Or, simplicity (that is, without any self-seeking motive or partiality), sincerity. **Y.** Or, managing, ruling, being at the head, presiding over.

Think And Diligently Act In Love, Faith, And Holiness

9 *I say*[A] *to let your* love *be* sincere[B], while abhorring the evil, clinging[C] *to* the good; **10** *to be* affectionate[D] to one another *in* brotherly-love, preferring[E] one another *in* honor; **11** *to* not *be* hesitant *in* diligence; *to be* boiling *in* spirit, serving the Lord, **12** rejoicing *in* hope, enduring *in* affliction, devoting-yourselves *to* prayer, **13** sharing *in* the needs *of* the saints, pursuing hospitality. **14** Be blessing the *ones* persecuting you— be blessing and not cursing[F]. **15** *I say* to rejoice with rejoicing *ones,* to weep with weeping *ones;* **16** *to be* thinking the same *thing* toward one another, not thinking lofty[G] things, but being carried-along-with[H] the lowly[I] (do not be wise among yourselves); **17** *to be* giving-back evil for evil *to* no one; *to be* providing-for[J] good *things* in the sight of all people, **18** living-in-peace with all people if possible— *as far as* from you; **19** *to* not *be* avenging yourselves, beloved, but give *a* place *to* the wrath *of* God. For it has been written: "Vengeance *is for* Me, I will repay, says *the* Lord" [Deut 32:35]. **20** "But if your enemy is hungry, feed him; if he is thirsty, give-a-drink *to* him. For doing this, you will heap coals *of* fire upon his head" [Prov 25:21-22]. **21** Do not be overcome by[K] evil, but be overcoming evil with good.

Be Subject To Authorities: They Are Established By God

13:1 Let every soul be subject[L] *to* superior authorities. For there is no authority except by God. And the existing *ones* are established[M] by God. **2** So then the *one* opposing[N] the authority has resisted[O] the ordinance[P] *of* God. And the *ones* having resisted will receive[Q] judgment *on* themselves.

Rulers are God's Servants To Reward Good And Punish Evil

3 For the rulers are not *a* fear *to* good work, but *to* evil[R]. Now do you want to not be fearing the authority? Be doing good, and you will have praise[S] from him[T]— **4** for he is God's servant *to* you for good. But if you are doing evil, be fearing! For he does not bear[U] the sword in-vain[V]— for he is God's servant, *an* avenger for wrath *on* the *one* practicing evil. **5** Therefore *it is a* necessity to be subject— not only because of the wrath[W], but also because of the conscience.

A. What follows is clearly a series of exhortations, so most make them all commands. Here they are given as Paul wrote them, with words supplied in italics to make the sense clear. Since there is no clear indication of a change of subject, they are listed as a continuation of what Paul wants to 'say to everyone being among you', v 3. **B.** Or, genuine, without-hypocrisy. **C.** Or, joining *oneself to,* associating *with.* **D.** Or, warmly-devoted, tenderly-loving. **E.** Paul may mean leading the way for one another in honor; or, being first to honor one another; or, esteeming one another more highly in honor. **F.** That is, calling down curses. **G.** Or, high, proud. **H.** Or, accommodating to, associating with. **I.** Or, humble. **J.** Or, planning for, taking thought for. **K.** That is, by the evil done to you. Do not be controlled or directed by it, but take the lead yourself with good. **L.** Or, submit *himself.* **M.** Or, put in place, stationed, arranged, assigned. **N.** Or, setting himself against. **O.** Or, stood against. **P.** Or, decree, direction. The authority of government is God's decree. Paul is commanding submission to this authority, however it is expressed in your nation. In some nations this includes active involvement in government; in others, citizens have little input. **Q.** That is, from God, whose decree you have resisted. Secondarily, from the authorities, if you are caught. **R.** That is, civil evil, crime. **S.** This is the general rule. Paul does not deal here with exceptions. Paul himself was persecuted for doing good, for proclaiming the gospel. **T.** Or, it, the authority. **U.** Or, wear. **V.** That is, for no purpose. Governments have God's authority to punish evil to the fullest extent, including death, and they serve God's purposes in doing so. Governments exercise this authority through the police, the courts, and the military, in ways and means and degrees of their own choosing. **W.** We submit out of fear of God's wrath expressed through government, and our own conscience toward God. Usually these are in agreement. In exceptional cases, which Paul does not address here, the conscience must be followed in spite of the threats from government.

So Give Them Their Due
6 For because of this also you pay tributes[A]. For they are ministers[B] *of* God devoting-themselves to this very *thing.* **7** Give-back *to* all *authorities* the *things* owed— the tribute *to* the *one owed* the tribute, the tax[C] *to* the *one owed* the tax, the fear[D] *to* the *one owed* the fear, the honor *to* the *one owed* the honor.

Pay Your Ongoing Debt of Love
8 Be owing[E] nothing *to* anyone except to be loving one another. For the *one* loving the other has fulfilled *the* Law. **9** For the *saying* "You shall not commit-adultery, you shall not murder, you shall not steal, you shall not covet" [Ex 20:13-17], and if *there is* any other commandment, is summed-up in this saying— in the "You shall love your neighbor as yourself" [Lev 19:18]. **10** Love does not work harm[F] *to* the neighbor. Therefore love *is the* fulfillment *of the* Law.

Put On The Weapons of The Light, And Make No Provision For The Flesh
11 And *do* this knowing the time, that *it is* already *the* hour *for* you to arise from sleep. For now our salvation *is* nearer than when we believed. **12** The night is advanced, and the day has drawn-near. Therefore let us lay-aside[G] the works *of* the darkness and let us put-on the weapons[H] *of* the light. **13** Let us walk properly[I] as in *the* day[J]— not *in* revelries[K] and drunkenness[L], not *in* beds[M] and sensualities, not *in* strife and jealousy, **14** but put-on[N] the Lord Jesus Christ and do not be making provision[O] *for* the flesh, for *its* desires.

Accept Those Weak In The Faith
14:1 Now be accepting the *one* being weak *in* the faith[P]— [but] not for disputes[Q] *about* opinions[R].

Don't Judge The Opinions of Fellow Servants of Your Master
2 One has faith to eat all *things,* but the *one* being weak eats vegetables[S]. **3** Let not the *one* eating be treating-with-contempt[T] the *one* not eating. And let not the *one* not eating be judging[U] the *one* eating— for God accepted him. **4** Who are **you**, the *one* judging *a* household-servant belonging-to-another? *To his* own master he stands or falls. And he will stand, for the Lord is able to make him stand.

A. Taxes paid by foreigners to ruling states, such as that paid by Israel to Rome. **B.** Or, public servants. Note that Paul is talking about Rome, which conquered and subjugated his nation and took away their freedom and right of self-government. **C.** That is, the local taxes. **D.** Or, respect. **E.** The owing and the loving refer to the same person or people. Paul is referring here to our personal relations with individuals. **F.** Or, evil, civil or personal. **G.** That is, like a garment. **H.** Or, tools, instruments. **I.** Or, decently, with propriety. **J.** Paul may mean the broad-daylight; or, the present daylight of the gospel; or, the future day when Jesus comes. **K.** Or, wild-parties with drunken antics. **L.** This word is plural, and may mean *episodes of* drunkenness, drinking bouts. **M.** That is, sex; in this context, perhaps orgies. **N.** Or, wear, clothe-*yourself*-in. **O.** Or, foresight, forethought, plan. **P.** Or, weak in faith. Their faith does not allow them to live in the full freedom of Christ. They are bound by customs and traditions from their former life. The weak sometimes judge a person who does not do as they do. The strong sometimes treat the weak with contempt because of their opinions. **Q.** This word means 'discernments, judgments', and then the 'disputes, quarrels' that result from this behavior. **R.** Or, reasonings, thoughts. **S.** The weak one's faith leads him to conclude that the meat has a negative spiritual significance and must be avoided. **T.** Or, despising, disregarding. **U.** Or, passing judgment on.

Live For The Lord As You Think Best, For Each of Us Will Give an Account To God
5 For one judges *a* day beyond *a* day[A], but another judges every day *alike*. Let each *one* be fully-convinced in *his* own mind[B]. **6** The *one* thinking[C] *as to* the day, is thinking *for the* Lord. And the *one* eating, is eating *for the* Lord— for he gives-thanks *to* God. And the *one* not eating, is not eating *for the* Lord— and he gives-thanks *to* God. **7** For[D] none *of* us lives *for* himself, and none dies *for* himself. **8** For if we live, we live *for* the Lord; and if we die, we die *for* the Lord. Therefore if we live and if we die, we are the Lord's. **9** For Christ died and came-to-life for this: that He might be-Lord both *of* dead and living *ones*. **10** But why are **you** judging your brother? Or why also are **you** treating your brother with contempt? For we will all stand before the judgment-seat *of* God. **11** For it has been written [in Isa 45:23]: "*As* **I** live", says *the* Lord, "every knee will bow *to* **Me**. And every tongue will confess-out *to* God". **12** So then, each *of* us will give *an* account for himself *to* God.

Don't Let Your Good Choices Cause Spiritual Harm To Others; Walk In Love
13 Therefore let us no longer be judging one another. But rather judge[E] this: not to be placing *an* opportunity-for-stumbling[F] or *a* cause-of-falling[G] *for* the brother (**14** I know[H] and am convinced in *the* Lord Jesus that nothing[I] *is* defiled[J] in itself[K], except *to* the *one* considering anything to be defiled— *to* that[L] *one it is* defiled). **15** For if your brother is grieved[M] because of food, you are no longer walking according-to love. Do not be destroying *with*[N] your food that *one* for whom Christ died. **16** Therefore do not be letting your good *thing* be blasphemed[O]. **17** For the kingdom *of* God is not eating and drinking, but righteousness[P] and peace and joy in *the* Holy Spirit. **18** For the *one* serving[Q] Christ in this *is* pleasing *to* God and approved *by* people.

Let Us Be Pursuing Peace And Things That Build Up, Not Things That Tear Down
19 So then, let us be pursuing the *things of*[R] peace and the *things of* edification for one another. **20** Do not be tearing-down the work *of* God for the sake of food. All *things are* clean— but *it is* evil *for* the person eating with *an* opportunity-for-stumbling. **21** *It is* good not to eat meats, nor to drink wine, nor *to do anything* by which your brother stumbles.

Hold To Your Convictions, But Carry The Weak. Don't Just Please Yourselves
22 *The* faith which **you** have, be having for[S] yourself in the sight of God. Blessed *is* the *one* not judging himself in what he is approving. **23** But the *one* doubting

---

A. That is, one day as spiritually more significant than another. **B.** Each should follow the course proceeding from their own faith in Christ. **C.** That is, thinking of it in a special way out of a desire to honor the Lord. **D.** Paul generalizes from these cases to the broad view. In all of life and death, we live for the Lord. **E.** That is, determine, decide, resolve. **F.** Or, an occasion to take offense or stumble into sin. **G.** The former case causes an unintended stumble; the cause of falling is a consciously chosen thing. The person deliberately proceeds with behavior known to be objectionable to the weak, perhaps even in defiance of them. **H.** As to knowledge, the strong are correct. But there is another way to view the matter besides 'in itself'. **I.** That is, nothing in the category of things being discussed here. **J.** Or, unclean, impure. **K.** That is, by means of being what it is. Even in the OT, pig was not unclean because it was pig. All God's creation is good. It was defined as unclean to Israel by God's Law. **L.** Regardless of what it is in itself or to God, it is defiled to the conscience of the one thinking it such. **M.** Or, distressed, caused pain, caused sorrow. **N.** Or, *for*. **O.** Or spoken against. **P.** It is the subjective experience of these three things that the strong can take from the weak. **Q.** That is, serving-as-slave to Christ. **R.** That is, *belonging to*; or, *leading to*. **S.** That is, in the interest of, in relation to.

has been condemned if he eats, because *it was* not from faith— and everything which *is* not from faith is sin. **15:1** But^A **we**, the strong *ones,* ought to be carrying^B the weaknesses *of* the *ones* not-strong, and not to be pleasing ourselves.

Be Pleasing Your Neighbor. For Even Christ Didn't Please Himself, As It Is Written
2 Let each *of* us be pleasing *his* neighbor for good, toward [his] edification. **3** For even Christ did not please Himself, but just as it has been written [in Ps 69:9]: "The reproaches *of* the *ones* reproaching You fell upon Me".

For Scripture Was Written To Give Us Hope As We Endure In This
4 For all that was written-before was written for our instruction, in order that we might have hope through endurance and through the encouragement *of* the Scriptures.

May God Help You All To Think The Same Thing, To His Glory
5 Now may the God *of* endurance and encouragement grant you to be thinking the same^C *thing* among one another according-to^D Christ Jesus, **6** in order that with-one-accord you may with one mouth be glorifying the God and Father *of* our Lord Jesus Christ.

Therefore Accept One Another As Christ Has Accepted You, Both Jew And Gentile
7 Therefore, be accepting one-another, just as Christ also accepted you— for *the* glory *of* God. **8** For I say *that* Christ has become *a* servant *of the* circumcised on behalf of *the* truth *of* God, so that *He might* confirm the promises *of*^E the fathers, **9** and the Gentiles *might* glorify God for *His* mercy just as it has been written: "For this reason I will praise You among *the* Gentiles and I will sing-praise *to* Your name" [Ps 18:49]. **10** And again he says, "Celebrate, Gentiles, with His people" [Deut 32:43]. **11** And again, "All Gentiles, be praising the Lord, and let all the peoples praise Him" [Ps 117:1]. **12** And again Isaiah says, "There will be the root of Jesse, even the *One* rising-up to rule^F *the* Gentiles. *The* Gentiles will put-*their*-hope upon Him" [Isa 11:10].

Peace And Joy To You All
13 Now may the God *of*^G hope fill you *with* all joy and peace in believing, so that you *may* be abounding in hope by *the* power *of the* Holy Spirit.

Brothers, I Wrote To You As a Minister of Christ To The Gentiles, Serving The Gospel
14 Now I am convinced, my brothers— even I myself concerning you— that you yourselves also are full *of* goodness, having been filled *with* all knowledge, being able also to admonish one another. **15** But I wrote more-boldly^H *to* you, in part^I as reminding you again, because of the grace having been given *to* me by God **16** so that I *might* be *a* minister *of* Christ Jesus to the

---

A. The strong would completely agree with 14:22-23. But Paul wants them to also see this point, which breaks the deadlock. **B.** Or, bearing, bearing with. The strong are not just to tolerate the weak, they are to help them, support them, carry their burden. **C.** Paul does not mean the same thing about foods and days, but about the treatment of one another. **D.** Or, in harmony with. **E.** That is, belonging to. **F.** Or, be-ruler *of.* **G.** That is, producing, granting. **H.** Or, more daringly. **I.** That is, in part reminding you, along with the reason stated in v 23-24. Or, I wrote more boldly in part; that is, in some parts of the book, such as chapter 14.

Gentiles, performing-priestly-service-for[A] the good-news *of* God in order that the offering *of*[B] the Gentiles might become acceptable[C], having been sanctified[D] by *the* Holy Spirit.

My Ministry of The Gospel To Gentiles Who Have Not Heard Is My Boast And My Ambition
[17] I then have *this* boasting[E] in Christ Jesus *as to* the *things* pertaining to God— [18] for I will not dare[F] to speak anything *of things* which Christ did not accomplish through me *in* word and deed for[G] the obedience *of the* Gentiles, [19] by *the* power *of* signs and wonders, by *the* power *of the* Spirit *of* God— so-that from Jerusalem and around as far as Illyricum[H] I have completed[I] the good-news *of* Christ, [20] and *was* thus being ambitious[J] to be announcing-the-good-news where Christ was not named in order that I might not be building upon *a* foundation belonging-to-another, [21] but just as it has been written [in Isa 52:15]: "*Ones to* whom it was not declared concerning Him will see, and they who have not heard will understand".

Pursuing This Ministry, I Hope To Come To You On The Way To Spain
[22] Therefore indeed I was hindered *as to* many[K] *things from* coming to you. [23] But now no longer having *a* place in these regions, and having *a* yearning for many years *that I should* come to you [24] whenever I am proceeding into Spain[L]— for I hope, while proceeding-through, to see you and to be sent-forward there by you, if I may first be filled in part *with* your *company*.

But First I Am Going To Jerusalem, Taking a Contribution To The Poor Saints There
[25] But now I am proceeding to Jerusalem, serving the saints. [26] For Macedonia[M] and Achaia were well-pleased to make *a* certain contribution for the poor *among* the saints in Jerusalem. [27] For they were well-pleased, and they are their debtors. For if the Gentiles shared *in* their spiritual *things*, they are indebted also to minister[N] *to* them in fleshly *things*. [28] Having then completed this, and having sealed[O] this fruit *to* them, I will go through you into Spain. [29] And I know that while coming to you, I will come in *the* fullness *of the* blessing *of* Christ.

Pray For Me, Brothers
[30] Now I appeal-to you, brothers, through our Lord Jesus Christ and through the love *of*[P] the Spirit, to struggle-with[Q] me in *your* prayers to God for me— [31] that I may be delivered from the *ones* disobeying in Judea, and *that* my service[R] for Jerusalem may prove-to-be acceptable *to* the saints, [32] in order that having come in joy to you by *the* will *of* God, I may rest-up-with you. [33] Now the God *of* peace *be* with you all, amen.

A. Or, serving-as-priest-for. Paul is doing temple duties in God's spiritual temple. **B.** That is, consisting of. **C.** Or, welcome. **D.** Or, made holy, set apart *to God*. **E.** Or, *my* boasting. That is, as to his God-given ministry. **F.** Stated positively, I will dare only to speak of what Christ accomplished through me. **G.** That is, for the purpose of; or, leading to; or, resulting in. **H.** In modern terms, from Israel up and around the Mediterranean to north of Greece in the area of the Balkans. **I.** That is, completed his proclamation of the good news about Christ. Paul finished his pioneering ministry, the task he was given to do. **J.** Or. making it my ambition, pursuing as my ambition. **K.** Or, many *times,* and thus, 'often'. **L.** Paul breaks off this sentence, and takes up this thought again in v 28. First he explains how the Romans fit into his yearning for Spain and his plans to get there. **M.** Compare 1 Cor 16:1; 2 Cor 8-9. **N.** Or, serve. This is the priestly service of the Gentiles. **O.** That is, secured and certified in accordance with its intention. **P.** That is, proceeding from; or, produced by. **Q.** Or, fight along with. **R.** Or, ministry.

Closing Remarks And Greetings:

I Commend Phoebe To You; Help Her
16:1 Now I commend *to* you our sister Phoebe[A]— *she* being also *a* servant[B] *of* the church in Cenchrea[C]— **2** in order that you may receive her in *the* Lord worthily *of* the saints, and may stand-by[D] her in whatever matter she may be having-need *of* you. For she herself indeed became *a* benefactor[E] *of* many, and *of* me myself.

Greet My Friends
3 Greet Prisca and Aquila— my fellow-workers in Christ Jesus, **4** who risked their *own* neck for my life, *to* whom not only am **I** giving-thanks, but also all the churches *of* the Gentiles— **5** and the church at their house. Greet Epaenetus, my beloved, who is *the* firstfruit *of* Asia for Christ. **6** Greet Mary, who labored-*at* many *things* for you. **7** Greet Andronicus and Junias[F], my kinsmen[G] and my fellow-captives[H], who are notable[I] among[J] the apostles, who also were in Christ before me. **8** Greet Ampliatus, my beloved in *the* Lord. **9** Greet Urbanus, our fellow-worker in Christ, and Stachys my beloved. **10** Greet Apelles, the approved *one* in Christ. Greet the *ones* from the *ones of* [K]Aristobulus. **11** Greet Herodion, my kinsman. Greet the *ones* from the *ones of* Narcissus, the *ones* being in *the* Lord. **12** Greet Tryphaena[L] and Tryphosa, the *ones* laboring in *the* Lord. Greet Persis[M] the beloved, who labored-*at* many *things* in *the* Lord. **13** Greet Rufus, the chosen *one* in *the* Lord, and his mother and mine. **14** Greet Asyncritus, Phlegon, Hermes, Patrobas, Hermas and the brothers with them. **15** Greet Philologus and Julia, Nereus and his sister, and Olympas, and all the saints with them. **16** Greet one another with *a* holy kiss.

The Churches Here Greet You
All the churches[N] *of* Christ greet you.

Watch Out For False Teachers
17 Now I urge you, brothers, to be watching-out-for the *ones* producing the dissensions and the causes-of-falling contrary to the teaching which **you** learned, and be turning-away from them. **18** For such *ones* are not serving our Lord Christ, but their *own* stomach. And by smooth-talk and flattery[O] they deceive the hearts *of* the guileless[P] *ones*. **19** For your obedience reached to all, therefore I am rejoicing over you. But I want you to be wise with-reference-to[Q] the good and innocent[R] with-reference-to the evil. **20** And the God *of* peace will crush Satan under your feet shortly. The grace *of* our Lord Jesus *be* with you.

My Companions Greet You
21 Timothy my fellow-worker greets you, and *so do* Lucius and Jason and Sosipater, my

A. She is probably the one carrying this letter. **B.** Or, deaconess. **C.** The eastern seaport of Corinth. **D.** Or, help, aid. **E.** Or, patron, protector, helper. **F.** This is a male name. Some manuscripts have it as a female name, Junia (perhaps as husband and wife, or brother and sister, as with Julia in v 15). **G.** That is, fellow Jews. **H.** Paul may mean they once shared an imprisonment with him; or, simply that they too were once jailed for Christ. **I.** Or, famous, distinguished. **J.** Paul may mean 'as apostles', in the wider sense of the word; or, 'to the apostles' (the twelve), their imprisonment having taken place in Judea where they were believers before Paul. **K.** Paul probably means the believers from the household-members of Aristobulus. **L.** The names of these women mean Delicate and Dainty. **M.** This is a woman. **N.** Perhaps Paul is referring to all the representatives with him in Act 20:4. This book was written from Corinth in Act 20:3. **O.** Or, false eloquence, good-sounding argument. Paul may mean their good speech about you (flattery); or their good-sounding but false speech regarding what they are teaching. **P.** Or, innocent, unsuspecting. **Q.** Or, for the purpose of. **R.** Or, pure.

kinsmen. **22** I, Tertius, greet you— the *one* having written the letter in^A *the* Lord. **23** Gaius, the host^B *of* me and *of* the whole church, greets you. Erastus, the steward^C *of* the city, greets you, and *so does* Quartus, *our* brother.   **24 D**

To God Be The Glory
25 Now^E *to* the *One* being able to establish^F you in-accordance-with^G my good-news and the proclamation *of* ^H Jesus Christ, [which is]^I in-accordance-with *the* revelation *of the* mystery having been kept-silent *for* eternal times, **26** but now having been revealed and **having been made-known to all the nations** through *the* prophetic Scriptures according to *the* command *of* the eternal God for *the* obedience *of* faith^J, **27** *to the* only wise God through Jesus Christ, *to* Whom^K *be* the glory forever, amen.

A. This is the Greek word order. This may mean 'greet you... in *the* Lord'; or, 'written... in *the* Lord'. Tertius served as Paul's secretary, writing down or copying this letter for him. **B.** Paul is apparently staying with Gaius in Corinth. This may be the Gaius of 1 Cor 1:14. **C.** Or, manager, administrator. **D.** Some manuscripts say 'The grace *of* our Lord Jesus Christ *be* with you all. Amen.' here instead of in v 20b. **E.** This doxology (v 25-27) appears in different places in the manuscripts. **F.** Same word as in 1:11. **G.** Or, based on, in relation to. **H.** That is, about. This proclamation is given in its greatest detail in this book. **I.** That is, the good news and proclamation are in accordance with the revelation of the mystery. **J.** Same phrase as in 1:5. **K.** This could refer back to the only wise God or to Jesus Christ.

1 Corinthians

Introduction   1:1-9

A.   I exhort you that there not be divisions among you over Paul, Apollos, Cephas, Christ   1:10-12

    1.   Has Christ been divided? Were you baptized into Paul? I give thanks I baptized none of you   1:13-16

       a.   For He sent me not to baptize, but to speak the gospel without wisdom of speech   1:17-31
       b.   And I having come to you, I did not proclaim God's mystery with human wisdom   2:1-5
       c.   Yet we are speaking wisdom to the mature, a wisdom God revealed through the Spirit   2:6-16
       d.   And I was not able to speak to you as to spiritual ones. I gave you milk. But even still   3:1-4
          you are fleshly, walking like mankind, saying I am of Paul, of Apollos

    2.   Therefore what is Apollos and Paul?— servants through whom you believed. We are   3:5-4:5
       co-workers of God. So let no one be boasting in people
    3.   I applied these things to Apollos and I that you may learn not to be puffed up about men   4:6-21

B.   Sexual immorality is being heard of among you. Remove the immoral person from among you   5:1-13
C.   Does any one of you dare to take your cases before the unrighteous judges and not the saints?   6:1-11
D.   Flee sexual immorality. Your body is for the Lord, a part of Christ, and a temple of the Spirit   6:12-20
E.   Now concerning the things which you wrote   7:1

    1.   Marital relations, marriage and singleness, divorce   7:1-24
    2.   Now concerning virgins, and the remarriage of widows   7:25-40
    3.   Now concerning foods sacrificed to idols. Some eat by the custom of the idol, staining   8:1-12
       their conscience

       a.   If food causes my brother to stumble, I will never eat meat again. Am I not an   8:13-9:23
          apostle? Nevertheless, I do not make use of my rights so as not to hinder the gospel
       b.   Run so as to lay hold of the prize and not become disapproved. Remember Israel!   9:24-10:22
       c.   All things are lawful, but not all are beneficial. Be seeking the good of the other   10:23-30
       d.   Therefore do all to the glory of God. Become blameless to all, imitators of me   10:31-11:1

    4.   Head coverings for women while publicly praying or prophesying   11:2-16
    5.   Proper conduct at the Lord's Supper   11:17-34
    6.   Now concerning spiritual gifts. There are differences of gifts, ministries, and things-   12:1-11
       worked, given by the one God. They are given to each for our benefit, just as He wills

       a.   For as the human body has many body-parts but is one body, so also is Christ   12:12-31
       b.   And I show you a way still beyond measure— love. Be pursuing love   12:31-14:1
       c.   Be zealous for spiritual gifts, but even more that you might be prophesying.   14:1-40
          In church, do all things for edification

    7.   Now I make known the good news I announced to you, that Christ died and was raised.   15:1-58
       But if Christ is proclaimed as raised, how is it some are saying there is no resurrection?
    8.   Now concerning the collection for the poor in Jerusalem, and Paul's next visit   16:1-11
    9.   Now concerning Apollos   16:12

Conclusion   16:13-24

1:1 Paul[A], *a* called apostle *of* Christ Jesus by *the* will *of* God, and Sosthenes *our* brother, **2** *to* the church *of* God being in Corinth, *to ones* having been sanctified[B] in Christ Jesus, called saints[C], with all the *ones* calling-upon the name *of* our Lord Jesus Christ in every place, their *Lord* and ours: **3** Grace *to* you and peace from God our Father and *the* Lord Jesus Christ.

4 I am giving-thanks *to* my God always for you for the grace *of* God having been given *to* you in Christ Jesus, **5** because you were enriched in everything in[D] Him— in all speech[E] and all knowledge, **6** even as the testimony *of*[F] Christ was confirmed[G] in[H] you— **7** so that you *are* not lacking in any gift while eagerly-awaiting the revelation *of* our Lord Jesus Christ, **8** Who also will confirm you until *the* end *so as to be* blameless[I] on the day *of* our Lord Jesus Christ. **9** God *is* faithful, through Whom you were called into fellowship *with* His Son, Jesus Christ our Lord.

Brothers, Be of One Mind; Stop Dividing Over Your Leaders
10 Now I exhort you, brothers, by the name *of* our Lord Jesus Christ, that you all be speaking the same *thing,* and *that* there not be divisions among you, but *that* you be made-complete[J] in the same mind[K] and in the same purpose[L]. **11** For it was made-clear *to* me concerning you, my brothers, by the *ones*[M] *of* Chloe, that there are quarrels among you. **12** Now I mean this: that each *of* you is saying "I am *of* Paul", and "I *of* Apollos", and "I *of* Cephas", and "I *of* Christ".

Has Christ Been Divided? Were You Baptized Into Paul? Thankfully, I Did Not Baptize You!
13 Has Christ been divided? Paul was not crucified for you, *was he*? Or were you baptized in the name *of* Paul? **14** I give-thanks *to* God that I baptized none *of* you, except Crispus and Gaius, **15** so that no one may say that you were baptized in my name! **16** Now I baptized also the household *of* Stephanas. *As to the* rest, I do not know if I baptized any other.

For I Was Not Sent To Baptize, But To Announce The Gospel Without Wisdom of Speech
17 For Christ did not send me forth to be baptizing, but to be announcing-the-good-news— not in wisdom *of* speech, in order that the cross *of* Christ may not be made-empty[N].

For God Intends The Gospel To Be Both Foolishness And Powerful
18 For the speech[O] *of* the cross is foolishness *to* the *ones* perishing, but is *the* power *of* God *to* us being saved. **19** For it has been written [in Isa 29:14]: "I will destroy the wisdom *of* the wise *ones,* and I will set-aside the intelligence[P] *of* the intelligent *ones*". **20** Where *is the* wise *one*? Where *is the* scribe[Q]? Where *is the* debater *of* this age? Did not God make-foolish the wisdom *of* the world?

For God Saves Those Who Believe The "Foolishness" of Christ Crucified
21 For since, in the wisdom *of* God, the world through *its* wisdom did not know[R] God, God was well-pleased through the foolishness *of*[S] the

---

A. On when this book was written, see Act 19:10. Paul was in Ephesus, 1 Cor 16:8. **B.** Or, set apart (to God), made holy. **C.** Or, holy *ones*. **D.** Or, in union with, by. **E.** Or, word, doctrine, speaking. **F.** That is, about. **G.** Or, established. **H.** Or, among. **I.** Or, unaccused. **J.** Or, put-in-order. **K.** Or, understanding. **L.** Or, intention, judgment. **M.** That is, servants or family members of her household. **N.** Or, made of no effect. **O.** Or, message, word. That is, the content of our speech about the cross. **P.** Or, understanding, cleverness. **Q.** That is, religious scholar. **R.** Or, come-to-know. **S.** That is, characterizing, belonging to.

proclamation to save the *ones* believing. **22** Because indeed Jews are asking-
for signs and Greeks are seeking wisdom, **23** but **we** are proclaiming Christ
crucified^A— *to* Jews, *an* offense; and *to* Gentiles, foolishness; **24** but *to* the
called *ones* themselves, both Jews and Greeks, Christ *the* power *of* God and
the wisdom *of* God. **25** Because the foolish *thing*^B *of* God is wiser *than*
humans, and the weak *thing of* God *is* stronger *than* humans.

God Chose To Save The Foolish And Weak To Shame Human Self-Effort
26 For look-*at*^C your calling, brothers— that *there are* not many wise
according-to^D *the* flesh, not many powerful, not many well-born^E. **27** But God
chose^F the foolish *things of* the world in order that He might be putting the
wise *ones* to shame. And God chose the weak *things of* the world in order
that He might be putting the strong *things* to shame. **28** And God chose the
low-born^G *things of* the world, and the *things* having been treated-with-
contempt^H— the *things* not being^I, in order that He might bring-to-nothing
the *things* being, **29** so that no flesh may boast in the sight of God. **30** But by
Him **you** are in Christ Jesus, Who became wisdom *to* us from God— both
righteousness and holiness^J, and redemption— **31** in order that just as it has
been written [in Jer 9:24], "Let the *one* boasting be boasting in *the* Lord".

And I Came To You Proclaiming Christ Crucified Without Human Eloquence Or Wisdom
2:1 And **I**, having come^K to you, brothers, did not come in accordance with
superiority^L *of* speech or *of* wisdom while proclaiming *to* you the mystery *of* God. **2** For
I determined not to know anything among you except Jesus Christ— and this *One*
having been crucified. **3** And **I** was^M with you in weakness and in fear and in much
trembling. **4** And my speech and my proclamation *was* not in persuasive words *of*
wisdom, but in demonstration^N *of*^O *the* Spirit and power, **5** in order that your faith
might not be in *the* wisdom *of* humans but in *the* power *of* God.

Yet We Are Speaking God's Wisdom To The Mature
6 Yet we are speaking wisdom among the mature, but *a* wisdom not *of* this age, nor
of the rulers *of* this age— the *ones* being brought-to-nothing. **7** Rather we are speaking
God's wisdom in *a* mystery; the *wisdom* having been hidden which God predestined
before the ages for our glory, **8** which none *of* the rulers *of* this age has understood.
For if they had understood, they would not have crucified the Lord *of* glory. **9** But *it*^P
is just as it has been written: "*Things* which *an* eye did not see and *an* ear did not
hear, and *which* did not come-up^Q on *the* heart *of a* human— which God prepared *for*
the *ones* loving Him".

God Revealed This Wisdom To Us Through His Spirit
10 And God revealed *it*^R **to us** through the Spirit. For the Spirit searches all *things,*

A. Or, *a* crucified Messiah. **B.** That is, this foolish proclamation. **C.** Or, you see. **D.** Or, with respect to, in
relation to. **E.** That is, not many are nobles. **F.** Or, called-out, selected. **G.** Or, base, not-noble, not-well-born.
H. Or, despised. **I.** That is, being anything in the eyes of the world. **J.** Or, sanctification. **K.** That is, in Act 18:1.
L. Or, preeminence, excellence. **M.** Or, came-to-be. **N.** Or, display, proof. **O.** Or, *from*. **P.** That is, But *this
wisdom is*; But *it happened*. **Q.** Or, arise. **R.** That is, the hidden wisdom. Or, *these things*.

even the deep *things of* God. **¹¹** For who *among* people knows the *things of* the person except the spirit *of* the person within him? In this manner also, no one has known the *things of* God except the Spirit *of* God. **¹²** And **we** did not receive the spirit *of* the world, but the Spirit from God, in order that we might know the *things* having been freely-given *to* us by God— **¹³** *things* which we also are speaking not in words taught *by* human wisdom, but in *words* taught *by the* Spirit, combining^A spiritual *things with* spiritual *words*. **¹⁴** But *a* natural person does not accept the *things of* the Spirit *of* God. For they are foolishness *to* him and he is not able to understand, because they are spiritually examined^B. **¹⁵** But the spiritual *person* examines all *things*, yet he himself is examined by no one^C. **¹⁶** For "who knew *the* mind *of the* Lord? Who will instruct Him?" [Isa 40:13], and **we** have *the* mind *of* Christ!

But You Are Still Acting Like Infants By Dividing Over Paul And Apollos
3:1 And **I**, brothers, was not able to speak *to* you as *to* spiritual *ones*, but as *to ones* made-of-flesh^D, as *to* infants in Christ. **²** I gave you milk to drink, not food, for you were not yet able. But not-even still now are you able, **³** for you are still fleshly^E. For where *there is* jealousy and strife among you, are you not fleshly and walking in accordance with human *thinking*^F? **⁴** For whenever one says "I am *of* Paul", and another "I *am of* Apollos", are you not [mere] humans?

So What Are Apollos And Paul? Servants Planting And Watering Seed For God
⁵ Therefore, what is Apollos? And what is Paul?— servants through whom you believed, even as the Lord gave *to* each *one*. **⁶** I planted, Apollos watered, but God was causing-growth. **⁷** So then neither is the *one* planting anything, nor the *one* watering, but God causing the growth. **⁸** And the *one* planting and the *one* watering are one^G, but each will receive *his* own reward according to *his* own labor.

We Are Workers In God's Building. Be Careful How You Build On The Foundation
⁹ For we are God's fellow-workers^H; you are God's farm, God's building. **¹⁰** I laid *a* foundation according-to^I the grace *of* God having been given *to* me as *a* wise master-builder, and another is building-upon *it*. But let each *one* be watching-out how he builds-upon *it*. **¹¹** For no one can lay another **foundation** other than the *one which* is laid, which is Jesus Christ. **¹²** And if one builds gold, silver, precious stones, wood, hay, straw upon the foundation, **¹³** each *one's* work will become evident. For the day will make *it* clear^J, because it is revealed by fire. And the fire itself will test what-sort each *one's* work is. **¹⁴** If one's work which he built-upon *it* shall remain, he will receive *a* reward. **¹⁵** If one's work shall be burned-up, he will suffer-loss^K. But he himself will be saved, yet so as through fire. **¹⁶** Do you not know that you are God's temple and the Spirit *of* God is dwelling in you? **¹⁷** If anyone ruins^L the temple *of* God, God will ruin this *one*. For the temple *of* God is holy— which **you** are!

A. Or, explaining spiritual *things to* spiritual *people*. **B.** Or, investigated, discerned. **C.** That is, no one without the mind of Christ. **D.** That is, as to ones like non-believers in their thinking. **E.** That is, living like non-believers. **F.** Or, with mankind. That is, with human logic, goals, ways of viewing things. **G.** That is, in purpose. Or, one *thing*, God's fellow workers. **H.** That is, co-workers *for* God, or *with* God. **I.** Or, based on. **J.** Or, reveal *it*, show *it* (for what it really is). **K.** Or forfeit (the reward). **L.** Or, corrupts, destroys, spoils.

Don't Be Deceived. The World's Wisdom Is Foolishness To God

18 Let no one be deceiving himself. If anyone among you thinks *that he* is wise in this age, let him become foolish in order that he may become wise. **19** For the wisdom *of* this world is foolishness with God. For it has been written [in Job 5:13], "*He is* the One catching the wise in their craftiness^A"; **20** and again [in Ps 94:11], "*The* Lord knows the thoughts^B *of* the wise, that they are futile".

So Don't Boast In People. All God's Servants Belong To You

21 So then, let no one be boasting in people. For all *things* are yours— **22** whether Paul or Apollos or Cephas or *the* world or life or death or *things* present or *things* coming— all *things are* yours. **23** And you *are* Christ's, and Christ *is* God's.

Consider Us As God's Assistants And Stewards. Don't Judge Anything Before The Time

4:1 Let *a* person be considering^C us in-this-manner: as attendants^D *of* Christ and stewards^E *of the* mysteries *of* God. **2** Here^F, furthermore, it is sought in^G stewards that one be found faithful^H. **3** Now *to* me, it is *a* very small *thing* that I should be examined^I by you, or by *a* human day *of judgment*. But I do not even examine myself ! **4** For I am conscious of nothing *against* myself, but I have not been declared-right^J by this, but the *One* examining me is *the* Lord. **5** So then do not be judging anything before *the* time, until the Lord comes, Who will both^K illuminate the hidden *things of* the darkness and reveal the motives^L *of* the hearts. And at-that-time the praise^M will come *to* each *one* from God.

Brothers, Learn From Apollos And Paul Not To Be Puffed Up About God's Ministers

6 Now brothers, I applied^N these *things* to myself and Apollos for your sakes, in order that in us you might learn the *saying* "*Do* not *go*^O beyond *the things* which have been written"— in order that you might not be puffed-up, one on behalf of the one against the other. **7** For who discerns^P you *to be superior*? And what do you have that you did not receive? But if indeed you received *it*, why do you boast as-*though* not having received *it*?

For God Has Displayed Us Apostles As Last And Lowest In This World

8 You are already satisfied^Q! You already became-rich! You became-kings^R without us! And o-that indeed you became-kings, in order that **we** also might reign with you. **9** For I think God displayed^S us the apostles *as* last^T, like *ones* condemned-to-death— because we were-made^U *a* spectacle^V *to* the world, both *to* angels and *to* people. **10** We *are* foolish *ones* for the sake of Christ, but you *are* wise *ones* in Christ. We *are* weak *ones*, but you *are* strong *ones*. You *are* distinguished *ones*, but we *are* dishonored *ones*. **11** Until the present hour indeed we hunger, and thirst, and are naked^W, and are beaten, and live-transiently^X, **12** and labor— working *with our* own hands. **13** While

---

A. Or, trickery, cunning. **B.** Or, opinions, reasonings. **C.** Or, estimating, counting, regarding. **D.** Or, assistants, underlings, helpers, servants. **E.** That is, household managers or administrators. **F.** That is, on earth; or, in this matter. **G.** That is, in the case of. **H.** Or, trustworthy, dependable. **I.** That is, as to his faithfulness, his execution of his stewardship. **J.** That is, before God. Or, vindicated. **K.** Or, also, indeed. **L.** Or, purposes, counsels, plans. **M.** Or, approval, commendation. **N.** Or, adapted. **O.** Or, *think*. **P.** Or, distinguishes, differentiates, judges; and thus, regards, makes. **Q.** Or, You already have enough; You already have all *you* want. **R.** Or, reigned. **S.** Or, exhibited. **T.** That is, last in status, like condemned criminals. **U.** Or, became. **V.** Or, *a* show, theater. **W.** That is, poorly clothed. **X.** Or, are unsettled, are unstable. That is, we move from place to place, with no permanent home.

being reviled^A, we bless; while being persecuted, we endure; while being slandered, we conciliate^B. We were-made^C like *the* sweepings^D *of* the world, *the* scum^E *of* all *things*, up to now.

I Am Writing To Admonish You As My Children. Be Imitators of Me

14 I am writing these *things* not shaming you, but admonishing *you* as my beloved children. **15** For if you should have ten-thousand tutors^F in Christ, yet *you do* not *have* many fathers. For **I** fathered you in Christ Jesus through the good-news. **16** Therefore I exhort you— be^G imitators *of* me. **17** For this reason I sent Timothy *to* you, who is my beloved and faithful child in *the* Lord, who will remind you *as to* my ways in Christ Jesus, just as I am teaching everywhere in every church. **18** Now some were puffed-up as-*if* I *were* not coming to you. **19** But I will come to you soon, if the Lord wills. And I shall come-to-know not the talk^H *of* the *ones* having been puffed-up, but the power. **20** For the kingdom *of* God *is* not in^I talk, but in power. **21** What do you want? Should I come to you with *a* rod, or with love and *a* spirit *of* gentleness?

Remove Sexually Immoral People From Your Church: A Little Leaven Leavens The Lump

5:1 Sexual-immorality is **actually** being heard-*of* among you— and such sexual immorality which *is* not even among the Gentiles, that someone has^J *the* wife *of his* father. **2** And **you** are puffed-up, and did not mourn instead, in order that the *one* having done this deed might be taken out of your midst. **3** For indeed **I**, being absent *in* the body but present *in* the^K spirit, have already judged— as-*though* being present— the *one* having thus committed this *thing*. **4** In the name *of* our Lord Jesus, you and my spirit having been gathered-together, with^L the power *of* our Lord Jesus, **5** *you are* to hand-over such *a one* to Satan for *the* destruction *of his* flesh, in order that *his* spirit may be saved on the day *of* the Lord. **6** Your boast *is* not good. Do you not know that *a* little leaven leavens the whole lump? **7** Clean-out the old leaven, in order that you may be *a* new lump, just as you are unleavened. For indeed, our Passover [Lamb] was sacrificed^M— Christ. **8** So then let us celebrate-the-feast not with old leaven, nor with *the* leaven *of* badness^N and evilness, but with *the* unleavened *loaves of* purity^O and truth.

Do Not Even Associate With So-Called Brothers Who Continue To Disobey God

9 I wrote you in the letter^P not to associate-with^Q sexually-immoral *ones*— **10** not at-all *meaning with* the sexually-immoral *ones of* this world, or *with* the greedy and swindlers^R, or *with* idolaters, because then you *would* have to go out of the world! **11** But now^S, I wrote^T *to* you not to associate-with *them* if anyone being named *a* brother should be *a* sexually-immoral *one,* or *a* greedy *one,* or *an* idolater, or *a* reviler, or *a* drunkard, or *a* swindler— not even to eat with such *a* one. **12** For what do I have to do with judging the *ones* outside? Are **you** not judging the *ones* inside? **13** But God judges^U the *ones* outside. Remove^V the evil *one* from-*among* you yourselves.

A. Or, insulted, reproached. **B.** Or, exhort, encourage, comfort. **C.** Or, became. **D.** Or, rinsings. **E.** Or, scrapings, dregs. **F.** Or, guardians, guides. **G.** Or, become. **H.** Or, message, word. **I.** That is, in the sphere of. **J.** That is, has his step mother as his wife. **K.** That is, *my* spirit, as in v 4. **L.** Or, along-with. **M.** Or, slaughtered, killed. Paul is applying the Passover celebration to the Corinthians. **N.** Or, malice. **O.** Or, sincerity. **P.** That is, some previous letter; or, *this* letter. **Q.** Or, keep company with. **R.** Or, robbers, plunderers. **S.** Or, But as-it-is. **T.** Or, did write. **U.** Or, will judge. **V.** Or, Purge, Expel.

Take Your Disputes With Brothers To Wise Judges In The Church, Not To The World's Courts
6:1 Does any one *of* you, having *a* matter against the other, **dare** to go-to-court[A] before the unrighteous *ones*, and not before the saints? **2** Or do you not know that the saints will judge the world? And if the world is judged by you, are you unworthy *of the* smallest cases[B]? **3** Do you not know that we will judge angels? *Shall I* not-indeed *mention things*-pertaining-to-*this*-life? **4** So indeed, if you have cases pertaining-to-*this*-life, are you seating[C] these [as judges]— the *ones* having been of-no-account[D] in the church? **5** I say *this* to your shame. So is there not among you anyone wise who will be able to discern[E] between his brother *and this brother?*— **6** but brother is going-to-court against brother, and this before unbelievers?

Better To Be Wronged Than To Wrong Your Brother With a Lawsuit
7 So indeed, it is **already** actually *a* defeat[F] *for* you that you have lawsuits with each other. Why not rather be wronged? Why not rather be defrauded[G]? **8** But **you** are wronging and defrauding— and this [your own] brothers!

Wrongdoers Will Not Inherit The Kingdom. But You Were Cleansed of Such Things
9 Or do you not know that wrongdoers will not inherit God's kingdom? Do not be deceived. Neither sexually-immoral *ones,* nor idolaters, nor adulterers, nor homo-erotic-partners[H], nor homosexuals[I], **10** nor thieves, nor greedy *ones*— not drunkards, not revilers, not swindlers— will inherit *the* kingdom *of* God. **11** And some *of you* were these *things.* But you washed-*them*-away[J], but you were sanctified[K], but you were declared-righteous in the name *of* the Lord Jesus Christ and in the Spirit *of* our God.

Do Not Be Sexually Immoral
12 "All[L] *things* are lawful[M] *to* me", but not all *things* are beneficial[N]. "All *things* are lawful *to* me", but **I** will not be mastered by any. **13** Foods[O] *are for* the stomach and the stomach *for* foods. But God will do-away-with[P] both this and these. But the body *is* not *for* sexual-immorality, but *for* the Lord, and the Lord *is for* the body. **14** And God both raised the Lord and will raise us up by His power.

Your Bodies Are Body-Parts of Christ: Flee Sexual Immorality
15 Do you not know that your bodies are body-parts[Q] *of* Christ? Therefore, having taken-away the body-parts *of* Christ, shall I make *them* body-parts *of a* prostitute? May it never be! **16** Or do you not know that the *one* joining *himself to a* prostitute is one body *with her*? For He says [in Gen 2:24] "the two will be one flesh". **17** But the *one* joining *himself to* the Lord is one spirit *with Him.* **18** Be fleeing sexual immorality.

Your Body Is The Temple of The Holy Spirit. Glorify God In Your Body
Every sin which *a* person may do is outside the body. But the *one* committing-sexual-immorality is sinning against *his* own body. **19** Or do you not know that your body is *the*

A. Or, to be judged. **B.** Or, courts. **C.** Or, seat these... church! (speaking sarcastically). **D.** Or, disdained, despised. **E.** Or, decide, judge. **F.** Or, failure. **G.** Or, robbed, deprived. **H.** Or, catamites. That is, males kept by older males for this purpose. **I.** That is, males who engage in sex with other males. **J.** Or, washed-away *your sins*; washed *yourselves.* **K.** Or, made holy. **L.** Paul may have said this to the Corinthians about Jewish food restrictions, as he does in 10:23. But they were wrongly applying it to sexual matters. **M.** Or, permitted. Paul may be quoting their slogan. **N.** Or, useful, profitable, advantageous. **O.** This too could be their slogan. **P.** Or, bring to nothing. **Q.** Or, limbs, members.

temple *of* the Holy Spirit in you, Whom you have from God? And you are not your *own*[A], [20] for you were bought *with a* price. Therefore glorify God in your body.

Answers To Your Questions:
7:1 Now concerning *the things* which you wrote—

Concerning Marriage And Singleness: Live According To Your Gift From God
It is good[B] *for a* man not to touch[C] *a* woman. [2] But because of sexual-immoralities, let each *man* have his *own* wife, and let each *woman* have *her* own husband. [3] Let the husband give-back *to his* wife *her* due[D], and likewise also the wife *to her* husband. [4] The wife does not have-authority[E] *over her* own body, but the husband *does*. And likewise also the husband does not have-authority *over his* own body, but the wife *does*. [5] Do not be depriving one another— except perhaps by agreement, for *a* time, in order that you may devote-yourselves *to* prayer and [then] be together again— in order that Satan may not tempt you because of your lack-of-self-control. [6] But I am saying this by way of concession, not by way of command. [7] And I wish *that* all people were as[F] indeed myself! But each has *his* own gift from God— one in this manner and another in this manner. [8] And I say *to* the unmarried and the widows— *it is* good *for* them if they remain as I also *am*. [9] But if they do not have-self-control, let them marry. For it is better to marry than to be burning[G].

But Do Not Divorce Your Christian Spouse
[10] But *to* the *ones* having married I command (not I, but the Lord), *that a* wife not be separated from *her* husband— [11] but if indeed she is separated, let her remain unmarried or let her be reconciled *to her* husband— and *that a* husband not leave[H] *his* wife.

Do Not Divorce an Unbelieving Spouse Who Chooses To Stay
[12] But *to* the rest I say, not[I] the Lord— if any brother has *an* unbelieving wife and this *one* consents to dwell with him, let him not leave her. [13] And if any woman has *an* unbelieving husband and this *one* consents to dwell with her, let her not leave *her* husband. [14] For the unbelieving husband has been sanctified[J] by *his* wife. And the unbelieving wife has been sanctified by the brother. Otherwise then your children are unclean, but now[K] they are holy. [15] But if the unbelieving *one* separates, let *such a one* separate. The brother or the sister has not been enslaved by such[L] *things,* but God has called you in peace. [16] For how do you know, wife, whether you will save *your* husband? Or how do you know, husband, whether you will save *your* wife? [17] Except *that*[M] as the Lord apportioned[N] *to* each *one,* as God has called each *one,* in this manner let him be walking. And thus I am directing[O] in all the churches.

A. That is, you do not belong to yourself. **B.** Or, commendable, praiseworthy. **C.** That is, to have sexual contact with, and thus, to marry. Paul extols singleness, in contradiction to the views of his day. **D.** That is, what is due her, physically and otherwise. **E.** Or, have-the-right. **F.** That is, single and pure, devoting themselves fully to God. **G.** That is, with sexual desire. **H.** Or, abandon, divorce. **I.** That is, this was not spoken of by the Lord, as was the last case. **J.** Or, consecrated, made holy. Rather than the believer being defiled by the unbeliever (who is probably an idolater), the reverse is true. **K.** Or, as-it-is. The children also are sanctified by the presence of the believer. **L.** Or, by such *ones.* Or, in such *cases.* **M.** That is, you are not enslaved... except that. Paul provides perspective. This is the general rule of Christian living of which the preceding is an exception. **N.** Or, distributed, assigned. **O.** Or, commanding, ordering.

In General, Remain With God In The Life Context In Which You Were Saved

[18] Was anyone called having been circumcised? Let him not conceal[A] *it*. Has anyone been called in uncircumcision? Let him not be circumcised. [19] Circumcision is nothing and uncircumcision is nothing, but *the* keeping *of the* commandments *of* God. [20] Each in the calling *in* which he was called— in this let him remain. [21] Were you called *as a* slave? Do not let it be *a* concern *to* you. But if also[B] you are able to become free, rather make-use-of *the opportunity*. [22] For the *one* having been called in *the* Lord *as a* slave is *a* freedperson *of the* Lord. Likewise the *one* having been called *as a* free *one* is *a* slave *of* Christ. [23] You were bought *with a* price; do not become slaves[C] *of* people. [24] Each in what he was called, brothers— in this let him remain with God.

Concerning The Unmarried: In General, It Is Good To Remain As You Are In Life

[25] Now concerning virgins, I do not have *a* command *from the* Lord, but I am giving *an* opinion as *one* having been shown-mercy by *the* Lord to be trustworthy. [26] I think then *that* this[D] is good because of the present necessity[E], that *it is* good *for a* person to be so[F]. [27] Have you been bound[G] *to a* woman? Do not be seeking *a* release[H]. Have you been released[I] from *a* woman? Do not be seeking *a* wife. [28] But even if you marry, you did not sin. And if the virgin marries, she did not sin. But such *ones* will have affliction *in* the flesh, and I am sparing[J] you.

We All Must Keep Our Earthly Life In Eternal Perspective

[29] And this I say, brothers— the time[K] is shortened, so that **henceforth** even the *ones* having wives should be as-*though* not having, [30] and the *ones* weeping as-*though* not weeping, and the *ones* rejoicing as-*though* not rejoicing, and the *ones* buying as-*though* not holding-on-to[L], [31] and the *ones* making-use-of the world as-*though* not making-full-use-of *it*. For the form[M] *of* this world is passing away.

Single People Can Be Solely Devoted To God; The Married Have a Dual Concern

[32] Now I want you to be free-from-concern. The unmarried *man* is concerned-*about* the *things of* the Lord— how he may please the Lord. [33] But the *man* having married is concerned-*about* the *things of* the world— how he may please his wife, [34] and he has been divided[N]. And the unmarried woman[O], and the virgin, is concerned-*about* the *things of* the Lord— that she may be holy both *in* the body and *in* the spirit. But the *woman* having married is concerned-*about* the *things of* the world— how she may please *her* husband.

A. Lit, pull-over the foreskin (a medical term). Do not hide your heritage. **B.** That is, if also (while not being concerned about it, but serving the Lord)... *the opportunity*. Or, if indeed... *your freedom*. Or, even if... *your present state*; that is, do not wait to be free to serve Christ. **C.** That is, sell yourselves as slaves; or, become slaves of the opinions of people regarding your status in life. **D.** That is, being a virgin; remaining unmarried. **E.** Or, constraint, pressure, distress. **F.** That is, unmarried. Or, as-follows. **G.** That is, promised, betrothed, in an arrangement usually made between the parents, according to their custom; or, bound (in marriage) to a wife. **H.** Or, unbinding, untying. That is, a release from your pledge, your commitment to marry; or, a release from your marriage, a divorce. **I.** Or, unbound, untied. That is, released from your commitment to marry; or, released from *your* wife; unbound from your marriage by any circumstance. **J.** That is, *trying to* spare you from the problems that will result due to the 'present necessity'. **K.** That is, the time remaining to serve Christ before you die or He comes is in a state of shortness. **L.** Or, retaining. **M.** Or, outward appearance. **N.** The divided interests are not sinful, but can dilute and distract (v 35) a person's service to the Lord. **O.** That is, the widowed, divorced, or abandoned.

Do What You Think Is Honorable For Your Virgin Daughter

35 Now I am saying this[A] for the benefit *of* you yourselves— not that I may throw *a* noose[B] on you, but toward good-order and devotion[C] *to* the Lord, undistractedly. **36** But if one[D] thinks *that he* is behaving-dishonorably[E] toward his virgin *daughter*— if she is beyond-the-bloom-of-youth[F], and it ought[G] to be so— let him do what he wants. He is not sinning. Let them marry. **37** But he who stands steadfast[H] in his heart, not having *a* necessity[I], and has authority[J] concerning[K] *his* own will, and has determined this in *his* own heart, to keep[L] his virgin *daughter*— he will do well[M]. **38** So then, both the *one* giving his virgin *daughter* in marriage is doing well, and the *one* not giving-in-marriage will do better.

Widows Are Free To Remarry, But May Be Happier Remaining As They Are

39 *A* wife has been bound for as much time as her husband lives. But if *her* husband falls-asleep, she is free to be married *to* whom she wishes— only in *the* Lord. **40** But she is happier if she remains thus[N], according to my opinion; and **I** also think *that I* have *the* Spirit *of* God.

Concerning Food Sacrificed To Idols: Let Love Guide Your Exercise of "Rights"

8:1 Now concerning the foods-sacrificed-to-idols, we know that we all have knowledge[O]. Knowledge puffs-up, but love builds-up. **2** If anyone thinks *that he* has come-to-know anything, he did not-yet know as *he* ought-to know. **3** But if one loves[P] God, this *one* has been known by Him. **4** Therefore concerning the eating *of* the foods-sacrificed-to-idols— we know that *an* idol *is* nothing[Q] in *the* world, and that *there is* no God except one. **5** For even if-indeed there are *ones* being called gods, whether in heaven or on earth— as-indeed there are many[R] gods and many lords— **6** yet *for* us *there is* One God the Father, from Whom *are* all *things*, and we *are*[S] for Him; and one Lord Jesus Christ, through Whom *are* all *things*, and we *are* through Him. **7** But *this* knowledge *is* not in all *people*. But some, *by* the accustomed-habit[T] *of* the idol until now, eat *this food* as[U] food-sacrificed-to-an-idol. And their conscience, being weak, is stained[V]. **8** But food will not bring us[W] near[X] *to* God— neither if we do not eat are we lacking, nor if we eat are we abounding. **9** But be watching-out *that* this right[Y] *of* yours does not somehow become *an* opportunity-for-stumbling *to* the weak *ones*. **10** For if someone sees you, the *one* having knowledge, reclining [to eat] in *an* idol-temple, will not his conscience, being weak, be built-up so as to eat the foods-sacrificed-to-idols? **11** For the *one* being weak is being destroyed[Z] by your

A. That is, that the unmarried should remain so. **B.** Or, halter, restraint, choke-chain. **C.** Or, service, attending. **D.** That is, a father who must decide what to do with his daughter. **E.** Or, behaving improperly, disgracefully, indecently. That is, by not permitting his daughter to wed. **F.** That is, she is of marriageable age. **G.** That is, if the marriage is right and ought to take place, all things considered. **H.** That is, believing it is best for his daughter to remain single. **I.** Or, constraint, obligation, compulsion. That is, outside forces, including his daughter's wishes, are not compelling the father to do otherwise. **J.** That is, freedom to act as he thinks best in the case of his daughter. **K.** Or, in relation to, with regard to. **L.** That is, keep her in his household, keep her as she is. **M.** That is, he is doing a good and commendable thing. **N.** That is, unmarried. **O.** Before Paul gives the content of such knowledge in v 4-6, he corrects the spirit of such a statement. **P.** Love is the heart of our relationship with God, not knowledge. **Q.** Or, that *there is* no idol (no genuine representation of any god). **R.** Paul later calls them demons, 10:20. **S.** Or, *exist*. **T.** Or, habitual-use. **U.** That is, as if the sacrifice, the eating, and the food still carry their old meanings. **V.** Or, soiled, dirtied. **W.** That is, us having knowledge, whose choices are the focus of the entire discussion in chapters 8-10. **X.** Or, present us *to* God(for reward or judgment). **Y.** That is, this right to eat such food. **Z.** Or, ruined.

knowledge— the brother for the sake of whom Christ died! **¹²** And in this manner sinning against the brothers and striking^A their conscience while being weak, you are sinning against Christ.

On The One Hand, I Will Not Do Anything That Hinders People's Spiritual Advance
¹³ For-this-very-reason, if food causes my brother to fall, I will never eat meats, ever— in-order-that I may not cause my brother to fall.

For Example, I Have The Right To Be Paid As God's Workman
9:1 Am^B I not free? Am I not *an* apostle? Have I not seen Jesus our Lord? Are **you** not my work in *the* Lord? **²** If *to* others I am not *an* apostle, yet indeed I am *to* you. For **you** are the seal *of* my apostleship in *the* Lord— **³** this^C is my defense *to* the *ones* examining me! **⁴** We do not fail to have *the* right to eat^D and drink, *do we?* **⁵** We do not fail to have *the* right to take along^E *a* sister *who is a* wife, *do we?*— as also the other apostles, and the brothers *of* the Lord, and Cephas. **⁶** Or I alone and Barnabas— do not we have *the* right not to be working^F?

Workers Always Partake of The Fruit of Their Labors
⁷ Who ever serves-as-a-soldier *with his* own rations? Who plants *a* vineyard and does not eat the fruit *of* it? Or who shepherds *a* flock and does not eat of the milk *of* the flock?

Does Not The Law Say This Very Thing?
⁸ I am not speaking these *things* according to [mere] human *thinking*^G, *am I?* Or does not the Law also say these *things?* **⁹** For in the Law *of* Moses it has been written [in Deut 25:4], "You shall not muzzle *a* threshing ox". God is not concerned *about* the oxen^H, *is He?* **¹⁰** Or is He surely speaking for our sake? Indeed it was written for our sake— because^I the *one* plowing ought to plow on the basis of hope, and the *one* threshing *to thresh* on the basis of hope *that he might* partake.

I Do Have This Right Over You
¹¹ If **we** sowed spiritual *things to* you, *is it a* great *thing* if **we** shall reap fleshly^J *things from* you? **¹²** If others partake of *this* right *over* you, *should* we not more?

But I Chose Not To Make Use Of This Right So As Not To Hinder The Gospel
Nevertheless, we did not make-use-of^K this right. But we are bearing^L all *things,* in order that we might not give any hindrance *to* the good-news *of* Christ.

A. Or, assaulting, wounding. **B.** To justify the bold statement just made, Paul uses himself (in foregoing his right to financial support) as an example of choosing not to use one's rights in order to advance the gospel. **C.** That is, you are the defense of my apostleship to any who would oppose it (making this a parenthetical comment). Or, "Lord. This is my defense (for the bold statement in 8:13) *to* the *ones* examining me— we" (making verse 2 parenthetical). **D.** That is, to sustain ourselves through our work among you. **E.** That is, to take a believing wife with us in our ministry to you, at your expense. **F.** That is, not to be working outside of our ministry to you in order to support ourselves. **G.** Or, according to mankind. **H.** No, God is not concerned whether oxen get fed before, during, or after threshing. This was an object-lesson. **I.** Or, [meaning] that. **J.** That is, material. **K.** Paul does not make use of rights from which he is in no way excluded. The Corinthians should also forego rights no one would ever deny are theirs. **L.** Or, enduring.

The Lord Even Commanded That Gospel Workers Live By Their Work

13 Do you not know that the *ones* working the temple-*duties* eat the *things* from the temple, *that* the *ones* serving *at* the altar divide-a-share *with* the altar? **14** So also the Lord directed[A] the *ones* proclaiming the good-news to be living from the good-news.

But My Boast Is That I Do Not Make Use of This Right

15 But **I** have not made-use-of any *of* these *things*. And I did not write these *things* in order that it might become so in my case, for *it would be* better *for* me to die rather than— no one shall empty my boast[B]! **16** For if I am announcing-the-good-news, it is not[C] *a* boast *for* me, for *a* necessity[D] is lying-upon[E] me; for woe is *to* me if I do not announce-the-good-news. **17** For if I am practicing this of-*my*-own-will, I have *a* reward; but if not-of-*my*-own-will, I have been entrusted *a* stewardship[F]. **18** What then is **my** reward? That while announcing-the-good-news, I might place the good-news free-of-charge, so as not to make-full-use-of my right in[G] the good-news.

For I Have Chosen To Enslave Myself To All For The Advance of The Gospel

19 For[H] while being free from all *people*, I enslaved myself *to* all in order that I might gain the more. **20** Indeed I became *to* the Jews as *a* Jew, in order that I might gain Jews; *to* the *ones* under *the* Law, as under *the* Law— not being myself under *the* Law— in order that I might gain the *ones* under *the* Law; **21** *to* the *ones* without-*the*-Law, as without-*the*-Law— not being without-*the*-law *of* God, but within-*the*-law *of* Christ— in order that I might gain the *ones* without-*the*-Law. **22** I became weak *to* the weak, in order that I might gain the weak. I have become all *things to* all *people*, in order that I might by all means save some. **23** And I am doing all *things* for the sake of the good-news, in order that I might become *a* co-partner *of* it.

On The Other Hand, I Will Do Everything Needed To Win My Race And Keep My Prize

24 Do[I] you not know that the *ones* running in *a* race all run, but one receives the prize? Be running in this manner: that you may take-hold-of *the* prize. **25** And everyone competing exercises-self-control *as* to all *things*. So those *do it* in order that they might receive *a* decayable crown, but we *an* undecayable *one*. **26** So-indeed **I** run in this manner, as not aimlessly[J]. I box in this manner, as not beating *the* air. **27** But I bruise my body and make *it my* slave, *that* having proclaimed *to* others, I myself should not somehow become disapproved[K].

A. Or, commanded, ordered. Paul does not make use of rights specifically commanded by the Lord. The Corinthians should also forego rights specifically granted in Scripture, rights based on knowledge. **B.** Paul's sacrifice of his right to financial support is a personal matter of boasting for which he would die rather than give up. **C.** Paul cannot boast *that* he is proclaiming the gospel, only in *how* he does it, sacrificially. **D.** Or, compulsion, constraint. **E.** Or, is pressing upon, is laid upon, is imposed upon. Paul *must* do it. **F.** That is, a position of management responsibility given him by his Master. **G.** That is, in connection with. **H.** Paul now expands his point beyond the financial arena. **I.** Paul now gives a positive reason. Do these things not only to not hinder the gospel (for the good of others, 8:13-9:23), but to take hold of your own reward (for your own good). **J.** Or, uncertainly, unknowingly. **K.** That is, for the prize, v 24. Or, disqualified. Positively stated, that I might receive my reward and keep it. The Corinthians could seem to win a reward based on knowledge, but lose it due to the impact of their behavior on others.

For Loss of The Prize Is Possible: Remember What Happened To Israel
10:1 For I do not want you to be unaware, brothers, that our fathers[A] were all under the cloud, and all went through the sea, **2** and all were baptized into Moses in the cloud and in the sea, **3** and all ate the same spiritual[B] food, **4** and all drank the same spiritual drink. For they were drinking from *a* spiritual[C] rock following *them.* And the rock was Christ. **5** But God was not well-pleased with the majority *of* them, for they were strewn in the wilderness.

Do Not Follow Their Example
6 Now these *things* took place *as* our examples, so that we *might* not be desirers *of* evil *things,* as those also desired. **7** And do not be idolaters, as some *of* them, as-indeed it has been written [in Ex 32:6], "The people sat-*down* to eat and drink, and stood up to play". **8** And let us not be committing-sexual-immorality, as some *of* them committed sexual immorality, and twenty three thousand fell *in* one day [Num 25:1-9]. **9** And let us not be putting Christ to the test, as some *of* them tested, and were being destroyed by the serpents [Num 21:5-6]. **10** And do not be grumbling, like some *of* them grumbled, and perished by the destroyer [Num 16:41-49]. **11** Now these[D] *things* were happening *to* those *ones* as-an-example. And it was written for our admonition, on whom the ends *of* the ages have come[E].

So Watch Out That You Do Not Fall
12 So then let the *one* thinking *that he* stands be watching-out *that* he may not fall. **13** *A* temptation has not seized you except *what is* common-to-humanity. And God *is* faithful, Who will not allow you to be tempted beyond what you are able, but also with the temptation will make the way-out, *that you may* be able to endure.

For This Very Reason, Flee From The Eating Connected With Idol Worship
14 For-this-very-reason, my beloved, be fleeing from idolatry[F]. **15** I speak as *to* wise *ones*; **you** judge what I say: **16** the cup *of* blessing which we bless, is it not *a* sharing[G] *of* the blood *of* Christ? The bread which we break, is it not *a* sharing *of* the body *of* Christ? **17** Because *there is* one bread, we the many are one body[H], for we all partake from the one bread. **18** Look-*at* Israel according to *the* flesh— are not the *ones* eating the sacrifices sharers *of* the altar? **19** Therefore what am I saying? That[I] food-sacrificed-to-an-idol is anything, or that *an* idol is anything? **20** On the contrary, that *the things* which they are sacrificing, they are sacrificing *to* demons, and not[J] *to* God. And I do not want you to be sharers *of* the demons. **21** You cannot drink *the* Lord's cup and *the* demons' cup. You cannot[K] partake *of*

A. Paul is a positive example, Israel a negative one. A fall into disapproval is not theoretical. It happened to Israel! **B.** That is, in origin. The manna came from God. Likewise next. **C.** That is, a rock from God, spiritual in origin; or, a supernatural, invisible rock, Christ Himself. **D.** That is, the consequences of sin just recounted. **E.** Or, arrived. The preceding ages ended in Christ, who began a new age. **F.** Paul now applies v 1-13 to eating in idols' temples, an issue mentioned but not addressed in 8:10. Your knowledge in which you think you stand will cause you to fall if you think you can do this without arousing the jealousy of God. **G.** Or, communion, partnership. **H.** Partaking of the bread and cup makes us one with Christ and one another. Paul's point is that the same is true in the idol's temple. **I:** That... that? These are the same two points of knowledge Paul began with in 8:4 and 8. **J.** Or, *to a* no God. **K.** That is, without provoking God to jealousy and bringing His judgment upon you.

the Lord's table and *the* demons' table. ²² Or do we provoke the Lord to jealousy? We are not stronger *than* He, *are we?*

So As To The Eating of Meat, Do What Is Beneficial And Edifying To Those Eating
²³ All *things* are lawful, but not all *things* are beneficial. All *things* are lawful, but not all *things* build-up. ²⁴ Let no one be seeking his *own thing,* but the *thing of* the other. ²⁵ Be eating anything being sold in *the* meat-market, examining nothing for the sake of conscience. ²⁶ For "The earth and the fullness *of* it *are* the Lord's" [Ps 24:1]. ²⁷ If one *of* the unbelievers invites you, and you want to go, eat anything being set-before you, examining nothing for the sake of conscience. ²⁸ But if one should say *to* you "This is offered-in-sacrifice", do not eat^A— for the sake of that *one* having disclosed *it,* and the conscience. ²⁹ Now *the* conscience I mean *is* not the *one of* oneself, but the *one of* the other. For why^B is my freedom being judged^C by another's conscience? ³⁰ If **I** am partaking *with* thanks, why am I being blasphemed for *that* which **I** am giving-thanks?

In Summary, Do All For God's Glory. Be Blameless To All And Seek Their Benefit
³¹ Therefore, whether you are eating or drinking or doing anything, be doing all for *the* glory *of* God. ³² Be blameless^D both *to* Jews and Greeks, and *to* the church *of* God— ³³ just as **I** also am pleasing all *people as to* all *things,* not seeking the benefit *of* myself, but the *benefit of* the many, in order that they might be saved. **11:1** Be imitators *of* me, just as I also *am of* Christ.

Concerning The Wearing of Veils In Public: God Has Established Heads of Authority
² Now I praise you because^E you have remembered^F me *as to* everything, and you are holding-on-to the traditions, just as I delivered *to* you. ³ And^G I want you to know that Christ is the head *of* every man^H, and the husband *is the* head *of a* wife, and God *is the* head *of* Christ.

Do Not Shame Your Head By How You Dress
⁴ Every^I man praying or prophesying while having *a covering* down *over his* head is shaming^J his head^K. ⁵ And every woman praying or prophesying *with* the head unveiled^L is shaming her head, for she is one and the same^M *with the one* having been shaved. ⁶ For if *a* woman is not veiling-*herself*, let her also^N have-*herself*-sheared. But if *it is* shameful *for a* woman to have-*herself*-sheared or shaved, let her be veiling-*herself.* ⁷ For *a* man ought not to be veiling the head, being *the* image and glory *of*

A. Or, stop eating. **B.** That is, (correcting the strong one) why should I allow my freely chosen behavior to come under condemnation? I should instead choose not to eat. Or, (supporting the strong one) why should I allow another person's conscience to judge my actions? They have no right to do so. My sacrifice of my right to eat is voluntary and for the sake of their conscience not mine, and not because I agree with their view. **C.** Or, condemned. **D.** Or, without-an-opportunity-for-stumbling, without-offense. **E.** Or, that. **F.** Or, kept me in mind. **G.** Paul begins to expound upon the next topic about which the Corinthians had kept him in mind in their letter (7:1). Or, But; Paul begins to correct them regarding an issue about which they had not kept him in mind or held on to his teaching. **H.** Or, husband. **I.** Now Paul applies the general principle in verse 3 to a question specific to their culture. **J.** Or, dishonoring. **K.** That is, Christ; or, his physical head, and thus, himself. Similarly next. **L.** Or, without-a-head-covering. **M.** She has identified herself with society's shameful. **N.** If you are going this far in violating proper decorum, why not go all the way and cut off your hair!

God— but the woman[A] is *the* glory *of* man. [8] For man is not from woman, but woman from man. [9] For indeed man was not created for the sake of the woman, but woman for the sake[B] of the man. [10] For this reason, the woman ought to be having authority[C] on *her* head because of the angels[D]. [11] Nevertheless[E] *there is* neither woman without man, nor man without woman in *the* Lord. [12] For just as the woman *is* from the man, so also the man *is* through the woman. And all *things are* from God.

Judge Among Yourselves Whether It Is Fitting To Ignore The Customs of The Churches
[13] Judge among[F] you yourselves— is it fitting[G] *that an* unveiled woman *should* pray *to* God? [14] Does not even nature[H] itself teach you that if *a* man has long hair, it is *a* dishonor *to* him— [15] but if *a* woman has long hair, it is *a* glory *to* her? Because[I] the long hair has been given *to* her for[J] *a* covering[K]. [16] But if anyone seems[L] to be contentious, **we** do not have such *a* custom[M], nor *do* the churches *of* God.

Concerning The Lord's Supper: Your Supper Is Unworthy of The Name
[17] But while commanding this, I do not praise[N]— because you are coming-together not for the better, but for the worse. [18] For first, while you *are* coming-together in church[O], I am hearing *that there* are divisions among you. And *a* certain part *of it* I believe— [19] for there indeed have-to[P] be factions among you in order that the approved *ones* may also[Q] become known among you. [20] So while you *are* coming-together at the same *place*, it is not *that you may* eat *the* Lord's Supper! [21] For at the eating[R], each *one* is taking *his* own dinner before *others*. And one is hungry, and another is drunk. [22] You do not indeed fail to have houses for eating and drinking, *do you*? Or are you treating the church *of* God with contempt, and humiliating the *ones* not having? What should I say *to* you? Shall I praise you? In this I do not praise.

A. That is, Adam and Eve reflect their Creator's glory, including the dominion they share as a pair, Gen 1:26-28. But Eve also reflects Adam's glory, having been created from him (v 8) as his counterpart (v 9). The aspects of her that reflect Adam's glory are specifically related to her as his counterpart and mate. Honoring her 'mateness' in whatever way her society deems appropriate is honoring him, herself, her marriage, and her Creator. So wear the veil. Or, man reflects the glory of God in a way woman does not, because he is in the position of authority and rule. **B.** That is, as his counterpart, as a mate suitable to him and completing the pair, Gen 2:18-24. **C.** That is, a symbol of her mate's authority over her in the God-given chain of relationships (v 3). Or, control over her head; that is, so as not to bring shame on herself and others. **D.** Compare 4:9. **E.** The creation of woman from man and for man is the order of the first creation, but not the new creation 'in the Lord'. At present we all live in both spheres. Balancing freedom 'in the Lord' with what was 'fitting' (v 13) in their culture so as not to bring unnecessary shame on Christ is Paul's goal in this discussion. **F.** Or, within. **G.** Or, proper, suitable, becoming, seemly. Our 'judgment' as to what is 'fitting' for this issue differs by culture. It would be just as unseemly for us in western cultures to force the wearing of veils upon women as it was for the women of Paul's day not to wear them. **H.** That is, the physical makeup of man and woman, woman generally having a richer endowment of hair; or, the natural disposition and preferences of men and women, as reflected in the customs regarding hair. **I.** Or, That, making this a second question. **J.** Or, corresponding to, answering to. **K.** That is, a woman's covering of hair honors her in a special way, and as such, shows that a veil is also honorable. **L.** Or, thinks, presumes. **M.** That is, if you want to debate this, we have no other custom. This is the practice we are accustomed to in the churches. Or, we have no custom of fighting about these things. **N.** Compare 11:2. **O.** Or, *an* assembly. That is, in home meetings. **P.** Or, must. **Q.** Or, indeed. Choices between right and wrong, good and bad, separate the approved from the disapproved. **R.** That is, the eating of the love feast, the dinner associated with the Lord's Supper in that day.

The Lord's Supper Is a Remembrance of What He Did For Us
23 For **I** received from the Lord what I also handed-over[A] *to* you— that the Lord Jesus, in the night *on* which He was being handed-over, took bread. **24** And having given-thanks, He broke *it* and said "This is My body, the *one being given*[B] for you. Be doing this for My remembrance". **25** Similarly also the cup after the dining[C], saying, "This cup is the new covenant in My blood. Be doing this, as-often-as you drink *it*, for My remembrance". **26** For as-often-as you eat this bread and drink the cup, you are proclaiming the death *of* the Lord, until which *time* He comes.

So Don't Partake of It In a Manner Unworthy of What He Did: Examine Yourselves
27 So then, whoever eats the bread or drinks the cup *of* the Lord unworthily[D] shall be guilty[E] *of* the body and the blood *of* the Lord. **28** But let *a* person examine himself, and in this manner let him eat of the bread and drink of the cup. **29** For the *one* eating and drinking while not rightly-judging the body[F] is eating and drinking judgment[G] *on* himself. **30** For this reason many among you *are* weak and sick, and many sleep. **31** But if we were rightly-judging ourselves, we would not be being[H] judged. **32** But while being judged, we are being disciplined[I] by the Lord in-order-that we might not be condemned with the world.

Partake of It Together With Proper Respect For One Another
33 So then, my brothers, while coming-together so as to eat, be waiting-for one another. **34** If one is hungry, let him eat at home, in-order-that you might not come-together for[J] judgment. And I will set-in-order the remaining *things* whenever I come.

Concerning Spiritual Gifts: God Distributes a Variety of Gifts For Our Mutual Benefit
12:1 Now concerning the spiritual *gifts,* brothers, I do not want you to be unaware. **2** You know that when you were Gentiles[K], *you were* being led-away[L] to the speechless idols, however[M] you were being led. **3** Therefore I make-known *to* you that no one speaking by *the* Spirit *of* God is saying "Jesus *is*[N] accursed". And no one is able to say "Jesus *is* Lord" except by *the* Holy Spirit. **4** Now there are differences[O] *of* gifts[P], but the same Spirit. **5** And there are differences *of* ministries[Q], and the same Lord. **6** And there are differences *of things*-worked[R], but the same God working all *things* in all *persons*. **7** And the manifestation[S] *of*[T] the Spirit is given *to* each *one* for *our* benefit. **8** For *to* one *a* word[U] *of*[V] wisdom is given through the Spirit; and *to* another, *a* word *of* knowledge according-to[W] the same

---

A. Or, delivered, handed-down. **B.** This is supplied from Lk 22:19. Or, *broken,* from earlier in this verse. **C.** That is, the eating of the Passover dinner. **D.** That is, in a manner unworthy of the Lord, such as what the Corinthians were doing, v 18-22. **E.** Or, liable *for,* answerable *for.* **F.** That is, the Lord's body being remembered by eating the bread; and thus, treating this Supper as common and failing to examine themselves in light of the full meaning of it. Or, the church, your fellow believers; and thus, failing to properly honor those with whom you are partaking. **G.** That is, discipline, as Paul says in v 32. **H.** Or, be experiencing judgment, as just described. **I.** Or, corrected, trained, educated, as His children. **J.** Or, resulting in, leading to. **K.** That is, non-believers. **L.** That is, by outside forces beyond your control. This is no longer so. In chapters 12-14 Paul explains how the Spirit of God is working in and through them. **M.** Or, whenever. **N.** Or, *be.* **O.** Or, divisions, varieties, distributions. **P.** That is, empowerments proceeding from God's grace. **Q.** That is, ways and spheres of service. **R.** Or, effects, products, results, activities. God accomplishes different things in and through us. **S.** Or, open-disclosure, public revelation. **T.** That is, given by; or, consisting of. **U.** Or, speech, saying, message, statement. **V.** That is, characterized by; or, resulting in. **W.** Or, based on, by way of.

Afghans

APPROX TIME **45** mins

MAKES **25**

By Jan Bilton

Afghans

 MAKES **25**

 APPROX TIME **45** mins

250g butter, softened

½ cup sugar

¼ cup brown sugar

1 ½ cups plain flour

½ cup dark cocoa powder

1 ½ cups cornflakes

Chocolate Icing: ½ cup cream

200g dark chocolate, finely chopped

25 walnut halves

Preheat the oven to 150°C. Line a large baking tray with baking paper.

Cream the butter and sugars, until light. Sift in the flour and cocoa. Mix well. Add the cornflakes. Mix, until just combined. Roll into 25 balls about 25g each. Place on the prepared tray. Flatten lightly with a fork. Bake for 25-30 minutes. Cool on a wire rack.

Icing: Bring the cream to the boil in a pan. Remove from the heat. Stir in the chocolate, until smooth. Cool, until thick. Spread over the biscuits. Top each with a walnut half. When set, store in an airtight container in a cool place.

freshchoice

www.freshchoice.co.nz

supervalue

just what you need

www.supervalue.co.nz

Spirit; **9** *to a* different *one,* faith by the same Spirit; and *to* another, gifts *of* [A] healings by the one Spirit; **10** and *to* another, *things*-worked[B] *by* miracles; and *to* another, prophecy[C]; and *to* another, discernments[D] *of* spirits; *to a* different *one,* kinds *of* tongues[E]; and *to* another, interpretation[F] *of* tongues. **11** But the one and the same Spirit works[G] all these *things,* distributing *to* each *one* individually[H], just as He wills[I].

For The Body of Christ Is Like The Human Body
12 For just as the [human] body is one [body]; and it has many body-parts; and all the body-parts *of* the [human] body, being many, are one body; so also *is* Christ.[J]

 It Is One Body With One Spirit
 13 For indeed with[K] one Spirit, **we** all were baptized into one body[L]— whether Jews or Greeks, whether slaves or free. And we all were given one Spirit to drink.

 It Has Many Body Parts Placed By God
 14 For indeed the body is not one body-part, but many. **15** If the foot should say "Because I am not *a* hand, I am not *a part* of the body", it is not for this *reason* not *a part* of the body. **16** And if the ear should say "Because I am not *an* eye, I am not *a part* of the body", it is not for this *reason* not *a part* of the body. **17** If the whole body *were an* eye, where *would* the hearing *be*? If *the* whole *were an* ear, where *would* the smelling *be*? **18** But now[M], God placed the body-parts— each one *of* them— in the body, just as He wanted. **19** And if all were one body-part, where *would* the body *be*?

 All Body Parts Are Needed For The Healthy Functioning of The One Body
 20 But now, *there are* many body-parts— but one body! **21** And the eye cannot say *to* the hand, "I do not have need *of* you". Or again the head *to* the feet, "I do not have need *of* you". **22** On the contrary, much rather the body-parts *of* the body seeming to be weaker are necessary. **23** And *the things of* the body which we are thinking to be more-without-honor, *on* these we are putting-on[N] more honor. Indeed our private[O] *parts* have more[P] presentability[Q], **24** but our presentable *parts* have no need[R]. But God blended-together the body, having given more honor *to* the *body-part* lacking, **25** in order that there should not be division in the body, but *that* the body-parts should be having the same concern for one another. **26** And if one body-part is suffering, all the body-parts are suffering-with *it*. If one body-part is being glorified, all the body-parts are rejoicing-with *it*.

 You Are The Parts of Christ's Body, Placed Where You Are By God
 27 And **you** are *the* body *of* Christ, and body-parts in part[S]. **28** And God placed

A. That is, resulting in; or, consisting of. **B.** Or, products *of* miracles. Or, workings *by Him of* miracles, workings *of His* powers. Or, results *characterized by* miracles, miraculous works. Verse 28 simply says 'miracles'. **C.** That is, speaking revelation from God confirmed by supernatural knowledge of past, present or future events; or, speaking revelation from God (but without such confirmation); or, speaking for God, forthtelling, preaching. **D.** Or, distinguishings. **E.** Or, languages. **F.** Or, translation. **G.** Or, produces, effects. **H.** Or, *his* own. **I.** Or, wants, wishes. **J.** Paul expands on the four parts of this verse in v 13-31. **K.** Or, in, by. **L.** This is what makes the body one body. **M.** Or, But as-it-is. **N.** Such as when we put on a ring or robe or fancy shoe. **O.** Or, shameful, un-honored. **P.** That is, because we cover them with clothing. **Q.** Or, decorum, decency, propriety. **R.** That is, of clothing. **S.** That is, body-parts [of it] in part; the Corinthians are part of Christ's worldwide body. Or, in [your

some[A] in the church *as* first, apostles[B]; second, prophets; third, teachers; then miracles; then gifts *of* healings, helps, administrations, kinds *of* tongues. **29** All *are* not apostles, *are*[C] they? All *are* not prophets, *are they*? All *are* not teachers, *are they*? All *do* not do miracles, *do they*? **30** All do not have gifts *of* healings, *do they*? All do not speak *in* tongues, *do they*? All do not interpret, *do they*? **31** But be zealous-for[D] the greater gifts.

The Value of Your God-Given Gift Is Measured By Your Love

And[E] I show you *a* way still[F] beyond measure[G]: **13:1** If I speak *in* the tongues *of* humans and *of* angels, but I do not have love, I have become *a* sounding brass [gong] or *a* clanging cymbal. **13:2** And if I have prophecy and know all mysteries and all knowledge, and if I have all faith so as to remove mountains, but I do not have love, I am nothing. **3** And if I dole-out[H] all my possessions, and if I hand-over[I] my body so that I may boast[J], but I do not have love, I am profited nothing.

The Way Love Behaves

4 Love is patient. Love shows-kindness. Love does not envy[K], does not brag, is not puffed-up, **5** does not behave-dishonorably[L], does not seek its *own things*, is not provoked[M], does not count[N] the bad, **6** does not rejoice over unrighteousness, but rejoices-with the truth, **7** bears all *things*, believes all *things*, hopes all *things*, endures all *things*.

Love Is Permanent; Gifts Are Temporary. Be Pursuing Love

8 Love never fails. But if *there are* prophecies, they will be set-aside[O]. If *there are* tongues, they will cease[P]. If *there is* knowledge, it will be set-aside. **9** For we know in part, and we prophesy in part— **10** but when the complete[Q] *thing* comes, the *thing* in part will be set-aside. **11** When I was *a* child, I was speaking like *a* child, thinking like *a* child, counting[R] like[S] *a* child— when I have become[T] *a* man, I have set-aside the *things of* the child. **12** For now we are seeing through[U] *a* mirror, in *an* enigma[V]— but then face to face. Now I know in part— but then I will know-fully, just as I also was fully-known. **13** But now[W] these three are remaining— faith, hope, love. But love *is the* greater *of* these. **14:1** Be pursuing[X] love.

---

assigned] part. Or, partially (not the eye, but part of the eye). **A.** Paul starts to say some... others, but then combines this with first, second, in order to rank the gifts. **B.** Or, sent ones, official representatives or messengers. That is, the twelve (or so) sent personally by Christ; or more broadly, ones sent out by churches. **C.** The grammar of all these questions expects a 'no' answer. **D.** The Spirit gives gifts as He wills. But since we do not know the works God has prepared for us (Eph 2:10), we should aim to be of maximum value to the body. **E.** Having completed his main explanation of gifts, Paul now puts them in a broader context. **F.** Or, And furthermore, I show you *a* way beyond measure. **G.** While some gifts are greater than others in edification value, love is beyond measure. God gives gifts; God is love. **H.** Or, give away (piece by piece). **I.** Or deliver. That is, deliver into slavery to help others; or as a martyr. **J.** Some manuscripts say 'be burned'. **K.** Or, behave jealously (in a negative sense). **L.** Or, -improperly, -disgracefully, -indecently. **M.** That is, to anger. Or, irritated. **N.** Or, account, calculate, impute. That is, keep account of it; or, count it against a person (be resentful); or, impute it to others. **O.** Or, done away, put to an end. **P.** Or, leave off, come to an end. **Q.** That is, in contrast to 'in part'. Or, perfect, mature, having attained its end or purpose. **R.** Or, calculating, evaluating. **S.** That is, with partial understanding. **T.** That is, attained the state of manhood. Paul is comparing the two states. **U.** Or, with, by means of. **V.** That is, in a form that is imperfectly seen, indistinctly reflected, as by a primitive polished-metal mirror. **W.** Or, But as-it-is. That is, in this life. Faith and hope are added because they are our connection to the next life. **X.** Or, running after, seeking after.

Be Zealous For Spiritual Gifts, But Especially To Prophesy And Edify The Church

Now be zealous-for the spiritual *gifts*, but even-more[A] that you might be prophesying. **2** For the *one* speaking *in a* tongue is not speaking[B] *to* people, but *to* God— for no one hears[C], but he speaks mysteries[D] *with his* spirit[E]. **3** But the *one* prophesying is speaking edification and exhortation and consolation[F] *to* people. **4** The *one* speaking *in a* tongue is edifying himself[G], but the *one* prophesying is edifying *the* church. **5** And I wish[H] *that* you all *were* speaking *in* tongues, but even-more[I] that you might be prophesying. But[J] the *one* prophesying *is* greater[K] than *one* speaking *in* tongues— unless[L] he interprets in order that the church may receive edification.

Speaking In Tongues Is Just Speaking Into The Air Unless It Is Understood

6 But now[M], brothers, if I come to you speaking[N] *in* tongues, what will I profit you unless I speak *to* you either[O] by[P] *a* revelation or by knowledge or by *a* prophecy or by *a* teaching? **7** Likewise the lifeless *things* giving *a* sound— whether *a* flute or harp— if it does not give *a* distinction *in* the tones, how will the *thing* being fluted or the *thing* being harped be known? **8** For indeed, if *a* trumpet gives *an* uncertain sound, who will prepare *himself* for battle? **9** So also you with the tongue— if you do not give *a* clear word, how will the *thing* being spoken be known? For you will be speaking into *the* air! **10** There are perhaps so-many kinds *of spoken* sounds[Q] in *the* world, and none *is* meaningless. **11** If then I do not know the force *of* the *spoken* sound, I will be *a* barbarian *to* the *one* speaking, and the *one* speaking *a* barbarian with me. **12** So also[R] you— since you are zealots[S] *for* spiritual *gifts*, be seeking that you may abound for the edification *of* the church.

So In Church, Tongues Must Be Interpreted If The Hearers Are To Be Edified

13 Therefore let the *one* speaking *in a* tongue pray in order that he might interpret. **14** For if I am praying *in a* tongue, my spirit[T] is praying, but my mind[U] is unfruitful[V]. **15** What then[W] is *to be done*? I will pray *with* the spirit, and[X] I will also pray *with* the mind. I will sing-praise *with* the spirit, and I will also sing-praise *with* the mind. **16** Otherwise, if you are blessing[Y] with *your* spirit[Z] [only], how will the *one* filling the place *of* the uninstructed[Z1] say the "Amen" at your thanksgiving, since he does not know what you are saying? **17** For you are giving-

---

A. Or, rather. **B.** That is, addressing himself to. **C.** That is, hears with understanding. **D.** That is, things not knowable by humans apart from a revelation by God. **E.** Or, *by the* Spirit; or, *with his* spiritual *gift* (as in v 12). **F.** Or, comfort, encouragement. **G.** That is, because God is speaking through him, not because he understands. **H.** That is, wish in theory (as this word is used in 7:7), since neither is possible, 12:11, 18, 30; or, wish it to truly happen. **I.** Or, rather. Same phrase as in v 1. **J.** Or, And, Now. **K.** That is, in ability to edify the church. **L.** Lit, except unless. That is, with this exception, unless. The interpretation is equivalent to prophecy in edification value. **M.** Or, But as-it-is. **N.** That is, as a tongues-speaker; or, as actually addressing you. **O.** That is, by one of these other gifts; or, by an interpretation of my tongues so as to yield one of these benefits. **P.** Or, with, in. **Q.** Or, voices, and thus, languages. **R.** Paul applies v 6-11 to them in a positive way. **S.** Or, zealous. **T.** Or, my spiritual *gift*, as in v 12. **U.** Or, understanding, intellect. **V.** Or, barren, unproductive, fruitless. My mind produces nothing for edification. **W.** That is, what is the tongues-speaker personally to do? Compare v 26. **X.** Or, but. That is, with one privately and the other publicly; or, with tongues in church and then with the interpretation to edify others; or, with both in church at the same time (meaning, in my native language). **Y.** This is equivalent to praying [a blessing] in a tongue, v 14. **Z.** Or, spiritual *gift*, as in v 12. **Z1.** Or, untrained, uninformed.

thanks well[A]— but the other *person* is not being edified. [18] I give-thanks *to* God I speak *in* tongues more *than* all *of* you. [19] But in church[B], I want to speak five words *with* my mind in order that I might also instruct others, *rather* than ten-thousand words in *a* tongue.

Tongues Are a Sign For Unbelievers; Prophecy Is For Believers
[20] Brothers, do not be children *in your* understanding. But be childlike *in* evilness, and be mature *in your* understanding. [21] It has been written in the Law [in Isa 28:11-12] that "I will speak *to* this people by *people of* other-tongues, and by *the* lips *of* others. And not even in this manner will they listen-to Me, says *the* Lord". [22] So then the tongues are for *a* sign[C]— not *for* the *ones* believing, but *for* the unbelievers. But the prophecy *is* not *for* the unbelievers, but *for* the *ones* believing.

So In Church, Tongues Not Understood Breed Confusion. Prophecy Edifies
[23] Therefore, if the whole church comes-together at the same *place*, and they all speak *in* tongues[D], and uninstructed *ones* or unbelievers come-in, will they not say that you are mad[E]? [24] But if they all prophesy[F], and some unbeliever or *an* uninstructed *one* comes in, he is convicted[G] by all. He is examined by all. [25] The hidden *things of* his heart become evident[H]. And thus, having fallen on *his* face, he will give-worship *to* God, declaring that God is really among you.

Brothers, Organize Your Church Service For Edification
[26] What then[I] is *to be done*, brothers? Whenever you come-together, each[J] *one* has *a* psalm, has *a* teaching, has *a* revelation, has *a* tongue, has *an* interpretation. Let all *things* be done for edification. [27] If anyone speaks *in a* tongue, *let it be done* by two or *at* the most three, and in turn, and let one[K] *person* interpret. [28] But if[L] there is no interpreter, let him be silent in church. And let him speak **to himself**[M] and *to* God. [29] And let two or three prophets speak, and let the others[N] discern[O]. [30] But if *a prophecy* is revealed *to* another being seated, let the first be silent. [31] For you can all prophesy individually[P], in order that all may learn, and all may be exhorted[Q]. [32] And *the* spirits[R] *of* prophets are subject[S] *to* prophets. [33] For God is not *the God of* disorder[T], but *of* peace.

This Also Includes Women Being Quiet During The Church Service
As[U] in all the churches[V] *of* the saints, [34] let the women be silent[W] in the

---

A. Or, commendably. **B.** This implies Paul either spoke in tongues to unbelievers, in accordance with v 22, or privately. **C.** That is, a sign of God's presence in the one speaking to the unbelievers, as seen in Acts 2; or more specifically, a sign of God's judgment on Israel, as in Isaiah 28. **D.** That is, without interpretation. **E.** Or, raving, out of your mind. In this case, none are edified. **F.** In this case, all are edified, even any unbeliever present. **G.** Or, exposed, rebuked. **H.** Or, known. **I.** That is, what is the church to do? **J.** That is, each has what God gives them, these being examples. **K.** That is, one for all three; or, one for each. **L.** This means the speaker must know in advance that the tongue will be interpreted. **M.** That is, silently; or, privately, somewhere else. **N.** That is, other prophets or gifted individuals. **O.** That is, discern whether God is the source. **P.** Or, one by one. **Q.** Or, encouraged. **R.** That is, human spirits; or, spiritual *gifts*, as in v 12. **S.** The prophets and tongue-speakers (as seen in v 28) are not in a state of uncontrollable ecstasy, possessed by the gods, as in the Corinthians' former pagan religions. **T.** Or, unruliness, commotions. **U.** Or, peace, as in all... saints. Let the. **V.** Or, churches, let the wives *of* the saints. **W.** Some think women prayed and prophesied in the church, subordinating this verse to

churches. For it is not permitted *for* them to speak[A]. But let them be subject, just as the Law also says[B]. **35** And if they want to learn anything, let them question *their* own husbands at home. For it is shameful *for a* woman to speak in church.

These Instructions Are The Lord's Commandments

36 Or did the word *of* God go-forth from you? Or did it reach to you only? **37** If anyone thinks *that he* is *a* prophet or *a* spiritual *person*, let him acknowledge *the things* which I am writing *to* you— that they are *a* commandment *of the* **Lord**. **38** But if anyone does not-know *this*, he is not-known[C].

Summary

39 So then, my brothers, be zealous-for the prophesying. And do not be forbidding[D] the speaking *in* tongues. **40** But let all *things* be done properly, and in accordance with order.

Concerning The Resurrection: Christ Was Raised From The Dead And Seen By Many

15:1 Now I make-known *to* you, brothers, the good-news which I announced-as-good-news *to* you, which you also received, in which you also stand, **2** through which you also are being saved— if[E] you are holding-on *in* that message I announced-as-good-news *to* you, unless[F] you believed in-vain. **3** For I delivered *to* you among *the* first[G] *things* what I also received: that Christ died for our sins in accordance with the Scriptures, **4** and that He was buried, and that He has been raised *on* the third day in accordance with the Scriptures, **5** and that He appeared *to* Cephas, then *to* the twelve. **6** After that He appeared *to* over five-hundred brothers at-one-time, of whom the majority are remaining until now. But some fell-asleep. **7** After that He appeared *to* James, then *to* all the apostles. **8** And last *of* all, as-if-indeed[H] *to* the untimely-born[I] *one*, He appeared *to* me also. **9** For I am the least *of* the apostles— who am not fit to be called *an* apostle, because I persecuted the church *of* God. **10** But *by the* grace *of* God I am what I am. And His grace toward me did not become[J] empty[K]. But I labored even more *than* them all— yet not I, but the grace *of* God with me. **11** So whether *it was* I or those, thus we are proclaiming, and thus you believed.

So If Christ Was Raised, Why Do Some of You Say There Is No Resurrection?

12 But if Christ is being proclaimed[L] that He has been raised from *the* dead, how *is it* some are saying among you that there is no resurrection *of* dead[M] *ones*?

11:4-5. Aside from such participation led by the Spirit, they are to remain quiet. General talking and asking questions is in view. Others think women prayed and prophesied elsewhere, subordinating 11:4-5 to this verse, meaning Paul is forbidding all speaking in church by women. **A.** Or, talk. That is, speak out of order, as with the prophets and tongue-speakers; or, speak at all. **B.** Compare 11:8-9; 1 Tim 2:13-14. **C.** That is, as a prophet or spiritual person. Or, not-recognize... not-recognized. **D.** Or, preventing, hindering, restraining. **E.** That is, assuming that. The uncertainty arises because of the issue of the resurrection addressed in this chapter. **F.** This would indeed be the case if Christ was not raised, v 17. **G.** Or, foremost. **H.** Or, as-it-were. Paul adds this word because he was not in fact born late in God's plan, but was separated from his mother's womb, Gal 1:15. **I.** Or, abnormally-born. **J.** Or, prove-to-be. **K.** Or, without result. **L.** That is, by all these witnesses in v 5-8, and others. **M.** That is, that their bodies will not be raised, but they will live as spirits.

If The Dead Are Not Raised, Christ Was Not Raised, And Your Faith Is Futile
13 Now if there is no resurrection *of* dead *ones,* neither has Christ been raised. **14** And if Christ has not been raised, then our proclamation *is* also **empty**; your faith *is* also **empty**; **15** and we are even found *to be* false-witnesses *of* ^A God, because we testified against^B God that He did raise Christ— Whom He did not raise if-indeed then dead *ones* are not raised. **16** For if dead *ones* are not raised, neither has Christ been raised. **17** And if Christ has not been raised, your faith *is* futile. You are **still** in your sins. **18** Then also the *ones* having fallen-asleep in Christ perished^C. **19** If we are *ones* having hoped in Christ **in this life only**, we are more pitiable^D *than* all people.

But Christ Has Been Raised As The Firstfruit of Those Yet To Be Raised
20 But now, Christ has been raised from *the* dead— *the* firstfruit^E *of* the *ones* having fallen-asleep. **21** For since death *came* through *a* man, *the* resurrection *of* dead *ones* also *came* through *a* man. **22** For just as in^F Adam all die, so also in Christ all will be given-life^G, **23** but each in *his* own order^H: Christ *the* firstfruit; after-that^I the *ones* of^J Christ at His coming. **24** Then^K *comes* the end— when He hands-over the kingdom *to* *His* God and Father, when He^L *has* abolished all^M rule and all authority and power. **25** For He^N must reign until which *time* He^O *has* put all the enemies under His feet. **26** Death, *the* last enemy, is abolished^P— **27** for "He^Q subjected **all *things*** under His^R feet" [Ps 8:6]. But when He says^S that "**All *things*** have been subjected", *it is* clear that *this is* except the One^T having subjected all *things to* Him. **28** But when all *things* **are subjected** *to* Him, then the Son Himself also will be subjected *to* the One^U having subjected all *things to* Him, in order that God may be all *things* in all.

Otherwise, Why Be Concerned About The Dead Or Risk Our Lives?
29 Otherwise^V, what will the *ones* being baptized for^W the dead do? If dead *ones* are not raised at-all, why indeed are they baptized for them? **30** Why indeed^X are **we** in danger every hour? **31** I die^Y daily— by^Z your boasting, brothers, which I have in Christ Jesus our Lord. **32** If in accordance with human^Z1 *thinking* I fought-wild-animals^Z2 at Ephesus, what *is* the profit *to* me? If dead *ones* are not raised, "Let us eat and drink, for tomorrow we die" [Isa 22:13].

A. That is, concerning. **B.** That is, against the truth of God. Or, by; that is, under oath. **C.** Or, were lost. **D.** That is, deserving of pity. **E.** Or, first-portion, representative. **F.** That is, in the sphere of, in connection with. **G.** That is, all bodies will be raised from the dead. This includes unbelievers, but they are not in view here. Or, just as all in Adam die, so also all in Christ will be given-life. In this case, Paul is comparing all humanity to all Christians, and 'given-life' has its full meaning. **H.** Or, group, class, division, turn. **I.** Or, then, next-in-order. **J.** That is, belonging to. **K.** Or, Next. **L.** That is, the Son (continuing from 'He hands-over'); or, the Father (as described in v 26-28). **M.** Or, every ruler and every authority. **N.** That is, the Son. **O.** That is, the Son; or, the Father. **P.** Or, done away with, put to an end, nullified. **Q.** That is, the Father, as in the psalm. **R.** That is, the Son. **S.** That is, when God says in the psalm; or, when God says at the end of time (note the change of tense to 'have been subjected'). **T.** That is, the Father... to the Son. **U.** That is, the Father. **V.** That is, if v 20-28 is not the case. **W.** Or, on behalf of, with reference to, for the sake of, because of. Paul's meaning is uncertain. Some think he is sarcastically referring to some pagan practice of proxy baptism familiar to the Corinthians, but otherwise unknown to us. Others think he means 'because of the dead', because of the influence of their lives, or to be with them. **X.** Or, also. **Y.** That is, face death. **Z.** Paul swears with an oath. I swear by the boasting I do concerning you. **Z1.** Or, with mankind. **Z2.** It was illegal to throw a Roman citizen like Paul to the animals. So this was either a mob action, or Paul is speaking of his enemies metaphorically.

Don't Be Deceived. Sober Up
33 Do not be deceived: bad companionships[A] corrupt good habits[B]. **34** Sober-up[C] righteously[D] and do not be[E] sinning, for some have *an* ignorance *of* God. I speak to your shame.

How Are The Dead Raised, And With What Kind of Body?
35 But someone will say, "How are the dead raised? And *with* what kind of body do they come?"

What You Sow Must Die, And Then God Gives It New Life In a Different Body
36 Foolish *one*! What **you** sow is not given-life unless it dies. **37** And *as to* what you sow— you do not sow the body *which* will come, but *a* bare seed, perhaps *of* wheat or *of* some *of* the rest. **38** And God gives it *a* body just as He willed— indeed, *to* each *of* the seeds *its* own body[F]. **39** Not all flesh *is* the same flesh. But *there is* one *of* humans, and another flesh *of* livestock, and another flesh *of* birds, and another *of* fish. **40** And *there are* heavenly[G] bodies and earthly bodies. But the glory *of* the heavenly *is* one *kind*, and the *glory of* the earthly *is* different. **41** *There is* one glory *of the* sun, and another glory *of the* moon, and another glory *of the* stars. For star differs *from* star in glory.

So Also Is The Resurrection of The Dead. We Are Raised In a Heavenly Body
42 So also *is* the resurrection *of* the dead. It is sown in decay[H]; it is raised in undecayability[I]. **43** It is sown in dishonor; it is raised in glory. It is sown in weakness; it is raised in power. **44** It is sown *a* natural[J] body; it is raised *a* spiritual body. If there is[K] *a* natural body, there is also *a* spiritual *body.* **45** So also it has been written [in Gen 2:7], "The first man, Adam, became *a* living soul". The Last Adam[L] *became a* life-giving[M] spirit. **46** But the spiritual *body is* not first— but the natural *body*, then the spiritual. **47** The first man *was* from earth, made-of-dust. The second Man *is* from heaven[N]. **48** Such[O] as *was* the *one* made-of-dust— such *ones* also *are* the *ones* made-of-dust. And such as *is* the heavenly *One*— such *ones* also *are* the heavenly *ones*. **49** And just as we bore[P] the image[Q] *of* the *one* made of dust, we shall also bear the image *of* the heavenly *One*.

Behold, I Tell You a Mystery: We Will Not All Die, But We Will All Conquer Death
50 Now I say this, brothers: that flesh and blood are not able to inherit *the* kingdom *of* God, nor does decay inherit undecayability. **51** Behold, I tell you *a* mystery[R]: we will not **all** fall-asleep. But we will **all** be changed— **52** in *a* moment, in *the* blink *of an* eye, at the last trumpet. For it will trumpet, and the dead will be raised undecayable[S], and **we** will be changed. **53** For this decayable *body* must put-on undecayability, and this

---

A. Or, associations. Paul is referring to those influencing 'some' in v 12. **B.** Or, customs, character. **C.** Or, Come-to-your-senses. **D.** Or, rightly. **E.** Or, stop sinning. **F.** These bodies God gives take many forms and have many degrees of glory, as seen by the following examples. **G.** That is, angelic; or, celestial. **H.** Or, corruption, ruin, destruction. **I.** Or, incorruptibility. **J.** Or, material, physical. **K.** Or, exists. **L.** Christ is the last progenitor or head of a race. **M.** That is, one giving resurrection life. **N.** That is, from the spiritual realm, even though He took a body like Adam's. **O.** That is, as to the composition and nature of their bodies, Adam's family takes after him, Christ's takes after Him. **P:** bore... bear. Or, wore... wear. **Q.** Or, likeness. **R.** That is, a truth formerly hidden, but now revealed. **S.** Or, imperishable, not-subject-to-decay, incorruptible.

mortal *body must* put on immortality[A]. **54** And when this decayable *body* puts-on undecayability, and this mortal *body* puts on immortality, then the saying having been written will come-about[B]: "Death was swallowed-up in victory" [Isa 25:8]. **55** "Death, where *is* **your** victory? Death, where is **your** stinger?" [Hos 13:14]. **56** Now the stinger[C] *of* death *is* sin, and the power *of* sin *is* the Law[D]. **57** But thanks *be to* God, the *One* giving us the victory through our Lord Jesus Christ.

So Abound In The Work of The Lord; Your Labor Is Not In Vain

58 So then my beloved brothers, be[E] steadfast, immovable, always abounding in the work *of* the Lord, knowing that your labor is not empty[F] in *the* Lord.

Concerning The Collection For Jerusalem: Store Up Your Gift And Be Ready When I Come

16:1 Now concerning the collection for the saints[G], just as I directed *in* the churches *of* Galatia, so **you** do also. **2** Every first *day of the* week[H], let each *of* you put-*aside*[I] beside[J] himself, storing-up[K] whatever thing he may be prospered, in-order-that when I come, collections might not be taking place at-that-time. **3** And when I arrive, whomever you approve, I will send these *ones* with letters[L] to carry-forth your grace-*gift* to Jerusalem. **4** And if it is fitting[M] *that* I also go, they will go with me.

I Will Stay In Ephesus For Now, And Come To You Before Winter

5 Now I will come to you whenever[N] I go through Macedonia, for I am going through Macedonia. **6** And perhaps I will continue with you, or even spend-the-winter, in order that **you** may send me forward wherever I may go. **7** For I do not want to see you now in passing, for I am hoping to stay with you *for* some time, if the Lord permits[O]. **8** But I will stay-on in Ephesus until Pentecost, **9** for *a* great and effective[P] door has opened *to* me, and *there are* many opposing.

Timothy May Come Before Me: Take Care of Him

10 But if Timothy comes, see that he may come-to-be with you fearlessly[Q]. For he is working the work *of the* Lord as I also. **11** Therefore let no one treat him with contempt. And send him forward in peace in order that he may come to me, for I am waiting-for him with the brothers.

Concerning Apollos: He Will Come When He Can

12 Now concerning Apollos *our* brother, I strongly urged him that he come to you with the brothers. And it was not at all *his* will that he come now, but he will come whenever he finds-an-opportunity.

A. Or, deathlessness. **B.** Or, take-place, come-to-pass, happen. **C.** Death delivers its poison through sin. Sin is what brings separation from God in death. Apart from sin, death is powerless. **D.** The Law establishes the line to cross, and the penalty for doing so. **E.** Or, become. **F.** Or, in vain. **G.** That is, the collection Paul was raising from the Gentile churches for the poor Christians in Jerusalem. Compare 2 Cor 8-9; Rom 15:25-27. **H.** That is, Sunday by Sunday. **I.** Or, lay-*away*. **J.** That is, at home. **K.** Or, treasuring-up. **L.** That is, with letters of introduction from Paul. Or, whomever you approve with letters, I will send. That is, with your letters of authorization as your official representatives. Some such people are named in Act 20:4. **M.** Or, worthy. That is, if the amount collected makes it appropriate for me to go; or, if it is fitting at the time in view of all the circumstances. **N.** This took place in Act 20:1-2. **O.** Paul spend three months with them, Act 20:3. **P.** Or, active. **Q.** Paul was really concerned about Timothy's age, since he writes 1 Tim 4:12 some eight to ten years later.

Closing Exhortations And Greetings

13 Keep-watching, be standing-*firm* in the faith, be acting-like-men[A], be growing-strong, **14** let all your *things* be done in love.

15 And I exhort you, brothers— you know the household *of* Stephanas, that it is *the* firstfruit *of* Achaia[B], and they appointed[C] themselves for ministry *to* the saints— **16** that **you** also be subject *to* such *ones,* and *to* everyone helping[D] and laboring. **17** Now I am rejoicing over the coming[E] *of* Stephanas and Fortunatus and Achaicus, because these *ones* filled-up your lack[F]. **18** For they refreshed my spirit and yours. Therefore be acknowledging such *ones*.

19 The churches *of* Asia[G] greet you. Aquila and Prisca[H] greet you earnestly in *the* Lord, along with the church at their house. **20** All the brothers greet you. Greet one another with *a* holy kiss.

21 The greeting *of* Paul *by* my *own* hand— **22** if anyone does not love the Lord, let him be accursed. Marana tha[I]. **23** The grace *of* the Lord Jesus *be* with you. **24** My love *be* with you all in Christ Jesus.

A. Or, be manly, be courageous. **B.** Corinth was located in this Roman province. **C.** Or, stationed, established, arranged. **D.** Or, working-with *us*. **E.** That is, to Ephesus, where Paul was, v 8. **F.** That is, your physical lack, your absence. **G.** Ephesus was located in this Roman province. **H.** Paul originally met this couple in Corinth in Act 18:1-2. **I:** Marana tha. This Aramaic phrase means Lord, come! Or, maran atha, The Lord has come!

2 Corinthians

Introduction   1:1-2

A.   Blessed be God who comforts us in all our affliction so that we may be able to comfort others   1:3-11

B.   Our conscience boasts that we conducted ourselves with you in simplicity and purity fromGod   1:12-14

     1.   And in this confidence I was intending to come to you first, on the way to Macedonia   1:15-16

     2.   Therefore while intending this, did I act with lightness? I changed plans to spare you!   1:17-2:11

     3.   Now having come to Troas, I had no rest at not finding Titus. I went to Macedonia   2:12-13

     4.   But thanks be to God who leads us and makes the aroma of Christ evident through us.   2:14-17
Because we are the fragrance of Christ— of death to some, of life to others

         a.   Are we commending ourselves? You are our letter of recommendation from Christ   3:1-3

         b.   And we have such a confidence through Christ. Our sufficiency is from God, who   3:4-18
made us ministers of a new covenant. Therefore we use much boldness, reflecting
the glory, not veiling it like Moses

         c.   For this reason, we do not lose heart. We are renewed daily by hope. Therefore we   4:1-5:11
are ambitious to please God, for we must all appear before Him

     5.   Now we have been made known to God, and I hope also in your consciences. We are   5:11-6:10
not commending ourselves, but giving you an opportunity to boast in us. For Christ's
love controls us. We are ambassadors for Christ, since God is appealing through us

     6.   Our mouth and heart have opened wide to you, Corinthians. You open wide also. Do not   6:11-7:4
become mis-yoked to unbelievers. Make room for us. I do not condemn you

     7.   I have been filled with comfort by the news of you brought by Titus   7:4-16

C.   Now we make known to you the grace of God granted in the churches of Macedonia— that their   8:1-6
abundance of joy and deep poverty abounded into their generosity

     1.   But just as you abound in everything, be abounding also in this grace. Complete the doing   8:7-15

     2.   I am sending Titus and two brothers to you so that you may be prepared when I come   8:16-9:5

     3.   Now this I say— the one sowing sparingly will reap sparingly. God will help you   9:6-15

D.   Now I beg to not have to be bold toward some considering us as walking according to the flesh.   10:1-6
For we do not wage war according to the flesh, but with God's weapons

     1.   You are looking at things according to appearance. For if I boast about our authority   10:7-17
which the Lord gave us, I will not be put to shame. But let us boast in the Lord

     2.   O that you would bear with me in a little bit of foolishness. For I am jealous for you. I   11:1-15
fear for you that your minds are being corrupted

     3.   Again I say, receive me even if as foolish, in order that I also may boast a little bit.   11:16-12:10
Since many are boasting according to the flesh, I also will boast— in my weaknesses!

     4.   I have become foolish— you compelled me! I ought to be being commended by you!   12:11-18
For I in no way come short of the superlative apostles— the signs prove it

     5.   All this time are you thinking we are defending ourselves? We are speaking before God.   12:19-21
For I fear that having come, we may not find each other such as we would want

         a.   If I come I will not spare you, since you are seeking proof of Christ in me. Prove   13:1-9
yourselves! We pray you not do anything bad, for your sakes, not mine

         b.   I am writing these things while absent so I may not have to act severely when I come   13:10

Conclusion   13:11-14

1:1 Paul[A], *an* apostle *of* Christ Jesus by *the* will *of* God, and Timothy *our* brother, *to* the church *of* God being in Corinth, together-with all the saints being in all Achaia[B]: **2** Grace *to* you and peace from God our Father and *the* Lord Jesus Christ.

Blessed Be God For Comforting Us In All Our Sufferings
3 Blessed *be* the God and Father *of* our Lord Jesus Christ, the Father *of* compassions[C] and God *of* all comfort[D], **4** the *One* comforting us concerning[E] all our affliction so that we *might* be able to comfort the *ones* in every affliction with the comfort *by* which we ourselves are being comforted by God. **5** Because just as the sufferings *of* Christ are abounding in us, so our comfort also is abounding through Christ. **6** And if we are being afflicted— *it is* for the sake of your comfort and salvation. If we are being comforted— *it is* for the sake of your comfort, the *comfort* being at-work[F] in *your* endurance *of* the same sufferings which **we** also are suffering. **7** And our hope for you *is* firm[G], knowing that as you are sharers *of* the sufferings, so also *of* the comfort.

For We Despaired Even of Living, But God Delivered Us, And Will Deliver Us
8 For we do not want you to be unaware, brothers, with-reference-to our affliction having taken place in Asia[H], that we were burdened[I] extremely beyond *our* power, so that we despaired[J] even *of* living. **9** But **we** had[K] the sentence *of* death in ourselves in order that we should not be trusting in ourselves, but in God, the *One* raising the dead, **10** Who delivered us from so great *a* death[L], and will deliver *us*; in Whom we have put *our* hope that He will indeed[M] still deliver *us*— **11** you also joining-in-helping *in your* prayer for us— in-order-that thanks might be given on our behalf by many faces[N] *as to* the gift *granted* to us through many *prayers.*

Our Boast As We Endure Our Suffering Is Our Blameless And Forthright Behavior Toward You
12 For our boasting is this: the testimony *of* [O] our conscience that we conducted-*ourselves* in the world, and especially toward you, in simplicity[P] and purity[Q] *from* God[R]; and not in fleshly wisdom, but in *the* grace *of* God. **13** For we are writing no other *things to* you other than *the things* which you read or indeed understand. And I hope that you will understand until *the* end[S]— **14** just as you also did understand us in part— that we are your boast, even as you also *are* ours, on the day *of* our Lord Jesus.

And In This Confidence I Was Intending To Come To You First, Then Go To Macedonia
15 And *in* this confidence, I was intending first[T] to come to you in order that you might have *a* second[U] benefit[V], **16** and[W] to go through you to Macedonia, and from Macedonia to come again to you, and to be sent-forward by you to Judea.

A. On when this book was written, see Act 20:2. **B.** This is the Roman province in which Corinth was located. **C.** That is, acts of compassion. **D.** Or, encouragement. **E.** Or, during, because of. **F.** Or, in-operation. **G.** Or, secure. **H.** That is, in Ephesus after 1 Cor 16:8-9. **I.** Or, weighed down. **J.** Or, were utterly at a loss. That is, they could not see how they would survive the danger facing them. **K.** The grammar implies it was true then and continues to be true now. **L.** That is, a peril of death. **M.** Or, also, even. **N.** That is, persons viewed as looking up to God in prayer. **O.** That is, proceeding from. **P.** Or, frankness. **Q.** Or, sincerity. **R.** Or, *before* God; or, godly, modifying one or both of the preceding terms. **S.** Or, fully, completely. **T.** Or, formerly. That is, intending formerly; or, to come to you first. This was Paul's original plan, which he changed in 1 Cor 16:3-6, apparently causing some Corinthians to question whether he was a divinely-directed apostle. **U.** That is, by virtue of a second visit by Paul. **V.** Or, grace, kindness, favor. **W.** Or, even, indeed.

I Do Not Make My Plans Lightly, But I Changed My Plans In Order To Spare You
17 Therefore, while intending this, I did not then act *with* lightness, *did I*? Or do I plan[A] *the things* which I plan according-to *the* flesh— so that[B] there is with me the yes, yes, and the no, no? **18** But *as* God *is* faithful[C], our message to you is not yes and no. **19** For God's Son Jesus Christ, the *One* having been proclaimed among you by us— by me and Silvanus and Timothy— did not become[D] yes and no, but has become yes in Him. **20** For as many as *there are* promises *of* God, in Him *is* the yes[E]! Therefore also through Him *is* [spoken] the amen[F] *to* God for *His* glory, through[G] us. **21** And the *One* establishing us with you for[H] Christ and having anointed us *is* God— **22** the *One* also having sealed us and given the pledge[I] *of* the Spirit in our hearts. **23** And **I** call-upon God *as* witness for my soul that sparing[J] you I no longer came to Corinth— **24** not that we are lording-over your faith, but we are fellow-workers *of*[K] your joy. For you stand *in*[L] *your* faith[M].

For I Did Not Want My Coming To Cause You Grief, So I Wrote To You Instead
2:1 For I determined this *for* myself: not to come to you again[N] in grief. **2** For if **I** grieve you, who indeed *is* the *one* cheering me except the *one* being grieved by me? **3** And I wrote this very[O] *thing* in order that having come, I should not have grief from *the ones of* whom I ought-to-have rejoicing— having confidence in you all that my joy[P] is *the joy of* you all.

I Wrote To You In Anguish Not To Grieve You, But Out of Love For You
4 For I wrote *to* you through many tears, out of much affliction and anguish *of* heart— not that you might be grieved, but that you might know **the love** which I have especially for you. **5** But[Q] if anyone has caused-grief, he has grieved not me, but in part[R] (that I not be *a* burden[S]), you all. **6** This[T] punishment by the majority *is* sufficient[U] *for* such *a one*, **7** so that on-the-contrary[V], instead you *should* forgive and comfort *him, that* such *a one* should not somehow be swallowed-up *by* more grief. **8** Therefore I urge you to confirm[W] *your* love for him.

I Also Wrote To Test Your Obedience To God
9 For I also wrote for this *purpose*: that I might know your approvedness, whether you are obedient in all *things.* **10** And *to* whom you are forgiving anything, I also. For indeed what **I** have forgiven, if I have forgiven anything, *is* for your sakes in *the* presence *of* Christ, **11** in order that we may not be exploited by Satan. For we are not unaware *as to* his schemes.

A. Or, decide, resolve. **B.** That is, so that my plans or my message are based on human uncertainty or whim. **C:** *as* God *is* faithful. This is an oath, like 11:10 and Rom 14:11. **D.** Or, was not; or, did not prove-to-be. **E.** That is, the fulfillment, confirmation, affirmation. **F.** That is, the amen of response and acceptance of God's message. **G.** Or, by. **H.** Or, in. **I.** Or, first-installment, down-payment. **J.** Sparing the Corinthians further grief over an incident that had occurred among them, as alluded to in 2:1-11, was Paul's motive for changing his plans. **K.** That is, producing. **L.** Or, *by*. **M.** Or, *in* faith. **N.** That is, come again; or, in grief again, implying a previous sorrowful interaction (whether in person, or by the letter mentioned in 2:4; 7:8). **O.** That is, this change of plans; or, my grief-causing letter. **P.** That is, obedience to Christ. **Q.** Paul pauses to comment on the case about which he wrote them in order to avoid coming to them and causing more grief. **R.** That is, partially (as to some of you, or some of the grief); or, to some degree. **S.** Or, weigh-heavily. That is, exaggerate the extent of the grief; or, burden him (by blaming him for everything); or, burden you (by detailing the matter). **T.** That is, this grief-causing punishment; or, this punishment about which Titus informed me upon his arrival, 7:6-13. **U.** Or, adequate, enough. That is, because it led to repentance. **V.** That is, contrary to punishing him further or more harshly. **W.** That is, publicly affirm.

So Instead I Went To Macedonia First To Find Titus
12 Now[A] having come to Troas for the good-news *of* Christ, and *a* door having been opened *for* me by *the* Lord, **13** I had no rest *in* my spirit *at* my not finding Titus my brother. But having said-goodbye *to* them, I went forth to Macedonia.

I Praise God That He Is Always Spreading The Aroma of Christ Through Us Everywhere
14 But thanks *be to* God, the *One* always leading us in triumph[B] in Christ, and making the aroma *of*[C] the knowledge *of* Him known through us in every place. **15** Because we are *the* fragrance *of* Christ *for*[D] God among the *ones* being saved, and among the *ones* perishing— **16** *to* the ones *an* aroma from death to[E] death, but *to* the others *an* aroma from life to life. And who *is* sufficient for these *things*? **17** For we are not like the many peddling[F] the word *of* God. But as from purity, but as from God, we are speaking in Christ before God.

You Yourselves Are Proof To Everyone That God Is Working Through Us
3:1 Are we[G] beginning to commend ourselves again? Or we do not have-need *of* letters *of* recommendation[H] to you or from you, like some, *do we*? **2** **You** are our letter— *it* having been inscribed in our hearts, *it* being known and being read by all people, **3** *you* being made-known[I] that you are *a* letter *from*[J] Christ having been served by us, having been inscribed not *with* ink but *with the* Spirit *of the* living God, not in tablets made-of-stone but in tablets[K] *which are* hearts made-of-flesh.

It Is God Who Makes Us Sufficient As Ministers of His New Covenant
4 And we have such[L] *a* confidence through Christ toward God— **5** not that we are sufficient[M] from ourselves to count anything as out of ourselves, but our sufficiency *is* from God, **6** Who indeed made us sufficient *as* ministers *of a* new covenant, not *of the* letter but *of the* Spirit. For the letter kills, but the Spirit gives-life.

And This Ministry Is More Glorious Than That of The Old Covenant
7 And if the ministry *of* death having been engraved in letters *on* stones came in glory (so that the sons *of* Israel could not look-intently at the face *of* Moses because of the glory *of* his face[N]— the *glory* passing-away), **8** how shall the ministry *of* the Spirit not be more in glory! **9** For if *in* the ministry *of* condemnation *there was* glory, *by* much more the ministry *of* righteousness is abounding *in* glory. **10** For indeed the [ministry of the letter][O] having been glorified has not[P] been glorified in this respect— because of the surpassing glory! **11** For if the [ministry of the letter] passing-away *was* with glory, *by* much more the [ministry of the Spirit] remaining *is* in glory.

A. Moving on from his aborted plans, Paul summarizes his travels before he met Titus returning from Corinth, with which he resumes in 7:4 after the lengthy reflection on his ministry in 2:14-7:4. **B.** That is, in a triumphal procession.**C.** That is, consisting of. **D.** Or, *to*. **E.** That is, originating in death and resulting in death; or, from Christ's death to their death. **F.** That is, selling it for personal gain. **G.** Paul pauses to answer a false conclusion that could be drawn from 2:14-17. **H.** That is, to prove we are authorized representatives of God. **I.** That is, through the letter recorded on your hearts. **J.** That is, from Christ to others; or, *about* Christ. **K:** in tablets... flesh. Or, in tablets made-of-flesh— *in* hearts. **L.** That is, such as described in 2:14-3:1. **M.** Or, adequate, worthy, competent. **N.** God made the face of Moses shine temporarily, Ex 34:29-30. **O.** Lit, the *thing*. Paul leaves it to the reader to supply the reference from the context. Likewise three more times below. **P.** That is, the ministry glorified in the face of Moses and other ways pales by comparison to the surpassing glory now.

We Don't Veil The Glory Like Moses. We Reflect It And Are Transformed By It
12 Therefore, having such *a* hope, we are using great boldness, **13** and *are* not like Moses. He was putting *a* veil on his face so that the sons *of* Israel *might* not look-intently at the end^A *of* the [face of glory]^B passing-away. **14** But^C their minds were hardened^D, for until this very day the same^E veil remains on the reading *of* the old covenant— *it* not being unveiled because^F it passes-away^G in Christ. **15** Indeed^H, until today whenever Moses is being read, *a* veil lies on their heart. **16** But whenever it^I turns to *the* Lord, the veil is taken-away. **17** Now the Lord^J is the Spirit, and where the Spirit *of the* Lord *is, there is* freedom! **18** But^K **we** all *with a* face having been unveiled, while reflecting^L the glory *of the* Lord as a mirror, are being transformed *into* the same image from glory^M to glory, just-as^N from *the* Lord^O, *the* Spirit.

So We Don't Lose Heart In This Ministry Or Its Reception; God Is Shining Through Us
4:1 For this reason, having this ministry even-as^P we received-mercy, we do not lose-heart. **2** But we renounced the hidden *things of* ^Q shame, not walking in craftiness^R, nor handling-deceitfully^S the word *of* God, but *by* the open-disclosure *of* the truth, commending^T ourselves to every conscience *of* mankind^U in the sight of God. **3** And if indeed our good-news is veiled, it is veiled in the *ones* perishing, **4** in whose case the god *of* this age blinded the minds *of* the unbelievers so that *they might* not see^V the illumination *of* the good-news *of* the glory *of* Christ— Who is *the* image *of* God. **5** For we are not proclaiming ourselves, but Jesus Christ *as* Lord, and ourselves *as* your slaves for the sake of Jesus, **6** because God, the *One* having said "Light will shine out of darkness", *is* He Who shined in our hearts for^W *the* illumination *of* ^X the knowledge *of* the glory *of* God in *the* face *of* Jesus Christ.

God Is Making Life Known Through Clay Vessels Handed Over To Death
7 But^Y we have this treasure in vessels made-of-clay, in order that the excess^Z *of* the power may be God's and not from us— **8** in every *way* being afflicted^Z1 but

A. Or, cessation, termination, finish, goal. **B.** For Paul, the fading glory on Moses' face symbolized the temporary nature of that covenant. Others supply [ministry of the letter]. **C.** Paul makes an application from Moses to Israel. **D.** That is, to the spiritual meaning of the fading glory, and thus to the true intent of the old covenant. **E.** Like the one on Moses, it hides the fading glory. **F.** Or, that; it not being unveiled (revealed) to them that it (the old covenant) passes away in Christ. **G.** Or, is done-away. **H.** Paul clarifies that the veil is not on the Law, but on their hearts. **I.** That is, such a veiled heart (v 15) or hardened mind (v 14); or, *a person, a Jew*. Or, he (Moses), as the type of one turning to the Lord, Ex 34:34. As with Moses physically then, so today spiritually. **J.** That is, the Lord in Moses' case (v 16) is the Spirit today; or, the Lord (Christ) is the OT 'Spirit of the Lord' in our experience of God today. **K.** Now Paul makes an application from Moses to us, completing what he began in v 13. We are not like Moses who veiled his face... But we all are being transformed. **L.** Or, looking at. Moses did both. **M.** That is, from glory to more glory (not fading); or, from *His* glory to *our* glory. **N.** That is, just as would be expected. **O.** That is, *the* Lord *who is the* Spirit; or, *the* Spirit *who is the* Lord; or, *the* Lord *of the* Spirit (that is, *who sends the* Spirit). **P.** That is, as a gift of His grace. **Q.** That is, proceeding from shameful motives; or, resulting in shame when they become known. It is failure to attain hidden self-focused motives that causes us to lose heart. **R.** Or, trickery. That is, using any means to gain our end. **S.** Or, adulterating, distorting, falsifying. **T.** Or, presenting. **U.** That is, every individual conscience of all people with whom we come in contact. **V.** Or, so that the illumination *of* the good-news *of* the glory *of* Christ *might* not shine-forth *on them*. **W.** That is, to create in us. **X.** That is, consisting of; or, produced by. **Y.** Paul now turns to the external causes of losing heart. **Z.** That is, abundance (in quantity); or, excellence (in quality). **Z1.** Or, pressed, squeezed.

not restrained[A], being perplexed but not utterly-perplexed, [9] being persecuted but not forsaken, being struck down but not perishing; [10] at-all-times carrying-around in *our* body the dying[B] *of* Jesus in order that the life *of* Jesus may also be made-evident[C] in our body. [11] For **we** the *ones* living are always being handed-over to death for the sake of Jesus, in order that the life *of* Jesus may also be made-evident in our mortal flesh. [12] So then, death is at-work in us, but life in you.

But We Believe And Speak Because We Know God Will Raise Us Up With Jesus
[13] But having the same spirit[D] *of* faith in accordance with the *thing* having been written, "I believed, therefore I spoke" [Ps 116:10]— **we** also believe, therefore we also speak, [14] knowing that the *One* having raised the Lord Jesus will also raise us with Jesus, and will present *us* with you. [15] For all *things are* for your sakes— in order that grace, having increased through the more *people*, may cause thanksgiving to abound to the glory *of* God.

And Our Affliction Is Producing an Eternal Weight of Glory For Us In Heaven
[16] Therefore we do not lose-heart. But even though our outer person is being destroyed[E], nevertheless our inner *person* is being renewed day *in* and day *out*. [17] For the momentary lightness *of* our affliction is producing *for* us *an* eternal weight *of* glory extremely beyond measure, [18] while we *are* not looking-for[F] the *things* being seen, but the *things* not being seen. For the *things* being seen *are* temporary, but the *things* not being seen *are* eternal. **5:1** For we know that if our earthly house— *our* tent[G]— is torn-down[H], we have *a* building[I] from God, *a* house not-made-by-*human*-hands, eternal, in the heavens.

We Do Indeed Groan In This Body And Would Prefer To Get Home To The Lord
[2] For indeed in this *tent* we are groaning, yearning to put-on-over[J] *ourselves* our dwelling from heaven— [3] inasmuch[K] as we, having taken-off[L] *this tent*, shall not be found naked[M]. [4] For indeed we, the *ones* being in the tent[N], are groaning, being burdened, because we do not want to take-off[O] *our earthly tent*, but to put on *our heavenly dwelling* over *it*, in order that the mortal may be swallowed-up by the life. [5] And the *One* having made us for this very *thing is* God, the *One* having given us *His* pledge: the Spirit. [6] So while always being confident[P], and knowing that while being-at-home in the body we are away-from-home, from the Lord [7] (for we walk by faith, not by appearance[Q])— [8] yet we are confident[R] and prefer rather to get-away-from-home, out of the body, and to get-at-home with the Lord.

A. Or, confined, crushed. **B.** Or, putting-to-death; or its result, the death, deadness. **C.** Or, revealed, made visible. **D.** That is, disposition *characterized by*. Or, Spirit *producing*. **E.** Or, ruined, spoiled, consumed, wasted. **F.** Or, looking-at, looking-to, watching-for. **G.** That is, our physical body. **H.** Or, taken-down. **I.** That is, a resurrection body; or, a place to stay (Jn 14:2). **J.** That is, like an outer garment. **K.** Or, since indeed. **L.** Some manuscripts say having put-on *the heavenly-dwelling*. **M.** That is, without a body; or, without a dwelling-place. The reverse of v 1. **N.** That is, physically alive on earth. **O:** to take off... to put on. That is, to die... to live with God. **P.** That is, in the present life we live by faith. **Q.** Or, sight, what is seen. **R.** That is, in the future life that awaits us when we die.

Therefore We Are Ambitious To Please Him By Persuading People

9 Therefore[A] we indeed are ambitious[B] to be pleasing *to* Him— whether being at-home or being away-from-home. **10** For we all must appear[C] before the judgment-seat *of* Christ in order that each *one* might receive-back[D] the *things done* in[E] the body, in-accordance-with *the things* which he practiced, whether good or bad. **11** Therefore knowing the fear[F] *of* the Lord, we are persuading[G] people.

Now Our Heart Has Been Made Known To God, And I Hope To You. Boast In Us

Now[H] we have been made known *to* God. And I hope *that we* also have been made known in your consciences. **12** We are not again commending ourselves *to* you, but *are* giving you *an* opportunity *for a* boast about us, in order that you may have *an answer* for the *ones* boasting in appearance and not in heart. **13** For if we lost-*our*-senses, *it is for* God! If we are sound-minded, *it is for* you!

For The Love of Christ Controls Us As We Live a New Life For Him

14 For the love *of*[I] Christ controls[J] us, *we* having determined this— that One died for all, therefore all died. **15** And He died for all so that the *ones* living might no longer be living *for* themselves, but *for* the One having died and been raised for them. **16** So then from now *on,* **we** regard[K] no one based-on[L] *the* flesh[M]. Even though we have known Christ based on *the* flesh, nevertheless now we no longer are knowing *Him* thus. **17** So then if anyone *is* in Christ, *he is a* new creation[N]. The old *things* passed-away; behold, new *things* have come-into-being[O].

And God Gave Us This Ministry of Reconciliation As His Ambassadors

18 And all *things are* from God, the *One* having reconciled us *to* Himself through Christ, and having given us the ministry *of* reconciliation: **19** how that God was in Christ reconciling *the* world *to* Himself— not counting their trespasses *against* them, and[P] having placed the message *of* reconciliation in us. **20** Therefore, we are ambassadors on behalf of Christ, since[Q] God *is* appealing through us.

We Are Begging People To Be Reconciled To God...

We are begging[R] on behalf of Christ: "Be reconciled *to* God! **21** He made the *One* not having known sin *to be* sin for us, in order that **we** might become *the* righteousness *of* God in Him"...

We Are Appealing To You Too!

6:1 And working-with *Him,* we also are appealing *that* **you** not receive the grace *of* God in vain. **2** For He says [in Isa 49:8], "I heard you *at the*

A. We do not lose heart, looking to the next life, 4:16-5:8. Now positively, we are ambitious, looking to what remains of earthly life. **B.** Or, make it our aim. **C.** Or be made-known (as in v 11). **D.** Or, get, obtain, receive-in-full. **E.** Or, during-the-time-of, by-means-of. **F.** That is, reverence for the Lord and the desire to please Him that this fact (v 10) elicits in us. **G.** That is, in accordance with what God commanded us to do. **H.** Or, But. Others begin this point with v 12. **I.** That is, proceeding from; or, for. **J.** Or, grips, governs, directs, compels. **K.** Or, know, recognize, take interest in, value. **L.** Or, in accordance with, in relation to. We regard people only in relation to the One who died for them: as living for Him or needing Him. **M.** That is, based on earthly viewpoints and distinctions. **N.** Or, creature. **O.** Or, come-to-pass, come-about. **P.** God 'was reconciling' in two senses, the 'not counting' which still continues and the 'having placed' which is finished. **Q.** Or, seeing-that. **R.** Or, pleading. What follows gives the content of the begging (Be reconciled), and the manner of it (6:3-10).

acceptable time. And I helped you on *the* day *of* salvation". Behold, now *is the* very-acceptable time. Behold, now *is the* day *of* salvation.

... In The Process Giving Them No Opportunity For Stumbling...
[3] ... in[A] nothing giving **any** opportunity-for-stumbling, in order that the ministry may not be faulted,

But Commending Ourselves While Enduring The Bad And Persevering In The Good
[4] ... but in everything, as God's servants, commending ourselves in great endurance— in afflictions, in constraints, in distresses, [5] in beatings, in prisons, in disturbances, in labors, in watchings[B], in fastings; [6] in purity, in knowledge, in patience, in kindness, in *a* holy[C] spirit, in sincere love, [7] in *the* word[D] *of* truth, in *the* power *of* God; through[E] the weapons *of* [F] righteousness *for* the right *hand* and[G] *the* left; [8] through[H] glory and dishonor, through evil-report[I] and good-report; as deceivers and true *ones,* [9] as being not-known and being fully-known; as dying and behold we live, as being disciplined and not being put-to-death, [10] as being grieved but always rejoicing; as poor but enriching many, as having nothing and holding-on-to all *things.*

Open Your Hearts To Us, Corinthians
[11] Our mouth has opened to you, Corinthians; our heart has been opened-wide. [12] You are not restrained[J] in us, but you are restrained in your *own* deep-feelings. [13] Now as[K] the same return[L]— I speak as *to my* children— **you** also open-wide.

Do Not Be Mis-Yoked To Unbelievers; Be Separated Out To God Your Father
[14] Do not be *ones* being mis-yoked *to* unbelievers[M]. For what partnership *is there for* righteousness and lawlessness? Or what fellowship *is there for* light with darkness? [15] And what *is the* harmony[N] *of* Christ with Beliar[O]? Or what share *is there for a* believer with *an* unbeliever? [16] And what agreement[P] *is there for the* temple *of* God with idols? For **we** are *the* temple *of the* living God, just as God said [in Lev 26:12], that "I will dwell in them, and I will walk-among *them,* and I will be their God, and **they** will be My people". [17] Therefore, "Come out of their midst and be separated[Q]", says *the* Lord, "and do not touch *an* unclean *thing*[R]. And **I** will take you in [18] and be *a* father *to* you, and **you** will be sons and daughters *to* me", says *the* Lord Almighty. **7:1** Therefore, having **these** promises, beloved, let us cleanse ourselves from every stain[S] *of* flesh and spirit, perfecting[T] holiness in *the* fear *of* God.

A. Paul continues on from 5:21. **B.** Or, sleepless-nights. **C.** That is, a holy disposition. Or, *the* Holy Spirit. **D.** Or, in *the* message *characterized by* truth (the gospel); or, in truthful speech; or, in *the* declaration *of* truth. **E.** Or, with, by-means-of. **F.** That is, belonging to, proceeding from, supplied by. **G:** right... and left. That is, offensive (a sword) and defensive (a shield); or more generally, fully armed for any fight. **H.** Or, by-way-of, with, amid. **I.** Or, ill-repute and good-repute; slander and praise. **J.** Or, cramped. There is no restraint of love or cramping of space for you in our hearts. **K.** Or, *give.* **L.** That is, the same return due me (love from one's children) as due you (love from one's father). What Paul has in mind requires both a turning from those misleading them (6:14-7:1) and a turning to Paul (7:2). **M.** This was one source of their mistaken attitudes and less-than wide-open feelings toward Paul. **N.** Or, agreement, shared interest. **O.** That is, Satan. **P.** Or, mutual decision, voted agreement. **Q.** Or, set apart. **R.** Or, *person.* **S.** Or, defilement. **T.** Or, finishing, bringing to completeness.

Make Room For Us In Your Hearts

2 Make-room-for us— we wronged no one, we corrupted[A] no one, we exploited[B] no one. **3** I am not speaking for *your* condemnation. For I have said-before that you are in our hearts so as to die-together and to live-together. **4** *There is* great confidence *in* me toward you. *There is* much boasting *by* me about you.

When I Found Titus In Macedonia, I Was Comforted By His Report About You

I have been filled *with* comfort. I am super-abounding *with* joy in all our affliction. **5** For indeed we having come to Macedonia[C], our flesh had no rest, but *we were* being afflicted in every *way*— battles[D] outside, fears inside. **6** But the *One* comforting the downcast[E], God, comforted us by the coming *of* Titus; **7** and not only by his coming, but also by the comfort *with* which he was comforted over you while reporting *to* us your yearning, your mourning, your zeal for me, so that I rejoiced more.

I Am Rejoicing At Your Repentance And Actions After You Received My Letter

8 Because even though I grieved you by the letter[F], I do not regret *it*. Even though I was regretting *it* (for I see that that letter grieved you, even though for *an* hour), **9** now I am rejoicing— not that you were grieved, but that you were grieved into repentance. For you were grieved in-accordance-with God, in order that you might suffer-loss in nothing by us. **10** For the grief in accordance with God works unregretted repentance leading-to salvation. But the grief *of* the world produces death. **11** For behold this very *thing*— the being grieved in accordance with God— how much earnestness[G] it produced *in* you; even *a* defense[H], even indignation[I], even fear, even yearning, even zeal, even punishment[J]. In everything you demonstrated yourselves to be pure *in* the matter. **12** So even though I wrote *to* you [causing grief], *it was* not[K] for the sake of the *one* having done wrong, nor for the sake of the *one* having been wronged, but for the sake of making your earnestness for us evident to you in the sight of God. **13** For this reason, we have been comforted.

I Rejoiced Even More At The Joy of Titus Over You

But in addition to our comfort, we rejoiced even more abundantly over the joy *of* Titus, because his spirit has been refreshed by you all. **14** Because if I have boasted anything *to* him about you, I was not put-to-shame. But as we spoke all *things to* you in truth, so also our boasting before Titus proved-to-be *the* truth. **15** And his deep-feelings are especially for you, while remembering the obedience *of* you all— how you received him with fear and trembling. **16** I am rejoicing because in everything I am confident in you.

Macedonia Gave Sacrificially, So We Urged Titus To Go Complete Your Gracious Gift

8:1 Now we make known *to* you, brothers, the grace *of* God having been granted in the churches *of* Macedonia[L]— **2** that in *a* great test *of*[M] affliction their abundance *of* joy and their

---

A. Or, ruined, destroyed. **B.** Or, defrauded. **C.** This resumes from 2:13. **D.** Or, fights, conflicts. **E.** Or, lowly, humble. **F.** That is, the one also mentioned in 2:3. **G.** That is, earnestness to obey God in response to the grief related to the incident in 2:1-11. **H.** That is, of God or Paul. **I.** That is, toward the sin committed. **J.** That is, for the man in 2:5-6. **K.** That is, not primarily. **L.** That is, where Paul was laboring at this time, 7:5. The churches we know about in this province are those at Philippi, Thessalonica, and Berea. **M.** That is, characterized by.

down deep poverty abounded into the riches *of* their generosity. **³** Because I testify *that they gave* in accordance with *their* ability and beyond *their* ability, of-*their*-own-accord, **⁴** with *a* great appeal begging *from* us the favor^A and the partnership^B *in this* ministry to the saints— **⁵** and not as we hoped^C, but they gave **themselves** first *to* the Lord and *to* us by *the* will *of* God— **⁶** so that we urged^D Titus that just as he previously-began, so also he should complete this grace^E with reference to you also.

I Urge You To Abound In This Grace of Giving Because It Is Beneficial For You!
⁷ But just as you are abounding in everything— *in* faith and speech and knowledge and all earnestness, and *in* the love from us in you— *I urge* that you also be abounding in this grace. **⁸** I am not speaking by way of command, but *am* proving^F through the earnestness *of* others the genuineness *of* your love also. **⁹** For you know the grace^G *of* our Lord Jesus Christ— that for your sakes He became-poor while being rich, in order that **you** might become-rich *by* the poverty *of* that *One*. **¹⁰** And I am giving *an* opinion in this *matter*, for this^H is beneficial *for* you, who began-beforehand from last year not only the doing, but the wanting *to do*. **¹¹** But now indeed complete the doing, so that just as *was* the eagerness *of* the wanting, so also *may be* the completing out of *what you* have.

A Gift Proportionate To Your Abundance Is Acceptable For Their Need
¹² For if the eagerness is there, *it*^I *is* acceptable to whatever degree *a person* may have, not to-the-degree he does not have. **¹³** For *it is* not in order that *there may be* rest^J *for* others, affliction^K *for* you, but out of^Lequality— **¹⁴** at the present time your abundance^M *being* for the need *of* those *ones,* in order that the abundance *of* those *ones* also may come-to-be for your need, so that there may be equality. **¹⁵** Just as it has been written [in Ex 16:18], "The *one gathering* much did not increase^N, and the *one gathering* little did not have-less".

Titus Was Eager To Go To You. So Demonstrate Your Love For All To See
¹⁶ Now thanks *be to* God, the *One* having given the same^O earnestness^P for you in the heart *of* Titus. **¹⁷** Because he welcomed the urging^Q— but being more^R earnest, went-out^S to you of-*his*-own-accord! **¹⁸** And we sent with him the brother^T whose praise in^U the good-news *is* through all the churches, **¹⁹** and not only *this,* but *who was* also appointed^V by the churches *to be* our fellow-traveler with this grace-*gift* being ministered by us for the glory *of* the Lord Himself, and *to show* our eagerness^W— **²⁰** avoiding this: *that* anyone should fault^X us in this abundance being ministered by us. **²¹** For we are providing-for^Y good *things* not only in the sight of *the* Lord, but also in the sight of people. **²²** And we sent with them our brother whom we often proved in many *things as* being diligent, but now *is* much

---

A. Or, grace. **B.** Or, participation. **C.** Or, expected. **D.** Or, appealed to. **E.** Or, grace-*gift, act-of-*grace. **F.** Or, testing, proving-by-test. **G.** Or, grace-*gift, act-of-*grace. **H.** That is, this participation in giving. **I.** That is, a gift, the concrete expression of your eagerness. **J.** Or, relief, abatement, relaxation. **K.** Or, pressure, trouble. **L.** Or, fairness, equity. **M.** Or, surplus, leftovers. **N.** That is, beyond their need. Likewise next. The Israelites gathered the same amount of manna for each person; none had an excess or a shortage. **O.** That is, the same kind as Paul's. **P.** Or, diligence, eagerness. **Q.** Or, the appeal. That is, the one mentioned in v 6. **R.** That is, more than Paul expected. **S.** That is, along with this letter, and the brothers mentioned next. **T.** Perhaps Paul is referring to one of those in Act 20:4. Paul wrote 2 Corinthians during Act 20:2. **U.** That is, in connection with. **V.** Or, chosen, elected. **W.** That is, to help those in Jerusalem. **X.** Or, blame, criticize. **Y.** Or, exercising-forethought-for.

more diligent *with* great confidence in you. **²³** If *any ask*^A about Titus— *he is* my partner and fellow-worker for you; if *as to* our brothers^B— *they are* delegates^C *of the* churches, *a* glory *of*^D Christ. **²⁴** Therefore, *be* demonstrating^E to them, to *the* face^F *of* the churches, the demonstration *of* your love and our boasting about you.

For I Have Boasted of Your Eagerness To Others, So I Want You Ready When I Come
9:1 For indeed, it is superfluous *for* me to write *to* you concerning *the* ministry^G to the saints. **²** For I know your eagerness, which I am boasting about you *to the* Macedonians— that "Achaia has been prepared [to give] since last year". And your zeal stirred-up the majority. **³** But I sent the brothers in order that our boast about you might not be made-empty in this respect: in order that, just as I was saying, you may be prepared, **⁴** *that* **we** should not somehow be put-to-shame (that I not say you) in this confidence^H if Macedonians come with me and find you unprepared. **⁵** Therefore I regarded *it* necessary to urge the brothers that they go-ahead to you and prepare-beforehand your previously-promised blessing^I, *that* this *may* be ready thus as *a* blessing and not as greediness^J.

Sow For Blessings, As You Freely Choose In Your Hearts: God Loves a Cheerful Giver
⁶ Now this^K *I say*: the *one* sowing sparingly will also reap sparingly. And the *one* sowing for^L blessings will also reap for blessings. **⁷** Each *should give* just as he has chosen-beforehand^M *in his* heart— not out of grief^N or out of compulsion. For God loves *a* cheerful giver. **⁸** And God is able to cause all grace to abound to you in order that in everything, always having all sufficiency, you may be abounding for every good work. **⁹** Just as it has been written [in Ps 112:9], "He scattered, he gave *to* the needy *ones*, his righteousness remains forever".

God Will Multiply Your Seed And Fruit, And Your Gift Will Abound To His Glory
¹⁰ And the *One* supplying seed *to* the *one* sowing^O, and bread for eating, will supply and multiply your seed, and will grow the fruits *of*^P your righteousness. **¹¹** In everything *you will* be enriched for all generosity, which through^Q us is *going to* produce thanksgiving *to* God, **¹²** because the ministry *of*^R this service^S is not only *going to be* filling-up the needs *of* the saints, but also abounding through many thanksgivings *to* God! **¹³** Through the approvedness *of* this ministry, *they will be* glorifying God for the obedience *of*^T your confession to^U the good-news *of* Christ, and *the* generosity^V *of* the contribution for them and for all, **¹⁴** while they also *are* yearning-for you *in* prayer for

---

A. Paul is giving a written commendation of these men. Titus represents Paul. **B.** That is, the ones in v 18 and 22. **C.** Or, official representatives, apostles. **D.** That is, to; or, proceeding from. This is a second description of these men. **E.** That is, through your reception of them and the assembling of your gift with their help. **F.** Or, presence. These men represent the churches who sent them. **G.** That is, the details of this ministry to the saints in Jerusalem. There is no need to promote this ministry. **H.** Or, project, undertaking. **I.** That is, blessing for those in Jerusalem. **J.** That is, as an exhibit of your blessing them by giving, and not as an exhibit of your greediness in withholding what you promised. **K.** Or, Now *as to* this *giving*. **L.** That is, for the purpose of. **M.** Or, preferred, purposed. **N.** That is, a heart grieving or pained over the loss of the money. **O:** sowing... multiply. Or, sowing, will both supply bread for eating and multiply. **P.** That is, consisting of; or, proceeding from. **Q.** That is, through our delivery of your gift. **R.** That is, consisting of. **S.** That is, public-service for God (for the believing public); or, priestly-service. **T.** That is, proceeding from; or, to. Or, the obedience to the good news *of* Christ *characterizing* your confession. **U.** Or, with reference to. **V.** Or, more broadly, *the* sincerity *of* the fellowship toward them and toward all.

you because of the surpassing grace *of* God upon you. **¹⁵** Thanks *be to* God for His indescribable gift^A.

Now Don't Make Me Have To Act Boldly Against Some of You, For My Weapons Are Powerful
10:1 Now I, Paul, myself, am appealing-to you by the gentleness and kindness *of* Christ— I who face-to-face *am* lowly among you, but while absent am-bold toward you! **²** And I am begging *that I may* not [have to] be bold^B while present *with* the confidence *with* which I am considering to dare [to act] against some considering us as walking in accordance with *the* flesh^C. **³** For [though] walking in *the* flesh, we are not waging-war in accordance with *the* flesh. **⁴** For the weapons *of* our warfare *are* not fleshly^D, but powerful *in*^E God for *the* tearing-down *of* fortresses. *We are* tearing-down^F considerations^G **⁵** and every height^H being raised-up against the knowledge *of* God, and taking-captive every thought^I to the obedience *of* Christ, **⁶** and being ready to punish^J all disobedience^K, when your obedience is fulfilled^L.

If I Boast In My Authority In Christ, I Will Not Be Put To Shame
⁷ You are^M looking *at things* according to appearance. If someone^N is confident *in* himself *that he* is Christ's^O, let him consider this again in himself: that just as he *is* Christ's, so also *are* we. **⁸** For if I should boast anything more about our authority, which the Lord gave for building-up and not for tearing you down, I shall not be put-to-shame— **⁹** in order that I may not seem^P as-*if I* would [merely] frighten you by *my* letters! **¹⁰** Because "The letters", he^Q says, "*are* weighty and strong, but the presence *of his* body *is* weak, and *his* speaking *is* treated-with-contempt^R". **¹¹** Let such *a one* consider this: that such as we are *in* word by letters while absent, such *ones we are* also *in* deed while present!

For I Do Not Commend Myself Or Compare Myself To Others
¹² For we do not dare to class or compare ourselves *with* some *of* the *ones* commending themselves. But **they**— measuring themselves by themselves, and comparing themselves *with* themselves— do not understand^S.

And I Do Not Boast In Unmeasured Things Or In The Labors of Others
¹³ And **we** will not boast in unmeasured^T *things*, but in-relation-to^U the measure *of*^V the standard^W which God apportioned *to* us *as a* measure: to reach as far as even you.

A. That is, gift of grace, referring either to that given in His Son, the model of all giving, or to the gift of grace enabling the Corinthians to abound (as in 8:1); or, to the anticipated result of the gift given by them. **B.** With this opening comment for this section compare the closing comment in 13:10. Paul is writing to correct a wrong attitude toward him on the part of some, the precise details of which are not stated but can only be inferred from what Paul says. His desire is to be bold in words here in order to avoid having to be bold in actions against them when he comes. **C.** That is, with mere human authority, motives, and power. **D.** That is, pertaining to the flesh, physical. **E.** Or, *for* God; or, *by* God, that is, divinely powerful. **F:** tearing down... punish (v 6). Warfare against a rebellious city in that day consisted of tearing down walls and defenses, then taking the people captive, then punishing the offenders. This is the metaphor here. **G.** Or, thoughts, reasonings; that is, the wrong thoughts raised up against God. **H.** Or, elevation, barrier, obstacle. **I.** Or, mind. **J.** Or, avenge. **K.** Or, every refusal-to-listen. **L.** After the full obedience of the majority, Paul will punish those remaining disobedient. **M:** You are... appearance. This sentence can be rendered in several ways, all implying 'Look deeper!' **N.** That is, one of the 'some' in v 2. **O.** That is, belongs to Christ; or, is Christ's servant. **P.** That is, as 'some' say. **Q.** That is, one of the 'some' in v 2. **R.** Or, despised, disdained. **S.** That is, understand the true reality of the matter, stated in v 18. **T.** Or, unmeasurable; things beyond measure or without measure. **U.** Or, based-on. **V.** That is, consisting of. **W.** Or, sphere. That is, the measuring rod or the measured out sphere or territory allotted to Paul by God. If Paul did boast, it would be in his own accomplishments as measured by what God gave him to do.

14 For we are not, as-*if* not reaching to you, overextending ourselves. For we arrived even as far as you in connection with the good-news *of* Christ!— **15** not boasting in unmeasured *things*, in labors belonging-to-others, but having *the* hope, while your faith *is* growing, *that we might* be enlarged^A in^B you in relation to our standard *of measure*, for *an* abundance; **16** *that we might* announce-the-good-news in the *regions* beyond^C you, not *that we might* boast in the prepared *things* in *the* standard *of measure* belonging-to-another.

The One The Lord Commends Is The Approved One
17 But "let the *one* boasting be boasting in *the* Lord" [Jer 9:24]. **18** For not that *one* commending himself is approved, but *the one* whom the Lord commends.

I Am Jealous For You, For I Fear That You Are Being Corrupted By False Messengers
11:1 O-that you *would* bear-with me *as to a* little bit^D *of* foolishness— but indeed, keep-bearing-with^E me! **2** For I am jealous-for^F you *with a* jealousy^G *of* ^H God. For I betrothed^I you *to* one husband, *that I might* present *you as a* pure virgin *to* Christ. **3** But I am fearing that as the serpent deceived Eve by his craftiness, your minds^J should somehow be corrupted^K from sincerity^L and purity for^M Christ. **4** For indeed if the *one* coming proclaims another Jesus whom we did not proclaim, or you receive *a* different spirit which you did not receive, or *a* different good-news which you did not accept— you bear-with *him* nicely!

For I Come Short of No Other Apostle, Especially In Knowledge
5 For I think *that I* have in no way come-short-of^N the superlative^O apostles. **6** But even though *I am* untrained *in* speech, nevertheless *I am* not *in* knowledge. But in every *way we* made *this* evident in all *things* to you.

Or Did I Sin By Not Letting You Pay Me?
7 Or^P did I commit *a* sin [by] humbling myself in order that **you** might be exalted— because I freely^Q announced-as-good-news *to* you the good-news *of* God? **8** I robbed^R other churches, having taken rations^S *from them* for your ministry! **9** And while being present with you and having been in-need, I did not burden anyone— for the brothers having come from Macedonia supplied my need. And in every *way* I kept and will keep myself unburdensome *to* you.

I Won't Stop This Boast, For It Cuts Off The Opportunity For False Apostles
10 As *the* truth *of* Christ is^T in me, this boasting^U will not be stopped for me in the regions *of* Achaia! **11** For what reason? Because I do not love you? God knows *I do.* **12** But what I am doing, I indeed will do in order that I may

---

A. Or, lengthened. **B.** Or, by. **C.** A few months later, Paul wrote Romans from Corinth in Act 20:2-3, setting his sights on Rome. **D.** Or, something. **E.** Or, you-are-bearing-with. **F.** Or, zealous-for. **G.** Or, zeal. **H.** That is, from God; or, a godly jealousy. **I.** Or, promised you in marriage, like a bride's father. **J.** Or, thoughts. **K.** Or, ruined, spoiled. **L.** Or, simplicity. **M.** Or, with regard to, towards. **N.** Or, been-inferior-to. **O.** That is, these 'super' apostles, as they think of themselves (who are false apostles, v 13); or, the chief, most-eminent apostles, such as Peter, James, and John. **P.** Paul brings up one way in which his opponents would have regarded him as inferior. **Q.** Paul did not earn his living from his teaching. He supported himself, taking no money from them. **R.** Or, plundered, sacked. Paul is sarcastically referring to the fact that he accepted money from other churches to support his work among the Corinthians. **S.** Or, wages. **T.** Same type of oath as in 1:18. **U.** That is, the boast in supporting himself as he serves Christ. Paul would rather die than give it up, 1 Cor 9:15.

cut-off the opportunity[A] *of* the *ones* wanting *an* opportunity that they might be found *to be* just as also we in what they are boasting. [13] For such *ones are* false-apostles, deceitful workers, transforming *themselves* into apostles *of* Christ. [14] And no wonder, for Satan himself transforms *himself* into *an* angel *of* light. [15] Therefore *it is* no great *thing* if also his ministers are disguising *themselves* as ministers *of* righteousness— whose end shall be according to their works.

Don't Think Me Foolish, But I Too Can Boast

[16] Again I say, let no one think me to be foolish. Otherwise indeed, receive me even if as foolish, in order that **I** also may boast *a* little bit! [17] In this confidence[B] *of* boasting[C], what I am speaking, I am not speaking according-to *the* Lord, but as in foolishness.

I Also Can Boast In My Heritage And My Service For Christ

[18] Since many are boasting according-to *the* flesh, **I** also will boast! [19] For with-pleasure you bear-with the unwise[D], being wise. [20] For you bear-with *it* if anyone enslaves[E] you, if anyone devours[F] *you,* if anyone takes *you,* if anyone lifts-up[G] *himself,* if anyone beats[H] you in *the* face. [21] I speak in-accordance-with *my* dishonor[I]— how that **we** have been weak! But in whatever anyone may dare *to boast*— I am speaking in foolishness— **I** also dare. [22] Are they Hebrews? I also. Are they Israelites? I also. Are they seed *of* Abraham? I also. [23] Are they servants *of* Christ? I speak being distraught[J], I more— in far-more labors, in far-more prisons, in many-more beatings, in deaths[K] often.

But I Will Boast In The Things Pertaining To My Weakness

[24] By Jews five-times I received forty *lashes* less one. [25] Three-times I was beaten-with-rods. Once I was stoned. Three-times I was shipwrecked. I have done *a* night-and-day in the deep. [26] *On* journeys often— *in* dangers *from* rivers, *in* dangers *from* robbers, *in* dangers from *my* nation[L], *in* dangers from Gentiles, *in* dangers in *the* city, *in* dangers in *the* wilderness, *in* dangers at sea, *in* dangers among false-brothers. [27] *In* labor and hardship, in watchings[M] often, in hunger and thirst, in fastings often, in cold and nakedness. [28] Apart from the external[N] *things, there is* the daily pressure[O] *on* me, the concern *for* all the churches— [29] who is weak, and I am not weak? Who is caused-to-fall, and **I** do not burn[P]? [30] If it-is-necessary[Q] to boast, I will boast the *things of* my weakness! [31] The God and Father *of* the Lord Jesus, the *One* being blessed[R] forever, knows that I am not

---

A. By not accepting money, Paul cuts off the opportunity for his opponents to be regarded as equal to him. **B.** Or, subject, undertaking. That is, this confidence in my status as apostle about which I am boasting; or, this subject of boasting forced upon me; or, this undertaking of boasting I will begin in v 21. **C.** Like his opponents, Paul will next boast in himself, in the flesh, rather than in the Lord; but Paul will boast in his weaknesses rather than his accomplishments. **D.** Or, foolish, as in v 16. **E.** Or, reduces you to bondage. **F.** Or, consumes. Compare Mk 12:40. **G.** Or, lifts *his hand* (in a threat); raises *his voice* (in anger). **H.** Paul may mean this literally (as in Jn 18:22; Act 23:2) or figuratively (insults you). **I.** That is, my weakness by comparison with my opponents, as they regard it. **J.** Or, deranged, mad, irrational. **K.** That is, perils of death. **L.** Or, people, kind; that is, Jews. **M.** That is, sleepless nights. **N.** Or, the *things* outside *these*; that is, the other things of this nature. **O.** Or, onset (of people). **P.** That is, with concern or anger. **Q.** Or, If *I* have to, If *I* must. **R.** Or, the *One Who* is blessed. This phrase refers back to the God and Father.

lying. [32] In Damascus, the ethnarch[A] *of* Aretas[B] the king was guarding the city *of the* Damascenes to seize me. [33] And I was lowered in *a* basket through *a* window through the wall and escaped his hands.

I Could Boast In My Visions And Revelations From The Lord

12:1 It-is-necessary to boast. *It is* not beneficial[C], but I will come to visions and revelations *from the* Lord. [2] I know *a* man in Christ, fourteen years ago— whether in *the* body, I do not know, or outside *of* the body, I do not know. God knows— *that* such *a one was* snatched-away[D] to *the* third heaven. [3] And I know such *a* man— whether in *the* body or apart from the body, I do not know. God knows— [4] that he was snatched away into paradise, and heard unspeakable words which *are* not permitted *for a* man to speak. [5] I will boast on behalf of such *a one*. But I will not boast on behalf of myself, except in the weaknesses. [6] For if I should desire to boast, I will not be foolish, for I will be speaking *the* truth; but I am sparing *you*, *that* no one might credit to me beyond what he sees *as to* me, or hears *as to* something from me.

But God's Power Is Perfected In Weakness, So I Will Boast In My Weaknesses

[7] And[E] *for* the excess[F] *of* the revelations— for-this-reason, in order that I might not be exalted[G], *a* thorn *in* the flesh was given *to* me; *a* messenger *of* Satan to[H] beat[I] me in order that I might not be exalted. [8] I appealed-to the Lord about this three-times, that it[J] might depart from me. [9] And He has said *to* me: "My grace is sufficient[K] *for* you. For *My* power is perfected[L] in weakness". Therefore most-gladly[M] I will rather boast in my weaknesses in order that the power *of* Christ may dwell upon me. [10] For this reason I am well-pleased with weaknesses, with insults[N], with constraints, with persecutions and distresses for the sake of Christ. For whenever I am weak, at that time I am powerful[O].

I Ought To Be Commended By You, For I Did The Signs of The Apostle Among You

[11] I have become foolish— **you** compelled me! For **I** ought to be being commended by you! For I in no way came-short-of the superlative[P] apostles, even though I am nothing; [12] the **signs**[Q] *of* the apostle were produced among you in[R] all endurance *in* both signs and wonders, and miracles.

My Only Shortcoming Is Not Letting You Pay Me! I Will Gladly Spend Myself For You!

[13] For what is it *as to* which you were worse-off[S] than the other churches?— except that **I** myself did not burden[T] you. Forgive me this wrong-doing! [14] Behold— this *is*

A. That is, governor. **B.** It was this king's daughter whom Herod (Mt 14:1) divorced to marry Herodias. **C.** Or, profitable, advantageous. Such talk exposes Paul to the charge of self-commendation. Perhaps for this reason he puts what follows in the third person. **D.** Or caught-up, carried-off. **E.** This points forward to "for-this-reason". Or, "beyond what he sees... or hears... and *for* the... revelations. For this reason", naming a second basis on which credit might come to Paul (v 6). **F.** Paul may mean excess of quality (excellence) or quantity (abundance). **G.** Or, exalt *myself*. **H.** Lit, in order that it (or, he) might beat me. **I.** Or, strike. **J.** That is, the thorn. Or, he; the messenger. **K.** Or, adequate, enough. **L.** Or, brought to completion or consummation. The greatness of God's power is seen in the weakness of the means He uses to accomplish His works. Jesus is the prime example. God's greatest victory came from the worst of human defeats. **M.** Or, with-the-greatest-pleasure. **N.** Or, violent mistreatment. **O.** Or, strong, mighty. **P.** See 11:5. **Q.** That is, that which authenticates someone as an apostle; the *true* signs *of* the apostle; or, the signs *of* the *true* apostle. **R.** That is, in connection with. **S.** Or, inferior, less. **T.** That is, financially. See 11:9.

the third *time* I am ready to come to you, and I will not be *a* burden. For I am not seeking your *things*, but you. For the children ought not to be storing-up *for* the parents, but the parents *for* the children. **15** But **I** will most gladly spend and be expended for your souls— though while loving you more, I am[A] loved less!

And Everyone I Sent You Did The Same As I
16 But let it[B] be— **I** did not weigh you down, but being crafty, I took you *by* deceit! **17** *As to* anyone *of* whom I have sent-out to you— I did not exploit you through him, *did I*? **18** I urged Titus *to go*, and I sent the brother with *him*. Titus did not exploit you, *did he*? Did we not walk *in* the same spirit? *In* the same footsteps?

In All This I Am Speaking To Edify You, Lest I Should Have To Come And Mourn Over You
19 All-this-time are you thinking[C] that we are defending-*ourselves to* you? We are speaking before God in Christ— and *speaking* all *things*, beloved, for the sake of your edification. **20** For I am fearing that having come, I may somehow find you *to be* not such as I want and **I** may be found *by* you *to be* such as you do not want— that somehow *there may be* strife, jealousy, rages[D], selfish-interests, slanders, whisperings, puffings [with pride], disorders[E]; **21** that I having come again[F], my God should humble me before you, and I should mourn many *of* the *ones* having previously-sinned and not having repented over[G] the impurity and sexual-immorality and sensuality which they practiced.

When I Come I Will Not Spare Those Seeking Proof of Christ Speaking In Me
13:1 This *is the* third *time* I am coming[H] to you. Every word shall be established based-on *the* mouth *of* two and three witnesses. **2** I have said-before and I am saying-beforehand, as being-present[I] the second *time* and being-absent now, *to* the *ones* having previously-sinned and *to* all the rest— that if I come again I will not spare *you,* **3** since you are seeking *a* proof *of* Christ speaking in me, Who is not weak toward you, but is strong in you. **4** For indeed He was crucified because-of weakness[J], but He lives because-of *the* power *of* God. For indeed **we** are weak in Him, but we will live with Him because of *the* power *of* God toward you.

Prove Yourselves, That Christ Is In You!
5 Test **yourselves** *to see* if you are in the faith! Prove[K] **yourselves**! Or do you not know yourselves, that Jesus Christ *is* in you?— unless indeed you are disapproved[L]. **6** But I hope that you will come-to-know that **we** are not disapproved.

We Are Praying For You
7 And we are praying to God *that* you *may* not do anything bad[M]— not in order

---

A. Or, am I loved less? **B.** That is, let someone's assertion be. Let their case be that I did not burden you, but I took you through those I sent. **C.** Or, you are thinking... you. **D.** Or, *fits of* rage. **E.** Or, disturbances. **F.** Or, that having come, my God should **again** humble me, perhaps implying a previous such sorrowful visit. **G.** Or, in relation to, concerning. **H.** That is, am *ready to* come, am *intending to* come, as clarified by 12:14 and 1:15 (the second planned visit never occurred because Paul changed his plans); or, am coming for an actual visit, implying two previous visits, this verse clarifying 12:14. **I.** That is, as when I was present; or, as though being present in spirit (as in 1 Cor 5:3). **J.** That is, our weakness (sin); or, Christ's weakness (His humiliation as a man). **K.** Or, Examine. Related to 'proof' in v 3. **L.** Or, failing-the-test. Related to 'Prove'. **M.** Or, wrong, harmful, evil. That is, such things as named in 12:20-21.

that **we** may appear approved[A], but in order that **you** may be doing the good, and **we** may be as[B] disapproved. [8] For we cannot *do* anything against the truth, but [only] for the truth. [9] For we are rejoicing whenever **we** are weak but **you** are strong. This also we are praying— your restoration[C].

I Am Writing So I Don't Have To Act Severely When I Come
[10] For this reason I am writing these *things* while absent— in order that while being-present, I may not act severely[D] according-to[E] the authority which the Lord gave me for building-up and not for tearing-down.

[11] Finally, brothers, be rejoicing[F], be restored[G], be exhorted[H], be thinking the same *thing*, be living-in-peace. And the God *of* love and peace will be with you. [12] Greet one another with *a* holy kiss. [13] All the saints greet you. [14] The grace *of*[I] the Lord Jesus Christ and the love *of*[J] God and the fellowship *of*[K] the Holy Spirit *be* with you all.

A. That is, because you submitted to and obeyed us. **B.** That is, appear disapproved (to some) because your right response eliminated any need for us to prove ourselves by displaying our disciplinary power. **C.** Or, completion, maturation. **D.** Or, sharply, harshly. **E.** Or, based on. **F.** Or, farewell. **G.** Or, put in order, made complete. **H.** Or, encouraged. **I.** That is, proceeding from, bestowed by Christ. **J.** That is, from; or, produced by God. **K.** That is, produced by; or, with the Spirit.

Galatians

Introduction   1:1-5

A.   I am marveling that you are turning away to a different gospel. If anyone announces a contrary   1:6-12
     gospel, let him be accursed. For I did not receive my gospel from humans, but by revelation

1.   For you heard of my former conduct in Judaism. When God revealed His Son to me, I did   1:13-17
     not immediately communicate with flesh and blood, but went to Arabia

   a.   After three years I went to Jerusalem to visit Cephas for fifteen days   1:18-24
   b.   After fourteen years, I went again to Jerusalem to lay before them the good news I   2:1-10
        was proclaiming. They gave me the right hand of fellowship

2.   And I rebuked Cephas for not walking straight with regard to the gospel and the Gentiles   2:11-14

   a.   We are all declared righteous by faith, not works of the Law   2:15-16
   b.   We have died to the Law, and live by faith in the Son of God   2:17-21

B.   O foolish Galatians, who bewitched you? Are you now perfecting yourselves with the flesh?   3:1-5

1.   Know then that the ones of faith are the sons of Abraham. Christ redeemed us from the Law   3:6-14

   a.   The promises to Abraham were not nullified by the Law which came later   3:15-18
   b.   Why then the law? It was added because of transgressions, until Christ came   3:19-20
   c.   Is the Law against the promises? No. It was our tutor leading to Christ. We are now   3:21-29
        not under a tutor, for we are sons of God, seed of Abraham, and heirs of the promise

2.   Now when we were minors we were slaves to the elemental things. But when God sent His   4:1-11
     Son, He adopted you as sons and heirs. Why are you turning back to slavery?
3.   I beg you, become as I. Have I become your enemy for speaking the truth to you?   4:12-20
4.   Tell me, do you not hear the Law? They are of the slave woman, we are of the free woman 4:21-31

C.   Christ set us free for freedom. So then stand firm, and do not again be held in a yoke of slavery   5:1-12
D.   For you were called for freedom, only do not use the freedom for an opportunity for the flesh   5:13-15

1.   And I say— be walking by the Spirit and you will never fulfill the desire of the flesh   5:16-18

   a.   Those who practice the works of the flesh will not inherit the kingdom of God   5:19-21
   b.   Those in Christ crucified the flesh and bear the fruit of walking in the Spirit   5:22-25

2.   Let us not become conceited, challenging one another. Restore those who have fallen.   5:26-6:5
     Each has a boast only in his own proven work

3.   Share all good things. We reap what we sow. Let us not grow weary while doing good   6:6-10

Conclusion   6:11-18

1:1 Paul[A]— *an* apostle not from humans nor through *a* human, but through Jesus Christ and God *the* Father, the *One* having raised Him from *the* dead— **²** and all the brothers with me, *to* the churches *of* Galatia: **³** Grace *to* you and peace from God our Father and *the* Lord Jesus Christ, **⁴** the *One* having given Himself for our sins so that He might rescue us out of the present evil age in accordance with the will *of* our God and Father, **⁵** *to* Whom *be* the glory forever and ever, amen.

Are You Turning Away From The Gospel I Received Through a Revelation From Christ?
⁶ I am marveling that you are so quickly[B] turning-away from the *One* having called you by *the* grace *of* Christ to *a* different good-news— **⁷** which is not another[C] [good news]— except there are some disturbing you and intending[D] to change[E] the good-news *of* Christ. **⁸** But even if we or *an* angel from heaven should[F] announce-a-good-news *to* you other-than[G] what we announced-as-good-news *to* you, let him be accursed[H]. **⁹** As we have said-before I am also now saying again— if anyone is[I] announcing-a-good-news-to you other-than what you received, let him be accursed. **¹⁰** For am I now *trying to* win-approval-of[J] humans or God? Or am I seeking to please humans? If I were still[K] *seeking to* please humans, I would not be *a* slave *of* Christ! **¹¹** For I make-known *to* you, brothers, *as to* the good-news having been announced-as-good-news by me, that it is not according-to[L] *a* human[M]. **¹²** For I neither received it from *a* human, nor was I taught *it*, but *I received it* through *a* revelation *of*[N] Jesus Christ.

For When God Was Pleased To Reveal Himself To Me, I Conferred With No One
¹³ For you heard-*of* my former conduct in Judaism— that I was persecuting the church *of* God extremely, and destroying[O] it. **¹⁴** And I was advancing in Judaism beyond many contemporaries in my nation, being far more *a* zealot *for* the traditions *of* my fathers. **¹⁵** But when God— the *One* having separated me from my mother's womb[P] and having called *me* through His grace— was well-pleased **¹⁶** to reveal His Son in me in order that I might be announcing Him as good news among the Gentiles, I did not immediately communicate[Q] *with* flesh and blood, **¹⁷** nor did I go up to Jerusalem to the apostles before me, but I went away to Arabia and returned back to Damascus.

Three Years Later I Went To Jerusalem And Visited Peter And James
¹⁸ Then after three years I went up to Jerusalem to visit Cephas, and stayed with him fifteen days. **¹⁹** But I did not see another *of* the apostles except[R] James, the brother *of* the Lord. **²⁰** Now *the things* which I am writing *to* you, behold— *I affirm* in the sight of God that I am not lying. **²¹** Then I went into the regions *of* Syria and Cilicia. **²²** And I was not-known *by* face *to* the churches *of* Judea in Christ, **²³** but they were only hearing that "the *one* once persecuting us is now announcing-as-good-news the faith which he was once destroying". **²⁴** And they were glorifying God in[S] me.

A. On when this book was written, see Act 14:28. **B.** Or, hastily. **C.** That is, another of the same kind. **D.** Or, wanting. **E.** Or, alter. **F.** That is, in the unlikely event that I or an angel should say this. **G.** Or, against, contrary-to. **H.** Lit, anathema. **I.** That is, assuming that someone is in fact now saying this. **J.** Or, win-over, *merely* persuade. Some accused Paul of reshaping the gospel to appeal to the Gentiles. **K.** That is, as Paul did when he was a Pharisee. **L.** Or, by way of, based on. **M.** Or, mankind; that is, the authority of mankind. **N.** Or, *from, given by.* **O.** Or, ravaging, pillaging. Same in v 23. **P.** That is, since birth. **Q.** Or, consult, confer. **R.** Or, apostles, only James. **S.** That is, in connection with.

Fourteen Years Later The Jerusalem Apostles Added Nothing To My Gospel
2:1 Then after fourteen years I again went up to Jerusalem with Barnabas, having also taken along Titus with *me.* **2** And I went up based-on[A] *a* revelation, and laid-before them the good-news which I am proclaiming among the Gentiles— but privately, *to* the *ones* having-the-reputation-of[B] *being something— that* somehow[C] I might not be running, or have run, in vain[D]. **3** But not even Titus, the *one* with me, being *a* Greek, was compelled to be circumcised. **4** Now[E] *this arose*[F] because of the false-brothers secretly-brought-in, who sneaked-in to spy-out our freedom which we have in Christ Jesus in order that they might enslave[G] us—**5** *to* whom we yielded *in* submission not-even for *an* hour, in order that the truth *of* the good-news might continue[H] with you. **6** And from the *ones* having-the-reputation-of being something— of-what-sort they ever[I] were makes no difference *to* me; God does not receive *the* face[J] *of a* human— indeed *to* me the *ones* having-the-reputation communicated nothing. **7** But on-the-contrary, having seen that I have been entrusted the good-news *for* the uncircumcised just as Peter *for* the circumcised— **8** for the *One* having worked[K] *in* Peter for *an* apostleship *of* the circumcised worked also *in* me for the Gentiles— **9** and having recognized the grace having been given *to* me, James and Cephas and John, the *ones* having-the-reputation-of being pillars, gave *the* right *hands of* fellowship *to* me and Barnabas, that we *should go* to the Gentiles and they to the circumcised. **10** *They asked* only that we should be remembering[L] **the poor**— *as to* which, I also was eager to do this very *thing.*

In Antioch I Rebuked Peter When He Erred With Respect To Gentile Christians
11 And when Cephas came to Antioch, I opposed *him* to his face— because he was condemned[M]. **12** For before certain *ones* came from James, he was eating with the Gentiles. But when they came, he was drawing-back and separating himself, fearing[N] the *ones* of *the* circumcision. **13** And the other Jews also joined-in-hypocrisy *with* him, so that even Barnabas was carried-away *by* their hypocrisy. **14** But when I saw that they were not walking-straight[O] with regard to the truth *of* the good-news, I said *to* Cephas in front of everyone— "If **you** being *a* Jew are living Gentile-ly[P] and not Jewish-ly[Q], how *is it* you are compelling the Gentiles to Judaize[R]?"

Even We Jews Are Declared Righteous By Faith In Christ, Not By Works of The Law
15 We[S] *are* Jews *by* nature, and not sinners from *the* Gentiles. **16** But knowing that *a* person[T] is not declared-righteous by works *of the* Law except[U] through faith *in* Jesus Christ, even **we** believed in Christ Jesus, in order that we might be declared-righteous

---

A. Or, in accordance with. **B.** Or, being-recognized-as, being-acknowledged-as. **C.** This rendering expresses Paul's fear that his work might come to no effect because of the opposition of some in Jerusalem. Or, 'whether somehow I am running or have run in vain', expressing the subject to be discussed. **D.** Or, for nothing, to no result. **E.** Or, But, And. **F.** Or, *we went up; it was.* **G.** Or, enslave us under *them*, reduce us to slavery. **H.** Or, remain continually. **I.** Or, once, formerly. **J.** That is, God is impartial. **K.** That is, *miraculously* worked. **L.** Or, keeping in mind. **M.** That is, in a state of condemnation, due to his actions. **N.** The issue here is not Gentiles keeping the Law (as in Acts 15), but Jewish Christians (like Peter) keeping the Law. **O.** Or, being-straightforward. **P.** That is, in a partially Gentile manner. **Q.** That is, in a totally Jewish manner. **R.** That is, live like Jews. **S.** Verses 15-21 may still be part of Paul's quotation of what he said that day; or it may be his present explanation of that event to the Galatians. **T.** That is, a Jewish person. **U.** Or, unless through, if not through. That is, if *he does* not *come* through. It is the faith, not the works, that bring the result.

by faith *in* Christ and not by works *of the* Law, because by works *of the* Law no flesh will be declared-righteous.

And We Died To The Law As a Rule of Life, And Now Live By Faith In The Son of God

[17] But if[A] while seeking to be declared-righteous in Christ, we also ourselves were found *to be* sinners[B], *is* then Christ *a* minister *of* sin[C]? May it never be! [18] For if I am building again these[D] *things* which I tore-down[E], I am demonstrating[F] myself *to be a* transgressor. [19] For through *the* Law I died *to the* Law in order that I might live *to* God. I have been crucified-with Christ! [20] And I no longer am living, but Christ is living in me. And what I am now[G] living in *the* flesh[H], I am living by[I] faith *in* the Son *of* God— the *One* having loved me and handed Himself over for me. [21] I am not setting-aside[J] the grace *of* God! For if righteousness *comes* through *the* Law, then Christ died without-a-reason!

Who Has Bewitched You? Do You Live By The Spirit And Faith, Or The Flesh And Law?

3:1 O foolish Galatians, who bewitched[K] you, before whose eyes Jesus Christ was portrayed[L] *as* crucified? [2] I want to learn only this from you: did you receive the Spirit by works *of the* Law or by *the* hearing[M] *of*[N] faith? [3] Are you so foolish? Having begun-with[O] *the* Spirit are you now perfecting-*yourselves*[P] with the flesh? [4] Did you suffer[Q] so many *things* in-vain— if indeed *it* really *was* in-vain? [5] *Did* then the *One* supplying[R] you the Spirit and working miracles among you *do it* because-of[S] works *of the* Law, or because-of *the* hearing *of* faith?

The Children of Abraham Are The Ones Living By Faith, Not By The Law

[6] Just as Abraham "believed God and it was credited *to* him for righteousness" [Gen 15:6], [7] know then that the *ones* of[T] faith— these are *the* sons[U] *of* Abraham. [8] Now the Scripture, having foreseen that God declares the Gentiles righteous by faith, announced-the-good-news-beforehand *to* Abraham: that "All the Gentiles will be blessed in[V] you"[Gen 12:3]. [9] So then the *ones* of faith are being blessed together-with Abraham, the *man-of*-faith[W]. [10] For all-who are of *the* works *of the* Law are under *a* curse, for it has been written that "Cursed *is* everyone who is not continuing-in[X] all the *things* having been written in the book *of* the Law, *that he might* do them"[Deut 27:26]. [11] And that no one is declared-righteous by[Y] *the* Law before God *is* evident[Z], because "The righteous *one* will live by faith" [Hab 2:4]. [12] But the Law is not of faith, but "The *one* having done these *things*

A. That is, assuming that. **B.** That is, equivalent to Gentiles in status before God. **C.** That is, for leading us to live Gentile-ly with our Gentile fellow-Christians. **D.** That is, these works of the Law as my rule of life and basis of relationship with others. **E.** That is, to be declared-righteous by God, since His only required condition is faith. **F.** Or, showing, exhibiting. That is, because I am erecting conditions in violation of God's only condition, faith. **G.** That is, as a Christian declared righteous by faith, with Christ living in me. **H.** That is, in my continued existence on earth. **I.** Or, in; that is, in the sphere of faith, not law. **J.** Or, nullifying, rejecting. **K.** Or, charmed. **L.** Or, placarded, publicly-posted. **M.** Or, report. **N.** That is, the subjective obedient hearing *proceeding from* or *characterized by* faith (was it by works or by your believing?); or, the objective report *concerning* faith (was it by works or by the proclaiming of the gospel to you?). **O.** That is, begun in the sphere of; or, begun by means of. Same next on 'with the flesh'. **P.** Or, being perfected, completed, finished. **Q.** That is, suffer negative consequences, persecutions. Or, experience, referring to positive benefits. **R.** Or, providing. **S.** Or, out-of, in the sense of originating in. **T.** That is, originating in and living by. So also in v 9, 10, 12, 18. **U.** That is, spiritual descendants. **V.** That is, in connection with, in union with. **W.** Or, the believer, the faithful *one*. **X.** Or, abiding-in; and thus, being-faithful-to, being-true-to. Only doers are justified, Rom 2:12-13. **Y.** Or, in the sphere of, under. **Z.** Or, clear, plain.

shall live by them" [Lev 18:5]. **13** Christ redeemed us from the curse *of* the Law, having become *a* curse for us— because it has been written, "Cursed *is* everyone hanging on *a* tree" [Deut 21:23]— **14** in order that the blessing *of* [A] Abraham might come to the Gentiles in Christ Jesus, in order that we might receive the promise *of* [B] the Spirit through faith.

God's Promises To Abraham Were Not Cancelled By The Law Which Came Later
15 Brothers, I speak in accordance with human *thinking*: Though *it is* [a covenant] *of a* human, no one sets-aside or adds-conditions-to *a* covenant having been ratified. **16** Now the promises were spoken *to* Abraham and *to* his seed [C]. He [D] does not say [in Gen 13:15] "and *to* seeds", as-*though speaking* in reference to many; but as-*though speaking* in reference to one, "and *to* your seed"— who is Christ. **17** And this I say: the Law, having come-about after four-hundred and thirty years, does not un-ratify [E] *the* covenant having been previously-ratified by God, so as to do-away-with [F] the promise. **18** For if the inheritance *is* of [G] *the* Law, *it is* no longer of *the* promise. But God has freely-given *it to* Abraham through *the* promise!

The Law Was Added Because of Transgressions, Until The Christ Should Come
19 Why then the Law? It was added because of the transgressions until which *time* the Seed should come *to* Whom the promise has been made, having been commanded [H] through angels by *the* hand *of a* mediator [I]. **20** Now a mediator is not [a mediator] *of* [only] one [party], but God is one [J].

The Law Served To Lead Us To Faith In Christ So As To Inherit The Abrahamic Promises
21 *Is* the Law then against the promises *of* God? May it never be! For if *a* Law being able to give-life had been given, righteousness really would have been by *the* Law! **22** But the Scripture confined all *things* under [K] sin, in order that the promise by faith [L] in Jesus Christ might be given *to* the *ones* believing. **23** And before the faith [M] came, we were being kept-in-custody [N] under *the* Law— being confined until [O] the faith destined to be revealed. **24** So then the Law has been [P] our tutor [Q] leading-to [R] Christ, in order that we might be declared-righteous by faith. **25** But the faith having come, we are no longer under *a* tutor! **26** For you all are sons [S] *of* God through faith in Christ Jesus! **27** For all you who were baptized into Christ put-on [T] Christ. **28** There is no Jew nor Greek, there is no slave nor free, there is no male and female. For **you** all are one in Christ Jesus. **29** And if you *are* Christ's, then you are seed *of* Abraham— heirs according-to *the* promise.

God Sent His Son To Redeem Us So We All Could Be Adopted As Sons And Heirs
4:1 Now I say— for as much time as the heir is *a* child [U], he is no different *from a* slave.

A. That is, promised to Abraham. **B.** That is, consisting of the Spirit. **C.** This word had the collective sense of offspring, descendants, posterity, but also the singular sense which Paul reminds us of next, linking Abraham and Christ. **D.** Or, It, meaning the Scripture. **E.** Or, nullify. **F.** Or, invalidate, set-aside, render-useless. **G.** That is, originating in. If this is the source of the inheritance. **H.** Or, ordained, set in order, arranged. **I.** That is, Moses. **J.** That is, a mediator stands between two parties. But God acted alone when He made His promise to Abraham and his seed. **K.** That is, under its power and consequence. **L.** Or, by *the* faithfulness *of* Jesus (to what God sent Him to do). **M.** That is, the faith just mentioned. Or, faith. **N.** Or, guarded. **O.** Or, to, for. **P.** Or, come-to-be. **Q.** Or, guardian, guide; our childhood custodian. **R.** Or, until. **S.** That is, descendants, children. **T.** Or, are dressed-in, are wearing. **U.** That is, a minor.

Being *the* [future] owner *of* all, **²** nevertheless[A] he is under guardians and stewards[B] until the pre-appointed *day of* the father. **³** In this manner also **we**, when we were children, were[C] enslaved under the elemental[D] *things of* the world. **⁴** But when the fullness *of* time came, God sent-forth His Son— having come[E] from *a* woman, having come under *the* Law **⁵** in order that He might redeem the *ones* under *the* Law, in order that we [all] might receive the adoption. **⁶** And because[F] you are sons, God sent-forth the Spirit *of* His Son into our hearts crying-out, "Abba! Father!" **⁷** So then you are no longer *a* slave, but *a* son— and if *a* son, also *an* heir through God!

Why Turn Back To Being Slaves Again? I Fear For You
⁸ But at that time not knowing God, you were-slaves *to* the *ones by* nature not being gods. **⁹** But now having known God, yet rather having been known by God, how *is it* you are turning-back again to the weak and poor elemental *things to* which again you are wanting to be-slaves anew? **¹⁰** You are observing days and months and seasons and years. **¹¹** I am fearing *for* you, that I somehow have labored in-vain for you.

I Beg You, Become As I Am. Have I Become Your Enemy By Speaking The Truth To You?
¹² I beg you, brothers, become as I, because I also *became* as you. You did me no wrong. **¹³** And you know that I first[G] announced-the-good-news *to* you because of *a* weakness[H] *of* the flesh. **¹⁴** And you did not treat-with-contempt nor loathe your trial in-connection-with my flesh, but you welcomed me as *an* angel[I] *of* God, as Christ Jesus. **¹⁵** Where then *is* your blessedness[J]? For I testify *concerning* you that, if possible, you *would* have given your eyes *to* me, having torn *them* out! **¹⁶** So then, have I become your enemy while speaking-the-truth *to* you? **¹⁷** They are zealously-seeking you— not commendably, but they want to shut you out[K] in-order-that you might be zealously-seeking them.

I Am Again Suffering Birth Pains For You Until Christ Is Formed In You
¹⁸ Now *it is* good to be zealously-sought in[L] *a* commendable *thing* at-all-times, and not only during my being present with you— **¹⁹** my[M] children, *as to* whom again I am suffering-birth-pains until which *time* Christ is formed in you. **²⁰** But I was [just now] wishing[N] to be present with you now and to change my tone, because I am perplexed with you.

Listen To The Law. We Are Children of The Free Promise, Not of The Slave Covenant
²¹ Tell me, the *ones* wanting to be under *the* Law, do you not hear *the* Law? **²²** For it has been written that Abraham had two sons— one by the slave-woman and one by the free *woman*. **²³** But the *one* by the slave-woman has been born according to *the* flesh, and the *one* by the free *woman* through *the* promise— **²⁴** which *things* are being allegorized[O], for these *women* are two covenants. One[P] *is* from Mount Sinai, bearing *children* for slavery,

---

A: slave... nevertheless he is. Or, slave, [though] being *the* [future] owner *of* all. But he is. **B.** Or, household managers. **C.** Or, had been. **D.** That is, the elementary knowledge of God available in the world before Christ came. Or, the elemental spiritual beings or angels associated with religions. Same in v 9. **E.** Or, 'having come-into-being' as a human, and in this sense, 'having been born'. **F.** Or, And that; meaning, 'And as proof that'. **G.** Or, formerly. **H.** Or, sickness. **I.** Or, messenger. **J.** That is, your feeling of blessing in my work among you. You had it then! **K.** Or, exclude you. **L.** That is, in connection with. **M.** Some start a new sentence here, omitting the 'But' at v 20. **N.** Or, I *would* wish, if it were possible. **O.** That is, which things contain an allegory; or, which things I am going to allegorize. **P.** That is, one woman representing one covenant.

which is Hagar ^{25} (now Hagar is Mount Sinai in Arabia). And she^A corresponds *to* the present Jerusalem, for she^B is *a* slave^C with her children. ^{26} But the Jerusalem above is free— which is our mother^D. ^{27} For it has been written, "Celebrate, barren *one,* the *one* not giving-birth. Break-forth and shout, the *one* not suffering-birth-pains. Because many more *are* the children *of* the desolate^E than *of* the *one* having the husband!"[Isa 54:1] ^{28} And **you**, brothers, are children *of the* promise in accordance with Isaac. ^{29} But just as at-that-time the *one* having been born according to *the* flesh was persecuting the *one born* according to *the* Spirit, so also now. ^{30} But what does the Scripture say? "Send-out the slave-woman and her son. For the son *of* the slave-woman shall by no means inherit with the son *of* the free *woman*" [Gen 21:10]. ^{31} Therefore, brothers, we are not children *of a* slave-woman, but *of* the free *woman.*

Christ Set Us Free, So Stand Firm In Faith. If You Pursue The Law, Christ Will Not Profit You
5:1 Christ set us free *for* freedom. Therefore be standing-*firm*, and do not again be held-in^F *a* yoke *of* slavery. ^{2} Behold— **I**, Paul, say *to* you that if you receive-circumcision, Christ will profit you nothing. ^{3} And I testify again *to* every man receiving-circumcision that he is *a* debtor to do the whole Law. ^{4} You who are [trying to be] declared-righteous by *the* Law were alienated^G from Christ. You fell-from grace^H. ^{5} For *by*^{I} *the* Spirit, by faith, **we** are eagerly-awaiting *the* hope *of* righteousness. ^{6} For in Christ Jesus neither circumcision nor uncircumcision can-do^J anything, but faith working^K through love.

Who Hindered You From Believing The Truth? He Will Bear His Judgment
^{7} You were running well. Who hindered^L you *that you should* not be persuaded^M *by* the truth? ^{8} The persuasion *is* not from the *One* calling you! ^{9} *A* little leaven leavens the whole lump. ^{10} **I** am persuaded^N with reference to you in *the* Lord that you will think no other *thing.* But the *one* disturbing you will bear the judgment, whoever he may be. ^{11} But **I**, brothers, if I am still proclaiming circumcision, why am I still being persecuted? Then the offense *of*^{O} the cross has been abolished. ^{12} O-that^P the *ones* upsetting you *would* indeed cut-*themselves*-off^Q!

Use Your Freedom To Serve One Another In Love, Not As an Opportunity For The Flesh
^{13} For **you** were called for freedom, brothers, only *do* not *use* the freedom for *an* opportunity *for* the flesh, but be serving one another through love. ^{14} For the whole Law has been fulfilled in one saying— in the "You shall love your neighbor as yourself " [Lev 19:18]. ^{15} But if you are biting and devouring one another, watch out *that* you may not be consumed by one another!

Walk By The Spirit And You Will Not Fulfill The Flesh's Desires Or Be Under The Law
^{16} And I say— be walking *by the* Spirit and you will never^R fulfill^S *the* desire *of*^{T} *the* flesh. ^{17} For the flesh desires against the Spirit and the Spirit against the flesh. For these are

---

A. That is, Hagar. **B.** That is, the present Jerusalem. **C.** Or, serves as slave. **D:** But... mother. Paul does not fully detail this side of the comparison, but jumps to his two main points from it. **E.** That is, unable to bear children, referring to Sarah. **F.** Or, caught-in, subject-to. **G.** Or, separated, severed, cut off. Christ is of no value to people seeking to relate to God based on works. **H.** Grace and works are mutually-exclusive paths. **I.** Or, *in.* **J.** Or, avails; has power for, has validity for. **K.** Or, being in operation, being at work. **L.** Or, cut-in-on. **M.** Or, be obeying. **N.** Or, confident. **O.** That is, consisting of. **P.** Or, Would-that. **Q.** That is, castrate themselves (a sarcastic response to their desire for circumcision); or, cut themselves off from the congregation. **R.** Or, by no means. **S.** Or, finish, bring to completion. **T.** That is, originating in.

contrary[A] *to* one another in-order-that you might not be doing these[B] *things* which you may be wanting. **¹⁸** But if you are being led *by the* Spirit, you are not under *the* Law.

Those Who Practice The Works of The Flesh Will Not Inherit God's Kingdom
¹⁹ Now the works *of* the flesh are evident, which are sexual-immorality, impurity, sensuality, **²⁰** idolatry, sorcery, hostilities, strife, jealousy, rages[C], selfish-interests, dissentions, factions, **²¹** envy[D], drunkenness, revelries, and the *things* like these— *as to* which *things* I tell you beforehand, just as I said-before, that the *ones* practicing such *things* will not inherit *the* kingdom *of* God.

Those In Christ Crucified The Flesh And Bear The Fruit of Living By The Spirit
²² But the fruit *of* [E] the Spirit is love, joy, peace, patience, kindness, goodness, faithfulness, **²³** gentleness, self-control. Against such *things* there is no law. **²⁴** And the *ones of* [F] Christ Jesus crucified the flesh, with *its* passions and desires. **²⁵** If we are living *by the* Spirit, let us also be walking-in-line[G] *with the* Spirit.

Don't Be Conceited. Humbly Care For One Another And You Will Fulfill Christ's Law
²⁶ Let us not become conceited[H] *ones*, challenging[I] one another, envying one another. **6:1** Brothers, even[J] if *a* person is overtaken[K] in some trespass, **you** spiritual *ones* be restoring[L] such *a* one in *a* spirit *of* gentleness, looking-out-for yourself *that* **you** also not be tempted. **²** Be carrying one another's burdens[M], and in this manner you will fulfill the law *of* Christ. **³** For if anyone thinks *that he* is something while being nothing, he is deceiving himself.

Each Person Has a Boast Only With Reference To His Own Proven Work
⁶ But let each *one* prove[N] his *own* work— and then he will have the boast with reference to himself alone, and not with reference to the other *person*. **⁵** For each *one* will carry *his* own load[O].

We Will Reap What We Sow. Plant Good Works To Reap a Good Harvest
⁶ And let the *one* being instructed-*in* the word share *with* the *one* instructing in all good *things*. **⁷** Do not be deceived— God is not mocked. For whatever *a* person sows, this he will also reap. **⁸** Because the *one* sowing to his *own* flesh will reap decay from the flesh. But the *one* sowing to *the* Spirit will reap eternal life from the Spirit. **⁹** And let us not grow-weary while doing good. For *in His* own time we not losing-heart[P] will reap. **¹⁰** So then, while we have[Q] opportunity[R], let us be working good to everyone, but especially to the family-members *of* the faith.

A. Or, opposed. But not as equals, for before Christ the flesh was dominant; after, the Spirit leads us into conformity to Him. **B.** That is, these desires of the flesh. The Spirit prevents us from living according to the flesh, proving the 'never' of v 16. Compare 1 Jn 3:9. **C.** Or, [fits of] rage. **D.** Or, [acts of] envy. It is plural, as is the next word. **E.** That is, produced by. **F.** That is, belonging to. **G.** That is, living in conformity *to*. **H.** This is defined by 6:3. **I.** Or, provoking, calling out (to fight). **J.** That is, even if one is caught in an explicit sin, do not respond in the conceit that you yourself are invulnerable. **K.** Or, caught, surprised. **L.** That is, be engaged in the process of restoring such a one. **M.** Or, weights, impediments. **N.** That is, prove by testing and examination. **O.** That is, load of work accomplished for Christ. **P.** Or, fainting, giving-out. **Q.** That is, in this life. **R.** Or, time.

Those Wanting Your Circumcision Are Seeking To Boast In Your Flesh, Not To Keep The Law
11 See *with* what large letters I wrote *to* you *with* my *own* hand! **12** All who want to make-a-good-showing[A] in *the* flesh— these *ones* are compelling you to receive-circumcision only in order that they may not be persecuted *for* the cross *of* Christ. **13** For not even the *ones* receiving-circumcision themselves are keeping *the* Law. But they want you to receive-circumcision in order that they might boast in your flesh.

I Will Boast Only In The Cross of Christ. Peace Be Upon All Who Do The Same
14 But *for* me, may it never be *that I should* boast except in the cross *of* our Lord Jesus Christ, through which[B] *the* world has been crucified *to* **me**, and I *to the* world. **15** For neither circumcision nor uncircumcision is anything, but *a* new creation. **16** And all who will walk-in-line *with* this standard[C]— peace and mercy *be* upon them, and[D] upon the Israel *of* God. **17** Henceforth[E] let no one be causing troubles *for* me. For **I** bear the brand-marks[F] *of* Jesus on my body.

18 *May* the grace *of* our Lord Jesus Christ *be* with your spirit, brothers. Amen.

A. Or, put-on-a-good-face. **B.** Or, Whom. **C.** Or, rule, norm. **D.** Or, even. **E.** Or, Finally. **F.** That is, of ownership.

Ephesians

Introduction   1:1-2

A. Blessed be the God who has blessed us with every spiritual blessing in Christ   1:3

   1. Even as He chose us in Him to be holy, having predestined us for adoption   1:4-6
   2. In Whom we have redemption through His blood and forgiveness by His grace   1:7-10
   3. In Whom we were allotted an inheritance, so that we might be for the praise of His glory   1:11-12
   4. In Whom you were sealed with the Holy Spirit, the pledge of our inheritance   1:13-14

B. For this reason, I do not cease giving thanks for you, making mention of you in my prayers so that you may know what is the hope of His calling, the riches of the glory of His inheritance among the saints, and the greatness of His power toward us—   1:15-19

   1. Which He worked in Christ, having raised Him from the dead and seated Him at His right hand in the heavens   1:19-23
   2. Indeed, you were dead in sins. But God made us alive and seated us with Christ in order to demonstrate His grace and kindness. For by grace you are saved   2:1-10

C. Therefore, remember that you Gentiles were excluded from God and His people   2:11-12

   1. But now you were made near by the blood of Christ, and we are one in Him   2:13-18
   2. So then, you are no longer strangers, but fellow-citizens and family-members of God   2:19-22
   3. For this reason I, Paul, a prisoner for you Gentiles—   3:1

      a. If indeed you heard of my stewardship to reveal God's promises to the Gentiles   3:2-7
      b. It was granted to me to enlighten everyone to see the Creator's long hidden plan   3:8-13

   4. For this reason I pray that you may be strengthened and know His love   3:14-19
   5. Now to the One able to do beyond what we ask or think be the glory forever   3:20-21

D. Therefore I exhort you to walk worthily, keeping the unity of the Spirit. There is one body and one Spirit, and each of us has been given gifts and grace to build up the body   4:1-16

E. Therefore walk no longer as the Gentiles walk, in the futility of their darkened minds   4:17-19

   1. Lay aside the old person, be renewed in your mind, and put on the new person   4:20-24
   2. Speak and live in truth and righteousness   4:25-32
   3. Be imitators of God, walking in love, with no kind of impurity or greed among you   5:1-7
   4. For you were formerly darkness, but now you are light. Walk as children of light   5:8-14

F. Therefore walk wisely. Understand God's will. Be filled with the Spirit in all relationships   5:15-21

   1. Wives, be subject to your husbands as the church is subject to Christ   5:22-24
   2. Husbands, love your wives as Christ loved the church   5:25-33
   3. Children, honor your parents   6:1-3
   4. Fathers, nourish your children in the Lord   6:4
   5. Slaves and masters, live as slaves of Christ   6:5-9

G. Finally, become strong in the Lord. Put on the full armor in our spiritual battle   6:10-20

Conclusion   6:21-24

1:1 Paul[A], *an* apostle *of* Christ Jesus by *the* will *of* God, *to* the saints being in Ephesus and faithful in Christ Jesus: **²** Grace *to* you and peace from God our Father and *the* Lord Jesus Christ.

Blessed Be The God Who Has Blessed Us In Christ With Every Spiritual Blessing
³ Blessed *be* the God and Father *of* our Lord Jesus Christ, the *One* having blessed us with every spiritual blessing in the heavenly *places* in Christ—

In Christ And By Grace He Chose Us To Be Holy, And Predestined Us For Adoption
⁴ ... even as He chose us in Him before *the* foundation *of the* world *that* we *might* be holy and without-blemish in His presence, in[B] love **⁵** having predestined us for adoption through Jesus Christ to Himself according-to[C] the good-pleasure *of* His will, **⁶** for *the* praise *of the* glory *of* His grace which He graciously-bestowed-on us in the Beloved[D] *One,*

In Christ And By Grace He Redeemed Us And Revealed The Mystery of His Will To Us
⁷ ... in[E] Whom we have the redemption through His blood, the forgiveness *of* trespasses, according to the riches *of* His grace **⁸** which He caused-to-abound to us, in[F] all wisdom and understanding **⁹** having made-known *to* us the mystery *of* His will according to His good-pleasure, which He purposed in Himself[G] **¹⁰** for *a* stewardship[H] *of*[I] the fullness *of* times, *that He might* sum-up[J] all *things* in Christ— the *things* at the heavens and the *things* on the earth, in Him,

In Christ He Predestined Us For an Inheritance
¹¹ ... in Whom also we were allotted *an inheritance*[K], having been predestined[L] according to *the* purpose[M] *of* the *One* working all *things* in accordance with the counsel[N] *of* His will **¹²** so-that we, the *ones* having previously-hoped[O] in the[P] Christ, *might* be for *the* praise *of* His glory,

In Christ He Sealed Us With The Holy Spirit As a Pledge of Our Inheritance
¹³ ... in Whom also you— having heard the word *of* truth, the good-news *of* your salvation, in which[Q] also having put-faith— you were sealed *with* the Holy Spirit *of* promise, **¹⁴** Who is *a* pledge *of* our inheritance until *the* [final] redemption *of* His possession[R] for *the* praise *of* His glory.

I Pray You May Understand The Hope of His Calling And The Greatness of His Power Toward Us
¹⁵ For this reason I also, having heard-*of* your faith in the Lord Jesus and love toward all the saints, **¹⁶** do not cease giving-thanks for you, making mention *of you* in my prayers, **¹⁷** that the

---

A. On when this book was written, see Acts 28:30. **B:** presence, in love having predestined. Or, presence in love, having predestined. **C.** Or, based on, in harmony with. **D:** the Beloved *One.* Lit, the *One* having been loved. **E.** Or, in connection with, by means of. **F:** caused-to-abound to us, in all wisdom. Or, caused to abound to us in all wisdom and understanding, having made known. **G.** Or, purposed in Him (Christ). Or, set forth in Him. **H.** Or, arrangement, mode of operation, administration, government. **I.** Or, *belonging to.* **J.** Or, gather-together into one. **K.** Were allotted *an inheritance,* and thus, obtained *an inheritance.* Or, were allotted *to God,* and thus, were made an inheritance *to God.* **L.** This refers back to 'we'. **M.** Or, plan, design. **N.** Or, determination, intention, resolution. **O.** Or, hoped-beforehand. **P:** in the Christ. Or, in Christ. **Q:** in which also having put faith— you were sealed. Or, in Whom also having believed, you were sealed. **R.** Or, acquisition, obtained *ones.* Or, until *the* redemption, the obtaining *of our inheritance* for *the* praise.

God *of* our Lord Jesus Christ, the Father *of* [A] glory, may give you *a* spirit[B] *of* [C] wisdom and revelation in[D] *the* knowledge *of* Him [18] so that you, **the eyes *of* your heart having been enlightened**, *may* know what is the hope *of* His calling, what *is* the riches *of* the glory *of* His inheritance among[E] the saints, [19] and what *is* the surpassing greatness *of* His power toward us, the *ones* believing

This Power Raised Christ From The Dead And Seated Him In Great Glory
... in-accordance-with the working *of* the might *of* His strength [20] which He worked in Christ, having raised Him from *the* dead and having seated *Him* at His right *hand* in the heavenly *places,* [21] far above all rule and authority and power and lordship and every name being named— not only in this age, but also in the *one* coming. [22] And He subjected all *things* under His feet. And He gave Him *as* head over all *things to* the church, [23] which is His body, the fullness *of* the *One* filling all *things* in all[F].

This Power Made Us Alive From The Dead And Seated Us With Christ As Recipients of Grace
2:1 Indeed, you *were* dead *in* your trespasses and sins [2] in which you formerly walked in accordance with the [present] age[G] *of* this world, in accordance with the ruler *of* the authority[H] *of* the air, *of* [I] the spirit[J] now being at-work in the sons *of* [K] disobedience, [3] among whom even **we** all formerly conducted-*ourselves*[L] in the desires *of* our flesh, doing the wants[M] *of* the flesh and *of* the thoughts, and were *by* nature children *of* [N] wrath, as also the rest. [4] But God, being rich in mercy, because of His great love *with* which He loved us, [5] even we being dead *in* trespasses, made-*us*-alive-with Christ— *by* grace you are saved— [6] and raised-*us*-with *Him* and seated-*us*-with *Him* in the heavenly-*places* in Christ Jesus, [7] in order that He might demonstrate[O] in the coming ages[P] the surpassing riches *of* His grace in *His* kindness toward us in Christ Jesus.

For We Are Saved By Grace For The Good Works Which God Prepared For Us
[8] For *by* grace you are saved through faith. And this[Q] *is* not from you. *It is* the gift *of* God— [9] not of works, in order that no one may boast. [10] For we are His workmanship, having been created in Christ Jesus for good works, which God prepared-beforehand in order that we might walk in them.

So Remember Your Hopeless Condition As Gentiles Without Christ And God's Promises
[11] Therefore remember that formerly you, the Gentiles in *the* flesh— the *ones* being called *"the* uncircumcised" by the *one* being called *"the* circumcised" (*one* done-by-*human*-hands in *the* flesh)—[12] that you were *at* that time without Christ, having been excluded *from* the citizenship[R] *of* Israel, and strangers *from* the covenants *of* promise, having no hope and without-God in the world.

A. Or, *characterized by.* **B.** Or, *a* disposition. Or, *the* Spirit. **C.** That is, *characterized by, leading to.* **D.** That is, in connection with. **E.** Or, in. **F.** That is, in all His people. Or, with all, filling all the universe with all things. **G.** Or, the course. **H.** Or, power, kingdom, empire. **I.** That is, and of the spirit; or, who is the spirit. **J.** That is, spirit *being,* spirit *world,* or spiritual *influence.* **K.** That is, characterized by; or, belonging to. **L.** Or, lived, behaved. **M.** Or, wishes, desires. **N.** That is, belonging to, destined for. **O.** Or, show, display, prove. **P.** Or, the ages coming-upon *us.* **Q.** That is, the being saved; all of v 4-8. **R.** Or, state, commonwealth. That is, the condition and rights of a citizen.

But Now Christ Made Peace And Reconciled Jews And Gentiles To God Through The Cross
13 But now in Christ Jesus **you**, the *ones* formerly being far-away, were made near by the blood *of* Christ. **14** For He Himself is our peace, the *One* having made both one and having broken-down the dividing-wall *of* partition[A], the hostility— in His flesh **15** having abolished[B] the Law *of* commandments in decrees[C] in order that He might create the two in Himself into one new man, making peace, **16** and reconcile both in one body *to* God through the cross, having killed the hostility by it[D]. **17** And having come, He announced-as-good-news peace *to* you, the *ones* far-away, and peace *to* the *ones* near, **18** because[E] through Him we both have the access in[F] one Spirit to the Father.

So You Are No Longer Strangers, But In Christ You Are Fellow Citizens And Family Members
19 So then, you are no longer strangers and foreigners, but you are fellow-citizens *with* the saints and family-members *of* God, **20** having been built upon the foundation *of*[G] the apostles and prophets— Christ Jesus Himself being *the* cornerstone, **21** in Whom *the* whole building being fitted-together[H] is growing into *a* holy temple in *the* Lord, **22** in Whom also **you** are being built-together into *a* dwelling-place *of* God in[I] *the* Spirit.

For This Reason, I Paul, a Prisoner of Christ For You Gentiles...
3:1 For this reason, I Paul, the prisoner *of* Christ Jesus for the sake of you the Gentiles—

For I Am a Steward of God's Plan To Make Gentiles Partakers of His Promises
2 ... if indeed you heard-*of* the stewardship[J] *of* the grace *of* God having been given[K] *to* me for you, **3** that by way of revelation the mystery was made-known *to* me (just as I wrote-before in brief, **4** with reference to which you are able, while reading, to perceive my understanding in[L] the mystery *of* Christ) **5** which *in* other generations was not made-known *to* the sons *of* humans as it was now revealed *to* His holy apostles and prophets by *the* Spirit— **6** *that* the Gentiles are fellow-heirs and fellow-body-members and fellow-partakers *of* the promise in Christ Jesus through the good-news, **7** *of* which I was made *a* minister[M] in-accordance-with the gift *of* the grace *of* God having been given[N] *to* me by-way-of the working *of* His power.

It Was Granted To Me To Enlighten Everyone To See The Creator's Long Hidden Plan
8 This grace was given **to me**, the less-than-least *of* all saints, *that I might* announce-as-good-news *to* the Gentiles the untraceable riches *of* Christ, **9** and enlighten everyone *to see* what *is* the stewardship[O] *of* the mystery having been hidden from the *past* ages in God, the *One* having created all *things*, **10** so that now the multifaceted wisdom *of* God might be made-known *to* the rulers and the authorities in the heavenly *places* through the church, **11** in-accordance-with *the* purpose *of* the ages[P] which He accomplished in Christ Jesus our Lord, **12** in Whom we have boldness and access in

---

A: partition... Law. Or, partition— in His flesh having abolished the hostility, the Law; or, partition, the hostility, in His flesh— having abolished the Law. **B.** Or, done away with. **C.** Or, regulations, ordinances. **D.** That is, the cross. Or, in Himself. **E.** Or, that. **F.** Or, by. **G.** That is, consisting of; or, laid by. **H.** Or, framed together, joined together, as stones were combined to make ancient buildings. **I.** Or, by; or, in spirit, in a spiritual manner. **J.** That is, the position of management responsibility; or, the arrangement or mode of operation in which Paul served. **K.** That is, the grace... given. **L.** That is, in connection with the mystery concerning Christ. **M.** Or, servant. **N.** That is, the grace... given. **O.** That is, mode of operation, arrangement. **P:** *the* purpose *of* the ages. Or, *the eternal purpose.*

confidence through faith[A] *in* Him. [13] Therefore I ask *that you* not lose-heart in connection with my afflictions for-your-sake, which is your glory!

For This Reason I Pray For You To Know The Love of Christ And The Fullness of God
[14] For this reason I bow my knees before the Father, [15] from Whom *the* whole[B] family in *the* heavens and on earth is named, [16] *asking* that He might grant *to* you in accordance with the riches *of* His glory *that you* be strengthened *with* power through His Spirit in *your* inner person [17] *so-that*[C] Christ *may* dwell[D] in your hearts through faith, [18] in-order-that[E] you, **having**[F] **been rooted and founded in love,** might be strong-*enough*[G] to grasp[H] together-with all the saints what *is* the width and length and height and depth, [19] and to know the love *of* Christ surpassing knowledge, in-order-that[I] you might be filled to all the fullness *of* God.

To God Be The Glory
[20] Now *to* the *One* being able to do super-abundantly beyond all *of the things* which we ask or think[J] according to the power being at-work[K] in us—[21] *to* Him *be* the glory in the church and in Christ Jesus for all generations forever and ever, amen.

Therefore I Exhort You To Walk Worthily of Your Calling, Keeping The Unity of The Spirit
4:1 Therefore **I**, the prisoner in *the* Lord, exhort you to walk worthily *of* the calling *with* which you were called, [2] with all humblemindedness and gentleness, with patience bearing-with one another in love, [3] being diligent to keep[L] the unity *of*[M] the Spirit in the bond *of*[N] peace—

God Made Us One, And Gave Gifts And Grace To Each One of Us
[4] *There is* one body and one Spirit, just as you also were called in one hope *of* your calling; [5] one Lord, one faith, one baptism; [6] one God and Father *of* all, the *One* over all and through all and in all; [7] and *to* each one *of* us grace was given according to the measure *of* the gift *of* Christ.

For Scripture Says Jesus Ascended On High And Gave Gifts To His People
[8] For this reason it says, "having ascended to on-high, He led captivity captive[O], He gave gifts *to* people" [Ps 68:18].

[9] Now what does the "He ascended" mean except that He also descended into the lower parts *of* the earth[P]? [10] The *One* having descended is Himself also the *One* having ascended far above all the heavens, in order that He might fill all *things*.

He Gave Gifted People To Equip The Saints To Build Up The Body of Christ To Maturity
[11] And He Himself gave some *as* apostles, and others *as* prophets, and others *as*

A: through faith *in* Him. Or, through His faithfulness. **B:** *the* whole. Or, every. **C:** *so that.* Or, *that,* parallel with '*that you* be strengthened'. **D.** Or, reside, live, have His home. **E:** in order that. Or, that, making this a second main thing he is '*asking* that'. **F:** having been ... in love. In the Greek word order, this phrase precedes 'in order that you' (it is part of v 17), making it emphatic. **G.** Or, fully able. **H.** Or, comprehend, lay hold of. Paul may be referring to the dimensions of God's plan and wisdom (v 10); or, the dimensions of Christ's love. **I:** in order that. Or, that, making this a third main thing he is '*asking* that'. **J.** Or, understand, imagine, perceive. **K.** Or, in-operation. **L.** Or, preserve, protect, guard. **M.** That is, produced by. **N.** That is, consisting of; or, leading to. **O:** led captivity captive. Or, took-prisoner prisoners of war. **P.** This may refer to Christ's incarnation, or to His descent into Hades after His death.

evangelists, and others *as* shepherds and teachers, **12** for[A] the equipping[B] *of* the saints for *the* work *of* ministry[C], for *the* building-up *of* the body *of* Christ **13** until we all attain to the unity *of* the faith and *of* the knowledge *of* the Son *of* God, to *a* mature[D] man, to *the* measure *of the* stature *of* the fullness *of* Christ, **14** so that we may no longer be children, being tossed-about and carried-around *by* every wind *of* teaching, by the trickery *of* people, by craftiness with-regard-to[E] the scheme *of* [F] error[G], **15** but *that* while speaking-the-truth in love, we may grow *as to* all *things* into Him Who is the head— Christ, **16** from Whom the whole body, being fitted-together[H] and held-together by every joint *of* supply according to *the* working in measure *of* each individual part, is producing the growth *of* the body for *the* building-up *of* itself in love.

So Walk No Longer In The Futile Darkness of The Gentiles, As They Pursue Impurity
17 Therefore this I say and testify in *the* Lord, *that* you be walking no longer as indeed the Gentiles are walking, in *the* futility *of* their mind, **18** being darkened *in their* understanding, having been excluded *from* the life *of* God because of the ignorance being in them, because of the hardness *of* their hearts— **19** who, having become callous, gave themselves over *to* sensuality for *the* practice[I] *of* every impurity with greed.

Lay Aside The Old Person. Be Renewed In Your Mind And Put On The New Person
20 But **you** did not learn Christ in this manner, **21** if indeed you heard Him and were taught in Him, even as it is *the* truth in Jesus **22** *that* in-relation-to *your* former way-of-life you lay-aside the old person being corrupted[J] in-accordance-with the desires *of* [K] deception, **23** and *that you* be being renewed *in* the spirit *of* your mind, **24** and *that you* put-on the new person having been created in accordance with God, in righteousness and holiness *of* [L] truth.

Live Out Righteousness And Truth
25 Therefore, having laid-aside the lie[M], each *of you* be speaking truth with his neighbor, because we are body-parts *of* one another. **26** Be angry and-*yet* do not be sinning. Do not let the sun go down upon your angriness[N], **27** nor give *a* place[O] *to* the devil. **28** Let the *one* stealing be stealing no longer. But rather let him be laboring, working the good *thing with his* own hands in order that he might have *something* to give *to* the *one* having *a* need. **29** Let every bad[P] word not proceed out of your mouth, but if *there is* something good for edification *of* the need, *speak* in order that it may give grace *to* the *ones* hearing. **30** And do not grieve the Holy Spirit *of* God with[Q] Whom you were sealed for *the* day *of* redemption. **31** Let all bitterness and anger and wrath and clamor and blasphemy[R] be taken-away[S] from you, along-with all malice. **32** And be kind to one another, tenderhearted, forgiving each other just as God in Christ also forgave you.

As Beloved Children, Be Imitators of God And Walk In Love
5:1 Therefore be imitators *of* God, as beloved children. **2** And be walking in love, just as

---

A. Or, with a view to. Not the same word as in the next two phrases. **B.** Or, preparing, furnishing, training. **C.** Or, service. **D.** Or, finished, complete. **E.** Or, with a view to. **F.** That is, leading to; or, proceeding from; or, characterized by. **G.** Or, deception. **H.** See 2:21. **I.** Or, pursuit, business, working. **J.** Or, corrupting *itself*. **K.** That is, proceeding from; or, belonging to; or, characterized by. **L.** That is, characterized by truth (true holiness); or, belonging to the truth. **M:** the lie. Or, falsehood. That is, the lie of the Gentile way of thinking and living, v 17-19 (introducing v 25-32); or, falsehood in general, in direct contrast to speaking truth next (and part of that point only). **N.** Or, irritation, exasperation, angry mood. **O.** That is, opportunity, chance. **P.** Or, corrupt, worthless, unfit. **Q.** Or, by, in. **R.** Or, harmful speech. **S.** Or, removed.

Christ also loved us and handed Himself over for us— *an* offering and *a* sacrifice *to* God for *an* aroma *of* fragrance.

But Don't Let Any Kind of Impurity Or Greed Exist Among You

3 But let sexual-immorality and all impurity or greed not even be named[A] among you, as is proper *for* saints— **4** and filthiness[B] and foolish-talk or coarse-joking[C], which are not fitting, but rather thanksgiving.

You Know This Is Right, So Don't Be Partakers With Those Inheriting Wrath

5 For you know this[D]— recognizing[E] that every sexually-immoral or impure or greedy *person* (that is, *an* idolater) does not have *an* inheritance in the kingdom *of* Christ and God. **6** Let no one deceive you *with* empty words, for because of these *things* the wrath *of* God is coming upon the sons *of*[F] disobedience. **7** Therefore do not be fellow-partakers *with* them.

For You Were Formerly Darkness, But Now You Are Light; Walk As Children of Light

8 For you were formerly darkness, but now *you are* light in *the* Lord. Be walking as children *of*[G] light (**9** for the fruit *of* the light *is* in[H] all goodness and righteousness and truth),**10** approving what is pleasing[I] *to* the Lord.

Expose The Works of Darkness To God's Light

11 And do not be participating *in* the unfruitful works *of* darkness, but rather even be exposing[J] *them*. **12** For it is shameful even to speak the *things* being done *in* secret by them, **13** but all *things* being exposed by the light become-visible[K]. **14** For everything becoming-visible is[L] light. Therefore he[M] says, "Awake, sleeping *one,* and rise-up from the dead, and Christ will shine-on you."

So Walk Wisely, Redeeming The Time. Be Filled With The Spirit, And Subject To One Another

15 Therefore be watching carefully how you walk— not as unwise, but as wise, **16** redeeming[N] the time, because the days are evil. **17** For this reason, do not be foolish *ones*, but understand what the will *of* the Lord *is*. **18** And do not get-drunk *with* wine, in[O] which is wild-living, but be filled with[P] *the* Spirit, **19** speaking *to* each other with[Q] psalms and hymns and spiritual songs, singing and making-melody *with* your heart *to* the Lord, **20** giving-thanks always for all *things* in *the* name *of* our Lord Jesus Christ *to* our God and Father, **21** being-subject[R] *to* one another in *the* fear[S] *of* Christ—

Wives, Be Subject To Your Husbands As The Church Is Subject To Christ

22 ... wives— *to your* own husbands, as *to* the Lord. **23** Because *a* husband is *the* head *of his* wife as also Christ *is the* head *of* the church, He *being the* Savior *of* the body.

A. That is, identified as part of your behavior. **B.** Or, indecency, obscenity, shamefulness in word or deed. **C.** Or, vulgar-wittiness. **D.** That is, v 3-4. **E:** For you know this— recognizing that. Or, For know this with certainty— that. **F.** See 2:2. **G.** That is, characterized by. **H.** That is, consisting of; or, in the sphere of. **I.** Or, acceptable. **J.** Or, bringing to light, rebuking. **K:** by the light become-visible. Or, are made-visible by the light. **L.** That is, reflects. **M.** Or, it. That is, the one exposing the sin says this; or, Paul may be referring to a written source, perhaps Isa 60:1. **N.** That is, buying up the time for the Lord, saving it from being lost or wasted; making the most of your time. **O.** That is, in connection with. **P.** Or, by. **Q.** Or, in, by means of. **R.** Or, subjecting *yourselves*, voluntarily-submitting. **S.** Or, respect, reverence.

24 Nevertheless[A], as the church is subject *to* Christ, in this manner also *let* the wives *be to their* husbands in everything.

Husbands, Love Your Wives As Christ Loved The Church

25 Husbands, be loving *your* wives just-as Christ also loved the church and handed Himself over for her **26** in order that He might sanctify[B] her, having cleansed[C] *her with*[D] the washing[E] *of* water by[F] *the* word, **27** in order that **He** might present the church *to* Himself *as* glorious— not having spot or wrinkle or any *of* such *things*, but that she might be holy and without-blemish. **28** In this manner[G], husbands ought also to be loving their wives as their *own* bodies. The *one* loving his wife is loving himself. **29** For no one ever hated his *own* flesh, but he nourishes and cherishes it, just as Christ also *does* the church, **30**because we are body-parts *of* His body. **31** "For this *cause a* man shall leave-behind *his* father and mother and shall be joined to his wife, and the two will be one flesh" [Gen 2:24]. **32** This mystery is great, but **I** am speaking with reference to Christ and with reference to the church. **33** Nevertheless, you also individually, let each in this manner be loving his wife as himself. And *let* the wife *see* that she be respecting *her* husband.

Children, Honor Your Parents

6:1 Children, be obeying your parents in *the* Lord, for this is right. **2** "Be honoring your father and mother"— which is *the* first commandment with *a* promise— **3** "in order that it may be well *with* you and you may be long-lived upon the earth" [Deut 5:16].

Fathers, Nourish Your Children In The Lord

4 And fathers, do not be provoking your children to anger, but be nourishing them in *the* training[H] and admonition[I] *of the* Lord.

Slaves And Masters, Live As Slaves of Christ

5 Slaves, be obeying *your* masters according-to *the* flesh with fear and trembling, in *the* sincerity *of* your heart, as *to* Christ— **6** not by way of eye-service as people-pleasers, but as slaves *of* Christ, doing the will *of* God from *the* soul, **7** serving with good-will as *to* the Lord and not *to* people, **8** knowing that each *one,* if he does anything good, will receive this back from *the* Lord, whether slave or free. **9** And masters, be doing the same *things* to them, giving-up the threatening, knowing that both their Master and yours is in *the* heavens, and there is no respect-of-persons with Him.

Finally, Put On The Full Armor of God So You Can Stand Against The Spiritual Forces of Evil

10 Finally, become-strong in *the* Lord and in the might *of* His strength. **11** Put-on the full-armor *of* God so-that you *may* be able to stand against the schemes[J] *of* the devil, **12** because the struggle[K] *for* us is not against blood and flesh, but against the rulers, against the authorities, against the world-powers[L] *of* this darkness, against the spiritual *forces*[M] *of* evilness in the

---

A. Or, But, However. That is, although your husband is not your savior. Or, So, Indeed. **B.** Or, make her holy. **C.** Or, cleansing, concurrently with the sanctifying. **D.** Or, *by, in.* **E.** Or, bath. **F.** Or, with, in. **G:** In this manner, husbands. That is, like Christ loved His body, the church, referring back to v 25. Or, In this manner husbands... wives: as their *own* bodies. **H.** Or, instruction, discipline. **I.** Or, warning, instruction. **J.** Or, stratagems, methods. **K.** Or, wrestling, conflict, one-on-one battle. **L.** Or, world forces, world rulers. **M.** Or, *beings, hosts.*

heavenly-*places.* **¹³** For this reason, take-up the full-armor *of* God in order that you may be able to resist^A on the evil day, and having worked^B everything, to stand.

> *Stand Armored With Truth, Righteousness, And Faith, Wielding God's Word And Prayer*
> **¹⁴** Stand [firm] therefore, having girded^C your waist with truth, and having put-on the breastplate *of* righteousness, **¹⁵** and having sandaled *your* feet with *the* readiness^D *of* the good-news *of* peace, **¹⁶** with all *these* having taken-up the shield *of* faith with which you will be able to quench all the flaming arrows *of* the evil *one.* **¹⁷** And take the helmet *of* salvation, and the sword^E *of*^F the Spirit, which is *the* Word *of* God, **¹⁸** praying with every-*kind-of* prayer and petition at every opportunity^G in *the* Spirit, and keeping-alert for it with all perseverance and petition concerning all the saints— **¹⁹** and for me, that *a* word may be given *to* me in connection with *the* opening *of* my mouth with boldness to make-known the mystery *of* the good-news **²⁰** for the sake of which I am-an-ambassador in *a* chain, that with^H it I may speak-boldly^I as I ought-to speak.

Closing Remarks
²¹ Now in order that **you** also may know the *things* concerning me, what I am doing, Tychicus will make everything known *to* you— the beloved brother and faithful minister^J in *the* Lord **²²** whom I sent to you for this very *reason,* in order that you may know the *things* concerning us and he may encourage your hearts. **²³** Peace *be to* the brothers, and love with faith from God *the* Father and *the* Lord Jesus Christ. **²⁴** Grace *be* with all the *ones* loving our Lord Jesus Christ with undecayability^K.

A. Or, oppose, withstand. **B.** Or, done, accomplished, overcome. **C.** Or, tied. **D.** Or, preparedness. **E.** Or, saber, dagger. **F.** Or, *belonging to*; *from.* **G:** at every opportunity. Or, at all times; or, on every occasion. **H.** That is, with the word, or, with my mouth; or, in order that in-connection-with it [the mystery of the good news]. **I.** Or, speak freely, speak openly. **J.** Or, servant. **K.** Or, immortality. That is, with a love that is unfading, undiminishing, and thus, sincere; or, a love in union with immortality, a forever love. Or, Grace with immortality *be* with all the *ones* loving our Lord Jesus Christ.

Philippians

Introduction   1:1-2

A.   I am thanking God for you for your partnership in the gospel, and praying your love abounds   1:3-11

B.   I want you to know that my circumstances have come for the advancement of the good news   1:12

   1.   So that my imprisonment in Christ has become visible in the whole Praetorium, and the majority of the brothers are more daring to speak the word   1:13-18
   2.   And I am rejoicing in this. But I will rejoice, for I know it will turn out for my deliverance   1:18-26
   3.   Only conduct yourselves worthily, so that I may be hearing of you whether I come or not   1:27-30
   4.   If then you have any encouragement, fill up my joy by being united in a love like Christ's   2:1-11
   5.   So then my beloved, be working out your salvation. For God is working in you   2:12-16
   6.   But if I even am poured out for you, I am rejoicing in it, and with you. Do the same   2:17-18

C.   Now I am hoping to send Timothy to you, and to come myself. But I sent Epaphroditus to you   2:19-30

D.   Finally my brothers, be rejoicing in the Lord. To write the same things is safe for you   3:1

   1.   Be watching out for the dogs. For we are the circumcision, the ones worshiping in the Spirit and not putting confidence in flesh   3:2-4

     a.   If any one thinks he may have confidence in the flesh, I more   3:4-6
     b.   But what things were gains to me, these I have regarded as loss for the sake of Christ. More than that, I regard all things a loss, and I forfeited them for the sake of the surpassing knowledge of Christ, so that I might gain Christ and be found in Him   3:7-14
     c.   Therefore, all who are mature— let us be thinking this. Be imitators of me   3:15-22
     d.   So then my beloved brothers, be standing firm in this manner   4:1-3

   2.   Be rejoicing in the Lord always. Let your kindness be known to all people. Be anxious for nothing, but let your requests be made known to God   4:4-7
   3.   Finally, be considering these things— the true, honorable, right, pure, lovely things. Be practicing these things which you learned and received and heard and saw in me   4:8-9

E.   Now I rejoiced over your gift to me through Epaphroditus. You did well to partner with me   4:10-14

   1.   In the beginning, you alone partnered with me   4:15-17
   2.   I have received everything and am abounding! And my God will fill up your every need   4:18-20

Conclusion   4:21-23

1:1 Paul[A] and Timothy, slaves *of* Christ Jesus, *to* all the saints in Christ Jesus being in Philippi, together-with *the* overseers[B] and deacons[C]: **2** Grace *to* you and peace from God our Father and *the* Lord Jesus Christ.

I Thank God For Your Partnership With Me In The Gospel
3 I am giving-thanks *to* my God upon every remembrance *of* you, **4** always in my every petition for you all making the petition with joy **5** on-the-basis-of your partnership[D] for the good-news from the first day until the present, **6** being confident-of this very *thing*: that the *One* having begun *a* good work in you will perfect[E] *it* until *the* day *of* Christ— **7** just as it is right *for* me to think this about you all because of my having you[F] in *my* heart, both in my imprisonment and in the defense and confirmation[G] *of* the good-news, you all being my co-partners[H] *of* grace. **8** For God *is* my witness how I am yearning-for you all with *the* deep-feelings[I] *of* Christ Jesus.

May Your Love Abound Still More In Knowledge Leading To Holiness
9 And I am praying this: that your love may be abounding still more and more in knowledge and all perception[J] **10** so that you *may* be approving the *things* mattering[K], in-order-that[L] you might be pure and blameless[M] for[N] *the* day *of* Christ, **11** having been filled *with the* fruit *of* righteousness which *comes* through Jesus Christ to *the* glory and praise *of* God.

Things Are Turning Out For The Good of The Gospel
12 Now I want you to know, brothers, that the *things* concerning me have come rather for *the* advancement *of* the good-news—

The Brothers Are More Fearlessly Speaking The Word
13 ... so that my imprisonment in[O] Christ became visible[P] in the whole Praetorium[Q] and *to* all the rest, **14** and *so that* the majority *of* the brothers, being confident[R] in the Lord *because-of* my imprisonment, are more daring to fearlessly speak the word.

Whatever Their Motives, Christ Is Being Proclaimed
15 Some indeed *speak* because of envy and strife, but some also are proclaiming Christ because of good-will. **16** The ones *speak* out of love, knowing that I am appointed for *the* defense *of* the good-news; **17** but the others are proclaiming Christ out of selfish-interest, not purely, supposing to raise trouble *in* my imprisonment. **18** What indeed *does it matter* except that[S] *in* every way, whether *in* pretense or *in* truth, Christ is being proclaimed!

Christ Will Be Magnified In Me, Whether I Live or Die
And I am rejoicing in this. But I also will rejoice, **19** for I know that this will turn-out *for* me for deliverance through your prayer and *the* provision *of* the Spirit *of* Jesus Christ,

A. On when this book was written, see Acts 28:30. **B.** Or, superintendents, guardians. **C.** Or, servants, assistants, ministers. **D.** Or, fellowship, participation, sharing, contribution. **E.** Or, complete, accomplish. **F.** Or, your having me in *your* heart. **G.** Or, establishment. **H.** Or, fellow-sharers, co-participants. **I.** Or, *the* affections; or *the* heart, as the location of these feelings or affections. **J.** Or, insight, discernment. **K.** Or, being worth more, and thus, being excellent, superior, or essential. **L.** Or, that, making this a second request, parallel with 'that your love'. **M.** Or, without an opportunity for stumbling. **N.** Or, in, until. **O.** That is, in connection with. **P.** Or, known. **Q.** Or, palace, governor's residence. **R.** Or, putting confidence, trusting. **S:** What... that. Or, What then? Only that.

20 in-accordance-with my eager-expectation and hope that I will in no way be put-to-shame, but *that* with all boldness, as always, even now Christ will be magnified in my body, whether by life or by death— **21** for *to* me, the living *is* Christ, and the dying[A] *is* gain.

Death Would Be Much Better For Me, But I Know I Will Continue To Live For Your Sake
22 Now if *it is* the living in *the* flesh, this *for* me *means* fruit *from* work. And I do not know[B] what I shall choose, **23** but am gripped[C] by the two— having the desire that *I might* depart and be with Christ, for *that is* better *by* much more, **24** but the remaining in the flesh *is* more-necessary for your sake. **25** And being confident-of this, I know that I will remain and continue *with* you all for your advancement and joy *of* faith, **26** in order that your boast may be abounding in Christ Jesus in me through my presence again with you.

But Conduct Yourselves Worthily of The Gospel, And Don't Be Frightened
27 Only be conducting-*yourselves*[D] worthily *of* the good-news *of* Christ in order that whether having come and seen you or being absent, I may be hearing-*of* the *things* concerning you— that you are standing-*firm* in one spirit, contending-together *with* one soul *for* the faith *of* the good-news, **28** and not being frightened[E] in any way by the *ones* opposing *you*— which is *a* sign[F] *of* destruction *for* them, but *of* your salvation, and this from God.

God Has Granted That We Should Both Believe In Christ And Suffer For Him
29 Because *to* you was granted the *thing*[G] for Christ's sake— not only the believing in Him, but also the suffering for His sake, **30** having the same struggle[H] such as you saw in me and now are hearing *to be* in me.

Fill Up My Joy By Being United In Love And Humility
2:1 If then *there is* any encouragement in Christ, if any consolation *of*[I] love, if any fellowship[J] *of the* Spirit, if any deep-feelings and compassions, **2** fill-up my joy, *which is* that you be thinking the same *thing*[K], having the same love, united-in-spirit, thinking[L] the one *thing*, **3** *doing* nothing based-on selfish-interest nor based on conceit, but *with* humble-mindedness regarding one another *as* surpassing[M] yourselves; **4** not each looking-out-for your *own things*, but also each the *things of* others.

Think And Behave Like Christ Did
5 Be thinking[N] this in you, which also *was* in Christ Jesus— **6** Who, while[O] being[P] in *the* form[Q] *of* God, did not regard the being equal *with* God *a* thing-to-be-grasped[R], **7** but emptied Himself, having taken *the* form *of a* slave, having come[S] in *the* likeness[T] *of* humans[U]. And having been found as *a* man *in* outward-appearance, **8** He humbled

---

A. That is, the death-event. **B.** Or, make-known. **C.** Or, controlled, governed. **D.** Or, living *your* citizenship, performing *your* duties as citizens (of heaven). **E.** Or, startled, scared, intimidated. **F.** Or, *a* proof *of, a* pointing *to*. **G.** That is, the two-fold thing following; or, the suffering in particular, emphasized by contrast to the believing. **H.** Or, conflict, fight. **I.** That is, proceeding from, originating in. **J.** Or, partnership *of* spirit. Or, participation *in the* Spirit. **K.** That is, be likeminded. **L.** Or, being intent on the one *thing*. **M.** Or, being superior to, being better than. **N.** Or, having this mind. **O.** Or, *although*. **P.** Or, existing. **Q.** Or, shape, appearance. **R.** Or, a treasure-to-be-hoarded. Or in another sense, a robbery, a usurpation. **S.** Or, having come-into-being, in the sense of having been born. **T.** Or, outward appearance. **U.** Or, mankind, people.

Himself, having become obedient to the point *of* death— and *a* death *of a* cross! **9** Therefore God also highly-exalted Him, and granted Him the name above every name **10** in-order-that every knee should bow at the name *of* Jesus— *of* heavenly *ones* and earthly *ones* and *ones* under-the-earth— **11** and every tongue should confess-out[A] that Jesus Christ *is* Lord, to *the* glory *of* God *the* Father.

Work Out Your Salvation As Shining Lights In The World, Holding Out The Word of Life
12 So then my beloved, just as you always obeyed— not as in my presence only, but now much more in my absence— be working-out your salvation with fear and trembling. **13** For God[B] is the *One* working in you both the wanting[C] and the working, for *His* good-pleasure. **14** Be doing all *things* without grumblings and arguments **15** in-order-that you may become[D] blameless[E] and innocent, children *of* God without-blemish amidst *a* crooked and perverted generation, among whom you are shining[F] as lights[G] in *the* world, **16** holding-out[H] *the* word *of* life— for *a* boast *for* me in *the* day *of* Christ that I did not run in vain nor labor in vain!

But Let Us Rejoice Together No Matter What Happens To Me
17 But if I even am being poured-out[I] upon the sacrifice and service *of* your faith, I am rejoicing [over it], and rejoicing-with you all. **18** And **you** also be rejoicing the same *way*, and be rejoicing-with me.

I Am Hoping To Send Timothy To You, And To Come Soon Myself
19 Now I am hoping in *the* Lord Jesus to send Timothy *to* you soon in order that **I** also may be cheered, having come-to-know the *things* concerning you. **20** For I have no one likeminded who will genuinely be concerned-*about* the *things* concerning you. **21** For the *ones* all are seeking their *own things*, not the *things of* Jesus Christ. **22** But you know his approvedness, because he served with me for the good-news as *a* child *with a* father. **23** So indeed I am hoping to send this *one* at-once, whenever I see the *things* with-respect-to me. **24** And I am confident in *the* Lord that I myself also will come soon.

I Sent Back Epaphroditus, Your Precious Servant To My Need. Rejoice In Him
25 But I regarded *it* necessary to send to you Epaphroditus— my brother and fellow-worker and fellow-soldier, and your delegate[J] and minister *of* my need— **26** because he was yearning-for you all, and *was* being distressed because you heard that he was sick. **27** For indeed he was sick nearly *to* death. But God had-mercy-on him— and not him only, but also me, in order that I should not have grief upon grief. **28** Therefore I sent him more-eagerly, in order that having seen him again you may rejoice, and **I** may be less-grieved. **29** So receive him in *the* Lord with all joy, and be holding such *ones* precious, **30** because he drew-near to the point *of* death for the sake of the work *of* Christ— having risked *his* life in order that he might fill-up your lack[K] *of* service to me.

Finally, Rejoice In The Lord
3:1 Finally, my brothers, be rejoicing in *the* Lord. To be writing the same *things to* you *is* not troublesome *for* me, and *is* safe *for* you—

A. Or, openly-acknowledge. **B.** Or, For the *One* working in you is **God**— both to will and to work for *His* good pleasure. **C.** Or, willing, desiring. **D.** Or, prove-to-be. **E.** Or, without fault, without guilt. **F.** Or, appearing, visible. **G.** Or, luminaries, light-givers. **H.** Or, holding forth, presenting; or, holding on to. **I.** That is, as a sacrificial offering. **J.** Or, representative, official-messenger, apostle. **K.** Or, shortcoming, deficiency.

Watch Out For The False Circumcision
2 Be watching-out-*for* the dogs^A, be watching out *for* the evil workers, be watching out *for* the mutilation^B. **3** For **we** are the circumcision, the *ones* worshiping *in the* Spirit *of* God and boasting in Christ Jesus and not putting-confidence in *the* flesh— **4** though myself having confidence even in *the* flesh!

If Anyone Can Put Confidence In The Flesh, I More
If any other *person* thinks *that he may* put-confidence in *the* flesh, I more— **5** *in* circumcision *the* eighth day; from *the* nation *of* Israel, *the* tribe *of* Benjamin, a Hebrew from Hebrews; in relation to *the* Law— *a* Pharisee; **6** in relation to zeal— persecuting the church; in relation to *the* righteousness in *the* Law— having been blameless^C.

But I Count All Such Things As Loss That I May Know Christ And His Power
7 But what *things* were gains *to* me, these I have regarded *to be a* loss for the sake of Christ. **8** But more than that, I am indeed regarding all *things* to be *a* loss for the sake of the surpassing *greatness of* the knowledge *of* Christ Jesus my Lord, for the sake of Whom I suffered-loss-of all *things* and am regarding *them as* garbage in order that I might gain Christ **9** and be found in Him, not having my *own* righteousness from *the* Law but the *one* through faith^D in Christ, the righteousness from God on the basis of faith— **10** *that I might* know Him and the power *of* His resurrection and the partnership^E *of* His sufferings, being conformed *to* His death **11** if somehow^F I might attain to [the power of] the resurrection-out from *the* dead.

Brothers, I Am Forgetting The Past And Pressing On Toward The True Prize
12 Not that I already obtained *it* or have already been made-perfect^G, but I am pressing-on *to see* if I may indeed take-hold-of^H *that* for which also I was taken hold of by Christ Jesus. **13** Brothers, **I** do not consider myself to have taken hold, but one *thing I do*: forgetting the *things* behind and stretching-toward the *things* ahead, **14** I am pressing-on toward *the* goal for the prize *of* the upward^I calling *from* God in Christ Jesus.

All Who Claim To Be Mature: Think This Same Way. Imitate Me
15 Therefore, all who *are* mature— let us be thinking^J this. And if you are thinking anything differently, God will reveal this also *to* you. **16** Nevertheless, to what *thinking* we attained, *by* the same *let us* be walking-in-line. **17** Be fellow-imitators *of* me, brothers, and be watching the *ones* walking in this manner, just as you have us *as a* pattern.

For There Are Many Enemies of The Cross. They Focus On Earthly Things
18 For many walk *as to* whom I was often saying *to* you, and now even weeping say, *they are* the enemies *of* the cross *of* Christ— **19** whose end *is* destruction,

---

A. All three descriptions here refer to the Judaizers. **B.** Paul harshly refers to the Judaizers with this word instead of the related word they use of themselves, the 'circumcision'. **C.** Or, without fault, without guilt (from the Jewish point of view). **D.** Or, through *the* faithfulness *of* Christ. **E.** Or sharing *of*, participation *in*. **F.** Or, if perhaps. **G.** Or, reached the goal, been made complete. **H.** Or, take hold, because I also was taken. **I.** That is, *consisting of* the upward calling *from* God; or, *belonging to my* calling *from* above *by* God. **J.** Or, having this mind.

whose god *is their* stomach and glory *is* in their shame— the *ones* thinking[A] the earthly *things*.

And Our Citizenship Is In Heaven
20 For our place-of-citizenship is in *the* heavens, from where also we are eagerly-awaiting *the* Savior, *the* Lord Jesus Christ, **21** Who will transform the body *of* our lowliness[B] *so as to be* similar-in-form[C] *to* the body *of* His glory, according-to the working *that* enables Him also to subject all *things to* Himself.

So My Beloved, Stand Firm In This Manner
4:1 So then, my beloved and yearned-for brothers, my joy and crown, be standing-*firm* in this manner in *the* Lord, beloved.

Help My Fellow-Workers To Think The Same Thing
2 I exhort Euodia and I exhort Syntyche to be thinking the same[D] *thing* in *the* Lord. **3** Yes, I ask you also, genuine comrade[E], be helping these *women* who contended-together[F] *with* me in connection with the good-news, along-with both Clement and the rest *of* my fellow-workers, whose names *are* in *the* book *of* life.

Be Rejoicing In The Lord, Kind To All, And Praying To God
4 Be rejoicing in *the* Lord always; again I will say, be rejoicing. **5** Let your kindness[G] be known *to* all people. The Lord *is* near. **6** Be anxious-*about* nothing, but in everything, *by* prayer and petition with thanksgivings, let your requests be made-known to God. **7** And the peace *of* God surpassing all understanding will guard[H] your hearts and your minds in Christ Jesus.

Be Considering And Practicing All That Is True And Commendable
8 Finally, brothers, be considering these *things*— whatever *things* are true, whatever *things are* honorable, whatever *things are* right, whatever *things are* pure, whatever *things are* lovely, whatever *things are* commendable, if *there is* any virtue, and if *there is* any praise. **9** Be practicing these *things* which you indeed learned and received and heard and saw in me, and the God *of* peace will be with you.

Thank You For The Gift Epaphroditus Brought, And Your Continuing Partnership With Me
10 Now I rejoiced in *the* Lord greatly that now at last you revived *your* thinking about me— upon which[I] indeed you were thinking, but you were lacking-opportunity. **11** Not that I speak in relation to *a* need, for **I** learned to be content in *the things in* which I am. **12** I indeed know-*how* to be humbled. I also know-*how* to abound. In anything and in all *things,* I have learned-the-secret[J]— both to be filled-to-satisfaction and to be hungry, both to abound and to be in-

---

A. Or, setting their minds on. B. Or, humble condition. C. Or, like-in-appearance. D. That is, the same mature thinking as himself, applying to them what he has been saying; or, the same thing as each other, referring to some personal dispute, making this a kind of private digression from his public letter to the church. E. Or, yoke-fellow, a man yoked together with Paul in the work of the gospel. F. That is, they fought in the battle alongside Paul. G. Or, gentleness, graciousness, reasonableness, fairness. H. Or, keep, protect. I. That is, my situation. Or, upon whom, referring to Paul. J. Or, been instructed, been initiated in.

need. **¹³** I can-do all *things* by-means-of^A the *One* strengthening me. **¹⁴** Nevertheless, you did well having co-partnered^B *in* my affliction.

You Alone Have Partnered With Me From The First

¹⁵ And **you** also know, Philippians, that in *the* beginning *of* the good-news when I departed from Macedonia, no church partnered^C *with* me in *the* matter *of* giving and receiving except you alone. **¹⁶** Because even in Thessalonica you sent *to* me both once and twice^D for *my* need. **¹⁷** Not that I am seeking-for the gift, but I am seeking-for the fruit increasing to your account.

I Have Received Your Pleasing Offering To God, And I Am Abounding

¹⁸ And I am receiving everything in full, and I am abounding. I have been filled-up, having received from Epaphroditus the *things* from you— *an* aroma *of* fragrance, *an* acceptable sacrifice, pleasing *to* God. **¹⁹** And my God will fill-up every need *of* yours in-accordance-with His riches in glory in Christ Jesus. **²⁰** Now *to* our God and Father *be* the glory forever and ever, amen.

²¹ Greet every saint in Christ Jesus. The brothers with me greet you. **²²** All the saints greet you, but especially the *ones* from Caesar's household. **²³** The grace *of* the Lord Jesus Christ *be* with your spirit.

A. Or, in union with. **B.** Or, shared-together, participated. **C.** Or, shared. **D.** That is, once and again, repeatedly.

Colossians

Introduction   1:1-2

A.   We are giving thanks to God always for you, having heard of your faith and love   1:3-8

     1.   For this reason we pray you may be filled with the knowledge of His will so that you may   1:9-14
walk worthily, bearing fruit in every good work and growing in the knowledge of God,
Who delivered us into the kingdom of His Son—

         a.   Who is the image of the invisible God, the firstborn of all creation, because all   1:15-18
things were created by Him

         b.   Who is the beginning, the firstborn from the dead, because the Father was pleased to   1:18-20
reconcile all things to Himself through the blood of His cross

             i.   Indeed you were formerly enemies, but He reconciled you through His death   1:21-23

B.   Now I am rejoicing in my sufferings for you and His church, of which I became a minister that 1:24-2:5
I might fulfill the Word of God— the mystery having been hidden, which is Christ in you

C.   As then you received Christ, be walking in Him— rooted, built, and established in the faith   2:6-7

     1.   Watch out no one takes you captive by human thinking not in accordance with Christ,   2:8-9
because in Him dwells all the fullness of the Deity

         a.   And in Him you are complete, Who is the head of all rule and authority   2:10-12

         b.   Indeed, you who were dead in sin God made alive with Christ   2:13-15

     2.   Therefore let no one judge you in eating and Sabbaths, shadows of coming things   2:16-19

     3.   If you died with Christ, why submit to decrees according to the teachings of humans?   2:20-23

     4.   If you were raised with Christ, be seeking the things above. Put to death the old person   3:1-11
and its practices, and put on the new person

D.   Therefore as chosen ones of God, put on compassion and love. And let the peace of Christ be   3:12-17
arbitrating in your hearts. Let the word be dwelling in you richly. Do all in the name of Jesus

     1.   Wives, be subject; husbands, loving; children, obeying. Fathers, do not be provoking   3:18-21

     2.   Slaves, be obeying. Masters, be granting to your slaves the just thing and equality   3:22-4:1

     3.   Be devoting yourself to prayer, and praying for us   4:2-4

     4.   Walk with wisdom toward outsiders, redeeming the time   4:5-6

Conclusion   4:7-18

1:1 Paul[A], *an* apostle *of* Christ Jesus by *the* will *of* God, and Timothy *our* brother, **2** *to* the saints[B] and faithful brothers in Christ in Colossae: Grace *to* you and peace from God our Father.

We Thank God For Your Faith And Love
3 We are giving-thanks *to* God, *the* Father *of* our Lord Jesus Christ, always while praying for you, **4** having heard-*of* your faith in Christ Jesus and the love which you have for all the saints **5** because of the hope being reserved *for* you in the heavens, which[C] you previously-heard-*of* in the word *of* the truth— the good-news **6** coming to you, just as also in[D] all the world it is bearing-fruit and growing, just as *it is doing* also in[E] you from which day you heard and understood the grace *of* God in truth[F], **7** just as you learned *it* from Epaphras, our beloved fellow-slave who is *a* faithful servant[G] *of* Christ on your behalf, **8** the *one* also having made-clear *to* us your love in[H] *the* Spirit.

May You Walk Worthily of God, Who Transferred Us Into The Kingdom of His Son
9 For this reason **we** also, from which day we heard, do not cease praying for you and asking that you may be filled *with* the knowledge[I] *of* His will in all spiritual wisdom and understanding[J], **10** so that *you may* walk worthily *of* the Lord, toward total[K] pleasing [of Him]— bearing-fruit in every good work and growing in[L] the knowledge *of* God; **11** being empowered with all power according-to[M] the might *of*[N] His glory, toward total[O] endurance and patience; with joy[P] **12** giving-thanks *to* the Father having qualified you for *your* part[Q] *of* the share[R] *of*[S] the saints[T] in the light[U], **13** Who delivered[V] us out of the authority[W] *of* darkness and transferred *us* into the kingdom *of* the Son *of*[X] His love, **14** in Whom we have the redemption, the forgiveness *of* sins—

The Son Is The Preeminent Head of All Creation, Because He Created All Things
15 ... Who is *the* image[Y] *of* the invisible God, *the* firstborn[Z] *of*[Z1] all creation[Z2], **16** because all *things* were created by[Z3] Him in the heavens and on the earth, the visible *things* and the invisible *things*— whether thrones or lordships or rulers or authorities. All *things* have been created through Him and for Him. **17** And He Himself is before all *things,* and all *things* have existence[Z4] in Him. **18** And He Himself is the head *of* the body, the church.

The Son Is First In Everything, Because God Reconciled All Things Through Him
... Who is *the* beginning[Z5], *the* firstborn from the dead, in order that He Himself might

---

A. On when this book was written, see Acts 28:30. **B.** Or, holy and. **C.** That is, which hope. **D.** That is, in the sphere of. **E.** Or, among you. **F.** That is, in reality, heard and truly understood. Or, the grace of God in its true form, as opposed to the false teaching; the true grace of God. **G.** Or, minister. **H.** That is, in the sphere of, in connection with, in union with. **I.** Or, full-knowledge. **J.** Or, wisdom and spiritual understanding. **K.** Or, for pleasing [Him] in every respect. **L.** Or, *by.* **M.** That is, based on, in accordance with. **N.** That is, belonging to; or, characterized by (His glorious might). **O.** Or, for endurance and patience in every respect. **P.** Or, patience with joy; giving thanks *to.* **Q.** Or, share, portion. **R.** Or, allotment, lot. **S.** That is, belonging to. **T.** Or, holy *ones.* **U.** That is, *your* share *of* the allotted inheritance... *found* in the *kingdom or realm of* light; or, having qualified you... by the light; or, *of* the saints *who are* in the light (heaven). **V.** Or, rescued. **W.** Or, jurisdiction, dominion. **X.** That is, the Son *who is the object of* His Love, and thus, His beloved Son. **Y.** Or, likeness, form. That is, the visible expression; or, the personal eternal likeness. **Z.** That is, the one having first status, holding first place; the preeminent one. **Z1.** That is, *before*; or, *in-relation-to.* **Z2.** Or, every created *thing.* **Z3.** Or, in, in relation to. **Z4.** Or, hold-together. **Z5.** Or, beginner (cause, source, founder); ruler.

come-to-be holding-first-place in all *things,* **¹⁹** because *the Father*ᴬ was well-pleased *that* all the fullnessᴮ *should* dwell in Him **²⁰** and *that He should* reconcile all *things* through Him to Himself, having made-peace through the blood *of* His cross— through Him, whether the *things* on the earth or the *things* in the heavens.

Indeed, You Yourselves Were Reconciled By Him

²¹ Indeed you *were* formerly being excluded, and *were* enemiesᶜ *in* the mind in-connection-with evil works. **²²** But now He reconciled *you* in the body *of* His fleshᴰ through *His* death, *that He might* present you holy and without-blemish and blameless in His presence— **²³** if indeedᴱ you continue *in* the faith, having been founded, and steadfast, and not being moved-away from the hope *of* the good-news which you heard, the *one* having been proclaimed inᶠ all creation under heaven, *of* which **I**, Paul, became *a* ministerᴳ.

I Am Suffering To Fulfill My Stewardship of God's Now Revealed Mystery: Christ In You

²⁴ Now I am rejoicing in *my* sufferings for your sake, and in my flesh I am filling-up-in-turnᴴ the *things* lacking *from* the afflictions *of* Christ,ᴵ for the sake of His body, which is the church, **²⁵** *of* which **I** became *a* minister according-toᴶ the stewardshipᴷ *of* God having been given *to* me for you, *that I might* fulfillᴸ the word *of* God— **²⁶** the mystery having been hidden from the *past* ages and from the *past* generations. But now it was revealed *to* His saints, **²⁷** *to* whom God willedᴹ to make-known what *is* the riches *of* the glory *of* this mystery among the Gentiles— which is Christ in you, the hope *of* glory, **²⁸** Whom **we** are proclaiming, admonishing every person, and teaching every person with all wisdom, in order that we may present every person matureᴺ in Christ, **²⁹** for whichᴼ I also am laboring, strugglingᴾ according to His working being at-workᵠ in me with power.

I Am Struggling Greatly For an Increase In Your Assurance And Knowledge of Christ

2:1 For I want you to know how great *a* struggle I am having for your sake and the *ones* in Laodicea, and all-who have not seen my face in *the* flesh, **²** in order that their hearts might be encouraged— *they* having been brought-togetherᴿ in love and forˢ all *the* riches *of* the full-assurance *of* understanding, forᵀ *the* full-knowledge *of* the mystery *of* God— Christ, **³** in Whom are all the treasures *of* wisdom and knowledge, hidden-awayᵁ. **⁴** I am saying thisⱽ in order that no one may be deluding you with persuasive-argument. **⁵** For even though I am absent *in* the flesh, nevertheless I am with you *in* the spirit, rejoicing and seeing your order and the firmness *of* your faith in Christ.

A. Or, because all the fullness was well-pleased to dwell in Him and to reconcile. **B.** That is, God in all His fullness. **C.** Or, hostile. **D.** That is, His fleshly body. **E.** That is, assuming that. **F.** That is, in the sphere of. **G.** Or, servant. **H.** That is, filling-up-on-my-part, in contrast to Christ's part. Or, filling-up. **I.** That is, lacking *from* the afflictions *belonging to* the Christ (Messiah's full measure of sorrows, suffered personally while He was on earth, and by His people now); or, lacking *from* Christ's afflictions (which He is now experiencing in union with His people); or, lacking *from* my afflictions *for* Christ. **J.** Or, based on, by way of. **K.** That is, position of management responsibility. **L.** Or, complete. **M.** Or, wanted, wished. **N.** Or, perfect, full-grown, finished. **O.** That is, to which end. **P.** Or, striving, fighting. **Q.** Or, in operation. **R.** Or, instructed. **S.** That is, for the purpose of or toward the goal of having what follows. **T.** Or, leading to, resulting in. **U.** Or, are hidden-away all the treasures *of* wisdom and knowledge; or, are all the hidden treasures *of* wisdom and knowledge. **V.** Or, the next paragraph may begin with this verse.

So Be Walking In Christ And Established In The Faith You Were Taught
6 As then you received Christ Jesus the[A] Lord, be walking in Him— **7** having been rooted, and being built-up in Him, and being established *in* the[B] faith just as you were taught, abounding in thanksgiving.

Don't Be Taken Captive By Human Thinking, Because All God's Fullness Is In Christ
8 Be watching-out *that* there will not be anyone taking you captive through philosophy and empty deception according-to[C] the tradition *of* humans, according to the elemental *things*[D] *of* the world, and not according to Christ, **9** because in Him dwells all the fullness *of* the Deity[E] bodily[F].

You Are Complete In Christ, With Whom You Have Been Buried And Raised Up
10 And in Him you are complete[G], Who is the head *of* all rule[H] and authority, **11** in Whom you also were circumcised *with a* circumcision not-done-by-*human*-hands, in[I] the taking-off[J] *of* the body[K] *of* the flesh in the circumcision *of*[L] Christ— **12** having been buried-with Him in baptism, in which[M] you also were raised-with *Him* through faith *in* the working *of* God, the *One* having raised Him from *the* dead.

Indeed, God Made Us Alive With Christ, Having Forgiven All Our Trespasses
13 Indeed, you being dead in the trespasses and the uncircumcision *of* your flesh— He made you alive-together with Him, having forgiven us all the trespasses, **14** having wiped-out[N] the written-document[O] against us *with*[P] its decrees, which was opposed *to* us. Indeed, He has taken it out of the middle, having nailed it *to* the cross! **15** Having stripped[Q] the rulers and the authorities, He exposed *them* in public, having celebrated-a-triumph-over[R] them in Him[S]!

Let No One Judge Your Behavior By False Standards
16 Therefore let no one judge you in eating and in drinking, or in respect to *a* feast or new-moon or Sabbath, **17** which are *a* shadow *of* the coming *things*, but the body[T] *is* Christ's. **18** Let no one decide-against you *while* delighting[U] in humility[V] and worship *of*[W] angels, dwelling-upon[X] *things* which he has seen, being puffed-up in-vain by the mind *of*[Y] his

---

A. Or, *as* Lord. **B.** Or, *in your* faith, *by* faith. **C.** Or, based on, by way of. **D.** That is, the elementary knowledge of God available in the world before Christ, the world's rudimentary teachings about God; or, the elemental spiritual beings or angels, the spirit powers. **E.** That is, the divine essence or nature. This is an abstract term for 'God'. **F.** That is, in bodily form, in a bodily manner. **G.** That is, are in a state of completeness. **H.** Or, every ruler. **I.** Or, in connection with. **J.** Or, removal. **K:** the body *of* the flesh. This corresponds to the foreskin in the literal case. **L.** That is, the spiritual circumcision belonging to Christ (Christian circumcision), or performed on our hearts by Christ. **M.** That is, baptism. Or, in Whom (Christ). **N.** Or, blotted out, erased. **O.** Or, handwriting; or more technically, certificate-of-debt. That is, the Law (God's requirements); or, the indictment against us; or, our personal certificate of debt to God. **P.** Or, in, *with reference to, by reason of, accompanied by*. Or, taking this with what follows, 'which *by its* decrees was opposed *to* us'. **Q.** Or, disarmed, spoiled. That is, having stripped away their power; or, having stripped these beings away from Himself. **R.** Or, led them *as captives* in a triumphant procession. **S.** Or, in it, by it (the cross). **T.** That is, the substance or reality casting the shadow belongs to Christ. Or, and the body [of Christ] is Christ's [to judge]. **U.** Or, desiring *to do so* by-means-of humility. **V.** That is, human lowliness, regarding humans as too insignificant to approach God except through angels; or, ascetic humility, self-abasement. **W.** That is offered to angels. Or, offered by angels (angels' worship), viewing themselves as mystically joining into the angels' worship of God. **X.** Or, taking *his* stand upon, entering in. Paul may be quoting their terms, delighting in 'humility' and 'angels' worship', *things* which he has seen while 'entering-in' [a mystical experience]. **Y.** That is, belonging to, characterized by, controlled by.

flesh, **19** and not holding-on-to^A the head— from Whom the whole body, being supplied^B and held-together by the joints and ligaments, is growing the growth *of* ^C God.

Since You Died With Christ, Do Not Submit To Human Decrees
20 If you died with Christ from^D the elemental^E *things of* the world, why, as-*though* living in *the* world, do you submit-to-decrees (**21** "Do not handle, nor taste, nor touch"; **22** *Things* which^F are all for^G perishing^H *in* the use'!) according-to the commandments and teachings *of* humans?— **23** which are indeed having the talk^J *of* wisdom in-connection-with will-worship^K and humility^L and harsh-treatment^M *of the* body, not^N in-connection-with any [real] value against *the* indulgence *of* the flesh.

Since You Were Raised With Christ, Be Seeking His Things
3:1 If then you were raised-with Christ, be seeking the *things* above where Christ is, sitting at *the* right *hand of* God. **2** Be thinking^O the *things* above, not the *things* upon the earth. **3** For you died, and your life has been hidden^P with Christ in God. **4** When Christ appears— your life— then **you** also will appear with Him in glory.

Put To Death The Practices of The Old Person And Put On The New Person
5 Therefore, put-to-death *your* body-part *things*^Q on earth— sexual-immorality, impurity, passion^R, evil desire, and greed, which is idolatry— **6** because of which *things* the wrath *of* God is coming upon the sons *of* ^S disobedience, **7** in which^T *things* **you** also formerly walked when you were living in these *things*. **8** But now **you** also, lay-aside all *these things*— wrath, anger, malice, blasphemy, filthy-language^U from your mouth; **9** do not be lying to one another— having stripped-off the old person with his practices, **10** and having put-on the new *person* being renewed to knowledge in-accordance-with *the* image *of* the One having created him, **11** where there is no Greek and Jew, circumcised and uncircumcised, barbarian^V, Scythian^W, slave, free, but Christ *is* all *things* and in all *persons*.

Therefore, Clothe Yourself In Love, Christ's Peace, God's Word, And Thankfulness
12 Therefore, as chosen^X *ones of* God, holy and having been loved, put-on^Y deep-feelings^Z *of* compassion, kindness, humblemindedness, gentleness, patience, **13** bearing-with one another, and forgiving each other— if anyone has *a* complaint against anyone. Just as indeed the Lord forgave you, so also you *forgive*. **14** And over^Z1 all these *things put on* love, which is *the* bond^Z2

A. Or, holding-tight, keeping-hold-of. **B.** Or, supported. **C.** That is, produced by. **D.** Or, away-from. **E.** See 2:8. **F.** Paul interjects his opinion of such teaching. **G.** That is, intended for, destined for. **H.** Or, destruction, ruin. **I.** Or, using-up, consumption. **J.** Or, report, reputation. **K.** Or, self-made religion, self-chosen religion, would-be religion. It is worship sourced in the will of the worshiper, not the will of the one worshiped. **L.** See v 18. **M.** Or, unsparing-treatment. **N:** not...flesh. Or, not in connection with any honor for *the* satisfaction *of* the flesh; or, not in connection with any honor, [but] for *the* indulgence *of their* flesh. **O.** Or, setting *your* mind on. **P.** That is, hidden safely, like a treasure. **Q.** That is, the sins associated with your body, the sins mentioned next. Or, your body-parts, members, limbs. That is, the physical members of your body insofar as they serve as instruments of sin; or, the metaphorical members of your 'old person', the old desires. **R.** Or, lustfulness. **S.** That is, characterized by. **T.** Or, among whom **you**. **U.** That is, obscene-language, foul-talk. Or, abusive-language, foul-mouthed-abusiveness. **V.** That is, uncivilized. **W.** These were brutal, feared, savage enemies from the East who attacked Palestine 600 years earlier. **X.** Or, elect, selected. **Y.** That is, like clothes. **Z.** Or, *a* heart. **Z1.** Or, upon, in addition to. **Z2.** Or, binding. Some think it binds together the virtues just mentioned; others, the people putting on these virtues, the church.

of [A] perfection. **15** And let the peace *of* [B] Christ be arbitrating[C] in your hearts— into which indeed you were called in one body. And be thankful. **16** Let the word *of* Christ be dwelling in[D] you richly, with all wisdom teaching and admonishing each other *with* psalms[E], hymns, spiritual songs; with gratitude[F] singing with[G] your hearts *to* God. **17** And everything, whatever thing you may do in word or in deed, *do* all *things* in *the* name *of the* Lord Jesus, giving-thanks *to* God *the* Father through Him.

Behave In a Godly Manner In Your Family
18 Wives, be subject *to your* husbands, as[H] it is fitting in *the* Lord. **19** Husbands, be loving *your* wives, and do not be bitter toward them. **20** Children, be obeying *your* parents in all *things*, for this is pleasing in *the* Lord. **21** Fathers, do not be provoking your children, in order that they may not be discouraged[I].

Work As For The Lord, Not For People
22 Slaves, be obeying *your* masters according-to[J] *the* flesh in all *things*, not with eye-service[K] as people-pleasers, but in sincerity *of* heart, fearing the Lord. **23** Whatever you do, be working from *the* soul as *for* the Lord and not *for* people, **24** knowing that from *the* Lord you will receive the payback[L] *of*[M] the inheritance. You are serving[N] the Lord Christ! **25** For the *one*[O] doing-wrong will receive-back what he did-wrong, and there is no respect-of-persons. **4:1** Masters, be granting *to your* slaves the just[P] *thing* and equality[Q], knowing that **you** also have *a* Master in heaven.

Devote Yourselves To Prayer
2 Be devoting-yourselves *to* prayer, keeping-watch[R] in it with thanksgiving, **3** praying at the same time also for us— that God may open *to* us *a* door *for* the word *that we may* speak the mystery *of* Christ because of which I also have been bound, **4** that[S] I may make it clear[T], as I ought-to-speak.

Walk With Wisdom And Grace In This World
5 Be walking with wisdom toward the *ones* outside, redeeming[U] the time, **6** your speech always *being* with grace, having been seasoned *with* salt, *that you may* know how you ought-to answer each one.

Closing Remarks And Greetings
7 All the *things* concerning me Tychicus will make-known *to* you, the beloved brother and faithful minister and fellow-slave in *the* Lord **8** whom I sent to you for this very *reason*— in

---

A. That is, *characterized by* (the perfect bond); or, *belonging to* (perfection's bond); or, *toward, leading to, resulting in, producing* perfection. **B.** That is, given by. **C.** Or, judging, deciding, ruling, umpiring. **D.** Or, among. **E:** *with* psalms, hymns, spiritual songs. Or, this phrase may go with the 'singing' that follows. **F.** Or, with the giving-of-thanks. **G.** Or, in (silently). **H.** That is, as it should be in union with the Lord; or, to the extent proper in the Lord; or, as appropriate among those who are in the Lord. **I.** Or, dispirited, despondent. **J.** Or, with respect to. **K.** That is, merely with an eye on the master to curry favor or avoid punishment. **L.** That is, reward. **M.** That is, consisting of. **N.** Or, You are a slave to. Or, this may be a command, Be serving. **O.** That is, whether the slave or the master. **P.** Or, right, righteous (before your Master). **Q.** That is, treat them as equals before your common Master. Or, equity, fairness (from your common Master's point of view). Paul is not directly referring to emancipation. **R.** Or, staying-alert. **S.** This is a second request. Or, in order that, giving the purpose of the request for an open door. **T.** Or, known. **U.** That is, buying up the time for the Lord; saving the time from being lost or wasted; making the most of your time.

order that you may know the *things* concerning us and he may encourage your hearts— [9] together-with Onesimus[A], the faithful and beloved brother who is from-*among* you. They will make all the *things* here known *to* you.

[10] Aristarchus, my fellow-captive, greets you, and *so does* Mark, the cousin *of* Barnabas, concerning whom you received commands (if he comes to you, welcome him), [11] and Jesus, the *one* being called Justus— the *ones* being from *the* circumcision[B] (these alone *are* fellow-workers for the kingdom *of* God, who proved-to-be[C] *a* comfort[D] *to* me). [12] Epaphras greets you— the *one* from-*among* you, *a* slave *of* Christ Jesus always struggling[E] for you in *his* prayers in-order-that[F] you might stand mature[G] and having been fully-assured in all *the* will *of* God. [13] For I testify *concerning* him that he has great pain[H] for you, and the *ones* in Laodicea, and the *ones* in Hierapolis. [14] Luke, the beloved physician, greets you, and Demas.

[15] Greet the brothers in Laodicea, and Nymphas and the church at her house. [16] And when *this* letter is read among you, cause that it also be read in the church *of the* Laodiceans, and that **you** also read the *letter* from Laodicea. [17] And say *to* Archippus— "See-*to* the ministry which you received in *the* Lord, in order that you may be fulfilling it".

[18] The greeting *of* Paul *by* my *own* hand— remember[I] my imprisonment[J]. Grace *be* with you.

A. That is, the one of whom Philemon was written. **B.** That is, Jewish Christians. **C.** Or, were, became. **D.** Or, consolation, assuagement. **E.** Or, striving, fighting. **F.** Or, that, giving the content of his prayers. **G.** Or, complete. **H.** That is, aching in his heart; or, toil, exertion (that is, he toils hard for you). **I.** That is, keep in mind. **J.** Or, bonds.

1 Thessalonians

Introduction 1:1

A. We are giving thanks to God for you, knowing your election, because our good news came to   1:2-10
    you in power and in the Spirit, and you became imitators of us and of the Lord

B. For you yourselves know our entrance to you— that it has not been empty. But we spoke the   2:1-16
    good news to you while conducting ourselves in a blameless manner. And we are giving thanks
    unceasingly because you accepted the message from us as the word of God

C. And we were very eager to see you again, and Satan hindered us. Therefore, we sent Timothy   2:17-3:5
    to establish and encourage you

    1.   Timothy having just now returned with good news about you, we were encouraged   3:6-10
    2.   Now may God direct our way to you and cause you to abound in love   3:11-13

D. Finally, we ask that as you received from us how to walk, that you be abounding more in it. For   4:1-8
    this is the will of God— your holiness, that you be abstaining from sexual immorality

    1.   But concerning brotherly love you have no need to be written, for you are God-taught   4:9-12

E. And we do not want you to be unaware concerning the ones falling asleep. For if we believe   4:13-18
    Jesus arose, God will bring with Him the ones having fallen asleep

    1.   But concerning the times and seasons you have no need to be written, for you know it   5:1-11

F. And we ask you to be esteeming those who labor among you superabundantly in love   5:12-13

G. Now we exhort you to admonish the disorderly, encourage the fainthearted, pursue good   5:14-22

Conclusion 5:23-28

1:1 Paul[A] and Silvanus[B] and Timothy *to* the church *of the* Thessalonians in God *the* Father and *the* Lord Jesus Christ: Grace *to* you and peace.

We Give Thanks For Your Faith And Love And Endurance
2 We are giving-thanks *to* God always for you all while making mention *of you* in our prayers, unceasingly[C] **3** remembering your work *of* [D] faith and labor *of* love and endurance *of* hope *in* our Lord Jesus Christ before our God and Father; **4** knowing, brothers having been loved by God, your election[E], **5** because our good-news did not come to you in word only, but also in power and in *the* Holy Spirit and with great fullness-of-conviction— just as you know what-kind-of *men* we proved-to-be among you for your sake.

For You Became Imitators of Us And Examples To All
6 And **you** became imitators *of* us and *of* the Lord, having accepted the word in much affliction with *the* joy *of the* Holy Spirit, **7** so that you became *an* example *to* all the *ones* believing in Macedonia and in Achaia. **8** For from you the word *of* the Lord has sounded-forth— not only in Macedonia and in Achaia, but in every place your faith toward God has gone-out— so that we *are* having no need to speak anything! **9** For they themselves are reporting about us *as to* what-sort-of entrance[F] we had with you, and how you turned to God from idols to be serving *the* living and true God, **10** and to be awaiting His Son from the heavens Whom He raised from the dead— Jesus, the *One* delivering us from the coming wrath.

You Know What Kind of Men We Were Among You When We Brought God's Message To You
2:1 For you yourselves know our entrance to you, brothers— that it has not been[G] empty[H]. **2** But having previously-suffered and been mistreated[I] in Philippi, as you know, we were bold in our God to speak the good-news *of* God to you in *a* great conflict. **3** For our exhortation[J] *is* not from[K] error, nor from impurity[L], nor in[M] deceit. **4** But just as we have been approved by God to be entrusted-*with* the good-news, so we speak— not as pleasing people, but God, the *One* testing our hearts. **5** For neither did we at-any-time come with *a* word *of* flattery, as you know; nor with *a* pretext *for* greed— God *is* witness; **6** nor seeking glory from people— neither from you, nor from others, **7** [although] being able to be with weight[N] as apostles *of* Christ. But we proved-to-be child-like[O] in your midst. As when *a* nurse[P] cherishes[Q] her children, **8** in this manner longing-affectionately *for* you, we were well-pleased to impart *to* you not only the good-news *of* God, but also our *own* lives[R], because you became beloved *ones to* us. **9** For you remember, brothers, our labor and hardship— working *by* night and *by* day so-as not to be *a* burden-on[S] any *of* you, we proclaimed to you the good-news *of* God. **10** You and God *are*

A. On when this book was written, see Acts 18:5. **B.** That is, the Silas in Acts 15:40-18:5. **C.** Or, prayers unceasingly, remembering. **D.** That is, proceeding from, characterized by. **E.** Or, selection, choosing. **F.** Or, reception. **G.** Or, proved-to-be, as in 1:5. **H.** Or, futile, in vain, without results on their part; or, without content on Paul's part. **I.** Or, treated in an arrogant manner. **J.** Or, appeal. **K.** That is, originating in. **L.** That is, impure motives; or, more narrowly, sexual immorality. **M.** That is, in connection with deceptive methods. **N.** That is, with weight of dignity or influence; or, with a weight/burden of financial support. **O.** Or, children, innocent *ones*. That is, as opposed to 'with weight'. Some manuscripts say 'gentle', making a single metaphor, 'gentle in your midst as when *a* nurse cherishes her children. In this manner'. **P.** Or, feeder. Paul is describing himself as their mother or wet nurse. **Q.** Or, gives warmth to, warms in her bosom. **R.** Or, souls. That is, expend our own lives; or, join our own souls with yours in love. **S.** Or, put a weight on, weigh heavily on. That is, a financial burden.

witnesses how devoutly and righteously and blamelessly we were *with*^A you, the *ones* believing— ¹¹ just-as you know how each one *of* you, as *a* father his *own* children, ¹² *we were* exhorting you and encouraging and testifying so-that you *might* walk worthily *of* God, the *One* calling you into His *own* kingdom and glory.

And We Thank God You Accepted Our Message As God's Word, Even Amidst Persecution
¹³ And for this^B reason **we** are indeed^C giving-thanks *to* God unceasingly: because having received *the* word *of* God heard from us^D, you accepted not *the* word *of* humans, but, as it truly is, *the* word *of* God, which also is at-work^E in you, the *ones* believing. ¹⁴ For **you** became imitators, brothers, *of* the churches *of* God existing in Judea in Christ Jesus, because **you** also suffered the same *things* by *your* own countrymen as they also by the Jews— ¹⁵ the *ones* also^F having killed **the Lord** Jesus and the prophets, and having driven us out, and not being pleasing *to* God, and *being* contrary^G *to* all people, ¹⁶ forbidding us to speak *to* the Gentiles in order that they might be saved, so that *they* fill-up^H *the measure of* their sins always. But the wrath^I came^J upon them to the uttermost^K.

We Sent Timothy To Establish You Amidst Your Afflictions, And That I Might Know Your Faith
¹⁷ And **we**, brothers, having been orphaned from you for *a* season *of an* hour *in* face, not *in* heart, were more eager^L with great desire to see your face. ¹⁸ Because we wanted^M to come to you— I, Paul, both once and twice^N— and Satan hindered us. ¹⁹ For what^O *is* our hope or joy or crown *of* boasting— or *is it* not indeed you!— before our Lord Jesus at His coming? ²⁰ For **you** are our glory and joy. **3:1** Therefore, bearing^P *it* no longer, we preferred^Q to be left-behind in Athens alone, ² and we sent Timothy, our brother and *a* fellow-worker *of* God in^R the good-news *of* Christ, so that *he might* establish^S you and encourage *you* concerning your faith, ³ *that* no one *might* be disturbed^T by these afflictions. For you yourselves know that we are appointed^U for this. ⁴ For even when we were with you, we were telling you beforehand that we were going to be afflicted, just as indeed it happened, and *just as* you know. ⁵ For this reason, and I bearing *it* no longer, I sent *Timothy* so as to know your faith— *that* the *one* tempting had not somehow tempted you and our labor proved-to-be in vain^V.

Timothy Now Returned With Encouraging News About Your Faith And Love. I Am Rejoicing!
⁶ And Timothy having just-now^W come to us from you, and having announced-the-good-news *to* us *as to* your faith and love, and that you have *a* good remembrance *of* us always^X, yearning to see us just as we also you— ⁷ because of this, brothers, we were encouraged over you in all our distress and affliction, through your faith. ⁸ Because now we live!— if **you** are standing-*firm* in *the* Lord. ⁹ For what thanksgiving can we return^Y *to* God for you for all the joy *with* which we are-rejoicing^Z because of you before our God?— ¹⁰ while

---

A. Or, *to, toward.* **B.** 'This reason' looks forward to 'because'. Or, if it looks backward, 'And for this reason, we are indeed giving-thanks *to* God unceasingly that'. **C.** Or, also (along with you). **D.** Or, 'having received from us *the* word heard *from* God'. **E.** Or, in operation. **F.** Or, both. **G.** Or, hostile, opposed. **H.** That is, these Jews fill fuller the measure of their sins at all times. **I.** That is, the hardening of their hearts and removal of the kingdom from them; or, the end-time wrath beginning with their hardening and looking toward the destruction of Jerusalem and the final wrath associated with the Second Coming. **J.** Or, arrived. **K.** That is, fully; or, continually; or, finally, at last. **L.** Or, made more effort. **M.** Or, intended. **N.** That is, repeatedly. **O.** Or, who. **P.** Or, enduring. **Q.** Or, were well-pleased, were delighted. **R.** That is, in connection with. **S.** Or, stabilize, support, strengthen. **T.** Or, shaken, moved. **U.** Or, destined. **V.** That is, without lasting result. **W.** This occurs in Act 18:5. **X.** Or, us, always yearning. **Y.** Or, give back, repay. **Z.** Or, are-joyful.

praying super-abundantly *by* night and *by* day that *we may* see your face and complete the *things* lacking *from* your faith.

May God And Our Lord Jesus Guide Our Ways And Cause Us To Abound In Love

11 Now may our God and Father Himself and our Lord Jesus direct our way to you. **12** And may the Lord cause you to increase and abound *in* love for one another and for everyone (just as we also for you), **13** so that *He may* establish your hearts *so as to be* blameless in holiness before our God and Father at the coming *of* our Lord Jesus with all His holy[A] *ones*. Amen.

Brothers, We Ask You To Abound Even More In Holiness, For This Is God's Will

4:1 Finally then, brothers, we ask you, and exhort in *the* Lord Jesus that just as you received from us how you ought-to be walking and pleasing God (just as you also are walking), that you be abounding more. **2** For you know what commands we gave *to* you through the Lord Jesus. **3** For this is *the* will *of* God: your holiness[B]— *that* you be abstaining[C] from sexual-immorality; **4** *that* each *of* you know-*how* to acquire[D] *control of* his *own* vessel[E] in holiness and honor, **5** not in *the* passion *of*[F] desire[G] as indeed the Gentiles not knowing God; **6** *that*[H] no *one* overstep[I] and exploit[J] his brother[K] in the matter[L]. Because *the* Lord *is the* avenger concerning all these *things*, just as we also told you before and solemnly-warned. **7** For God did not call us for[M] impurity, but in[N] holiness. **8** So-therefore[O] the *one* rejecting is not rejecting *a* human, but God, the *One* also giving His Holy Spirit to you.

But You Know From God To Love One Another. We Exhort You To Abound Even More

9 But concerning brotherly-love, you have no need *that anyone should* be writing *to* you. For **you** yourselves are God-taught so-that *you might* be loving one another. **10** For indeed you are doing it toward all the brothers in all Macedonia. But we exhort you, brothers, to be abounding more, **11** and to be ambitious[P] to be quiet[Q], and to be doing[R] *your* own *things* and working *with* your own hands just as we commanded you, **12** in order that you may walk properly toward the *ones* outside and may have need *of* nothing[S].

Do Not Grieve Over The Dead In Christ. We Will Rise Together To Be With Him Forever

13 And we do not want you to be unaware, brothers, concerning the *ones* falling-asleep[T], in-order-that you may not grieve as indeed the others— the *ones* not having *a* hope. **14** For if we believe that Jesus died and rose-up, so also[U] God will bring with Him the *ones* having fallen asleep through[V] Jesus. **15** For we say this *to* you by *the* word *of the* Lord, that **we**— the *ones*

A. That is, saints; or, angels; or, both. **B.** Or, sanctification. **C.** Or, keeping away, avoiding, holding back. **D.** Or, get, obtain, procure, gain. **E.** That is, his own body. In this case, Paul is referring to self-mastery with regard to sexual desires, and 'each *of* you' means 'all of you' all the time. Or, 'acquire his *own* vessel'; that is, his own wife. In this case Paul is referring to premarital purity, and 'each *of* you' means 'the unmarried'. **F.** That is, proceeding from; or, belonging to (lustful passion). **G.** Or, lust. **H.** There is a grammatical change here from the previous two '*that*' statements. Paul may be restating the previous two points from a different perspective. Or, this may indicate he is changing to a new subject, business relations. **I.** Or, transgress. **J.** Or, take advantage of, cheat, defraud. **K.** That is, fellow-believer, whether male or female. **L.** That is, this matter of sexual relations; or, the matter of business. **M.** That is, for the purpose of. **N.** That is, in connection with, in the sphere of. **O.** Or, Therefore-for-that-very-reason. **P.** Or, make it *your* ambition. **Q.** Or, lead a quiet life. **R.** Or, tending-to *your* own *affairs*. **S.** Or, no one. **T.** That is, dying. Or, sleeping; that is, dead. **U.** That is, so also *we believe that*. **V.** Or, by means of. That is, having entered into God's rest through what Jesus has done. Or, so also through Jesus God will bring with Him the *ones* having fallen-asleep.

living, the *ones* remaining^A^ until the coming *of* the Lord— will in-no-way precede the *ones* having fallen asleep. **16** Because^B^ the Lord Himself will descend from heaven with *a* shouted-command^C^, with *a* voice *of an* archangel^D^, and with *a* trumpet *of* God, and the dead in Christ will rise-up first. **17** Then **we**— the *ones* living, the *ones* remaining— will be snatched-up^E^ together^F^ with them in *the* clouds^G^ to meet the Lord in *the* air. And so we shall always be with *the* Lord. **18** So then, be encouraging^H^ one another with these words.

But You Know The Day of The Lord Will Come Like a Thief In The Night. Keep Watching
5:1 But concerning the times and the seasons, brothers, you have no need *that anything should* be written *to* you. **2** For you yourselves accurately know that *the* day *of the* Lord comes in this manner— like *a* thief in *the* night. **3** When they are saying "peace and security", then unexpected^I^ destruction suddenly-comes-upon^J^ them, just as the birth-pain *on* the *one* having *a child* in *the* womb. And they will by no means escape. **4** But **you**, brothers, are not in darkness, so that the day should overtake you like *a* thief. **5** For **you** all are sons *of*^K^ light and sons *of* day. We are not *of* night, nor *of* darkness. **6** So then, let us not be sleeping like the others, but let us be keeping-watch^L^ and being sober. **7** For the *ones* sleeping are sleeping *at* night. And the *ones* getting-drunk are-drunk *at* night. **8** But let **us**, being *of the* day, be sober, having put on *a* breastplate *of* faith and love, and *a* helmet: *the* hope *of* salvation. **9** Because God did not appoint^M^ us for wrath, but for *the* obtaining^N^ *of* salvation through our Lord Jesus Christ— **10** the *One* having died for us in order that whether we are keeping-watch or sleeping^O^, we may live together with Him. **11** Therefore be encouraging one another and building-up one the other, just as you are also doing.

Esteem Your Leaders in Love
12 And we ask you, brothers, to know^P^ the *ones* laboring among you and leading you in *the* Lord and admonishing you, **13** and to be esteeming them super-abundantly^Q^ in love because of their work. Be living-in-peace among yourselves.

Closing Exhortations
14 Now we exhort you, brothers— be admonishing the disorderly *ones*, be encouraging^R^ the fainthearted *ones*, be holding-on-to^S^ the weak *ones,* be patient with everyone. **15** See *that* no one gives-back evil for evil *to* anyone, but always be pursuing the good, both for one another and for everyone. **16** Be rejoicing always, **17** be praying unceasingly, **18** be giving-thanks in everything. For this *is the* will *of* God in Christ Jesus for you. **19** Do not be quenching^T^ the Spirit, **20** do not be treating prophecies with contempt, **21** but be testing all *things.* Be holding-on-to the good^U^, **22** be abstaining from every form^V^ *of* evil.

A. Or, being left behind. That is, remaining alive at that time. **B.** Or, asleep; that. In this case, this is a second thing Paul 'says' to them. **C.** Or, signal-call. **D.** That is, ruling or chief angel. **E.** Our word 'rapture' comes from the Latin translation of this word. **F.** Or, at the same time. **G.** Or, in clouds, on clouds. **H.** Or, comforting. **I.** Or, sudden, unforeseen. **J.** Or, springs-upon. **K.** That is, belonging to. **L.** Or, staying awake, keeping alert. **M.** Or, make, destine. **N.** Or, possession. **O.** That is, physically alive (living, remaining at the end, and thus watching) or dead. Or, prepared (keeping watch) or unprepared, as in v 6. **P.** That is, in the sense of stand in close relationship with, recognize and respect. **Q.** Or, immeasurably, surpassingly. **R.** Or, consoling. **S.** Or, clinging-to, devoted to, supporting. **T.** Or, stifling, suppressing. **U.** That is, the beautiful, commendable, praiseworthy. **V.** Or, outward appearance; or, kind, species, class, sort.

[23] Now may the God *of* peace Himself sanctify[A] you wholly[B]. And may your whole[C] spirit and soul and body be preserved[D] blamelessly at the coming *of* our Lord Jesus Christ. [24] Faithful *is* the *One* calling you, Who also will do *it*. [25] Brothers, be praying also for us. [26] Greet all the brothers with *a* holy kiss. [27] I adjure[E] you *by* the Lord *that this* letter be read *to* all the brothers. [28] The grace *of* our Lord Jesus Christ *be* with you.

A. Or, make you wholly holy. **B.** Or, through and through, in every part, altogether. **C.** Or, taking this with the verb, complete, sound, intact: 'May your spirit and soul and body be preserved **complete**' (it would have Paul's emphasis). **D.** Or, kept, guarded, protected. **E.** That is, make you swear, put you under oath.

2 Thessalonians

Introduction 1:1-2

A. We ought to be giving thanks always for you because your faith and love are growing 1:3-4

   1. Which is evidence that you will be considered worthy of the kingdom 1:5-10
   2. For which also we pray always concerning you, that God may consider you worthy of the 1:11-12
      calling, and fulfill your every desire of goodness and work of faith with power

B. Now we ask you not to be alarmed as though the day of the Lord is present. The apostasy must 2:1-6
   come first, and the man of lawlessness. You know what is restraining him now

   1. For the mystery of lawlessness is already at work, only there is one restaining now 2:7-12
   2. But we ought to be giving thanks always concerning you, brothers loved by the Lord, 2:13-17
      because God chose you to be the firstfruit for salvation. So then, be standing firm

C. Finally, be praying for us. And may the Lord direct you into His love and endurance 3:1-5

D. Now we command you to be keeping away from every brother walking disorderly 3:6-16

Conclusion 3:17-18

1:1 Paul[A] and Silvanus[B] and Timothy *to* the church *of the* Thessalonians in God our Father and *the* Lord Jesus Christ: **²** Grace *to* you and peace from God our Father and *the* Lord Jesus Christ.

We Thank God For Your Faith And Love, And Boast of Your Endurance Amidst Afflictions
³ We ought to be giving-thanks *to* God always for you, brothers, just as it is fitting, because your faith is growing-abundantly and the love *of* each one *of* you all toward one another is increasing, **⁴** so that we ourselves *are* boasting in you among the churches *of* God with reference to your endurance and faith in all your persecutions and afflictions which you are bearing-with—

These Are Evidence of God's Righteous Judgment Concerning You And Those Afflicting You
⁵ ... *which is* evidence[C] *of* the righteous judgment *of*[D] God that you *will* be[E] considered-worthy *of* the kingdom *of* God for the sake of which you also[F] are suffering, **⁶** since *it will be a* righteous *thing* with[G] God to repay[H] affliction *to* the *ones* afflicting you **⁷** and *to give* you, the *ones* being afflicted, rest[I] along with us at the revelation *of* the Lord Jesus from heaven with angels *of*[J] His power **⁸** in flaming fire, giving[K] punishment[L] *to* the *ones* not knowing God and[M] the *ones* not obeying the good-news *of* our Lord Jesus— **⁹** who will pay *the* penalty: eternal destruction from[N] *the* presence *of* the Lord and from the glory *of*[O] His strength, **¹⁰** when He comes to be glorified in[P] His saints and marveled-at[Q] among[R] all the *ones* having believed— because[S] our testimony to you was believed— on that day,

We Pray For God To Fulfill Your Every Desire To Express Your Goodness And Faith
¹¹ ... for which[T] also[U] we are praying always for you in order that our God may consider you worthy *of* the calling, and may fulfill every desire[V] *of* goodness[W] and work *of*[X] faith with [His] power, **¹²** so that the name *of* our Lord Jesus may be glorified in you and you in Him, according-to[Y] the grace *of* our God and *the* Lord Jesus Christ.

Now Don't Be Alarmed: The Day of The Lord Has Not Yet Come
2:1 Now we ask you, brothers, concerning the coming *of* our Lord Jesus Christ and our gathering-together to Him, **²** that you not be quickly shaken from *your* understanding nor alarmed— neither by *a* spirit[Z], nor by *a* word, nor by *a* letter as-*if* through us, how that the day *of* the Lord is present[Z1]. **³** Let no one deceive you in any way, because *it will not be present* unless the apostasy[Z2] comes first and the man *of* lawlessness is revealed[Z3]— the son *of*[Z4] destruction, **⁴** the *one* opposing and exalting *himself* over[Z5] everything being called god or *an* object-of-worship[Z6], so that he sits-down[Z7] in the temple[Z8] *of* God displaying[Z9] himself that he

---

A. On when this book was written, see Acts 18:11. **B.** That is, the Silas of Acts 15:40-18:5. **C.** Or, *a* clear-indication, *a* proof. **D.** That is, by. **E.** Or, that you are. Or, so that you *may* be. Or, so that you *will* be. **F.** That is, along with us. Or, indeed. **G.** Or, in the sight of. **H.** Or, give back, return. **I.** Or, relief, refreshment. **J.** That is, proceeding from; or, characterized by (His powerful angels). **K.** That is, the Lord Jesus... giving. **L.** Or, vengeance. **M.** That is, Gentiles and Jews. Or, even, making one group with two descriptions. **N.** That is, away from. Or, proceeding from. **O.** That is, originating in. **P.** Or, among, by. **Q.** Or, admired. **R.** Or, in, by. **S.** Or, because our testimony to you in-connection-with that day was believed. **T.** That is, their faith and love (v 3-4), or worthiness (v 5). Or, With-a-view-to-which *event* (v 6-10). Or, For which *believing* (v 10). **U.** Or, indeed. **V.** Or, good-pleasure. **W.** That is, *for* goodness. Or, fulfill all *the* good-pleasure *of* [God's] goodness; that is, His good will for you. **X.** That is, proceeding from, characterized by faith. **Y.** Or, based on, in accordance with. **Z.** That is, a spoken spiritual manifestation. **Z1.** Or, has come, is here. **Z2.** Or, rebellion, falling away, abandonment. **Z3.** Or, disclosed, made known. **Z4.** That is, belonging to, destined for. **Z5.** That is, above, against. **Z6.** Or, object-of-veneration. **Z7.** Or, takes *his* seat. **Z8.** That is, the visible church; or, the Jerusalem temple. **Z9.** Or, showing, exhibiting, proving, attesting.

is god. **⁵** Do you not remember that while still being with you I was telling you these *things*? **⁶** And you know the *thing* restraining^A **now**, so that he *might* be revealed in his *own* time.

For Lawlessness Is Being Restrained Right Now, But The Lawless One Will Come Later
⁷ For the mystery *of* lawlessness is already at-work^B, only *there is* the *one* restraining right-now until he comes^C out of *the* midst^D. **⁸** And then the lawless *one* will be revealed, whom the Lord Jesus will kill *with* the breath *of* His mouth and do-away-with^E *by* the appearance *of* His coming^F— **⁹** whose coming is in accordance with *the* working *of* Satan, with all power and signs and wonders *of*^G falsehood, **¹⁰** and with every deception *of*^H unrighteousness *for* the *ones* perishing because they did not receive the love *of* the truth so that they *might* be saved. **¹¹** And for this reason, God sends them *a* working *of*^I error^J so that they *will* believe the falsehood^K, **¹²** in order that all the *ones* not having believed *in* the truth but having taken-pleasure^L *in* unrighteousness may be condemned.

But God Chose You To Be The Firstfruits of Salvation. Stand Firm And Hold On To The Truth
¹³ But^M **we** ought to be giving-thanks *to* God always for you, brothers having been loved by *the* Lord, because God chose you *to be the* firstfruit^N for salvation in^O *the* holiness *of*^P *the* Spirit and faith^Q *in the* truth— **¹⁴** to which also He called you through our good-news, for *the* obtaining^R *of the* glory *of* our Lord Jesus Christ. **¹⁵** So then, brothers, be standing-firm, and be holding-on-to the traditions which you were taught— whether by word [of mouth] or by our letter. **¹⁶** And may our Lord Jesus Christ Himself and God our Father, the *One* having loved us and having given *us* eternal comfort and good hope by grace, **¹⁷** comfort your hearts and establish *you* in every good work and word.

Pray That The Word May Spread Quickly And That We May Be Protected From Evil People
3:1 Finally, brothers, be praying for us that the word *of* the Lord may run^S and be glorified, just as also with you, **²** and that we may be delivered from out-of-place^T and evil people. For faith^U is not *possessed by* everyone. **³** But the Lord is faithful— Who will establish you, and protect *you* from the evil one^V. **⁴** And we are confident in *the* Lord concerning you that *the things* which we are commanding, you also^W are doing and will do. **⁵** And may the Lord direct your hearts into the love *of*^X God and into the endurance *of*^X Christ.

Imitate Us, And Keep Away From Those Who Don't
⁶ Now we command you, brothers, in *the* name *of* our Lord Jesus Christ, *that* you be keeping-away^Y from every brother walking disorderly^Z and not according to the tradition which they received from us. **⁷** For you yourselves know how *you* ought-to be imitating us. Because we

---

A. That is, the Holy Spirit; or, God's own acts of restraint; or, some agent of God such as government or the church. **B.** Or, in-operation. **C.** Or, comes-to-be, becomes. **D.** Or, middle. **E.** Or, bring-to-an-end. **F.** Or, presence. **G.** That is, characterized by falsehood (false wonders). Or, proceeding from. **H.** That is, proceeding from unrighteousness; or, leading to. **I.** That is, characterized by error (a delusion); or, leading to error. **J.** Or, deception. **K.** Or, lie. **L.** Or, delighted *in*, been well-pleased *with*. **M.** That is, in contrast to this concern about you being shaken, v 1-2; or, in contrast to such people as in v 10-12. **N:** *to be the* firstfruit. Some manuscripts instead say 'from *the* beginning'. **O.** That is, in the sphere of. Or, by means of. **P.** That is, produced by the Spirit. Or, *characterizing your* spirit. **Q.** Or, belief. **R.** Or, possession. That is, for our obtaining of His glory; or, for our becoming a possession of His glory. **S.** That is, run speedily ahead. **T.** Or, improper, unnatural, wrong. **U.** Or, the faith. **V.** Or, from evil. **W.** Or, indeed. **X.** That is, for God; or, from God. Same next. **Y.** Or, standing aloof. **Z.** Or, out of order, out of ranks, undisciplined.

were not disorderly among you, [8] nor did we eat bread as-a-gift[A] from anyone, but *were* working with labor and hardship *by* night and *by* day so-as not to be *a* burden-on any *of* you— [9] not because we do not have *the* right, but in order that we might give ourselves *as a* pattern *to* you, so that *you may* be imitating us. [10] For even when we were with you, we commanded this *to* you— that "if anyone does not want to work, neither let him eat". [11] For we are hearing *of* some among you walking disorderly, not working at all, but being-busybodies[B]. [12] Now *to* such *ones* we command and exhort in *the* Lord Jesus Christ that while working with quietness, they eat their *own* bread. [13] But **you**, brothers, do not grow-weary while doing-good. [14] And if anyone does not obey our word through *this* letter, be taking-note-of[C] this *one*— to not be associating-with him, in order that he may be ashamed. [15] And do not be regarding *him* as *an* enemy, but be admonishing *him* as *a* brother. [16] And may the Lord *of* peace Himself give you peace continually[D] in every way. The Lord *be* with you all.

[17] The greeting *of* Paul *by* my *own* hand, which is *a* sign in every letter— I write in this manner. [18] The grace *of* our Lord Jesus Christ *be* with you all.

A. Or, freely, without-payment. **B.** Lit, working-around, a play on words. That is, puttering around, meddling. **C.** Or, marking. **D.** Or, through all *things*.

1 Timothy

Introduction   1:1-2

A.   Just as I urged you, stay in Ephesus in order to command certain ones not to teach different   1:3-11
     doctrines. The goal is love— from a pure heart, a good conscience, and a sincere faith

B.   I have gratitiude for the One having strengthened me, having put me into service by His grace   1:12-17

C.   I am depositing this instruction with you, Timothy, in order that you may fight the good fight,   1:18-20
     having faith and a good conscience

     1.   First of all then, I urge that prayers be made for all people by the men in every place   2:1-8
     2.   Similarly, I urge that women adorn themselves fittingly. Let them be learning in quietness   2:9-15
     3.   Overseers must be above reproach, meeting godly character qualifications   3:1-7
     4.   Deacons similarly must be honorable, faithful people   3:8-13

D.   I am writing these things to you hoping to come to you soon, but in case I am slow, in order   3:14-15
     that you may know how to behave in the church, the pillar and support of the truth

     1.   And the mystery of godliness is confessedly great. But the Spirit says that in later times   3:16-4:7
          some will depart from the faith. While pointing out these things, you will be a good
          servant of Christ Jesus
     2.   But you be training yourself for godliness. For godliness is profitable for all things.   4:7-16
          Become a pattern in speech, conduct, love, faith, purity. Be paying attention to reading,
          exhortation, teaching
     3.   Be appealing to older men as fathers, younger men as brothers, older women as   5:1-2
          mothers, younger women as sisters
     4.   Honor real widows. Families have first responsibility. Put qualified widows on the list   5:3-16
     5.   Let elders having led well be considered worthy of double honor. Rebuke the ones sinning   5:17-25
          in the presence of all
     6.   Let all who are slaves be regarding their masters as worthy of all honor   6:1-2

E.   Be teaching and exhorting these things. If anyone teaches differently, he is diseased about   6:2-10
     controversies and riches

     1.   But you, O man of God, flee these things and pursue godly virtues. Fight the good fight. I   6:11-16
          command you in the sight of God and Jesus to keep the commandment until He comes
     2.   Command the rich ones to be rich in good works, that they may take hold of real life   6:17-19
     3.   O Timothy, guard the deposit, turning aside from the empty chatterings of false   6:20-21
          knowledge

1:1 Paul, *an* apostle *of* Christ Jesus according to *the* command *of* God our Savior and Christ Jesus our hope, **²** *to* Timothy, genuine child in *the* faith: Grace, mercy, peace from God *the* Father and Christ Jesus our Lord.

Stay On In Ephesus To Turn Certain "Law-Teachers" From Worthless Talk To Love
³ Just as I urged you to stay-on in Ephesus while *I was* proceeding to Macedonia, *do so* in order that you might command[A] certain *ones* not to be teaching-different-*doctrines*, **⁴** nor paying-attention-to myths[B] and endless genealogies, which cause speculations rather than *a* stewardship[C] *of* [D] God, *which is* by[E] faith. **⁵** And the goal *of your* command[F] is love from *a* pure heart and good conscience and sincere faith, **⁶** having departed[G] *from* which *things* some turned-aside into worthless-talk[H]— **⁷** wanting to be Law-teachers, not understanding either *the things* which they are saying or about what *things* they are speaking-confidently.

> *The Law Is Useful When It Is Used Properly: To Correct The Ungodly*
> **⁸** Now we know that the Law *is* good[I] if one is using it lawfully, **⁹** knowing this: that law is not laid-down[J] *for a* righteous *one* but *for* lawless *ones* and rebellious *ones,* ungodly *ones* and sinful *ones,* unholy *ones* and profane[K] *ones,* father-thrashers[L] and mother-thrashers, man-slayers[M], **¹⁰**sexually-immoral *ones,* homosexuals[N], slave-traders[O], liars, perjurers[P], and if any other *thing* is contrary *to* healthy[Q] teaching **¹¹** in accordance with the good-news *of* the glory *of* the blessed God which **I** was entrusted.

I Thank The Lord Jesus For Showing Mercy To Me And Appointing Me To Serve Him
¹² I have gratitude *to* Christ Jesus our Lord, the *One* having strengthened me, because He regarded me trustworthy[R], having appointed *me* for service— **¹³** *I* formerly being *a* blasphemous *one* and *a* persecutor and violent[S] *one*! But I was shown-mercy because being ignorant, I acted in unbelief. **¹⁴** And the grace *of* our Lord overflowed, along with *the* faith and love *which are* in Christ Jesus. **¹⁵** The saying *is* trustworthy and worthy *of* full acceptance— that Christ Jesus came into the world to save sinners, *of* whom **I** am foremost[T]. **¹⁶** But for this reason I was shown-mercy: in order that in me, *the* foremost, Christ Jesus might demonstrate[U] all patience, for *a* pattern *for* the *ones* going to put-faith upon Him for eternal life. **¹⁷** Now *to* the King *of* the ages[V], *to the* immortal invisible only God, *be* honor and glory forever and ever, amen.

I Am Giving You This Instruction, My Child, So You Can Fight The Good Fight
¹⁸ I am depositing[W] this instruction[X] *with* you, *my* child Timothy, in accordance with the preceding[Y] prophecies about you, in order that by them[Z] you may fight the good fight, **¹⁹** having faith and *a* good conscience, which[Z1] having pushed-aside[Z2], some suffered-shipwreck with respect to the[Z3] faith— **²⁰** *of* whom are Hymenaeus and Alexander, whom I handed-over *to* Satan in order that they may be trained not to blaspheme.

A. Or, instruct, direct. **B.** Or, fables, tales. **C.** Or, arrangement, mode of operation. **D.** That is, proceeding from. **E.** Or, in the sphere of. **F.** Or, instruction. **G.** Or, deviated. **H.** Or, futile-talk, useless-talk, pointless-talk. **I.** That is, advantageous, useful. **J.** Or, set-in-place. **K.** Or, godless, irreligious. **L:** -thrashers. Or, -abusers, -assaulters, -killers. It depends on how extreme a violation of the fifth commandment Paul has in mind. **M.** Or, murderers. **N.** See 1 Cor 6:9. **O.** Or, man-stealers. **P.** Or, oath-breakers. **Q.** Or, sound, correct. **R.** Or, faithful. **S.** Or, insolent. **T.** Or, first, chief. **U.** Or, display, show. **V.** Or, the King *of* eternity; the eternal King. **W.** Or, committing, entrusting. **X.** Or, command, as in v 5. **Y.** That is, preceding Timothy's ministry. **Z.** Or, in them. That is, by following the contents of this instruction; or, in living out the prophecies. **Z1.** That is, a good conscience. **Z2.** Or, rejected. **Z3.** Or, *their* faith. That is, having ignored their conscience, they ran aground the Christian faith; or, their personal faith.

First, I Urge That Prayers And Thanksgivings Be Made For All People

2:1 First *of* all then, I urge *that* petitions, prayers, intercessions, thanksgivings be made for all people, **2** for kings and all the *ones* being in *a place of* superiority, in order that we may spend^A *a* tranquil and quiet life in all godliness and dignity. **3** This^B *is* good and acceptable^C in the sight of our Savior God, **4** Who desires^D all people to be saved and to come to *the* knowledge *of the* truth.

For Jesus Gave Himself As a Ransom For All

2 For *there is* one God, and one mediator *of* God and people— *the* man Christ Jesus, **6** the *One* having given Himself *as a* ransom for all, the testimony *given in His*^E own times **7** for which **I** was appointed *a* proclaimer and *an* apostle (I am telling *the* truth; I am not lying), *a* teacher *of the* Gentiles in^F faith and truth. **8** So I want the men in every place to be praying, lifting-up holy hands without anger and argument.

Women's Appearance And Behavior Should Be Fitting For Ones Professing Godliness

9 Similarly also, *I urge that* women be adorning themselves in well-ordered^G apparel with modesty and sound-mindedness^H— not in braided *hair* and gold or pearls or very-expensive clothing, **10** but through^I good works, which is fitting *for* women professing godliness^J. **11** Let *a* woman be learning in quietness with all submission. **12** And I do not permit *a* woman to teach nor have-authority-over^K *a* man, but to be in quietness. **13** For Adam was formed first, then Eve. **14** And Adam was not deceived^L, but the woman, having been completely-deceived, has come-to-be in transgression. **15** But she^M will be saved by^N The Childbearing, if they^O continue in faith and love and holiness with sound-mindedness.

Overseers Must Be Above Reproach

3:1 The saying *is* trustworthy— if anyone aspires-to *the* office-of-overseer, he desires *a* good work. **2** Therefore the overseer must be above-reproach^P, *a* man *of* one woman^Q, sober^R, sound-minded^S, respectable^T, hospitable, skillful-at-teaching, **3** not *a* drunken^U *one*, not *a* brawler^V, but kind, non-quarrelsome^W, not-a-money-lover, **4** leading *his* own household well^X, having children in submission, with all dignity (**5** but if one does not know-*how* to lead *his* own household, how will he take-care-of *a* church *of* God?), **6** not *a* new-convert, in order that he may not fall into *the* judgment *of*^Y the devil, having become conceited^Z. **7** And *he* must also have *a* good testimony from the *ones* outside, in order that he may not fall into reproach and *a* snare *of* the devil.

A. Or, lead, pass, live. **B.** That is, such prayer. **C.** Or, pleasing. **D.** Or, wants, wishes. **E.** Or, *its.* **F.** That is, in connection with. **G.** Or, respectable, modest, appropriate. **H.** Or, good-sense, moderation, discretion. **I.** Or, by way of. **J.** Or, piety, reverence. **K.** Or, have independent rule over; or, domineer over. **L.** Adam sinned by deliberate choice. **M.** That is, the generic 'woman' of v 11, 12; or, Eve, v 14. **N.** Or, through. That is, directly and independently through Christ, just like the men. Or, through *her* childbearing; that is, while living in her childbearing role, just as men are saved in their toil, Gen 3:16-17. **O.** That is, the individual women represented by 'she' earlier in the verse. **P.** Or, without blame, beyond criticism. **Q.** Or, husband *of* one wife. Some think this refers in some sense to marital status; others, to marital fidelity. **R.** That is, sober in judgment, serious. **S.** Or, prudent, moderate, self-controlled. **T.** Or, well-ordered, as in 2:9; honorable. **U.** That is, known for drunken behavior and exhibitions. **V.** Or, belligerent, combative. **W.** Or, peaceable. **X.** Or, commendably. **Y.** That is, the kind of judgment made by the devil, a judgmental spirit; or, the condemnation pronounced upon the devil. **Z.** Or, clouded with pride.

Deacons Must Be Honorable And Tested

8 Deacons similarly *must be* honorable[A], not double-tongued[B], not paying-attention-to[C] much wine, not fond-of-shameful-gain, **9** holding the mystery *of* the faith with *a* clean conscience. **10** And let these also first be tested, then let them be serving[D], being blameless. **11** *Their* wives[E] similarly *must be* honorable, not slanderous, sober, faithful in all *things*. **12** Let deacons be men *of* one woman, leading *their* children and *their* own households well. **13** For the *ones* having served well obtain *for* themselves *a* good standing[F] and great confidence[G] in *their*[H] faith in Christ Jesus.

I Am Writing So You Will Know How To Conduct Yourself In The Church

14 I am writing these *things to* you hoping to come to you quickly, **15** but in-case I am slow[I], in order that you may know how *you* ought-to conduct-*yourself* [J] in *the* household *of* God— which is *the* church *of the* living God, *the* pillar and support[K] *of* the truth.

God Was Revealed In The Flesh, But Some Will Depart From The Faith And Good Teaching

16 And the mystery *of* godliness is confessedly great: Who[L] was revealed[M] in *the* flesh, was declared-righteous[N] in *the* spirit[O]; was seen[P] *by* messengers[Q], was proclaimed among *the* nations; was believed in *the* world, was taken-up in glory. **4:1** But the Spirit explicitly says that in later times some will depart[R] *from* the faith, paying-attention-to deceitful spirits and teachings *of* demons **2** by means of *the* hypocrisy *of* liars having been seared *as to their* own conscience— **3** forbidding to marry, *commanding* to abstain *from* foods which God created for *a* receiving with thanksgiving *by* the *ones who are* believers and know[S] the truth. **4** Because every creature *of* God *is* good. And nothing being received with thanksgiving *is to be* rejected, **5** for it is sanctified[T] by *the* word *of* God and prayer. **6** While pointing-out these *things to* the brothers, you will be *a* good servant *of* Christ Jesus, while being nourished in the words *of* the faith and the good teaching which you have closely-followed. **7** But be declining[U] the profane[V] and old-womanish myths.

But You Be Training Yourself For Godliness In Your Character And Teaching

But be training[W] yourself for godliness. **8** For bodily training is profitable for *a* little, but godliness is profitable for all *things*— having promise *for* the present life and the *one* coming. **9** The saying *is* trustworthy and worthy *of* full acceptance. **10** For we are laboring and struggling[X] for this[Y], because we have put *our* hope upon *the* living God, Who is *the* Savior *of* all people— especially *of* believers. **11** Be commanding and teaching these *things*. **12** Let no one be-looking-down-on[Z] your youth, but be *a* pattern *for* the believers in speech, in conduct, in love, in faith, in purity. **13** Until I come[Z1], be paying-attention-to the reading[Z2], the exhortation, the teaching. **14** Do not be careless[Z3] *of* the gift in you, which was given *to* you through *a* prophecy with *the* laying-on *of* the hands *of* the council-of-elders. **15** Be

---

A. Or, worthy of respect, dignified. **B.** That is, insincere. **C.** Or, devoting-*themselves*-to, and thus, being addicted to. **D.** Or, serving-as-deacons. **E:** *Their* wives. Or, Women *deacons*. **F.** Or, rank, degree *of respect*. **G.** Or, boldness. **H.** Or, in *the* faith *which is* in. **I.** That is, choose to proceed slowly. **J.** Or, behave, live. **K.** Or, mainstay, foundation. **L.** Some manuscripts say 'God'. **M.** Or, appeared. **N.** Or, vindicated, proved-righteous. **O.** Or, in *His* spirit; or, by *the* Spirit. **P.** Or, appeared *to*. **Q.** Or, angels, if heavenly messengers are in view. **R.** Or, withdraw, revolt, apostatize. **S.** Or, have come-to-know. **T.** Or, made holy, set apart to God's use. **U.** Or, refusing. **V.** Or godless, irreligious. **W.** Or, exercising. **X.** Or, competing, striving, contending. **Y.** That is, to experience God's promise for this life and the next. **Z.** Or, treating-with-contempt, because of your conduct. **Z1.** Or, While I am coming. **Z2.** That is, the public reading of Scripture. **Z3.** Or, Do not neglect the gift.

taking-care-with these *things,* be in these *things,* in order that your progress may be evident *to* everyone. [16] Be fixing-*your*-attention-on yourself and *your* teaching. Be continuing *in* them. For while doing this, you will save both yourself and the *ones* hearing you.

Speak To Everyone As You Would Your Own Family Members

5:1 Do not sharply-rebuke *an* older *man,* but be appealing-to[A] *him* as *a* father, younger *men* as brothers, [2] older *women* as mothers, younger *women* as sisters in all purity.

Provide Church Support For Real Widows Attested By Faith And Good Works

[3] Be honoring widows— the real[B] widows. [4] Now if any widow has children or grandchildren, let them first learn to reverence[C] *their* own household and to give-back *a* return *to their* ancestors. For this is acceptable[D] in the sight of God. [5] But the *one who is a* real widow and has been left-alone[E] has put *her* hope upon God, and continues-in petitions and prayers *by* night and *by* day. [6] But the *one* living-indulgently is-dead while living. [7] Indeed be commanding these *things* in order that they may be above-reproach. [8] But if anyone does not provide-for *his* own *relatives,* and especially family-members, he has denied the faith and is worse *than an* unbeliever. [9] Let *a* widow be put-on-the-list[F] having become not fewer *than* sixty years *old, a* woman *of* one man[G], [10] being attested by good works: if she brought-up-children, if she received-strangers[H], if she washed *the* feet *of* saints, if she aided *ones* being afflicted, if she followed-after every good work.

But Decline To Include The Young Widows; Let Them Marry

[11] But be declining[I] younger[J] widows. For when they grow-sensual[K] *against* Christ, they want to marry— [12] having condemnation [upon themselves] because[L] they set-aside *their* first pledge. [13] And at the same time also they are learning *to be* idle[M], while going-around the houses. And not only idle, but also babblers and busybodies— speaking the *things* not being proper. [14] Therefore, I want younger *widows* to marry, to bear-children, to manage-the-house[N], to give *to* the *one* opposing no opportunity for the sake of reviling[O]. [15] For some already turned-aside after Satan. [16] If any believing-*woman* has widows, let her be aiding them, and let the church not be burdened in order that it may aid the real widows.

Give Unbiased Church Support And Respect To Elders Leading Well

[17] Let the elders having led well be considered-worthy *of* double[P] honor, especially[Q] the *ones* laboring in word[R] and teaching. [18] For the Scripture says "You shall not muzzle *a* threshing ox" [Deut 25:4], and "The worker *is* worthy *of* his wages" [Lk 10:7]. [19] Do not be accepting *an* accusation against *an* elder unless on the basis of two or three witnesses.

A. Or, urging. **B.** As seen next, Paul means widows dependent on God alone in contrast to those with relatives, or whose character has not demonstrated a relationship to God or His family, or who are of marriageable age. **C.** That is, treat with reverence, show devotion to, respect. **D.** Or, pleasing. **E.** Or, made-alone. **F.** Or, enrolled, enlisted. That is, as financially supported by the church; or, as a deaconess serving the church. **G.** Or, *a* wife *of* one husband. Some think this refers in some sense to marital status; others, to marital fidelity. **H.** Or, showed-hospitality. **I.** That is, declining to put on the list. **J.** That is, such as would bear children, v 14. **K.** That is, desire the pleasures of marriage. Their desire for children and a home will lead them to pursue things other than the service to Christ as a widow to which they pledged themselves. **L.** Or, *the* condemnation that. **M.** Or, lazy, unproductive. **N.** Or, be-master-of-the-house. **O.** Or, insulting, abusing the church or the faith. **P.** Or, two-fold, twice-as-much. **Q.** That is, in contrast to elders excelling in other forms of leadership. **R.** That is, the Word; or, speech.

²⁰ Be rebuking the *ones* sinning in the presence of all^A, in order that the rest also may have fear. ²¹ I solemnly-charge *you* in the sight of God and Christ Jesus and the chosen angels that you keep these *things* without pre-judgment, doing nothing according-to^B partiality^C. ²² Be laying hands^D on no one hastily, nor sharing^E *in the* sins belonging-to-others; be keeping yourself pure. (²³ No longer be-a-water-drinker, but be using *a* little wine for the sake of *your* stomach and your frequent sicknesses). ²⁴ The sins *of* some^F people are clear-beforehand, going ahead-of *them* to judgment, but indeed *for* some they follow-after. ²⁵ Similarly also the good works *are* clear-beforehand, and the *ones* having it otherwise^G are not able to be hidden.

Slaves Are To Honor Their Masters

6:1 Let all-who are under *a* yoke *as* slaves be regarding *their* own masters *as* worthy *of* all honor, in order that the name *of* God and the teaching may not be blasphemed^H. ² And let the *ones* having believing masters not be disregarding *them* because they are brothers, but let them be serving *them* more^I, because the *ones* being helped^J *by* the good-work are believers and beloved *ones*.

Anyone Who Teaches Differently Is Spiritually Diseased And Pursuing Personal Gain

Be teaching and exhorting these *things*. ³ If anyone teaches-different-*doctrines*, and does not come-to^K healthy^L words— the *ones of* our Lord Jesus Christ— and *to* the teaching in accordance with godliness, ⁴ he has become conceited^M, understanding nothing, but being diseased^N with respect to controversies and word-battles, out of which comes envy, strife, blasphemies, evil suspicions, ⁵ constant-frictions, *from* people having been corrupted *as to* the mind and robbed^O *of* the truth, while supposing *that* godliness is *a* means-of-gain. ⁶ Now godliness with contentment **is** *a* means of great gain. ⁷ For we brought-in nothing to the world; *it is clear* that neither can we bring-out anything. ⁸ But having sustenance and coverings, *with* these *things* we shall be content. ⁹ But the *ones* wanting to-be-rich fall into temptation and *a* snare, and many foolish and harmful desires which plunge^P people into ruin and destruction. ¹⁰ For the love-of-money is *a* root^Q *of* all evils— aspiring-to which, some were led-astray^R from the faith and pierced themselves *with* many pains.

But You, O Man of God, Fight The Good Fight And Keep The Command Unspotted

¹¹ But **you,** O man *of* God, be fleeing these *things,* and be pursuing righteousness, godliness, faith, love, endurance, gentleness. ¹² Be fighting the good fight *of* faith. Take-hold-of eternal life, into which you were called, and confessed the good confession in the presence of many witnesses. ¹³ I command you in the sight of God, the *One* giving-life-to all *things*, and Christ Jesus, the *One* having testified the good confession before^S Pontius Pilate, ¹⁴ *that* you keep the commandment unspotted, above-reproach, until the appearance *of* our Lord Jesus Christ, ¹⁵ which *in His*^T own times, the blessed and only

---

A. That is, all the elders; or, all the church. **B.** Or, by way of. **C.** Or, bias, partisanship. **D.** That is, to commission elders; or, to restore elders. **E.** Such is the case if one appoints leaders who turn out to be unqualified due to sin. **F.** That is, some on whom you might consider laying hands. **G.** That is, not openly apparent to people. These works will not stay hidden upon examination. Good character is verifiable. **H.** Or, slandered, insulted, spoken-against. **I.** Or, but rather let them be serving *them*. **J.** Or, benefitting. **K.** That is, agree with. **L.** Or, sound, correct. **M.** Or, clouded with pride. **N.** Or, ailing. **O.** Or, deprived. **P.** Or, sink. **Q.** Or, *the* root *of* all *kinds of* evil. **R.** Or, wandered away. **S.** Or, in the time of. **T.** Or, *its*.

Ruler will show[A]— the King *of* the *ones* being-kings[B] and Lord *of* the *ones* being-lords[C], [16] the only *One* having immortality, dwelling *in* unapproachable light, Whom none *of* mankind saw nor is able to see, *to* Whom *be* honor and eternal dominion, amen.

Command The Rich To Be Rich In Good Works And To Take Hold of Real Life

[17] Be commanding the *ones* rich in the present age not to be-high-minded, nor to have put-hope on *the* uncertainty *of* riches, but upon God, the *One* richly granting us all *things* for enjoyment; [18] to be working-good, to be-rich in good[D] works, to be generous, sharing *ones*, [19] treasuring-up *for* themselves *a* good foundation for the future[E], in order that they may take-hold-of real life.

Guard The Deposit, Timothy

[20] O Timothy, guard the deposit[F], turning-aside-*from* the profane empty-chatterings and opposing-arguments *of* the falsely-named "knowledge"— [21] professing which, some missed-the-mark[G] with respect to the faith. Grace *be* with you[H] *all*.

A. Or, display, exhibit. **B.** Or, reigning. **C.** Or, ruling. **D.** Or, commendable, praiseworthy. **E.** Lit, the *thing* coming. **F.** That is, this book (1:18); or, the ministry entrusted to you; or, the Gospel. **G.** Or, deviated, departed. **H.** This word is plural.

2 Timothy

Introduction   1:1-2

A. I have gratitude to God as I have unceasing remembrance concerning you in my prayers, for   1:3-7
    which reason I am reminding you to rekindle the gift of God in you

B. Therefore do not be ashamed of the testimony of our Lord nor of me His prisoner, but suffer   1:8-18
    hardship with me for the gospel. Be holding the pattern of healthy words which you heard
    from me. Guard the good deposit. You know that all the ones in Asia turned away from me

C. Therefore you, my child, become strong in the grace in Christ Jesus. And the things you heard   2:1-3
    from me, deposit these with faithful people who can teach others. Suffer hardship with me like a
    good soldier of Christ Jesus

    1. No one serving as soldier entangles himself in the affairs of life   2:4-7
    2. Remember Jesus Christ, for whose gospel I suffer hardship that others may obtain   2:8-14
        salvation. If we endure, we will reign with Him
    3. Be diligent to present yourself approved to God as an unashamed worker cutting straight   2:15
        the word of truth

        a. Be shunning empty chatterings. Cleanse yourself of this and be a vessel of honor   2:16-21
        b. Be fleeing youthful desires and pursuing righteousness, love, faith, peace   2:22
        c. Be declining foolish controversies. Correct with gentleness and kindness   2:23-26

    4. But know this— that the last days will be difficult. Turn away from the corrupted ones   3:1-9

D. Now you closely followed my teaching, way of life, persecutions and sufferings for the gospel.   3:10-15
    We will all be persecuted. But you be continuing in the things which you have learned and
    have known since babyhood from the sacred writings

    1. All Scripture is God-breathed and profitable for teaching, training, and equipping   3:16-17

E. I solemnly charge you in the sight of God and Christ— Proclaim the word, rebuke, warn,   4:1-5
    exhort. Be sober, suffer hardship, do the work of an evangelist, fulfill your ministry

    1. For the time of my departure is near. I have fought the good fight   4:6-8

Conclusion   4:9-22

1:1 Paul, *an* apostle *of* Christ Jesus by *the* will *of* God in-relation-to *the* promise *of* life in Christ Jesus, **2** *to* Timothy, beloved child: Grace, mercy, peace from God *the* Father and Christ Jesus our Lord.

I Give Thanks For Your Sincere Faith, And Remind You To Rekindle The Gift of God In You
3 I have gratitude *to* God, Whom I *have* served[A] from *my* ancestors[B] with *a* clean conscience, as I have unceasing remembrance concerning you in my prayers *by* night and *by* day— **4** yearning to see you, having remembered your tears, in order that I may be filled *with* joy; **5** having received *a* reminder *of* the sincere faith in you which first dwelt in your grandmother Lois and your mother Eunice. And I am convinced that *it is* also in you, **6** for which reason I am reminding you to be rekindling[C] the gift *of* God which is in you through the laying-on *of* my hands. **7** For God did not give us *a* spirit *of* fearfulness[D], but *of* power and love and *a* sound-mind[E].

Suffer Hardship With Me For The Gospel. Hold The Teachings In Faith And Love
8 Therefore, do not be[F] ashamed-of the testimony *of* our Lord nor me His prisoner, but suffer-hardship-with *me for* the good-news according-to[G] *the* power *of* God: **9** the *One* having saved us and called *us with*[H] *a* holy calling, not according-to our works but according to *His* own purpose and grace— *it* having been given *to* us in Christ Jesus before eternal times **10** but now having been revealed through the appearance *of* our Savior Christ Jesus, *He* having abolished[I] death and brought-to-light life and immortality through the good-news **11** for which **I** was appointed *a* proclaimer and apostle and teacher, **12** for which reason I also am suffering these *things*. But I am not ashamed, for I know *in* Whom I have believed and am convinced that He is able to guard my deposit until that day. **13** Be holding *the* pattern *of* healthy words which you heard from me in[J] *the* faith and love *which are* in Christ Jesus. **14** Guard the good deposit through *the* Holy Spirit dwelling in us.

    For Some Have Turned Away From Me. But Not All
    15 You know this— that all the *ones* in[K] Asia turned-away-from me, *among* whom are Phygelus and Hermogenes. **16** May the Lord grant mercy *to* the household *of* Onesiphorus, because he often refreshed me and was not ashamed-of my chain, **17** but having come-to-be in Rome, he sought me diligently and found *me*. **18** May the Lord grant him to find mercy from *the* Lord on that day. And **you** know very-well how many *things* he ministered in Ephesus.

Become Strong In Grace, My Child, And Suffer Hardship With Me Like a Good Soldier
2:1 Therefore **you**, my child, become-strong in[L] the grace in Christ Jesus. **2** And *the things* which you heard from me through many witnesses, these *things* deposit[M] *with* faithful people who will be competent[N] to teach others also. **3** Suffer-hardship with *me* like *a* good soldier *of* Christ Jesus.

    Consider the Soldier, Athlete And Farmer
    4 No one while serving-as-a-soldier entangles *himself in* the affairs *of* life, in order that he

---

A. Or, worshiped. **B.** Or, forefathers. **C.** Or, fanning to a flame, keeping in full flame. **D.** Or, timidity, being afraid to act. **E.** Or, sound-judgment; or its result, self-discipline, self-control. **F.** The grammar means, Do not become ashamed, Do not start being ashamed (that is, because of my suffering, v 12; my chain, v 16). **G.** Or, based on, by way of. Likewise twice in v 9. **H.** Or, to. **I.** Or, done away with, rendered powerless. **J.** Or, in-connection-with; in-the-sphere-of. That is, holding... in; or, heard... in. **K.** Or, in-connection-with. Compare 4:16. **L.** Or, by. **M.** Or, entrust *to*. **N.** Or, fit, adequate, worthy, able.

may please the *one* having enlisted *him*. **⁵** And also if one competes [in an athletic contest], he is not crowned unless he competes lawfully. **⁶** The laboring farmer must[A] *be* first to receive-a-share *of* the fruits. **⁷** Be considering what I am saying, for the Lord will give you understanding in everything.

Remember Jesus Christ And The Gospel For Which I Am Imprisoned
⁸ Be remembering Jesus Christ having been raised from *the* dead, from *the* seed *of* David, according to my good-news— **⁹** in connection with which[B] I am suffering-hardship to the point of imprisonment like *a* criminal. Nevertheless the Word *of* God has not been bound[C]! **¹⁰** For this reason, I am enduring all *things* for the sake of the chosen *ones,* in order that **they** also may obtain salvation in Christ Jesus with eternal glory.

If We Endure, We Will Reign With Him. He Will Be Faithful To Us
¹¹ The saying *is* trustworthy— for if we died-with *Him,* we will also live-with *Him;* **¹²** if we are enduring, we will also reign-with *Him;* if we shall deny *Him,* that *One* also will deny us; **¹³** if we are faithless[D], that *One* remains faithful, for He cannot deny Himself. **¹⁴** Be reminding *them* of these *things,* solemnly-warning in the sight of God not to battle-about-words for nothing useful[E], to[F] *the* overthrow[G] *of* the *ones* hearing.

Be Diligent To Present Yourself As an Approved Worker of The Word of Truth
¹⁵ Be diligent to present yourself approved *to* God, *a* worker not-needing-to-be-ashamed, cutting-straight[H] the word *of* truth.

Shun Worthless Talk. Be an Honorable, Useful Vessel Prepared For Good Works
¹⁶ But be shunning the profane[I] empty-chatterings. For they[J] will advance further *in* ungodliness, **¹⁷** and their talk[K] will have *a* spreading like gangrene— *of* whom are Hymenaeus and Philetus, **¹⁸** who missed-the-mark with regard to the truth, saying *that* the resurrection has already taken place, and are overturning[L] the faith *of* some. **¹⁹** Nevertheless, the firm foundation *of* God stands, having this seal— "*The* Lord knows the *ones* being His" and "Let everyone naming the name *of the* Lord depart from unrighteousness". **²⁰** Now in *a* large house there are not only golden and silver vessels, but also wooden and made-of-clay— even some for honor and others for dishonor. **²¹** If then one cleanses himself from these *things,* he will be *a* vessel for honor— having been sanctified[M], useful *to* the Master, having been prepared for every good work.

Flee Youthful Desires. Pursue Righteousness, Faith, Love And Peace
²² And be fleeing the youthful desires, and be pursuing righteousness, faith, love, peace, with the *ones* calling-upon the Lord from *a* pure heart.

A. Or, has to, ought to. Lit, It is necessary *that* the laboring farmer *be* first. **B.** Or, Whom. **C.** That is, imprisoned. **D.** Or, without faith, unfaithful, unbelieving. **E.** Or, beneficial, profitable. That is, for no useful purpose, goal, result. **F.** Or, tending toward, resulting in. **G.** Or, ruin, destruction. **H.** That is, cutting true, accurately handling, as a skilled worker (a stonecutter, a farmer, a roadbuilder) would perform their job. **I.** Or, godless, irreverent, worldly. **J.** That is, those who engage in this profane chattering. **K.** Or, word, message. **L.** Or, upsetting. **M.** Or, made holy, set apart.

Decline Foolish Controversies. Be Kind, Skillful At Teaching, Gentle At Correcting
23 And be declining the foolish and ignorant controversies, knowing that they breed battles. **24** And *a* slave *of the* Lord must not battle, but *must* be kind to everyone, skillful-at-teaching, forbearing[A], **25** correcting the *ones* opposing with gentleness, if perhaps God may grant them repentance leading-to *the* knowledge *of the* truth **26** and they may return-to-*their*-senses from the snare *of* the devil, having been caught[B] by him, for the will *of* that *one*[C].

Know That Difficult Times Will Come, And Turn Away From The Ungodly
3:1 But know this— that during *the* last days difficult[D] times will be present. **2** For the people will be self-lovers, money-lovers, boasters, proud, blasphemous, disobedient *to* parents, ungrateful, unholy, **3** unaffectionate, unreconcilable[E], slanderous, without-self-control, untamed[F], not-lovers-of-good, **4**traitors, reckless, having become conceited, pleasure-lovers rather than God-lovers, **5** holding *a* form *of* godliness but having denied the power *of* it. Indeed, be turning-away-from these *ones*.

For They Deceive The Ignorant And Oppose The Truth
6 For from these are the *ones* creeping into the houses and taking-captive little-women[G]— *women* having been heaped *with* sins, being led *by* various desires, **7** always learning and never being able to come to *the* knowledge *of the* truth. **8** And the way Jannes and Jambres opposed Moses, in this manner these also oppose the truth— people having been corrupted *as to* the mind, disapproved with respect to the faith. **9** But they will not advance further, for their folly will be very-evident *to* everyone, as also the *folly of* those *two* came-to-be[H].

Continue In The Teaching And Lifestyle You Have Seen In Me And Learned From The Scriptures
10 Now **you** closely-followed my teaching, way-of-life, purpose, faith, patience, love, endurance, **11**persecutions, sufferings— such as happened *to* me at Antioch, at Iconium, at Lystra. Such persecutions I endured! And the Lord delivered me out of *them* all! **12** And indeed all the *ones* wanting to live godly in Christ Jesus will be persecuted. **13** And evil people and impostors will advance to the worse, deceiving and being deceived. **14** But **you**, be continuing in *the things* which you learned and were convinced-of, knowing from whom[I] you learned, **15** and that from babyhood you *have* known the sacred writings being able to make you wise for salvation through faith in Christ Jesus!

All Scripture Is God-Breathed, And Profitable For Equipping Us For Good Works
16 All[J] Scripture *is* God-breathed[K], and profitable for teaching, for rebuking[L], for correcting[M], for training[N] in righteousness, **17** in order that the person *of* God may be complete[O], having been equipped for every good work.

A. That is, bearing evil against oneself without resentment. **B.** Or, captured-alive. **C.** Or, that *One*. **D.** Or, hard, hard to bear, troublesome. **E.** That is, unwilling to be reconciled. **F.** Or, savage, brutal. **G.** Paul may be referring negatively to the women, *weak*-women, *silly*-women, *gullible*-women; or, this may be derogatory of the creepers who prey on *helpless*-women, *vulnerable*-women. The following three phrases describe the women. **H.** Or, proved-to-be. **I.** This word is plural. **J.** Or, Every. **K.** That is, God-inspired. **L.** Or, refuting, exposing. **M.** Or, amending, restoring, reforming. **N.** Or, discipline, instruction, education. **O.** Or, proficient, fitted to God's purpose.

I Solemnly Charge You To Proclaim The Word, For People Will Turn Away From The Truth
4:1 I solemnly-charge *you* in the sight of God and Christ Jesus, the *One* going-to judge *the* living and *the* dead, and *by* His appearance and His kingdom— **2** proclaim the Word. Stand-at^A *it* in-season, out-of-season. Rebuke, warn, exhort^B, with all patience and instruction. **3** For there will be *a* time when they will not bear-with healthy teaching, but while itching^C *with respect to* the hearing, they will heap-up teachers *for* themselves in accordance with *their* own desires. **4** And they will turn the hearing away from the truth and be turned-aside to myths. **5** But **you**, be sober in all *things*, suffer-hardship, do *the* work *of an* evangelist, fulfill^D your ministry.

For The Time of My Departure Is Near. I Have Finished My Course
6 For **I** am already being poured-out^E, and the time *of* my departure^F has stood-near^G. **7** I have fought the good fight. I have finished the course. I have kept the faith. **8** Henceforth, the crown *of* righteousness is reserved *for* me, which the Lord, the righteous judge, will render *to* me on that day— and not only *to* me, but also *to* all the *ones* having loved His appearance.

Closing Words
9 Be diligent to come to me quickly. **10** For Demas deserted^H me, having loved the present age^I, and went to Thessalonica. Crescens *has gone* to Galatia, Titus to Dalmatia. **11** Luke only is with me. Having picked-up Mark, bring *him* with yourself, for he is useful *to* me for service. **12** And I sent-forth Tychicus to Ephesus. **13** While coming, bring the cloak which I left-behind in Troas with Carpus, and the books— especially the parchments.

14 Alexander the coppersmith^J showed^K many evil *things against* me— the Lord will render *to* him according to his works— **15** *as to* whom **you** also be guarding *yourself*, for he greatly opposed our words.

16 At my first defense no one was present^L *with* me, but they all deserted me. May it not be counted *against* them. **17** But the Lord stood-by me and strengthened me, in order that through me the proclamation might be fulfilled and all the Gentiles might hear. And I was delivered out of *a* lion's mouth. **18** The Lord will deliver me from every evil work and save^M *me* into His heavenly kingdom— *to* Whom *be* the glory forever and ever, amen.

19 Greet Prisca and Aquila, and the household *of* Onesiphorus. **20** Erastus remained in Corinth, but I left-behind Trophimus sick in Miletus. **21** Be diligent to come before winter. Eubulus greets you, and [so do] Pudens, and Linus, and Claudia, and all the brothers. **22** The Lord *be* with your^N spirit. Grace *be* with you^O *all*.

A. Or, Stand by, and therefore, Attend to, Be ready. **B.** Or, encourage. **C.** Or, being tickled. **D.** Or, accomplish, bring to completion. **E.** Or, offered up. That is, poured out like a drink offering of wine at the foot of the altar, Num 28:7. **F.** That is, death. **G.** Or, is imminent, is impending. **H.** Or, abandoned. **I.** Or, world. **J.** Or, more generally, blacksmith, metalworker. **K.** Or, displayed, declared, exhibited, charged. **L.** Or, stood *by* me, approached *with* me. **M.** Or, bring *me* safely. **N.** This word is singular. **O.** This word is plural.

Titus

Introduction   1:1-4

A.   I left you in Crete in order that you might set straight the things lacking, and appoint elders as I directed you— if one is blameless, a man of one woman, having believing children   1:5-9

    1.   For there are many rebellious ones whom it is necessary to silence. Rebuke them severely   1:10-16

B.   But you be speaking the things fitting for healthy teaching— that old men be sober, that old women be reverent, younger men sound minded, slaves subject   2:1-10

    1.   For the grace of God appeared bringing salvation for all people, instructing us how to live righteously in the present age   2:11-14

    2.   Be speaking these things, and be exhorting, and be rebuking with all authority   2:15

C.   Remind them to be subject to rulers, ready for good works, not quarrelsome but gentle to all   3:1-2

    1.   For we also were once foolish, disobedient, deceived, and slaves to various desires. But when the kindness and love-for-mankind of our Savior God appeared, He saved us   3:3-8

    2.   And concerning these things I want you to be speaking confidently. But be shunning foolish controversies and genealogies and quarrels and battles about the Law   3:8-11

Conclusion   3:12-15

1:1 Paul, *a* slave *of* God and apostle *of* Jesus Christ in-relation-to[A] *the* faith *of the* chosen *ones of* God and *the* knowledge *of the* truth *which is* in-accordance-with[B] godliness, **2** on-the-basis-of *the* hope *of* eternal life which the non-lying God promised before eternal times— **3** but He revealed His word *in His*[C] own times, in *the* proclamation which **I** was entrusted-*with* according-to *the* command *of* our Savior God; **4** *to* Titus, genuine child according-to[D] *a* common[E] faith: Grace and peace from God *the* Father and Christ Jesus our Savior.

Set Things Straight And Appoint Qualified Elders In Each City On Crete
5 For this reason I left you behind in Crete: in order that you might set-straight[F] the *things* lacking[G], and appoint[H] elders in each city as **I** directed you— **6** if one is blameless[I], *a* man *of* one woman[J], having believing children *who are* not under *an* accusation[K] *of* wild-living or rebellious *ones*. **7** For the overseer must be blameless as God's steward[L], not self-willed[M], not quick-tempered, not *a* drunken *one*, not *a* brawler, not fond-of-shameful[N]-gain, **8** but hospitable, *a* lover-of-good, sound-minded[O], just[P], holy, self-controlled, **9** holding-on-to[Q] the faithful word in accordance with the teaching, so that he may be able both to exhort with[R] healthy teaching and refute[S] the *ones* contradicting[T].

For There Are Many Deceivers Teaching Falsehood For Personal Gain
10 For there are indeed many rebellious *ones,* worthless-talkers[U], and deceivers— especially the *ones* from the circumcision— **11** whom it-is-necessary to silence, who are overturning whole households, teaching *things* which *they* ought not to *teach* for the sake of shameful gain. **12** One of them, their own prophet[V], said "Cretans *are* always liars[W], evil beasts, lazy gluttons". **13** This testimony is true. For which reason, be rebuking them severely in order that they may be healthy in the faith, **14** not paying-attention-to Jewish myths and commandments *of* people turning-away-from the truth. **15** All *things are* clean[X] *to* the clean. But *to* the *ones* having been defiled[Y] and *who are* unbelieving, nothing *is* clean, but both their mind and conscience have been defiled. **16** They are confessing to know God, but *by their* works they are denying *Him,* being detestable and disobedient and disapproved[Z] for every good work.

Speak Healthy Teaching To All Groups of People
2:1 But **you** be speaking *the things* which are fitting[Z1] *for* healthy teaching— **2** *that* old-men[Z2] be sober[Z3], honorable[Z4], sound-minded, being healthy *in* faith, *in* love, *in* endurance; **3** *that* old-women similarly *be* reverent in behavior, not slanderous, not having been enslaved *to* much wine, teachers-of-good[Z5], **4** in order that they may train the young *women* to be husband-lovers[Z6], children-lovers, **5** sound-minded, pure, working-at-home[Z7], good, while being subject

---

A. Or, in the interest of, for. **B.** Or, leading to. **C.** Or, *its*. **D.** Or, in relation to, based on, in the interest of. **E.** Or, shared. **F.** Or, set in order, correct. **G.** Or, falling short. **H.** Or, put in charge. **I.** Or, 'unaccused' of doing wrong. **J.** Or, husband *of* one wife. Some think this refers in some sense to marital status; others, to marital fidelity. **K.** Or, charge. **L.** Or, household manager, administrator. **M.** Or, stubborn, obstinate, self-pleasing. **N:** -shameful. Or, -dishonorable-, -dishonest-. **O.** Or, prudent, moderate, temperate. **P.** That is, law-abiding, observant of right. **Q.** Or, being-devoted-to. **R.** Or, in, by. **S.** Or, correct, rebuke. **T.** Or, opposing, speaking-against. **U.** That is, ones talking of worthless, futile, vain, pointless things. **V.** Paul quotes Epimenides, a Cretan poet/philosopher born in 659 B.C. **W.** The Cretans were notorious for lying. **X.** Or, pure. **Y.** Or, stained, polluted. **Z.** Or, rejected, disqualified. **Z1.** Or, proper. **Z2:** old men... old women. These words refer to what we call middle-aged and senior people, the generations that should be an example to the younger generation. **Z3.** Or, serious, temperate. **Z4.** Or, dignified, worthy of respect. **Z5.** Or, teaching-what-is-good. **Z6.** Or, husband-loving. Likewise next. **Z7.** The emphasis is on working, on not being idle busybodies (compare 1 Tim 5:13).

to *their* own husbands, in order that the word *of* God may not be blasphemed. 6 Be exhorting
the younger *men* similarly to be sound-minded 7 with-respect-to all *things*[A], while showing[B]
yourself *as a* pattern *of* good works— in *your* teaching *showing* uncorruptness[C], dignity, 8 healthy
uncondemnable[D] speech— in order that the *one* from *the* contrary *side* may be ashamed, having
nothing bad to say about us. 9 *Be exhorting* slaves to be subject *to their* own masters in all
things[E], to be pleasing, not contradicting, 10 not pilfering, but demonstrating all good faith[F], in
order that they may adorn the teaching *of* our Savior God in all *things*.

For Salvation Trains Us To Live Righteously And Godly As Zealots For Good Works

11 For the grace *of* God appeared[G] *bringing*-salvation *for* all people, 12 training us that
having denied ungodliness and worldly desires, we should live sound-mindedly[H] and
righteously and godly in the present age, 13 while waiting-for the blessed hope and
appearance *of* the glory *of* our great God and Savior Jesus Christ, 14 Who gave Himself for
us in order that He might redeem us from all lawlessness and cleanse *for* Himself *a* special[I]
people— zealots[J] *for* good works.

Speak With Authority; Let No One Disregard You

15 Be speaking these *things*, and be exhorting, and be rebuking with all authority. Let no one be disregarding you.

Remind Everyone How To Behave Toward Other People

3:1 Be reminding them to be subject *to* rulers, *to* authorities; to be obedient[K]; to be ready for
every good work; 2 to blaspheme no one; to be non-quarrelsome, kind, demonstrating all
gentleness toward all people.

For We Also Were Once Foolish And Deceived, But God Saved Us By His Mercy And Grace

3 For **we** also were once foolish[L], disobedient, being deceived, being-slaves[M] *to* various
desires and pleasures, spending *life* in malice and envy, detested[N], hating one another. 4 But
when the kindness and love-for-mankind *of* our Savior God appeared, 5 **He saved us**[O]—
not by works which **we** did in [our] righteousness, but according-to[P] His mercy, through
a washing[Q] *of*[R] regeneration[S] and *a* renewing[T] *of*[U] *the* Holy Spirit, 6 Whom He richly
poured-out upon us through Jesus Christ our Savior, 7 in order that having been declared-
righteous *by* the grace *of* that *One*, we might become heirs according-to[V] *the* hope *of*
eternal life. 8 The saying *is* trustworthy.

Speak With Confidence, So That Believers Take The Lead In Good Works

And concerning these *things* I want you to be speaking-confidently, in order that the *ones*

A. Or, sound-minded, while with respect to all *things* showing. **B.** Or, presenting, offering. **C.** Or, lack of corruption, and thus, soundness, purity. **D.** That is, not blameworthy. **E.** Or, masters, to be pleasing in all *things*. **F.** Or, faithfulness, fidelity. **G.** Or, showed-itself, made its appearance. Or, the grace *of* God *bringing*-salvation appeared *for* all people. **H.** Or, sensibly, moderately, prudently. **I.** Or, chosen. **J.** Or, zealous. **K.** That is, to obey ones in authority. **L.** Or, senseless, without-understanding. **M.** Or, serving-as-slaves. **N.** Or, loathed; or, detestable, loathsome; or, hateful. **O.** In the Greek word order, this comes after 'mercy'. It has Paul's emphasis. **P.** Or, based-on, by-way-of. **Q.** Or, bath. **R.** That is, a spiritual washing consisting of, proceeding from; or, a water baptism leading to. **S.** Or, rebirth. **T.** Or, renewal. **U.** That is, proceeding from, performed by. **V.** Or, with respect to, based on, in accordance with.

having believed *in* God may be careful[A] to take-the-lead[B] *in* good works. These *things* are good and profitable *for* people. **9** But be shunning foolish[C] controversies and genealogies and quarrels and battles pertaining-to-the-Law. For they are unprofitable and worthless[D]. **10** Be declining[E] *a* divisive person after *a* first and second admonition, **11** knowing that such *a one* has been perverted[F] and is sinning, being self-condemned.

12 When I send Artemas or Tychicus to you, be diligent to come to me in Nicopolis, for I have determined to spend-the-winter there. **13** Diligently[G] send-forward[H] Zenas the lawyer[I] and Apollos, in order that nothing may be lacking *for* them. **14** And let our *people* also be learning to take-the-lead[J] *in* good works for necessary[K] needs, in order that they may not be unfruitful. **15** All the *ones* with me greet you. Greet the *ones* loving us in *the* faith. Grace *be* with you all.

A. Or, be intent, be concerned, give thought. **B.** Or, busy *themselves with.* **C.** Or, stupid, silly. **D.** Or, useless, pointless, futile. **E.** Or, refusing, and therefore, rejecting, avoiding. **F.** Or, turned-aside, turned-from [the right path]. **G.** Or, Urgently. **H.** Or, accompany. **I.** Or, law-expert. Whether Paul is referring to Jewish law or Roman law is unclear. **J.** See v 8. **K.** Or, indispensible, pressing, required.

Philemon

Introduction 1-3

A.   I am making mention of you in my prayers so the fellowship of your faith may become effective   4-7

B.   Therefore, although having boldness to command you, I rather am appealing to you for Onesimus 8-16

C.   Therefore, if you hold me as a partner, accept him as me. May I profit from you in the Lord   17-20

Conclusion 21-25

[1] Paul[A], *a* prisoner *of* Christ Jesus, and Timothy *our* brother, *to* Philemon, our beloved *one* and fellow-worker, [2] and *to* Apphia *our* sister, and *to* Archippus our fellow-soldier, and *to* the church at your house: [3] Grace *to* you and peace from God our Father and *the* Lord Jesus Christ.

I Thank God For Your Love, And Pray That Your Faith May Become Effective
[4] I am giving-thanks *to* my God always while[B] making mention *of* you in my prayers, [5] hearing-*of* your love and the faith[C] which you have toward the Lord Jesus and for all the saints, [6] so that the fellowship[D] *of*[E] your faith may become effective[F] in[G] *the* knowledge *of* every good *thing* in us for Christ. [7] For I had much joy and encouragement in your love, because the deep-feelings *of* the saints have been refreshed through you, brother.

A. On when this book was written, see Act 28:30. **B.** Or, while always. **C.** Or, faithfulness. Some regroup this as 'your love for all the saints and the faith which you have toward the Lord Jesus'. **D.** Or, participation, contribution, communion, sharing; or, the material contribution, generosity. **E.** Or, *with, springing from, produced by.* **F.** Or, powerful, productive. Or, active, operative. **G.** Or, by.

I Appeal To You For Onesimus, Your Slave And Our Beloved Brother
8 Therefore, [although] having much boldness in Christ to be commanding you *to do* the fitting *thing*, **9** for the sake of love I am rather appealing— being such *a one* as Paul, *an* old-man[A], and now also *a* prisoner *of* Christ Jesus. **10** I am appealing to you concerning my child whom I fathered in *my* imprisonment, Onesimus,**11** the *one* formerly useless[B] *to* you but now useful both *to* you and *to* me, **12** whom I sent-back *to* you (him! That is, my *own* deep-feelings[C]!), **13** whom **I** was wishing to hold-back with myself in order that on behalf of you he might be serving me in *my* imprisonment *for* the good-news. **14** But without your consent I wanted to do nothing, in order that your good *deed* should not be as-*if* based-on[D] compulsion[E], but based-on willingness[F]. **15** For perhaps for this reason he was separated for *an* hour: in order that you might receive him in full forever, **16** no longer as *a* slave, but beyond *a* slave, *a* beloved brother— especially *to* me, but how much more *to* you, both in *the* flesh and in *the* Lord!

Accept Him As Me, And Charge His Debts To My Account
17 Therefore if you hold me *as a* partner, accept him as me. **18** And if *as to* anything he wronged[G] you or owes *you*, charge this *to* my account— **19** I, Paul, wrote *this with* my *own* hand, **I** will repay— in order that I may not be saying *to* you that you indeed owe[H] yourself *to* me! **20** Yes, brother, may **I** profit[I] *from* you in *the* Lord. Refresh my deep-feelings in Christ.

I Have Confidence In Your Response, And Hope To See You Soon
21 I wrote *to* you having confidence *in* your obedience, knowing that you will do even beyond *the things* which I am saying. **22** And at the same time also, prepare lodging *for* me, for I hope that through your prayers I shall be granted *to* you. **23** Epaphras, my fellow-captive in Christ Jesus, greets you, **24** *as do* Mark, Aristarchus, Demas, Luke, my fellow-workers. **25** The grace *of* the Lord Jesus Christ *be* with your spirit.

A. Or, *an* ambassador. **B.** This is a play on words. The name Onesimus means 'useful'. **C.** Onesimus represents Paul's own deep feelings (or, heart) sent back to Philemon to be 'refreshed' (v 20). **D.** Or, by-way-of. **E.** Or, force, necessity. **F.** Or, voluntary-choice. **G.** Or, harmed. **H.** In other words, I will repay any debt of his so that the issue does not arise, because if you hold Onesimus responsible for any debt to you, I will be forced to speak to you about the even greater debt you owe to me. **I.** Or, may I be favored *by* you; may I benefit *from* you.

Hebrews

A. God, having spoken long ago by the prophets, spoke to us in these latter days by a Son — 1:1-2

  1. Who, being the radiance of His glory and exact representation of His essence, having made purification of sins, sat down on high, having become better than the angels — 1:3-4

    a. For God calls Him His own Son, and commands the angels to worship Him — 1:5-6
    b. And God says the Son will rule forever — 1:7-12
    c. And God is making all the Son's enemies His footstool — 1:13-14

  2. For this reason we must pay attention to what we have heard, that we may not drift away — 2:1-4
  3. For God did not subject to angels the coming world, but we see Jesus crowned with glory and honor because of the suffering of death — 2:5-9
  4. For it was fitting for God to perfect the Author of our salvation through sufferings — 2:10-13

    a. So the Son took on blood and flesh that through death He might defeat the devil — 2:14-16
    b. The Son became our merciful high priest so as to make an offering for our sins — 2:17-18

  5. Hence, brothers, consider Jesus as faithful to God. He is worthy of more glory than Moses — 3:1-6
  6. Therefore "Today, do not harden your hearts against God as Israel did in the wilderness" — 3:7-11

    a. Watch that there will never be an evil heart of unbelief in you in departing from God — 3:12-19
    b. Let us fear lest any of you should seem to have come short of entering His rest — 4:1-10
    c. Let us be diligent to enter that rest. For the word of God is living and effective — 4:11-13

B. Therefore having a great High Priest— Jesus, the Son of God— let us hold on to the confession. For we have One tempted like us, without sin. So let us be approaching to receive grace — 4:14-16

  1. For every human priest is appointed to offer gifts and sacrifices for sin — 5:1-4
  2. So also, Christ was appointed by God — 5:5-8
  3. And having been perfected, He became the cause of eternal salvation to all obeying Him, having been designated as High Priest according to the order of Melchizedek — 5:9-10

    a. Concerning whom, our message is great and hard to explain to you — 5:11

      i. For although you ought to be teachers, you again need to be taught the milk — 5:12-14
      ii Therefore let us be carried on to maturity, not again laying the foundation — 6:1-2
      iii. And this we will do if God permits. For it is impossible to renew to repentance those having fallen aside, crucifying Him again and publicly disgracing Him — 6:3-8
      iv. But concerning you, we are convinced of better things, of your salvation. But we desire you to be imitators of those who inherit the promises through faith — 6:9-20

    b. For this Melchizedek remains a priest perpetually. Observe how great he is — 7:1-4

      i. He collected a tithe from Abraham. He is greater than Abraham — 7:5-7
      ii. He serves a priest perpetually, unlike the Levitical priests — 7:8
      iii. Levi paid a tithe to him through Abraham. He is greater than Levi — 7:9-10

    c. Now what need was there for another priesthood? It indicates a setting aside of the old one and a bringing in of a better hope through which we draw near to God — 7:11-19
    d. And His priesthood has God's oath-swearing, so Jesus guarantees a better covenant — 7:20-22
    e. And unlike Levitical priests, He remains forever. Hence He can save completely — 7:23-25
    f. For such a High Priest was fitting for us— having offered Himself once for all — 7:26-28

4. The main point is that we have such a High Priest, minister in the true tabernacle of God — 8:1-2

   a. Now indeed, if He were on earth He would not be a priest according to the Law — 8:3-5
   b. But He has obtained a more excellent ministry as mediator of a better covenant — 8:6

      i. For if that first covenant was faultless, God would not have made a second — 8:7-13
      ii. Now indeed, the first covenant had its ministry, which is unable to perfect us — 9:1-10
      iii. But Christ entered the heavenly tabernacle once for all by His own blood — 9:11-14
      iv. And for this reason He is mediator of a new covenant, so that we may receive the promise of the eternal inheritance, a death having occurred for redemption — 9:15-28
      v. For the Law is never able to perfect us through the yearly sacrifice. Therefore Jesus came and God did so through the offering of His body once for all — 10:1-10
      vi. And every priest stands offering daily sacrifices unable to take away sins. Jesus offered one sacrifice for all time and sat down, having perfected us — 10:11-14
      vii. And the Spirit also testifies to us, for there is no longer an offering for sin — 10:15-18

5. Therefore, having confidence to enter by His blood and a great High Priest, let us be approaching with a true heart in full assurance of faith. Let us be holding on to the confession of our hope and provoking one another to love and good works — 10:19-25

   a. For if we disregard Jesus, no sacrifice for sin remains, only fearful judgment — 10:26-31

C. Now remember the former days when you endured a great struggle of sufferings. For indeed you accepted your plundering with joy. Do not throw away your confidence. For you have need of endurance by faith in order that you may receive the promise — 10:32-39

  1. Now faith is the assurance of the things being hoped. In this the elders were attested — 11:1-2

    a. In the early times: Abel, Enoch, Noah — 11:3-7
    b. In the time of the patriarchs: Abraham, Isaac, Jacob, Joseph — 11:8-22
    c. In the time of the Exodus: Moses, Joshua, Rahab — 11:23-31
    d. What more shall I say? For time will fail me if I tell about all the rest — 11:32-38
    e. These all lived by faith, and died not yet receiving the promise — 11:39-40

  2. So therefore let us run our race with endurance, looking to Jesus who endured the cross — 12:1-2

    a. For consider He having endured such opposition, that you may not lose heart — 12:3-4
    b. And have you forgotten the Lord's discipline? You are enduring as sons — 12:5-11

  3. Therefore, straighten up your feeble knees, and make straight paths for your feet — 12:12-13

    a. Be pursuing peace and the holiness without which no one will see the Lord. For you have not come to a mountain being touched, but to the heavenly Jerusalem. Watch out that you do not refuse the One warning from heaven — 12:14-29
    b. Let brotherly love continue. Do not forget hospitality. Remember the prisoners. Let marriage be honored by all. Let character be without the love of money. — 13:1-6
    c. Remember the ones leading you. Do not be carried away by strange teachings. We have a spiritual altar. Let us go out to Him and offer a sacrifice of praise — 13:7-16
    d. Be obeying and yielding to the ones leading you — 13:17
    e. Be praying for us — 13:18-19

  4. Now may the God of peace prepare you in every good thing so that you may do His will — 13:20-21

Conclusion — 13:22-25

God Has Spoken To Us Through Not a Prophet, But a Son
1:1 God, having spoken long-ago in-many-portions and in-many-ways *to* the fathers by the prophets, **²** spoke *to* us at *the* last^A *of* these days by *a* Son^B, Whom He appointed inheritor *of* all *things,* through Whom also He made the worlds^C,

The Son Sat Down At God's Right Hand, Having Become Better Than Angels
³ ...Who— being *the* radiance^D *of His* glory and exact-representation^E *of* His essence^F, and upholding all *things by* the word *of* ^G His power— having made purification *of* sins, sat-*down* at *the* right *hand of* the Majesty on high, **⁴** having become so-much better *than* the angels *by*-as-much-as He has inherited *a* more-excellent name than they.

For God Commands The Angels To Worship His Son
⁵ For *to* which *of* the angels did He ever say "**You** are my Son. Today **I** have fathered you"? [Ps 2:7]; and again, "**I** will be *a* father *to* Him, and **He** will be *a* son *to* Me"? [1 Chron 17:13]. **⁶** And again^H, when He brings the Firstborn into the world He says [in Deut 32:43] "And let all *the* angels *of* God give-worship *to* Him".

And God Says His Son Will Rule Forever Over What He Created
⁷ And with regard to the angels He says [in Ps 104:4] "The *One* making His angels winds and His ministers *a* flame *of* ¹ fire". **⁸** But with regard to the Son *He says:*

"Your throne, God^J, *is* forever and ever. And the scepter *of*^K straightness^L *is the* scepter *of* Your kingdom. **⁹** You loved righteousness and hated lawlessness. For this reason God, your God, anointed You *with the* oil *of* gladness beyond Your companions" [Ps 45:6-7].

¹⁰ And, "You^M, Lord, laid-the-foundation-of the earth at *the* beginnings, and the heavens are works *of* Your hands. **¹¹** **They** will perish, but **You** continue^N. Indeed they will all become-old like *a* garment, **¹²** and You will roll them up as-if *a* cloak. They will indeed be changed like *a* garment. But **You** are the same, and Your years will not end" [Ps 102:25-27].

And God Will Make His Son's Enemies His Footstool
¹³ And with regard to which *of* the angels has He ever said "Be sitting on My right *side* until I put Your enemies *as a* footstool *of* Your feet"? [Ps 110:1]. **¹⁴** Are they not all ministering spirits being sent-forth for service for the sake of the *ones* going to inherit salvation?

Therefore We Must Pay More Attention To What God Said Through His Son
2:1 For this reason^O, we must pay more attention to the *things* having been heard, that we

---

A. Or, end. **B.** That is, one whose essential quality is that He is God's Son (as in 3:6; 5:8; 7:28), not just a prophet. **C.** Or, ages. That is, the universe of time and space. **D.** Or, reflection. **E.** As the imprint matches the die, so Christ matches the very 'essence' of God. **F.** Or, substance, actual being, reality. **G.** That is, characterized by; His powerful word. **H.** Or, And when He again brings. **I.** That is, characterized by; a fiery flame. **J.** The Son is addressed as God here; as Lord in v 10. The angels, who serve, are compared to the Son, who rules forever. **K.** That is, characterized by. **L.** That is, moral straightness; uprightness. **M.** That is, the Son. The created angels are compared to the Son who created the universe and will bring it to an end. **N.** Or, remain continually. **O.** That is, because God spoke (1:2) and because of who the Son is (1:3-14).

may not-ever drift-away. **²** For if the word having been spoken through angels proved-to-be firm, and every transgression and disobedience received *a* just penalty, **³** how shall **we** escape, having neglected^A **so great** *a* salvation?— which, having begun to be spoken by the Lord, was confirmed to^B us by the *ones* having heard, **⁴** God testifying-with both signs and wonders and various miracles and distributions *of the* Holy Spirit according to His will.

For The Coming World Is Subject To Jesus, Who Tasted Death For All And Was Crowned
⁵ For He^C did not subject *to* **angels** the coming world concerning which we are speaking. **⁶** But one solemnly-testified somewhere saying, "What is man that You remember^D him, or *the* son^E *of* man that You look-after him? **⁷** You made him lower^F than angels *for* a little^G *while*. You crowned him *with* glory and honor. **⁸** You subjected all *things* under his feet" [Ps 8:4-6]. For^H in the subjecting all *things to* him, He left **nothing** not-subject *to* him. But now we do not yet see all *things* having been subjected *to* **him**. **⁹** But^I we see the *One* having been made lower than angels *for* a little *while*— Jesus— having been crowned *with* glory and honor because-of the suffering *of* the death, so-that *by the* grace *of* God He might taste death for everyone.

For It Was Fitting For God To Perfect The Author of Salvation Through Sufferings
¹⁰ For it was fitting^J *for* Him^K for-the-sake-of Whom *are* all *things* and through Whom *are* all *things, that in* bringing many sons to glory *He should* perfect^L the Author^M *of* their salvation through sufferings. **¹¹** For both the *One* making-holy and the *ones* being made holy *are* all from one *Father^N*, for which reason He is not ashamed to be calling them **brothers**, **¹²** saying "I will declare Your name *to* My brothers. I will sing-praise to You in *the* midst *of the* congregation" [Ps 22:22]; **¹³** and again [in Isa 8:17], "**I** will be trusting^O in Him"; and again [in Isa 8:18], "Behold— I and the children whom God gave *to* Me".

So The Son Took On Mortal Flesh And Died To Release Us From The Power of Death
¹⁴ Therefore, since the children have shared *of* blood and flesh, He Himself also similarly partook *of* the same *things* in order that through death He might do-away-with^P the *one* having the power *of* death (that is, the devil), **¹⁵** and release these: all-who *by the* fear *of* death were subject-to^Q slavery through all *their* living. **¹⁶** For He surely does not take-hold-of^R angels, but He takes hold of *the* seed *of* Abraham.

He Had To Become Like Us In All Things In Order To Become a Merciful High Priest
¹⁷ Hence, He had-to become-like *His* brothers in all *things* in order that He might become *a* **merciful** and faithful High Priest *in the things* pertaining to God, so as to

---

A. Or, paid no concern *to*, been careless *of.* **B.** Or, for. **C.** That is, God. The writer continues his description of the Son. Rulership was not given to angels. **D.** That is, keep him in mind for his benefit. **E.** The OT verse is an example of Hebrew parallelism, so this may mean the same as 'man' earlier; humanity or the offspring of humanity. The writer then applies this OT quote to Christ in v 9. Or, Son *of* Man, referring to Jesus; the writer applies this quote to Christ beginning right here. In this case, 'his' and 'him' in v 7-8 refer to Jesus. **F.** That is, in physical status, being mortal. **G.** Or, *a* little bit lower than angels. **H.** The writer draws his point from the psalm. God did not subject the coming world to angels, for He left nothing not subject to man (or, to Jesus). **I.** The writer contrasts the present lack of fulfillment in man (or in Jesus, referring to His presently unsubdued enemies) to the present fulfillment in Jesus. **J.** Or, suitable, proper. **K.** That is, God. **L.** Or, complete, finish. **M.** Or, Beginner, Originator, Founder. **N.** Or, *ancestor* (Adam or Abraham); or, *nature* (blood and flesh, v 14). **O.** The Messiah shares our trust in the Father. **P.** Or, render-powerless. **Q.** Or, held-in. **R.** That is, to help.

make-an-offering-for-satisfaction[A] [of God's wrath] *as to* the sins *of* the people. **18** For having Himself[B] been tempted[C] in what He has suffered, He is able to help the *ones* being tempted.

So Consider Jesus As Faithful, Like Moses. But He Is Worthy of More Glory Than Moses
3:1 Hence[D] holy brothers, partakers[E] *of a* heavenly calling, consider[F] the Apostle and High Priest *of* our confession— Jesus— **2** *as* being faithful[G] *to* the *One* having appointed Him, as also *was* Moses in His[H] whole house. **3** For this *One* has been considered-worthy *of* **more** glory than Moses— to the degree that the *One*[I] having built *the house* has more honor *than* the house.

For Moses Was Faithful As a Servant, But Christ Was Faithful As a Son
4 For every house is built by someone, but[J] the *One*[K] having built all *things is* God. **5** And **Moses** *was* faithful in His[L] whole house as *a* servant[M], for[N] *a* testimony *of* the *things which* will[O] be spoken. **6** But Christ *was faithful* as *a* Son over His house, whose house **we** are, if-indeed we hold-on-to *our* confidence and *our* boast *of* the hope.

Therefore Do Not Harden Your Hearts As Israel Once Did
7 Therefore, just as the Holy Spirit says[P] [in Ps 95:7-11]: "Today, if you hear His voice, **8** do not harden your hearts as in the rebellion during the day *of* testing in the wilderness, **9** where your fathers tested *Me* with *a* trial and saw My works **10** *for* forty years. Therefore I was-angry *with* this generation and said, 'They are always going-astray *in* the heart, and **they** did not know My ways'. **11** As I swore in My wrath, they will *never*[Q] enter into My rest".

Watch Out For an Evil Heart of Unbelief As Long As It Is Called "Today"
12 Be watching-out, brothers, so that there will not-ever be in any *of* you *an* evil heart *of* unbelief in departing[R] from *the* living God. **13** But be exhorting yourselves each day, as long as it is called "Today", in order that none of you may be hardened *by the* deceitfulness *of* sin.

For We Are Partakers of Christ If We Hold On Until The End
14 For we have become[S] partakers[T] *of* Christ if-indeed we hold-on-to the beginning *of* our assurance[U] firm until *the* end— **15** in *that it* is[V] said [in Ps 95:7-8]: "Today, if you hear His voice, do not harden your hearts as in the rebellion".

A. Or, make-propitiation. That is, make a sacrificial offering to satisfy God's wrath against sin and gain His mercy. Jesus offered Himself, 7:27; 9:26. Compare Rom 3:25. **B.** Or, For having been tempted in what He Himself has suffered. **C.** Or, tested. **D.** This begins the conclusion and application of 1:1-2:18. **E.** Or, partners, sharers. **F.** Or, think carefully about. **G.** Jesus did not die an unfortunate death. He was faithful to what God appointed Him to do, just like Moses. **H.** That is, in God's whole household. Or, Moses in his whole house. **I.** That is, Jesus, making Him the builder of the house of which Moses was a part. Or, the *one*, referring to a general proverb which illustrates the magnitude of Christ's glory. **J.** Or, and. **K.** That is, the Son, the builder of the house (v 3), naming Him God; or, the Father, who is building His house through the Son. **L.** That is, God's. Or, his. **M.** Or, freely serving assistant (not a slave). God used this term of Moses in Num 12:7. **N.** That is, to give. **O.** That is, in future days when the types given to Moses become reality in the Messiah. **P.** The writer concludes this section by quoting from Ps 95 and applying it to the subject at hand. **Q.** Lit, if they will enter. This is the conclusion of a Hebrew oath, May [?] happen to me if they will enter. **R.** Or, withdrawing, deserting. **S.** The grammar means have become and continue to be. **T.** Or, partners *of*, sharers *in*. **U.** That is, our initial subjective confidence in God; or, the objective hope in which we initially believed. **V.** That is, in light of it being said; or, while it is being said. We must hold on until the end because the psalm says as long as it is called

For Israel Did Not Enter God's Rest Because of Unbelief
16 For who having heard rebelled? But *was it* not all the *ones* having come out of Egypt through Moses? **17** And *with* whom was He angry *for* forty years? *Was it* not *with* the *ones* having sinned, whose corpses fell in the wilderness? **18** And *to* whom did He swear *that they* will not enter into His rest, except *to* the *ones* having disobeyed? **19** And we see that they were not able to enter because of unbelief.

Fear Falling Short of Entering God's Promised Rest
4:1 Therefore, let us fear that at any time while *a* promise to enter into His rest *is* left-remaining [open], any of you should seem to have come-short[A]— **2** for indeed, we have had-good-news-announced[B], just as those[C] also.

In Moses' Day Only Those Who Believed Entered The Promised Physical Rest
But the word[D] *of* hearing did not profit those *ones*, they[E] not having been united *in* faith *with* the *ones*[F] having heard. **3** For we, the *ones* having believed[G], enter into the rest, just as He has said: "As I swore in My wrath, they shall *never* enter into My rest" [Ps 95:11].

And Yet God's Rest Began On The Seventh Day, Not In Moses' Day
And-yet, *His* works have been done since *the* foundation *of the* world. **4** For He has spoken somewhere about the seventh *day* as follows: "And God rested on the seventh day from all His works" [Gen 2:2], **5** and in this [Ps 95:11] again: "They shall *never* enter into My rest".

And David Still Calls Us To Enter God's Rest "Today"
6 Since then it remains *that* some *may* enter into it, and the *ones* formerly having had-good-news-announced *to them* did not enter because of disobedience, **7** He again designates *a* certain day— "Today"— saying by[H] David after so much time just as it has been said-before: "Today, if you hear His voice, do not harden your hearts" [Ps 95:7-8]. **8** For if Joshua had given them rest, He would not be speaking after these *things* about **another** day[I].

So God's Spiritual Rest Remains Open For Us To Enter
9 Therefore *a* Sabbath-rest remains *for* the people *of* God. **10** For the *one* having entered into His rest also himself rested from his works, just as God *did* from *His* own.

Be Diligent To Enter His Rest, For God Knows Your Heart
11 Therefore, let us be diligent to enter into that[J] rest, in order that no one may fall in

---

'Today' we must not harden our hearts. **A.** That is, due to unbelief. What is said negatively here is said positively in v 11. **B.** That is, the word spoken by God about His Son (1:2), to which we must pay more attention (2:1). **C.** That is, those in Moses' day. **D.** That is, their subjective hearing of the message. Or, the objective message itself which they heard. **E.** That is, Moses' generation. **F.** That is, heard in faith; Moses, Joshua, and Caleb. **G.** Then as now, we enter by faith; we are excluded by unbelief. **H.** Or, in David; in the Psalms. **I.** If the rest was merely a physical rest in Moses' day, David would not be offering it 'Today' in the psalm. **J.** That is, the rest mentioned in v 1 and proven to exist in v 3-10.

the same example *of* disobedience. **¹²** For the word *of* God *is* living and effective^A and sharper than any double-edged sword, and piercing as-far-as *the* division *of* soul and spirit, and joints and marrows, and able-to-judge *the* thoughts and intentions *of the* heart^B. **¹³** And there is no creation^C hidden in His sight, but all *things are* naked and having been laid-open^D *to* His eyes to Whom the account *will be given by* us.

Jesus The Son of God Is Our Great High Priest

¹⁴ Therefore, having *a* great High Priest having gone through the heavens^E— Jesus, the Son *of* God— let us be holding-on-to the confession. **¹⁵** For we do not have *a* high priest not being able to sympathize-with our weaknesses, but *One* having been tempted^F in all *things*^G in accordance with *our* likeness, without sin. **¹⁶** So let us be approaching the throne *of* grace with confidence^H, in order that we may receive mercy and find grace for well-timed^I help.

High Priests Are Called By God From Among Men To Offer Sacrifices For Sins

5:1 For every high priest being taken from-*among* men is appointed for people *in* the *things* pertaining to God, in order that he might offer both gifts and sacrifices for sins— **²** being able to deal-gently *with* the *ones* being ignorant and going-astray since he himself is also surrounded *with* weakness. **³** And because of it^J, he is obligated to be offering *sacrifices* for sins— just as for the people, so also for himself. **⁴** And one does not take the honor *to* himself, but *receives it* being called by God, just as also Aaron.

So Also Jesus Was Made High Priest By God

⁵ So also, Christ did not glorify Himself to become High Priest, but the *One* having said to Him [in Ps 2:7] "**You** are My Son. Today **I** have fathered You" *did,* **⁶** just as also in another *place* He says "You *are a* priest forever according to the order *of* Melchizedek" [Ps 110:4],

Although Being a Son, He Learned Obedience From His Sufferings

⁷ ... Who, in the days *of* His flesh^K having offered both petitions and supplications^L with *a* strong outcry and tears to the *One* being able to save Him from^M death^N, and having been heard because of *His* reverence^O, **⁸** although being *a* Son^P, learned obedience from *the things* which He suffered^Q.

And Jesus Became The Cause of Salvation, As High Priest In The Order of Melchizedek

⁹ And having been perfected^R, He became *the* cause^S of eternal salvation *to* all the *ones* obeying Him, **¹⁰** having been designated^T by God *as* High Priest according to the order *of* Melchizedek—

A. Or, at-work, in-operation. **B.** Thus, God can distinguish between unbelief and genuine faith. **C.** Or, creature. **D.** Or, laid-bare, exposed. **E.** That is, back to His throne, 1:3. **F.** Or, tested. **G.** Or, *respects.* **H.** Or, boldness, freedom of speech. **I.** Or, opportune, seasonable, strategic. **J.** That is, his weakness. **K.** Or, in His days *of* the flesh. **L.** Or, pleadings. **M.** Or, out of. **N.** That is, peril of death; or, dying; or, physical death (through resurrection). **O.** Or, piety, devotion, godly fear. **P.** That is, One whose essential quality is that He is God's own Son. **Q.** Jesus learned obedience to God's will from undeserved suffering, rather than from the consequences of personal sin. **R.** That is, as a human, by the sufferings. **S.** Or, source, grounds. **T.** Or, addressed, named.

This Is Hard To Explain To You
11 ... concerning whom[A] our message-*to-speak* is great[B] and hard-to-interpret[C] *so as* to speak, since you have become sluggish[D] *in* the hearing.

For You Are Still Immature In The Word
12 For indeed, [although] being obligated to be teachers because of the time, you again have *a* need *that* someone be teaching you the elements[E] *of*[F] the beginning[G] *concerning* the oracles[H] *of* God. And you have become *ones* having *a* need *of* milk and not *of* solid[I] food. **13** For everyone partaking *of* milk *is* inexperienced *in the* word *of*[J] righteousness, for he is *an* infant. **14** But the solid food is *for the* mature— the *ones* because of habit[K] having *their* faculties[L] trained for discernment *of* both good and evil.

So Let Us Move Along Toward Maturity
6:1 Therefore, having left the message *of* the beginning[M] *concerning* Christ, let us be carried-along to maturity— not again laying-down *a* foundation *of* repentance from dead works and faith toward God, **2** *of* instruction *about* cleansings[N] and laying-on *of* hands, and *about the* resurrection *of the* dead and eternal judgment.

And We Will Do This As God Permits, For It Is Impossible For Us To Help Some
3 And this[O] we will do if-indeed God permits. **4** For *it is* impossible **to renew**[P] **again to repentance** the *ones* having once been enlightened[Q] and having tasted[R] the heavenly gift, and having been made[S] partakers[T] *of the* Holy Spirit, **5** and having tasted *the* **good** word *of* God and *the* powers[U] *of the* coming age, **6** and having fallen-away— crucifying-again[V] *for* themselves the Son *of* God, and publicly-disgracing *Him.* **7** For land having drunk the rain coming often upon it, and producing *a* plant useful *to* those for whose sake it is also farmed, receives *a* blessing from God. **8** But *land* bringing-forth thorns and thistles *is* disapproved[W] and near *a* curse[X], whose end[Y] *is* for burning.

But As For You, Beloved, Diligently Imitate The Inheritors Of The Promises
9 But concerning you, beloved, we are **convinced-of** better *things*, and *things* having salvation— even though we are speaking in this manner. **10** For God *is* not unjust *so as* to forget your work and the love which you demonstrated for His name, having served[Z] the saints and [still] serving. **11** But we desire *that* each *of* you be demonstrating the **same** diligence toward the full-assurance *of* hope until

A. That is, Melchizedek. Or, which; that is, Christ as High Priest. **B.** That is, great in length (long); or, great in quality (deep, profound). **C.** That is, difficult to put in words you will understand. **D.** Or, lazy, dull. **E.** Or, fundamentals, basics. **F.** That is, belonging to. **G.** Or, first thing. **H.** Or, sayings. **I.** In this context, solid food refers to teaching about Christ as High Priest. **J.** That is, about, leading to. **K.** Or, practice, constant use. **L.** That is, moral senses. **M.** See 5:12. **N.** That is, the Christian view of Jewish washings (same word as in Mk 7:4), certainly a foundational issue for these Hebrews. Or, baptisms. **O.** That is, carry you on toward maturity. **P.** Or, restore. In the Greek word order, 'to renew again to repentance' is in v 6, just before 'crucifying-again', placing emphasis on it. **Q.** Or, illuminated, given light. **R.** That is, experienced; or, partaken of. **S.** Or, come-to-be, become, been. **T.** Or, partners, sharers. **U.** Or, miracles, as in 2:4. **V.** Or, re-crucifying. That is, *since they are* crucifying-again, defining the sense in which they have fallen away. **W.** Or, rejected. **X.** That is, near to being cursed. **Y.** That is, destiny. **Z.** Compare 10:32-34.

the end, ¹² in order that you may not be sluggish, but imitators *of* the *ones* inheriting the promises through faith and patience.

For Abraham Waited Patiently And Obtained The Promise
¹³ For God, having promised *to* Abraham, swore by Himself— since He had by no one greater to swear— ¹⁴ saying [in Gen 22:17]: "Surely while blessing I will bless you, and while multiplying I will multiply^A you". ¹⁵ And so, having waited-patiently, he obtained the promise.

God Even Guaranteed His Promise To Encourage Those Waiting For It
¹⁶ For people swear by the greater *one*. And *for* them the oath for confirmation *is the* end^B *of* every dispute, ¹⁷ by which *custom* God, intending even more to show the unchangeableness *of* His intention^C *to* the heirs *of* the promise, guaranteed *with an* oath, ¹⁸ in order that by two^D unchangeable things in which *it is* impossible *for* God to lie, we^E— the *ones* having fled to take-hold-of the hope being set-before *us*— may have strong encouragement^F, ¹⁹ which *hope* we have as *an* anchor *of* the soul, both secure and firm and entering into the inner *side of* the curtain, ²⁰ where *a* forerunner for us went in— Jesus— having become High Priest forever according to the order *of* Melchizedek.

Now Observe How Great This Melchizedek Is
7:1 For this Melchizedek^G, king *of* Salem, priest *of* the Most-High God, **remains**^H *a* **priest perpetually**^I— the *one* having met Abraham returning from the defeat *of* the kings and having blessed him; ² *to* whom also Abraham divided *a* tenth from everything; *who is* first ([his name] being translated), king *of* righteousness; and then also king *of* Salem, which is^J king *of* peace; ³ fatherless, motherless, genealogy-less, having^K neither *a* beginning *of* days nor *an* end *of* life, but having been made-like^L the Son *of* God. ⁴ Now observe how great this *one is to* whom indeed Abraham the patriarch gave *a* tenth from the choicest-spoils:

He Is Greater Than Abraham
⁵ Indeed, the *ones* from the sons *of* Levi receiving the priestly-office have *a* commandment to be collecting-a-tenth-from the people according to the Law (that is, *from* their brothers, even though *their brothers* have come-out of the loins *of* Abraham)— ⁶ yet the *one* not tracing-*his*-genealogy from them has collected-a-tenth *from* Abraham, and has blessed the *one* having the promises! ⁷ And apart from all dispute, the lesser *one* is blessed by the better *one*.

A: while blessing... multiply. This literal reflection of a Hebrew way of speaking means 'I will surely bless and I will surely multiply'. **B.** Or, conclusion. **C:** intending... intention. Or, purposing... purpose, determining... determination. **D.** That is, the promise and the oath. **E:** we... encouragement. Or, we, the *ones* having fled-for-refuge, may have strong encouragement to take-hold-of the hope being set-before *us*. **F.** That is, to wait patiently like Abraham. **G.** The meaning of this man is explained by examining the two places he is mentioned in the OT, Gen 14:17-20 (in v 1-10) and Ps 110 (in v 11-28). **H:** remains *a* priest perpetually. In the Greek word order this phrase is at the end of v 3, placing emphasis on it. **I.** Or, continually, and in this sense, for all time, forever. **J.** That is, means. **K.** That is, in the OT record. **L.** Or, made-to-resemble, copied-from. He is made to appear as a prefigurement of Christ.

He Is Living As a Priest Perpetually

8 And here, dying men[A] receive *the* tenths— yet there, *it is* being attested[B] that he is living!

He Is Greater Than Levi And His Priesthood

9 And so to speak, through Abraham even Levi[C], the *one* receiving *the* tenths, has paid-a-tenth. **10** For he was still in the loins *of his* father when Melchizedek met him!

Now Why Did Another Priesthood Need To Arise After Aaron?

11 Now indeed, if perfection had been through the Levitical priesthood (for the [Jewish] people have received-the-Law on the basis of it) what further need *would there have been that* another priest *should* arise according to the order[D] *of* Melchizedek, and not be named according to the order *of* Aaron?

For This New Priesthood Also Brings a Change of Law

12 For the priesthood being changed, of necessity there is[E] also *a* change *of* law.

For Its High Priest Is From The Tribe of Judah

13 For *the One* about Whom these[F] *things* are spoken has partaken *of* another tribe from which no one has attended-to the altar. **14** For *it is* clear that our Lord has risen from Judah— for which tribe Moses spoke nothing concerning priests.

And He Became High Priest Based On His Indestructible Life

15 And it is still even-more very-clear[G] if Another Priest arises in accordance with the likeness *of* Melchizedek, **16** Who has become *such* not based-on *the* law *of a* fleshy[H] commandment, but based on *the* power *of an* indestructible life! **17** For it is attested that "You *are a* priest forever according to the order *of* Melchizedek" [Ps 110:4].

The New Sets Aside The Old And Brings In a Better Hope

18 For *a* setting-aside[I] *of the* preceding commandment takes place because of its weakness and unprofitableness **19** (for the Law perfected nothing)— and *a* bringing-in *of a* better hope through which we draw-near *to* God.

Jesus Is a Better Priest Because His Priesthood Is Based On God's Oath

20 And[J] to the degree that *it was* not without *an* oath-swearing (for the *ones* have become[K] priests without *an* oath-swearing, **21** but the *One* with *an* oath-swearing,

---

A. That is, Levitical priests, who all eventually die. **B.** That is, because Genesis records no end of life, v 3. **C.** Thus, the entire Levitical priesthood is inferior to the priesthood of Melchizedek. **D.** This new priestly order is mentioned in Ps 110, long after the establishment of the Levitical priesthood. This implies that the Levitical priesthood was imperfect and temporary. **E.** Or, occurs. **F.** That is, Ps 110:4. **G.** That is, that there is a change of law. **H.** That is, a law pertaining to the flesh, to the candidate's physical lineage. **I.** Or, annulment, abolishment, abrogation. The conclusion is that Ps 110 predicts a new High Priest in a new priesthood, which requires a new law. This means the old is set aside and the new brought in by Jesus. **J.** Now an inference is drawn from 'swore' in Ps 110. **K.** The grammar implies have become and continue to be.

through the *One* saying to Him [in Ps 110:4]: *"The* Lord swore and He will not change-*His*-mind, You *are a* priest forever")— **22** to that degree also **Jesus** has become *the* guarantee^A *of a* better covenant.

Jesus Serves As High Priest Forever
23 And^B the many have been [Levitical] priests because of *their* being prevented from continuing *by* death— **24** but the *One,* because of His remaining forever, has *a* permanent^C priesthood. **25** Hence also, He is able to save completely^D the *ones* coming-to God through Him, always living so as to intercede for them.

God's Son Perfected Forever Is a Fitting High Priest For Us
26 For such *a* High Priest was indeed fitting *for* us— holy, innocent, undefiled, having been separated^E from sinners, and having become higher *than* the heavens— **27** Who does not have *the* daily necessity (as indeed the high priests) to be offering sacrifices first for *His* own sins, then the *sins of* the people. For He did this once-for-all, having offered Himself. **28** For the Law appoints men having weakness *as* high priests, but the word *of* the oath-swearing after^F the Law *appoints a* Son having been perfected forever.

Jesus Is Our High Priest In The True Heavenly Temple
8:1 Now^G *the* main-point in the *things* being said *is:* we have such *a* High Priest, Who sat-*down* at *the* right *hand of* the throne *of* the Majesty in the heavens, **2** Minister *of* the Holies^H, indeed^I *of* the true tabernacle (which the Lord pitched^J, not *a* human).

Earthly Priests Serve In a Copy And Shadow of The Heavenly Things
3 For every high priest is appointed that *he might* be offering both gifts and sacrifices. Hence *it is*^K necessary *that* this One also have something which He may offer. **4** Now indeed, if He were on earth He would not even be *a* priest— *there* being the *ones* offering the gifts according-to *the* Law, **5** who are serving *a* copy and *a* shadow *of* the heavenly *things,* just as Moses has been warned, being about to complete the tabernacle: for "See", He says [in Ex 25:40], *"that* you make everything according to the pattern having been shown *to* you on the mountain".

But Jesus Has a Better Ministry As Mediator of a Better Covenant With Better Promises
6 But He has now obtained *a* **more-excellent** ministry^L, *by* as much as He is indeed *the* mediator *of a* **better** covenant, which has been enacted on better promises!

For God Promised a New Covenant
7 For if that first *covenant* had been faultless, no place would have been sought *for a* second. **8** For, finding-fault-with^M them, He says [in Jer 31:31-34]: "Behold— days are coming, says *the* Lord, and I will consummate^N *a* new

---

A. Or, pledge, security. **B.** Now an inference is drawn from 'forever' in Ps 110. **C.** Or, unchangeable. It does not pass to another. **D.** That is, in contrast to the Law, which perfected nothing. Or, forever. **E.** That is, in character, taking this with what precedes; or, physically, to heaven, taking it with what follows. **F.** That is, written after, in Ps 110. **G.** At this point the writer turns from Christ's person as High Priest in the order of Melchizedek to His work as High Priest. **H.** Or, Holy *places.* **I.** Or, and. **J.** Or, set up, erected. **K.** Or, *was;* making this a specific reference to the cross instead of a general statement of principle. **L.** Or, priestly-service. **M.** Or, blaming. **N.** Or, accomplish, complete, execute.

covenant for the house *of* Israel and for the house *of* Judah; [9] not in accordance with the covenant which I made *with* their fathers on *the* day I took-hold-of their hand to lead them out of *the* land *of* Egypt, because **they** did not continue in My covenant, and **I** did not-care-for them, says *the* Lord. [10] Because this *is* the covenant which I will covenant *with* the house *of* Israel after those days, says *the* Lord: Giving My laws into their mind, I will also write them upon their heart. And I will be God *to* them and **they** will be *a* people *to* Me. [11] And they will by no means each teach his *fellow*-citizen and each his brother, saying 'Know[A] the Lord', because they all will know Me from *the* small[B] *one* up to their great *one*. [12] Because I will be merciful[C] *to* their wrong-doings, and I will never remember[D] their sins again".

God Has Thus Made The First Covenant Old
[13] In *that He* says "New", He has made the first old[E]. And the *thing* becoming old and growing-aged *is* near disappearance.

The First Covenant Allowed Entrance Into The Holy of Holies Once a Year
9:1 Now indeed, the first *covenant* also had regulations *of* service and the earthly Holy *Place*. [2] For the first[F] tabernacle was prepared[G]— in which *were* both the lampstand and the table, and the Presentation *of* the bread— which is called *the* Holies. [3] And behind the second curtain *was the* tabernacle being called *the* Holies *of* Holies, [4] having *a* golden altar-of-incense[H], and the ark[I] *of* the covenant having been covered on-all-sides *with* gold, in which *was a* golden jar having the manna and the rod *of* Aaron having budded and the tablets *of* the covenant, [5] and above it *were the* cherubim[J] *of* glory overshadowing the mercy-seat[K]— concerning which *things* there is not *time* now to be speaking in detail. [6] And these *things* thus having been prepared, the priests accomplishing the services are continually going into the first tabernacle.[7] But into the second only the high priest *goes* once *a* year, not without blood, which he offers for himself and the ignorances[L] *of* the people—

God Was Making Clear That The Way Into The Holies Was Not Yet Revealed
[8] ... the Holy Spirit making this clear: *that* the way *of*[M] the Holies has not yet been made-known while the first tabernacle[N] *was*[O] still having[P] *a* standing, [9] which[Q] *is*[R] a symbol for the present[S] time, according to which both gifts and sacrifices are offered not being able to perfect the *one* worshiping in relation to *the* conscience, [10] being[T] only (in-addition-to foods

---

A. Or, Come-to-know. **B.** Or, little. That is, insignificant. Or, least... greatest. **C.** Or, propitious, gracious. **D.** That is, call-to-mind, keep-in-mind. **E.** Or, obsolete. **F.** That is, the first room of the two-room tabernacle tent, the part the priests entered. **G.** Or, built, erected, furnished. **H.** Or, censer. **I.** Or, box, chest. **J.** Or, winged-creatures. **K.** Or, place-of-propitiation. **L.** That is, sins of ignorance. **M.** That is, leading into. **N.** That is, the outer room of the tabernacle, as in v 2 and 6; or, the tabernacle as a whole, the sanctuary of the first covenant. **O.** Or, *is*. **P.** That is, *was* having an appointed place in the divine order, a standing with God (this ended when Christ died and the curtain was torn); or, *is* physically standing (this ended in A.D. 70). **Q.** This refers back to 'first tabernacle'. **R.** Or, *was*. **S.** That is, which *is* a symbol for the now present NT times, pointing to the better reality Christ brought; or, which *was* a symbol for the then present OT times, pointing to the fact that the Levitical system could not gain the people free access to God. **T:** *being* only... regulations. That is, the gifts and

and drinks and different cleansings[A]) regulations *of* [B] flesh being imposed until *the* time *of* reformation.

But Christ Entered The True Holy of Holies Once For All And Obtained Redemption
11 But Christ, having arrived[C] *as* High Priest *of* the good *things* having come, **entered[D] once-for-all into the Holies** through[E] the greater and more-perfect tabernacle not made-by-*human*-hands— that is, not *of* this creation; **12** and not through[F] *the* blood *of* goats and calves, but through *His* own blood, having obtained[G] eternal redemption.

For Through The Spirit He Offered Himself Without Blemish To God
13 For if the blood *of* goats and bulls and *the* ashes *of a* heifer sprinkling the *ones* having been defiled sanctifies for the cleansing *of* the flesh, **14** *by* how much more will the blood *of* Christ, Who through *the* eternal Spirit[H] offered Himself without-blemish *to* God, cleanse our conscience from dead works so that *we may* worship[I] *the* living God!

Thus Christ Mediates a New Covenant Inaugurated By His Own Blood
15 And for this reason He is *the* mediator *of a* new covenant, so that the *ones* having been called may receive the promise *of* the eternal inheritance— *a* death having taken-place for *the* redemption *from* the transgressions *committed* under[J] the first covenant. **16** For where *there is a* will[K], *it is a* necessity *that the* death *of* the *one* having made-the-will be brought-forth. **17** For *a* will over dead *ones is* firm, since it does not ever have [legal] power when the *one* having made-the-will is living. **18** Hence, not even the first *covenant* has been inaugurated[L] without blood. **19** For every commandment having been spoken *to* all the people by Moses according-to[M] the Law— having taken the blood *of* the calves and the goats along with water and scarlet wool and hyssop, he sprinkled both the book itself and all the people, **20** saying "This *is* the blood *of* the covenant which God commanded to you" [Ex 24:8]. **21** And he likewise sprinkled *with* the blood both the tabernacle and all the objects *of* the ministry. **22** Indeed according-to[N] the Law almost everything is cleansed[O] with blood, and forgiveness does not take-place[P] apart-from blood-shedding[Q]. **23** Therefore *it was a* necessity *that* the copies[R] *of* the *things* in the heavens be cleansed *with* these[S] *things*— but the heavenly *things* themselves *with* better sacrifices than these.

---

sacrifices offered by the priests, like laws about food, drink, and cleansings, were only temporary outward regulations. Compare v 13-14. The sacrifices outwardly cleansed the flesh, but could not inwardly cleanse the heart. **A.** Or, washings, baptisms. **B.** That is, for the flesh. **C.** Or, appeared, come. **D:** entered... Holies. In the Greek word order, this phrase is in v 12, just before 'having obtained', giving it the emphasis. **E.** That is, passing through the heavenly tabernacle. Or, by means of, meaning the tabernacle in view is Christ's resurrection body. **F.** Or, by means of. **G.** That is, on the cross. Or, obtaining (at the time of His entering). **H.** Or, *His* eternal spirit. **I.** Or, serve. **J.** That is, at the time of. **K.** By way of illustration, the writer refers to a will, which is a special kind of covenant. The Greek word is the same for both. **L.** Or, dedicated, ratified. That is, put into effect. **M.** Or, in-harmony-with. **N.** Or, based-on. **O.** Or, purified. **P.** Or, come-about, happen. Or, and there is no forgiveness. **Q.** Or, blood-pouring (on the altar). **R.** That is, earthly copies. **S.** That is, the things in v 18-22; the applied blood of animals.

He Entered The Heavenly Temple

24 For Christ did not enter into *the* Holies made-by-*human*-hands— copies *of* the true *things*— but into heaven itself, now to appear *in* the presence *of* God for us.

He Offered Himself Once For All As a Sacrifice To Set Aside Sin

25 Nor *did He enter* in order that He might offer Himself often— as indeed the high priest enters into the Holies yearly with *the* blood belonging-to-another— **26** otherwise He *would* had-to-have suffered often since *the* foundation *of the* world. But now He has appeared once-for-all at *the* conclusion[A] *of the* ages for *the* setting-aside *of* sin by the sacrifice[B] *of* Himself.

He Will Appear To Us a Second Time For Salvation

27 And just as it is destined *for* people to die once and after this *comes the* judgment, **28** so also[C] Christ, having been offered once so as to bear[D] *the* sins *of* many, will appear for *a* second *time* without *reference to* sin to the *ones* eagerly-awaiting Him, for salvation.

For The Law Could Never Take Away Sins, So Jesus Came To Offer His Body

10:1 For the Law— having *a* shadow *of* the coming good *things*, not the very image[E] *of* the things— is never able to perfect the *ones* approaching yearly *with* the same sacrifices which they offer perpetually[F]. **2** Otherwise would they not have ceased being offered, because of the *ones* worshiping no longer having *a* consciousness *of* sins, having been cleansed once-for-all? **3** But in them[G] *there is a* yearly reminder *of* sins. **4** For *it is* impossible *for the* blood *of* bulls and goats to take-away sins. **5** Therefore, while entering into the world, He says [in Ps 40:6-8]: "You did not desire sacrifice and offering, but You prepared *a* body *for* Me. **6** You were not well-pleased *with* whole-burnt-offerings and *offerings* for sin. **7** Then I said, Behold, I have come— in *the* roll[H] *of a* book it has been written about Me—*that I might* do Your will, God".

Thus God Has Done Away With Animal Offerings And Established Christ's

8 Saying above that "You did not desire nor were You well-pleased *with* sacrifices and offerings and whole-burnt-offerings and *offerings* for sin" (which are being offered according-to[I] *the* Law!), **9** then He has said, "Behold, I have come *that I might* do Your will"— He does-away-with[J] the first in-order-that He might establish the second,

And By God's Will We Are Made Holy By The Offering of Christ's Body

10 ... by which will we have been made-holy through the offering *of* the body *of* Jesus Christ once-for-all.

A. Or, end, consummation, close. All the past ages are brought to a conclusion in Christ. **B.** Or, sacrificial-offering. **C.** For Christ's side of the comparison, the writer does not merely say Christ died and was favorably judged by God; he states the deeper significance of each event. Christ's death was an offering for sin, and since this offering was accepted by God, He will appear for salvation to those awaiting Him. **D.** Or, take-up, take-upon *Himself*. **E.** Or, likeness, form. **F.** Or, continually. That is, year after year. **G.** That is, the sacrifices. **H.** That is, the book-roll, the book's scroll, the OT. **I.** Or, in keeping with, based on. **J.** Or, abolishes. God does away with the Levitical system of animal sacrifices in order to establish His will.

The Priests Offer Sacrifices Daily, But Jesus Offered One Sacrifice For All

11 And every priest stands ministering daily and offering often the same sacrifices which are never able to take-away sins— **12** but this *One,* having offered **one** sacrifice for sins[A] for all time, sat-*down* at *the* right *hand of* God, **13** henceforth waiting until His enemies are put *as a* footstool *of* His feet.

For By One Offering Jesus Perfected Us For All Time

14 For *by* one offering He has perfected for all time the *ones* being made-holy.

The New Covenant Says That God Will Never Remember Our Sins Again

15 And the Holy Spirit also testifies *to* us; for after the *statement* [in Jer 31:33] having said **16** "This *is* the covenant which I will covenant with them after those days, says *the* Lord: Giving My laws upon their hearts, I will also write them upon their mind", **17** *then He says* "And I will never remember their sins and their lawless-*deeds* again".

God's Permanent Forgiveness Makes Further Offerings For Sin Unnecessary

18 Now where *there is* forgiveness *of* these *things, there is* no longer *an* offering for sin!

Therefore Let Us Approach God In Full Assurance of Faith And Hold On Without Wavering

19 Therefore, brothers, having confidence for the entering *of* the Holies by the blood *of* Jesus— **20** which fresh[B] and living way He inaugurated *for* us through[C] the curtain, that is[D], His flesh— **21** and *having a* great Priest over the house *of* God, **22** let us be approaching *God* with *a* true heart in full-assurance *of* faith, having *our* hearts sprinkled[E] from *an* evil conscience, and having *our* body washed[F] *with* clean water. **23** Let us be holding-on-to the confession *of our* hope without-wavering, for the *One* having promised *is* faithful. **24** And let us be considering[G] one another for *the* provoking[H] *of* love and good works, **25** not forsaking the gathering-together *of* ourselves as *is a* habit *with* some, but exhorting[I] *one another*, and so-much more *by*-as-much-as you see the day drawing-near.

To Now Do Otherwise Is To Trample Underfoot The Son of God

26 For while[J] we *are* willfully[K] sinning[L] after the receiving *of* the knowledge *of* the truth, *a* sacrifice no longer remains[M] for sins, **27** but some fearful expectation[N] *of* judgment and *a* zeal *of* fire going to consume the adversaries. **28** Anyone having set-aside[O] *the* Law *of* Moses dies without compassions upon *the testimony of* two or three witnesses. **29** *For* how much worse punishment[P] do you think he will be considered-worthy— the *one* having trampled-underfoot the Son *of* God, and having regarded

---

A. Or, sins, sat-*down* for all time. **B.** Or, new, recent. **C.** Or, by-means-of. **D.** That is, 'which fresh and living way... that is, His flesh'; Christ's body on the cross is the living way through the curtain into the Holies. Or, 'by-means-of the curtain, that is, His flesh'; Christ's flesh is a curtain or veil on His true identity. **E.** As the priests sprinkled animal blood on things to cleanse them, so Christ sprinkles our hearts with His own blood. **F.** As the high priest was to bathe before entering the Holy of Holies, so we have been spiritually bathed so as to enter the heavenly Holy of Holies. **G.** Or, thinking carefully about, fixing attention on. **H.** Or, inciting, stirring up. **I.** Or, encouraging. **J.** That is, if. **K.** Or, willingly, deliberately, by our own choice. **L.** The kind of sinning in view is seen in v 29. **M.** If Christ's sacrifice is rejected, there is no other that can be made that will satisfy God's wrath upon our sin. **N.** Or, reception. **O.** Or, rejected. **P.** Or, vengeance, retribution.

as defiled[A] the blood *of* the covenant by which[B] he was sanctified[C], and having insulted[D] the Spirit *of* grace? [30] For we know the *One* having said [in Deut 32:35]: "Vengeance *is for* Me, **I** will repay"; and again [in Deut 32:36]: *"The* Lord will judge His people". [31] *It is a* fearful *thing* to fall into *the* hands *of the* living God.

You Need To Endure By Faith Until You Receive The Promises
[32] Now[E] remember the former days during which, having been enlightened[F], you endured *a* great struggle[G] *of* sufferings— [33] on this *hand* being made-a-spectacle[H] *by* both reproaches[I] and afflictions, and on this *hand* having become partners *of* the *ones* living in this manner[J]. [34] For indeed you sympathized-with the prisoners, and you accepted with joy the plundering *of* your possessions, knowing *that you*-yourselves have *a* better and abiding possession. [35] So do not throw-away your confidence, which has *a* great reward. [36] For you have need *of* endurance, in order that having done the will *of* God, you might receive the promise. [37] For yet *in a* very little *while,* "the *One* coming will come and will not delay. [38] But My righteous *one* will live by faith. And if he draws-back[K], My soul is not well-pleased[L] with him" [Hab 2:3-4]. [39] But **we** are not *of* [M] *a* drawing-back resulting-in destruction, but *of a* faith resulting in *the* preserving *of the* soul.

The Saints Have Always Endured By Faith
11:1 Now[N] faith is *the* assurance[O] *of things* being hoped-for[P], *the* conviction[Q] *of* things not being seen[R]. [2] For in this the elders[S] were attested.

The Early Times
[3] *By* faith we understand *that* the worlds have been prepared *by the* word *of* God, so that the *thing* being seen *has* not[T] come-into-being from *things* being visible. [4] *By* faith Abel offered *to* God *a* greater sacrifice than Cain, through which he was attested to be righteous— God testifying about his gifts. And through it, [although] having died, he is still speaking. [5] *By* faith Enoch was removed[U], *so as* not to see death: "And he was not found because God removed him" [Gen 5:24]. For before the removal, he has been attested to have pleased God. [6] And without faith *it is* impossible to please *Him.* For the *one* coming-to God must **believe** that He is, and He becomes *the* rewarder *to* the *ones* seeking Him out. [7] *By* faith Noah, having been warned about the *things* not yet being seen, having been reverent, prepared *the* ark for *the* salvation[V] *of* his household, through which he condemned the world and became *an* inheritor *of* the righteousness according-to faith.

The Time of The Patriarchs
[8] *By* faith Abraham, being called, obeyed to go out to *a* place which he was going-to

---

A. Or, common. **B.** That is, the blood... by which. **C.** Or, set-apart to God, consecrated, treated-as-holy. **D.** Or, arrogantly-treated. **E.** Or, But. **F.** Or, given-light, illuminated. **G.** Or, contest. **H.** Or, publicly-exposed *to.* **I.** Or, insults, disgraces. **J.** That is, amid reproach and affliction for Christ. **K.** Or, shrinks-back, withdraws. **L.** Or, takes no pleasure in. **M.** That is, characterized by. **N.** The writer now proves by example that God's people have always endured by faith (10:36-39). **O.** That is, our subjective confidence about the future things. Or, substance, reality; that is, the objective present reality of the future things. **P.** That is, future realities. **Q.** Or, *the* certainty, *the* being-convinced. Or, *the* proof, *the* evidence, the thing-convincing. **R.** That is, unseen realities, past, present, and future. **S.** That is, the OT saints mentioned next. **T:** has not... visible. Or, *has* come-into-being from *things* not being visible. **U.** Or, transferred, changed. **V.** Or, deliverance.

receive for *an* inheritance. And he went out not knowing where he was going. **⁹** *By* faith he stayed^A in *the* land *of* the promise as *a land* belonging-to-another, having dwelled in tents with Isaac and Jacob, the fellow-heirs *of* the same promise. **¹⁰** For he was waiting-for the city having foundations, *of* which^B God *is* designer^C and maker^D. **¹¹** *By* faith— and Sarah herself *being* barren— he^E received power for *the* foundation^F *of a* seed^G even beyond *the* time *of* mature-age, since he regarded the *One* having promised *to be* faithful. **¹²** Therefore indeed from one *man*— and *he* having become impotent *as to* these^H *things*— were born^I *seed* as the stars *of* heaven *in* number, and countless as the sand by the shore *of* the sea. **¹³** In accordance with faith, these^J all died not having received the promises, but having seen them from a distance, and having greeted *them*, and having confessed that they are strangers and pilgrims^K on the earth. **¹⁴** For the *ones* saying such *things* are making-clear that they are seeking-for *a* homeland. **¹⁵** And if they had been remembering that *homeland* from which they came out, they would have had opportunity to return—**¹⁶** but as-it-is, they are aspiring-to *a* better *homeland*; that is, *a* heavenly *one*. Therefore God is not ashamed-of them, to be called their God. For He prepared *a* city *for* them. **¹⁷** *By* faith Abraham has offered Isaac while being tested. And the *one* having received the promises was offering *his* only-born^L, **¹⁸** with-regard-to whom^M it was said [in Gen 21:12] that "In Isaac *a* seed will be called *for* you", **¹⁹** having considered^N that God *was* able to raise *him* even from *the* dead, from-which^O he also received him back in *a* symbol^P. **²⁰** *By* faith Isaac blessed Jacob and Esau even concerning coming *things*. **²¹** *By* faith Jacob, while dying, blessed each *of* the sons *of* Joseph and "worshiped [leaning] on the top *of* his staff " [Gen 47:31]. **²²** *By* faith Joseph, while coming-to-an-end^Q, mentioned concerning the departure^R *of* the sons *of* Israel and gave-commands concerning his bones.

The Time of The Exodus

²³ *By* faith Moses, having been born, was hidden *for* three months by his parents, because they saw the child *was* beautiful and did not fear the edict *of* the king. **²⁴** *By* faith Moses, having become great^S, refused to be called son *of* Pharaoh's daughter, **²⁵** having chosen rather to be mistreated-with the people *of* God than to be having *a* temporary enjoyment *of* sin, **²⁶** having regarded the reproach *of* ^T the Christ *to be* greater riches *than* the treasures *of* Egypt. For he was looking-away^U to the reward. **²⁷** *By* faith he left Egypt, not having feared the fury *of* the king. For he persevered^V as seeing^W the invisible *One*. **²⁸** *By* faith he has performed the Passover^X and the sprinkling *of* the blood in order that the *one* destroying the firstborns might not touch them. **²⁹** *By* faith they crossed^Y the Red Sea as through dry land— *of* which having

---

A. Or, lived-as-a-foreigner. **B.** That is, which city. **C.** Or, craftsman, artisan. **D.** Or, builder. **E:** *By* faith... he received... he regarded. Or, *By* faith also, barren Sarah herself received... she regarded. **F.** Or, beginning. Or, deposit (of sperm). **G.** That is, a posterity; or, sperm. **H.** That is, his powers of procreation. **I.** Or, fathered. **J.** That is, the four mentioned in v 8-12. **K.** Or, temporary-residents. **L.** That is, with reference to the promise; through Sarah. **M.** That is, Isaac. Or, to whom; that is, Abraham. **N.** Or, calculated, accounted. **O.** That is, from the dead. Or, 'dead. Hence, ...'. That is, Hence (by his faith), he received him back. **P.** That is, in an illustration of the Father and Christ; or simply, in a figure of speech. **Q.** That is, dying. **R.** Or, exodus. **S.** That is, in stature (meaning, grown up); or, in status. **T.** That is, belonging to; or, for. **U.** Or, focusing-attention-on. **V.** Or, persisted, endured, was steadfast. **W.** That is, as though he saw; or, as one who saw. **X.** Having made reference to the entire exodus event, the writer now singles out one crucial and enduring aspect of it. **Y.** Or, went-through, stepped-across.

taken *the* test[A], the Egyptians were swallowed-up. [30] *By* faith the walls *of* Jericho fell, having been encircled for seven days. [31] *By* faith Rahab the prostitute did not perish- with the *ones* having disobeyed, having welcomed the spies with peace.

What More Shall I Say?

[32] And what more may I say? For time will fail me while telling about Gideon, Barak, Samson, Jephthah, both David and Samuel, and the prophets, [33] who through faith conquered kingdoms, worked righteousness[B], obtained[C] promises, stopped *the* mouths *of* lions, [34] quenched *the* power *of* fire, escaped *the* edges *of the* sword, were strengthened from weakness, became mighty in battle, put-to-flight armies *of* foreigners. [35] Women received their dead by resurrection— but others were tortured, not accepting redemption[D], in order that they might obtain *a* better resurrection. [36] And others received *a* trial *of* mockings and whippings, and furthermore *of* bonds and prison. [37] They were stoned, they were sawn-in-two, they died by murder *of the* sword. They went-around in sheepskins, in skins of-goats, being in-need, being afflicted, being mistreated— [38] *of* whom the world was not worthy— wandering in desolate-places and mountains and caves and openings *of* the earth.

They Did Not Receive The Promise, For God Had a Better Promise For Us

[39] And these all, having been attested through *their* faith, did not receive the promise— [40] God having provided[E] something better for us, in order that they should not be perfected[F] apart from us.

So Run Your Race With Endurance, Looking To Jesus

12:1 So-therefore we also[G], having **so large** *a* cloud *of* witnesses[H] surrounding us, having laid-aside every weight[I] and the easily-entangling[J] sin, let us be running the race being set- before us with endurance [2] while looking-away toward the author and perfecter[K] *of* the faith[L]— Jesus— Who endured *a* cross for[M] the joy being set-before Him, having disregarded[N] *the* shame[O], and has sat-*down* at *the* right *hand of* the throne *of* God.

Consider His Endurance

[3] For consider[P] the *One* having endured **such** opposition[Q] by sinners against Himself, in order that you may not be weary *in* your souls, losing-heart— [4] you did not yet resist to the point *of* blood while struggling against sin!

And Have You Forgotten That God Disciplines Those He Loves?

[5] And have[R] you completely-forgotten[S] the exhortation which speaks[T] *to* you as sons?: "My son, do not be thinking-lightly[U] *of the* discipline[V] *of the* Lord, nor losing-heart

---

A. Or, *an* attempt. **B.** Or, justice. **C.** Or, attained. **D.** Or, deliverance, release. **E.** Or, foreseen. **F.** Or, completed, finished. **G.** The writer now applies the lesson from chapter 11, returning to the exhortation of 10:36-39. **H.** That is, witnesses of endurance by faith while awaiting the promises, such as those just mentioned. **I.** That is, such as would impede a runner. **J.** Or, easily-ensnaring, besetting, clinging. **K.** Or, finisher, consummator, completer. **L.** Or, *of* faith, *of our* faith. **M.** That is, to obtain; or, instead-of (the joy He had or could have had). **N.** Or, cared-nothing-for. **O.** Or, humiliation, disgrace. **P.** Or, compare, calculate in comparison. **Q.** Or, dispute, hostility, rebellion. **R.** Or, And you have. **S.** If the readers thought they should be exempt from suffering for their faith, they must have utterly-forgotten Prov 3:11-12, and they must have failed to consider the Son, v 3. **T.** Or, reasons *with*. **U.** Or, making-little-of. **V.** Or, training, correction, corporal punishment.

while being rebuked by Him. **6** For *the one* whom *the* Lord loves He disciplines, and He whips[A] every son whom He accepts" [Prov 3:11-12].

God Is Dealing With You As Sons
7 You are enduring[B] [your trials] for discipline; God is dealing *with* you as *with* sons. For what son *is there* whom *his* father does not discipline? **8** But if you are without discipline, *of* which all have become partakers[C], then you are illegitimate[D] *children* and not sons.

And God Is Disciplining You For Your Benefit
9 Furthermore, we had fathers *of* our flesh[E] *as* discipliners and were respecting *them*— but shall we not much more be subject *to* the Father *of* [our] spirits and live? **10** For the *ones* were disciplining *us* for *a* few days according to the *thing* seeming *good to* them; but the *One does so* for *our* benefit[F], so that *we may* share-in His holiness.

And His Discipline Will Yield The Fruit of Righteousness
11 And all discipline for the present does not seem to be *a thing of* joy, but *of* grief— but later it yields[G] *the* peaceful fruit *of* righteousness *to* the *ones* having been trained by it.

Therefore Straighten Up And Walk Straight Paths
12 Therefore straighten-up[H] the hands having been slackened[I] and the knees having been made-feeble[J], **13** and be making straight paths *for* your feet, in order that the lame *part* may not be dislocated[K] but rather may be healed.

Pursue Peace And Holiness
14 Be pursuing peace with[L] all *people*, and the holiness without which no one will see the Lord, **15** while exercising-oversight *that* someone *may* not *be* coming-short of the grace *of* God; *that* some root *of*[M] bitterness growing[N] up may not be causing-trouble and many be defiled[O] by it; **16** *that* someone *may* not *be* sexually-immoral or[P] profane like Esau, who sold his *own* firstborn-rights[Q] for one meal[R]. **17** For you know that indeed afterward, while wanting to inherit the blessing, he was rejected— for he did not find *a* place *of*[S] repentance— even-though having sought-for it[T] with tears.

For You Have Come To The City of God, The Heavenly Jerusalem
18 For you have not come-to *a mountain* being touched[U], and *a* fire having been burning, and darkness and gloom and *a* storm, **19** and *a* blast *of a* trumpet, and *a* sound *of* words— *of* which, the *ones* having heard begged *that a* word not be

---

A. Or, scourges. **B.** Or, Be enduring. **C.** Or, sharers. **D.** Or, born-out-of-wedlock. That is, children not part of the father's family, not having a father to train them, not heirs. **E.** That is, human fathers. **F.** Lit, for the *thing* being beneficial (from our Father's viewpoint). **G.** Or, pays back. **H.** Or, set straight. **I.** Or, relaxed, weakened. **J.** Or, lame, paralyzed. **K.** Or, turned-out *of joint*. **L.** Or, together-with. **M.** That is, characterized by. Some bitter root, referring to a person. **N.** Or, springing. **O.** Or, polluted, stained. **P.** Or, sexually-immoral, or profane like Esau (so that only 'profane' applies to Esau). **Q.** That is, the status and inheritance rights of the firstborn son. **R.** Or, eating; one act of eating. **S.** That is, for. **T.** That is, the blessing. Or, repentance. **U.** That is, a physical mountain.

added *to* them. **20** For they were not bearing the *thing* being commanded: "If even *a* wild-animal should touch the mountain, it shall be stoned" [Ex 19:12-13]. **21** And so fearful was the *thing* appearing^A, Moses said "I am terrified and trembling". **22** But you have come to Mount Zion; and *the* city *of the* living God, *the* heavenly Jerusalem; and *the* myriads *of* angels, *a* festive-gathering^B; **23** and *the* church^C *of the* firstborn *ones* having been registered^D in *the* heavens; and *the* Judge, God *of* all; and *the* spirits *of* righteous *ones* having been perfected; **24** and *the* mediator *of the* new covenant, Jesus; and *the* blood *of* sprinkling speaking better than Abel.

Do Not Refuse The One Warning From Heaven, But Worship Him With Gratitude
25 Be watching-out *that* you not refuse^E the *One* speaking. For if those did not escape, having refused the *One* warning on earth, much more we *will not escape*: the *ones* turning-away-from the *One warning* from *the* heavens— **26** Whose voice shook the earth at that time, but now He has promised, saying [in Hag 2:6] "**I** will shake once more not only the earth, but also the heaven". **27** And the *phrase* "once more" indicates the removal *of* the *things* being shaken— as *of things* having been made— so that the *things* not being shaken may continue. **28** Therefore while receiving *an* unshakable kingdom, let us have gratitude, through which we may worship^F God pleasingly^G, with reverence and awe. **29** For indeed our God *is a* consuming fire.

Be Loving, Pure, and Content
13:1 Let brotherly-love continue. **2** Do not be forgetting hospitality, for through this some having entertained^H angels did not know *it.* **3** Remember^I the prisoners, as-*though* having been imprisoned-with *them;* the *ones* being mistreated, as-*though*^J also yourselves being in *their* body. **4** *Let* marriage *be*^K honored^L by all^M, and the bed undefiled. For God will judge *the* sexually-immoral-*ones* and adulterers. **5** *Let* character *be* without-love-of-money, being content *with* the present *things.* For He Himself has said [in Deut 31:6] "I will never^N let you go^O, nor will I by any means forsake^P you", **6** so that while being confident we say "*The* Lord *is a* helper *for* me and I will not fear. What^Q will *a* human do *to* me?" [Ps 118:6].

Imitate The Faith of Your Leaders. Do Not Be Carried Away By Strange Teachings
7 Remember the *ones* leading you, who spoke the word *of* God *to* you, whose faith^R be imitating while looking-carefully-at the result^S *of their* way-of-life^T. **8** Jesus^U Christ *is* the same yesterday and today and forever. **9** Do not be carried-away^V by various^W and strange^X teachings. For *it is* good *for* the heart to be established^Y *by* grace, not *by* foods in-connection-with^Z which the *ones* walking were not profited.

A. That is, the sight Moses saw. **B.** Or, public festival, general assembly. **C.** That is, assembly. **D.** Or, enrolled, listed. **E.** Or, decline, shun, beg-off. **F.** Or, let us worship. **G.** Or, acceptably (to God). **H.** Or, lodged, received as guests. This is referring to Abraham in Gen 18-19. **I.** That is, keep in mind. **J.** Or, as also yourselves being in *a* body. **K.** In this list of ten commands, note that this one has the same grammar as the next one (v 5). **L.** Or, respected. **M.** Or, among all; or, in all *respects.* **N.** Or, by no means. **O.** Or, turn you loose, give you up. **P.** Or, desert, abandon. **Q.** Or, fear what *a* human will do *to* me. **R.** Or, faithfulness. **S.** Or, end, outcome. **T.** Or, behavior, conduct. **U.** This may end the thought of v 7, or begin the thought of v 9. **V.** Or, taken-away. **W.** Or, diverse. Or, intricate, riddling, ambiguous. **X.** Or, foreign. **Y.** Or, strengthened, confirmed. **Z.** Or, by-means-of.

We Have a Spiritual Altar. Let Us Go Out And Offer Sacrifices of Praise

10 We have *an* altar[A] from which the *ones* serving[B] *in* the tabernacle have no right[C] to eat. **11** For *of* animals *from* which the blood is brought into the Holies by the high priest for sin— the bodies *of* these are burned-up[D] outside *of* the camp. **12** Therefore[E] Jesus also, in order that He might make the people holy with *His* own blood, suffered outside[F] *of* the gate. **13** So-indeed[G], let us go-out[H] to Him outside *of* the camp, bearing His reproach. **14** For here we do not have *an* abiding city, but we are seeking-for the *one* coming. **15** Therefore through Him let us be continually offering *a* sacrifice *of* [I] praise *to* God— that is, *the* fruit *of* lips praising[J] His name. **16** And do not be forgetting good-doing and sharing. For *with* such sacrifices God is pleased.

Yield To Your Leaders

17 Be obeying[K] the *ones* leading you and be yielding[L], for **they** are keeping-watch for your souls as *ones who* will render *an* account— in order that they may be doing this with joy, and not while groaning, for this *would be* unprofitable *for* you.

Pray For Us

18 Be praying for us. For we are persuaded that we have *a* good conscience, wanting to conduct-*ourselves* well[M] in all[N] *things.* **19** And I especially appeal-to *you* to do this in order that I may be restored *to* you sooner.

May God Prepare You To Do His Will

20 Now may the God *of* peace— the *One* having brought-up from *the* dead the Great Shepherd *of* the sheep in-connection-with[O] *the* blood *of the* eternal covenant, our Lord Jesus— **21** prepare[P] you in every good *thing* so that *you may* do His will, while doing *in* us the pleasing *thing* in His sight through Jesus Christ, *to* Whom *be* the glory forever and ever, amen.

22 Now I exhort you, brothers, bear-with the word *of* exhortation. For indeed I wrote-to you with *a* few[Q] *words.* **23** Take-notice-of [R] our brother Timothy having been released[S], with whom if he comes quicker[T], I will see you. **24** Greet all the *ones* leading you and all the saints. The *ones* from Italy greet you. **25** Grace *be* with you all.

A. That is, a spiritual altar. **B.** That is, Jewish priests. **C.** The reason this is the case is explained in v 11-12. **D.** No one had the right to eat any of the sacrifice made on the Day of Atonement. **E.** That is, because Jesus is the fulfillment of that sacrifice. **F.** As the fulfillment of that sacrifice, there is no sacrificial body remaining. There is no physical eating associated with the sacrifice of Jesus. We are established by grace, not by any connection with foods or eating. So do not be carried away by teachings linking physical eating to spiritual benefits. **G.** The writer makes another application of Jesus being outside the gate. **H.** The readers must identify themselves with Jesus where He was sacrificed for sin, outside the earthly Jewish system. Worship there is spiritual, not physical. **I.** That is, consisting of. **J.** Or, confessing. **K.** That is, be persuaded by, and thus, obeying, following. **L.** Or, deferring, giving way. **M.** Or, rightly, honorably, commendably. **N.** Or, among all *people.* **O.** Or, by-means-of. **P.** Or, equip, furnish, complete. **Q.** That is, compared to what the writer could have said about these subjects; or, this may be an understatement, meaning he wrote at length. **R.** Or, You know of. **S.** Or, having departed. **T.** Or, sooner, as in v 19. That is, quicker than Timothy's progress so far would indicate; or, sooner that the writer himself intends to depart. Or, soon, quickly.

James

Introduction   1:1

A.   Regard it all joy, my brothers, when you fall into various trials, knowing endurance is produced   1:2-12

     1.   But let no one say he is being tempted to do evil by God. This comes from within   1:13-16

B.   My beloved brothers, every good giving and perfect gift comes down from the Father of lights. He brought us into being by the word of truth. Therefore receive with gentleness the implanted word being able to save your souls   1:16-21

     1.   But be doers of the word, not hearers only. Bridle your tongue. Help widows and orphans   1:22-27

C.   My brothers, do not be holding your faith with respect of persons, or favoring the rich   2:1-4

     1.   Did not God chose the poor to be rich in faith? So love your neighbor as yourself   2:5-13

D.   What is the profit, my brothers, if someone claims to have faith but does not have works?   2:14-17

     1.   Show me your faith without works. Even demons have that kind of faith!   2:18-19
     2.   Abraham's faith was perfected by his works. Likewise also Rahab   2:20-26

E.   Do not become many teachers, my brothers, knowing that we will receive a greater judgment. If one does not stumble in speech, he is a perfect man. For the tongue is small but powerful   3:1-5

     1.   The tongue is the world of unrighteousness, staining the whole body, setting on fire the course of our existence   3:6-10
     2.   My brothers these things ought not to be so. The tree is known by its fruit   3:10-12
     3.   Who is wise among you? Your works reveal whether your wisdom is from above   3:13-18

         a.   Fights and quarrels proceed from your worldly desires   4:1-5
         b.   But God gives grace to the humble, so submit to God and resist the devil   4:6-10

     4.   So do not speak against one another, brothers. There is one Judge, but who are you?   4:11-12

F.   Come now, ones making plans apart from God. You boast in your pretensions. This is evil   4:13-17

G.   Come now, rich ones, weep over your miseries coming upon you   5:1-6

H.   Be patient, brothers, until the coming of the Lord. Endure hardship like the prophets   5:7-11

     1.   Above all, do not be swearing. Be praying. Be singing praise   5:12-13
     2.   Confess your sins to one another and pray for one another that you may be healed   5:14-18
     3.   Turn back the sinner from the error of his way   5:19-20

1:1 James, *a* slave *of* God and *the* Lord Jesus Christ, *to* the twelve tribes in the dispersion: Greetings.

Endure Your Trials With Joy, Asking God For Wisdom And Viewing Life From His Standpoint
2 Regard *it* all joy, my brothers, whenever you fall-into[A] various trials, **3** knowing that the testing *of* your faith is producing endurance. **4** And let endurance be having *its* complete[B] work in order that you may be complete and whole, lacking in nothing. **5** And if any *of* you is lacking wisdom, let him be asking from the God giving generously *to* all and not reproaching[C], and it will be given *to* him. **6** But let him be asking in faith, not doubting[D] at all. For the *one* doubting is like *a* surge *of the* sea being blown-by-wind and tossed. **7** For let that person not be supposing that he will receive anything from the Lord— **8** *a* double-minded man, unstable in all his ways. **9** And let the lowly[E] brother be boasting in his height, **10** and the rich *one* in his lowliness, because he will pass-away like *a* flower *of* grass. **11** For the sun rose with the burning-heat and dried-up the grass, and its flower fell-off and the beauty *of* its appearance perished. In this manner also the rich *one* will fade-away in his pursuits. **12** Blessed[F] *is the* man who endures *the* trial, because having become[G] approved, he will receive the crown *of*[H] life which He promised *to* the *ones* loving Him.

But Temptation To Evil Comes From Within, Not From God
13 Let no one being tempted be saying that "I am being tempted by[I] God". For God is not-tempted *by* evils. And He Himself tempts no one, **14** but each *one* is tempted by[J] *his* own desire while being drawn-away[K] and enticed[L]. **15** Then the desire, having conceived, gives-birth to sin. And the sin, having been fully-formed[M], brings-forth death. **16** Do not be deceived!

Receive God's Lifegiving Gift of The Implanted Word With Gentleness Toward Others, Not Anger
My[N] beloved brothers, **17** every good gift-giving[O] and every perfect gift-given is from-above, coming down from the Father *of* lights[P], with Whom there is no variation[Q] or shadow[R] *of* turning. **18** Having willed[S] *it*, He brought[T] us forth *by the* word *of* truth so that we *might* be *a* kind-of firstfruit *of* His creatures. **19** You know[U] *this*, my beloved brothers, but[V] let every person be quick to listen, slow to speak, slow into anger. **20** For *the* anger *of a* man does not produce[W] *the* righteousness *of* God. **21** Therefore having laid-aside all filthiness and abundance[X] *of* badness, receive with gentleness the implanted word being able to save your souls.

But Be Doers of The Word, Not Hearers Only
22 But be[Y] doers *of the* word and not hearers only, deluding[Z] yourselves. **23** Because if

---

A. Or, encounter. **B.** Or, perfect, finished. **C.** Or, reprimanding, scolding. **D.** Or, being divided *in the mind, wavering, disputing with himself.* **E.** Or, materially poor, humble. **F.** Or, Fortunate (from God's point of view). **G.** Or, been. **H.** That is, consisting of, belonging to. **I.** Or from. **J:** by *his* own desire... enticed. Or, while being drawn-away and enticed by *his* own desire. **K.** Or, pulled-out. **L.** Or, baited, lured, entrapped. **M.** Or, having been brought to completion, having run its course. **N.** Others start this next main section with v 19. See the note there. **O.** Or, *act-of-*giving. **P.** That is, Creator of sun, moon, and stars. **Q.** Or, change. **R.** That is, shadow caused by turning, such as when a light moves around an object. In other words, the changing creation does not cause changes in God. **S.** Or, wished, wanted, desired. **T.** That is, gave us spiritual birth. **U.** Others start the new point here, taking this as a command ('Know *this*') to know or understand what follows, and omitting 'but'. **V.** That is, you know the gift of salvation comes down from God, who brought us forth by the word of truth, but receive this word not with anger toward others, but with gentleness. As seen in Acts 11, 15 and 21, this was an issue for some Jewish Christians. **W.** Or, accomplish, work, bring about. **X.** Or, overflow, surplus. **Y.** Or, become. **Z.** That is, deluding yourselves that you have genuinely received God's word.

anyone is *a* hearer *of the* word and not *a* doer, this *one* is like *a* man considering[A] the face *of* his birth[B] in *a* mirror. [24] For he considered himself and has gone-away and immediately forgot[C] what-sort *of man* he was. [25] But the *one* having looked into *the* perfect law *of* liberty and having continued, not having become *a* forgetful[D] hearer, but *a* doer *of* work— this *one* will be blessed in his doing. [26] If anyone thinks *that he* is religious while not bridling[E] his tongue, but deceiving his heart, the religion[F] *of* this *one is* worthless[G]. [27] This is pure and undefiled religion before *our* God and Father— to be looking-after orphans and widows in their affliction; to be keeping oneself unspotted by the world.

Do Not Show Partiality Based On Earthly Status

2:1 My brothers, do not be holding the faith *of*[H] our Lord Jesus Christ *of*[I] glory with respect-of-persons[J]. [2] For if *a* gold-ringed man in shining clothing enters into your gathering, and *a* poor *man* in filthy clothing also enters, [3] and you look-upon[K] the *one* wearing the shining clothing and say "**You** be sitting here honorably[L]", and you say *to* the poor *man* "**You** stand there, or be sitting under[M] my footstool", [4] did you not make-distinctions among yourselves and become judges *with*[N] evil thoughts?

God Does Not Base His Actions On Human Distinctions. Love Your Neighbor

[5] Listen, my beloved brothers— did not God choose the poor *in* the world *to be* rich in faith and inheritors *of* the kingdom which He promised *to* the *ones* loving Him? [6] But **you** dishonored the poor *man*. Do not the rich oppress you and themselves drag you into courts? [7] Do not **they** blaspheme the good name having been called[O] upon you? [8] If indeed[P] you are fulfilling *the* royal law according to the Scripture [in Lev 19:18], "You shall love your neighbor as yourself", you are doing well[Q]. [9] But if you are showing-respect-of-persons you are working[R] *a* sin, being convicted[S] by the Law as transgressors. [10] For whoever keeps the whole Law but stumbles in one *thing* has become guilty *of* all. [11] For the *One* having said "Do not commit-adultery" also said "Do not murder". Now if you do not commit-adultery, but you murder, you have become *a* transgressor *of the* Law. [12] So speak and so do as *ones* going to be judged by *the* law *of* liberty. [13] For judgment *will be* merciless *to* the *one* not having done[T] mercy. Mercy vaunts[U] *over* judgment.

Faith Without Works Is Dead

[14] What *is* the profit, my brothers, if someone claims to have faith but does not have works[V]? The[W] faith is not able to save him, *is it*? [15] If brother or sister are naked and lacking daily food [16] and one of you says *to* them "Go in peace; be warmed and filled", but you do not give them the necessities *of* the body, what *is* the profit[X]? [17] In this manner also faith, if it does not have works, is dead by[Y] itself.

A. Or, looking-closely-at. **B.** Or, existence. That is, his natural face. **C.** He saw himself as he is, but it had no lasting effect on him. **D.** Lit, hearer *characterized by* forgetfulness. **E.** Or, restraining, controlling. **F.** Or, worship, religious service. **G.** Or, futile, pointless. **H.** That is, in; or, originated by. **I.** That is, *characterized by* glory (our glorious Lord Jesus Christ); or, *from* glory; or, Christ, [the Lord] *of* glory. **J.** Or, partiality, favoritism. **K.** That is, look with favor upon. **L.** Or, fitly, well, appropriately. **M.** Or, at. That is, under the shadow cast by it. **N.** Or, *characterized by*. **O.** Or, named. That is, the good name your Owner has given you, Christian. **P.** Or, however. **Q.** Or, acting commendably. **R.** Or, carrying-out. **S.** Or, exposed, rebuked. **T.** That is, shown. **U.** Or, boasts, exults; that is, in triumph. **V.** That is, works, actions, deeds, as the fruit of the faith. **W.** That is, the faith just mentioned; *That* faith. A negative answer is expected. **X.** Or, use, benefit. **Y.** That is, *being* by itself. Or, faith by itself is dead.

Faith Cannot Be Seen Apart From Works

18 But someone will say "**You** have faith, and **I** have works". Show me your faith without[A] the works, and **I** will show you the faith by my works. **19** **You** believe that God is one[B]? You do well. Even the demons believe and shudder!

Faith Is Perfected By Works

20 But do you want to know[C], O empty[D] person, that faith without works is useless[E]? **21** Abraham our father— was he not declared-righteous by works[F], having offered Isaac his son on the altar? **22** Do you[G] see that faith was working-with his works, and the faith was perfected[H] by the works? **23** And the Scripture was fulfilled, the *one* saying [in Gen 15:6] "And Abraham believed God, and it was credited *to* him for righteousness". And he was called *a* friend *of* God. **24** Do you[I] *all* see that *a* person is declared-righteous by works, and not by faith alone[J]? **25** And likewise also Rahab the prostitute— was she not declared-righteous by works, having received the messengers and sent-*them*-out *by a* different way? **26** For just as the body without spirit[K] is dead, so also faith without works is dead.

Control Your Tongue And You Will Control Your Life

3:1 Do not become[L] many[M] teachers, my brothers, knowing that we will receive *a* greater judgment. **2** For we all stumble many[N] *ways*. If one does not stumble in speech, this *one is a* perfect man able to bridle[O] also the whole body. **3** Now if we put bridles into the mouths *of* horses so-that they obey us, we also guide their whole body. **4** Behold also ships being so large and being driven by hard winds— they are guided by *a* very small rudder where the impulse *of* the *one* steering wants. **5** So also the tongue is *a* small body-part, and boastfully-declares great *things*. Behold how-small *a* fire kindles how-great *a* forest!

An Untamed Tongue Stains And Burns And Poisons Life

6 And the tongue *is a* fire! The[P] tongue is made[Q] the world *of* [R] unrighteousness among our body-parts— the *thing* staining the whole body and setting-on-fire the course *of our* existence, and being set-on-fire by Gehenna[S]. **7** For every nature[T] *of* both wild-animals and birds, *of* both reptiles and sea-creatures, is tamed and has been tamed *by* the human nature. **8** But none *of* mankind is able to tame the tongue— *a* restless evil, full *of* death-bringing poison. **9** With it we bless the Lord and Father, and with it we curse the people having been made in accordance with *the* likeness *of* God; **10** *a* blessing and *a* curse come out of the same mouth.

A. Or, apart-from. This could only be done by pointing to one's beliefs, which James addresses next. **B.** Or, this may be a statement. 'Believe' is the same root word as 'faith'. Even the demons have this kind of faith. **C.** Or, are you willing to recognize, or acknowledge. **D.** Or, senseless. **E.** Or, inactive, unproductive, idle. **F.** That is, by faith with works, the subject under discussion. A 'Yes' answer is expected. **G.** Or, You see (a statement). That is, you empty person. **H.** Or, completed, fulfilled, brought to its goal. **I.** This 'you' is plural. Or, You *all* see (a statement). **J.** Or, only. That is, by faith with works, and not by faith alone. Faith alone is the faith of hearers only (1:22) and demons (2:19). Works as the inevitable fruit of genuine faith are in view here, not works done to earn salvation (as in Romans). **K.** Or, breath. **L.** Or, be. **M.** That is, a multitude of teachers. Or, Do not many *of you* become teachers. **N.** Or, many *times*, greatly. **O.** Or, restrain, control, hold in check. **P.** Or, fire, the world *of* unrighteousness! The tongue is set among our body-parts *as* the *thing*. **Q.** Or, is set, is constituted. Or, makes-*itself*, renders-*itself*. **R.** Or, *characterized by, belonging to, used by, ruled by.* **S.** Or, Hell. **T.** That is, natural disposition. Or, species, both times in this verse.

Such Destruction Ought Not To Proceed From Us

My brothers, these *things* ought[A] not to be so. **11** The spring does not gush out of the same opening the sweet and the bitter, *does it*? **12** *A* fig tree is not able, my brothers, to make olives, or *a* grapevine figs, *is it*? Neither *is* salty water *able* to make sweet *water.*

Your Speech And Conduct And The Fruit They Produce Reveal The Source of Your Wisdom

13 Who[B] *is* wise and knowledgeable among you? Let him show from *his* good conduct his works *done* in *the* gentleness *of* wisdom. **14** But if you have bitter jealousy and selfish-interest[C] in your heart, do not be vaunting[D] and lying against the truth. **15** This wisdom is not coming down[E] from-above, but *is* earthly, natural, demonic. **16** For where jealousy and selfish-interest *are*, in-that-place *there is* disorder[F] and every bad thing[G]. **17** But the wisdom from-above is first pure, then peaceful, kind, yielding[H], full *of* mercy and good fruits, impartial, sincere. **18** And *the* fruit *of* righteousness is sown in peace *by* the *ones* making peace.

Fights And Battles Come From Your Pursuit of Worldly Desires

4:1 From-what-source *are* fights and from-what-source *are* battles among you? *Are they* not from-here— from your pleasures waging-war in your body-parts? **2** You desire and do not have; you[I] murder. And you are jealous and are not able to obtain; you battle and fight. You do not have because of your not asking! **3** You ask and do not receive because you ask badly[J], in order that you may spend *it* in connection with your pleasures. **4** Adulterous[K] *ones*, do you not know that friendship *with* the world is hostility *toward* God? Therefore, whoever wants to be *a* friend *of* the world makes-himself[L] *an* enemy *of* God. **5** Or do you think that the Scripture[M] speaks vainly? He yearns jealously for the spirit[N] which He made-to-dwell in us!

But God Gives Grace To The Humble. So Submit To God And Purify Your Hearts

6 But He gives greater grace. Therefore it says [in Prov 3:34], "God opposes *the* proud, but gives grace *to the* humble". **7** Therefore, submit *to* God, but resist the devil and he will flee from you. **8** Draw-near *to* God and He will draw-near *to* you. Cleanse *your* hands, sinners, and purify *your* hearts, double-minded *ones*. **9** Be miserable[O] and mourn and weep. Let your laughter be turned into mourning and *your* joy into dejection[P]. **10** Humble-*yourselves*[Q] in the presence of *the* Lord, and He will exalt you.

So Do Not Be Speaking Against Or Judging One Another

11 Do not be speaking-against one another, brothers. The *one* speaking-against *a* brother or judging his brother is speaking-against *the* Law and judging *the* Law. But if you are

---

A. Or, must not. It is true for mankind in general, but not for doers of the word (1:26). A tree is known by its fruit. **B.** Do you claim to have wisdom and knowledge? What does your fruit say about you? **C.** Or, selfish-ambition, party-spirit. **D.** That is, in claiming to be wise. **E.** The source of the wisdom in your heart will be known by the actions it produces in you and in your listeners. **F.** Or, instability, confusion, disturbance. **G.** Or, evil matter, deed, work. **H.** Or, compliant, ready to obey, reasonable. **I:** have; you murder... fight. Or, have. You murder and envy and cannot obtain. You battle and fight. **J.** Or, wrongly. That is, with bad motives. **K.** James is referring to spiritual adultery. **L.** Or, is made, is constituted. **M.** That is, does Scripture in general speak to no purpose about spiritual adultery and God's response to it? Or, Scripture as summarized and paraphrased in v 5b; or, Scripture as quoted in v 6. **N.** Or, Spirit. This may also be rendered 'The Spirit which He caused-to-dwell in us yearns jealously for *us*'; or, 'the spirit which he caused-to-dwell in us yearns enviously' for the world. **O.** Or, Lament. **P.** Or, gloominess, depression. **Q.** Or, Be humbled.

judging *the* Law, you are not *a* doer *of the* Law, but *a* judge. [12] There is one Lawgiver and Judge— the *One* being able to save and to destroy. But who are **you**, the *one* judging *your* neighbor?

Do Not Presume To Direct Your Life Apart From God

[13] Come now, the *ones* saying "Today or tomorrow we will travel to such-and-such city and do *a* year there, and we will do-business and make-a-gain"— [14] who do not know the *thing of* [A] tomorrow! What *is* your life? For you are *a* vapor appearing for *a* little *while,* then indeed disappearing!— [15] instead of you saying, "If the Lord wills, we indeed[B] will live and do this or that". [16] But as-it-is, you are boasting in your pretensions. All such boasting is evil. [17] Therefore, *to one* knowing[C] to be doing good and not doing *it, to* him it is *a* sin.

Ill-Gotten Riches Will Yield a Treasure of Miseries

5:1 Come now, rich *ones,* weep while wailing over your miseries coming-upon *you.* [2] Your riches have rotted and your garments have become moth-eaten. [3] Your gold and silver have become corroded[D]. And their corrosion will be for *a* testimony *against* you, and will eat your flesh like fire. You stored-up *treasure*[E] in *the* last days! [4] Behold— the wages *of* the workers having mowed your fields, the *wages* having been fraudulently-withheld by you, cry-out. And the outcries *of* the *ones* having reaped have entered into the ears *of the* Lord *of* Sabaoth[F]. [5] You lived-in-luxury upon the earth, and you lived-indulgently[G]. You fattened your hearts in[H] *a* day *of* slaughter. [6] You condemned, you murdered the righteous. He does not oppose[I] you!

Be Patient and Endure Hardship Until The Lord Comes

[7] Therefore be patient, brothers, until the coming *of* the Lord. Behold— the farmer waits-for the precious fruit *of* the land, being-patient with it until it receives *the* early and late *rain.* [8] **You** also be-patient. Establish your hearts, because the coming *of* the Lord has drawn-near. [9] Do not be groaning against one another, brothers, in order that you may not be judged. Behold— the Judge stands in front of the doors. [10] Take *as an* example *of* suffering-hardship and patience, brothers, the prophets who spoke in the name *of the* Lord. [11] Behold— we consider-blessed the *ones* having endured! You heard *of* the endurance *of* Job, and you saw the outcome *from the* Lord: that the Lord is large-hearted[J] and compassionate.

Above All, Be True To Your Word. Be Praying And Singing-Praise

[12] And above all, my brothers, do not be swearing[K]— neither *by* heaven nor *by* earth nor *by* any other oath. But let your yes be yes and *your* no *be* no, in order that you may not fall under judgment. [13] Is anyone among you suffering-hardship? Let him be praying. Is anyone cheerful? Let him be singing-praise.

Pray For One Another So That You May Be Healed

[14] Is anyone among you sick? Let him summon the elders *of* the church, and let them pray over him, having anointed[L] him *with* oil in the name *of the* Lord. [15] And the prayer *of*[M] faith

---

A. That is, belonging to. In other words, what will happen tomorrow. **B.** Or, both. **C.** This general rule applies in this case. **D.** Or, tarnished. **E.** Or, *wrath, witnesses.* **F.** Or, hosts, armies. **G.** Or, lived-for-pleasure. **H.** That is, in connection with. **I.** Or, resist, set himself in array against. **J.** Or, very-affectionate, very-kind. **K.** That is, swearing an oath to strengthen or guarantee your word. **L.** Or, rubbed, smeared. A medicinal use of oil may be in view here, as in Lk 10:34; or, a symbolic use of oil, as in Mk 6:13. In the latter case, the oil may be symbolic of the healing power of the Holy Spirit. **M.** That is, characterized by; or, proceeding from.

will restore[A] the *one* being ill, and the Lord will raise him. And if he has committed[B] sins, it will be forgiven him. **¹⁶** Therefore be confessing-out[C] *your* sins *to* one another, and be praying for one another so that you may be healed. *A* prayer[D] *of a* righteous *person* can-do much while working[E]. **¹⁷** Elijah was *a* person of-like-nature *to* us, and he prayed *with* prayer[F] *that it* not rain. And it did not rain upon the land *for* three years and six months. **¹⁸** And he prayed again and the heaven gave rain, and the earth produced its fruit.

Try To Turn Back Those Who Stray From The Truth
¹⁹ My brothers, if anyone among you errs[G] from the truth and someone turns him back, **²⁰** let him know that the *one* having turned-back *a* sinner from *the* error *of* his way will save his[H] soul[I] from death, and will cover *a* multitude *of* sins.

A. Or, save *from disease*. **B.** That is, if he is in a state of having committed sins, resulting in his sickness. **C.** Or, openly acknowledging. **D.** That is, prayer request, petition. **E.** Or, while at-work. Or this may be rendered 'the working prayer *of a* righteous *person* can do much', in which case the working (or, effective) prayer means the prayer that God answers. **F:** he prayed *with* prayer. This is a Hebrew way of speaking, meaning he prayed earnestly. **G.** Or, wanders, goes astray, is led astray. **H.** That is, the sinner's. **I.** Or, life.

1 Peter

Introduction   1:1-2

A.   Blessed be God, the One having caused us to be born again to a living hope, in which you are   1:3-12
     rejoicing greatly, though right now having been grieved by various trials

B.   Therefore: 1:13

     1.   Put your hope completely on the grace being brought to you at the revelation of Christ   1:13
     2.   As children of obedience, be holy in all your conduct, just as He is holy   1:14-16
     3.   Conduct the time of your stay with fear, knowing you were redeemed with His blood   1:17-21
     4.   Love one another from a pure heart, having been born again through the word of God   1:22-25
     5.   Yearn like babies for the milk of the Word, if you tasted that the Lord is good,   2:1-3

          a.   Coming to Whom as the Living Cornerstone, you also as living stones are being   2:4-8
               built as a spiritual house for a holy priesthood to offer spiritual sacrifices
          b.   And you are a chosen family, a royal priesthood to report His virtues   2:9-10

     6.   Beloved, I exhort you to be abstaining from fleshly desires   2:11-12
     7.   Be subject to every human institution for the Lord's sake   2:13-15
     8.   As free ones, honor everyone—   2:16-17

          a.   Servants, being subject to your masters. For you were called to suffer like Christ   2:18-25
          b.   Likewise wives, being subject to your own husbands   3:1-6
          c.   Husbands likewise, showing honor to the feminine one as to a fellow heir   3:7
          d.   And finally, everyone— being likeminded, sympathetic, brother-loving, humble   3:8-12

C.   Who will do you evil for doing good? But though you might be suffering, you are blessed!   3:13-14

     1.   But do not fear them, but set apart Christ as Lord in your hearts, being ready always for a   3:14-17
          defense to everyone asking a reason for the hope in you, having a good conscience
     2.   Because Christ also suffered for sins, in order that He might bring you to God   3:18-22
     3.   Therefore, Christ having suffered, you also arm yourselves with the same intention   4:1-7
     4.   Therefore be sound-minded, sober in prayer, loving, hospitable, ministering your gift   4:7-11
     5.   Beloved, do not think your fiery trials strange, but be rejoicing to share His sufferings!   4:12-18
     6.   So then, let the ones suffering according to the will of God be entrusting their souls in   4:19
          good-doing to a faithful Creator

          a.   Therefore I exhort the elders— Shepherd the flock of God among you by example   5:1-4
          b.   Likewise, younger men—Be subject to the elders   5:5
          c.   And everyone,— Clothe yourselves with humblemindedness. Resist the devil   5:5-9
          d.   And having suffered *a* little, the God *of* all grace will Himself restore you   5:10-11

Conclusion   5:12-14

1:1 Peter, *an* apostle *of* Jesus Christ *to the* chosen pilgrims[A] *of the* dispersion *of* Pontus, Galatia, Cappadocia, Asia, and Bythinia, **²** according-to[B] *the* foreknowledge *of* God *the* Father, in[C] *the* sanctification[D] *of the* Spirit, for[E] obedience and *the* sprinkling *of the* blood *of* Jesus Christ: May grace and peace be multiplied *to* you.

Blessed Be God For Our Present And Future Salvation, Which Was Prophesied Long Ago
³ Blessed *be* the God and Father *of* our Lord Jesus Christ, the *One* having caused us to be born-again[F] according to His great mercy to *a* living hope through *the* resurrection *of* Jesus Christ from *the* dead, **⁴** to *an* undecayable[G] and undefiled and unfading inheritance having been reserved[H] in *the* heavens for you— **⁵** the *ones* being guarded by *the* power *of* God through faith for[I] *a* salvation ready to be revealed in *the* last time,

> **⁶** ... in which you are rejoicing-greatly, [although] right-now *for a* little *while,* if it is necessary, having been grieved by various trials **⁷** in order that the genuineness *of* your faith— *being* more-valuable *than* gold (*which is* perishing), though being tested by fire— may be found resulting-in praise and glory and honor at *the* revelation *of* Jesus Christ,

>> **⁸** ... Whom not having seen, you are loving; in Whom— right-now not seeing *Him,* but believing— you are rejoicing-greatly *with* inexpressible[J] and glorified joy **⁹** while receiving[K] the outcome[L] *of* your faith, *the* salvation *of your* souls,

>>> **¹⁰** ... concerning which salvation prophets sought-out and searched-out— the *ones* having prophesied about the grace for[M] you— **¹¹** searching for what *person*[N] or what manner of time the Spirit *of* Christ in them was indicating while predicting the sufferings for Christ and the glories after these, **¹²** *to* whom it was revealed that they were ministering them not *for* themselves, but *for* you,

>>> ... which *things* now were declared *to* you through the *ones* having announced-the-good-news-to you by *the* Holy Spirit having been sent-forth from heaven, into which *things* angels desire to look.

In Light of What God Has Done:
¹³ Therefore:

> *Put Your Hope Completely Upon Your Coming Salvation*
> Having girded-up the waist *of* your minds[O], being sober[P]— put-*your*-hope completely[Q] upon the grace being brought *to* you at *the* revelation *of* Jesus Christ.

> *Be Holy In All Your Conduct*
> **¹⁴** As children *of*[R] obedience not being conformed[S] *to* the former desires in-connection-with your ignorance, **¹⁵** but in accordance with the holy *One* having called you— be holy

---

A. That is, temporary residents. **B.** Or, based on. **C.** Or, in connection with, in the domain of. **D.** Or, holiness, holy-making. **E.** Or, resulting in. **F:** caused us to be born again. Or, regenerated us, fathered us again, given us a new birth. **G.** Or, imperishable. **H.** Or, kept, protected, held. **I.** Or, until. **J.** Or, untellable, unspeakable. **K.** Or, obtaining. **L.** Or, goal, end. **M.** Or, the grace *that would come* to you. **N.** Or, *time.* **O.** That is, having prepared your minds for exertion or work. **P.** Or, well-balanced, clear-headed. **Q.** Or, fully, totally. **R.** That is, characterized by. **S.** Or, conforming *yourselves.*

yourselves also in all *your* conduct^A. ^16 Because it has been written that "You shall be holy, because **I** am holy" [Lev 19:2].

Live Out Your Days In The Fear of God
^17 And if you are calling-upon *as* Father the *One* judging without-respect-of-persons according to the work *of* each *person*— conduct the time *of* your stay^B with fear^C, ^18 knowing that you were redeemed from your futile^D way-of-life handed-down-from-your-fathers not *with* perishable *things,* silver or gold, ^19 but *with the* precious blood *of* Christ, as *of a* lamb without-blemish and without-spot; ^20 *He* having been foreknown before *the* foundation *of the* world but having appeared^E at *the* last *of* times for your sake, ^21 the believers through Him in God— the *One* having raised Him from *the* dead and having given Him glory— so that your faith and hope are in God.

Love One Another From a Pure Heart
^22 Having purified your souls in^F obedience *of* the truth for *a* sincere^G brotherly-love— love one another fervently from *a* pure heart, ^23 having been born-again not from perishable seed but imperishable, through *the* living and abiding word *of* God. ^24 Because "All flesh *is* like grass and all its glory like *a* flower *of* grass. The grass was dried-up and the flower fell-off. ^25 But the word *of the* Lord abides forever" [Isa 40:6-8]— and this is the word having been announced-as-good-news to you.

Yearn For His Word So That You May Grow
2:1 Having then laid-aside all badness^H, and all deceit and hypocrisies and jealousies, and all slanders—^2 yearn like newborn babies for the deceitless^I milk of-the-Word^J in order that by it you may grow in^K [your] salvation, ^3 if^L you tasted that the Lord *is* good—

For You Are Being Built Upon The Living Cornerstone As a Holy Priesthood
^4 ... coming to Whom *as the* living Stone having been rejected by people, but chosen, precious with God, ^5 you yourselves also as living stones are being built^M *as a* spiritual house for *a* holy priesthood, to offer spiritual sacrifices acceptable *to* God through Jesus Christ. ^6 Because it is contained in Scripture: "Behold, I am laying *a* Stone in Zion— *a* chosen, precious Cornerstone. And the *one* putting-faith upon Him will never be put-to-shame" [Isa 28:16]. ^7 The *precious*-value then *is for* you, the *ones* believing. But *for ones* not-believing: "*The* Stone which the *ones* building rejected, this became *the* head^N *of the* corner" [Ps 118:22] ^8 and "*a* Stone *of* stumbling and *a* Rock *of* ^O falling" [Isa 8:14]— who stumble while^P disobeying the word, to which indeed they were appointed^Q.

And You Are Chosen By God To Report His Virtues To The World
^9 And you *are a* chosen family^R, *a* royal priesthood, *a* holy nation, *a* people for *His*

A. Or, behavior, way of life. **B.** That is, stay as foreigners. **C.** Or, reverence. **D.** Or, useless, pointless, worthless. **E.** Or, having been made known. **F.** Or, by. **G.** Or, unhypocritical. **H.** Or, evilness, malice. **I.** Or, pure, unadulterated. **J.** Or, pertaining-to-the-Word. Or, pertaining-to-the-real-nature-of-things, and thus, 'spiritual' milk. **K.** Or, in relation to, into. **L.** That is, assuming that. **M.** Or, are building *yourselves*. Or this may be a command, be built, build *yourselves*. **N.** See Mk 12:10. **O.** That is, causing a fall. **P.** That is, because they are disobeying; or, by disobeying. **Q.** Or, destined. **R.** Or, race, people, nation.

possession, so that you may report the virtues^A *of* the *One* having called you out of darkness into His marvelous light— **10** who once *were* not *a* people, but now *are the* people *of* God; the *ones* not having received-mercy, but now having received-mercy.

Beloved, Keep Your Conduct Praiseworthy In The World So That God May Be Glorified
11 Beloved, I exhort *you* as foreigners^B and pilgrims to be abstaining *from* fleshly desires which wage-war against the soul, **12** holding your conduct good^C among the Gentiles in order that in what they are speaking-against you as evil-doers^D, they may by observing *your* good works glorify God on *the* day *of* visitation^E.

Be Subject To Human Institutions For The Lord's Sake
13 Be subject *to* every human institution for the Lord's sake— whether *to a* king as being superior, **14** or *to* governors as being sent by him^F for *the* punishment *of* evil-doers and praise *of* good-doers. **15** Because thus is the will *of* God, *that* while doing-good *you may* be silencing the ignorance *of* foolish people.

Honor Everyone
16 As^G free *ones,* and not having the freedom as *a* covering *of* evilness, but as slaves *of* God, **17** honor everyone: be loving the brotherhood^H, be fearing God, be honoring the king;

Be Subject To Your Masters, Whether Good Or Bad, Following Christ's Example
18 ... servants, being subject *to your* masters with all fear^I, not only *to* the good and kind *ones,* but also *to* the crooked^J *ones.* **19** For this *finds* favor— if for the sake of *a* consciousness^K *of* God one bears-up^L while suffering sorrows unjustly. **20** For what-kind-of credit^M *is it* if while sinning and being beaten, you will endure? But if while doing-good and suffering you will endure, this *finds* favor with God. **21** For you were called to this^N. Because Christ also suffered for you, leaving-behind *a* pattern *for* you in order that you might follow-after His footsteps—

Christ Suffered Unjustly, Entrusting Himself To God
22 ... Who "did not commit sin, nor was deceit found in His mouth" [Isa 53:9]; **23** Who while being reviled, was not reviling-in-return; while suffering, was not threatening, but was committing *Himself*^O to the *One* judging righteously; **24** Who Himself bore our sins in His body on the cross in order that we, having died^P *to* sins, might live *for* righteousness; *by* Whose bruise you were healed. **25** For you were going-astray like sheep, but now you returned to the Shepherd and Overseer *of* your souls.

Be Subject To Your Husbands, Adorning Yourself With Things Precious To God
3:1 Likewise wives, being subject *to your* own husbands, in order that even if any are disobeying the word, they may be gained without *a* word by the conduct *of their*

A. Or, excellencies, praises, mighty acts. **B.** Or, resident aliens. **C.** Or, commendable, praiseworthy. **D.** Or, criminals (in living as Christians). **E.** That is, the day when God visits them with salvation or judgment; or, the day when they judge you. **F.** Or, Him. **G.** Or, [Live] as free *ones.* **H.** That is, the community of believers. **I.** That is, with all respect; or, in all reverence *of God.* **J.** Or, dishonest, unscrupulous. That is, toward you, v 19. **K.** Or, conscience *toward* God. **L.** Or, endures. **M.** Or, fame, glory. **N.** That is, to bear up under unjust suffering for Christ. **O.** Or, *them, it.* **P.** Or, being dead.

wives, **2** having observed your pure conduct with fear[A]— **3** *of* whom let *what is observed*[B] be not the outside adornment *consisting of a* braiding *of* hair and *a* wearing *of* gold *things* or putting-on *of* garments, **4** but the hidden person *of* the heart in[C] the imperishable *adorning consisting of* the gentle and quiet spirit, which is very-precious in the sight of God. **5** For in this manner formerly also the holy wives putting-hope in God were adorning themselves, being subject *to their* own husbands,**6** as Sarah obeyed Abraham, calling him lord[D]— *of* whom[E] you became children while[F] doing-good and not fearing any terror[G].

Honor Your Wives As Fellow Heirs of The Gift of Life
7 Husbands likewise, living-with *them*[H] according-to[I] knowledge[J], showing honor *to* the feminine[K] *one* as to[L] *the* weaker vessel[M], as indeed *to your* fellow-heirs *of the* grace[N] *of* life, so that your prayers *may* not be hindered.

Everyone Be Loving, Humbleminded, And Doing Good
8 And finally, everyone— *being* likeminded[O], sympathetic, brother-loving, tender-hearted[P], humbleminded, **9** not giving-back evil for evil or reviling[Q] for reviling, but on the contrary, blessing *them*. Because you were called to this, in order that you might inherit *a* blessing. **10** For "the *one* desiring[R] to love life and see good days— let him stop *his* tongue from evil and *his* lips *that they* not speak deceit; **11** and let him turn-away from evil and do good. Let him seek peace and pursue it. **12** Because *the* eyes *of the* Lord *are* upon *the* righteous, and His ears *are open* to their prayer. But *the* face *of the* Lord *is* against *ones* doing evil *things*" [Ps 34:12-16].

You Are Blessed If You Suffer For Righteousness
13 And who *is* the *one who* will do you evil[S] if you become zealots[T] *for* good? **14** But even though you might be suffering[U] for the sake of righteousness, *you are* blessed[V] ones!

Make Christ Lord In Your Heart As You Suffer For Doing Good
But do not fear their fear[W], nor be disturbed, **15** but set Christ apart *as* Lord in your hearts, *being* ready always for *a* defense *to* everyone asking you *a* reason for the hope in you, **16** but with gentleness and fear[X], having *a* good conscience in order that in what you are spoken-against[Y], the *ones* maligning your good conduct in Christ may be put-to-shame. **17** For *it is* better to be suffering while doing-good, if the will *of* God should [so] will *it*, than while doing-evil.

A. Or, with respect *for them*. Or, with reverence *for God*. **B:** *what is observed*. Or, *their adornment*. Lit, *it*. **C.** That is, dressed in. **D.** Or, sir. See Gen 18:12. **E.** That is, Sarah. **F.** That is, by, as long as you are, since you are, as ones. **G.** Or, intimidation, fright. **H:** living with *them...* fellow-heirs. Or, living with the feminine *one* according-to knowledge, as *with the* weaker vessel, showing honor as indeed *to* fellow heirs. **I.** Or, in harmony with, based on. **J.** That is, Christian knowledge of her status before God. Or, understanding; that is, in an understanding way, with consideration. **K.** Or, womanly *one*, female. **L.** That is, as appropriate to. **M.** This describes her as God's creation, rather than the husband's partner. **N.** That is, the grace-gift of spiritual life, which they possess equally. **O.** Or, harmonious. **P.** Or, good-hearted. **Q.** Or, insult, abuse. **R.** Or, wanting, intending. **S.** Or, harm you, mistreat you. **T.** Or, zealous. **U:** even though you might be suffering... *you are* blessed. Or, if you even should suffer... *you would be* blessed. **V.** Or, fortunate, from God's point of view. **W.** That is, their intimidation; or, what they fear. **X.** That is respect; or, fear of God. **Y.** Or, slandered.

Because Christ Himself Suffered To Bring Us To God, And Is Now Glorified By God
18 Because Christ also suffered once-for-all for sins— *a* righteous *One* for unrighteous *ones*— in order that He might bring you to God, having been put-to-death *in the* flesh but made-alive[A] *by the* Spirit[B],

> **19** ... by Whom[C] also[D] having gone, He proclaimed[E] *to* the spirits[F] in prison— **20** *ones* having disobeyed formerly when the patience *of* God was waiting in *the* days *of* Noah while *an* ark *was* being prepared,

> > ... in which *a* few (that is, eight souls) were brought-safely through *the* water,

> > > **21** ... which[G] also *as to* you *a* corresponding-*thing*[H] now saves— baptism (not *a* putting-off[I] *of* dirt *from the* flesh, but *an* appeal[J] to God *for*[K] *a* good conscience) through *the* resurrection *of* Jesus Christ,

> > > > **22** ... Who is at *the* right *hand of* God, having gone into heaven, angels and authorities and powers having been subjected *to* Him.

Therefore Arm Yourselves With The Same Intention
4:1 Therefore, Christ having suffered *in the* flesh, **you** also arm-*yourselves with* the same intention[L]. Because the *one* having suffered *in the* flesh has ceased *from* sin, **2** so as to live the remaining time in *the* flesh no longer *for*[M] the desires *of* humans, but *for*[M] the will *of* God. **3** For the time having passed *is* enough *for you* to have worked-out the will *of* the Gentiles, having walked in sensualities, lusts, drunkenness, revelries, drinking-parties and unlawful idolatries, **4** in connection with which they are thinking-*it*-strange *that* you *are* not running-with *them* into the same excess[N] *of* wild-living, while *they continue* blaspheming— **5** who shall render *an* account *to* the One being ready to judge *the* living and *the* dead. **6** For to this *end* it[O] was announced-as-good-news even *to the* dead[P]: that they might be judged according-to[Q] people *in the* flesh[R], but be living according to God *in the* spirit[S]. **7** And[T] the end *of* all *things* has drawn-near.

So Be Sober In Prayer, Loving One Another, And Good Stewards of God's Gifts To You
Therefore be sound-minded and be sober in[U] *your* prayers— **8** above all, having fervent

---

A. Or, given life. **B.** Or, *in the* Spirit; or, *in* spirit, *in His* spirit; or, *in the realm of the* spirit. **C.** That is, the Spirit. Or, in which. That is, in His spirit; or, in the state of being dead in the flesh but alive in spirit. **D.** Or even; that is, by Whom having gone, He even proclaimed. **E.** Or, made a proclamation. **F.** That is, people; or, angels. **G.** That is, which event (Noah being brought safely through the water); or, which water. **H.** Or, a fulfillment; or, a reflection, echo, copy. **I.** Or, removal. **J.** Or, request. Or, pledge, answer; that is, *the* pledge *to keep a* good conscience toward God, or, *the* pledge to God *from a* good conscience. **K.** Or, *from*. **L.** Or, thought, way of thinking. That is, to suffer for righteousness (3:14) like Christ (3:18). **M.** Or, *in, by*. **N.** Or, flood, pouring-out. **O.** That is, the gospel. Or, He; that is, Christ (as the judge in v 5; Act 17:31). **P:** *the* dead... spirit. That is, to spiritually dead ones, that having become Christians, they might be judged in accordance with human standards while living on earth (and thus suffer for righteousness like Christ), but be living in accordance with God's standards now and forever (continuing the main argument from v 1-4); or, to now dead Christians while they were still alive, that they might have been judged by human standards while on earth, but now be living with God as He desires, in accordance with His nature and likeness (continuing on from v 5). **Q.** Or, by way of, in keeping with. **R.** That is, *in the sphere of the* flesh, *in connection with* mankind's human fleshly nature. **S.** Or, Spirit. **T.** A final reason we should arm ourselves with this intention. Or, Now; the beginning of the next paragraph. **U.** Or, for, for the purpose of.

love for each other, because love covers *a* multitude *of* sins; **9** *being* hospitable to one another without grumbling; **10** as each received *a grace*-gift, ministering it to each other as good stewards[A] *of the* diversified grace *of* God— **11** if anyone speaks, as *speaking* oracles[B] *of* God; if anyone serves, as *serving* by strength which God supplies— in order that God may be glorified in all *things* through Jesus Christ, *to* Whom is the glory and the dominion forever and ever, amen.

Beloved, Be Rejoicing To Share In The Sufferings of Christ

12 Beloved, do not be thinking-strange the fiery[C] *suffering* among you coming *upon* you for *a* trial[D], as-*though a* strange *thing were* happening *to* you, **13** but be rejoicing to-the-degree you are sharing *in* the sufferings *of* Christ, in order that you may also rejoice while being overjoyed at the revelation *of* His glory! **14** If you are being reproached[E] in[F] *the* name *of* Christ, *you are* blessed[G] *ones*!— because the Spirit *of* glory and *of* God is resting upon you. **15** For let none *of* you be suffering as *a* murderer or thief or evil-doer, or as *a* meddler[H]. **16** But if *one suffers* as *a* Christian, let him not be ashamed, but let him be glorifying God in this name. **17** Because *it is* time *that* the judgment begin from the household[I] *of* God. But if *it begins* first from us, what *will be* the outcome *of* the *ones* disobeying the good-news *of* God? **18** "And if the righteous *one* is saved with-difficulty, where will the ungodly and sinner appear[J]?" [Prov 11:31].

Entrust Your Souls To God While Doing Good

19 So then, let indeed the *ones* suffering according to the will *of* God be entrusting their souls in good-doing *to a* faithful Creator.

So Elders, Lead By Example

5:1 Therefore[K] I exhort the elders among you, *I* the fellow-elder and witness *of* the sufferings *of* Christ, the sharer[L] also *of* the glory going-to be revealed: **2** Shepherd the flock *of* God among you, exercising-oversight— not by-compulsion[M], but willingly[N], according to God; nor greedily, but eagerly; **3** nor as lording-over[O] *your* lots[P], but being patterns *for* the flock. **4** And the Chief-shepherd having appeared, you will receive the unfading crown *of*[Q] glory.

Young Men, Follow

5 Likewise, younger *men*— be subject *to the*[R] elders.

Everyone, Be Humble And Keep Watch For The Adversary

And everyone— clothe-*yourselves*-with humblemindedness *toward* one another. Because "God opposes *the* proud, but He gives grace *to the* humble" [Prov 3:34].

A. Or, managers, administrators. **B.** Or, sayings, pronouncements, declarations. **C.** That is, painful, intense. **D.** Or, test. **E.** Or, insulted, scolded. **F.** That is, in connection with. **G.** Or, fortunate, from God's point of view. **H.** Or, busybody. **I.** Or, family. **J.** Or, show-*themselves*, make-*their*-appearance. If Christians suffer such fiery trials on earth while entering into the kingdom of God, where in God's kingdom will unbelievers be seen? **K.** In these circumstances and to this end, I exhort you as follows. **L.** That is, former sharer (at the transfiguration, 2 Pet 1:17); or, future sharer with you. **M.** Or, out of obligation, by necessity; by being forced into this role. **N.** Or, by-choice, voluntarily. **O.** Or, domineering, ruling-over. **P.** That is, the ones allotted to your charge by God; those for whom you are responsible. **Q.** That is, consisting of, belonging to, characterized by. **R.** Or, *your*. That is, your leaders just mentioned; or, your elders in general, older people.

⁶ Therefore humble *yourselves* under the mighty hand *of* God in order that He may exalt you at *the* proper-time, ⁷ having cast all your anxiety^A upon Him, because He is concerned^B about you. ⁸ Be sober, keep-watch. Your adversary *the* devil is walking-around like *a* roaring lion, seeking someone to devour— ⁹ whom resist, firm *in* the^C faith, knowing *that* the same *kinds of* sufferings *are* being accomplished^D *by* your brotherhood *in* the world.

And The God of All Grace Will Establish You After Your Sufferings
¹⁰ And the God *of* all grace, the *One* having called you into His eternal glory in Christ Jesus— *you* having suffered *a* little— will Himself restore, support, strengthen, establish *you.* ¹¹ *To* Him *be* the dominion forever, amen.

¹² I wrote *to* you through Silvanus, the faithful brother, as I count *him,* with *a* few *words* exhorting and bearing-witness *that* this^E is *the* true grace *of* God— in which, stand [firm]. ¹³ *She* in Babylon^F chosen-with *you* greets you. Also Mark, my son. ¹⁴ Greet one another with *a* kiss *of* love. Peace *to* you, *to* all the *ones* in Christ.

A. Or, care, concern, worry. **B.** Lit, it is *a* concern *to* Him about you. **C.** Or, *in your* faith. **D.** Or, paid; that is, knowing *that* the same *debt of* sufferings *is* being paid. **E.** That is, this of which Peter has written and taught in this letter. **F.** Peter may be referring to a church in Rome.

2 Peter

Introduction   1:1-2

A.   Because of His divine power having granted us all things for life and godliness, and indeed for   1:3-7
this very reason you having applied all diligence, in your faith supply virtue, knowledge, love

    1.   For these qualities make you neither useless nor unfruitful in the knowledge of Christ   1:8-9
    2.   Therefore brothers, be more diligent to be making your calling and election firm   1:10-11

B.   I will always remind you about these things, even though you have known the truth   1:12-15

    1.   For we made known to you the power and coming of our Lord Jesus as eyewitnesses   1:16-18
    2.   And we have the prophetic word more firm, to which you are doing well to pay attention   1:19-21
    3.   But there will also be false teachers among you, and many will follow them   2:1-3

        a.   God knows how to deliver the godly and reserve the unrighteous for judgment   2:4-10
        b.   They are self-willed slaves of corruption with hearts trained in greed   2:10-22

C.   Beloved, I am writing this to arouse you to remember the words of the prophets and apostles,   3:1-4
knowing this first— that mockers will come denying the coming of the day of the Lord

    1.   For this escapes their notice, that God destroyed the ancient world with a flood, and the   3:5-7
present heavens and earth have been stored up for fire at the judgment of the ungodly
    2.   But do not let it escape your notice, beloved, that one day with God is like a thousand years.   3:8-13
The Lord is not slow about the promise, but is patient, not wishing any to perish. But the
day of the Lord will come like a thief, so what kind of people should you be?
    3.   Therefore beloved, while looking for these things, be diligent to be found unspotted   3:14-16
    4.   You therefore be guarding yourselves. And be growing in the grace of our Lord   3:17-18

1:1 Simeon[A] Peter, *a* slave and apostle *of* Jesus Christ, *to* the *ones* having received *an* equally-precious faith *with* us by-means-of[B] *the* righteousness *of* our God and Savior Jesus Christ: **²** May grace and peace be multiplied *to* you in[C] *the* knowledge *of* God and Jesus our Lord.

Because of All That God Has Given Us, Diligently Add To Your Faith These God-Like Qualities
³ Because-of His divine power having granted[D] us **all** *things* pertaining-to life and godliness through the knowledge *of* the *One* having called us *by*[E] *His* own glory and virtue[F], **⁴** through which *qualities*[G] He has granted us the precious and greatest *things*-promised in order that through these[H] you might become sharers *of the* divine nature[I], having escaped-from the corruption in the world by *evil* desire; **⁵** and indeed *for* this very *reason you* having applied all diligence— in[J] your faith supply[K] virtue; and in *your* virtue, knowledge; **⁶** and in *your* knowledge, self-control; and in *your* self-control, endurance; and in *your* endurance, godliness; **⁷** and in *your* godliness, brotherly-love; and in *your* brotherly-love, love.

These Qualities Make You Useful And Fruitful
⁸ For these *qualities* being-present *in* you and increasing make[L] *you* neither useless[M] nor unfruitful in the knowledge *of* our Lord Jesus Christ. **⁹** For *the one in* whom these *qualities* are not present is blind, being shortsighted[N], having forgotten[O] the purification *of* his former sins.

So Be Diligent To Make Your Calling And Election Firm
¹⁰ Therefore brothers, be **more** diligent to be making your calling and election[P] firm[Q]. For while doing these *things* you will by no means ever stumble. **¹¹** For in this manner the entrance into the eternal kingdom *of* our Lord and Savior Jesus Christ will be richly supplied *to* you.

I Will Always Be Reminding You of These Things As Long As I Live
¹² Therefore, I will-certainly[R] always be reminding you about these *things,* even though *you are ones* knowing and having been established in *the* truth being present *with you.* **¹³** And I regard *it* right for as long as I am in this [bodily] tent to be arousing you with *a* reminder, **¹⁴** knowing that the putting-off *of* my [bodily] tent is imminent, just as indeed our Lord Jesus Christ made-clear *to* me. **¹⁵** And I will also be diligent *that* at-any-time after my departure[S], you *may* have *the ability* to produce the memory *of* these *things.*

For We Were Eyewitnesses of Christ's Majesty And Glory
¹⁶ For we made-known *to* you the power and coming *of* our Lord Jesus Christ— not having followed-after cleverly-devised myths, but having been made[T] eyewitnesses *of* the majesty *of* that *One.* **¹⁷** For *He* having received from God the Father *the* honor and glory *of* such *a* voice[U] having been carried[V] *to* Him by the Majestic Glory— "This is My Son, My Beloved, in Whom **I** was[W] well-pleased"— **¹⁸** we ourselves also heard this voice having been carried out of heaven, being with Him on the holy mountain.

A. This is the Aramaic spelling of 'Simon', found also in Act 15:14. **B.** Or, through. **C.** Or, by, in the sphere of. **D.** Or, bestowed, given as a gift. **E.** Or, *to.* **F.** Or, moral-excellence, excellence of character. **G.** That is, the glory and virtue. **H.** That is, the things promised. **I.** That is, God's character qualities. **J.** That is, in connection with; or, in the sphere of. **K.** Or, provide, furnish. **L.** Or, render. **M.** Or, idle, unproductive. **N.** Such ones do not see the distant reality. **O.** Lit, received forgetfulness *of.* **P.** Or, choosing, selection. **Q.** Or, secure, sure, steadfast, reliable. **R.** Or, must. **S.** That is, his death. **T.** Or, having come-to-be. **U.** That is, such a unique voice. Or, *of an* utterance such-as-this. **V.** Or, borne-along, brought-forth. **W.** Or, I delighted, I took-pleasure. See Mt 3:17.

And We Have God's Prophetic Word More Firm

19 And we have the prophetic^A word *as* more-firm^B, *to* which you are doing well *to be* paying-attention as *to a* lamp shining in *a* dismal^C place, until which *time the* day dawns and *the* morning-star rises in your hearts, **20** knowing this first— that no prophecy *of* Scripture comes^D *from one's* own^E interpretation^F. **21** For no prophecy was ever carried^G *by the* will *of a* human, but people being carried by *the* Holy Spirit spoke from God.

And There Will Be False Teachers Among You, Exploiting You

2:1 But false-prophets also came among the people, as there will also be false-teachers among you who will secretly-bring-in heresies *of*^H destruction— even denying the Master having bought them, bringing swift destruction upon themselves. **2** And many will follow-after their sensualities^I, because of whom the way *of* the truth will be blasphemed. **3** And in greed they will exploit^J you *with* fabricated words, *for* whom the judgment from-long-ago is not idle, and their destruction is not asleep.

God Will Reserve Them For Punishment And Protect The Righteous

4 For if God did not spare angels having sinned but handed-*them*-over *to* chains *of* gloom, having cast-*them*-into-hell, being reserved for^K judgment; **5** and He did not spare *the* ancient world but protected *the* eighth^L *one*, Noah, *a* proclaimer *of* righteousness, having brought *a* flood upon *the* world *of* ungodly *ones*; **6** and He condemned *the* cities *of* Sodom and Gomorrah, having reduced-*them*-to-ashes *by an* overthrow, having made *them an* example *of things* coming *to* ungodly *ones*; **7** and He delivered Lot, *a* righteous *one* being oppressed^M by the conduct *of* the lawless^N *ones* in connection with sensuality (**8** for *by* sight and hearing the righteous *one* dwelling among them day^O after day was tormenting *his* righteous soul *with their* lawless^P works)— **9** *then the* Lord knows-*how* to deliver godly *ones* from *a* trial^Q and reserve unrighteous *ones* for *the* day *of* judgment while being punished, **10** and especially the *ones* proceeding after *the* flesh in^R *a* lust^S *for*^T defilement, and despising^U authority^V.

They Are Self-Willed Slaves of Corruption Speaking Against The Things of God

Daring^W, self-willed *ones*— they do not tremble while blaspheming glories^X, **11** where^Y angels being greater *in* strength and power do not bring *a* blasphemous judgment against them from *the* Lord. **12** But these *ones are* like unreasoning animals having

---

A. That is, the words written by the prophets; in particular, about the Messiah. **B.** That is, more certain as to its meaning, because we were eyewitnesses of its fulfillment. Or, we have the more-firm prophetic word, the OT prophecies, an even stronger witness than our eyewitness account of the voice from heaven. **C.** Or, squalid, dark. **D.** That is, comes to be written; or, comes to pass; or, comes to be understood. **E.** Or, personal, private. **F.** Or, explanation. God is the author and fulfiller of prophecy. The key to Isa 53, for example, is how God fulfilled it, not how humans interpret it. Thus, Peter has the prophetic word more firm because he was an eyewitness of its fulfillment. **G.** That is, carried out of heaven, as in v 18. **H.** That is, *leading to*; or, *characterized by* (destructive heresies). **I.** Or, indecent conduct, lustful indulgences. **J.** Or, make merchandise of. **K.** Or, until. **L.** That is, eighth along with seven others. **M.** Or, worn out. **N.** That is, ones who rebel against what is 'set down'. **O:** dwelling... day after day. Or, was day after day tormenting. **P.** That is, contrary to law. **Q.** Or, from temptation. **R.** That is, in connection with. Or, with. **S.** Or, desire. **T:** *a* lust *for* defilement. Or, *a* desire *characterized by* defilement, *a* defiled desire. **U.** Or, scorning, disregarding. **V.** Or, lordship, dominion. That is, authority in general; or, the lordship of Christ (denying the Master, 2:1); or, the rule of angels; or, the authority of church leaders. **W.** Or, Bold, in a negative sense, Presumptuous. **X.** Or, dignities, majesties. Compare Jude 8-9. **Y.** Or, whereas.

been born *as creatures*-of-instinct[A] for capture and destruction. While blaspheming in[B] *things* which they are ignorant, they will also be destroyed in their[C] destruction[D], [13] being wronged *as the* wages *of* wrong-doing. Regarding the reveling during *the* day *to be a* pleasure, *they are* spots and blemishes reveling in their deceptions while feasting-with you, [14] having eyes full *of an* adulteress[E] and restless[F] *of* sin, enticing[G] unstable souls, having *a* heart trained in[H] greed. Children *of* [I] *a* curse!— [15] leaving-behind *the* straight way, they went-astray, having followed-after the way *of* Balaam the *son of* Bosor, who loved *the* wages *of* wrong-doing. [16] But he had *a* rebuke *of his* own law-violation: *a* speechless donkey having uttered in *the* voice *of a* human restrained the madness *of* the prophet. [17] These *ones* are waterless springs, and mists being driven by *a* storm, *for* whom the gloom *of* the darkness has been reserved. [18] For while uttering pompous[J] *words of* [K] futility[L], they entice by *the* desires *of the* flesh, by[M] sensualities, the *ones* barely[N] escaping-from the *ones* living in error, [19] promising them freedom, themselves being slaves *of* corruption. For *by* what one has been defeated, *by* this he has been enslaved.

Their Slavery Now Is Worse Than Ever

[20] For if— having escaped-from the defilements *of* the world by *the* knowledge *of* our Lord and Savior Jesus Christ, and again having been entangled *by* these *things*— they[O] are defeated, *then* the last *state* has become worse *for* them *than* the first. [21] For it *would* be better *for* them not to have known the way *of* righteousness than having known, to turn-back from the holy commandment having been delivered *to* them. [22] The *thing* of the true proverb has happened *to* them— "*The* dog having returned to *its* own vomit", and, "*The* sow having washed *herself returns* to *a* wallowing *of the* mire".

Beloved, Remember That People Will Come Mocking Christ's Future Coming

3:1 Beloved, I am now writing this second letter *to* you, in which *letters* I am arousing your pure mind with *a* reminder [2] to remember the words having been spoken-beforehand by the holy prophets and the commandment *of* the Lord and Savior *from* your apostles, [3] knowing this first— that mockers will come with mocking in *the* last days, proceeding in accordance with their own desires, [4] and saying "Where is the promise[P] *of* His coming? For from which *day* the fathers[Q] fell-asleep, everything is continuing in-this-manner[R] from *the* beginning *of* creation".

But God Has Destroyed The Ungodly Before, And He Will Do So Again

[5] For this escapes-notice-of those *who are* willing[S]— that *by* the word *of* God there were heavens from-long-ago, and *an* earth having existence out of water and by water, [6] through

---

A. That is, they live like animals led by their physical appetites to their destruction. Or, of-nature; like unreasoning animals of-nature, having been born for capture. They live like part of the animal kingdom and share their fate. **B.** That is, in connection with, in the sphere of. **C.** That is, their own; or, the animals'. **D.** Or, corruption (as in v 19), taking this word differently here than earlier in the verse. **E.** That is, full of desire for a woman with whom to commit adultery. **F.** Or, unceasing, not-resting. That is, eyes restless to continue sinning, or never resting from sinning. **G.** Or, luring, baiting, entrapping. **H.** Or, *from, by*. **I.** That is, *characterized by* (accursed children); or, *destined to*. **J.** Or, swollen, excessive, bombastic. **K.** That is, *characterized by*. **L.** Or, uselessness, worthlessness. **M.** Or, *for*. Or, by *the* sensual desires *of the* flesh. **N.** That is, just beginning to. **O.** That is, the false teachers (v 17-18a); or, their victims (v 18b-19); or, this may be a general principle referring to all. **P.** That is, the fulfillment of the promise He would come. **Q.** That is, the ones who wrote of the promise. **R.** That is, as it has been. **S.** That is, those who willingly ignore what follows.

which[A] the world at that time was destroyed[B], having been flooded *with* water. [7] And *by* the same word the present heavens and earth have been stored-up *for* fire, being reserved for *the* day *of the* judgment and destruction *of* ungodly people.

He Is Being Patient Now, But The Day of Destruction Will Come Like a Thief
[8] But do not let this one *thing* be escaping your notice, beloved— that one day with *the* Lord *is* like *a* thousand years, and *a* thousand years *is* like one day. [9] *The* Lord is not being slow *about*[C] the promise as some regard slowness, but He is being patient toward you, not wishing[D] any to perish, but all to make-room[E] for repentance. [10] But *the* day *of the* Lord will come like *a* thief— during which the heavens will pass-away with-a-roar, and *the* elements will be destroyed while burning, and *the* earth and the works in it will be found[F]. [11] All these *things* thus being destroyed, what-kind-of *people* ought you to be in holy behaviors and *acts of* godliness, [12] looking-for and hastening[G] the coming *of* the day *of* God, because of which *the* heavens will be destroyed, being set-on-fire, and *the* elements are melted while burning. [13] But in accordance with His promise we are looking-for new heavens and *a* new earth, in which[H] righteousness dwells.

So Be Diligent To Be Unspotted And Unblemished In This Day of Salvation
[14] Therefore beloved, while looking-for these *things*, be diligent to be found unspotted[I] and unblemished[J] *by*[K] Him, in peace. [15] And be regarding the patience *of* our Lord *to be* salvation, just as also our beloved brother Paul wrote *to* you according-to[L] the wisdom having been given *to* him, [16] as also *he writes* in all *his* letters, speaking in them concerning these *things*, in which *letters* are some *things* hard-to-understand which the untaught and unstable twist[M]— as also the other[N] Scriptures— to their own destruction.

Beloved, Be Guarding Yourselves And Growing In Christ
[17] **You** therefore, beloved, knowing-*this*-beforehand, be guarding *yourselves* in order that you may not fall-from *your* own steadfastness, having been carried-away-by[O] the error *of* the lawless *ones*. [18] And be growing in *the* grace and knowledge *of* our Lord and Savior Jesus Christ. *To* Him *be* the glory both now, and to *the* day *of* eternity. Amen.

A. This is plural, referring to the water and the word, or to the waters. **B.** Or, perished. **C:** *about* the promise. Or, *The* Lord *of* the promise is not being slow. **D.** Or, wanting, willing. **E.** Or, give-way for, have room for, go forward to, come to. **F.** Or, discovered, found out. Some manuscripts say 'will be burned up'. **G.** Or, hurrying, advancing, promoting zealously, seeking eagerly. **H.** This is plural. **I.** Or, without-stain. **J.** Or, without-defect. **K.** Or, *in*. **L.** Or, based on, by way of. **M.** Or, distort, wrench. For example, they changed grace into sensuality, Jude 4. **N.** Or, the rest-of-the Scriptures. That is, the other books in the category of 'Scriptures.' **O.** Or, carried-along-with. In other words, led astray by.

1 John

A.   That which we have witnessed concerning the word of life, we announce to you   1:1-4

B.   And this is the message we have heard from Him and are declaring to you: God is light   1:5

     1.   If we are walking in the light, we have fellowship, and He cleanses us from all sin   1:6-10
     2.   My little children, I am writing that you may not sin. By this we know we are in Him   2:1-6
     3.   Beloved, I am not writing a new command to you, but an old one— the message you   2:7-11
          heard. Yet I am writing a new command, because the darkness is passing away and the
          true Light is already shining
     4.   I am writing because your sins are forgiven, you know Him, and you overcame Satan   2:12-13
     5.   I wrote to you because you know the Father, and the Word of God is abiding in you   2:14
     6.   Do not be loving the world nor the things in it. It is not from Him and it is passing away   2:15-17

C.   Children, it is the last hour. And many antichrists have arisen   2:18-19

     1.   And you have an Anointing from the Holy One, and you all have knowledge. I did not   2:20-27
          write because you do not know the truth, but because you know it. Let what you heard
          from the beginning abide in you. As His Anointing is teaching you, abide in it
     2.   And now little children, abide in Him, that we may have confidence and not be put to shame   2:28

          a.   You know everyone doing righteousness has been born from Him. By this the   2:29-3:10
               children of God and the children of the devil are evident
          b.   Everyone not doing righteousness is not from God— and the one not loving. Let   3:10-24
               us be loving in deed and truth. By this we will persuade our heart before Him

     3.   Beloved, do not believe every spirit, but test them, because many false prophets went out   4:1-6

D.   Beloved, let us be loving one another. Everyone loving has been born from God and knows God   4:7-8

     1.   By this God's love was made known: He sent His Son that we might live through Him   4:9-10
     2.   Beloved, if God loved us in this manner, we also ought to be loving one another   4:11

          a.   No one has ever seen God; if we are loving one another, God is abiding in us   4:12-16
          b.   God is love; the one abiding in the love is abiding in God, and God is abiding in him   4:16-19
          c.   If one says he loves God and hates his brother, he is a liar. God commanded love   4:20-21

     3.   Everyone believing Jesus is the Christ has been born from God, and loves God, and loves   5:1-3
          God's children, and keeps God's commandments

          a.   Because faith in Jesus Christ is the victory over the world   5:4
          b.   Who is victorious over the world if not the one believing Jesus is the Son of God!   5:5

               i.   Because Jesus has the threefold witness of God   5:6-9
               ii.   Because God's testimony is that He gave us eternal life in His Son   5:9-12

     4.   I wrote these things to you who believe that you may know that you have eternal life   5:13-14

          a.   And this we know with confidence: That God answers our prayer, that God's   5:14-21
               children are not sinning, that we are from God, that the Son came and gave us
               understanding that we might know the True One

We Are Announcing To You What We Have Personally Witnessed Concerning The Word of Life
1:1 *That*-which[A] was from *the* beginning, *that* which we have heard, *that* which we have seen *with* our eyes, *that* which we looked-*at* and our hands touched, concerning the word[B] *of* life— [2] indeed[C] life[D] was made-known! And we have seen and are testifying and are announcing *to* you the eternal life[E] which was with the Father and was made-known *to* us!— [3] *That*-which[F] we have seen and heard we are announcing also *to* you so that **you** also may have fellowship[G] with us. And indeed our fellowship *is* with the Father, and with His Son Jesus Christ. [4] And **we** are writing these *things* in order that our joy may be full.

The Message We Heard Is That God Is Light
[5] And this is the message which we have heard from Him and are declaring *to* you: that God is light, and there is not any darkness in Him.

If We Walk In The Light And Confess Our Sins, Jesus Cleanses And Forgives Us
[6] If we claim that we have fellowship with Him and are walking in the darkness, we are lying and not doing the truth. [7] But if we are walking in the light as **He** is in the light, we have fellowship with one another and the blood *of* Jesus His Son cleanses us from all sin. [8] If we claim that we do not have[H] sin, we are deceiving ourselves and the truth is not in us. [9] If we are confessing[I] our sins, He is faithful and righteous to forgive us the sins and cleanse us from all unrighteousness. [10] If we claim that we have not sinned, we are making Him *a* liar and His word is not in us.

Jesus Is Our Advocate With God. We Know That We Know Him If We Keep His Commands
2:1 My little-children, I am writing these *things to* you in order that you may not sin. And if anyone sins, we have *an* advocate[J] with the Father: Jesus Christ *the* Righteous. [2] And He Himself is *the* satisfaction[K] for our sins; and not for ours only, but also for the whole world's. [3] And by this we know that we have come-to-know Him: if we are keeping His commandments. [4] The *one* claiming that "I have come-to-know Him" and not keeping His commandments is *a* liar, and the truth is not in this *one*. [5] But whoever is keeping **His** word, truly the love *of* God has been perfected[L] in this *one*. By this we know that we are in Him: [6] the *one* claiming to be abiding in Him ought just as that *One* walked also himself thus to be walking.

If We Are Loving One Another, We Are Abiding In The Light
[7] Beloved, I am not writing *a* new commandment *to* you, but *an* old[M] commandment which you had from *the* beginning. The old commandment is the word which you heard. [8] Yet-again I am writing *a* new[N] commandment *to* you, which[O] is true[P] in Him and in you,

---

A. Or, What. **B.** Or, message. **C.** Or, and. Before John completes the thought that he is declaring his eyewitness testimony, he leaps ahead to exclaim the result produced by the Christ he witnessed. **D:** life was made-known. Or, the Life (Christ) appeared! **E:** life... was made-known *to* us. Or, Life which was with the Father and appeared *to* us. **F.** This resumes from v 1 after the emphatic placement of v 2. **G.** Or, partnership, communion. **H.** That is, have no need for a Savior. **I.** Or, admitting, agreeing about. **J.** Or, defender, intercessor. **K.** Or, propitiation; the sacrifice offered to remove God's wrath against our sin. **L.** Or, brought-to-completion. **M.** Some think it is old in the sense that it is in the Law of Moses; others, in that it was spoken by Jesus Himself; others, in that the readers have had it since they first became Christians. **N.** That is, 'new' in that it is Christ's 'new commandment', Jn 13:34. Or, 'new' in that John gives us here a fresh statement of the old command they heard from the beginning. **O.** This does not refer back to 'new commandment', as it appears in English. John may mean '*all of* which' (everything included in what I am writing here); or, '*the newness of* which'. **P.** That is, genuinely

because[A] the darkness is passing-away and the true Light[B] is already shining. **9** The *one* claiming to be in the light and hating his brother is in the darkness until now. **10** The *one* loving his brother is abiding in the light, and there is no cause-of-falling in him. **11** But the *one* hating his brother is in the darkness, and is walking in the darkness, and does not know where he is going because the darkness blinded his eyes.

I Am Writing To You Because of What Has Already Happened In Your Life
12 I am writing *to* you, little-children[C], because *your* sins have been forgiven you for-the-sake-of His name. **13** I am writing *to* you, fathers, because you have known the *One* from *the* beginning. I am writing *to* you, young-men, because you have overcome the evil *one.*

I Wrote To You Because of Who And What You Already Know
14 I wrote[D] *to* you, children, because you have known the Father. I wrote *to* you, fathers, because you have known the *One* from *the* beginning. I wrote *to* you, young-men, because you are strong *ones,* and the word *of* God is abiding in you, and you have overcome the evil *one.*

So Don't Love The World Or Pursue Its Desires. The One Doing God's Will Abides Forever
15 Do not be loving the world, nor the *things* in the world. If anyone is loving the world, the love *of* the Father is not in him. **16** Because everything in the world— the desire *of*[E] the flesh, and the desire *of* the eyes, and the boastful-pride *of* life[F]— is not from the Father, but is from the world. **17** And the world is passing-away, and its desire. But the *one* doing the will *of* God abides forever.

Children, Antichrists Have Arisen
18 Children, it is *the* last[G] hour. And just as you heard that *the* Antichrist is coming, even now many antichrists have arisen— from which we know that it is *the* last hour. **19** They went out from us, but they were not of[H] us. For if they had been of us, they would have remained with us. But *they went out* in order that they might be made-evident that[I] they all are not of us.

You Have God's Anointing And You Know The Truth. Let It Abide In You And You In It
20 And **you** have *an* Anointing[J] from the Holy *One*, and you all have-knowledge[K]. **21** I did not write *to* you because you do not know the truth, but because you know it, and that[L] every lie is not from[M] the truth. **22** Who is the liar if not the *one* denying that Jesus is the

present, truly seen. **A.** John may be explaining why he is writing (as in v 12-14); or, why it is true in Him and in you (because His light is shining in you). **B.** Or, light. **C:** little children... fathers... young-men. Some think John is referring to all Christians from three viewpoints; others, that 'little children' refers to all Christians (as elsewhere in the letter), who are then divided into two groups; others, that three groups are intended. In the last two views, some think the groups represent stages of spiritual growth; others, tenure as a Christian; others, physical age. **D.** John may mean 'wrote' from the readers viewpoint when they receive the letter, 'writing' (v 12-13) from his viewpoint as he writes; or, 'wrote' what he has already written, 'writing' the whole letter. Some think the change in tense is merely stylistic. **E.** That is, belonging to; or, proceeding from. **F.** That is, the manner of living, the things or goods of life. **G.** That is, the final period of time, which extends from when antichrists first appear until Christ returns. **H.** That is, belonging to us. **I.** That is, that none of those who left are of us. Or, made-evident, because. That is, because not all the people in the church are of us. **J.** That is, the Holy Spirit. **K.** That is, you all have the knowledge you need to discern between truth and error. **L.** Or, and because. This may be a second thing they know; or, a second reason John wrote to them. **M.** That is, originating from, belonging to.

Christ? This *one* is the antichrist, the *one* denying the Father and the Son. **²³** Everyone denying the Son does also-not have the Father. The *one* confessing[A] the Son also has the Father. **²⁴** Let what **you heard** from *the* beginning be abiding in you. If what you heard **from *the* beginning** abides in you, **you** also will abide in the Son and in the Father. **²⁵** And this is the promise which He Himself promised *to* us: eternal life. **²⁶** I wrote these *things to* you concerning the *ones* deceiving you. **²⁷** And the Anointing which **you** received from Him is abiding in you. And you have no need that anyone should be teaching[B] you; but as **His** Anointing is teaching you about all *things,* and is true and is not *a* lie, and just as it[C] taught you, be abiding[D] in it[E].

Abide In Christ So That If He Appears You May Have Confidence And Not Shame
²⁸ And now little-children, be abiding[F] in Him so that if He appears, we may have confidence and not be put-to-shame[G] by Him at His coming.

> *Abiding Means Doing Righteousness, Which Characterizes All Those Born From God*
> **²⁹** If you know[H] that He[I] is righteous, you know that everyone also doing righteousness has been born[J] from Him. **3:1** See what-kind-of love the Father has given *to* us: that we should be called children *of* God! And we are! For this reason the world does not know us, because it did not know Him. **²** Beloved, we are **now** children *of* God, and what we will be has not yet appeared[K]. We know that if He appears, we will be like Him, because we will see Him just as He is. **³** And everyone having this hope in[L] Him is purifying himself, just as that *One* is pure. **⁴** Everyone doing sin also is doing lawlessness. Indeed sin is lawlessness. **⁵** And you know that that *One* appeared in order that He might take-away sins. And there is no sin in Him. **⁶** Everyone abiding in Him is not sinning[M]. Everyone sinning has not seen Him nor known Him. **⁷** Little-children, let no one be deceiving you— the *one* doing righteousness is righteous, just as that *One* is righteous. **⁸** The *one* doing sin is of the devil, because the devil is sinning[N] from *the* beginning. The Son *of* God appeared for this: that He might destroy the works *of* the devil. **⁹** Everyone having been born[O] from God is not doing sin— because His seed[P] is abiding in him, and he is not able to be sinning[Q] because he has been born from God. **¹⁰** By this, the children *of* God and the children *of* the devil are evident.

> *Abiding Means Loving In Deed And Truth, As Jesus Commanded Us*
> Everyone not doing[R] righteousness is not from God— and the *one* not loving his brother! **¹¹** Because this is the message which you heard from *the* beginning: that we should be loving one another. **¹²** Not as Cain. He was of the evil *one,* and slew his brother. And for what reason did he slay him? Because his works were evil, but the *ones of* his brother *were* righteous. **¹³** And do not be marveling, brothers, if the world

---

A. Or, declaring. **B.** That is, teaching you about God beyond what the Anointing and Christ through His servants (Eph 4:11) are teaching you. **C.** That is, just as His Anointing taught you from the beginning. Or, as He (Jesus) taught you when He was on Earth. **D.** Or, you are abiding. **E.** That is, in the teaching, as in v 24. Or, in Him, as in v 28. **F.** John turns from abiding in His truth to abiding in His character, His righteousness (2:29-3:10) and love (3:10-24). **G.** Or, shrink-in-shame from Him. **H.** Or, understand, recognize. **I.** That is, the Father; or, Jesus. **J.** Or, fathered by. **K.** Or, been revealed, been made known. **L.** That is, fixed on Him. **M.** Or, *continuing to* sin. **N.** Or, *continuing to* sin since. **O.** Or, fathered. **P.** That is, His nature, His life. It is transforming us from within, growing into His likeness. **Q.** That is, to be continuing in sin as a pattern of life. We all still sin, 1:8-10. **R.** What John said positively in 2:29, he says negatively here.

hates you! **14** **We** know that we have passed from death into life because we are loving the brothers. The *one* not loving is abiding^A in death. **15** Everyone hating his brother is *a* murderer, and you know that every murderer does not have eternal life abiding in him. **16** By this we have come-to-know love: because that *One* laid-*down* His life for us. And **we** ought to lay-*down our* lives for the brothers. **17** But whoever has the goods *of* the world and sees his brother having *a* need and shuts his deep-feelings from him, how is the love *of* God abiding in him? **18** Little children, let us not be loving *with* word nor tongue, but in deed and truth. **19** And by this, we will know that we are of^B the truth, and we will persuade^C our heart before Him. **20** Because^D if our heart **is condemning**^E *us, we know* that God is greater^F *than* our hearts, and He knows all *things*. **21** Beloved, if **our heart** is not condemning *us*, we have confidence^G before God. **22** And whatever we are asking, we are receiving from Him, because we are keeping His commandments and doing the pleasing *things* in His sight. **23** And this is His commandment: that we believe *in* the name *of* His Son Jesus Christ, and *that* we be loving one another, just as He gave us *the* commandment. **24** And the *one* keeping His commandments is abiding in Him, and He in him. And by this we know that He is abiding in us: from the Spirit Whom He gave *to* us.

Test The Spirits. The Spirit From God Confesses Christ
4:1 Beloved, do not be believing every spirit, but be testing the spirits^H *to see* if they are from God, because many false-prophets have gone out into the world. **2** By this you know^I the Spirit^J *of* God: every spirit that is confessing Jesus Christ *as* having come in *the* flesh is from God. **3** And every spirit that is not confessing Jesus is not from God. And this is the *spirit of* the Antichrist— which, you have heard that it is coming, and now it is already in the world. **4** **You** are from^K God, little children, and you have overcome them, because greater is the *One* in you than the *one* in the world. **5** **They** are from^L the world. For this reason they are speaking from the world, and the world is listening-to them. **6** **We** are from God. The *one* knowing God is listening-to us. He who is not from God is not listening-to us. From this, we know the Spirit^M *of* truth and the spirit *of* error^N.

Be Loving One Another, Because The Love Is From God
7 Beloved, let us be loving one another. Because the love^O is from God! And everyone loving has been born^P from God, and knows God. **8** The *one* not loving did not know God, because God is love.

God Made His Love Known To Us By Sending His Son
9 By this God's love was made-known among^Q us: that God has sent-forth His only-born^R

A. Or, remaining. **B.** That is, belonging to or originating from the truth. **C.** Or, conciliate, set at ease. **D:** before Him. Because if... *we know* that God. Or, before Him— whatever thing our heart is condemning— because God. **E.** Or, blaming, laying a charge against, convicting. **F.** We persuade ourselves by our love in action, because it proves we are His in spite of some failure our heart may be throwing up to us. God knows our hearts and our pattern of life. **G.** That is, the confidence sought in 2:28. **H.** That is, spiritual manifestations; expressions of a professed 'spiritual *gift*', as this word is used in 1 Cor 14:12. **I.** Or, recognize. **J.** Or, spirit *from* God, maintaining the same sense as the other four uses of 'spirit' in v 1-3. **K.** That is, you belong to Him, having been fathered by Him. **L.** They belong to the world which is passing away. This is the source of their words. **M.** Or, spirit. **N.** Or, deception. **O.** That is, *this* love, the love just mentioned. Or, love, in an abstract sense. **P.** Or, fathered. This love flows from a living relationship with God. **Q.** Or, in-connection-with; or, in. **R.** Or, unique, one-and-only, only-begotten.

Son into the world in order that we might live through Him. **10** In this is love— not that **we** have loved God, but that **He** loved us, and sent-forth His Son *to be the* satisfaction[A] for our sins.

We Ought To Be Loving As He Loved Us

11 Beloved, if God loved us in-this-manner[B], **we** also ought to be loving one another.

Love Makes the Unseen God Visible In Us, Together With Our Confession of Christ

12 No one has ever seen God; if we are loving[C] one another, God is abiding in us, and His love[D] has been perfected[E] in us. **13** By this[F] we know that we are abiding in Him and He in us: because He has given *to* us of His Spirit. **14** And **we** have seen, and are testifying that the Father has sent-forth the Son *to be* Savior *of* the world. **15** Whoever confesses that Jesus is the Son *of* God, God is abiding in him and he in God. **16** And **we** have come-to-know and have believed the love which God has in us.

Love Demonstrates Our Mutual Relationship With God, And Gives Us Confidence

God is love; and the *one* abiding in the love is abiding in God, and God is abiding in him. **17** By this[G], the love has been perfected with[H] us in order that we may have confidence on the day *of* judgment. Because just as that *One* is[I], **we** also are, in this world. **18** Fear[J] is not in love— rather, perfect love throws fear out, because fear has punishment. And the *one* fearing has not been perfected in love. **19** **We** are loving because[K] **He** first loved us.

Not Loving One Another As He Commanded Proves That We Do Not Love God

20 If someone claims that "I love God" and is hating his brother, he is *a* liar. For the *one* not loving his brother whom he has seen cannot be loving God Whom he has not seen. **21** And we have this commandment from Him: that the *one* loving God should be loving his brother also.

Everyone Born of God Believes Jesus Is His Son, Loves His People, Keeps His Commands

5:1 Everyone believing that Jesus is the Christ has been born[L] from God. And everyone loving the One[M] having fathered is loving also the *one* having been born[L] from Him. **2** By this we know that we are loving[N] the children *of* God: when we are loving God and doing

---

A. See 2:2. **B.** Or, to such an extent. **C.** That is, with the love from God (v 7) made known to us in His Son (v 9). **D.** Or, *our* love *for* Him. **E.** Or, brought to its goal, brought to full development. **F.** John knows love cannot stand alone as a witness that God is abiding in us, so he now inseparably links it to two other witnesses, the Spirit and our confession of Christ. **G.** That is, by this mutual abiding just mentioned, God's love has been brought to its goal with us, that we may have confidence. **H.** That is, together with us, along with our cooperation; or, among us, in our mutual love as Christians. **I:** is... we also are. That is, abiding in the Father's love; or, reflecting God's love or character. **J.** This is a negative reason why such love produces confidence (v 17). Fear is part of a performance-based relationship, with penalties for failure. A mutually-abiding love relationship has no such fear, but rather brings confidence. This is the Greek word order. Or, There is no fear in-connection-with love. **K.** This is a positive reason why such love produces confidence. Our love is the result of the relationship, not the cause of it. **L.** Or, fathered. **M:** the *One* having... Him. That is, the [God] having fathered [us] is loving also [the children] having been born from Him. **N.** That is, with love flowing from an abiding relationship with God. In this section, John inseparably binds together love for God, love for His children, believing in His Son, and obeying His commandments. We cannot claim to have one apart from any of the others.

His commandments. **³** For this is the love *of* God: that we be keeping His commandments. And His commandments are not burdensome.

Because The One Born of God Is Victorious Over The World By Faith In Jesus
⁴ Because everything having been born from God is being-victorious-over the world. And this is the victory having been-victorious-over the world: our faith!

Who Indeed Is Victorious If Not The One Believing Jesus Is The Son of God!
⁵ And who is the *one* being-victorious-over the world if not the *one* believingᴬ that Jesus is the Son *of* God!

Because Jesus Christ Has The Three-Fold Witness of God
⁶ This *One* is the *One* having come by water and bloodᴮ: Jesus Christ (not inᶜ the water only, butᴰ in the water and in the blood). And the Spirit is the *One* testifying, becauseᴱ the Spirit is the truth. **⁷** Becauseᶠ the *ones* testifying are threeᴳ: **⁸** the Spirit and the water and the blood. And the three are for theᴴ one *thing.* **⁹** If we receive the testimony *of* humans, the testimony *of* God is greater!

Because God Himself Has Testified That He Has Given Us Eternal Life In His Son
Becauseᴵ this is the testimony *of* God: thatᴶ He has testified about His Son! **¹⁰** The *one* believing in the Son *of* God has the testimony in himself. The *one* not believing God has made Him *a* liar, because he has not believed in the testimony which God has testified about His Son. **¹¹** And this is the testimonyᴷ: that God gave us eternal life, and this life is in His Son. **¹²** The *one* having the Son has the life. The *one* not having the Son *of* God does not have the life.

I Wrote These Things That You May Know You Have Eternal Life
¹³ I wrote theseᴸ *things to* you, the *ones* believing in the name *of* the Son *of* God, in order that you may know that you have eternal **life.**

And This We Know With Confidence:
¹⁴ And this is the confidence which we have before Him:

That God Hears Our Prayers
... that if we request anything according to His will, He hears us. **¹⁵** And if we

---

A. Or, having-faith, to show the relationship to 'faith' in v 4. **B.** These two historical witnesses may refer to Christ's baptism (where the Father testified) and death (where the resurrection gave the Father's testimony); or, His birth (He came in real flesh) and His death (He died a real death); or, the blood and water that came from His side (Jn 19:34, giving testimony to His real humanity and death). **C.** Or, in-connection-with, by, with. **D.** John denies some false teaching of his day, the details of which are not certain. We know some denied that God died. They taught that the Spirit of God came on the human Jesus at His baptism and left in Gethsemane. Jesus was not God come in the flesh (4:2), and His death had no significance. Perhaps John is refuting some such teaching here. **E.** The Spirit is presently adding His testimony to the two historical witnesses because it is His nature to testify to the truth. **F.** The one believing Jesus is the Son of God is victorious (v 5) because Jesus has the threefold divine testimony to His identity, sufficient proof even in a human court. **G:** three: the Spirit. Some manuscripts say 'three in heaven: the Father, the Word, and the Holy Spirit. And these three are one. And the *ones* giving testimony on earth are three: the Spirit'. **H.** That is, they are in agreement. **I.** The one believing is victorious because he is believing God's own testimony. **J.** God's testimony is that He has testified. **K.** The content of God's testimony regarding His Son is now given. **L.** That is, 4:7-5:12; or, 5:1-12; or, 5:5-12; or, the whole book.

know that He hears us— whatever we request— we know that we have the requests which we have requested from Him.

But I Am Not Implying You Should Pray About a Sin Leading To Death
16 If anyone sees his brother sinning *a* sin not *leading* to death, he shall request, and He will give him life— *for* the *ones* sinning *a sin* not *leading* to death. There is *a* sin *leading* to death^A. I am not saying that he should pray about that. **17** All unrighteousness is sin, and there is sin not *leading* to death.

That God's Children Are Not Sinning, And Are Protected From Satan
18 We know that everyone having been born^B from God is not sinning^C. But the One^D having been fathered from God is keeping^E him. And the evil *one* is not touching^F him.

That We Are Born From God
19 We know that we are from God, and the whole world lies in^G the evil *one*.

That We Know The True God And Have Eternal Life In Him
20 And we know that the Son *of* God has come, and has given us understanding in order that we might know the true^H *One*. And we are in^I the true *One*, in His Son Jesus Christ. This *One*^J is the true God and eternal life. **21** Little-children, guard yourselves from idols!

A. If John means physical death, any sin leading to this level of discipline from God could be in view, as in Act 5:5; 1 Cor 11:30. If John means spiritual, eternal death, some think he means the knowing and deliberate rejection of Christ, as in 2:19, 22, and Heb 6:4-6; 10:26-29. **B.** Or, fathered. **C.** See 3:9. **D:** the *One* having been fathered... him. Or, the *one* having been born from God is keeping himself [from sin]. **E.** Or, guarding, keeping watch over, preserving. **F.** That is, to bring him harm. **G.** That is, in the sphere of, in the domain of. **H.** That is, the real, genuine God. **I.** That is, in union with, in the domain of. **J.** Grammatically, this could refer to Jesus Christ or the true *One*. Some think it would redundant to say the true *One*... is the true God, and so John says here what he says in Jn 1:1: Jesus is God. Others think John repeats himself for emphasis as he prepares for the command regarding idols.

2 John

Introduction   1-3

A.   I rejoiced greatly that I have found some of your children walking in the truth. And now I ask you,   4-6
     lady, that we be loving one another

     1.   Because many deceivers went out into the world. Be watching yourselves in order that you   7-11
          may receive a full reward

Conclusion   12-13

¹ The elder *to the* chosen lady and her children, whom **I** love in truth^A— and not only I, but also all the *ones* having known the truth— ² because-of^B the truth abiding in us. And it will be with us forever. ³ Grace, mercy, peace from God *the* Father, and from Jesus Christ the Son *of* the Father, will be with us in^C truth and love.

I Rejoiced To Find You Walking In The Truth. Be Loving One Another
⁴ I rejoiced greatly that I have found *some* of your children walking in *the* truth, just as we received commandment from the Father. ⁵ And now I ask you, lady— not as-*if* writing you *a* new commandment, but *the one* which we had from *the* beginning— that we be loving one another. ⁶ And this is love: that we be walking according to His commandments. This is the commandment, just as you^D *all* heard from *the* beginning, that you should be walking in it.

Because There Are Many Deceivers. Watch Out, And Abide In The Teaching of Christ
⁷ Because many deceivers went-out into the world— the *ones* not confessing Jesus Christ *as* coming in *the* flesh. This is the deceiver and the antichrist. ⁸ Be watching yourselves in order that you^E may not lose^F *the things* which we^G accomplished, but may receive *a* full reward. ⁹ Everyone going-ahead^H and not abiding in the teaching *of* Christ does not have God; the *one* abiding in the teaching— this *one* has both the Father and the Son. ¹⁰ If anyone comes to you^I and does not bring this teaching, do not receive him into *the* house^J and do not speak greetings *to* him. ¹¹ For the *one* speaking greetings *to* him shares *in* his evil works.

¹² Having many *things* to write *to* you^K *all*, I did not want *to do so* with paper and ink. But I hope to come-to-be with you and to speak mouth to mouth, in order that our joy may be full. ¹³ The children *of* your chosen sister greet you^L.

A: in truth. Or, in *the* truth, in-connection-with *the* truth. **B.** Or, for-the-sake-of. **C.** That is, in the sphere of; in connection with. **D:** you... you. This is plural. John turns from addressing the lady in v 5, to them all. **E.** Some manuscripts say 'we'. **F.** Or, ruin, waste. **G.** Some manuscripts say 'you'. **H.** Or, leading-forth, advancing. **I.** This is plural. **J.** That is, the church in your house. **K.** This is plural both times in this verse. **L.** This is singular.

3 John

Introduction 1

A. Beloved, I pray that you may prosper and be healthy, just as your soul is prospering 2-4

B. Beloved, you are doing a faithful thing for the brothers, whom you will do well to send forward 5-8

C. I wrote something to the church, but Diotrephes is not accepting us. Beloved, imitate the good 9-11

D. With regard to Demetrius, he has been attested by all, by the truth, and we also are testifying 12

Conclusion 13-14

---

1 The elder *to* the beloved Gaius, whom **I** love in truthᴬ.

May You Prosper In All Things, Just As Your Soul Is Prospering Because You Walk In The Truth
2 Beloved, I prayᴮ *that* with respect to all *things* you *may* prosper and be healthy, just as your soul is prospering. **3** For I rejoiced greatly while brothers *were* coming and testifying *concerning* your truth— howᶜ **you** are walking in *the* truth. **4** I have no joy greater *than* these *things*: that I may be hearing-*of* my children walking in the truth.

Beloved, Support Fellow Workers For The Truth
5 Beloved, you are doing *a* faithful *thing*— whatever you may accomplishᴰ— for the brothers (and this, *for* strangers!) **6** who testified *concerning* your love before *the* church, *as to* whom you will do well having sent-*them*-forward worthily *of* God. **7** For they went out for the Name, taking nothing from the Gentiles. **8** Therefore **we** ought to be supporting such *ones*, in order that we may beᴱ fellow-workersᶠ *for* the truth.

Diotrephes Is Not Accepting Us. Beloved, Imitate The One Doing Good
9 I wrote something *to* the church, but Diotrephes, the *one* loving-to-be-firstᴳ *among* them, is not acceptingᴴ us. **10** For this reason, if I come I will call-to-mindᴵ his deeds which he is doing— talking-nonsense-aboutᴶ us *with* malicious words. And not being content with these *things,* neither is he himself accepting the brothers. And he is forbidding and putting-outᴷ of the church the *ones* wanting *to do so.* **11** Beloved, do not be imitating the evil, but the good. The *one* doing-good is from God. The *one* doing-evil has not seen God.

Demetrius Is Attested By Everyone
12 *With regard to* Demetrius, he has been attested by everyone, and by the truth itself. And **we** also are testifying, and you know that our testimony is true.

13 I had many *things* to write *to* you, but I do not wish to write *to* you with ink and pen. **14** But I hope to see you at-once, and we will speak mouth to mouth. Peace *to* you. The friends greet you. Greet the friends by name.

A. Or, in *the* truth, in-connection-with *the* truth. **B:** I pray... be healthy. Or, I pray *that* you *may* prosper with respect to all *things*, and be healthy. **C.** Or, just as, in as much as. **D.** Or, do, carry out, work out. **E.** Or, become. **F.** Or, co-workers. **G.** Or, loving-to-have-preeminence. **H.** Or, receiving. **I.** Or, remember. **J.** Or, more formally, bringing-unjustified-charges-against. **K.** Or, expelling, driving-out.

Jude

Introduction   1-2

A.   I had the necessity to write exhorting you to be contending for the faith delivered once for all   3-4

B.   Now I want to remind you that God judges unbelief and immorality   5-7

C.   Yet these dreaming ones defile the flesh, reject authority, and blaspheme glories. Woe to them   8-11

D.   These ones are spots, waterless clouds, fruitless trees, wild waves, wandering stars. But Enoch   12-15
     prophesied their judgment

E.   These ones are grumblers, faultfinders, proceeding according to their own desires. But you,   16-18
     beloved, remember that the apostles said mockers would come

F.   These ones are the ones causing divisions— natural ones, not having the Spirit. But you,   19-23
     beloved, keep yourselves in the love of God

Conclusion   24-25

---

¹ Jude[A], *a* slave *of* Jesus Christ and brother *of* James, *to* the called *ones* having been loved by[B] God *the* Father and kept[C] by[D] Jesus Christ: ² May mercy and peace and love be multiplied *to* you.

Beloved, Fight For The Faith Against Those Seeking To Change Grace Into License
³ Beloved, while making every effort to be writing *to* you concerning our common salvation, I had *the* necessity to write *to* you exhorting *you* to be contending[E] *for* the faith having been delivered once-for-all *to* the saints. ⁴ For certain persons sneaked-in[F]— the *ones* formerly[G] having been portrayed[H] for this judgment, ungodly *ones*— changing[I] the grace *of* our God into sensuality and denying our only Master and Lord, Jesus Christ.

Remember: The Lord Punished The Unbelieving And The Immoral
⁵ Now I want to remind you— you knowing[J] all *things*— that the Lord[K], having once[L] saved[M] *the* people out of *the* land *of* Egypt, afterwards destroyed the *ones* not having believed. ⁶ And He has kept[N] angels— the *ones* not having kept their *own* domain[O], but having left-behind[P] *their* own dwelling[Q]— *in* eternal bonds[R] under gloom for *the* judgment *of the* great day.

A. Or, Judas, Judah. **B.** Or, in. **C.** Or, protected, guarded. **D.** Or, *for, in.* **E.** Or, fighting, struggling. **F.** Or, crept-in. **G.** Or, already, long-ago, all-this-time. The word can refer to hours or centuries in the past. **H.** Or, written-of. **I.** Or, more negatively, perverting. **J.** Jude may mean *although* you *are* knowing; or, *since you are* knowing. **K:** that the Lord. Some manuscripts say 'that Jesus'. **L.** Or, once-for-all, as in v 3. Some manuscripts instead have this word earlier, 'knowing all *things* once-for-all'. **M.** Or, delivered. **N.** Or, reserved. **O.** Or, rule. That is, their sphere or position or place of rule and authority. **P.** Or, more negatively, abandoned. **Q.** Or, home, abode, habitation, dwelling-place. **R.** Or, bindings.

7 *Just* as Sodom and Gomorrah and the cities around them *in* like manner *to* these^A— having indulged-in-sexual-immorality and gone after other flesh— are set-forth *as an* example, undergoing *the* penalty^B *of* eternal fire.

Yet These People Defile The Flesh And Reject God's Authority. Woe To Them
8 Yet in the same way also these dreaming *ones* are defiling *the* flesh and rejecting authority^C and blaspheming^D glories^E! **9** Now Michael the archangel^F, when he was speaking concerning the body *of* Moses while disputing *with* the devil, did not dare to bring^G a judgment *of* blasphemy, but said, "May *the* Lord rebuke you". **10** But these *ones*— whatever *things* they do not understand, they blaspheme; and whatever *things* they know instinctually like unreasoning animals, by these they are being destroyed. **11** Woe *to* them, because they went *in* the way *of* Cain, and they poured-forth^H *in* the error *of* Balaam *for* wages, and they perished^I *in* the rebellion *of* Korah.

Enoch Prophesied God Would Execute Judgment Against These Ungodly Stains
12 These *ones* are the *ones who are* spots^J in your love-*feasts*, feasting-with^K *you* fearlessly, tending^L themselves; waterless clouds being carried-along by winds; fruitless autumn trees having died twice, having been uprooted; **13** wild waves *of the* sea foaming-up their shames; wandering stars *for* whom the gloom *of* darkness has been reserved forever. **14** But indeed Enoch, *the* seventh from Adam, prophesied *with regard to* these *ones,* saying, "Behold— *the* Lord came with His holy myriads **15** to execute judgment against all, and to convict every soul concerning all their works *of* ^M ungodliness which they did-godlessly, and concerning all the harsh *things* which ungodly sinners spoke against Him".

Remember That The Apostles Prophesied of These Mockers Pursuing Their Ungodly Desires
16 These *ones* are grumblers^N, faultfinders, proceeding in accordance with their *own* desires. And their mouth speaks pompous *words,* marveling-at^O faces for the sake of advantage. **17** But **you**, beloved, remember the words having been spoken-beforehand by the apostles *of* our Lord Jesus Christ— **18** that they were saying *to* you that "In *the* last time there will be mockers proceeding in accordance with their *own* desires *of* ^P ungodliness".

But You, Beloved, Keep Yourselves In The Love of God
19 These *ones* are the *ones* causing-divisions^Q— natural *ones,* not having *the* Spirit. **20** But **you**, beloved, while building-up yourselves *on*^R your most holy faith, while praying in^S *the* Holy Spirit, **21** keep yourselves in *the* love *of* God while waiting-for the mercy *of* our Lord Jesus Christ for eternal life. **22** And be having-mercy-on^T some doubting^U *ones.* **23** And be

A. That is, *in* like manner *to* these [previous two examples]... are set forth. The similarity is in their judgment by God, as in 2 Pet 2:6. Or, *in* like manner *to* these [angels] having indulged in sexual immorality and gone after other flesh. The similarity is in their sin. **B.** Or, punishment. **C.** Or, lordship, dominion. **D.** Or, speaking-against. **E.** Or, dignities, majesties. **F.** That is, ruler of angels, chief angel. **G.** Or, pronounce. **H.** Or, poured-*themselves into,* rushed *into.* **I.** Or, lost-*themselves,* were destroyed. **J.** Or, stains. Or, reefs, hidden-rocks. **K:** love-*feasts*, feasting with *you* fearlessly, tending themselves. Or, love-*feasts* while feasting-with *you,* tending themselves without-fear. **L.** Or, feeding, pasturing. **M.** That is, characterized by; ungodly works. **N.** Or, complainers. **O.** Or, admiring; and thus, flattering. **P.** That is, characterized by, proceeding from, for. **Q.** Or, making separations. **R.** Or, *in, by.* **S.** Or, by, in-the-sphere-of, in-connection-with. **T.** Or, showing-mercy-to. **U.** Or, wavering. Some manuscripts say, Be having mercy on some, making a distinction; that is, separating them out for special attention, as this word is used in Jam 2:4.

saving[A] others, snatching *them* out of *the* fire. And be having-mercy-on others with fear while hating even the tunic[B] having been stained by the flesh.

24 Now *to* the *One* being able to keep[C] you from-stumbling[D] and to make *you* stand in the presence *of* His glory without-blemish with gladness[E], **25** *to the* only God our Savior through Jesus Christ our Lord, *be* glory, majesty, dominion, and authority before[F] every age, and now, and for[G] all ages, amen.

A. Some manuscripts say as v 23, And be saving others with fear, snatching *them* out of *the* fire, while hating...flesh. **B.** That is, undershirt. **C.** Or, guard, protect. **D.** Or, not-stumbling. **E.** Or, great-joy. **F:** before every age. Or, before all time. **G:** and for all ages. Or, and forever.

Revelation

Introduction   1:1-8

A.   I, John, was on the island of Patmos because of the word of God and the testimony of Jesus. I   1:9-12
     heard a voice saying, Write in a book what you see and send it to the seven churches

     1.   And having turned, I saw One like a son of man standing amidst seven golden lampstands. 1:12-20
          And when I saw Him, I fell as dead. He laid His right hand upon me, saying, Do not fear.
          Write the things which you saw, which are, and which are destined to take place

          a.   To Ephesus, write— Remember, and repent, and do the first works   2:1-7
          b.   To Smyrna, write— Don't fear what you are about to suffer. Be faithful until death 2:8-11
          c.   To Pergamum, write— Repent of the teaching of the Nicolaitans   2:12-17
          d.   To Thyatira, write— Repent of tolerating Jezebel. Hold on until I come   2:18-29
          e.   To Sardis, write— You are dead. Remember what you heard, keep it, and repent   3:1-6
          f.   To Philadelphia, write— I have given you an open door, hold on to your crown   3:7-13
          g.   To Laodicea, write— You are lukewarm. Be zealous and repent. Open the door to Me 3:14-22

B.   After these things, the voice said, Come up here to heaven, and I will show the things which must 4:1-2
     take place after these things. Immediately I came-to-be in the Spirit

     1.   And behold— a throne, One sitting on the throne, 24 elders, 7 torches, 4 living creatures   4:2-11

          a.   I saw on the right hand of the One upon the throne a scroll sealed with seven seals.   5:1-7
               Who is worthy to open the scroll? And I saw a Lamb, and He came and took it
          b.   And when He took the scroll, every created thing in heaven and earth worshiped Him   5:8-14
          c.   And I saw when the Lamb opened the first seal— a white horse with one conquering   6:1-2
          d.   And when He opened the second seal— a fire-red horse with one removing peace   6:3-4
          e.   And when He opened the third seal— a black horse with one setting famine prices   6:5-6
          f.   And when He opened the fourth seal— a pale-green horse with Death and Hades   6:7-8
          g.   And when He opened the fifth seal— martyrs under the altar crying for vengeance   6:9-11
          h.   And when He opened the sixth seal— an earthquake, the sky darkened, all hide   6:12-17
          i.   After this I saw four angels restrained from harming the land, sea, and trees, until 7:1-8
               another angel sealed 144,000 slaves of God on their foreheads
          j.   After these things I saw a multitude in heaven, coming out of the great affliction   7:9-17
          k.   And when He opened the seventh seal— silence in heaven for half an hour   8:1

     2.   And I saw the seven angels who stand before God, and seven trumpets were given to them   8:2-6

          a.   And the first angel trumpeted— hail and fire with blood burn a third of vegetation   8:7
          b.   And the second angel trumpeted— a third of sea life and ships are destroyed   8:8-9
          c.   And the third angel trumpeted— a third of rivers and springs are made bitter   8:10-11
          d.   And the fourth angel trumpeted— a third of sun, moon, and stars darkened   8:12
          e.   And I saw and I heard an eagle say, Woe because of the 3 remaining trumpets   8:13
          f.   And the fifth angel trumpeted— locusts torment for 5 months. The first woe passed   9:1-12
          g.   And the sixth angel trumpeted—   9:13

               i.   And I heard a voice tell the sixth angel to release the four angels at the   9:13-21
                     Euphrates to lead an army of 200,000,000 to kill a third of mankind
               ii.   I saw another angel holding a little scroll stand on land and sea and swear that 10:1-11
                     when the seventh angel is about to trumpet, the mystery of God was finished.
                     The angel said to eat the little scroll. It was sweet and bitter. Prophesy again

428

iii. And a rod was given to me to measure the temple. Two witnesses described   11:1-13

iv. The second woe passed away. Behold, the third woe is coming quickly   11:14

h. And the seventh angel trumpeted. And loud voices were saying, The kingdom of   11:15-18
the world became His kingdom. The time came to judge and reward

3. And the temple of God in heaven was opened, and the ark of His covenant appeared   11:19

a. And a great sign appeared in heaven— a woman with Child, in torment to give birth   12:1-2

b. And another sign appeared in heaven— a great fire-red dragon with seven heads and   12:3-6
ten horns. The dragon wanted to devour her child. She gave birth to a Son, who was
caught up to His throne. She fled and was nourished for 1260 days

i. And there was a war in heaven. The dragon was thrown to earth   12:7-12

ii. And the dragon pursued the woman on earth, and made war with her seed   12:13-18

iii. I saw a beast coming up out of the sea. The dragon gave him his power. The   13:1-10
world worshiped him, and he made war with the saints, and overcame them

iv. And I saw another beast come up out of the land. And he made all the world   13:11-18
worship the first beast, performing great signs, and deceiving the whole world

v. And I saw the Lamb standing on Mt Zion with the 144,000 singing a new song   14:1-5

vi. And I saw three angels proclaiming an eternal gospel, judgment and a warning   14:6-13

vii. I saw one on a white cloud told to reap the harvest of the earth, and another   14:14-20
angel was told to gather the grapes into the winepress of God's fury

c. And I saw another sign in heaven, great and marvelous— seven angels with seven   15:1-4
plagues— the last, because the fury of God was finished. And I saw the victors
from the beast standing on a sea of glass, singing to God

4. After these things I saw, and the temple of the tabernacle of testimony in heaven was   15:5-16:1
opened. Seven angels came out of the temple and were given 7 bowls of God's wrath

a. And the first poured his bowl into the land— a sore on the beast's followers   16:2

b. And the second poured his bowl into the sea— all sea life died   16:3

c. And the third poured his bowl into the rivers and springs— they became blood   16:4-7

d. And the fourth poured his bowl on the sun— it scorches people   16:8-9

e. The fifth poured his bowl on the beast's throne— his kingdom is darkened   16:10-11

f. The sixth poured his bowl on the Euphrates— it is dried up and three demons   16:12-16
gathered the kings of the earth at Har-magedon for the great day of God Almighty

g. The seventh angel poured his bowl on the air— It is done! A great earthquake takes   16:17-21
place. Babylon the Great receives the wrath of God. Hail falls

i. One of the seven angels takes me to see the judgment of the great prostitute. I   17:1-6
saw a woman sitting on a beast, drunk with the blood of the saints

ii. And I wondered. The angel tells me the mystery of the woman and beast   17:6-18

iii. After these things I saw an angel say, Babylon the Great fell, it fell   18:1-3

iv. And I heard a voice say, Come out of her, and call for judgment. Earth laments   18:4-20

v. A strong angel threw a millstone into the sea and pronounced her judgment   18:21-24

h. After these things I heard a great multitude in heaven rejoice over her downfall   19:1-4

i. And a voice came from the throne saying, Give praise to God, all his slaves. And I   19:5-9
heard a great multitude saying, Hallelujah, He reigns. Rejoice, because the wedding
of the Lamb came. Write— Blessed are those called to the wedding of the Lamb

j. And he says to me, These words are true ones of God. And I fell to worship him   19:9-10

5. And I saw heaven having been opened 19:11

    a. And behold— Christ riding a white horse, and His armies following Him 19:11-16

    b. And I saw an angel call the birds to eat the flesh of the armies of the beast 19:17-18

    c. And I saw the beast and the kings and their armies gathered against Christ. The beast and false prophet were thrown into the lake of fire. The the rest were killed 19:19-21

    d. And I saw an angel coming down with the key of the abyss, and a great chain. He seized the dragon and bound him and threw him into the abyss for 1000 years 20:1-3

    e. And I saw thrones, and the souls who did not worship the beast. And they came to life and reigned 1000 years 20:4-6

    f. Then Satan is released, deceives the nations, and is thrown into the lake of fire 20:7-10

6. And I saw a great white throne, and One sitting on it, from Whom heaven and earth fled. 20:11-15
The dead were judged. Those not in the book of life were thrown into the lake of fire

7. And I saw a new heaven and earth, for the first passed away. And I saw the new Jerusalem. 21:1-8
God dwells with mankind, and makes all things new.

    a. And one of the seven angels showed me the new Jerusalem coming down from heaven. The Lord God and the Lamb are its temple and its light 21:9-27

    b. And he showed me a river of the water of life. And God's slaves will serve Him and reign forever 22:1-5

C. And he said to me, These words are trustworthy and true. Blessed is the one obeying this book. 22:6-9
And I, John, am the one hearing these things. I fell to worship him. He said, Worship God

D. And he says to me, Do not seal up the words of the prophecy of this book. I am coming 22:10-20
quickly, and My recompense is with me. Let the one thirsting come Do not add to this book

Conclusion 22:20-21

1:1 *The* revelation[A] *of*[B] Jesus Christ, which God gave Him to show His slaves *the things* which must take-place quickly, and He signified[C], having sent-forth through His angel *to* His slave John, **2** who testified-to the word *of* God and[D] the testimony *of* Jesus Christ— *to* all that he saw. **3** Blessed *is* the *one* reading[E], and the *ones* hearing the words *of this* prophecy and keeping the *things* having been written in it, for the time *is* near.

4 John, *to* the seven churches in Asia: Grace *to* you and peace from the *One Who* is and *Who* was and *Who* is coming, and from the seven Spirits[F] that *are* before His throne, **5** and from Jesus Christ— the Faithful Witness, the Firstborn *of* the dead, and the Ruler *of* the kings *of* the earth.

To the *One* loving us and having released[G] us from our sins by His blood— **6** and He made us *a* kingdom, priests *to* His God and Father— *to* Him *be* the glory and the dominion forever and ever, amen. **7** Behold, He is coming with the clouds, and every eye will see Him— even they who pierced Him. And all the tribes *of* the earth[H] will beat-their-breasts over Him. Yes! Amen!

8 "I am the Alpha and the Omega", says the Lord God, "the *One Who* is and *Who* was and *Who* is coming, the Almighty".

I, John, Heard a Voice Say, Write What You See And Send It To The Seven Churches
9 I, John, your brother and co-partner in the affliction and kingdom and endurance in[I] Jesus, came-to-be on the island being called Patmos because of the word *of* God and[J] the testimony *of* Jesus. **10** I came-to-be in *the* Spirit[K] on the Lord's day, and I heard behind me *a* loud voice like [the sound] *of a* trumpet, **11** saying "Write in *a* book what you see, and send *it to* the seven churches— to Ephesus, and to Smyrna, and to Pergamum, and to Thyatira, and to Sardis, and to Philadelphia, and to Laodicea". **12** And I turned to see the voice which was speaking with me.

I Saw One Like a Son of Man Amidst Seven Lampstands, Which Are Seven Churches
And having turned, I saw seven golden lampstands. **13** And in *the* midst *of* the lampstands *I saw One* resembling[L] *a* son[M] *of* man having been dressed-in *a* robe reaching-to-the-feet, and having been girded-with *a* golden belt at the breasts. **14** And His head and hair *were* white like white wool, like snow. And His eyes *were* like *a* flame *of* fire. **15** And His feet *were* resembling brass[N], like *something* having been refined[O] in *a* furnace. And His voice *was* like *the* sound *of* many waters. **16** And *He was* holding seven stars in His right hand. And *a* sharp double-edged sword *was* coming-out of His mouth. And His face[P] *was* like the sun shines in its power. **17** And when I saw Him, I fell at His feet as-*though* dead. And He placed His right *hand* upon me, saying "Do not be fearing. I am the First and the Last, **18** and the *One* living. And I became dead, and behold— I am living forever and ever. And I have the keys *of* death and Hades. **19** Therefore write *the things* which you saw, and[Q] *the things* which are, and *the things* which are destined[R] to take place after these *things*. **20** As to the mystery *of* the seven stars which you saw upon My right *hand* and the seven golden

---

A. Or, disclosure, unveiling. **B.** That is, given by; or, about. **C.** Or, showed by signs. **D.** Or, even. **E.** That is, publicly. **F.** That is, the sevenfold fullness of the Holy Spirit; or, spirits, meaning angels. **G.** Or, freed. **H.** Or, land. **I.** That is, in connection with. **J.** Or, even. **K.** That is, under the Spirit's power. Or, in *the* spirit; that is, in a trance, outside the body. **L.** Or, like, similar to. **M.** That is, a human, as this phrase is used in Dan 7:13. Or, *the* Son *of* Man, the person to whom this phrase refers in Dan 7:13. **N.** Or, metal. **O.** Or, made fiery-hot. **P.** Or, outward appearance. **Q.** Or, even. **R.** Or, going-to.

lampstands— the seven stars are angels[A] *of* the seven churches, and the seven lampstands are seven churches.

Write To Ephesus: You Left Your First Love. Repent And Do The First Works
2:1 "*To* the angel *of* the church in Ephesus, write— These *things* says the *One* holding-on-to the seven stars in His right *hand*, the *One* walking in *the* midst *of* the seven golden lampstands. **²** I know your works and[B] labor and your endurance, and that you cannot bear-with evil *ones*. And you tested the *ones* calling themselves apostles (and they are not) and you found them *to be* false. **³** And you have endurance, and bore-up for the sake of My name, and have not become-weary. **⁴** But I have against you that you left your first love. **⁵** Therefore, be remembering[C] from where you have fallen, and repent, and do the first works. Otherwise, I am coming *to* you. And I will move[D] your lampstand from its place unless you repent. **⁶** But this you have— that you hate the works *of* the Nicolaitans, which **I** also hate. **⁷** Let the *one* having *an* ear hear what the Spirit is saying *to* the churches. *To* the *one* overcoming[E], I will give him *authority* to eat from the tree *of* life which is in the paradise *of* God.

Write To Smyrna: You Are Going To Suffer. Be Faithful
⁸ "And *to* the angel *of* the church in Smyrna, write— These *things* says the First and the Last Who became dead and came-to-life. **⁹** I know your affliction, and[F] poverty (but you are rich), and the blasphemy by the *ones* saying *that* they are Jews (and they are not), but *are a* synagogue *of* Satan. **¹⁰** Do not be fearing at all *the things* which you are about to suffer. Behold— the devil is going to throw *some* of you into prison so that you may be tested. And you will have affliction *for* ten days. Be[G] faithful until[H] death, and I will give you the crown *of* life. **¹¹** Let the *one* having *an* ear hear what the Spirit is saying *to* the churches. The *one* overcoming will never be harmed by the second death.

Write To Pergamum: You Have Some Holding On To False Teachings. Repent
¹² "And *to* the angel *of* the church in Pergamum, write— These *things* says the *One* having the sharp double-edged sword. **¹³** I know where you dwell: where Satan's throne *is*. And you are holding-on-to My name. And you did not deny My faith[I], even during the days *of* Antipas, My witness, My faithful *one*, who was killed among you where Satan dwells. **¹⁴** But I have *a* few *things* against you, because you have there *ones* holding-on-to the teaching *of* Balaam, who was teaching Balak to put *a* cause-of-falling before the sons *of* Israel to eat foods-sacrificed-to-idols and to commit-sexual-immorality. **¹⁵** So **you** also have *ones* holding-on-to the teaching *of* the Nicolaitans likewise. **¹⁶** Therefore repent. Otherwise, I am coming *to* you[J] quickly. And I will fight[K] against them with the sword *of* My mouth. **¹⁷** Let the *one* having *an* ear hear what the Spirit is saying *to* the churches. *To* the *one* overcoming— I will give him *some of* the hidden manna, and I will give him *a* white pebble. And having been written upon the pebble *is a* new name which no one knows except the *one*[L] receiving *it*.

A. Or, messengers. **B.** Or, even. **C.** Or, keeping in mind. **D.** Or, shake, remove. **E.** Or, conquering, being victorious. **F.** Or, even. **G.** Or, Prove-to-be faithful *ones*. **H.** Or, as far as, to the extent of. **I.** That is, your faith in Me; or, My gospel. **J.** That is, the church. This word is singular. **K.** Or, wage war. **L.** Or, the *One*; that is, Jesus, 19:12.

Write To Thyatira: You Are Tolerating a False Teacher. Repent From Her Works
18 "And *to* the angel *of* the church in Thyatira, write— These *things* says the Son *of* God, the *One* having His eyes like *a* flame *of* fire and His feet resembling brass[A]. **19** I know your works and[B] love and faith[C] and service and your endurance. And your last works *are* greater[D] *than* the first. **20** But I have against you that you are tolerating the woman Jezebel— the *one* calling herself *a* prophet. And she is teaching and misleading My slaves to commit-sexual-immorality and eat foods-sacrificed-to-idols. **21** And I gave her time in order that she might repent. And she is not willing to repent from her sexual-immorality. **22** Behold— I am throwing[E] her into *a* bed[F], and the *ones* committing-adultery with her into *a* great affliction, unless they repent from her works. **23** And I will kill her children[G] with *a* death[H]. And all the churches will know[I] that I am the *One* searching[J] minds and hearts, and I will give *to* you, *to* each *one*, according to your works. **24** But I say *to* you, *to* the rest in Thyatira— all-who are not holding this teaching, who did not know the deep *things of* Satan (as they say): I am not putting[K] another burden upon you. **25** However, hold-on-to what you have until whenever I come. **26** And the *one* overcoming and[L] the *one* keeping My works[M] until *the* end— I will give him authority over the nations. **27** And he will shepherd[N] them with *an* iron rod like clay vessels are broken-to-pieces, **28** as I also[O] have received from My Father. And I will give him the morning[P] star. **29** Let the *one* having *an* ear hear what the Spirit is saying *to* the churches.

Write To Sardis: You Are Alive In Name Only. Remember What You Received. Repent
3:1 "And *to* the angel *of* the church in Sardis, write— These *things* says the *One* having the seven Spirits[Q] *of* God and the seven stars. I know your works: that you have *a* name[R] that you are alive[S], and you are dead. **2** Be[T] keeping-watch, and establish[U] the remaining *things* which were-about-to die, for I have not found your works fulfilled[V] in the sight of My God. **3** Therefore be remembering how you have received and you heard, and be keeping *it*, and repent. Therefore if you do not keep-watch, I will come like *a* thief. And you will never know at what hour I will come upon you. **4** But you have *a* few names[W] in Sardis who did not stain their garments. And they will walk with Me in white *garments*, because they are worthy. **5** The *one* overcoming will in-this-manner clothe *himself* in white garments. And I will never[X] wipe-out[Y] his name from the book *of* life. And I will confess[Z] his name before My Father and before His angels. **6** Let the *one* having *an* ear hear what the Spirit is saying *to* the churches.

Write To Philadelphia: You Have Kept My Word. I Am Giving You an Opened Door
7 "And *to* the angel *of* the church in Philadelphia, write— These *things* says the Holy

---

A. Or, metal. **B.** Or, even. **C.** Or, faithfulness. **D.** That is, in quantity (more) or quality (better, superior). **E.** Or, putting. **F.** That is, of sickness; or, of judgment. **G.** That is, followers. **H:** kill... with *a* death. That is, I will surely kill. Or, I will kill... with pestilence. **I.** Or, come-to-know. **J.** Or, examining. **K.** Or, throwing, as in v 22. **L.** Or, even. **M.** As opposed to her works, v 22. **N.** That is, rule. **O.** Compare 19:15. **P.** That is, the light of a new day; or, Myself, since this phrase is used of Christ in 22:16. **Q.** See 1:4. **R.** Or, reputation. **S.** Or, are living (spiritually). **T.** Or, Prove-to-be *ones who are* keeping watch. **U.** Or, stabilize. **V.** Or, completed. Jesus has not found their faith fulfilled in their actions. **W.** That is, people. **X.** Or, by no means. **Y.** Or, smear-out, blot-out, erase. **Z.** Or, declare, acknowledge.

One, the True *One*, the *One* having the key[A] *of* David, the *One* opening and no one will shut, and shutting and no one opens. [8] I know your works[B]. Behold— I have given before you *an* opened door[C] (which, no one is able to shut it). Because[D] you have *a* little[E] power[F], and you kept My word, and you did not deny My name, [9] behold— I am giving *some*[G] from the synagogue *of* Satan, the *ones* saying *that* they are Jews (and they are not), but they are lying. Behold— I will make them so that they will come and worship[H] before your feet, and they may know that **I** loved you. [10] Because you kept the word *of* My[I] endurance, **I** also will keep[J] you from[K] the hour *of* testing, the *hour* going-to come upon the whole world to test the *ones* dwelling upon the earth[L]. [11] I am coming quickly. Be holding-on-to what you have in order that no one may take your crown. [12] The *one* overcoming— I will make him *a* pillar in the temple *of* My God, and he will never go outside again. And I will write upon him the name *of* My God, and the name *of* the city *of* My God— the new Jerusalem, the *one* coming down out of heaven from My God— and My new name. [13] Let the *one* having *an* ear hear what the Spirit is saying *to* the churches.

Write To Laodicea: You Are Lukewarm. Get What You Need From Me. Repent
[14] "And *to* the angel *of* the church in Laodicea, write— These *things* says the Amen, the Faithful and True Witness, the Beginning[M] *of* the creation *of* God. [15] I know your works: that you are neither cold nor hot. O-that you were cold or hot. [16] So because you are lukewarm and neither hot nor cold, I am about-to spew you out of My mouth. [17] Because you say that "I am *a* rich *one*, and I have become-rich, and I have *a* need *for* nothing", and you do not know that **you** are the *one* wretched and pitiable and poor and blind and naked— [18] I counsel you to buy from Me gold having been refined by fire in order that you may become-rich, and white garments in order that you may clothe *yourself* and the shame *of* your nakedness may not be revealed, and eye-salve to rub-in your eyes in order that you may see. [19] **I** rebuke and discipline[N] all whom I love. Therefore be zealous, and repent. [20] Behold— I stand at the door. And I am knocking. If anyone hears My voice and opens the door, I also[O] will come-in to him. And I will have-dinner with him, and he with Me. [21] The *one* overcoming— I will give him *authority* to sit *down* with Me on My throne, as **I** also overcame and sat *down* with My Father on His throne. [22] Let the *one* having *an* ear hear what the Spirit is saying *to* the churches".

A Voice Says, Come Up To Heaven And See Things Which Must Take Place After These Things
4:1 After these *things* I saw, and behold— *there was an* opened door in heaven, and the first voice which I heard speaking with me like [the sound] *of a* trumpet saying, "Come-up here and

A. That is, the authority to open David's house, the Messiah's kingdom, the New Jerusalem. **B.** The content of their works are contained in the two 'Because' statements that follow. **C.** That is, a door of service; or, a door of salvation, a door into Messiah's city. **D.** This gives the reason for giving them their enemies. Or, 'shut it), because... name. Behold', giving the reason for the open door. Or, 'I know your works (Behold... shut it), that', giving the content of their works. **E:** *a* little power, and. That is, some power, which you are using effectively. Or, little power, yet; that is, hardly any power. **F.** Or, strength. That is, spiritual power; or, number of people. **G.** That is, some converts; or short of that, some who will submit to you as follows. **H.** That is, worship Me. Or, prostrate-*themselves* [to you]; that is, in submission. **I.** That is, the message proceeding from Christ's endurance. Or, My word *of* endurance; that is, My command to endure. **J.** Or, preserve, protect, guard. **K.** Or, out-of, away-from. That is, preserve you through the hour; or, keep you out of the hour. **L.** Or, land. **M.** That is, origin, first cause (as in 'the beginning and the end', 22:13). Or, Ruler. **N.** Or, train, correct. **O.** Or, indeed.

I will show you *the things* which must take-place after these *things*". ² Immediately I came-to-be in *the* Spirit^A.

Vision 1: The Scroll With Seven Seals. The Heavenly Scene
And behold— *a* throne was setting *there* in heaven, and *One* sitting on the throne. ³ And the *One* sitting *was* resembling^B *a* jasper stone and *a* carnelian *in* appearance. And *a* rainbow^C *was* around the throne resembling *an* emerald *in* appearance. ⁴ And around the throne *I saw* twenty four thrones. And on the thrones *I saw* twenty four elders sitting, having been clothed in white garments, and golden crowns^D on their heads. ⁵ And lightnings^E and voices^F and thunders^G are coming-out from the throne. And seven torches^H *of* fire *are* burning before the throne (which are the seven^I Spirits *of* God). ⁶ And before the throne *is something* like *a* sea of-glass^J, resembling crystal. And in *the* midst *of* the throne and around the throne *are* four living-creatures^K being full *of* eyes on the front and on the back. ⁷ And the first living-creature *is* resembling *a* lion. And the second living-creature *is* resembling *a* calf. And the third living-creature *is* having the face like *of a* man^L. And the fourth living-creature *is* resembling *a* flying eagle. ⁸ And the four living-creatures, each one *of* them having six wings apiece, are full *of* eyes around and inside^M. And they do not have *a* rest^N *by* day and *by* night, saying "Holy, holy, holy *is* the Lord God Almighty, the *One Who* was and *Who* is and *Who* is coming". ⁹ And whenever the living-creatures will give glory and honor and thanks *to* the *One* sitting on the throne, *to* the *One* living forever and ever, ¹⁰ the twenty four elders will fall before the *One* sitting on the throne, and will give-worship *to* the *One* living forever and ever, and will cast^O their crowns before the throne, saying ¹¹ "You are worthy, our Lord and God, to receive the glory and the honor and the power, because **You** created all *things*. And they existed and were created because-of Your will".

Who Is Worthy To Open The Scroll? A Lamb Takes It From The One On The Throne
5:1 And I saw upon the right *hand of* the *One* sitting on the throne *a* scroll having been written inside and on-the-back, having been sealed-down *with* seven seals. ² And I saw *a* strong angel proclaiming with *a* loud voice, "Who *is* worthy to open the scroll and to break its seals?" ³ And no one in heaven nor on earth nor under the earth was able to open the scroll, nor to look-*at*^P it. ⁴ And I was weeping greatly because no one worthy was found to open the scroll, nor to look-*at* it. ⁵ And one *of* the elders says *to* me, "Do not be weeping. Behold— the Lion from the tribe *of* Judah, the Root *of* David, **overcame** *so as* to open the scroll and its seven seals". ⁶ And I saw in *the* midst *of* the throne and the four living-creatures, and in *the* midst *of* the elders, *there was a* Lamb as-*if*^Q having been slain, standing, having seven horns, and seven eyes (which are the seven Spirits^R *of* God having been sent-forth into all the earth). ⁷ And He came, and He has taken *it* out of the right *hand of* the *One* sitting on the throne.

A. See 1:10. **B.** That is, in color. **C.** Or, halo. **D.** Or, wreaths. That is, victor's-crowns. **E.** That is, bolts or flashes of lightning. **F.** Or, sounds. **G.** That is, crashes or peals of thunder. **H.** Or, lamps. **I.** See 1:4. **J.** That is, made of glass. **K.** Or, living-beings, living-ones. **L.** Or, human. **M.** That is, under their wings. **N.** Or, cessation. That is, they say this both daytime and nighttime, with no stopping for sleep (not, over and over without any pause). **O.** Or, throw, put. They repeatedly cast their crowns, v 9. **P.** That is, look at its contents. **Q.** That is, having the marks of having been slain, a throat which was cut and a bloodied body. **R.** See 1:4.

Then The One On The Throne And The Lamb Are Worshiped By All Creation

[8] And when He took the scroll, the four living-creatures and the twenty four elders fell before the Lamb— each *one* holding *a* harp and golden bowls being full *of* incense (which are the prayers *of* the saints). [9] And they are singing *a* new song, saying "You are worthy to take the scroll and to open its seals, because You were slain, and You bought[A] *for* God with Your blood *some* from every tribe and tongue and people and nation, [10] and You made them *a* kingdom and priests *to* our God, and they will reign upon[B] the earth". [11] And I saw, and I heard *the* voice *of* many angels around the throne, and *of* the living-creatures, and *of* the elders— and the number *of* them was myriads *of* myriads, and thousands *of* thousands— [12] saying *with a* loud voice "Worthy is the Lamb having been slain to receive the power and riches and wisdom and strength and honor and glory and blessing". [13] And I heard every creature which *is* in the heaven and on earth and under the earth and on the sea, and[C] all the *things* in them, saying "*To* the *One* sitting on the throne and *to* the Lamb *be* the blessing and the honor and the glory and the dominion forever and ever". [14] And the four living-creatures were saying "amen". And the elders fell and worshiped.

The Lamb Opens The First Six Seals

6:1 And I saw when the Lamb opened *the* first of the seven seals, and I heard one of the four living-creatures saying like *a* voice *of*[D] thunder, "Come[E]". [2] And I saw, and behold— *there was a* white horse, and the *one* sitting on it having *a* bow. And *a* crown was given *to* him. And he went out conquering, and[F] in order that he might conquer.

[3] And when He opened the second seal, I heard the second living-creature saying, "Come". [4] And another horse— *a* fire-red *one*— went out. And *to* the *one* sitting on it, *authority* was given *to* him to take the peace[G] from the earth, and[H] that they will slay one another. And *a* great sword was given *to* him.

[5] And when He opened the third seal, I heard the third living-creature saying, "Come". And I saw, and behold— *there was a* black horse, and the *one* sitting on it holding *a* balance-scale in his hand. [6] And I heard *something* like *a* voice in *the* midst *of* the four living-creatures, saying "*A* quart[I] *of* wheat *for a* denarius[J], and three quarts *of* barley *for a* denarius. And do not harm the olive-oil and the wine".

[7] And when He opened the fourth seal, I heard *the* voice *of* the fourth living-creature saying, "Come". [8] And I saw, and behold— *there was a* pale-green horse, and the one sitting on it. Death *was the* name *for* him. And Hades was following with him. And authority[K] was given *to* them over *a* fourth *of* the earth[L], to kill with sword and with famine and with pestilence and by the wild-beasts *of* the earth.

[9] And when He opened the fifth seal, I saw under the altar the souls *of* the *ones* having been slain because of the word *of* God and[M] because of the testimony which they were holding[N]. [10] And they cried-out *with a* loud voice, saying "How long, holy and true

---

A. Or, purchased. **B.** Or, over. **C.** Or, even. **D.** That is, characterized by. **E.** Or, Go. **F.** Or, even. **G.** That is, the peace following the first horseman. Or, peace; that is, peace in general. **H.** Or, even. **I.** This was the daily allowance for a slave. **J.** That is, the daily wage for a laborer. That is, it will cost all one can earn to buy food to survive. **K.** Or, power, freedom-to-act. **L.** Or, land. **M.** Or, even. **N.** Or, having.

Master, are You not judging and avenging^A our blood from the *ones* dwelling upon the earth?" **11** And *a* white robe was given *to* them, *to* each *one*. And it was told *to* them that they shall^B rest^C *a* short time longer, until also^D *the number of* their fellow-slaves and^E their brothers going to be killed as also they, may be completed^F.

12 And I saw when He opened the sixth seal. And *a* great earthquake took place. And the sun became black like *a* sackcloth made-of-hair, and the whole moon became like blood^G, **13** and the stars *of* the heaven fell to the earth— as *a* fig tree being shaken by *a* great wind throws its late-figs. **14** And the heaven was split^H like *a* scroll being rolled-up. And every mountain and island were moved out of their places. **15** And the kings *of* the earth and the princes and the commanders and the rich and the powerful and every slave and free *one* hid themselves in the caves and in the rocks *of* the mountains. **16** And they are saying *to* the mountains and the rocks, "Fall upon us and hide us from *the* face^I *of* the *One* sitting on the throne, and from the wrath *of* the Lamb, **17** because the great day *of* Their wrath came, and who is able to stand?".

Angels Seal 144,000 Slaves of God On Their Foreheads With The Seal of God
7:1 After this^J I saw four angels standing at the four corners *of* the earth, holding-back the four winds *of* the earth in order that *a* wind might not blow on the land, nor on the sea, nor against any tree. **2** And I saw another angel coming-up from *the* rising *of* the sun^K, having *a* seal *of the* living God. And he cried-out *with a* loud voice *to* the four angels *to* whom *authority* was given *to* them to harm the land and the sea, **3** saying "Do not harm the land nor the sea nor the trees until we seal^L the slaves *of* our God upon their foreheads". **4** And I heard the number *of* the *ones* having been sealed, one-hundred forty four thousand, having been sealed from every tribe *of the* sons *of* Israel— **5** from^M *the* tribe *of* Judah, twelve thousand having been sealed; from *the* tribe *of* Reuben, twelve thousand; from *the* tribe *of* Gad, twelve thousand; **6** from *the* tribe *of* Asher, twelve thousand; from *the* tribe *of* Naphtali, twelve thousand; from *the* tribe *of* Manasseh, twelve thousand; **7** from *the* tribe *of* Simeon, twelve thousand; from *the* tribe *of* Levi, twelve thousand; from *the* tribe *of* Issachar, twelve thousand; **8** from *the* tribe *of* Zebulun, twelve thousand; from *the* tribe *of* Joseph, twelve thousand; from *the* tribe *of* Benjamin, twelve thousand having been sealed.

A Multitude Having Died In The Great Affliction Worship God Before His Throne
9 After these *things* I saw, and behold— *there was a* great multitude (which, no one was able to number it) from every nation and *all* tribes and peoples and tongues, standing before the throne and before the Lamb, having been clothed-with^N white robes, and palm-branches in their hands. **10** And they are crying-out *with a* loud voice, saying "Salvation^O *belongs to*^P our God sitting on the throne and *to* the Lamb". **11** And all the angels were standing around the throne and the elders and the four living-creatures. And they fell on their faces before the throne and gave-worship *to* God, **12** saying "Amen. The blessing and the glory and the wisdom and the thanksgiving and

---

A. Related to 'Vengeance' is Mine. **B.** Or, should. **C.** That is, from their labors; or, from crying for vengeance. **D.** Or, both. **E.** Or, even. **F.** Or, fulfilled, filled-full. **G.** That is, red. **H.** Or, parted. That is, split in two like a scroll being rolled up sometimes tears in two; or, parted from earth, like a scroll being rolled up. **I.** Or, presence. **J.** That is, the next thing to happen; or, the next thing I saw. **K.** That is, from the east. **L.** It is a seal of protection. 9:4. **M.** Or, out-of. **N.** Or, having put-on. **O.** Or, The deliverance; that is, the victory. **P.** Or, *is in*.

the honor and the power and the strength *be* to our God forever and ever, amen". **¹³** And one of the elders responded, saying *to* me, "These *ones* having been clothed-with the white robes— who are they, and from where did they come?" **¹⁴** And I have said *to* him, "My lord, **you** know". And he said *to* me, "These are the *ones* coming out of the great affliction^A^. And they washed their robes and made them white^B^ in the blood *of* the Lamb. **¹⁵** For this reason, they are before the throne *of* God, and they are serving^C^ Him *by* day and *by* night in His temple. And the *One* sitting on the throne will dwell over them. **¹⁶** They will not hunger anymore, nor thirst anymore, nor may the sun fall upon them, nor any scorching-heat. **¹⁷** Because the Lamb at *the* center *of* the throne will shepherd them, and guide them to springs *of the* waters *of* life. And God will wipe-away^D^ every tear from their eyes".

The Lamb Opens The Seventh Seal

8:1 And when^E^ He opened the seventh seal, *a* silence took place in heaven *for* about *a* half hour.

Vision 2: The Seven Trumpets

² And I saw the seven angels who stand before God, and seven trumpets were given *to* them. **³** And another angel came and stood at the altar, holding *a* golden censer. And much incense was given *to* him so-that he will give *it with*^F^ the prayers *of* all the saints upon the golden altar before the throne. **⁴** And the smoke *of* the incense, *with* the prayers *of* the saints, went up from *the* hand *of* the angel before God. **⁵** And the angel has taken the censer, and he filled it from the fire *of* the altar and threw *it* to the earth. And there came thunders and voices and lightnings^G^ and *an* earthquake. **⁶** And the seven angels having the seven trumpets prepared themselves in order that they might trumpet.

Angels Blow The First Four Trumpets

⁷ And the first trumpeted, and there came hail and fire having been mixed with blood, and it was thrown to the land^H^. And *a* third *of* the land was burned-up, and *a* third *of* the trees was burned-up, and all *the* green grass was burned-up.

⁸ And the second angel trumpeted, and *something* like *a* great mountain burning *with* fire was thrown into the sea. **⁹** And *a* third *of* the sea became blood. And *a* third *of* the creatures in the sea, the *ones* having life, died. And *a* third *of* the ships were destroyed.

¹⁰ And the third angel trumpeted, and *a* great star fell from heaven, burning like *a* torch. And it fell on *a* third *of* the rivers, and on the springs *of* waters. **¹¹** And the name *of* the star is called Wormwood^I^. And *a* third *of* the waters became wormwood. And many *of* the people died from the waters, because they were made-bitter.

¹² And the fourth angel trumpeted, and *a* third *of* the sun was struck^J^, and *a* third *of* the moon, and *a* third *of* the stars, so-that *a* third *of* them might be darkened, and the day might not shine *for a* third *of* it, and the night likewise.

A. Or, tribulation, oppression, trouble, distress. **B.** Or, whitened them. **C.** Or, worshiping. **D:** wipe-away... eyes. Same phrase as in 21:4. **E.** Or, whenever. **F.** That is, along with. Or, *for*; that is, representing. **G.** See 4:5 on these three items. **H.** That is, in contrast with sea in v 8. Or, earth. **I.** That is, bitter. **J.** Or, hit (with a blow).

Three Woes Remain For The Ones Dwelling On The Earth

13 And I saw, and I heard one eagle[A] flying in mid-heaven[B], saying *with a* loud voice. "Woe, woe, woe *for* the *ones* dwelling upon the earth, because-of the remaining blasts *of* the trumpet *of* the three angels being about to trumpet!"

The Fifth Trumpet. The First Woe

9:1 And the fifth angel trumpeted, and I saw *a* star from heaven having fallen to the earth. And the key *of* the shaft *of* the abyss was given *to* him. **2** And he opened the shaft *of* the abyss. And smoke went-up from the shaft like *the* smoke *of a* great furnace. And the sun and the air was darkened by the smoke *of* the shaft. **3** And locusts came out of the smoke to the earth. And authority was given *to* them as the scorpions *of* the earth have authority. **4** And it was told *to* them that they shall not harm the grass *of* the land, nor any green *thing*, nor any tree, but only the people who do not have the seal *of* God on *their* foreheads. **5** And *authority* was given *to* them so that they might not kill them, but so that they will be tormented *for* five months. And their torment *was* like *the* torment *of a* scorpion when it strikes *a* person. **6** And during those days the people will seek death, and will by no means find it; and they will desire to die, and death flees from them. **7** And the likenesses[C] *of* the locusts *were* like horses having been prepared for battle. And on their heads *were something* like crowns resembling gold. And their faces *were* like faces *of* people[D]. **8** And they had hair like *the* hair *of* women[E]. And their teeth were like *ones of* lions. **9** And they had breastplates like iron breastplates. And the sound *of* their wings *was* like *the* sound *of* chariots, *of* many horses running into battle. **10** And they have tails like scorpions, and stingers. And their authority to harm people *for* five months *is* in their tails. **11** They have *a* king over them: the angel *of* the abyss. *The* name *for* him *in* Hebrew *is* Abaddon[F]. And in Greek he has *the* name Apollyon.

12 The first woe passed-away. Behold— two woes are still coming after these *things.*

The Sixth Trumpet. The Second Woe

13 And the sixth angel trumpeted.

Four Angels Are Released To Kill a Third of Mankind

And I heard one voice from the four horns *of* the golden altar before God **14** saying *to* the sixth angel, the *one* having the trumpet, "Release the four angels having been bound at the great river Euphrates". **15** And the four angels were released, the *ones* having been prepared for the hour and day and month and year, in order that they might kill *a* third *of* mankind. **16** And the number *of* the troops *of* cavalry *was* two hundred million. I heard the number *of* them. **17** And I saw the horses and the *ones* sitting on them in the vision as follows— having[G] breastplates [the color] of-fire and of-hyacinth[H] and of-sulphur. And the heads *of* the horses *are* like heads *of* lions. And fire and smoke and sulphur is coming-out of their mouths.

A. Or, vulture. **B.** That is, where birds fly. **C:** likenesses... *were* like. Or, the resemblances... resembled. **D.** Or, men (males), humans. **E.** That is, long hair. **F:** Abaddon... Apollyon. Both names mean 'destroyer'. **G.** This may refer to the rider, the horse, or both. **H.** This precious stone is dark blue or dark red. Sulphur is yellow. The breastplates may be tri-colored; or, each having one of these colors.

18 *A* third *of* mankind were killed from these three plagues— by the fire and the smoke and the sulphur coming-out of their mouths. **19** For the authority *of* the horses is in their mouth and in their tails. For their tails *are* like snakes, having heads, and with them they do harm. **20** And the rest *of* mankind who were not killed by these plagues, they did not-even repent from the works *of* their hands, so-that they will not worship demons and idols— the golden *ones* and the silver *ones* and the brass *ones* and the stone *ones* and the wooden *ones*— which are neither able to see, nor to hear, nor to walk. **21** And they did not repent from their murders, nor from their sorcerer's-potions^A, nor from their sexual-immorality, nor from their thefts.

An Angel With a Scroll Says The Mystery Will Be Finished With The Seventh Trumpet
10:1 And I saw another strong angel coming down from heaven, having been clothed-with *a* cloud. And the rainbow^B *was* over^C his head, and his face *was* like the sun, and his feet *were* like pillars *of* fire. **2** And *he was* holding^D in his hand *an* opened little-scroll. And he placed his right foot upon the sea and the left *one* upon the land, **3** and he cried-out *with a* loud voice— as indeed *a* lion roars. And when he cried-out, the seven thunders spoke their voices. **4** And when the seven thunders spoke, I was about to write. And I heard *a* voice from heaven saying, "Seal *the things* which the seven thunders spoke, and do not write them". **5** And the angel whom I saw standing upon the sea and upon the land lifted-up his right hand to heaven **6** and swore by the *One* living forever and ever— Who created the heaven and the *things* in it, and the land and the *things* in it, and the sea and the *things* in it— that there will be no more time^E [of delay]. **7** But during the days *of* the sound *of* the seventh angel, when he is about-to trumpet, the mystery *of* God was indeed finished^F, as He announced-as-good-news-to His slaves, the prophets. **8** And the voice which I heard from heaven *was* again speaking with me, and saying "Go, take the opened scroll in the hand *of* the angel standing upon the sea and upon the land". **9** And I went to the angel, telling him to give me the little-scroll. And he says *to* me, "Take, and eat^G it up. And it will make your stomach bitter. But in your mouth it will be sweet like honey". **10** And I took the little-scroll out of the hand *of* the angel, and I ate it up. And it was like sweet honey in my mouth. And when I ate it, my stomach was made-bitter. **11** And they^H say *to* me, "You must prophesy again for^I many peoples and nations and tongues and kings".

Two Witnesses Prophesy And Torment The Earth For 1260 Days
11:1 And *a measuring*-rod resembling *a* staff was given^J *to* me, saying "Arise, and measure^K the temple^L *of* God, and the altar, and the *ones* worshiping in it. **2** And put the court outside *of* the temple on-the-outside, and do not measure it, because

A. This word refers to the drugs, charms, and potions used by sorcerers. Some manuscripts instead say 'sorceries'. **B.** That is, the well-known multi-colored rainbow; or, the emerald rainbow of 4:3. **C.** Or, upon. **D.** Or, having. **E.** This answers the question of 6:10. Or, time, in an absolute sense. **F.** Or, completed, accomplished, fulfilled. It is stated as an accomplished fact. **G.** Or, consume it, devour it. **H.** That is, the voice from heaven and the angel, v 8. Or, this may be an indefinite 'they' meaning 'it was said'. **I.** That is, things destined to occur to them. Or, against, about, before. **J.** That is, by the angel in 10:9; or, the giver is not named. **K.** That is, to mark off what belongs to God. **L.** That is, the inner sanctuary, the Holy Place and Holy of Holies.

it was given *to* the Gentiles[A]. And they will trample the holy city *for* forty and two months. **3** And I will give *authority to* my two witnesses, and they will prophesy *for* one-thousand two-hundred sixty days, having been clothed-with[B] sackcloth. **4** These are the two olive-trees and the two lampstands standing in the presence of the Lord *of* the earth. **5** And if anyone is intending[C] to harm them, fire comes-out of their mouth and devours their enemies. Indeed, if anyone should intend to harm them, in this manner he must be killed. **6** These *ones* have the authority to shut the heaven in-order-that no rain may fall *for* the days *of*[D] their prophecy. And they have authority over the waters— to be turning them into blood— and *authority* to strike the earth[E] with every plague, as often as they may want. **7** And when they finish their testimony, the beast coming up out of the abyss will make war against them, and overcome them, and kill them. **8** And their corpse *will be* on the wide-road *of* the great city which spiritually is called Sodom and Egypt— where also their Lord was crucified. **9** And *some* from the peoples and tribes and tongues and nations look-*at* their corpse *for* three and *a* half days. And they do not permit their corpses to be put in *a* tomb. **10** And the *ones* dwelling upon the earth[F] rejoice over them and celebrate. And they will send gifts *to* one another, because these two prophets tormented the *ones* dwelling upon the earth. **11** And after the three and *a* half days, *a* breath[G] *of* life from God entered in them, and they stood on their feet. And great fear fell upon the *ones* seeing them. **12** And they heard *a* loud voice from heaven saying *to* them, "Come-up here". And they went-up into heaven in the cloud, and their enemies watched them. **13** And at that hour *a* great earthquake took place, and *a* tenth *of* the city fell. And seven thousand names *of* people were killed in the earthquake, and the rest became terrified and gave glory *to* the God *of* heaven".

14 The second woe passed-away. Behold— the third woe is coming quickly.

The Seventh Trumpet, The Third Woe
15 And the seventh angel trumpeted. And there came loud voices in heaven, saying "The kingdom *of* the world became[H] *the kingdom of* our Lord and *of* His Christ. And He will reign forever and ever". **16** And the twenty four elders sitting on their thrones in the presence of God fell on their faces and gave-worship *to* God, **17** saying "We give-thanks *to* You, Lord God Almighty, the *One Who* is and *Who* was[I], because You have taken Your great power, and You *began to* reign[J]. **18** And the nations became-angry. And Your wrath came, and the time *for* the dead to be judged, and to give the reward *to* Your slaves the prophets, and the saints, and[K] the *ones* fearing Your name, the small and the great, and to destroy the *ones* destroying[L] the earth".

Vision 3: The Three Signs In Heaven
19 And the temple *of* God in heaven was opened. And the ark *of*[M] His covenant appeared in His temple. And there came lightnings[N] and voices and thunders and *an* earthquake and *a* great hail.

A. Or, nations. **B.** Or, having put-on. **C.** Or, wanting. **D.** That is, of their prophetic activity. **E.** Or, land. **F.** Or, land. **G.** Or, spirit. **H.** Or, was made. **I.** Note that 'and *Who* is coming' is not stated this time (compare 1:4, 8; 4:8), perhaps because He has now come. **J.** Or, You became king, You [openly, publicly] reigned. **K.** Or, even. **L.** Or, corrupting. **M.** That is, the box *containing*. **N.** See 4:5; 8:5.

Sign 1: A Woman About To Give Birth
12:1 And *a* great sign appeared in heaven: *there was a* woman, having been clothed-with the sun, and the moon *was* under her feet and *a* crown *of* twelve stars on her head, **2** and having *a child* in *her* womb. And she is crying-out, suffering-birth-pains and being-in-torment to give-birth.

Sign 2: A Red Dragon Tries To Devour The Woman And Her Newborn Son, But Fails
3 And another sign appeared in heaven. And behold— *there was a* great fire-red dragon, having seven heads and ten horns, and seven diademsᴬ on his heads. **4** And his tail sweeps-awayᴮ *a* third *of* the stars *of* heaven and threw them to the earth. And the dragon is standing before the woman being about to give-birth, in order that when she gives-birth he might devour her child. **5** And she gave-birth to *a* Son, *a* male *Child,* Who is going to shepherdᶜ all the nations with *an* iron rod. And her Child was snatched-up to God, and to His throne. **6** And the woman fled into the wildernessᴰ where she has *a* place there having been prepared by God, in order that theyᴱ might nourishᶠ her there *for* one-thousand two-hundred sixty days.

There Is a War In Heaven: The Dragon Is Thrown Down To Earth
7 And there was *a* warᴳ in heaven. Michael and his angels *were* to fight against the dragon. And the dragon and his angels fought. **8** And he did not prevail, nor was *a* place *for* them still found in heaven. **9** And the great dragon was thrown-down— the ancient serpent, the *one* being called *the* devil and Satan, the *one* deceiving the whole world— he was thrown-*down* to the earth. And his angels were thrown-*down* with him. **10** And I heard *a* loud voice in heaven, saying "Nowᴴ the salvationᴵ and the power and the kingdom *of* our God and the authority *of* His Christ cameᴶ, because the accuser *of* our brothers was thrown-*down*— the *one* accusing them before our God *by* day and *by* night. **11** And **they** overcameᴷ him because-of the blood *of* the Lamb and because of the word *of*ᴸ their testimony. And they did not love their life untilᴹ death. **12** For this reason— celebrate, heavens, and the *ones* dwelling in them. Woe *for* the land and the sea, because the devil went down to you having great fury, knowing that he has *a* short time".

The Dragon Pursues The Woman, And Then Makes War Against Her Children
13 And when the dragon saw that he was thrown-*down* to the earth, he pursuedᴺ the woman who gave-birth to the male *Child.* **14** And the two wings *of* the great eagle were given *to* the woman in order that she might fly into the wilderness, into her place where she is nourished there *for a* time and times and half *of a* time from *the* presence *of* the serpent. **15** And the serpent threwᴼ water from his mouth after the woman like *a* river, in order that he might cause her *to be* swept-away-by-a-river. **16** And the earth helpedᴾ the woman. Indeed the earth opened its mouth and swallowed-up the river which the dragon threw from his mouth. **17** And the dragon became-angry at the woman, and he went to make war against

---

A. That is, king's crowns. **B.** Or, drags-away. **C.** That is, rule. **D.** Or, desert. **E.** That is, ones send by God, but otherwise undefined by John. **F.** Or, feed, provide for. **G.** Or, battle. **H.** Or, At-this-moment, At-this-time. **I.** Or, deliverance. **J.** Or, came-to-pass, became-*reality*. **K.** Or, were victorious over. **L.** That is, consisting of. Or, the Word *to which they bore* testimony. **M.** Or, as far as, up to. That is, they loved Jesus more than their lives, until their death. **N.** Or, persecuted. **O.** Or, cast. **P.** Or, came-to-the-aid-of.

the rest *of* her seed^A— the *ones* keeping the commandments *of* God and holding the testimony *of*^B Jesus. **18** And he stood on the sand *of* the sea.

A Beast Comes From The Sea: The Dragon Gives Him Power And Authority

13:1 And I saw *a* beast coming-up out of the sea, having ten horns and seven heads, and ten diadems upon his horns, and names *of*^C blasphemy on his heads. **2** And the beast which I saw was resembling *a* leopard, and his feet *were* like *ones of a* bear, and his mouth *was* like *a* mouth *of a* lion. And the dragon gave him his power and his throne and great authority. **3** And *I saw* one of his heads as-*if*^D having been slain to^E death. And his wound *of*^F death was cured. And the whole earth was caused-to-marvel [while following] after the beast. **4** And they gave-worship *to* the dragon, because he gave the authority *to* the beast. And they gave worship *to* the beast saying, "Who *is* like the beast, and who can wage-war against him?" **5** And *a* mouth was given *to* him speaking great *things* and^G blasphemies. And authority to act *for* forty and two months was given *to* him. **6** And he opened his mouth for blasphemies against God, to blaspheme His name, and His dwelling^H— the^I *ones* dwelling in heaven. **7** And *authority* was given *to* him to make war against the saints, and to overcome^J them. And authority was given *to* him over every tribe and people and tongue and nation. **8** And all the *ones* dwelling upon the earth will worship him— *each* whose name has not been written in the book *of* life *of* the Lamb having been slain since^K *the* foundation *of the* world. **9** If anyone has *an* ear, let him hear: **10** if anyone *is* for^L captivity, he is going into captivity; if anyone *is* to^M be killed with *a* sword, he *is* to be killed with *a* sword. Here^N is the endurance and the faith^O *of* the saints.

A Beast Comes From The Land. He Makes Everyone Worship The First Beast

11 And I saw another beast^P coming-up out of the land^Q. And he had two horns like *a* lamb. And he was speaking like *a* dragon. **12** And he exercises all the authority *of* the first beast in his presence. And he makes the earth and the *ones* dwelling in it so that they will worship the first beast whose wound *of* death was cured. **13** And he does great signs, so that he even makes fire to come-down out of heaven to the earth in the presence of *the* people. **14** And he deceives the *ones* dwelling upon the earth because-of the signs which it was given him to do in the presence of the beast— telling the *ones* dwelling upon the earth to make *an* image *to* the beast who has the wound *of* the sword and lived^R. **15** And *authority* was given *to* him to give breath *to* the image *of* the beast, in order that the image *of* the beast might even^S speak and cause that all-who do not give-worship *to* the image *of* the beast should be killed. **16** And he causes everyone— the small and the great, and the rich and the poor, and the free and the slaves— that they^T

A. That is, her offspring, her spiritual descendants, Christians. **B.** That is, given by; or, concerning. **C.** That is, characterized by. **D.** That is, having the marks of one slain. **E.** Or, resulting in, leading to. **F.** That is, characterized by (his death wound); or, leading to. **G.** Or, even. **H.** That is, place of dwelling, defined next. **I.** Some manuscripts make this a third thing, 'and the *ones*'; others combine it with what precedes as 'His dwelling in heaven'. **J.** Or, conquer. **K.** That is, slain since; or, written... since, as in 17:8. **L.** That is, destined for. **M.** That is, destined to. **N.** Or, At-this-point. **O.** Or, faithfulness. **P.** He is called the false prophet in 16:13; 19:20; 20:10. **Q.** Versus the sea in v 1. Or, the earth. **R.** Or, came-to-life, became alive. **S.** Or, both. **T.** That is, the authorities who do such things.

should give them *a* mark on their right hand or on their forehead, [17] and that no one should be able to buy or to sell except the *one* having the mark: the name *of* the beast or the number *of* his name. [18] Here[A] is wisdom. Let the *one* having understanding calculate the number *of* the beast, for it is *the* number[B] *of a* man. And his number *is* six-hundred sixty six.

The Lamb And The 144,000 Stand On Mt. Zion, Singing a New Song

14:1 And I saw, and behold— the Lamb *was* standing on Mount Zion, and with Him one-hundred forty four thousand having His name and the name *of* His Father having been written on their foreheads. [2] And I heard *a* sound from heaven like *a* sound *of* many waters, and like *a* sound *of* loud thunder. And the sound which I heard *was* like *that of* harpists harping with their harps. [3] And they[C] are singing *something* like *a* new song before the throne and before the four living-creatures and the elders. And no one was able to learn the song except the one-hundred forty four thousand, the *ones* having been bought[D] from the earth. [4] These are *ones* who were not stained[E] with women, for they are virgins. These *are*[F] the *ones* following the Lamb wherever He goes. These were bought from mankind *to be the* firstfruit *to* God and *to* the Lamb. [5] And falsehood was not found in their mouth. They are without-blemish.

Three Angels Proclaim God's Message To The Earth

[6] And I saw another angel flying in mid-heaven[G], having eternal good-news to announce-as-good-news to[H] the *ones* sitting on the earth— indeed, to every nation and tribe and tongue and people, [7] saying with *a* loud voice "Fear God and give Him glory, because the hour *of* His judgment came[I]. And give-worship *to* the One having made the heaven and the land and sea and springs *of* waters". [8] And another angel, *a* second, followed, saying "Babylon the great fell[J], it fell— she who has given-a-drink-*to* all the nations from the wine *of* the passion[K] *of* her sexual-immorality". [9] And another angel, *a* third, followed them, saying with *a* loud voice, "If anyone worships the beast and his image and receives *a* mark on his forehead or on his hand, [10] he himself will also drink from the wine *of* the fury *of* God having been mixed undiluted in the cup *of* His wrath. And he will be tormented with fire and sulphur in the presence of holy angels, and in the presence of the Lamb. [11] And the smoke *of* their torment goes up forever and ever. And they do not have *a* rest *by* day and *by* night[L]— the *ones* worshiping the beast and his image, and if anyone receives the mark *of* his name. [12] Here[M] is the endurance *of* the saints, the *ones* keeping the commandments *of* God and the faith *of*[N] Jesus. [13] And I heard *a* voice from heaven saying, "Write— 'Blessed[O] *are* the dead dying in *the* Lord from-now-on! Yes, says the Spirit, so that they will rest from their labors, for their works are following with them".

A. Or, At-this-point. **B.** Or, *a* number *of* man; a human number. **C.** That is, the unidentified group in heaven before the throne. **D.** Or, purchased. **E.** Or, soiled, defiled. They never engaged in sexual-immorality. **F.** Or, *were*. **G.** See 8:13. **H.** Or, across, over, for. **I.** That is, has arrived. **J.** This further announcement of judgment is given as if the falling had already occurred. **K.** Or fury, as in v 10; meaning, the wine *consisting of* the fury [of God] *belonging to* her sexual-immorality. **L.** Same phrase as in 4:8. **M.** Or, At-this-point. **N.** That is, given by; or, in. **O.** Or, Fortunate (from God's point of view).

The Reaping of Mankind

14 And I saw and behold— *there was a* white cloud, and *one* sitting on the cloud resembling *a* son[A] *of* man, having *a* golden crown[B] upon his head and *a* sharp sickle in his hand. **15** And another angel came out of the temple, crying-out with *a* loud voice *to* the *one* sitting on the cloud, "Send your sickle and reap, because the hour to reap came, because the harvest *of* the earth was dried-up[C]". **16** And the *one* sitting on the cloud cast his sickle over[D] the earth, and the earth was reaped. **17** And another angel came out of the temple in heaven, he also having *a* sharp sickle. **18** And another angel came-out from the altar— the *one* having[E] authority over the fire. And he called-out *with a* loud voice *to* the *one* having the sharp sickle, saying, "Send your sharp sickle and gather the clusters *from* the grapevine *of* the earth, because its grapes became ripe". **19** And the angel cast his sickle into the earth, and gathered the grapevine *of* the earth, and threw *it* into the great winepress *of* the fury *of* God. **20** And the winepress was trodden outside the city. And blood came out of the winepress up to the bridles *of* the horses, one-thousand six-hundred stades[F] away.

Sign 3: Seven Angels With The Seven Last Plagues, And The Overcomers Singing

15:1 And I saw another sign in heaven, great and marvelous: seven angels having seven plagues— the last, because the fury *of* God was finished[G] in them. **2** And I saw *something* like *a* sea of-glass[H] having been mixed *with* fire, and the *ones* overcoming[I] from the beast and from his image and from the number *of* his name standing upon the sea of-glass, holding harps *of* God. **3** And they are singing the song *of* Moses the slave *of* God, and the song *of* the Lamb, saying "Your works *are* great and marvelous, Lord God Almighty. Your ways *are* righteous and true, King *of* the nations. **4** Who will never come-to-fear, Lord, and glorify Your name? Because *You* alone *are* holy. Because all the nations will come and worship[J] before You, because Your righteous-acts were revealed".

Vision 4: The Seven Bowls of Wrath

5 And after these *things* I saw, and the temple *of*[K] the tabernacle[L] *of*[M] testimony[N] in heaven was opened[O]. **6** And the seven angels having the seven plagues[P] came out of the temple, having been dressed-in clean shining linen and having been girded-with golden belts around the chests. **7** And one of the four living-creatures gave *to* the seven angels seven golden bowls being full *of* the fury *of* God, the *One* living forever and ever. **8** And the temple was filled *with* smoke from the glory *of* God, and from His power. And no one was able to enter into the temple until the seven plagues *of* the seven angels were finished. **16:1** And I heard *a* loud voice from the temple saying *to* the seven angels, "Go and pour-out the seven bowls *of* the fury *of* God into the earth".

A. See 1:13. **B.** That is, a victor's crown or wreath, as in 4:4. **C.** Or, became dry. That is, ready to harvest. **D.** Or, upon, across, to. Some think believers are harvested here, unbelievers next. **E.** John may be referring to the angel in 8:3-5. **F.** 1600 stades is about 184 miles or 296 kilometers. **G.** This third sign in heaven is carried out in detail beginning in v 5. John refers to it here as if it were already accomplished, as in 10:7. **H.** That is, made of glass, as in 4:6. **I.** Or, coming off victorious from. **J.** Or, prostrate-*themselves*. **K.** That is, containing; or, consisting of. **L.** Or, tent *of* witness. **M.** That is, containing. **N.** Or, witness. That is, the ark of the covenant. **O.** This scene resumes from 11:19. This may be a reopening of that temple, or a new opening of an inner or outer temple. **P.** This phrase refers back to what was seen in v 1, the sign there now actually taking place here.

2 And the first went and poured out his bowl into the land^A— and *a* bad and evil sore came upon the people having the mark *of* the beast and the *ones* giving worship *to* his image.

3 And the second poured out his bowl into the sea— and it became blood like *of a* dead *man*. And every soul *of* life died— the *things* in the sea.

4 And the third poured-out his bowl into the rivers and the springs *of* waters— and it^B became blood. **5** And I heard the angel *of* the waters saying, "You are righteous^C, the *One Who* is and *Who* was^D, the holy *One*, because You judged these *things*. **6** Because they shed *the* blood *of* saints and prophets, and You have given them blood to drink. They are worthy^E *of it*". **7** And I heard *a voice from* the altar saying, "Yes, Lord God Almighty, Your judgments *are* true and righteous".

8 And the fourth poured out his bowl upon the sun— and *authority* was given *to* it to scorch the people with fire. **9** And the people were scorched *with a* great scorching-heat. And they blasphemed the name *of* God, the *One* having the authority over these plagues. And they did not repent so° *as* to give Him glory.

10 And the fifth poured out his bowl upon the throne *of* the beast— and his kingdom became darkened. And they were biting their tongues because-of the pain. **11** And they blasphemed the God *of* heaven because of their pains, and because of their sores. And they did not repent from their works.

12 And the sixth poured out his bowl upon the great river Euphrates— and its water was dried-up in order that the way might be prepared *for* the kings from *the* rising *of the* sun^F. **13** And I saw three unclean spirits like frogs *come* out of the mouth *of* the dragon, and out of the mouth *of* the beast, and out of the mouth *of* the false-prophet. **14** For they are spirits *of* demons doing signs, which go out to the kings *of* the whole world to gather them together for the battle *of* the great day *of* God Almighty. **15** "Behold^G— I am coming like *a* thief. Blessed *is* the *one* keeping-watch^H, and keeping his garments in order that he not be walking-around naked and they see his shame". **16** And they gathered them together to the place being called Har-Magedon *in* Hebrew.

17 And the seventh poured out his bowl upon the air— and *a* loud voice came out of the temple from the throne saying, "It is done^I". **18** And there came lightnings^J and voices and thunders. And *a* great earthquake took place such as did not take place from which *time a* human^K came-to-be^L upon the earth— so-large *an* earthquake, so great. **19** And the great city^M came-to-be in three parts. And the cities *of* the nations fell. And Babylon the great was remembered^N in the presence *of* God— to give her the cup *of* the wine *of* the fury *of* His wrath. **20** And every island fled, and *the* mountains were not found. **21** And great hail weighing about *a* talent^O comes down from heaven

---

A. Or, earth. **B.** That is, the water. **C.** Or, just. **D.** Note that 'and *Who* is coming' is omitted, as in 11:17. **E.** Or, deserving. **F.** That is, from the east. **G.** This interjection to the readers of this book is similar to the one in 22:7. **H.** Or, staying-alert. **I.** Or, It has come-to-pass. **J.** See 4:5. **K.** Or, mankind. **L.** Or, came-into-being. **M.** That is, Jerusalem; or, Babylon. **N.** That is, was kept in mind. **O.** That is, about 58-94 pounds or 26-43 kilograms,

upon the people. And the people blasphemed God because of the plague *of* the hail, because its plague is extremely great.

One of The Seven Angels Takes John To See The Judgment of Babylon The Great
17:1 And one of the seven angels having the seven bowls came and spoke with me, saying, "Come, I will show you the judgment *of* the great prostitute sitting on many waters, [2] with whom the kings *of* the earth committed-sexual-immorality, and the *ones* dwelling-in the earth[A] got-drunk from the wine *of* her sexual-immorality". [3] And he carried me away in *the* Spirit[B] to *a* wilderness. And I saw *a* woman sitting on *a* scarlet beast being-full-of names *of* [C] blasphemy having seven heads and ten horns. [4] And the woman had been clothed-with[D] purple and scarlet, and gilded *with* gold, and *with* precious stone and pearls, having *a* golden cup in her hand being-full *of* abominations[E] and[F] the impure *things of* her sexual-immorality, [5] and *a* name having been written upon her forehead, *a* mystery[G]: "Babylon the Great, the mother *of* the prostitutes and *of* the abominations *of* the earth". [6] And I saw the woman being-drunk from the blood *of* the saints, and[H] from the blood *of* the witnesses *of* Jesus.

The Angel Explains The Mystery of The Great Prostitute And The Beast
And having seen her, I wondered *with* great wonder. [7] And the angel said *to* me, "For what reason do you wonder? I will tell you the mystery *of* the woman, and *of* the beast carrying her— the *one* having the seven heads and the ten horns. [8] The beast which you saw was and is not and is going to come-up out of the abyss. And he goes to destruction. And the *ones* dwelling upon the earth whose name has not been written on the book *of* life since *the* foundation *of the* world will be caused-to-marvel while seeing the beast, because he was and is not and will be present[I]. [9] Here[J] *is* the mind having wisdom: the seven heads are seven mountains where the woman sits on them, and they are seven kings. [10] The five fell, the one is, the other did not yet come. And when he comes, he must remain *a* short *time*. [11] And the beast which was and is not, is himself also *an* eighth. And he is from[K] the seven. And he goes to destruction. [12] And the ten horns which you saw are ten kings[L] who did not-yet receive *a* kingdom, but they receive authority as kings with the beast *for* one hour[M]. [13] These have one purpose, and they give their power and authority *to* the beast. [14] These will wage-war against the Lamb. And the Lamb[N] will overcome them, because He is Lord *of* lords and King *of* kings, and the *ones* with Him *are* called *ones* and chosen *ones* and faithful *ones*". [15] And he says *to* me, "The waters which you saw where the prostitute sits, are peoples and multitudes and nations and tongues. [16] And the ten horns which you saw, and the beast— these will hate[O] the prostitute and they will make her desolated[A]

depending on the system of measurement. **A.** Or, land. **B.** Or, in spirit. See 1:10. **C.** That is, characterized by. **D.** Or, had put-on. **E.** Or, detestable *things*, loathsome *things*. This word is used of things associated with idolatry. **F.** Or, even. **G.** Or, forehead: "Mystery Babylon the Great. **H.** Or, even. **I.** Or, be here. **J.** Or, At-this-point. **K.** That is, *one* of the seven; or, out-of the seven. **L.** Note that these ten kings help destroy Babylon (v 16-17) and the 'kings of the earth' weep over this (18:9). **M.** This short period of time ends when the Lamb overcomes them, v 14. **N:** And the Lamb... faithful *ones*. Or, And the Lamb and the called and chosen and faithful *ones* with Him will overcome them, because He is Lord... kings. **O.** The ten kings will turn against the prostitute.

and naked, and they will eat her flesh, and they will burn her up with fire. **¹⁷** For God gave *it* into their hearts to do His purpose, and to do one purpose, and to give their kingdom *to* the beast— until the words *of* God will be finished. **¹⁸** And the woman whom you saw is the great city having *a* kingdom over the kings *of* the earth".

Another Angel Says, Babylon The Great Fell, It Fell!

18:1 After these *things* I saw another angel coming down from heaven, having great authority. And the earth was illuminated by his glory. **²** And he cried-out with *a* strong voice, saying "Babylon the great fell, it fell! And it became *a* dwelling-place *of* demons, and *a* prison *of* every unclean spirit, and *a* prison *of* every unclean bird, and *a* prison *of* every unclean and hated wild-beast. **³** Because all the nations have drunk from**ᴮ** the wine *of* the passion**ᶜ** *of* her sexual-immorality, and the kings *of* the earth committed-sexual-immorality with her, and the merchants *of* the earth became-rich by the power *of* her luxury".

A Voice Says, Come Out of Her, My People. Babylon's Judgment Comes In One Day

⁴ And I heard another voice from heaven, saying "Come out of her, my people, so-that you will not participate *in* her sins, and so that you will not receive of her plagues, **⁵** because her sins reached as far as heaven, and God remembered her wrongs. **⁶** Render**ᴰ** *to* her as indeed she herself rendered, and double**ᴱ** the doubles in accordance with her works. Mix double *for* her in the cup *in* which she mixed. **⁷** To the degree she glorified herself and lived-luxuriously**ᶠ**, to that degree give her torment and mourning. Because she says in her heart that 'I sit *as* queen and I am not *a* widow, and I will never see mourning', **⁸** for this reason her plagues will come in one day— death**ᴳ** and mourning and famine— and she will be burned-up with fire, because the Lord God, the *One* having judged her, *is* strong**ᴴ**.

The Kings of The Earth Weep

⁹ "And the kings *of* the earth having committed-sexual-immorality with her and lived-luxuriously will weep and beat-their-breasts over her when they see the smoke *of* her burning, **¹⁰** while standing at *a* distance because of the fear *of* her torment, saying 'Woe, woe, the great city, Babylon, the strong city— because your judgment came *in* one hour'.

The Merchants of The Earth Weep

¹¹ "And the merchants *of* the earth weep and mourn over her because no one buys their cargo**ᴵ** anymore— **¹²** cargo *of* gold and *of* silver and *of* precious stone and *of* pearls, and *of* fine-linen and *of* purple and *of* silk and *of* scarlet, and everything made-of-citron wood, and every object made-of-ivory, and every object from very-precious wood and brass and iron and marble, **¹³** and cinnamon and spice and incense and perfume and frankincense, and wine and olive-oil and fine-flour and wheat and cattle and sheep, and *of* horses

---

A. That is, render her desolate. **B.** Some manuscripts say, fallen because-of. **C.** See 14:8. **D.** This may be addressed to God's agents for Babylon's destruction (17:16-17); or, this may be a prayer to God by the voice in v 4. **E.** That is, give back to her double for the things she doubled to others. **F.** Or, lived-sensually. **G.** Or, pestilence. **H.** Or, mighty, powerful. **I.** Or, freight.

and *of* carriages, and *of* bodies^A— even^B souls *of* people. **14** And^C the fruit *of*^D the desire *of* your soul departed from you; indeed all the rich *things* and shining *things* perished from you, and *people* will never find them anymore. **15** The merchants *of* these *things,* the *ones* having become-rich from her, will stand at *a* distance because of the fear *of* her torment, weeping and mourning, **16** saying 'Woe, woe, the great city, the *one* having been clothed-with fine-linen and purple and scarlet, and having been gilded with gold, and *with* precious stone and pearl— **17** because so much wealth was desolated *in* one hour!'

All Who Work The Sea Weep

"And every helmsman^E and everyone sailing to *a* place and sailors and all-who work the sea stood at *a* distance, **18** and were crying-out while seeing the smoke *of* her burning, saying 'What *city is* like the great city?' **19** And they threw dirt on their heads and were crying-out, weeping and mourning, saying 'Woe, woe, the great city by which all the *ones* having ships at sea became-rich because-of her preciousness^F— because she was desolated *in* one hour!'

Saints Celebrate

20 "Celebrate^G over her, heaven and saints and apostles and prophets— because God judged your judgment^H from her!"

A Strong Angel Says Babylon Will Never Be Seen Again

21 And one strong angel picked-up *a* stone like *a* large millstone and threw *it* into the sea, saying "In this manner, Babylon the great city will be thrown-*down with* violence and never found again. **22** And *a* sound *of* harpists and musicians and flute-players and trumpeters will never be heard in you again. And every craftsman *of* every craft will never be found in you again. And *a* sound *of a* mill will never be heard in you again. **23** And *a* light *of a* lamp will never shine in you again. And *a* sound *of a* bridegroom and bride will never be heard in you again. Because your merchants were the princes *of* the earth. Because all the nations were deceived by your sorcery, **24** and in her *the* blood *of* prophets and saints was found, even *of* all the *ones* having been slain upon the earth".

Heaven Rejoices Over God's Judgment

19:1 After these *things* I heard *something* like *a* loud voice *of a* great multitude in heaven^I *of ones* saying "Hallelujah— the salvation and the glory and the power *of*^J our God! **2** Because His judgments *are* true and righteous. Because He judged the great prostitute who corrupted^K the earth with her sexual-immorality, and He avenged the blood *of* His slaves from her hand". **3** And *a* second *time* they have said, "Hallelujah! And her smoke goes up forever and ever". **4** And the twenty four elders

---

A. That is, slaves, human livestock. **B.** Or, bodies, and. **C.** Here the voice of v 4 addresses Babylon directly. **D.** That is, sought by. **E.** That is, pilot of a ship. **F.** Or, costliness. That is, because of the costly nature of Babylon's things. **G.** The voice directly addresses believers again, as in v 4. **H.** That is, exacted your verdict. **I.** John's perspective changes from earth (17:3-18:24) back to heaven, where he hears heaven's response to the events in 16:17-21. **J.** Or, *belonging to, belongs to.* Or, *of our God came,* as in 12:10. **K.** Or, was corrupting.

and the four living-creatures fell and gave-worship *to* God, the *One* sitting on the throne, saying "Amen. Hallelujah!"

Heaven Rejoices Over The Wedding of The Lamb

5 And *a* voice came out from the throne, saying "Give-praise[A] *to* our God, all His slaves, and[B] the *ones* fearing Him— the small and the great". **6** And I heard *something* like *the* voice *of a* great multitude and like *the* sound *of* many waters and like *the* sound *of* strong thunders, saying "Hallelujah! Because *the* Lord our God, the Almighty, *began*[C] *to* reign. **7** Let us rejoice and be overjoyed, and give the glory *to* Him, because the wedding[D] *of* the Lamb came, and His wife prepared herself". **8** And[E] *authority* was given *to* her to[F] clothe *herself* with shining clean fine-linen. For the fine-linen is the righteous-acts *of* the saints. **9** And he[G] says *to* me, "Write— 'Blessed *are* the *ones* having been called[H] to the banquet *of* the wedding *of* the Lamb' ".

These Words Are True Words of God

And he says *to* me, "These[I] words are true *ones of* God". **10** And I fell in front of his feet to give-worship[J] *to* him. And he says *to* me "See *that you* not *do it*. I am *a* fellow-slave *of* you and your brothers— the *ones* holding the testimony *of*[K] Jesus. Give-worship *to* God. For the testimony *of*[L] Jesus is the spirit[M] *of* prophecy".

Vision 5: Heaven Is Opened. The King of Kings Comes To Earth On a White Horse

11 And I saw heaven having been opened. And behold— *there was a* white horse, and the *One* sitting on it being called Faithful and True. And He judges and wages-war in righteousness. **12** And His eyes *are* like *a* flame *of* fire, and upon His head *are* many diadems[N]— *He* having *a* name having been written which no one knows except Himself, **13** and having clothed *Himself* with *a* garment having been dipped *in* blood[O]. And His name has been called "The Word *of* God". **14** And the armies in heaven were following Him on white horses, *the riders* having been dressed-in white clean fine-linen. **15** And *a* sharp sword comes out of His mouth, in order that He may strike the nations with it. And He Himself will shepherd[P] them with *an* iron rod. And He Himself treads the winepress *of* the wine *of* the fury *of* the wrath *of* God Almighty. **16** And He has *a* name having been written on the garment and[Q] on His thigh: "King *of* kings, and Lord *of* lords".

An Angel Calls The Birds To Feast On Human Flesh

17 And I saw one angel standing in the sun, and he cried-out with *a* loud voice, saying *to* all the birds flying in mid-heaven, "Come, be gathered-together for the great banquet *of* God, **18** in order that you may eat *the* flesh *of* kings, and *the* flesh *of* commanders,

---

A. Note that verses 6 and 7 come in response to this command. Or, this command may be in response to v 4, concluding that paragraph; verse 6 then beginning a second thing John 'heard' (v 1). **B.** Or, even. **C.** Or, reigned, became king, as also in 11:17. **D.** Or, wedding-celebration. **E.** The preceding quotation may extend to 'fine-linen' or 'saints' in this verse. **F.** Or, that she might. **G.** That is, the angel who has been guiding John since 17:1; or, the voice in 19:5, who is now with John in person. **H.** Or, summoned, invited. **I.** That is, all that this angel has been a part of since 17:1; or, the words in verse 9 in particular. **J.** John takes the preceding declaration to mean God is directly speaking to him. **K.** That is, given by; or, about. **L.** That is, given by. **M.** Or, breath. That is, the testimony given by Jesus is the inspiration producing what the prophets speak. **N.** That is, royal crowns. **O.** The blood could be Christ's own (at the Cross), that of the martyrs, or that of His enemies. **P.** That is, rule. He will herd this flock to its destiny in a way that permits no opposition or deviation. **Q.** Or, even.

and *the* flesh *of* powerful *ones,* and *the* flesh *of* horses and *of* the *ones* sitting on them, and *the* flesh *of* everyone— both free and slaves, both^A small and great".

The Beast And His Followers Are Conquered. The Birds Are Satisfied

19 And I saw the beast and the kings *of* the earth and their armies having been gathered-together to make^B war against the *One* sitting on the horse, and against His army. **20** And the beast was seized, and with him the false-prophet having done the signs in his presence, by which he deceived the *ones* having received the mark *of* the beast, and the *ones* giving-worship *to* his image. While living, the two were thrown into the lake *of* fire burning with sulphur. **21** And the rest were killed with the sword *of* the *One* sitting on the horse, the *sword* having come-out of His mouth. And all the birds were filled-to-satisfaction from their flesh.

The Thousand Years: Satan Is Bound

20:1 And I saw *an* angel coming down from heaven, having the key *of* the abyss, and *a* great chain on his hand. **2** And he seized the dragon— the ancient serpent, who is *the* devil and Satan^C— and bound him *for a* thousand^D years. **3** And he threw him into the abyss, and shut and sealed *it* over him in order that he might not deceive the nations anymore until the thousand years are finished. After these *things* he must be released *for a* short time.

The Thousand Years: Saints Reign With Christ

4 And I saw thrones— and they^E sat-*down* on them, and judgment^F was given *to* them— and the souls *of* the *ones* having been beheaded^G because of the testimony *of* Jesus and because of the word *of* God, and^H they who did not worship the beast nor his image, and did not receive the mark upon the forehead and upon their hand. And they came-to-life^I and reigned with Christ *for a* thousand years. **5** The rest *of* the dead did not come-to-life until the thousand years were finished. This *is* the first^J resurrection. **6** Blessed and holy *is* the *one* having *a* part in the first resurrection. The second death does not have authority over these, but they will be priests *of* God and *of* Christ, and will reign with Him *for* the thousand years.

The End of The Thousand Years: Satan Is Defeated Forever

7 And when the thousand years are finished, Satan will be released from his prison. **8** And he will go out to deceive the nations in the four corners *of* the earth— Gog and Magog— to gather them together for the battle, whose number *is* like the sand *of* the sea. **9** And they went-up over the breadth^K *of* the earth, and surrounded^L the camp^M *of* the saints and^N the city having been loved. And fire came down from heaven and

---

A. Or, and. **B.** Or, make the war; that is, the one previously mentioned in 16:14, 16; 17:14. **C.** These four names are also in 12:19. **D.** Some think 20:1-10 continues on in time from 19:21, describing a thousand year period after Christ's return. Others think 20:1-10 gives another overview of the time between the two comings of Christ. **E.** That is, Christ and His army, 19:19, the souls named next being a subgroup of them. Or, this may anticipate the souls John speaks of next. **F.** That is, authority to judge and the work of judging. **G.** That is, executed. **H.** Or, even. This is either describing a second group who were not beheaded, or giving further details about the beheaded group. **I.** Or, lived, became alive. This can refer to resurrection life or to spiritual life with God. **J.** The second may be the physical resurrection of a different group; or, the physical resurrection of this same group raised spiritually to God here. **K.** Or, width. **L.** Or, encircled. **M.** This word can have a general or a military sense here. **N.** Or, even.

devoured them. [10] And the devil, the *one* deceiving them, was thrown into the lake *of* fire and sulphur— where both[A] the beast and the false prophet *are*. And they will be tormented *by* day and *by* night forever and ever.

Vision 6: The Great White Throne Judgment

[11] And I saw *a* great white throne, and the *One* sitting on it, from Whose presence the earth fled, and the heaven, and *a* place was not found *for* them. [12] And I saw the dead[B]— the great and the small— standing before the throne. And books[C] were opened. And another book was opened, which is *the book of* life. And the dead were judged from the *things* having been written in the books, according-to[D] their works. [13] And the sea gave the dead in it, and death and Hades gave the dead in them, and they were judged— each *one*— according-to their works. [14] And death and Hades were thrown into the lake *of* fire. This is the second death— the lake *of* fire. [15] And if anyone was not found having been written in the book *of* life, he was thrown into the lake *of* fire.

Vision 7: The New Heaven And New Earth And New Jerusalem

21:1 And I saw *a* new heaven and *a* new earth, for the first heaven and the first earth passed-away. And there is no longer *a* sea[E]. [2] And I saw the holy city— *the* new Jerusalem— coming down out of heaven from God, having been prepared like *a* bride having been adorned *for* her husband. [3] And I heard *a* loud voice from the throne, saying "Behold— the dwelling[F] *of* God *is* with mankind. And He will dwell with them. And they themselves will be His peoples[G]. And God Himself with them will be their God. [4] And He will wipe-away every tear from their eyes[H]. And there will no longer be death, nor will there be mourning nor crying nor pain any longer, because the first *things* passed away". [5] And the *One* sitting on the throne said, "Behold— I am making all *things* new". And he[I] says, "Write, because these words are trustworthy[J] and true". [6] And He said *to* me, "They[K] are done[L]. I am the Alpha and the Omega, the Beginning and the End. *To* the *one* thirsting, I will give from the spring *of* the water *of* life as-a-gift[M]. [7] The *one* overcoming will inherit these *things,* and I will be God *to* him and **he** will be *a* son *to* Me. [8] But *for* the cowardly[N] *ones,* and unbelieving[O] *ones,* and *ones* having been abominable[P], and murderers, and sexually-immoral *ones,* and sorcerers, and idolaters, and all the liars— their part[Q] *will be* in the lake burning *with* fire and sulphur, which is the second death".

The Home of The Bride of The Lamb: The New Jerusalem

[9] And one of the seven angels[R] having the seven bowls being-full *of* the seven last plagues came and spoke with me, saying "Come, I will show you the bride[S], the wife *of* the Lamb". [10] And he carried me away in *the* Spirit[T] to *a* great and high mountain, and showed me the holy city Jerusalem, coming down out of heaven from God, [11] having

---

A. Or, also. **B.** That is, the whole human race (this is the final and only judgment); or, 'the rest' in v 5 (this is the final phase of judgment). **C.** That is, books of deeds or works. **D.** Or, based-on. **E.** This may refer to the sea on the 'first' earth, completing that idea (passed-away, and...); or it may be referring to the state of things on the new earth. **F.** Or, tent, tabernacle. **G.** That is, people groups. Or, people. **H.** Same phrase as in 7:17. **I.** That is, the angel with John. Note the change of tense from "said." Or, He says. **J.** Or, faithful. **K.** That is, all things in v 5. **L.** Or, have taken place, have come to pass. These things stand as done from God's point of view. **M.** Or, freely. **N.** Or, timid, afraid to act on what God has said. **O.** Or, faithless. **P.** Or, detestable, abhorrent, vile. **Q.** Or, share. That is, inheritance. **R.** That is, another of the angels from 17:1-3 again gives John a guided tour to show him more detail. **S.** That is, the destiny of the bride, the place where she will be. **T.** Or, in spirit. See 1:10.

the glory *of* God, the brilliance *of* it resembling *a* very-precious stone like *a* jasper stone, shining-like-crystal[A]; **12** having *a* great and high wall; having twelve gates, and twelve angels at the gates, and names having been inscribed— which are the names *of* the twelve tribes *of the* sons *of* Israel. **13** Three gates from *the* east, and three gates from *the* north, and three gates from *the* south, and three gates from *the* west. **14** And the wall *of* the city has twelve foundations, and on them *are the* twelve names *of* the twelve apostles *of* the Lamb. **15** And the *one* speaking with me had *a* golden measuring rod, in order that he might measure the city and its gates and its wall. **16** And the city lies square— indeed its length *is* as much as also the width. And he measured the city *with* the rod, a-matter-of twelve thousand stades[B]. Its length and width and height are equal. **17** And he measured its wall— *a* hundred forty four cubits[C] (*a* human's measure, which is *an* angel's [also]). **18** And the material *of* [D] its wall *is* jasper, and the city *is* pure gold resembling pure[E] glass. **19** The foundations *of* the wall *of* the city have been adorned *with* every precious stone. The first foundation *is* jasper; the second, sapphire; the third, chalcedony; the fourth, emerald; **20** the fifth, sardonyx; the sixth, carnelian; the seventh, chrysolite; the eighth, beryl; the ninth, topaz; the tenth, chrysoprase; the eleventh, hyacinth; the twelfth, amethyst. **21** And the twelve gates *are* twelve pearls— individually, each one *of* the gates was from one pearl. And the wide-road *of* the city *is* pure gold, like transparent glass. **22** And I did not see *a* temple in it, for its temple[F] *is* the Lord God Almighty and the Lamb. **23** And the city has no need *of* the sun nor the moon, in order that they might shine *on* it. For the glory *of* God illuminated it, and its lamp *is* the Lamb. **24** And the nations will walk by its light. And the kings *of* the earth bring their glory into it. **25** And its gates will never be shut *by* day[G]— for night will not exist there. **26** And they will bring the glory and the honor *of* the nations into it. **27** And every defiled *thing*, and the *one* doing abomination and falsehood, will never enter into it, but only the *ones* having been written in the Lamb's book *of* life.

The River of Life Flowing From The Throne of God

22:1 And he showed[H] me *a* river *of the* water *of* life, shining[I] like crystal, proceeding out from the throne *of* God and *of* the Lamb, **2** in *the* middle *of* its wide-road. And on this *side* and on that *side of* the river *is* a tree *of* life producing twelve fruits, yielding its fruit[J] every month. And the leaves *of* the tree *are* for *the* service[K] *of* the nations. **3** And there will no longer be any accursed[L] *thing*. And the throne *of* God and *of* the Lamb will be in it. And His slaves will serve[M] Him, **4** and see His face. And His name *will be* on their foreheads. **5** And there will be no more night. And they do not have *a* need *of the* light *of a* lamp and *the* light *of the* sun, because the Lord God will give-light upon them. And they will reign forever and ever.

A. Or, being-clear-like-crystal. **B.** 12,000 stades is about 1,380 miles or 2,220 kilometers. **C.** 144 cubits (forearms) is about 216 feet or 66 meters. **D.** That is, making up; or, built into. **E.** That is, clear; or, bright. **F.** That is, God is worshiped in person, face to face, not in a special place. **G.** That is, during the daytime, in anticipation of darkness. **H.** Now the angel turns from a city-tour point of view, to things of special importance to believers. **I.** Or, bright, radiant. **J.** That is, its twelve fruits monthly; or, one fruit each month. **K.** Or, attendance *on*, care *of*, healing *for*. John could mean *the* 'attendance upon' *God* by the nations (that is, for worship); or, *the* healing *for* the nations, or service in some other sense. 'Service' is intended to be a neutral rendering. **L.** Or, cursed. That is, thing under a curse. **M.** Or, worship.

The Angel Says, These Words Are Trustworthy And True. I, John, Heard And Saw These Things
6 And he[A] said *to* me, "These words *are* trustworthy[B] and true. And the Lord, the God *of* the spirits[C] *of* the prophets, sent-forth His angel[D] to show[E] His slaves *the things* which must take place quickly. **7** And behold— I[F] am coming quickly. Blessed *is* the *one* keeping the words *of* the prophecy *of* this book". **8** And I, John, *am* the *one* hearing and seeing these *things*. And when I heard and saw, I fell to worship[G] in front of the feet *of* the angel showing me these *things*. **9** And he says *to* me, "See *that you* not *do it*. I am *a* fellow-slave *of* you and *of* your brothers the prophets, and *of* the *ones* keeping the words *of* this book. Give-worship *to* God".

Behold, I Am Coming Quickly To Render To Each His Due. Come, Take The Water of Life
10 And he[H] says *to* me, "Do not seal the words *of* the prophecy *of* this book, for the time is near. **11** Let the *one* doing-unrighteousness still do-unrighteousness. And let the filthy[I] *one* still be-filthy. And let the righteous *one* still do righteousness. And let the holy *one* still be made-holy. **12** 'Behold— I am coming quickly. And My recompense[J] *is* with Me, to render to each *one* as his work is. **13** I *am* the Alpha and the Omega, the First and the Last, the Beginning and the End. **14** Blessed *are* the *ones* washing[K] their robes so that their right[L] over the tree *of* life will exist[M], and they may enter[N] into the city *by* the gates. **15** Outside *are* the dogs[O] and the sorcerers, and the sexually-immoral *ones,* and the murderers, and the idolaters, and everyone loving and doing falsehood. **16** I, Jesus, sent My angel[P] to testify these *things to* you[Q] for the churches. I am the Root and the Offspring *of* David, the bright Morning Star[R]'. **17** And the Spirit and the bride say, 'Come[S]'. And let the *one* hearing say, 'Come'. And let the *one* thirsting, come. Let the *one* wanting[T], take[U] *the* water *of* life as-a-gift[V]. **18** I testify *to* everyone hearing the words *of* the prophecy *of* this book: if anyone adds to them, God will add to him the plagues having been written in this book. **19** And if anyone takes-away from the words *of* the book *of* this prophecy, God will take his part[W] away-from the tree *of* life, and out-from the holy city— the *ones* having been written in this book. **20** The *One* testifying these *things* says, 'Yes, I am coming quickly' ".

Amen. Come, Lord Jesus. **21** The grace *of* the Lord Jesus *be* with all.

A. That is, the angel speaking the words of Jesus to John. **B.** Or, faithful. **C.** That is, human spirits; or, spiritual *gifts*, as in 1 Cor 14:12. **D.** That is, the one speaking here. **E:** to show... quickly. Same phrase as in 1:1. This is the conclusion of the whole book. **F.** As in 16:15, Christ interjects through the angel speaking for Him; or, Christ is speaking directly to John. **G.** If the angel stated v 7 on behalf of the One who sent him (v 6), John's confusion is understandable. **H.** That is, the angel speaking Christ's words here, as explained in v 6 and 16. Or, He, Christ Himself speaking. Likewise throughout this paragraph. **I.** That is, morally filthy. The point of this verse is, Do what you are going to do. Make your choices in life. I will render to you according to your works. **J.** That is, whether positive (reward) or negative (punishment). **K.** That is, in the blood, as in 7:14. **L.** Or, authority. **M.** That is, so they will have the right to eat from the tree of life. **N.** Only those written in the book of life can enter, 21:27. **O.** That is, morally impure. **P.** That is, the one speaking to John here. **Q.** That is, you all. This word is plural. **R.** That is, the precursor of the new day, visible before the sunrise. **S.** That is, Come, Lord Jesus!; or, Come to Jesus (addressing unbelievers). **T.** Or, wishing, desiring, being willing. **U.** Or, receive. **V.** Or, freely, without-payment. **W.** Or, share.

Appendix:
Details About This Translation

Notes on the Greek Translation

Vocabulary. In general, the renderings given to the Greek words in the *Disciples' Literal New Testament* are of a simple, standardized nature, and are not as finely nuanced as in other translations. Most translations try to reflect the particular shade or nuance of meaning in each place a certain word is used, minimizing footnotes. The *Disciples' Literal New Testament* tries to use the same rendering in all places a Greek word is used. It tries to render different forms of a Greek word (a noun, adjective, adverb, and verb of the same root word, for example) in a way that reflects the relationship between them. For example, "If the salt became tasteless, by what will it be salted?" (Mt 5:13); "the good-news which I announced-as-good-news" (1 Cor 15:1). "Think" is used three times in Phil 2:2, 5. By this method the *Disciples' Literal New Testament* displays more of the interrelationships and connections between the Greek words than is normally seen in English. The Greek student can find the more finely-tuned renderings in a lexicon, and English readers can see them in their standard English translations.

Word order. Greek words have different endings that determine the part of speech of each word, so they can be placed almost anywhere in the sentence. English words do not have such endings, so word order is critical. Normal English word order is subject, verb, object, prepositional phrase, as in "Fred hit the ball with the bat." In Greek the word order could be "The ball hit Fred with the bat" or "Hit Fred with the bat the ball." Clearly these must be placed in English word order to be understood in English. Sometimes the Greek word order could be kept in English, but it sounds like poetry to us. For example, "Imitators of me be, brothers," Phil 3:17. Since the writers of the New Testament wrote in the common language of the people, not poetry, the *Disciples' Literal New Testament* places words in normal English word order when it would be confusing to do otherwise. "Brothers, be imitators of me." Thus the word order of the Greek is not fully retained in the *Disciples' Literal New Testament*, in the interests of understandability. Using English word order in general allows the *Disciples' Literal New Testament* to include other literal aspects of the Greek without overwhelming the English reader with foreignness. But in those cases where the word order is a factor in understanding what is being said, the Greek word order is retained.

Italics. Words in *italics* in the *Disciples' Literal New Testament* are a vital part of the literal translation into English. They are not optional words, but words required or implied by the use in context of various aspects of Greek grammar and sentence construction. Do not skip over them when reading. **Warning:** Italics are used in a different way in the *Disciples' Literal New Testament* and are not directly comparable to their use in other translations! The need to use italics at all illustrates the fact that Greek and English express certain matters in different ways. The Greek can express things through the grammar of the words that the English can express only with additional words. In the *Disciples' Literal New Testament*, the *expressed*

Greek words are in plain type; the words *implied by the grammar* of the Greek word, phrase, or sentence structure are in *italic* type. Both together make up a literal translation into English. Using italics to display these words is not a perfect solution, but it does permit more visibility of the Greek word relations than has previously been available to the English reader. Taking this approach, instead of putting all the implied words in plain type as is usually and properly done in English translations, allows the *Disciples' Literal New Testament* to more precisely display the forms of the Greek word relations. This allows the English reader to see things a little more from the Greek perspective. The English reader will understand *that* these words are implied; the reader who knows Greek will understand *why*. In the vast majority of cases, there is no dispute whatsoever about what word is implied by the grammar, or about the alternate ways to express it accurately in English. It is all quite routine. Here are a few examples of the use of italics.

In Greek, the relationship that a noun, pronoun, adjective or article has to the sentence is indicated by the ending on the word, and its use in the context. For example, one ending can imply "of " or "from" or "than"; another, "for" or "to" or "with" or "by" or "in," depending on how the word is used. Thus, the Greek says "the disciples *of* the Pharisees," "*of* " being part of the article "the," so to speak, not an independent word. These implied helping words are in *italics* in the *Disciples' Literal New Testament*, since which one to use is based on the use of the word in context. But Greek also separately expresses these helping words (prepositions), for various reasons. When this is the case, they are in plain type. Thus, the difference in the form of expression chosen by the biblical writer can be clearly seen by the English reader in cases like Luke 1:55, "just as He spoke to [an expressed preposition] our fathers—*to* [implied by the grammar] Abraham and *to* [implied by the grammar] his seed forever."

In Greek, the pronoun "you" has different endings for the singular and the plural. In English, it is not always clear in the context which is being used. So in order to make clear that the "you" is plural, sometimes the word "all" or "people" is added in *italics*. For example, "Do not marvel that I said to you 'You *all* must be born again' " (Jn 3:7). "If I told you *people* earthly things" (Jn 3:12).

In Greek, a writer may deliberately leave routine words out of a phrase or sentence, expecting the reader to supply them from the context. The structure of the phrase or sentence demands that the reader supply the necessary word to make it complete. This is a very common feature of Greek, but not English, which requires more explicitness. For example, the writer may intend that the reader supply the verb, as Peter does in 1 Peter 1:3, "Blessed *be* the God"; "and His ears *are open*" in 3:12; "But if *one suffers*" in 4:16; "Because *it is* time" in 4:17, etc. Or, the reader may be expected to supply the object, as in "I exhort *you*" in 2:11; "blessing *them*" in 3:9; or a possessive pronoun, as in "observing *your* good works" in 2:12; "for *His* possession" in 2:9.

In Greek, the grammar of a participle in context often implies a personal subject, expressed in the *Disciples' Literal New Testament* with the word "one" in *italics*. For example, Peter says "the *One* having caused" in 1 Peter 1:3; "the *ones* being guarded" in 1:5. The "one" is implied by the usage of the participle. These are commonly and properly rephrased in English as "who caused," "who are being guarded."

In Greek, the gender relation of a word is implied by the ending of the word as used in context. For example, Peter says the work of "each *person*" (1:17), the grammar of the adjective "each" in context implying the word "person," or "one" (NASB), or "man" in a generic sense (NIV). The NRSV rephrases "each person" here as "their." Peter's intent is perfectly clear and may be properly expressed in English in these various ways. "Free *ones*" (2:16) and "all *things*" (4:7) are other examples.

In Greek, purpose and result are expressed in several ways, as in English. There are words that are translated "that," "in order that," and "so that." Take for example, "He died in order that He might save us." But many times the word "that" is not stated or is represented by another word. The required words are added in *italics*. For example, "He died *that* He *might* save us," "He died *that He might* save us," "He died *so as* to save us." These all mean the same basic thing, but represent different grammatical constructions.

In Greek, the usage of the article "the" is not like English. There are many places where Greek includes the article, but it is not needed in English (for example, "I thank God always" would read "I thank the God always"). In these cases, the article is not included in the *Disciples' Literal New Testament*. On the other hand, there are many places where Greek implies an article but does not write it (such as the object of a preposition, "for *the* praise of *the* glory of His grace"). If it is needed in English, it is included in *italics*. Finally, in many places smooth English simply prefers an article where the Greek does not have one for various reasons ("having taken *the* form of *a* slave"). These are also included in *italics*. Since Greek has no indefinite article, "*a*" or "*an*," they are always included in *italics*.

Brackets. When words are added to clarify the meaning of a word, phrase or sentence, they are added in brackets. These words are not implied by the grammar or sentence structure, but by the intended meaning of the biblical writer. If one skips over them, the actual words expressed in Greek may be read. For example, the word "deep feelings" in Mt 9:36 can refer to several specific emotions. The phrase "[of compassion]" is added to clarify the word, but the word is understandable without this clarification. In the phrase "reclining back [to eat]" in Mt 26:20, "[to eat]" is added to the word "reclining back" to bring out its meaning in this context. Others rephrase this idiom as "sat down," since we do not recline to eat in our society as people did in that day. In Mt 9:31, "[the news about]" is added to clarify the meaning. As with words in italics, these words are rarely in dispute. Most are usually in plain type in the other translations; some are in italics.

The gender issue. Words such as 'sons,' 'brothers,' 'man,' and the pronoun 'he' are often used in the New Testament when both men and women are in view, a custom also followed in English until recent times. Since the *Disciples' Literal New Testament* is reflecting the ancient Greek, these words are rendered as the biblical writers wrote them. Although this is not the modern gender-explicit way of speaking, it accurately reflects the Greek point of view. The modern reader can easily make the transition between how the Greek states it, and how we in the 21st century prefer to state it. In the case of "brother" and "son," the reader can discern from the context whether physical brothers/sons are meant, or fellow-members of Abraham's physical family (Israelites, male and female), or fellow-members of God's spiritual family (fellow-believers, brothers and sisters in the Lord). In the case of "man," there are Greek words that always refer specifically to a male or a female, and they are translated as such. But there is another Greek word (*anthropos*, from which we get "anthropo"-logy) which means "man" in the sense of "male" and "mankind, a person, whether male or female." In order to clearly reflect the writers' intended meaning in English, this word is translated "man" when a male person is intended. Otherwise, it is rendered "person, mankind, human." This permits the English reader to see the meaning in places like Jn 6:10, which uses two different words to say that the "people" (*anthropos*) sat down to eat, and the "men" were counted.

Verbs. In English we use helping words to convey the meaning of the verb. For example, consider the verb "walk." We say "to walk," "he has walked," "I have been walking," "having walked," "while walking," "he will walk," "he had walked," "I am walking," "I was walking," etc. The words "to, has, have been, having, while, will, had, am, was," and the pronouns, are helping words. In Greek there are no helping words. Whether the verb means "I am walking," "You will walk," or "They have walked" is indicated by the form of the verb, by the ending on the verb itself (the context indicates whether the third person singular means "he," "she," or "it"). In the *Disciples' Literal New Testament*, the helping words are considered to be part of the verb form itself and are not placed in italics. If the pronoun (I, we, you, he, she, they) is separately expressed in Greek, it is done for emphasis. In the *Disciples' Literal New Testament*, such words are in **bold**.

The Greek tenses do not correspond precisely to English tenses. This is especially true of the Perfect tense. For example, consider "It has been written." Put simply, the Greek perfect tense can either lay the stress on a past completed action (as in English, translated as "it has been written"), or on the continuing result of that completed action (translated as "it is written," which sounds like a present tense in English). There is no clear way to bring both senses into English. Most translations choose which emphasis to bring across in each specific case. In general, the *Disciples' Literal New Testament* renders the tenses in an artificially strict fashion. Present tense, "I walk" or "I am walking." Imperfect tense, "I was walking." Future tense, "I will walk." Aorist tense, "I walked" or "I walk." Perfect tense, "I have walked." Pluperfect tense, "I had walked." This method displays the difficult cases in which the meaning of the Greek tense must be interpreted. For example, "I was well pleased" in Mt 3:17.

The Greek participle is one of the rich features of the Greek language and is used in various ways. For example, consider the participle "having come." Based on the context, this could mean "when he came," "after he came," "since he came," "although he came," "if he comes," "because he came," "by his coming," etc. In the *Disciples' Literal New Testament*, however, the participle is translated in an artificially strict fashion in order to communicate to the English reader that a participle is being used and to retain the Greek sentence structure. To illustrate using the word "walk," the verbal use of the participle for the present tense is translated "walking" or "while walking"; for the aorist and perfect tenses, "having walked." The substantive use of the participle for the present tense is translated "The *one* walking" (one is in italics because it is implied in the usage of the participle with the article); for the aorist and perfect tense, "The *one* having walked." The reader can easily discern in most cases which nuance to place on the "while" or "having." While the result may not sound like the way we would normally speak in English, it allows the English reader to "hear" the text from the Greek perspective. For example, note Matthew 2:10-12, and Mt 27:48.

The *Disciples' Literal New Testament* rendering of verbs and participles is deliberately standardized with a non-nuanced, basic significance, reflecting the Greek form of the word. In other words, they are rendered in a "raw" form, to which a translator would then add a more explicit nuance in English, based on the implications of the context. English simply prefers more explicitness than Greek. In most cases, these nuances from the context are clear and obvious to everyone, and can be supplied by the reader, as intended by the Greek. In some places, there are different opinions about which grammatical nuance the context implies. In general, the intent of the *Disciples' Literal New Testament* is to remain one step short of interpreting the grammatical nuance, allowing the reader to see the raw data from which such interpretation proceeds. For example, based on the context, the usage of the participle in "having known God, they did not glorify Him as God" in Rom 1:21 more explicitly means "although they knew"; the verb in "He was teaching them, saying" in Mt 5:2 may mean "He began to teach"; the verb in "I was compelling them to blaspheme" in Act 26:11 may mean "I was trying to compel"; the participle in "how shall we escape, having neglected" in Heb 2:3 more explicitly means "if we neglect."

This does not mean that the *Disciples' Literal New Testament* rendering of verbs and participles is "more accurate" or "more literal." Rather, the *Disciples' Literal New Testament* has more simple, more rudimentary, less explicit renderings that follow the Greek forms more closely. The renderings in other translations are fuller, more explicit expressions of the meaning of the word together with its contextual implications, in normal English forms. The one contains the raw data; the other, the finely tuned and polished end-product. But this does mean that the other versions are more interpretive, since they seek to make explicit what is implied by the context, although in the vast majority of cases the interpretation required is minimal, routine, obvious, and undisputed. And this explains, in part, why we see differences of phrasing in the various standard translations. There is simply more than one way to correctly rephrase these things in English!

The reader who knows Greek will understand the *Disciples' Literal New Testament* renderings for what they are, and will immediately begin considering how to properly nuance them. The English reader can also do this, to some degree. But with English readers, the renderings in the *Disciples' Literal New Testament* face a danger from their "rawness" and standardization, a danger of not being fully understood or perhaps of even being misunderstood. The English reader can avoid such dangers by using the other translations as a guide to the various ways in which the verbs and participles can be properly nuanced.

The Gospels. Because the Gospels each present the details of the life of Christ, there are many parallel accounts of the same events or words. Special care has been taken to ensure that when two Gospels use the same words and grammar, it is translated the same way in both. When they use different words or grammar, the *Disciples' Literal New Testament* reflects it.

The Greek Text Underlying This Translation

The history of the Greek text. The books of the New Testament were written in Greek. In His wisdom, God did not think it necessary to preserve for us the original copy of these books. Instead, we have thousands of handwritten copies—Greek manuscripts and papyrus fragments produced from the second century up to the invention of the printing press. There is far more manuscript evidence for the New Testament documents than for any other document of ancient history. We also have ancient translations of the New Testament, and quotations of New Testament verses in ancient writings, dating from the second to the sixth century and beyond. These and other sources form the raw material from which the Greek New Testament is constructed. Soon after the invention of the printing press, Greek New Testaments began to be printed. Among others were those of Erasmus (1527), Stephanus (1551), and Beza (1598). In fact, it was Robert Stephanus, in his fourth edition of the Greek New Testament published in 1551, who first added the verse numbers which we now use. These Greek texts were the sources used to produce the King James translation in 1611. In 1633, the Greek text behind the KJV began to be called the "Textus Receptus"—the received or standard Greek text. It remained the standard Greek text for 250 years, although other Greek texts continued to be produced. Even today, some still prefer to follow this time-honored text, or one similar to it. The situation changed as a result of the great manuscript discoveries of the 19th and 20th centuries. These resulted in new Greek texts incorporating this important new manuscript evidence. Most modern translations are based upon one of these updated Greek texts. Today's standard Greek text was prepared by a committee of scholars and is used worldwide by Protestants and Catholics, liberals and conservatives, scholars and pastors (though other Greek texts do exist). Except for punctuation, the New Testament TransLine follows this Greek text exactly—not because any (including those who produced it) consider it the final word on the subject, but so that the starting point of this translation is clear to everyone.

Textual variants— the differences between the Greek manuscripts. The handwritten copies contain all the types of errors which any honest hand-copier would make. Some were accidental, as when one's eye skips from one line to a similar word in the next line. Some were intentional, as when a difficult idiom or word order or spelling was smoothed out. Sometimes explanatory marginal notes were incorporated into the text by a subsequent copier because he thought the previous copier had accidentally left them out. Each change was then included in all the subsequent copies made from that manuscript. These differences between the Greek manuscripts are called "textual variants." Most of these variances relate to differences of spelling and similar matters of no significance to the meaning of the text. But some are significant or interesting.

All the textual variants have been identified and studied by scholars. Many unsung heroes over the centuries have toiled over the thousands of Greek manuscripts and other writings in multiple languages, in a painstaking effort to produce the most accurate Greek text possible. Textual scholars have analyzed every minute detail in all the copies, making the text of the New Testament far more reliable than any other document of antiquity. The result of their work is contained in the Greek New Testament in footnotes listing the significant variants, and detailing the manuscripts that contain them. These textual details may not be important to the average Bible reader. He or she may even ignore the subject and continue to use whatever Bible version is most familiar—a perfectly acceptable choice. But should he or she ever desire to know more about the subject, the laborers have been in the field for centuries, and their work is available for public examination.

Only a few of these variants are mentioned in the notes of the *Disciples' Literal New Testament*. But for those who are interested, over 3,000 variants are detailed in the companion volume, the *New Testament TransLine*. This is a substantial but not exhaustive list providing an accurate picture of the nature of the issue, with particular focus on the variants that are reflected in the major translations and that might be of interest to the English reader. Because this translation is a very literal translation, it is able for the first time to allow the English reader to personally examine these variants in detail. As you examine them, you will see that most of them make little if any difference to the meaning of the verse. Some are important, such as Mk 16:8-20 and Jn 7:53-8:11. Some will help you understand a difference between English translations such as the NKJV and the NIV. And some will help you in your understanding of the verse. You will also notice the extreme detail and precision reflected in the variants. For example, does it say "Jesus Christ" or "Christ Jesus"; "Spirit" or "Holy Spirit"; "His hands" or "*His* hands"; "He said" or "Jesus said." .

In order to truly understand what lies behind a variant reading, the Greek sources must be studied. Since the English reader cannot do so, he or she will not be able to assess the manuscript evidence for the variants or the theories for weighing it. However, the English reader can understand what the variants are and observe their potential significance to the meaning of the verse. It is not the place of the *Disciples' Literal New Testament* or the *New Testament TransLine* to express its own opinion regarding any variant, but simply to present the textual facts for the reader's consideration. The standard Greek text serves best as the starting point for this purpose.

Primary Sources Used For This Translation

Greek text:

> Aland, Aland, Karavidopoulos, Martini, Metzger, *The Greek New Testament*, Fourth Revised Edition (UBS4), United Bible Societies, 1994.
>
> Nestle, Aland, *Novum Testamentum Graece*, 27th Edition, Deutsche Bibelgesellschaft (German Bible Society), 1993.

Greek-English lexicons:

> Danker, *A Greek-English Lexicon of the New Testament and Other Early Christian Literature*, Third Edition of Bauer, Arndt, and Gingrich, The University of Chicago Press, 2000.
>
> Liddell, Scott, Jones, McKenzie, Glare, *A Greek-English Lexicon*, Ninth Edition, Clarendon Press (Oxford University Press), 1996.

Concordances:

> Bushell, *BibleWorks 5.0*, Hermeneutika Computer Bible Research Software, 2001. (A computer program linking multiple Greek and Hebrew texts and lexicons, and English and other translations, with a powerful search engine. Based on UBS4).
>
> Kohlenberger, Goodrick, Swanson, *The Greek English Concordance to the New Testament*, Zondervan, 1997. (The Greek word with English excerpts from the NIV, based on UBS4).

CPSIA information can be obtained at www.ICGtesting.com
Printed in the USA
LVOW11*1506310314

379674LV00013B/354/P